LAW AND (DIS)ORDER IN THE ANCIENT NEAR EAST

## RENCONTRE ASSYRIOLOGIQUE INTERNATIONALE

### *Proceedings*

1. *Language in the Ancient Near East*, edited by L. Kogan, N. Koslova, S. Loesov, and S. Tischchenko. 2 volumes (RAI 53)
2. *City Administration in the Ancient Near East*, edited by L. Kogan, N. Koslova, S. Loesov, and S. Tischchenko (RAI 53)
3. *Organization, Representation, and Symbols of Power in the Ancient Near East*, edited by Gernot Wilhelm (RAI 54)
4. *La famille dans le Proche-Orient ancien: Réalités, symbolismes et images*, edited by Lionel Marti (RAI 55)
5. *Time and History in the Ancient Near East*, edited by Lluis Feliu, J. Llop, A. Millet Albà, and Joaquin Sanmartín (RAI 56)
6. *Tradition and Innovation in the Ancient Near East*, edited by Alfonso Archi (RAI 57)
7. *Private and State in the Ancient Near East*, edited by R. DeBoer and J. G. Dercksen (RAI 58)
8. *Fortune and Misfortune in the Ancient Near East*, edited by Olga Drewnowska and Małgorzata Sandowicz (RAI 60)
9. *Ur in the Twenty-First Century CE*, edited by Grant Frame, Joshua Jeffers, and Holly Pittman (RAI 62)
10. *Law and (Dis)Order in the Ancient Near East*, edited by Katrien De Graef and Anne Goddeeris (RAI 59)

### *Associated Volumes*

1. *Divination in the Ancient Near East*, edited by Jeanette C. Fincke (RAI 54)
2. *Divination as Science*, edited by Jeanette C. Fincke (RAI 60)
3. *Studying Gender in the Ancient Near East*, edited by Saana Svärd and Agnès Garcia-Ventura (RAI 59 and 60)
4. *Distant Impressions: The Senses in the Ancient Near East*, edited by Ainsley Hawthorn and Anne-Caroline Rendu Loisel (RAI 61)
5. *Patients and Performative Identities: At the Intersection of the Mesopotamian Technical Disciplines and Their Clients*, edited by J. Cale Johnson (RAI 60 and 61)

# Law and (Dis)Order in the Ancient Near East

*Proceedings of the 59th Rencontre Assyriologique Internationale Held at Ghent, Belgium, 15–19 July 2013*

EDITED BY KATRIEN DE GRAEF AND ANNE GODDEERIS

EISENBRAUNS | University Park, Pennsylvania

Library of Congress Cataloging-in-Publication Data

Names: Rencontre assyriologique internationale (59th : 2013 : Ghent, Belgium), author. | Graef, Katrien de, editor. | Goddeeris, Anne, editor.
Title: Law and (dis)order in the ancient Near East : proceedings of the 59th Rencontre assyriologique internationale held at Ghent, Belgium, 15-19 July 2013 / edited by Katrien De Graef and Anne Goddeeris.
Description: University Park, Pennsylvania : Eisenbrauns, [2021] | Includes bibliographical references and index. | Essays chiefly in English, some in French and German.
Summary: "A collection of 26 essays delivered at the 2013 yearly meeting of the Rencontre Assyriologique Internationale on archaeological, philological, and historical topics related to order and chaos in the Ancient Near East"—Provided by publisher.
Identifiers: LCCN 2020044814 | ISBN 9781575068428 (cloth)
Subjects: LCSH: Law, Ancient—Congresses. | Law—Middle East—History—To 1500—Congresses. | Law enforcement—Middle East—To 1500—Congresses. | LCGFT: Conference papers and proceedings.
Classification: LCC KL135 2013 | DDC 340.5/394—dc23
LC record available at https://lccn.loc.gov/2020044814


Printed in the United States of America
Published by The Pennsylvania State University Press,
University Park, PA 16802-1003

Eisenbrauns is an imprint of The Pennsylvania State University Press.

The Pennsylvania State University Press is a member of the Association of University Presses.

It is the policy of The Pennsylvania State University Press to use acid-free paper. Publications on uncoated stock satisfy the minimum requirements of American National Standard for Information Sciences—Permanence of Paper for Printed Library Material, ANSI Z39.48–1992.

# CONTENTS

# PREFACE: LAW AND (DIS)ORDER IN GHENT (AND THE ANCIENT NEAR EAST)

## Disorder

When one sets out to organize an RAI, especially for the first time, it is safe to say one does not have an idea what one is getting into: Will the colleagues respond to the invitation, will the lecture halls you have in mind be available, will the financial side of things be manageable—these were all questions that haunted our nights for quite some time.

A first big decision which had to be made, even before we started making practical preparations was of course the most important one: choosing a central theme. Going over the themes of previous Rencontres one finds a multitude of topics, going from rather specific ones such as the cultic function of ziggurats (Paris 1950) and Sumerian and Akkadian terminology for bronze (Paris 1951), over Mesopotamia's relations with its neighbors, specifically or in general (Heidelberg 1959, Paris 1961, Berlin 1978, Leningrad 1984, Istanbul 1987, Ghent 1989, and Leuven 1995), to more general themes such as life (Vienna 1981), death (Copenhagen 1979), war (London 1963, and Münster 2006), women (Paris, 1956 and 1986), sex and gender (Helsinki and Tartu 2001), and time and history (Barcelona 2010).

In fact, so many aspects of ancient Mesopotamian civilization were chosen that it was not easy to find one that had not been chosen already. And then we thought of law and this was indeed a theme that had never been chosen before. This is somewhat astonishing since so many studies have been devoted to this subject. Having chosen law and aiming to widen the perspective so as to not only include studies of law corpora, law and order, meaning the law and its application in society, resulting in some form of order, sprang to mind. The last touch was added when we considered not only the reality of ancient Mesopotamia, which knew as many periods of some disorder as ones of some order, but also when we thought of our colleagues, fellow Assyriologists, some exhibiting a clear penchant for order and others more in favor of a sound portion of disorder.

## Order

So it was decided that law and (dis)order would be the theme of the 59th Rencontre. I must add that when the titles of papers and the abstracts started coming in, I was pleasantly surprised to see that so many, in fact most of them, were connected to the theme. As can be seen in the program, not only papers on law and its application in ancient Near Eastern societies, but also papers on order and disorder in ancient Near Eastern literature, linguistics, mathematics and medicine, astronomy and divination, geography, and iconography were presented.

In addition to this, we also welcomed workshops on the study of ancient Near Eastern history (organized by Marc Van De Mieroop), chronology (organized by Klaas R. Veenhof and Gojko Barjamovic), Neo-Assyrian imperial administration (organized by Saana Svärd and Natalie N. May), gender (organized by Saana Svärd and Agnès Garcia-Ventura), and Ugarit (organized by Wilfred van Soldt).

A second important step was to find the appropriate location to organize the Rencontre. After considering various options, our eye fell on the beautifully renovated Emile Braun School, not only for its architectural charm or location in the very heart of Ghent, but also for its link to law and order, both past and present. It is a renovated Jesuit cloister, originally built in the middle of the seventeenth century, used as a tribunal after the abolition of the Order of Jesuits at the end of the eighteenth century by Joseph the Second. The cloister itself later became a school, named after a mayor of Ghent, Emile Braun, and finally, the building was completely renovated by Ghent University and is now part of the Law Faculty.

## Law

So it came to happen that the 59th Rencontre on law and (dis)order took place in the buildings of the Law Faculty of Ghent University, whose dean, Piet Taelman, welcomed us warmly, for which I wish to express my deep gratitude.

The annual apogee of Assyriology did indeed live up to its name, as we enjoyed a very fruitful week full of interesting and innovative papers, as well as fine and productive discussions, not only in and around the courtyards of the Emile Braun School but also in many a sunny sidewalk café of Ghent, for Shamash granted us both judicial insight and sunny weather. All of this would of course not have been possible without the dedicated, enthusiastic and very efficient organizing team around me, whom I want to thank wholeheartedly: Lotte Oers, Guido Suurmeijer, Michel Tanret, and Astrid Verhulst.

Finally, a third and last step was the publishing of the proceedings, which took a while, but has been completed successfully, especially thanks to the help of my co-editor Anne Goddeeris.

It was a great honor and pleasure to host the 59th Rencontre Assyriologique Internationale in Ghent.

Katrien De Graef
July 2019

# ABBREVIATIONS

The abbreviations used in the volume are those used by the Cuneiform Digital Library Initiative (http://cdli.ox.ac.uk/wiki/abbreviations_for_assyriology).

| | |
|---|---|
| 2ms | 2nd-person masculine singular |
| 3ms | 3rd-person masculine singular |
| *AArH* | *Acta Archaeologica Academiae Scientiarum Hungaricae* |
| AASOR | Annual of the American Schools of Oriental Research |
| ÄAT | Ägypten und Altes Testament |
| AbB | Altbabylonische Briefe in Umschrift und Übersetzung |
| ADOG | Abhandlungen der Deutschen Orient-Gesellschaft |
| ADPV | Abhandlungen des deutschen Palästina Vereins |
| *AEPHE* | *Annuaire de l'École pratique des Hautes-Études* |
| *AfO* | *Archiv für Orientforschung* |
| AfOB | Archiv für Orientforschung: Beiheft |
| *AHw* | W. von Soden. *Akkadisches Handwörterbuch.* Wiesbaden 1959–1981. |
| AIL | Ancient Israel and Its Literature |
| *AJA* | *American Journal of Archaeology* |
| ANESup | Ancient Near Eastern Studies Supplement |
| AnOr | Analecta Orientalia |
| AO | Antiquités orientales (Museum siglum Louvre) |
| AOAT | Alter Orient und Altes Testament |
| *AoF* | *Altorientalische Forschungen* |
| AOS | American Oriental Series |
| ARCANE | Associated Regional Chronologies for the Ancient Near East and the Eastern Mediterranean |
| ARM | Archive Royales de Mari |
| ARMT | Archive Royales de Mari Texts |
| ARN | Altbabylonische Rechtsurkunden aus Nippur |
| AS | Assyriological Studies |
| *ASJ* | *Acta Sumerologica* |
| *AuOr* | *Aula Orientalis* |

| | |
|---|---|
| AuOrSup | Aula Orientalis Supplementa |
| *BAAL* | *Bulletin d'Archéologie et d'Architecture Libanaises* |
| BaF | Baghdader Forschungen |
| *BaM* | *Baghdader Mitteilungen* |
| BAP | Beiträge zum altbabylonischen Privatrecht |
| BARIS | British Archaeological Reports International Series |
| BBVO | Berliner Beiträge zum Vorderen Orients |
| *BCSMS* | *Bulletin of the Canadian Society for Mesopotamian Studies* |
| BDB | Brown, Francis, S. R. Driver, and Charles A. Briggs. *A Hebrew and English Lexicon of the Old Testament*. Oxford: Clarendon, 1907. |
| BE | Babylonian Expedition of the University of Pennsylvania |
| BEATAJ | Beiträge zur Erforschung des Alten Testaments und des antiken Judentums |
| BETL | Bibliotheca Ephemeridum Theologicarum Lovaniensium |
| *Bib* | *Biblica* |
| BibOr | Biblica et Orientalia |
| BibSem | The Biblical Seminar |
| BIN | Babylonian Inscriptions in the Collection of J. B. Nies |
| BIWA | Borger, R. *Beiträge zum Inschriftenwerk Assurbanipals. Die Prismenklassen A, B, C = K, D, E, F, G, H, J und T sowie andere Inschriften. Mit einem Beitrag von Andreas Fuchs*. Wiesbaden: Harrassowitz. |
| BJSUCSD | Biblical and Judaic Studies from the University of California, San Diego |
| BMes | Bibliotheca Mesopotamica |
| *BO* | *Bibliotheca Orientalis* |
| BZABR | Beihefte zur Zeitschrift für altorientalische und biblische Rechtsgeschichte |
| BZAW | Beihefte zur Zeitschrift für die alttestamentliche Wissenschaft |
| *CAD* | Gelb, Ignace J., et al. *The Assyrian Dictionary of the Oriental Institute of the University of Chicago*. 21 vols. Chicago: Oriental Institute of the University of Chicago, 1956–2010. |
| *CANE* | *Civilizations of the Ancient Near East*. Edited by J. M. Sasson. 4 vols. New York, 1995. Repr. in 2 vols. Peabody, MA: Hendrickson, 2006. |
| *CBQ* | *Catholic Biblical Quarterly* |
| CBS | Catalogue of the Babylonian Section |
| CCEM | Contributions to the Chronology of the Eastern Mediterranean |
| *CDLB* | *Cuneiform Digital Library Bulletin* |
| CE | Laws of Eshnunna |
| CH | Codex Hammurabi |
| CHANE | Culture and History of the Ancient Near East |
| CM | Cuneiform Monographs |
| CNIP | Carsten Niebuhr Institute Publications |
| coll. | collated |

| | |
|---|---|
| *COS* | Hallo, William W., and K. Lawson Younger Jr., eds. *The Context of Scripture*. 4 vols. Leiden: Brill, 1997–2016. |
| CST | Catalogue of Sumerian Tablets in the John Rylands Library |
| *CT* | *Cuneiform Texts from the Babylonian Tablets in the British Museum*. London: British Museum, 1896–. |
| CUNES | Cornell University Near Eastern Section |
| CUSAS | Cornell University Studies in Assyriology and Sumerology |
| DBAT | Dielheimer Blätter zum Alten Testament |
| DMOA | Documenta et Monumenta Orientis Antiqui |
| EN | Excavations at Nuzi |
| *Esar.* | *Annals of Esarhaddon* |
| *ETCSL* | Black, J. A., Cunningham, G., Ebeling, J., Flückiger-Hawker, E., Robson, E., Taylor, J., and Zólyomi, G. *The Electronic Text Corpus of Sumerian Literature*. Oxford, 1998–2006. http://etcsl.orinst.ox.ac.uk. |
| FAOS | Freiburger altorientalische Studien |
| FCB | Feminist Companion to the Bible |
| FM | Florilegium marianum |
| FRLANT | Forschungen zur Religion und Literatur des Alten und Neuen Testaments |
| GAAL | Göttinger Arbeitshefte Altorientalischen Literatur |
| *GAG* | *Grundriss der Akkadischen Grammatik*. W. von Soden; with the cooperation of W. R. Mayer. 3rd ed. AnOr 33. Rome: Pontifical Biblical Institute. |
| GAT | Grundrisse zum Alten Testament |
| HANE/M | History of the Ancient Near East/Monographs |
| HCOT | Historical Commentaries on the Old Testament |
| HdO | Handbuch der Orientalistik |
| hemer. | hemerology |
| HEO | Hautes études orientales |
| *HR* | *History of Religions* |
| HS | Tablet siglum of the Hilprecht Collection in Jena |
| HSAO | Heidelberger Studien zum Alten Orient |
| HSS | Harvard Semitic Studies |
| *HTR* | *Harvard Theological Review* |
| *IEJ* | *Israel Exploration Journal* |
| IM | Museum siglum of the Iraq Museum in Baghdad |
| ITT | Inventaire des tablettes de Tello |
| *JA* | *Journal Asiatique* |
| *JANES(CU)* | Journal of the Ancient Near Eastern Society (of Columbia University) |
| *JAOS* | *Journal of the American Oriental Society* |
| *JBL* | *Journal of Biblical Literature* |
| *JCS* | *Journal of Cuneiform Studies* |
| JEN | Joint Expedition with the Iraq Museum at Nuzi |

| | |
|---|---|
| *JEOL* | *Jaarbericht van het Vooraziatisch-Egyptisch Genootschap Ex Oriente Lux* |
| *JESHO* | *Journal of the Economic and Social History of the Orient* |
| *JFA* | *Journal of Field Archaeology* |
| *JNES* | *Journal of Near Eastern Studies* |
| JSJSup | Supplements to the Journal for the Study of Judaism |
| JSNTSup | Journal for the Study of the New Testament Supplement |
| JSOTSup | Journal for the Study of the Old Testament Supplement |
| *JSS* | *Journal of Semitic Studies* |
| *KAR* | E. Ebeling. *Keilschrifttexte aus Assur religiösen Inhalts I/II.* WVDOG 28, 34. Leipzig: Zeller, 1919, 1923. |
| KAT | Kommentar zum Alten Testament |
| KStTh | Kohlhammer Studienbücher Theologie |
| LANE | Languages of the Ancient Near East |
| LAOS | Leipziger altorientalistische Studien |
| LAPO | Littératures anciennes du Proche-Orient |
| LB | Late Bronze Age |
| MC | Mesopotamian Civilizations |
| *MDOG* | *Mitteilungen der Deutschen Orient-Gesellschaft* |
| MHET | Mesopotamian History and Environment: Texts |
| *MIOF* | *Mitteilungen des Instituts für Orientforschung* |
| *MNAW.L* | Mededelingen der Koninklijke Nederlandse Akademie van Wetenschappen; Afd. letterkunde |
| MS(S) | manuscript(s) |
| MT | Masoretic Text |
| MVN | Materiali per il vocabulario neosumerico |
| *NABU* | *Nouvelles assyriologiques brèves et utilitaires* |
| NATN | Owen, D. S. Neo-Sumerian Archival Texts Primarily from Nippur. Winona Lake, IN: Eisenbrauns, 1982. |
| NBC | Nies Babylonian Collection, siglum of the Yale Babylonian Collection |
| NBL | Neo-Babylonian Laws |
| ND | Field numbers of tablets excavated at Nimrud |
| *NedTT* | *Nederlands theologisch tijdschrift* |
| OB | Old Babylonian |
| OBO | Orbis Biblicus et Orientalis |
| OECT | Oxford Editions of Cuneiform Texts |
| OIP | Oriental Institute Publications |
| OIS | Oriental Institute Seminars |
| OLA | Orientalia Lovaniensia Analecta |
| OLP | Orientalia Lovaniensia periodica |
| *Or* | *Orientalia NS* |
| *OrAnt* | *Oriens Antiquus* |
| OTS | Old Testament Studies |
| PBS | Publications of the Babylonian Section |
| pers. comm. | personal communication |

| | |
|---|---|
| PIHANS | Publications de l'Institut historique-archéologique néerlandais de Stamboul |
| PLO | Porta Linguarum Orientalium |
| pl(s). | plural; plate(s) |
| PRAK | Premieres recherches archeologiques a Kich |
| *RA* | *Revue d'assyriologie et d'archéologie orientale* |
| *RB* | *Revue biblique* |
| rev. | reverse |
| *RHR* | *Revue de l'histoire des religions* |
| RIMA | The Royal Inscriptions of Mesopotamia, Assyrian Periods |
| RIME | Royal Inscriptions of Mesopotamia, Early Periods |
| RINAP | Royal Inscriptions of the Neo-Assyrian Period |
| *RlA* | *Reallexikon der Assyriologie und vorderasiatischen Archäologie.* Edited by Erich Ebeling et al. Berlin: de Gruyter, 1928–. |
| RS | Ras Shamra tablet |
| *RSO* | *Rivista degli Studi Orientali* |
| *RTP* | *Revue de théologie et de philosophie* |
| SAA | State Archives of Assyria |
| SAACT | State Archives of Assyria Cuneiform Texts |
| SAAS | State Archives of Assyria Studies |
| SANER | Studies in Ancient Near Eastern Records |
| SAOC | Studies in the Ancient Oriental Civilization |
| SB | Sources Bibliques |
| SBA | Saarbrücker Beiträge zur Altertumskunde |
| SBH | Sumerisch-babylonische Hymnen nach Thontafeln griechischer Zeit |
| SBLDS | Society of Biblical Literature Dissertation Series |
| SBLMS | Society of Biblical Literature Monograph Series |
| SCCNH | Studies on the Civilization and Culture of Nuzi and the Hurrians |
| *SEL* | *Studi epigrafici e linguistici* |
| sg. | singular |
| SHCANE | Studies in the History and Culture of the Ancient Near East |
| SLTN | Sumerian Literary Texts from Nippur in the Museum of the Ancient Orient at Istanbul |
| SMN | Museum siglum of the Semitic Museum of the Harvard University (Nuzi Tablets) |
| *StOr* | *Studia Orientalia* |
| StSem | Studi Semitici |
| suff. | suffix |
| TAVO | Tübinger Atlas zum vorderen Orients Beiheft |
| TCS | Texts from Cuneiform Sources |
| TIM | Texts in the Iraq Museum |
| TLB | Tabulae Cuneiformes a F.M.Th. de Liagre Böhl collectae |
| TMH | Texte und Materialien der Frau Professor Hilprecht Collection |
| *TUAT* | Kaiser, Otto, et al., eds. *Texte aus der Umwelt des Alten Testaments*. Gütersloh: Mohn; Gütersloher Verlagshaus, 1984–. |

| | |
|---|---|
| UET | Ur Excavations Texts |
| *UF* | *Ugarit-Forschungen* |
| UN | Laws of Ur-Namma |
| VAB | Vorderasiatische Bibliothek |
| VAS | Vorderasiatische Schriftdenkmaler |
| VAT | Vorderasiatische Abteilung. Tontafeln (museum siglum of the Vorderasiatisches Museum) |
| *VT* | *Vetus Testamentum* |
| VTSup | Supplements to Vetus Testamentum |
| WAW | Writings from the Ancient World |
| *WO* | *Welt des Orients* |
| WVDOG | Wissenschaftliche Veröffentlichungen der Deutschen Orient-Gesellschaft |
| *WZKM* | *Wiener Zeitschrift für die Kunde des Morgenlandes* |
| YJS | Yale Judaica Series |
| YNER | Yale Near Eastern Researches |
| YOS | Yale Oriental Series |
| *ZA* | *Zeitschrift für Assyriologie und vorderasiatische Archäologie* |
| *ZABR* | *Zeitschrift für Altorientalische und Biblische Rechtsgeschichte* |
| *ZAW* | *Zeitschrift für die alttestamentliche Wissenschaft* |
| *ZDPV* | *Zeitschrift des Deutschen Palästina-Vereins* |

# PROGRAM

## Sunday, July 14

4:00–7:00 Registration

## Monday, July 15

8:30–10:00 Registration (continuation)

***Welcoming Session and Plenary Papers***

*10:00–11:00 Welcoming Session*

Vice-Rector UGent, Luc Moens

Honorary Dean Humanities Faculty UGent, Johnny Devreker

Chair Organizing Committee 59e RAI, Katrien De Graef

President International Association for Assyriology (IAA), Piotr Michalowski

*Plenary Papers*

11:00–11:30 Sophie Démare-Lafont, Unjust Law: Royal Rhetoric of Social Reality?

11:30–12:00 Marc Van De Mieroop, The Conception of Order in Mesopotamian Culture

12:00–12:30 Piotr Michalowski, The Pleasures of Contingency and Chaos: Mesopotamian Vistas

*12:30–2:00 Lunch Break*

***Session 1: Law and (Dis)Order in the Ancient Near East (General Approaches, Epigraphy)***

*Chair: Antoine Cavigneaux*

2:00–2:30 Jacob Klein, From Agade to Samaria: The Inflationary Price of Barley in Situations of Famine

2:30–3:00 Daniel Bonneterre, Lorsque les généraux prêtent serment . . . Quelques remarques sur l'usage du serment rituel de loyauté (depuis la documentation d'Ur III jusqu'à l'époque néo-assyrienne)

3:00–3:30 Sandra Jacobs, Made to Measure? Proportioning Punishment to Fit the Crime

***Workshop "The Study of Ancient Near Eastern History: Methods and Approaches"***
*Organized by Marc Van De Mieroop*
*Chair: Marc Van De Mieroop*

2:00–2:15 Steven Garfinkle, Introduction
2:15–2:40 Seth Richardson, Mesopotamian Political History: Some Perversities
2:40-13:05 Daniel Fleming, Chasing Down the Mundane: The Near East with Social Historical Interest
3:05–3:30 Niek Veldhuis, Intellectual History and Assyriology

*3:30–4:00 Coffee Break*

***Session 2: Law and (Dis)Order in Ancient Near Eastern Chronicles and Astronomical Diaries***
*Chair: Theo J. H. Krispin*

4:00–4:30 Yasuyuki Mitsuma, Compilation of the Late Babylonian "Standard" Astronomical Diaries
4:30–5:00 Geert de Breucker, Order or Just Disorder? The Babylonian Chronicles and the Development of a Historical Canon

***Session 3: Law and (Dis)Order in Ancient Near Eastern Iconography***
*Chair: Michael Roaf*

4:00–4:30 Agnete Wisti Lassen, Seal Collecting and Recarving in the Old Assyrian Period: Representation Strategies in Glyptic Imagery
4:30–5:00 Astrid Verhulst, "Order! Order!" On the Standardization of Old Babylonian Seal Scenes from Sippar through the Reconstruction of Two Families and their Seals
5:00–5:30 Noemi Colombo, Plaque Kh. VI:81: Transition from Ancient Laws to a New (Dis)Order

**Tuesday, July 16**

***Session 4a: Law and (Dis)Order in Ancient Near Eastern Literature***
*Chair: Benjamin Foster*

9:00–9:30 Nathan Wasserman, "Je t'aime . . . moi non plus": New Perspectives on Akkadian Love Lyrics
9:30–10:00 Michela Piccin, Strategies of Persuasion in the Hymn to Marduk (Ludlul I, 1–40)
10:00–10:30 Joanna Töyräänvuori, The Sea and Monarchic Legitimation in the Ancient Near East

***Session 5: Law and (Dis)Order in the Ancient Near East (General Approaches, Archaeology)***
*Chair: Katrien De Graef*

9:00–9:30 Elisabeth Wagner-Durand and Julia Linke, Putting Life in Order: The Architecture of the New Excavations in Kamid el-Loz, Lebanon
9:30–10:00 Michela Piccin, Strategies of Persuasion in the Hymn to Marduk (Ludlul I, 1–40)

***Workshop "Toward an Absolute Chronology of the Ancient Near East"***
*Organized by Klaas R. Veenhof and Gojko Barjamovic*

9:00–9:10 Gojko Barjamovic, Welcome
9:10–9:20 Klaas R. Veenhof, Current Problems in the Study of the Absolute Chronology of the Ancient Near East
9:20–9:30 Felix Höflmayer, Integrating Chronologies: Egypt, the Aegean, and the Ancient Near East in the Mid-Second Millennium BCE
9:30–9:40 Walther Sallaberger, Third Millennium BCE Chronologies of the Near East
9:40–9:50 Jared Miller, Chronological Synchronisms between Babylon and Assyria, Egypt, and Hatti
9:50–10:00 Werner Nahm, The Case for the Lower Middle Chronology
10:00–10:10 Teije de Jong, Astronomical Fine-tuning of the Chronology of the Hammurabi Age
10:10–10:20 Michael Roaf, Toward the Lower Middle Chronology but Not Yet There
10:20–10:30 Gojko Barjamovic, A New Look at the KEL G

*10:30–11:00 Coffee break*

***Session 4b: Law and (Dis)Order in Ancient Near Eastern Literature***
*Chair: Niek Veldhuis*

11:00–11:30 Daniel Bodi, Does the Human "Noise" (*ḫubūru, rigmu*) in Some Akkadian Myths Stand for Disorder?
11:30–12:00 Michela Piccin, Strategies of Persuasion in the Hymn to Marduk (Ludlul I, 1–40)
12:00–12:30 Joanna Töyräänvuori, The Sea and Monarchic Legitimation in the Ancient Near East

***Session 6: Law and (Dis)Order in Achaemenid Babylonia***
*Chair: Jan Tavernier*

11:00–11:30 Malgorzata Sandowicz, Babylonian Judges, Persian Kings: Court System under Regime Change
11:30–12:00 Michela Piccin, Strategies of Persuasion in the Hymn to Marduk (Ludlul I, 1– 40)

***Workshop "Toward an Absolute Chronology of the Ancient Near East"***
*Organized by Klaas R. Veenhof and Gojko Barjamovic*

11:00–11:10 Denis Lacambre, The Eponym Ahiyaya in the Chagar Bazar Documentation
11:10–11:20 Yigal Bloch, The Eponyms Dating the Conquests of Shamshi-Adad I in the Assyrian King List and Their Apparent Absence from the Kültepe Eponym List
11:20–12:30 Discussion

*12:30–12:40 Group photo (Central Court Emile Braun School)*

*12:40–2:00 Lunch Break*

***Session 7a: Law and (Dis)Order in the Old Babylonian Period***

*Chair: Brigitte Lion*

2:00–2:30 Dalila Bendellal, Le vol à l'époque Paléo-Babylonienne: L'Application de la loi à travers la jurisprudence

2:30–3:00 Cristina Simonetti, When the Trial Does Not Work: Pathological Elements in the Judicial Procedure in the Old Babylonian Period

3:00–3:30 Marie-France Scouflaire, L'Institution des nipûtum dans les royaumes paléo-babyloniens

***Workshop "Change in Neo-Assyrian Imperial Administration: Evolution and Revolution"***

*Organized by Saana Svärd and Natalie N. May*

*Chair: Saana Svärd*

2:00–2:30 Rajia Mattila, Change or Chance? Studying Change in Neo-Assyrian Administration

2:30–3:00 Simonetta Ponchia, Neo-Assyrian Imperial Offices and Officials: Places, Roles, and Actors of a Political Mentality Change

3:00–3:30 Natalie May, Administrative Reforms of Sargon II and Tiglath-Pileser III

***Session 8a: Law and (Dis)Order in Sumer***

*Chair: Steven Garfinkle*

2:00–2:30 Manuel Molina, Law and Order in Irisagrig

2:30–3:00 Walther Sallaberger, Transparency in Ancient Sumer? Discussing the Role of Administrative Documents

3:00–3:30 Sarah Clegg, Capacity Measures, the Temple and the State: Ordering Metrology at the End of the Third Millennium

*3:30–4:00 Coffee Break*

***Session 7b: Law and (Dis)Order in the Old Babylonian Period***

*Chair: Michel Tanret*

4:00–4:30 Wiebke Meinhold, Erbrechtliche Regelungen und ihre Umsetzung im altbabylonischen Nippur

4:30–5:00 Anne Goddeeris, A Tangled Framework: A Calendric Innovation by Rim-Sîn

5:00–5:30 Virginie Muller, Rétablir l'ordre social par la mort dans les textes législatifs du début du IIème millénaire av. J.C.

***Workshop "Change in Neo-Assyrian Imperial Administration: Evolution and Revolution"***

*Organized by Saana Svärd and Natalie N. May*

*Chair: Natalie May*

4:00–4:30 Kazuko Watanabe, Esarhaddon's "Religious Reformation" as Seen through his Vassal Treaties

4:30–5:00 Saana Svärd, Changes in Neo-Assyrian Queenship
5:00–5:30 Melanie Gross, Food and Drink for the Palace: The Management of Foodstuffs in Neo-Assyrian Times

***Session 8b: Law and (Dis)Order in Sumer***
*Chair: Manuel Molina*
4:00–4:30 Steven Garfinkle, What the "Man of One Mina" Wanted: Law and Commerce in the Ur III Period
4:30–5:00 Christina Tsouparopoulou, Ordering the Archival Rooms at Puzrish-Dagan
5:00–5:30 Daniele Umberto Lampasona, Putting Some Order in Ur III Letter-orders

*7:00–10:00 Board Meeting International Association for Assyriology (IAA)*

**Wednesday, July 17**
***Session 9a: Law and (Dis)Order in Ancient Near Eastern Language and Linguistics***
*Chair: Alfonso Archi*
9:00–9:30 Leonid Kogan, Waw sargonicum: Creating Syntactic Order in Early Akkadian
9:30–10:00 Hans Neumann, Eid und Ordal als Beweismittel im Rahmen des gerichtlichen Beweisverfahrens der Akkade-Zeit
10:00–10:30 Ainsley Dicks, IGI $DU_8$ vs. IGI BAR: Semantics, Subject-Specific Usage, and Theological Implications

***Workshop "Gender, Methodology and Assyriology"***
*Organized by Saana Svärd and Agnès Garcia-Ventura*
*Chair: Dina Katz*
9:00–9:10 Saana Svärd/Agnès Garcia-Ventura, Introductory Remarks
9:10–9:40 Julia M. Asher-Greve, Sex and Gender Classification: The Potential of New Methods for Ancient Near Eastern Studies
9:40–10:10 Ann Guinan, Querying the Sounds of Silence: Mesopotamian Texts and Queer Theory
10:10–10:30 Discussion

***Workshop "The Religion and Society of Ancient Ugarit"***
*Organized by Wilfred van Soldt*
*Chair: Pierre Bordreuil*
9:00–9:05 Wilfred van Soldt, Introduction
9:05–9:35 Valérie Matoïan, The So-Called House of Rashapabu
9:35–10:05 Hedwige Rouillard-Bonraisin, Aspects sociologiques et religieux de la presence hourrite à Ougarit, d'après les textes alphabétiques
10:05–10:35 Françoise Ernst-Pradal, Paléographie des tablettes musicales hourrites

*10:30–11:00 Coffee break*

***Session 9b: Law and (Dis)Order in Ancient Near Eastern Language and Linguistics***
*Chair: Bert Kouwenberg*

11:00–11:30 C. Jay Crisostomo, Bilingualism and "Laws" of Translation: Knowledge, Scholarship, and Language in Old Babylonian Lexicography
11:30–12:00 Rodrigo Hernáiz, A Variationist Approach to Peculiarities of the Language in the Code of Hammurabi
12:00–12:30 Hanadah Tarawneh, Legal Themes in the Amarna Letters

***Workshop "Gender, Methodology, and Assyriology"***
*Organized by Saana Svärd and Agnès Garcia-Ventura*
*Chair: Jack Sasson*

11:00–11:30 Kathleen Mccaffrey, (Mis)Translating Gender: The Scribes Couldn't Have Been Competent in Akkadian, They Didn't Go to Yale
11:30–12:00 Maria Rosa Oliver and Eleonora Ravenna, Who Imposes and Who Disposes? Ordering the Disorder in the Palace of Mari: Gender Relationships and the Assyriological Prospective
12:00–12:30 Luciana Urbano, Marriage Policy in Mari as Field of Domination and Resistance: Some Reflections from the Gender Perspective

***Workshop "The Religion and Society of Ancient Ugarit"***
*Organized by Wilfred van Soldt*
*Chair: Valérie Matoïan*

11:00–11:30 Pierre Bordreuil, Les preoccupations religieuses des diverses composantes de la société ougaritaine à partir des textes et de l'iconographie: Quelques exemples
11:30–12:00 Wilfred van Soldt, Divinities in Personal Names at Ugarit
12:00–12:30 Meindert Dijkstra, El-Kunirsha in Hatti, Ugarit, and Elsewhere

*12:30–2:00 Lunch Break*

***Session 9c: Law and (Dis)Order in Ancient Near Eastern Language and Linguistics***
*Chair: Leonid Kogan*

2:00–2:30 Mojca Cajnko, Akkadian Prepositions and the Hittite Writing System
2:30–3:00 Aline Distexhe, A Study in Assyrian Lexicography: The Vocabulary of Rebellion in Neo-Assyrian Letters
3:00–3:30 Anna Meskhi, Sumerian, Kartvelian, and Theory of Information

***Workshop "Gender, Methodology, and Assyriology"***
*Organized by Saana Svärd and Agnès Garcia-Ventura*
*Chair: Christina Tsouparopoulou*

2:00–2:30 Brigitte Lion, Gender and Methodology in the Study of the IInd Millennium BCE Private Archives
2:30–3:00 Saana Svärd, Female Agency and Authorship in Mesopotamian Texts
3:00–3:30 Agnès Garcia-Ventura, Past and Present or How to Apply Some Proposals from Post-Feminism to Assyriology

***Session 10: Law and (Dis)Order in the Middle Assyrian Period***
*Chair: Heather Baker*
2:00–2:30 Yigal Bloch, Restoring Law and Order: The Weakening of the Assyrian Power in Hanigalbat in the Reign of Tukulti-Ninurta I and the King's Efforts to Restore Control over the Region
2:30–3:00 Jaume Llop, The Traveling King in the Middle Assyrian Archival Documentation
3:00–3:30 Jo Ann Scurlock, Not Even Her Own Jewelry: A Woman's Property in the Middle Assyrian Laws

*3:30–4:00 Coffee break*

***Session 11: Law and (Dis)Order in Ancient Near Eastern Geography***
*Chair: Hartmut Waetzoldt*
4:00–4:30 Karlheinz Kessler, Kar Assur and Artemita
4:30–5:00 Olof Pedersén, Digital Near East and Digital Babylon: Two Projects and Their Integration

***Workshop "Gender, Methodology, and Assyriology"***
*Organized by Saana Svärd and Agnès Garcia-Ventura*
*Chair: Eva Von Dassow*
4:00–4:30 Project Presentations
4:30–5:30 Round Table Discussion

***Session 12: Law and (Dis)Order in Ancient Near Eastern Mathematics and Medicine***
*Chair: Jo Ann Scurlock*
4:00–4:30 Maddalena Rumor, From Iqīšâ to Pliny the Elder: A Case of Dreckapotheke
4:30–5:00 Mathieu Ossendrijver, The Powers of 9 and 12: New Mathematical Discoveries from Babylon
5:00–5:30 Jan Tavernier, Disorder in the Head! Alcohol Abuse and Hangovers in the Ancient Near East
5:30–6:00 Mark Geller, Order and Algorithms in Babylonian Medicine

*7:00–11:00 Oriental Walking Dinner*

**Thursday, July 18**
***Session 13a: Law and (Dis)Order in the Neo-Assyrian Period***
*Chair: Mark Geller*
9:00–9:30 Eckart Frahm and Grant Frame, Some New Discoveries Related to the Inscriptions of Sargon II
9:30–10:00 Heather D. Baker, Disordered States? Homeland Security in the Neo-Assyrian Empire
10:00–10:30 Jon Taylor, The Library of Ashurbanipal Online

***Session 14a: Law and (Dis)Order in the Ancient Near Eastern Periphery***
*Chair: Hans Neumann*

9:00–9:30 Amanda Podany, Royal Involvement in Late Bronze Age Contracts from Syria

9:30–10:00 Eva Von Dassow, Alalah between Mittani and Hatti, c. 1400–1330 BCE

10:00–10:30 Lena Fijalkowska, Legal Fiction in Emar and Ekalte: A Source of Order or Disorder in the Legal System?

***Session 15a: Law and (Dis)Order in Ancient Near Eastern Divination and Omina***
*Chair: Wilfred van Soldt*

9:00–9:30 Netanel Anor, Foreseeing the Future, Controlling the Present: Omens as a Tool to Help Conceptualize Social Order

9:30–10:00 Alexandre Loktionov and Christoph Schmidhuber, Luminous Oils and Waters of Wisdom: Shedding New Light on Lecanomancy and Its Place in the Mesopotamian Intellectual Milieu

10:00–10:30 Gina Konstantopoulos, UDUG and LAMA: The Dual Nature of the *āšipu*'s Protective Spirits

*10:30–11:00 Coffee Break*

***Session 13b: Law and (Dis)Order in the Neo-Assyrian Period***
*Chair: Eckart Frahm*

11:00–11:30 Amitai Baruchi-Unna, Maintaining the Order: Gestures Toward Babylonia in the Imgur-Enlil Inscription of Shalmaneser III of Assyria

11:30–12:00 Krzysztof Hipp, For Each Runaway Assyrian Fugitive, Let Me Replace Him One Hundred-Fold: Fugitives/Runaways in the Neo-Assyrian Empire

12:00–12:30 Andrew Knapp, Why Did Esarhaddon Commission His Apology? Examining the Role of the Failed Egyptian Campaign

***Session 14b: Law and (Dis)Order in the Ancient Near Eastern Periphery***
*Chair: Richard Beal*

11:00–11:30 Lucia Mori, The Places of Order: Notes on the Legal Landscape of the Land of Ashtata

11:30–12:00 Paola Negri Scafa, To Be Guilty in Nuzi

***Session 15b: Law and (Dis)Order in Ancient Near Eastern Divination and Omina***
*Chair: Grant Frame*

11:00–11:30 Jeanette Fincke, Problems of Disorder: The Different Numbering Systems of the Omen Series Enuma Anu Enlil Revisited

11:30–12:00 Strahil Panayotov, New Features of Tablets with a Handle ("Amulet-Shaped Tablets"): Toward an Understanding of Their Function

*12:30–2:00 Lunch Break*

***Session 13c: Law and (Dis)Order in the Neo-Assyrian Period***
*Chair: Jon Taylor*
2:00–2:30 Stefania Ermidoro, The "Protocol for the Royal Banquet": Keeping Order at the King's Table
2:30–3:00 Reettakaisa Sofia Salo, Fremde Götter—eigene Götter: Zu den neuassyrischen Götterbeschreibungen
3:00–3:30 Sanae Ito, References to Treaties in a Letter from Assurbanipal

***Session 16: Archaeology Session***
*Chair: Amanda Podany*
2:00–2:30 Dlshad Marf Zamua, New Archaeological Evidence from the Land of Muṣaṣir (Preliminary Report on Fieldwork 2005–2012)
2:30–3:00 Simin Piran, A Steatite Axe Head from the Bronze Age Civilization in the Halil Rud River Basin, Jiroft

*3:30–4:00 Coffee Break*

*4:00–5:30 General Meeting International Association for Assyriology (IAA)*

## Friday, July 19

***Session 17: Law and (Dis)Order in the Old Babylonian Period***
*Chair: Anne Goddeeris*
9:00–9:30 Jared Miller, "May Inanna and Belet-Agade Set the Base of Your Throne": New Evidence on King Iluni of Eshnunna in the Old Babylonian Period
9:30–10:00 Rients De Boer, The Ikun-piša Letter Archive from Early Old Babylonian Sippar
10:00–10:30 Olga Drewnowska, Il était une fois à Ešnunna . . . : Un désordre dans le panthéon local de l'époque paléo-babylonienne

***Session 18: Law and (Dis)Order in Hatti***
*Chair: Jeanette Fincke*
9:00–9:30 Elena Devecchi, How Many Treaties? Considerations on the Corpus of the Hittite Treaties
9:30–10:00 Ilknur Tas and Veysel Dinler, The Assessment of Hittite Criminal Law According to Modern Paradigms
10:00–10:30 Vladimir Shelestin, The Parity Treaties Between Hatti and Kizzuwatna in the Light of Earlier Traditions

*10:30–11:00 Coffee Break*

***Session 19: Law and (Dis)Order in the Old Babylonian and Kassite Periods***
*Chair: Michel Tanret*
11:00–11:30 Sheyda Jalilvand Sadafi, Frauen als Erben in Susa
11:30–12:00 Elyze Zomer, Enmity Against Samsu-ditana

12:00–12:30 Susanne Paulus, Self-help, Prison, and Water Ordeal: A New Outlook on Kassite Trials

*12:30–1:00 Closing Session*

Wilfred van Soldt, Secretary International Association for Assyriology (IAA)

CHAPTER 1

# Foreseeing the Future, Classifying the Present: On the Concepts of Law and Order in the Omen Literature

Netanel Anor

THIS PAPER EXAMINES whether omen compendia were understood in ancient Mesopotamia as collections of divine laws. The second part discusses the concept of order as an important principal behind the composition of these compendia.

In ancient Mesopotamia the different phenomena in the universe were understood to be signs written by the gods and as rules that explain cosmic order or its possible destabilization. Understanding the meaning of these signs was of great value to Mesopotamian scholars. Therefore, in Old Babylonian times they initiated the great enterprise of collecting these signs into omen compendia. These sequences of omens were collections of signs revealed on earth or in the sky, in the sheep's liver or in the shapes of oil. So important was this literature that it was spread all over the ancient Near East. The dimensions of the omen series were impressive as well. One single composition could sometime gather thousands of omens on a collection of dozens of tablets.

These massive compendia remind us of another type of collections of entries that were also popular in the ancient Near East, the law collections. For this reason Jeannette Fincke (2006/2007) proposed that in antiquity omens were understood to be the "divine laws of divination." In her article "Omina, Die göttlichen 'Gestze' der Divination" she used several arguments in order to illustrate this point:

1. Both the omen compendia and the collections of laws are collections of *šumma* conditional sentences.
2. The namburbi ritual is understood in Mesopotamia as a juridical procedure. The metaphor, as Stefan Maul has pointed out, is of an appeal to the sun god against a former verdict. The incantation priest, *āšipu*, serves as an advocate of the man who is affected by the bad sign, the bad sign itself is seen as his opponent and the sun god serves as the judge.
3. Both omens and laws are based on precedents. The laws on former verdicts of human judges, and the omens on verdicts of the gods. Therefore the omens have to be seen as rules that gods gave to man in order to correctly interpret the ominous signs.

The trial metaphor is indeed made clear by the *ikribu* prayers, which are prayers that have an important role in the extispicy ritual. Ivan Starr (1983: 26), who edited the *ikribu*s, described them as "extispicy-prayer-cum-ritual." Since these prayers are often cited, I will only cite here a short passage from YOS 11, 22 that demonstrates this setting well:[1]

1. . . . $^{d}$utu *be-el di-nim*
2. $^{d}$iškur *be-el ik-ri-bi ù bi-ri-im*
3. *wa-ši-ib* $^{giš}$gu.za$^{meš}$ kù.zi *a-ki-il* $^{giš}$banšur $^{na4}$za.[gìn]
4. *tu-ur-ra-da-am ta-ak-ka-al tu-uš-ša*[*-ab*]
5. *i-na* $^{giš}$gu.za *ta-di-a-an di*[*-nam*]
6. *i-na ik-ri-ib a-ka-ra-bu*
7. *i-na te-er-ti e-pu*[*-šu*]
8. *ki-it-tam šu-uk-n*[*am*]

$^{26b}$Oh Shamash, lord of judgment, $^{27}$Oh Adad, lord of prayers and divination, $^{28}$who sit on the golden thrones and eat from the lapis-lazuli table. $^{29}$You will come down to us, eat and sit down. $^{30}$Then, on the golden throne you will give judgment. In the offering that I dedicate and in the oracle that I perform, place justice for me.[2]

No doubt, the ritual of evoking signs was understood in terms of a juridical procedure in which the sun god places his verdict in the different offering the *bārû* was using as medium to the gods' decision.[3] But how did this actually work? Were the marks themselves perceived as the verdict? The queries to the sun god suggest a more complex procedure. Those so-called queries are records of questions the Assyrian kings addressed to the sun god. Sometimes, the questions are followed or preceded by a report of the different features observed on the examined entrails, as could be observed in the following example (see Starr 1990: 265–266 n. 282):

K4

| | |
|---|---|
| 1. [be suhuš na] *šá-miṭ* gír gar | $^{1}$[The base of the "station"] is protruding pointedly. The "path" is present. |
| 2. [x x x] gar 150 ze *ṣa-mid* | $^{2}$[. . .] is present. The left of the gall bladder is attached. |
| 3. [be *ina* s]ag e[di]n 150 u $^{giš}$tukul<br>4. gar-*ma*<br>[sag] u igi [z]i-*ib*$^{?}$ kúr *kaš-du* | $^{3}$[If in the t]op of the left surface of the "finger" there is a "weapon"-mark that faces the [top] of the "finger": the enemy's [ons]laught will be successful. |
| 5. [be *ina* u]gu máš $^{giš}$tukul gar-*ma* ta<br>6. 15<br>[*ana* 1]50 *te-bi* erín-*ni hi-im-ṣa-ta* erín kúr kú | $^{5}$[If] there is a "weapon"-mark [abo]ve the "increment" which rises from right [to l]eft: my army will take the enemy's booty. |

1. The most recent publications are Steinkeller 2005, Wilcke 2007, and again Fincke 2009.
2. Unless otherwise noted, all translations are by the author.
3. Ulla Jeyes pointed out that different media for provoked divination are actually materials used as offering to the gods. See Jeyes 1991–1992: 23.

| | |
|---|---|
| 7. be *gíp-ši* 150 zé u$_5$ *gíp-ši* erín kúr *ana* kur-mu | [7]If the "mass" rides upon the left of the gall bladder: the mass of the enemy's army (will march) against my country. |
| 8. be *an.ta-ti* du-*ik* | [8]The upper part is *elevated.* |
| 9. be sa-*ti* ugu u.sag u$_5$ | [9]The "outside" rides upon the "cap." |
| 10. be *ina* 150 mur gìr gag.zag.ga sag-*sà* du$_8$ | [10]In the left side of the lung there is a "foot"-mark. The top of the breast-bone is split. |
| 11. be šà.nigin 14 šà udu.nitá *šá-lim* | [11]The coils of the colon are 14 in number. The heart of the ram is normal. |

---

| | |
|---|---|
| 12. be suhuš na *sa-miṭ ina* sag edin 150 u<br>13. $^{\text{giš}}$tukul gar-*ma* sag u igi | [12]The base of the "station" is protruding pointedly. In the top of the left surface of the "finger" there is a "weapon"-mark which faces the top of the "finger." |
| 14. be *gíp-ši* 150 zé u$_5$ | [14]The "mass" rides upon the left side of the gall bladder. |
| 15. be *ina* 150 mur gìr gag.zag.ga sag-*sà* du$_8$ | [15]There is a "foot"-mark in the left side of the lung. The top of the breast-bone is split. |
| 16. be *ina* dagal 150 u *ana* á edin u murub$_4$ bùr | [16]There is a hole in the wide part of the left side of the "finger" at the side of the middle surface of the "finger." |
| 17. [šu]b-*di* 5 tag$^{\text{meš}}$ *ina* šà | [17]There are 5 unfavorable features in the extispicy. |
| 18. [$^{\text{md}}$giš.nu$_{\text{II}}$]-mu-gi.na šeš *lá* gin<br>19. [*šá* kur] *i-dal-la-hu-ma* | [18][Šamaš]-šumu-ukin, unfaithful brother, who stirred up [the country] and caused major uprising, [. . .] . . . not good— |

r.

| | |
|---|---|
| 1. [sù]h gal-*ú i-pu-*[*šú*]<br>2. [x x x x]-*un-ni-i la ṭa-a-bu*<br>3. *i-*‹$^{\text{d}}$šeš$^{!}$›.ki-*na* $^{\text{m}}$an.šár-du-a man<br>4. *kur-aš-šur*<br>5. man dù-*ut* šu$^{\text{II}}$-*ka šá ana* tu$_{15}$-*ka* dùg.<br>6. ga<br>*ú-paq-qu u ki-di-in šá* zi-*ka*<br>*šit-ku-na* igi$^{\text{II}}$-*šu iš-mu-ú um-ma* | [3r.]now Assurbanipal, king of Assyria, a king created by you, who is attentive to your gentle breath and whose eyes are set on your personal protection, has heard: |
| 7. $^{\text{mgiš}}$nu$_{\text{II}}$-mu-gi.na *ana* kur.nim.ma$^{\text{ki}}$<br>8. *i-hal-liq a-mat-ú ša-lim-tu ši-i*<br>9. *ana* kur.nim.ma$^{\text{ki}}$ *i-hal-li-qí* | 7 "Šamaš-šumu-ukin is fleeing to Elam." Is the rumor true? Is he indeed fleeing to Elam? |
| 10. 4 tag$^{\text{meš}}$ *ina* šà *ul* dùg.ga | [10]5(!) unfavorable features in the extispicy. It is unfavorable. |

| | |
|---|---|
| 11. iti.du$_6$ ud-15-kám *lim-mu* $^{m}$ud-*gab* | [11]Month Tishri (VII), 15th day, eponym year of Sagab (651 ). |
| 12. $^{m}$*dà-ri*-lugal $^{m}$*dan-a-a* en-umuš | [12]Dari-šarru (and) Dannaya, reporters. |
| 13. dingir$^{meš}$ gal$^{meš}$ en$^{meš}$ eš.bar | [13]May the great gods, lords of decision, send their favorable decision daily to the king, my lord. |
| 14. ud-*mu-us-su* eš.bar-*šú-nu* | |
| 15. *šá* sig$_5$ *a-na* lugal *be-lí-iá* | |
| 16. *liš-tap-pa-ru-ú-ni* | |

Analyzing the structure of this text can give an idea of how ancient diviners might have come up with answers for the oracular questions they posed. We can see that this query is composed of several distinct elements. Lines 1, 2, 8–16 consist of a description of some sixteen elements of the entrails of the sacrificial lamb. Lines 3–4, 5–6, and 7 consist of citations from the omen compendia *Bārûtu*, which also deals with such elements. In line 17 the scribes refer to the sum of unfavorable signs. Lines 18 and 19 of the obverse and lines 1–9 of the reverse describe the rumors regarding Shamash-shumu-ukin and asking whether they are true. In other words, they consist of the oracular question and its background. The most important line is line 10 of the reverse, as it repeats the sum of the unfavorable signs and concludes whether the query is positive or negative. The end of the tablet consists of a date, the names of the scribes and greetings to the king.

In short, this suggests that not one sign was used in order to obtained an oracular decision. It was rather the combination of several signs that allowed the diviners to reach an answer of yes or no, to reach, if using the trial metaphor, a verdict. How to combine those signs is described in the last chapter of the series of liver omens, *bārûtu*, which is in a sense, a sort of manual for the diviner (Livingstone 1993: 108). Among other matters this chapter deals with the combination of the different protases and with matters of different meaning of protases according to context.[4]

When taking this into account it becomes harder to understand omens strictly in terms of divine laws. Laws are generally understood to have universal validity and their meaning is unaffected by context. But the case of omens is different since their meaning is of a more complex nature. The same sign can change, and sometimes even reverse its meaning when evaluated in context with other signs and can change validity according to time. The above-mentioned queries always report a sequence of ominous signs, because only the combination of such signs can lead to an oracular decision. In other words, an omen only has meaning in relation to another omen and by evaluating them, a judgment is obtained. On the other hand, it is impossible to find such application of laws in the ancient juridical procedure. The way laws were actually applied in trials is not entirely clear. But, what is clear is that laws were never cited in legal documents (Charpin 2010: 80). Still, it is hard to imagine that a combination of laws was taken into account, or that a judge thought that one law can reverse its meaning according to context.

Understanding omens as a witness or evidence in the trial is perhaps a better analogy. The earthly judge takes the different witnesses and exhibits into consideration in order to reach a verdict (Glassner 2012: esp. 39–46, dealing with *dīnum*). The oracular

4. Koch 2005: text nos. 34–89. For a discussion of those tablets, see pp. 48–52.

verdict could be thought to have been handled in a similar manner. Several omens would be combined into one decision understood to be that of the heavenly judge, Shamash. But, this does not necessarily means that omen compendia were considered to be collections of laws.

Now, back to the two literary genres in question, indeed, both laws and omens are phrased as a conditional sentence preceded by the particle *šumma*. But, recent studies have shown that this conditional structure functions differently in omens and in laws. Eran Cohen (2012) has thoroughly investigated the conditional structure in the Old Babylonian dialect. His commutation table (table 1.1) shows that in laws the hypothetical factor of the *šumma* construction is essentially missing. In other words, what happens in the apodosis is a direct result of what is described in the protasis and the question of whether the event described in the protasis occurred or not is essentially irrelevant (Cohen 2012: 151–152). Hence, Cohen understands laws in terms of "generic expressions" and as such he perceives them to be timeless (170).

On the other hand, Cohen finds the *šumma* construction to function differently in omen collections, as shown in table 1.2. First, he stresses that this table describing the different strategies to construct an omen sentence is unique (2012: 170). Second, he mentions that the generic nature of this structure is weaker in omens than in laws and that: "It is as though the abstraction phase, which takes place when formulating a specific case as a case of general validity, took place only partially" (154).

This could help to explain two other phenomena that are quite common in omens, but do not occur in law collections, and which, indeed, could be understood as exposing the preliminary phases of the art of phrasing the omen. The first is the use of

TABLE 1.1. Legal *šumma* structures: no tense involved.

<table>
<tr><th colspan="3">protasis</th><th colspan="3">apodosis</th></tr>
<tr><th>exponent</th><th>value</th><th>categories</th><th>exponent</th><th>value</th><th>categories</th></tr>
<tr><td>iprus</td><td>event(s)</td><td rowspan="4">aspect and modality</td><td>predicative</td><td>factual</td><td rowspan="4">modality</td></tr>
<tr><td>iptaras</td><td>chain-final event</td><td rowspan="3">iparras<br>NVC</td><td rowspan="3">modal (obligation / permission)</td></tr>
<tr><td>paris</td><td>state</td></tr>
<tr><td>iparras</td><td>intent (CH durative too)</td></tr>
</table>

TABLE 1.2. Omen *šumma* structures: No modality.

<table>
<tr><th colspan="3">protasis (= theme)</th><th colspan="3">apodosis (= rheme)</th></tr>
<tr><th>exponent</th><th>value</th><th>categories</th><th>exponent</th><th>value</th><th>categories</th></tr>
<tr><td>iprus/iptaras</td><td>resultative pf.</td><td rowspan="4">aspect</td><td>iprus</td><td>past</td><td rowspan="4">tense</td></tr>
<tr><td>iparras</td><td>durativity</td><td>paris</td><td>present</td></tr>
<tr><td>paris</td><td rowspan="2">unmarked state</td><td>iparras</td><td>future</td></tr>
<tr><td>NVC</td><td>NVC</td><td>future?</td></tr>
</table>

the first and second person in the two parts of the conditional sentence (Anor 2017). Although, some laws introduce direct speech, the description of the offence and the penal act are always given in the third person. But, in omens, the configuration of the ominous signs and their possible consequences are often described in relation to the diviner and his client and are therefore formulated in the first or second person. The second phenomenon occurs in the apodosis of an omen. Sometimes the apodosis is not a formal sentence at all. It consists of nothing other than a noun or a construction of two nouns in the nominative case. In this structure, which is unique for omens, the apodosis functions as the predicate, or the rheme, in Cohen's (2012: 161–163, 168–169) terminology, while the protasis is the subject, or the theme. The following sequence demonstrates this point well, since both phenomena are represented here:

64. DIŠ Ì *a-na ḫa-al-li-ka ir-ta-qí-iq uz-za-tum ṣi-bi-it ku-bi*
    If the oil thins up toward your thigh, (it is) rage, (or) the grasp of the "Kūbu-demon."
65. DIŠ Ì *a-na ḫa-al-li-ka pa-ṭi-ir ma-an-za-az* dNANNA
    If the oil is dispersed toward your thigh, (it is) the presence of Sîn.

This example demonstrates an additional difference between the phraseology of laws and omens. Sometimes, one sign can have two results. This could mean that one ominous sign can have more than one meaning and therefore have more than one implication on the human sphere. This actually fits well with a suggestion recently proposed by Mark Geller (2011) that the *šumma* sentence could sometimes express probability rather than causality. First, he points out the fact that this is often the case in medical texts that also use the *šumma* construction. Second, both he and Nils Heeßel (2010) understand at least some of the omens to be ambiguous regarding the certainty of their result, since they could have different validity according to time, as mentioned.[5] Laws, on the other hand, do not depend on timing. They are timeless. No matter when the offence took place the corrective act will remain the same (Cohen 2012: 122). They are, then, of a causal nature, and lack any aspect of probability. In other words, there is a constant mutual dependency between the protasis and the apodosis in laws and a causal nexus between the crime and its punishment. But, as far as omens are concerned, a relation of this kind is far from being the rule.

Now, let us summarize the different arguments:

Just like evidence and exhibits in a trial, the omens have different meaning according to the context and the time they are examined. Mesopotamian law on the other hand was perceived to be blind and depended neither on time nor context.

Omens contain several grammatical features that are absent in laws, namely the use of the first and second person as well as protases with a bare noun as a predicate.

Omens and law are both phrased as a *šumma* conditional sentence, but the syntactic structure in omens is different than that of the laws. Laws function as a generic expression; they are timeless and have no context. Therefore the *šumma* construction in the laws has strictly a causal meaning while in omen it could also express probability. This

5. For the edition of this chapter of the omen series *bārûtu*, see Koch 2005.

is also sustained by the fact that sometimes one protasis is followed by more than one apodosis.

The conclusion, therefore, is that the perspective that examines the omen compendia as a code of law does not provide us with the entire picture. The association between those genres seems to be of a more complex nature that is not unquestionably a relation of direct analogy. The notion that really links the two genres together is rather found in the second notion of this Rencontre's title, the notion of order. As Jean Bottéro (1974: 153) has pointed out:

> une divination fondée avant tout sur les efforts de l'homme, l'analyse des choses, leur étude en quelque sorte désintéressée et rationnelle, est tout à fait à sa place; même la forme littéraire qu'elle a finalement prise, celle des traités et des listes classifiées des présages, rejoint l'énorme littérature de " mise en ordre" dont les plus vieux témoins sont contemporains des tout premiers débuts de l'écriture.

The notion of order was indeed a basic principle that led the Mesopotamian society to the invention of writing. It is not by accident that in the beginning written documents were used in order to organize work and economy. This fact reveals the very nature of the written document in the context of its invention as a tool for establishing social order. Omen series were composed under similar conditions.

Up to this point, we have only discussed omen compendia in relation to extispicy. The omen compendia are often thought to belong to the domain of the *bārû*. But one has to keep in mind that performing extispicy is one task and collecting omens is another. In fact omens had a purpose in other circumstances than that of the oracular inquiry, since they seem to be useful in the process of the interpretation of unprovoked signs. Hence, it is perhaps better to understand the compendia as a tool for organizing this kind knowledge.

Indeed, we find that a big portion of this literature has little to do with evoking signs and was related to the occupation of various other experts. Many series actually relate to the expertise of the *ṭupšarru*, the astrologer/scribe. The activity of this kind of scholar is well known from the reports on astrological phenomena they sent to the Assyrian kings.[6]

A standard report would usually begin with a citation of an astrological omen, thus referring to the series *Enūma Anu Enlil*. Moreover, those experts were more than just astrologers. Sometimes, they would also cite terrestrial omens while referring to two additional series: *šumma ālu* and *šumma izbu* (Hunger 1992: xviii). Since the above mentioned namburbi ritual was sometimes appended to those same series (Maul 1994: 163), they should also be associated with yet a third expert, the *āšipu*, magician/exorcist, as this ritual was his responsibility.

The variety of scholars using these compendia and the way they refer to them reveal their function as a handbook or even better, an encyclopedia. Their main purpose is to organize knowledge into a scheme and thus give meaning to the phenomena in the cosmos. Just as man had achieved the ability to control society by means of the

6. For the edition of these reports see Hunger 1992.

administrative document, he attempted to grasp the universe by writing down omens. The very content of the omens alludes to the purpose of their composition. Good omens are related to the concept of order and they result in peace, stability, and victories for the king, with fertility of the land, or good health. Following the same logic, bad omens were generally associated with disorder. They result in rebellion, plague, invasion, and chaos. The main concept behind ancient law is the notion of the corrective act. It describes how order is reestablished after it had been breached. Omens, on the other hand lack this notion, because they have other purposes, they intend to reveal the rules of the cosmos and as such, they function as a tool of description and interpretation.

The act of extispicy is indeed perceived as a process of decision, but it also lacks the notion of correction, since it does not discuss an offence, but rather an answer to a specific question. Nevertheless, omens and laws do share a common ground, the notion of order. The first collection represents an attempt to understand the universal order of things while the last aims to idealize and thus maintain social order. The conclusion, therefore is that it is more effective to understand both genres as exhibiting different aspects of the notion of order, rather than to understand omens merely as divine laws.

## BIBLIOGRAPHY

Anor, N.
2017 Mesopotamian Divinatory Inquiry: A Private or a State Matter? Pp. 71–78 in *Private and State in the Ancient Near East: Proceedings of the 58th Rencontre Assyriologique Internationale at Leiden, 16–20 July 2012*. Edited by R. de Boer and J. G. Dercksen. University Park, PA: Eisenbrauns.

Bottéro, J.
1974 Symptômes, signes, écritures en Mésopotamie ancienne. Pp. 70–197 in *Divination et rationalité*. Edited by J.-P. Vernant. Paris: Éditions du Seuil.

Charpin, D.
2010 *Writing, Law, and Kingship in Old Babylonian Mesopotamia*. Translated by J. M. Todd. Chicago: University of Chicago Press.

Cohen, E.
2012 *Conditional Structures in Mesopotamian Old Babylonian*. LANE 4. Winona Lake, IN: Eisenbrauns.

Fincke, J.
2006/2007 Omina, Die göttlichen "Gestze" der Divination. *JEOL* 40: 131–147.
2009 Ist die mesopotamische Opferschau ein nächtlisches Ritual. *BO* 66: 519–558.

Geller, M.
2011 Review of *Divinatorische Texte I: Terrestrische, teratologische, physiognomische und oneiromantische Texte*, by N. Heeßel. *WO* 41: 117–121.

Glassner, J.-J.
2012 Droit et divination: Deux manières de rendre la justice; à propos de *dīnum*, *uṣurtum* et *awatum*. *JCS* 64: 39–56.

Heeßel, N.
2010 The Calculation of the Stipulated Term in Extispicy. Pp. 163–175 in *Divination and Interpretation of Signs in the Ancient World.* Edited by A. Annus. OIS 6. Chicago: Oriental Institute of the University of Chicago.

Hunger, H.
1992 *Astrological Reports to the Assyrian Kings*. SAA 8. Helsinki: Helsinki University Press.

Jeyes, U.
1991–1992 Divination as a Science in Ancient Mesopotamia. *JEOL* 32: 23–41.

Koch, U.
2005 *Secrets of Extispicy: The Chapter Multābiltu of the Babylonian Extispicy Series and Niṣirti bārûti Texts Mainly from Aššurbanipal's Library*. AOAT 326. Münster: Ugarit-Verlag.

Livingstone, A.
1993 The Case of the Hemerologies: Official Cult, Learned Formulation and Popular Practice. Pp. 97–113 in *Official Cult and Popular Religion in the Ancient Near East: Papers of the First Colloquium on the Ancient Near East; the City and Its Life, Held at the Middle Eastern Culture Center in Japan (Mitaka, Tokyo), March 20–22, 1992*. Edited by E. Matsushima. Heidelberg: Winter.

Maul, S.
1994 *Zukunftsbewältigung: Eine Untersuchung altorientalischen Denkens anhand der babylonisch-assyrischen Löserituale (Namburbi)*. BaF 18. Mainz: Zabern.

Starr, I.
1983 *The Ritual of the Diviner*. BMes 12. Malibu, CA: Undina, 1983.
1990 *Queries to the Sungod: Divination and Politics in Sargonid Assyria*. SAA 4. Helsinki: Helsinki University Press.

Steinkeller, P.
2005 Of Stars and Men: The Conceptual and Mythological Setup of Babylonian Extispicy. Pp. 11–47 in *Biblical and Oriental Essays in Memory of William L. Moran*. Edited by A. Gianto. BibOr 48. Rome: Pontificio Istituto Biblico.

Wilkce, C.
2007 Das Recht: Grunlage des sozial und politischen Diskurses im Alten Orient. Pp. 209–244 in *Der geistige Erfassen der Welt im Alten Orient: Sprache, Religion, Kultur und Gesellschaft*. Edited by C. Wilcke. Wiesbaden: Harrassowitz.

CHAPTER 2

# Le vol à l'époque paléo-babylonienne : L'application de la loi à travers la jurisprudence

Dalila Bendellal-Younsi

DANS LE DROIT moderne, le vol couvre un large éventail d'infractions allant du vol à l'étalage au vol à main armée. Cela est encore plus visible dans le Proche-Orient ancien. Pour le législateur mésopotamien, le vol recouvre plusieurs notions, telles que l'enlèvement, la fraude ou le recel. Il ne fait pas explicitement la distinction entre le vol simple, soit la prise de possession d'un bien appartenant à un tiers, et le vol aggravé, même s'il semble que ces notions lui étaient connues.

Cet article, s'intéresse avant tout au traitement réservé aux voleurs dans le droit de l'époque paléo-babylonienne, soit les quatre premiers siècles du deuxième millénaire avant notre ère, en Mésopotamie et en Syrie. Le code de Hammu-rabi (cité ci-après CH) et les lois d'Ešnunna (LE) donnent de nombreuses informations sur la manière dont les Mésopotamiens traitaient les affaires de vol (Roth 1995). Les études se sont beaucoup intéressées à cette documentation, ne citant que de manière ponctuelle les actes de la pratique. L'ambition du présent article de s'intéresser aux sources normatives et à la documentation de la pratique qui traitent du vol. Un grand nombre de documents de la pratique est en effet désormais accessible sur la base informatique ARCHIBAB, créée en 2008 (Charpin 2014), elle a permis de réunir de nombreux textes, de l'époque paléo-babylonienne, dont l'exploitation était difficile à cause de leur nombre (plus de mm32000 publiés à ce jour [Jacquet 2013: 65]) et de la dispersion de leur publication dans de nombreux recueils.

Nous examinerons, la manière dont le vol était exposé dans les lois, les procès et la documentation épistolaire, en insistant tout particulièrement sur les peines prévues (Charpin 2000: 69–111). Notre propos s'organisera en trois temps : la présentation du corpus disponible, l'étude des peines : peine capitale et amendes, enfin l'interprétation de ce corpus.

Le vol est, l'une des infractions, les plus documentées à l'époque paléo-babylonienne.[1] Cet article présente une partie du corpus disponible : quatre lois dans le recueil de lois d'Ešnunna. Des vols sont mentionnés dans au moins 5 procès et 41 documents épistolaires. La difficulté que l'on rencontre, lors de l'étude de la documentation épistolaire et des procès, provient de leur nature allusive : si les lettres retracent principalement les détails des affaires juridiques, ce que les procès ne font pas et donnent des éléments

*Note de l'auteur :* Cet article est un extrait de ma thèse intitulée : « Le droit pénal dans la première moitié du IIe millénaire: L'example du vol » dirigé par D. Lacambre et B. Lion à l'université de Lille (France). Je tiens à remercier D. Lacambre et B. Lion pour leur relecture de cet article.

1. Good 1967: 951. Il suggère que de nombreux cas de vol ne sont jamais allés jusqu'à une cour de justice et étaient réglés entre les parties.

TABLE 2.1. La présentation du corpus.

| **Les Lois** | |
|---|---|
| **LE** | § 12, § 13, § 40, § 60 |
| **CH** | § 6, § 7, § 8, § 9, § 10, § 12, § 13, § 21, § 22, § 23, § 24, § 25, § 34 |
| **Les Lettres** | |
| **Babylone** | AbB 6 181, AbB 9 109, AbB 10 192, AbB 14 107, TCL 1 164 |
| **Larsa** | AbB 1 76, AbB 9 266, AbB 13 12, AbB 14 144, AbB 14 146, TCL 11 245[a] |
| **Ešnunna** | DCS 115[b], TIM 4 33 |
| **Mari** | ARM 14 51, ARM 14 111, ARM 26/2 332, ARM 27 32, ARM 27 70, FM 6 4 |
| **Šaduppum** | SUMER 14 n° 28[c], YOS 14 40 |
| **Sippar** | AbB 1 30, AbB 1 101, AbB 7 85 |
| **Ur** | UET 5 254[d] |
| **Uruk** | AbB 8 82 |
| **Lieu de découverte incertain** | AbB 1 47, CT 48 23, TLB 1 144 |
| **Les Proces** | |
| **Ašdubba** | Riftin 46[e] |
| **Dilbat** | YOS 13 28 |
| **Larsa** | YOS 12 325 |
| **Nerebtum** | UCP 10/1 107 |
| **Nippur** | IM 28051[f] |

[a] Wilcke 1992: 59 et 73; Fortner 1997, 948–50; www.archibab.fr.
[b] Charpin 2000: 106–7.
[c] Charpin 2000: 106 ; Goetze 1958: 52–53 (n°28) [trs.], pl. 14–15 (n°28) [copie]; voir également Bendellal 2013: 79–80.
[d] Charpin 1986: 106.
[e] Démare-Lafont 2002am 74–75.
[f] Démare-Lafont 1999: 494 (trs. et trd.); Van Dijk 1962: 70–77 (trs., trd. et copie).

essentiels sur la procédure engagée, en revanche elles permettent rarement de connaître l'issue du litige. Or, il s'agit de la documentation la plus abondante concernant le vol.

## Le vol et son châtiment d'après les recueils de lois

En préambule à notre étude des actes de la pratique, il convient de revenir sur la résolution des affaires de vol à travers les textes législatifs. Les affaires se présentaient généralement dans une structure faisant intervenir trois personnes : le voleur, l'acheteur soupçonné de recel et la victime (Démare-Lafont 1999: 292). Le propriétaire d'un bien était dépossédé frauduleusement de son bien. Le voleur cédait à un tiers – innocent ou complice – l'objet qu'il avait dérobé. L'acheteur était accusé d'avoir commis le méfait, à charge pour lui de prouver le contraire en apportant des témoignages pour appuyer ses allégations. Les témoins des deux parties devaient prêter serment. Les juges étudiaient les dépositions. Dans le cas où les allégations de l'acheteur étaient vérifiées, le propriétaire de l'objet récupérait celui-ci, et l'acheteur pouvait prendre dans la maison de son vendeur l'équivalent de la somme qu'il avait perdue. Le vendeur, qui se révélait être le voleur, était condamné à la peine de mort. Enfin, l'acheteur qui aurait agi par complicité avec le vendeur était également condamné à la peine capitale.

Il s'agit d'un cadre général dont il convient de relever les exceptions :

- Le contrevenant pris en flagrant délit de vol en pleine journée devait s'acquitter de la somme de 10 sicles d'argent. Tandis que s'il était pris la nuit, il était condamné à la peine capitale (LE §12).
- Le voleur d'un bien rattaché à un temple ou au palais avait la possibilité de s'acquitter d'une peine du multiple, s'il ne pouvait pas payer, il était condamné à la peine capitale (CH §8).
- Lorsque le voleur mourrait, la victime pouvait prendre 5 fois la valeur du bien dérobé directement dans les biens du voleur (CH §12).
- Si le délinquant n'était pas pris, il incombait à la ville de compenser pécuniairement les pertes de la victime (CH §23).

En outre, le mode d'exécution de la peine de mort n'est jamais cité, en dehors des cas de vol en flagrant délit. Lors d'un incendie, par exemple, le coupable de vol pris sur le fait était directement jeté dans le feu.[2]

Enfin, la terminologie permet dans certains cas de distinguer le vol simple du vol aggravé. Le vol simple, exprimé par le verbe *šarāqum,* désigne la prise d'un objet ou d'un esclave par un tiers à l'insu de son propriétaire (Leemans 1957: 661–662).[3] Le vol aggravé, exprimé par le verbe *habātum,* désigne le cambriolage par la force, avec violence ou le pillage.[4] Cependant, le vol aggravé est souvent déduit de la peine infligée (plus sévère que pour un vol simple), de l'usage de la violence ou de la qualité de la victime.[5]

Les sources sont nombreuses pour l'étude de cette infraction. Nous avons donc choisi, dans ce qui suit, de nous limiter à l'étude des peines prévues, en laissant de côté les éléments permettant de comprendre ou d'analyser les affaires judiciaires.

## Les peines encourues d'après les documents de la pratique

Il s'agit de présenter les différentes peines prévues par les textes de manière à en déterminer les modalités d'applications.

2. Cf. CH § 25. Sur ce type de peine, voir Démare-Lafont 2005: 107. Noter également LE § 60 ; un garde est assigné à la surveillance d'une maison. Pendant son service un voleur entre dans la maison. Le garde n'ayant pas accompli son devoir correctement est condamné à être mis à mort, son corps est laissé sans sépulture devant l'endroit de la violation. De même CH § 21, le contrevenant perce le mur d'une maison : s'il est pris sur le fait, il doit être mis à mort et son corps est exposé devant l'endroit de l'infraction.

3. Pour une étude du verbe *šarāqum* voir Badamchi 2016.

4. Pour une étude du verbe *habātum* voir Cavigneaux 2017.

5. Cf. CH § 6, il s'agit du vol d'un bien d'un temple ou d'un palais, le contrevenant est condamné à la peine de mort. Dans cette affaire, le facteur aggravant concerne le fait que le dieu ou le palais sont visés, donc des institutions et non des personnes privées. Westbrook 2003: 120. Etudes sur les § 6 et 8 du CH : Driver et Miles 1956: 320.

### *La peine capitale*

La peine capitale n'est que peu attestée pour les affaires de vol. On examinera deux textes qui évoquent cette peine.

Tout d'abord, une lettre trouvée dans le palais de Mari, **FM 6 4 (= A. 402)**[6] concernant une exécution sommaire suite à un vol de grand chemin. Une tribu benjaminite, les Yahruréens, attaquait régulièrement les convois passant dans la région de Tuttul. Le roi de Mari Zimri-Lîm est informé de la situation, il a demandé de réunir l'assemblée locale, de ligoter les coupables et de les lui faire conduire afin qu'il se charge de les punir. Lanasûm, représentant du roi de Mari à Tuttul et expéditeur de la lettre, réunit donc l'assemblée, mais voyant que les pillards ne sont pas entravés et ne se dirigent pas vers Mari, il les fait exécuter.

> (22–30) A propos de cette affaire, j'ai rencontré ces hommes en pleine route. Il n'y avait pas une corde à leur taille. Je n'ai rien pris dans leurs mains. En outre, il n'y avait pas leur « jugeur ». J'ai étranglé ces hommes afin qu'ainsi, à l'avenir, un autre redoute de porter la main sur quoi que ce soit.
> (31–37) J'ai donné 5/6e de mine et 1 sicle d'argent aux marchands pillés. Et, le jour même, j'ai terminé leur affaire. Et à partir du moment où le marchand avait fait entrer son argent dans le temple de Dagan, c'est devant Dagan que l'argent reposait. J'ai fait ce qu'il y avait à faire.

Ensuite, dans une lettre d'Ešnunna, TIM 4 33, il s'agit d'une affaire de vol de sésame.[7] Le voleur ne garde pas la marchandise volée pour lui et la remet à une femme de sa connaissance. Cette dernière transmet à son tour le sésame à un tiers. Le propriétaire retrouve le voleur initial et la femme. Il les mène devant la cour, le voleur admet avoir commis le méfait alors que sa complice présumée nie toute connaissance de ce vol.

> (12–14) Šamaš-muštepiš (a dit) ceci : « J'ai volé le sésame et je l'ai transporté dans la maison de Ahatum. » [...] (29–33) Du fait que Šamaš-muštepiš a volé le sésame la nuit, qu'il a reconnu le vol par sa déclaration, il payera [...] sicles d'argent [*et s'il ne peut pas payer*] il sera tué.

### *Les amendes*

La sanction qui prédomine pour le vol est finalement la compensation pécuniaire, qui est d'ailleurs aussi envisagé dans TIM 4 33 présenté ci-dessus. On examinera trois textes concernant cette peine.

Tout d'abord, une lettre de Šaduppum (actuelle Tell Harmal), **YOS 14 40 (JCS 14 60 ; NBC 82 57)**.[8] Un certain Sîn-eribam a été pris en possession d'un bien volé à un

6. Charpin 2012: 1–22. Traduction de S. Démare-Lafont 2002: 89. Voir également www.archibab.fr (consulté 03/2014).

7. Passage cité dans Roth (2001: 411). Voir également H. Petschow 1972–1975: 249.

8. Première édition par Simmons 1978: 28–29 (n°60). Voir également www.archibab.fr (consulté 03/2014).

certain Ilšu-naṣir. Il a tenté de se disculper en affirmant que son associé lui avait donné l'objet avant de s'enfuir à Babylone.

> (6–7) Les juges lui ont rendu un verdict et lui ont infligé une amende de 1/3 de mine d'argent et 4 sicles d'argent.
> (8–11) Igihluma, le maire de Zaralulu, est venu à Šaduppum. Concernant Sîn-eribam, sur (la somme de) 1/3 de mines d'argent et 4 sicles d'argent, il a mesuré 10 GUR d'orge.

Ce même type de sanction est évoqué dans deux procès. Le premier est un procès pour vol de l'époque d'Ibal-pî-El II d'Ešnunna, provenant de Nerebtum (actuel Ischali) **UCP 10/1 107** (Roth 2001: 412):

> (7–9) Taribum [son fils] devant la ville et les Anciens a dit: « je suis le voleur ! ».
> (10–14) Du fait qu'il a déclaré « j'ai volé ! » et que le bien volé a été saisi [dans sa main], la ville et les Anciens devant la hache de Sîn et l'arme [d']Išarkidiššu, l'ont donné en compensation à Ilušunaṣir.

Le deuxième, **YOS 12 325 (=YBC 5577)**,[9] concerne un vol de grains, de sésame et de tablettes appartenant à un certain Ibbi-Anna à Ešnunna. La tablette est datée de l'an 10 de Samsu-iluna. Le contrevenant, Ali-banišu, a prêté serment de ne pas avoir fait entrer chez lui les marchandises volées. Cependant, il ne s'est pas présenté devant la cour au terme fixé, il est donc condamné à donner à la victime ce qu'elle lui demandera.

> (20–22) « Il n'est pas venu le 10/xi et n'a pas offert de compensation: il (=Ali-banišu) devra (donc) lui fournir tout ce qu'il (=Ibbi-Anna) lui a réclamé ».

Nous avons sélectionné ces textes, afin de donner une vue d'ensemble de la matière étudiée. Toutefois, un corpus plus large pourrait bien évidemment permettre d'apporter certaines nuances.

## Interprétation du corpus

### *La peine capitale*

En définitive, la peine de mort serait la sanction encourue en cas de vol commis dans des circonstances aggravantes: vol de grand chemin, vol commis la nuit (Westbrook 2003: 419) ou impliquant un certain type de victimes.

En effet, comme on a pu le voir dans la lettre de Mari, le vol avec violence, implique des facteurs différents de ceux du vol simple. Ces exactions étaient perpétrées par des brigands généralement étrangers, ou du moins de passage. Ils étaient donc rarement attrapés

9. Voir www.archibab.fr (consulté 03/2014).

et, lorsque c'était le cas, il convenait d'agir avec rigueur.[10] D'ailleurs, la justice est rendue directement par le gouverneur. Il n'y a pas de jugement et le gouverneur dédommage les victimes de leurs pertes. De même, les codes de lois appliquent une procédure différente lorsqu'il s'agit de vol avec violence. En effet, si les voleurs ne sont pas retrouvés, la victime, après avoir prêté serment, peut se faire compenser ses pertes par le maire de la ville sous la juridiction duquel le méfait a été commis. Enfin, si, durant ce vol, le voleur a commis un meurtre, la ville doit donner une compensation financière à la famille de la victime.[11] Au contraire, lors d'un vol simple, il appartient aux victimes de saisir la justice et d'obtenir gain de cause. Il n'y a pas d'indemnisation prévue (Westbrook 2003: 421) en dehors du cas où la victime se rembourse directement sur les biens du voleur.

En ce qui concerne les exactions commises la nuit, les textes législatifs sont très clairs, le fautif doit être condamné à la peine de mort : LE §12 et LE §13 stipulent qu'un homme pris en flagrant délit de vol dans la maison ou le champ d'un *muškenum* en plein jour doit payer une amende, mais surpris en pleine nuit, il doit mourir.[12] La journée, le prétendu voleur pouvait avoir des circonstances atténuantes, il avait le droit à un interrogatoire et à un jugement. Par contre, de nuit, l'intrus n'avait aucune raison de se trouver sur une propriété privée, le propriétaire pouvait et avait même le devoir de défendre ses biens et sa vie, conformément au droit coutumier qui veut qu'un chef de famille doive protéger ce qui lui appartient. Cependant, le texte d'Ešnunna permet au contrevenant de payer une compensation au lieu d'être condamné à la peine capitale. Cette peine serait probablement un châtiment dissuasif, destiné à empêcher que ce genre d'infractions ne se produise régulièrement. Il s'agit d'un vestige de la justice privée, lorsque l'homme devait assurer seul sa survie et celle de sa famille.

Les sources ne permettent pas de déterminer pourquoi la peine de mort n'était que peu appliquée dans la documentation épistolaire ou dans les procès. Deux possibilités s'offrent à nous : d'une part attribuer cela à la nature lacunaire des sources qui ne fournissent que rarement la peine infligée. D'autre part, on peut supposer que la peine de mort ne serait finalement qu'une peine d'exception.

## *Les amendes*

Les amendes infligées aux voleurs représentaient un montant assez élevé. Elles avaient un rapport direct avec la valeur du bien volé. Dans la lettre de Šaddupum, la somme demandée, 1/3 de mine d'argent et 4 sicles, n'est pas ronde, ce qui suggère qu'elle est liée au prix de la marchandise volée.

D'ailleurs, le concept même d'amende suppose qu'elle excède largement le dommage ou qu'elle s'ajoute à l'indemnité. Effectivement, si le contrevenant n'avait qu'à compenser le dommage que son acte illicite a causé à autrui, il ne serait pas vraiment

10. Exemple de vol avec violence : la lettre AbB 13 181 relate l'affaire d'un individu qui vole une dague de bronze pendant un affrontement, commet un meurtre, puis s'enfuit avec l'arme. Dans cette affaire c'est le verbe *habātum* qui est employé, il s'agit donc d'un vol avec violence. Le contrevenant s'enfuit et n'est vraisemblablement pas rattrapé.

11. Cf. CH § 22 à 24.

12. Le caractère aggravant de l'infraction commise la nuit se retrouve également dans l'Ancien Testament, Exode 22: 1–3 envisage une affaire de vol d'animaux ; il est stipulé que (de nuit) le voleur peut parfaitement être frappé à mort sans que son agresseur risque d'être pénalisé, tandis que, si ce vol a lieu en plein jour et que le propriétaire de la maison tue le voleur, il est considéré comme coupable d'agression.

puni. Cependant, la peine pécuniaire, lorsqu'elle est de 10 fois le prix du bien substitué, est définitivement punitive. D'autres facteurs, plus « moraux » entrent en considération dans la conclusion des affaires (cf. CH §253 à §255), tels que le statut social de la personne volée, la valeur du bien volé ou même le lien existant entre la victime et le voleur (Versteeg 2000: 113).

L'amende peut également être remplacée par la mise en esclavage (UCP 10/1 107) du délinquant ou de l'un ses proches, pour compenser de sa personne la perte occasionnée.[13] Tout comme dans un esclavage pour dette, le voleur était probablement libéré dès qu'il avait remboursé la somme convenue avec la victime.

### *Peine capitale et/ou amende*

En somme, la question qui se pose est : dans quel cas appliquer la peine de mort, l'amende ou même les deux ? Le choix recoupe-t-il la distinction entre vol simple ou vol aggravé, l'amende s'appliquant au vol simple et la peine de mort au vol aggravé ? Cela pourrait être une réponse, d'après l'étude des textes législatifs. Cependant, le procès d'Ešnunna qui concerne un vol aggravé, laisse tout de même la possibilité au coupable de régler une amende. Il peut s'agir ici de l'expression de deux traditions juridiques distinctes :[14] l'une basée sur la peine capitale et les châtiments corporels et l'autre basée sur les amendes. Il convient d'ailleurs de souligner que plusieurs traditions juridiques ont coexisté lors de la période paléo-babylonienne. C'est pour cela que géographiquement, on ne peut pas parler d'un droit unitaire pour une infraction donnée. En effet, il faut avoir à l'esprit que nous avons affaire à plusieurs « environnements juridiques » et de ce fait à plusieurs droits. Autrement dit, les règles régissant la vie dans la société n'étaient pas uniformes, les droits cunéiformes ne s'inscrivaient pas dans un seul système global mais dans des sociétés plurielles.

La priorité est donnée au paiement d'une somme pécuniaire mais le châtiment corporel ou la mise à mort demeure le dernier recours. Bien que les sources soient peu nombreuses à faire état de la peine capitale, on ne peut pas dire qu'elle n'était pas appliquée. Les amendes étant souvent d'un montant assez élevé, tous les contrevenants ne pouvaient certainement pas s'en acquitter.

## Conclusion

Le traitement du vol dans les textes législatifs trouve un écho partiel dans les actes de la pratique. Toutefois, la peine capitale est loin d'être aussi présente que le laissent supposer les codes de lois. La confrontation de la documentation de la pratique aux textes normatifs prend toute son importance dans l'étude du droit pénal.

13. On peut comparer cette situation à l'esclavage pour dette mentionné dans CH § 117, dans les deux cas, la force de travail de la personne asservie compense ou remplace un payement. Voir également Westbrook 1996.

14. Westbrook et Wilcke 1974–1977: 112 ; Westbrook 2003: 420. Dans cette étude des § 6 et 8 du CH, R. Westbrook évoque cette existence de deux traditions juridiques distinctes. En effet, dans le § 6 le voleur devait savoir qu'il s'appropriait les biens d'une institution alors que dans le § 8, il pouvait arguer ne pas savoir d'où venaient les marchandises volées. Ainsi la différence est due au statut de la victime du vol.

Une étude plus poussée des sources permettrait peut-être de répondre à plusieurs interrogations : La répartition géographique des sources permet-elle de déterminer une zone d'influence des lois de Babylone et Ešnunna ? De même, en quoi l'environnement géographique influe-t-il sur les sanctions des infractions pénales ? Enfin, le contexte influe-t-il sur la peine infligée ? Il serait intéressant de répondre à ces interrogations non seulement pour une infraction précise mais aussi pour le droit pénal mésopotamien en général.

## BIBLIOGRAPHIE


Badamchi, H.
2016. The Meaning of "Theft" in Ancient Near Eastern Law. *Folio Orientalia* 53: 369–386.

Bendellal, D.
2013 Les lois d'Ešnunna, un recueil de lois destiné à être appliqué? *NABU* 2013.3: 79–80.

Cavigneaux, A.
2017 À tâtons dans le noir. À la recherche du sens de *ḫabātum*. Pp. 12–36 in *The First Years: A Sumerian Celebration in Honor of Miguel Civil*. Édité par F. Lluis, K. Fumi, et R. Gonzalo. SANER 12. Berlin: de Gruyer.

Charpin, D.
1986 *Le Clergé d'Ur au siècle d'Hammurabi: (XIXe–XVIIIe siècles av. J.-C.)*. HEO 22. Genève: Droz.

2000 Lettres et procès paléo-babyloniens. Pp. 69–111 dans *Rendre la justice en Mésopotamie, archives judiciaires du Proche-Orient ancien (IIIe–Ier millénaires avant J.-C.)*. Édité par F. Joannès. Temps et Espaces. Saint-Denis: Presses Universitaires de Vincennes.

2012 Amendes et châtiments prévus dans les contrats paléo-babyloniens. Pp. 1–22 dans *La Faute et sa punition: Colloque Collège de France, CNRS, Société Asiatique de juin 2010*. Édité par J.-M. Durand, T. Römer et J.-P. Mahé. Publications de l'Institut du Proche-Orient ancien du Collège de France 1. Louvain: Peeters.

2014 The Historian and the Old Babylonian Archives. Pp. 24–58 dans *Documentary Sources in Ancient Near Eastern and Greco-roman Economic History: Methodology and Practice*. Édité par H. D. Baker et M. Jursa. Oxford: Oxbow.

Démare-Lafont, S.
1999 *Femmes, droit et justice dans l'Antiquité orientale: Contribution à l'étude du droit pénal au Proche-Orient ancien*. OBO 165. Fribourg: Éditions Universitaires; Göttingen: Vandenhoeck & Ruprecht.

2002a Enlèvement et séquestration à l'époque paléo-babylonienne. Pp. 69–88 dans *Recueil d'études à la mémoire d'André Parrot*. Édité par D. Charpin et J.-M. Durand, FM 6. Paris: Société pour l'étude du Proche-Orient ancien.

2002b Un cas d'exécution sommaire à Tuttul. Pp. 89–92 in *Recueil d'études à la mémoire d'André Parrot*. Édité par D. Charpin et J.-M. Durand. FM 6. Paris: Société pour l'étude du Proche-Orient ancien.

2005 La peine par le feu dans les droits cunéiformes. *Ktema* 30: 107–116.

Dijk, J. van.
1962 Neusumerische Gerichtsurkunden in Bagdad. *ZA* 55: 70–90.

Driver, G. R. and Miles, J. C.
1956 *The Babylonian Laws*, vol. 1: *Legal Commentary*; vol. 2: *Transliterated Text*. Ancient Codes and Laws of the Near East. Oxford: Clarendon, 1956.

Fortner, J. D.
1997 Adjucating Entities and Levels of Legal Authority in Lawsuit Records of the Old Babylonian Era. Thèse. Hebrew Union College—Jewish Institute of Religion.

Goetze, A.
1958 Fifty Old Babylonian Letters from Harmal. *Sumer* 14: 1–76.

Good, E. M.
1967 Capital Punishment and Its Alternatives in Ancient Near Eastern Law. *Stanford Law Review* 19: 947–977.

Jacquet, A.
2013 Family Archives in Mesopotamia During the Old-Babylonian Period. Pp. 63–86 dans *Archives and Archival Documents in Ancient Societies.* Édité par M. Faraguna. Trieste: Edizioni Università di Trieste.

Leemans, W. F.
1957 Some Aspects of Theft and Robbery in Old Babylonian Documents. Pp. 661–666 in vol. 2 of *Scritti in onore di Giuseppe Furlani 2*. Édité par G. Bardi. *RSO* 32. Rome: Università di Roma. Istituto di Studi Orientali.

Petschow, H.
1972–75 Hehlerei. *RlA* 4: 247–251.

Roth, M. T.
1995 *Law Collections from Mesopotamia and Asia Minor.* WAW 6. Atlanta: Scholars Press.
2001 The Because Clause: Punishment Rationalization in Mesopotamian Laws." Pp. 407–412 in *Veenhof Anniversary Volume: Studies Presented to Klaas R. Veenhof on the Occasion of His Sixty-Fifth Birthday*. Édité par W. H. van Soldt. Leyde: Nederlands Instituut voor het Nabije Oosten.

Schorr, M.
1971 *Urkunden des Altbabylonischen Zivil und Prozessrechts.* Édition revisée. VAB 5. Hildesheim: Olms.

Simmons, S. D.
1978 *Early Old Babylonian Documents*. YOS 14. New Haven: Yale University Press.

Versteeg, R.
2000 *Early Mesopotamian Law*. Durham, NC: Carolina Academic Press.

Westbrook R.
1996 ziz.da/*kiššâtum*. *WZKM* 86: 449–459.
2003 *A History of Ancient Near Eastern Law*. 2 vols. HdO 72. Leiden: Brill.

Westbrook, R. et Wilcke, C.
1974–77 The Liability of an Innocent Purchaser of Stolen Goods in Early Mesopotamian Law. *AfO* 25: 111–121.

Wilcke, C.
1992 Dieber, Räuber und Mörder. *Xenia* 32: 53–78.

CHAPTER 3

# "Let the Sleeping Dogs Lie" or the Taboo (NÍG.GIG=*ikkibu*) of the Sacredness of Sleep as Order and Noise at Night ("*tapage nocturne*") as Disorder in Some Ancient Near Eastern Texts

Daniel Bodi

## Elements from the History of Research

The earlier scholarly discussion on the topic of noise in Akkadian texts centered in particular on the meaning of the term *ḫubūru* "din, clamor" in the Old Babylonian Atraḫasis epic. The Assyriologists and biblical scholars interested in the reasons for the flood debated whether the term has a moral or metaphorical connotation like "*Böses treiben*," "to practice evil" as suggested by G. Pettinato (1968: 165–200), subsequently given the status of "*mythologème*" of human rebellion against the gods by V. Afanasieva (1996: 89–96) and reiterated as "*sündhaftes Lärm*" by E. Cancik-Kirschbaum (2009: 141–150). In her PhD dissertation, A.-C. Rendu Loisel (2010) analyzed most of the sound and noise vocabulary like *ḫabāru* "to make noise, clamor," *hawû* (*AHw*, "to howl") "to buzz, to drone," *ḫabābu* "to twitter" also applied to water, *hazû* "to whistle," *ramāmu* "to growl," *šagāmu* "to roar," and a plethora of different bird sounds.

Building on P. Machinist's (1983: 221–226) insight with respect to the Poem of Erra where noise and silence are symbols of action and inaction, P. Michalowski (1990: 381–396) analyzed the two Akkadian words for "noise" in Enuma Elish: *rigmu* and *ḫubūru*. He concentrates in particular on the statement found in Enuma Elish I 133//II 19 *ummu ḫubur pātiqat kalama* "Mother *ḫubur* who fashions all things." He explains *ḫubur* as the absolute state from *ḫubūru*, just as Ti'amat is the absolute state of *tâmtu*. "Hence, when Ti'amat springs into action she is 'mother noise, who fashions all things'" (Michalowski 1990: 386). He points out the homonymic and synonymic relationships between terms by placing these lines in conjunction with Enuma Elish I 4 seen as being semantically parallel: *mummu ti'āmat muallidat gimrīšun* "(And) *mummu* Ti'amat who bore them all." In his view, *mummu* would be another word for noise, a synonym of *ḫubūru* and *rigmu* as well as an anagram, and in a sense a homonym for *ummu*, while *gimrīšun* is taken as an anagram for *rigmu*. His reasoning is based on two texts, first on CT 13 32 rev.10, that equates *mu-um-mu*/*rig-mu* and second, on a bilingual text where the Sumerian word for noise is $MU_7$-$MU_7$. Michalowski understands the noise in Enuma Elish as a metaphor for activity and creation. In this context one may add a Louvre Sumerian text which prompted A. Cavigneaux (1987: 46) to put in parallel DÉ = $ABZU_X$ with DÉ = ÚMUN, where Sumerian ÚMUN corresponds to Akkadian *mummu*, understood as "*science technique*," the technical knowledge or the know-how, being also the epithet of Ti'amat as in Enuma Elish and of Enki/Ea.[1]

In my work on *The Book of Ezekiel and the Poem of Erra* (Bodi 1991), I compared the Hebrew term *hāmôn* in Ezekiel meaning both "noise, clamor" and "crowd," which prompts YHWH to destroy Jerusalem's population, with Akkadian *ḫubūru*, which provokes the destruction of humans in Erra and Atraḫasis. My chapter 5 (117–161) on "Hebrew *hāmôn* and Akkadian *ḫubūru/rigmu* 'noise, din,'" provides the history of research with an analysis of about twenty authors and a summary of the debate at that time (Kilmer, von Soden, Cassin, Moran, Oden, etc.). Here I will analyze the terms *ḫubūru* and *rigmu* in their connotation of "disorder, mayhem, uproar, night racket" in relationship with an ancient Near Eastern taboo of the sacredness of sleep.

There are a couple of articles dealing with the motif of the sleeping god: one by B. Batto (1987: 153–177), a joint article by A. Mrozek and S. Votto (1999: 415–419), another by T. Oshima (2014: 271–289), and a long article on Sumerian and Akkadian terms for sleep, beds, divine abodes, and for the sleep motif by U. Steinert (2010: 245), bearing on our topic. Steinert mentions Weidner Chronicle describing Marduk's wrath against Sargon I of Agade. Marduk made people rebel against his rule and punished him with sleeplessness *la ṣalāla īmid*[*su*] (Grayson 1975: 149 [Chronicles 19:52–53b]; 154 [Chronicles 20:20–23]). This conjunction between rebellion and sleeplessness is significant and could be seen as an outworking of a curse and punishment on someone who committed a sacrilege. Weidner Chronicle 51–56, blames Sargon for having built a city "in front of Akkad" and naming it Babylon (Grayson 1975: 145–151 Chronicle 51–56). Sargon's building activity is considered as a sacrilegious act. Batto has combined the divine complaint about being deprived of sleep and the divine rest *nâḫu* "to rest." He interprets the disturbance of the divine sleep in Mesopotamia as a challenge to divine authority. However, it is more than this. As I will try to show, in the ancient Near East, to disturb divine or human sleep at night amounts to transgressing a major taboo. The night racket and sleep taboo relationship might be the key that opens our correct understanding of the noise motif and the divine punishment related to the flood in the Atraḫasis epic.

Mrozek and Votto tried to differentiate between two literary motifs: (1) the topos of the god who wants to sleep but cannot do so because of the riot and (2) the god who has to be awakened because the rebels are at his door. This distinction is somewhat artificial since in both cases the god Enlil or Enki have to be awakened because the rioters, human or divine, are either besieging their abode or are at the door. The basic underlying theme is disturbing someone's sleep at an inappropriate moment, due to some form of racket and upheaval. They brought into discussion the Sumerian composition Enki and Ninmah, where the lower gods refuse to dig the canals, rebel, and break their tools. Namma, the primordial mother who gave birth to the gods goes to wake up her son Enki and tell him to create humans who would assume the corvée type of work of digging the canals (Kramer 1989: 31–7).

1. The term *ḫubur* in Enuma Elish I 133//II 19 would stand for "*la matière première de creation*" (A. Cavigneaux pers. comm.).

## The Taboo of the Sacredness of Sleep ("Heiligkeit des Schlafes") as Order

There is an Akkadian text in a mythological explanatory work that confirms the existence of a taboo of not waking the sleeper.

> 28 $^{\text{giš}}$I.DIB É $^{d}$*en-me-šár-ra ina* ⌜É⌝.[S]IG$_4$ *i-lul*
> 29 *ṣal-lu id-ki* NÍG.GIG $^{d}$*en-me-šár-ra*
>
> He hung the ladders of the house of Enmesharra on the wall,
> and woke up the sleeper: Taboo of Enmesharra.
> SAA 3: 100, no. 39 (= *KAR* 307), obv. 28–29:[2]

A. Livingstone (1989: 100; 1991: 1) explains the expression *ṣallu idki*, "woke up the sleeping one," as a euphemism for "the dead," and "to wake the sleeper" means "to disturb the dead." He attempts to prove his point in a roundabout way. That the Mesopotamian literary tradition likens sleep to death is known already from the Gilgamesh epic. The hero Gilgamesh who desired immortality was unable to fend off sleep (XI 200–4), intimating that his quest was going to end in failure; death is his fate.

The taboo of not waking up the sleeper, however, before applying to the dead first concerns the living. The taboo applies in both cases: do not disturb the sleeper either dead or alive and particularly at night. Enmesharra is a chthonic, underworld divinity, and to call this transgression the NÍG.GIG $^{d}$*Enmešarra* "Taboo of Enmesharra," indicates that if you wake a sleeping person you may end up raising hell.[3] This is one of the ways the taboo functions, designated by another term *assakku*. The one who transgresses the *assakku*-taboo is attacked by the *assakku*-demon. D. Charpin (1997: 85–96) has clarified this conjunction in his article on "Manger un serment."[4]

The expression "do not wake the sleeper: Taboo of Enmesharra" should be compared with similar expressions about prohibited behavior like, *nāra la ibbir . . . ikkib* $^{d}$*Ea* "do not cross the river: Taboo of Ea" (sin against Ea) (*KAR* 178 rev. iv 42).

> *ṭuppī la taṭappil girgin[akku] la taparraru* [NÍG.GI]G=*ikkibu* $^{d}$*Ea šar apsî* "do not get my tablet dirty, do not scatter my library: Taboo of Ea, king of the Apsû (*Anatolian Studies* 6 158:11–13).

> *summata tarlugalla la ikkal qāt ili iṣabbasu ikkib* $^{d}$*Nedu* "he shall eat neither pigeon not rooster, or else pestilence will seize him: Taboo of Nedu (sin against Nedu, the chief doorkeeper of the netherworld) (*KAR* 178 rev. iv 54, hemer.).[5]

2. The verb is *ṣalālu, CAD* Ṣ, s.v., 1, "to lie asleep," "to remain inactive," but also "to sleep with a woman."

3. The English metaphor, "Let the sleeping dogs lie," captures some of this meaning of raising hell, and of incurring big trouble if you wake a sleeping dog. I thank JoAnn Scurlock for this suggestion.

4. The expression in *ARMT* 26/1 52:10 *a-sa-ak be-lí-ia a-na pí-šu-nu aš-ku-u*[*n*] "I have put in their mouth the taboo of my lord," means to commit a major fault (Durand 1988: *ARMT* 26.1, 195 n. b).

5. *CAD* I and J, s.v. "*ikkibu,*" 1. Another example quoted on p. 56, "*la ta-pa-šiṭ* (NÍG.GIG=*ikkibu*) $^{d}$*Nisaba* do not efface (the tablet) it is a sin against Nisaba (the patron goddess of scribes) *RA* 15 75:14" does not match the reference in *RA*.

Akkadian texts known as the Prayers to the Gods of the Night, dating from Old Babylonian times, describe the order of the world at night (Dossin 1935: 179–187; von Soden 1936: 305–308; Horowitz 2000: 194–206; Oshima 2014: 279 n. 42). The noise and the busyness of the day with it humming sound of bustling human activity cease during the night. That should be the usual state of affairs and represents the norm: (line 3) *ḫa-ab-ra-tum ni-šu-ú ša-qú-um-ma-a* "The noisy/busy people (during the daytime) are (now) silenced (at night)."[6] The bolts of cities and houses are lowered, rings set in place, gates closed.

The great gods who ordinarily control the affairs of the world Shamash, Sîn, Adad and Ishtar, are resting at night, they "have betaken themselves to the 'lap of heaven'" an unseen interior portion of heaven (lines 6–7). "The temple and the most holy places are quiet and dark" (line 11) For the act of divination carried out at night the gods of the night represented by several stars and constellations (Gibil, Erra, Pleiades, Orion, Ursa major, lines 17–20), are invited to witness the performance and reveal the truth in the sacrificed lamb. M. Weippert (1983: 279–289; 1984: 75–87), compared this apparent inactivity of the great gods at night with Enlil not exercising his divine jurisdiction during the night in Atraḫasis I 57–84. When in the midst of the night the Igigi with their torches approach and besiege his temple, Kalkal the bolt-keeper slides the bolt, peeps through the door and observes the riot going on outside. He first warns Enlil's vizier Nusku who in turn wakes up his master, the god Enlil.

For the ancient Mesopotamians, however, when Ishtar goes to sleep she does not really sleep. She is only retiring to her chambers and continues keeping an eye on human lovemaking, protecting it, which is one of her major divine activities.

One should not attribute to the ancient Mesopotamians extreme naïveté and assume that they believed their gods needed to sleep. They understood that at least the high gods did not sleep in the way humans sleep. One of the most common titles of Enlil ($^{d}$Mu-ul-líl) in Sumero-Akkadian lamentations is "the one who sleeps a false sleep" (ù-lul-la ku-ku) (M. Cohen 1988: 1, 96:8; 148:182; 159:a+114; 163:b+201; 176:10). In other words, "although Enlil appears to be sleeping, he is not really asleep, instead he is paying attention to the world order. This could well be a Mesopotamian expression for the omniscience of the supreme god" (Oshima 2014: 280 n. 44). In a Sumerian proverb the "false sleep" is applied to a human being: GEME$_2$-KAR-KA Ù-LUL-LA KU-KU "the runaway slave sleeps a false sleep" he remains constantly on his guard, or "with one eye open" (Falkowitz 1980: 199 col. 3.79; Steinert 2010: 264). It could also stand for Enlil's sly and shrewd nature; he is an always vigilant god. Something similar is expressed in the Hebrew Bible about God's eternal vigilance in Ps 121:3–4 "He will not let your foot be moved; he who keeps you will not slumber [*ʾal yānûm*]. He who keeps Israel will neither slumber nor sleep [*lōʾ yānûm welōʾ yîšān*]." This statement should be seen in a dialectic polarity with laments or prayers in times of duress found in Pss 7; 35; 44; 59; and 74 (Batto 1987: 169 n. 47). The one praying pleads in standardized terms for God to "rise up//awake" *qûmâ//ʿûrâ* (Ps 7:7; 44:23) in the sense hear my plight, do not remain inactive in respect to my predicament.

6. Stephens 1969: 390. The adjective in the nominative *ḫubrātum*, from *ḫubru* "clamorous, busy," agrees with *nišû*, "people."

Already the ancient Sumerians expressed their bafflement in the official belief in an all-powerful, all-knowing, all-seeing, eternally vigilant Enlil and their dismal condition in a destroyed city:

> Enlil, father of the nation, how long . . .
> Shepherd of the black-headed people, how long . . . ?
> He who witnesses everything first-hand, how long . . . ?
> Bull who causes the troops to wander, how long . . . ?
> He who sleeps a false sleep, how long [Ù-LUL-LA KU-KU ME-NA]?
> (M. Cohen 1988: 1, 168 a+114).

The reclining of the gods at night and their rising in the morning was accompanied by cultic rituals implying that the expression might have arisen from the daily ritual in the Mesopotamian temples. There were specific rituals related to the care of the divine statue, changing their garments, bringing a bowl of water to Anu and his spouse for their morning toilette, and bringing breakfast and supper to the gods through offerings in Mesopotamia and in Egypt (Oppenheim 1977: 184; Erman 1927: 12). In Greece gods required regular sleep each night for refreshment and revitalization, as depicted in *Iliad* 1.605–611.

The goddess Ishtar, whose star is Venus, in the Iddin-Dagan's Sacred Marriage Hymn (lines 103–104) continually supervises human lovemaking:

> 103 "The young man makes love to his spouse.
> 104 Upon him my lady looks in a friendly way from the midst of heaven."
> (Sumerian text, Römer 1965: 131 and 139; trans. Reisman 1973: 188).

Why is it so important to protect humans during lovemaking? This activity is closely linked with procreation since humans could be hurt by the demons, creatures that never sleep and hate human lovemaking. In Inanna's Descent to the Netherworld the nefarious action of the demons is described in the following way: (ID 303) DAM ÚR-LÚ-KA BA-RA-AN-SI-IL-SI-IL-EŠ "But tear the wife away from her husband during intercourse" (Sladek 1974: 176).

According to Inanna's Descent, the demons seize away the wife from her husband while they make love, they snatch away children from the knees of their fathers and take away the young bride from the nuptial chamber (ID 303; 366). Sladek's comments are to the point,

> Sexual intercourse is especially hated by the demons not only because it is fun, but because it creates life which is the antithesis of the netherworld. The demons will do everything in their power to prevent it. This inimical attitude of the netherworld towards sex is also found in the AV [=the Akkadian Version]. When Ištar descends into the netherworld, all sexual activity ceases on earth," (Sladek 1974: 66).

Moreover, demons never sleep, night doesn't bother them, they seem to be active all the time. Anyone who disturbs the sleep is demonized, perceived as a hostile and potentially threatening force. The night thugs and rioters are assimilated to demons. In his study on dreams, S. Butler states that for the ancient Mesopotamians, oppressive sleep, restless sleep, nightmares, and sleeplessness were considered as symptoms of illness, an expression of divine wrath on an individual (cf. Sargon of Akkad) or visitation by demons. When someone fell ill, it was because an angry deity had touched that person (*qāt ili* "hand of god" referring to illness) or allowed evil demons and ghosts to attack the person as a punishment (Butler 1998: 43; see also 50, an incantation against a demon who "crossed the edge" of the sleeper's bed; 59–60 a ghost assimilated to a demon). Even today, sleep deprivation is used as an enhanced interrogation technique aiming in breaking down the resistance of prisoners.

The first tablet of the Atraḫasis epic relates the institution of the nuptial night with newly created human race where again the goddess Ishtar plays a role:

Atraḫasis I
299 *i-na* [. . .] x *na-de-e e-er-ši*
When [. . .]. the bed is laid
300 *li-*⌜*i*⌝*-ti-*[*lu aš-ša*]*-tum ù mu-sà*
Let the wife and her husband lie together
301 *i-nu-ma* <*a-na*> *aš-š[u-ti] ù mu-tu-ti*
When, to institute marriage,
302 *i-na bi-it* [*e-mi ra-bé*]-⌜*e*⌝ *i-ta-'i-du Iš-tar*
They heed Ishtar in the house of [the father-in-law]
303 9(tišti) $u_4$*-mi* [*li-iš-ša*]*a-ki-in ḫi-du-tum*
Let there be rejoicing for 9 days
304 *Iš-tar* [*li-it-ta-a*]*b-bu-ú* $^{d}$*Iš-ḫa-ra*
Let them call Ishtar Ishḫara
305 *i-na* [. . . . . .] x*-ti si-ma-nu ši-im-ti*
. . [. . . .] . . at the destined moment.

The Erra epic sheds additional light on what the gods are doing while they are "sleeping," or better, "reclining in their chamber." Although the entire Erra epic breathes war and destruction, the opening scene is highly significant. The first tablet presents the god Erra lying in his bedroom (*uršu*) and making love (*epēšu ulṣam* I 20) with his consort Mami. Erra appears as a married person more concerned with his love life than with the furor of war. He is undecided about breaking his rest and dalliance with Mami, neglecting his main activity, which is war.

However, it is more than just enjoying soft life and bourgeois indulgences. This sexual aspect has its importance in understanding the sacredness of sleep. One should not disturb the neighbor at night because he might be in his bedroom making love to his wife, an activity essential to the act of procreation, something so important that it had to be under special divine protection. This is one of the permanent roles of Ishtar and Ishum.[7]

7. Roberts 1971, 11–16, explains the marital relationship between Erra and Mami in the following way: Erra personifies the destructive power of fire. Mami is the goddess of fertility and procreation. Roberts suggests that the ancient Mesopotamians were using the common agricultural technique of burning fields

The god Erra/Nergal, stands for war and plague, activities that bring death to humans. The god's destructive feature is compensated by his lieutenant Ishum who also acts as a protective buffer between Erra and the humans.

In Erra I 19–20 his lieutenant, Ishum, goes to wake up his master, to pull him out of his bedroom from the embrace of his female companion and remind him that he has work to do.

I 19 *adi atta taddekū-šu ṣālil uršuš-šu*
I 20 *itti Mami ḫīratuš ippuša ulṣam-ma*[8]

I 19 Until you (Ishum) rouse him, he will (remain) lying in his bedroom,
I 20 with Mami, his consort, he will make love (Cagni 1969: 60–61; Farber 2008: 262–267).

The terms *ḫubūru* occurs four times (Erra I 41, 73, 82; and IV 68), as well as *rigmu* (Erra I 61, Erra's "battle cry"; IIB 43 "loud cry"; IIC 45 "clamor"; and IIIA 18 *rigim* $^{d}$*Alala* "the alala song" or the workers in the field), each time with different meanings (Bodi 1991: 151–155). Hence the noise motif is very present and should not be seen as sporadic in Erra. The Sebetti, Erra's hypostatized weapons, impatient to go to war, bring up the old charge that human clamor disturbs the sleep of the Anunnakū, the chthonic gods.

Ere the whole land outgrows us,
do a kindly deed for the Anunnakū,
who delight in deadly silence.
The Anunnaku cannot fall asleep for the clamor of humankind
(*Anunnakī ina ḫubūr nišī ul ireḫḫû šittim*) (Erra I 79–82).

The reason why Erra punishes the inhabitants of Babylon and destroys Mesopotamian cities is expressed together with another *Leitmotiv*, a stereotypical phrase *leqû šēṭūtu* (I 77, 120; IIID 15; IV 133). Erra complains that humans scorn him, "hold him in contempt" and do not fear his divinized weapons, the Sebetti (Bodi 1991: 77–79). This is why he decides to punish humans and teach them a lesson. The motif of waking up the god Erra reclining in his bedchamber while making love to his divine lover is used in a particular way. Ishum is Erra's faithful lieutenant, he enjoys privileged access to his master, and part of his explicit job is to supervise and protect divine and human lovemaking. In the Erra epic, Ishum is not breeching the holiness of sleep

in order to increase their yield. The initial rest of Erra and Mami resembles the beginning of Enuma Elish where Apsû and Ti'âmat intermingle their waters, enjoying tranquility. Seux 1977, 73, translates the term *uršu* with "*chambre à coucher*" = "bedroom" as over against Cagni's "*letto*" = "bed." One is probably dealing here with the figure of speech called *pars pro toto*.

8. The verb *dekûm* II, *dakû* means "to raise, lift" or "wake up" a person; *tadekkū-šu* is a G-stem present 2ms + 3ms suff.; cf. *ṣallu idki*, "woke up the sleeping one," mentioned in Livingstone 1989 (SAA 3), 100 n. 39; *ṣalālum* means "to lie (down), sleep" but also "to lie with sexually" as in this precise context; here a G-stem participle; *uršum* I "bedroom" *uršum-ma –um locative adverbialis* "in the bedroom" + *šu* 3ms suff. "his" which becomes *uršuššu* due to assimilation.

taboo. He is simply doing his job reminding his lord that for the god who incarnates war and destruction the usual agenda is inversed: "Make war not love."

The name Mami is an abbreviated form of *Māmītu*, an underworld divinity better known as one of the wives of Nergal. This element favors the identification of Erra with the netherworld god Nergal. Her name should not be confused with that of the creator goddess Mami (Edzard 1965: 95).[9] The expression, *epēšum ulṣam*, literally means "to take pleasure, to enjoy oneself" and is a euphemism for "making love." Ishum, Erra's lieutenant, is presented as the guardian of prince Erra and other humans. In times of peace when both gods and humans make love, Ishum's role is to watch over them, love-making being an activity exposed to potentially nefarious demonic influences or to forces intent on hurting the lovers.

I 21 *Engidudu bēlu muttallik mūši mutarrû rube*
I 22 *ša eṭla u ardatu ina šul*[*m*]*i i*[*tt*]*anarru unammaru kīma ūmi*

The divine night watchman, the lord who goes about in the night, who watches over the prince (Erra),
who watches out for the well-being of lads and girls and makes (them) radiant as day(light).

Being the time of repose, peace, and sleep, in the ancient Near East the night is closely related to the sexual life of humans and gods.

## The Taboo of the Sacredness of Sleep in the Hebrew Bible and in the Life of Muhammad

This taboo is also found in the Hebrew Bible. In Gen 19, the night racket and attempted rape by the inhabitants of Sodom upon Lot's visitors was divinely punished by wiping out the whole city. In Judg 19 in Gibeah, the night racket and gang rape of the Levite's concubine by the Benjaminites resulted in a collective punishment inflicted by other Hebrew tribes having exterminated almost the entire tribe of Benjamin. In 1 Sam 26 David refrains from killing Saul who sleeps in a cave at night, respecting the taboo of the sacredness of sleep (the doublet in 1 Sam 24 is a later elaboration where the same occurs but with a scatological twist, Saul was not sleeping but relieving himself in a cave).[10] In Judg 16:1–2 in Gaza, Samson was ambushed in a harlot's house; he skillfully used the taboo of the sacredness of the sleep of not being attacked by the Philistines while he was with a woman in order to escape at midnight. Similarly,

9. *Mami, Māmītu* was originally a personification of the oath. Taken as an appellative, her Akkadian name means "oath, curse," Following the breaking of an oath, the curse appears as a demon provoking a disease in the perjurer and is called *qāt māmīti* "Māmīti's hand." A similar operation was already noted with *assaku*.

10. Two cases belong to a different category: The first in 1 Kgs 18:27 at midday the prophet Elijah derides the prophets of Baal urging them to disturb their god who might be sleeping or relieving himself (a scatological twist as in 1 Sam 26). And the second in Judg 4:17–22, Yael killed the Canaanite warlord Sisera, asleep on her knees but that happened during the day, and by driving a peg through his head, Yael made him pass from a deep slumber into eternal sleep.

in 1 Sam 19:10–18, David was ambushed in his house with his wife Michal. Saul sends henchmen to Michal's house in order to kill David when he comes out in the morning. The way the conspirators wait in ambush the whole night without entering the house follows the same pattern as the Samson incident in Judg 16:1–3, where he went to Gaza to see a harlot. The townspeople surrounded the place to ambush him, and during the entire night they made plans to kill him, without, however, storming the house. Samson stayed in bed with the prostitute until midnight (*ḥṣy hlylh*) when he escaped. As demonstrated by L. Köhler (1916: 22) there is a reason why Samson and David felt safe at night in the shelter of a home and with a woman. Owing to the Near Eastern taboo-like social customs, David was protected as long as he stayed with Michal in the house and the night was not yet over. Köhler cites a similar situation from the life of Muhammad belonging to the traditions of the prophet's escape from his hometown Mecca. A handpicked group of young men from several prominent Meccan families were sent under the cover of the night to kill him in his house. When they tried to force their way into Muhammad's house, the henchmen were greeted by a cry for help by a screaming woman. Thereupon one of the henchmen said, "If we enter by force, the whole of Arabia will say that we are that kind of heroes who at night climb over the walls of their neighbors and disturb the daughters of their kin in their sleep, and desecrate the sacrosanct premises of the women."[11]

German commentators describe this Near Eastern custom with the expression "*Heiligkeit des Schlafes*," (Holiness of Sleep), that is, during the night the neighbor should not be disturbed, his or her sleep being considered sacred (Stoebe 1973: 357). In the two examples of the "Sodomite theme" in Gen 19 and Judg 19 (Niditch 1982: 365–378), the assault of the rapists occurred during the night, a breach of this Near Eastern "*Heiligkeit des Schlafes*" taboo that aggravated the offense. The outrage committed by the rapists is twofold: They disturb the sleep of their neighbors and they make a breach of the custom of hospitality. Setting these biblical stories in Gen 19, Judg 19, and 1 Sam 19:10–18 at night shows that something unusual is happening. One author calls this "the atmosphere-charged potential of the night-time motif." For "apart from battle scenes in which armies make use of darkness for tactical purposes, the rule for normal life seems to have been, start a task early in the morning, continue during the day, and finish it in time to be home before darkness" (Fields 1992: 21 n. 11).

## The Multiple Meanings of *ḫubūru* and *rigmu*—"Noise, Clamor, Din"—in the Atraḫasis Epic

The terms *ḫubūru* and *rigmu* do not have a uniform meaning in the Atraḫasis epic. Their precise meaning depends on the context. The epic dates from the time of the First Babylonian Dynasty (Laessoe 1956: 90–102; Shehata 2001).[12] Both *ḫubūru* and *rigmu* occur in the Atraḫasis epic, although the latter term predominates (Lambert and

11. ". . . die Töchter ihrer nächsten Verwandten im Schlafe stön und die Unantastbarkeit des Frauengemaches entheiligen," A. Sprenger, *Das Leben und die Lehre des Moḥammad*, 3 vols. (Berlin: Nikolai, 1862), 2:543–544, available online: https://books.google.fr/books?id=yJwPAAAAQAAJ.

12. Some tablets of the Atraḫasis epic are datable to the time of the scribe Kasap-Aya, in the service of the King Ammiṣaduqa (1646–1626 BCE), while the Assyrian recension comes from Aššurbanipal's library in

Millard 1969: glossary). The terms run like a *Leitmotiv* throughout the epic (von Soden 1978: 50–94; 1979: 1; Bottéro and Kramer 1989: 527–567). *Rigmu* has a variety of connotations and only the context allows precise determination. The most common meanings of the term *rigmu* are those of "sound of thunder" in association with the storm god Adad, and that of "cry of complaint," also in the sense of "legal complaint."

1. At the outbreak of the flood *rigmu* stands for **the thunder of the storm**, *ištagna* $^{d}$*Adad ina erpetī ila išmu rigim-šu* = "Adad roared in the clouds. As soon as he (Atraḫasis) heard his voice" (i.e., thunder) (Atraḫasis 3 ii 49–50).

2. The term *rigmu* also appears as **a "cry of complaint."** Mother-goddess Mami hears humans crying (*rigmu*), overwhelmed by the flood. Their bodies are carried away like flies on the surface of the water. Touched by compassion for her creation she too cries until she has no more tears, and her cry (*rigmu*) died away. To the cry of the humans corresponds the cry of the goddess who created them.

> III iii
> 43 And to my own hurt I have listened to their cry
> [*rigim-šina ešme*] (Lambert and Millard, 1969, 95 "noise")
> 44 my offspring—cut off from me have become like flies!
> 46 And as for me, like the occupant *u anāku kî ašābi*
> 47 of a house of lamentation, my cry has died away *ina bīt dimmati šaḫurru rigim*.

The noise of the land is contrasted with the noise of the flood,

> III iii
> 10 [*kīma karpati r*]*igimša iḫpi*
> and shattered its noise [like a pot]
> 11 [. . . *itaṣa*] *abūbu*
> [. . .] the flood [set out]
> 23 *rigim a*[*būb*]*i*
> the noise of the flood.

The term *rigmu* connotes a "complaint" in the context of the forced labor of the gods, Atraḫasis I 179, [*tukku kab*]*i*[*t ni?še*]*me rigma*. Although W. G. Lambert and A. R. Millard translate: "[The lamentation was] heavy, [we could] hear the noise," in this line it might be more appropriate to translate *rigmu* with "complaint" in the light of what is said in Atraḫasis I 177 *kabit dulla-šun m*[*âd*] *šapšāq-šun* = "Their work was heavy, their distress was much!" Here *rigmu* is a synonym of *tukku*. J. R. Kupper takes the basic meaning of *tukku* to be "*cri bruyant*," and in certain contexts "*cri d'alarme*" (1951: 120–125; *tukku* appears as a synonym of *rigmu* as attested in lists of synonyms).

In the following context, *rigmu* might be a complaint out of distress as the gods feel oppressed by heavy labor, Atraḫasis I 242–243 *tašta'ita (=taštêta) rigma ana awēlūti*

Nineveh (668 BCE). Fragments were found at Ugarit (thirteenth century BCE) and at Megiddo (fourteenth century BCE, a Gilgamesh fragment). However, the epic probably originated in the eighteenth century BCE.

*aptur ulla andurā[ra ašku]n* = "You have raised a complaint (asking for) humankind (to be created), I have loosened the yoke, I have established freedom."

3. The term *rigmu* and the **breech of the sacredness of sleep taboo at night** by the revolt of the gods. In the first tablet of the Atraḫasis epic, before the creation of human beings, the term *rigmu* acquires a particular meaning of night racket and mayhem occurring in a context of an overt conflict between the gods Igigi and Annunaki. The first tablet of the Atraḫasis epic together with its precursor found in Enki and Ninmaḫ have something remarkable, while depicting the revolt of the inferior against the superior gods, they describe the only workers' revolt in the entire ancient Near East, this theme being, apparently, not very common in ancient Near Eastern literature (Bodi 2009: 83–100). The beginning of the epic depicts the junior gods, the Igigi, doing the menial work, digging the beds of the waterways, carrying heavy baskets (*š/tupšikka*) at the behest of the senior gods, the Anunnaki (Kienast 1965: 141–158; von Soden 1966: 140–145). The younger gods found their corvée type of work unbearable.[13] They held a meeting, decided to implement a revolution and to overthrow their taskmaster Enlil. (I ii 61–62) "Now proclaim war. Let us mingle hostilities and battle." Similar to the modern-day revolutionary slogan, "burn, baby, burn," they burned their tools (I ii 65–66) and in the night they went to besiege Enlil's temple. The god slept but his watchman Kalkal observed the approach of the attackers. He woke Nusku the vizier "and they listened to the noise" (I ii 77). In this context *rigmu* may stand for mayhem, a violent public disturbance of the peace, and for hostility. It corresponds to modern-day delict technically called, "*tapage nocturne*," and punishable by law. The young gods were breaking an ancient social taboo, the sacredness of sleep ("*Heiligkeit des Schlafes*").

Atraḫasis I 70–73
70 *mi-ši-il ma-aṣ-ṣa-ar-ti mu-šum i-ba-aš-ši*
71 *bītu la-wi i-lu ú-ul i-di*
72 *mi-ši-il ma-aṣ-ṣa-ar-ti mu-šum i-ba-aš-ši*
73 é-kur *la-wi* $^{d}$en-líl *ú-ul i-di*

It was night, halfway through the watch,
The temple was surrounded, but the god did not know,
It was night, halfway through the watch,
Ekur was surrounded, but Enlil did not know
(Lambert and Millard 1969: 46–47).

Here the Akkadian expression *mišil maṣṣarti* means "half of the watch," (from *mišlu* "half"), has a direct counterpart in the Hebrew *ḥ$^{a}$ṣî hal-laylâ* "middle of the night" in Judg 16:3. The context is that of upheaval and radical modification of the

13. According to von Soden (1969: 429) this part of the Atraḫasis epic may reflect the relationship between the Sumerian overlords and the various Semitic immigrants, called the Martu-people. During the Ur III period the latter were employed as canal diggers as well as for various building projects. According to Bottéro (1967–1968: 116; 1966: 14 n. 3) the passage shows that in ancient Mesopotamia corvée workers were occasionally instigating strikes and revolts (Atraḫasis 2 1–7). (Garelli 1959: 100, "les révoltes," and 102, "les grêves"; Evans 1963: 65–78; Brinkman 1980: 17–22; Picchioni 1974: 83–111).

social order instigated by the junior gods. Hence, the assembly of the gods holds an extraordinary session and sends a messenger to inquire into the cause of the riot. The junior gods respond, "[Excessive] toil [has killed us], [our] work was heavy, [the distress much]" (I ii 149–150). The divine assembly decides to create humans as substitutes to do the work. The birth-goddess Mami is enjoined to supervise the creation of humankind. She asked for Enlil's assistance. He prepared the clay by mixing it with the flesh and blood of a slaughtered god Wê or Wê-ila, and gave it to the mother goddess Mami. In connection with her work she is called *Bēlet-kala-ilī* = "Mistress-of-All-the Gods."

4. The terms *ḫubūru* and *rigmu* and the **encroachment on the sacredness of sleep taboo** by the humans

The epic continues with the motif of human encroachment and defiance of the limits set by the assembly of the gods. The human race multiplied and their noise became such that Enlil, who still dwelt on earth among humans, could not sleep. The term *ḫubūru* occurs seven times and always in parallelism with *rigmu*. Lambert and Millard translate them by "noise" and "uproar" respectively (I 355, 358–359; II i 7–8; S iv 2–3, 6–8, 40–41; X i 2′–3′). The rest of the Atraḫasis epic describes Enlil's different control devices to reduce the human population and to silence their din. However, the humans did not heed the warnings sent by Enlil in the form of plague, famine, drought, and blight. Enlil finally decides that the human race should be exterminated by the flood. Warned by Enki, Atraḫasis, the hero of the epic, precursor of the biblical Noah, builds an ark and survives the flood (Klein 2011: 151–176).

The following quotation comes from the introduction to Enlil's complaint before the first and second plague.

Atraḫasis II
1 *ul illik-ma* 600.600 *šanāti*
Twelve hundred years had not yet passed,
2 *mātum irtapiš niš[ū im]tīdā*
When the land extended and the peoples multiplied
3 *[mā]tum kīma lî išabbu*
The land was bellowing like a bull,
4 *[in]a ḫubūrī-šina ilu itta'dar*
The god became disturbed with their uproar.
5 *[dEnl]il išteme rigim-šin*
Enlil heard their noise,
6 *issaqar ana ilī rabûtim*
and addressed the great gods,
7 *iktabta rigim awēlūti*
'The noise of humankind has become too intense for me
8 *ina ḫubūrī-šina ina uzamma šitta*
With their uproar I am deprived of sleep.'
(Lambert and Millard 1969:73; Smith 1925: 67 on *uzamma šitta*).

Since the term "day" is not employed as in Enuma Elish, it is implied that Enlil is disturbed in his night sleep not in his day rest. In this manner the breach of the taboo of the sacredness of sleep by the humans is put in parallelism with the previous breach and uproar made by the gods.

As pointed by Michalowski (1990: 388 n. 27), in addition to its function as one of the causes of the flood in Atraḫasis, the noise of humankind, disturbing the god Enlil, also occurs in the Myth of Labbu (CT 13, 33–34).

## Rigmu in Enuma Elish

In Enuma Elish only the term *rigmu* is used. While it occurs in a context of conflict between older and younger generations of gods, the taboo of the sacredness of sleep at night is modified since the epic states that Apsû "cannot rest by day nor sleep by night." The trouble goes beyond uniquely night riot and mayhem, it is permanent, implying that something else is the matter. A clear contrast is established between the younger and the older generation of gods. The older gods have become like old people who increasingly need to rest, nap during the day and sleep at night. The younger gods, teeming with vigor and energy are active day and night. In this context the term *rigmu* is the result of their bustling and unstoppable activity. According to E. Cassin (1968: 32), the need for sleep in connection with gods indicates that they are losing an essential quality: vigilance.

The Babylonian Epic of Creation enjoyed considerable popularity beginning with the eleventh century BCE.[14] The first tablet depicts the primordial condition when the heavens and the earth were not yet named (i.e., created I 1–2). The only thing that existed was the immobile, stagnant, and dormant watery mass called Apsû (the subterranean sweet water) and Ti'amat (the salt water). Their waters intermingled creating a fertile life-giving milieu. The couple Ti'amat and Apsû beget children who represent the new generation of gods, carriers of a new world. The junior gods are active and agitated as over against the senior ones who are inert, silent, and immobile. To the need of quietude and sleep of the otiose older gods is opposed to the noisy turbulence of the younger ones. The latter with their movements and dancing roil violently Ti'âmat's interior. This excessive agitation annoys Apsû: (I 25) "Apsû could not subdue their clamor" (*lā našir Apsû rigim-šun*). Prompted by one of his descendants, Mummu, he decides to exterminate his progeny (I 21–28). Apsû is alarmed,

Enuma Elish I
37 *imtarṣāmma alkassun elīya*
38 *uriš lā šupšuḫāku mūšīš lā ṣallāku*

37 Their ways have become noisome to me!
38 I am allowed no rest by day, by night no sleep.

14. In the course of the New Year (Akitu) festival at Babylon a battle in which Marduk ritually defeated Ti'âmat was ritually enacted (Lambert 1968: 104–112), and Enuma Elish was recited to the statue of Marduk by a priest (Thureau-Dangin 1921: 136). According to Lambert, the only period when one can be sure that this ritual took place is from 625 to 539 BCE under the late Babylonian kings. Late Assyrian sources confirm that the festival was essentially the same from about 750 BCE. No evidence exists to ascertain how much farther back the festival went (Lambert 2013; Talon 2005).

39 I will destroy, I will wreck their ways.
40 That quiet may be restored, that we may sleep [*qūlu liššakin-ma i niṣlal nīni*].
(Lambert and Parker 1966; Wilcke 1977: 153–216; Jacobsen, 1975: 170)

However, the younger gods gain the upper hand and Apsû, the father, is killed by a sly trick of the all-wise Enki/Ea. The god Ea's artful spell put Apsû into a sleep-trance and turned his vizier Mummu into a zombie: "Sleep came upon him, he slept soundly, (Ea) caused Apsû to sleep, sleep having overtaken him. Mummu the counselor though awake was in a daze" (*šit-tu ir-te-ḫi-šu ṣa-lil ṭu-ub-ba-tiš ú-šá-aṣ-lil-ma* ABZU *ri-ḫi št-tu* [d]*mu-um-mu tam-la-ku da-la-piš ku-ú-ru* [Enuma Elish I 64–65]). In an attempt to revenge Apsû's death Ti'âmat will be defeated by Ea's formidable son Marduk. Out of the dead carcass of one of the parents the world is created.

According to T. Jacobsen (1975: 186), the passage reflects "the parricide theme": "An open conflict of generations follows and ends in parricide, after which the slayer founds his own house upon the body of the dead parent." The context is that of a theomachy, a war and power-struggle between the younger and the older gods. The former want to seize power, and the very foundation of heaven is challenged. Their dance culminates in a parricide. It is a foreboding dance akin to a *danse macabre*.

With reference to Enuma Elish, we may speak of the conflict of generations where *rigmu* stands for incipient disorder, because the younger gods are calling the existing order into question. They initiate the disorder and manage to establish a new one. In this context, in Enuma Elish, the term *rigmu* may also stand for hostility, threat, and disrespect. H. R. Cohen (1978: 138 n. 78) points out a text where Akkadian *ikkillu* "noise, clamor" (a synonym of *rigmu*) is identified with hostility, *šumma bītu ikkil*[*la*] *īšu āšib libbīšu nakru* šumma *bītu ikki*[*la*] *lā īšu libbīšu ṭâb* = "If a house is noisy, its residents will be hostile; If a house is not noisy, its residents will be contented (*CT* 40, 5, 13–14).

## Conclusion

The sleep taboo and the religious-literary discourse about sleep of the gods found in Akkadian epics should probably be seen as human activities and customs being projected on the behavior of the Mesopotamian gods. The long scholarly tradition of looking for a human model with socio-historical explanations of Mesopotamian mythological accounts, themes, and motifs seems justified. This article has tried to show that the Atraḫasis epic did not suggest that the flood and the destruction of humankind happened as the result of a malicious, otiose, and completely arbitrary decision by the supreme deity Enlil. The flood was sent because a major ancient Near Eastern taboo was breached. It is more than a petty reason of the loss of physical sleep. The Atraḫasis epic with the initial episode of the Igigū gods besieging Enlil's temple at night, raising the *ḫubūru* noise, gives the clue about the meaning of the term. It reflects the breach of an ancient Near Eastern taboo of the sacredness of sleep. Neither gods nor humans should be disturbed at night when they retreat to their bed chamber. This taboo probably stems from fear of disturbing humans while involved in the act of procreation insuring the continuity of the human race. In Enuma Elish Apsû complains that he cannot rest during the day nor sleep at night, indicating that he is in need of quietude while the younger gods are bustling with vigor and activity. The motif serves to underline the contrast between peace, immobile condition, and incipient growth on the one hand and activity related to setting creation in motion on the other hand. It indicates that the old order is about to be superseded. The taboo of the sacredness of sleep is also found in the Hebrew Bible and in the life of Muhammad. This latter example confirms the continuation of the sacredness of sleep taboo in medieval times among the Arabic tribes. The individuals who show disrespect for this taboo are demonized, and assimilated to thugs, rapists, troublemakers, and lawless groups.

## BIBLIOGRAPHY


Afanasieva, V.
1996 Die irdische Lärm des Menschen (nochmals zum Atramḫasīs-Epos). *ZA* 86: 89–96.

Batto, B. F.
1987 The Sleeping God: An Ancient Near Eastern Motif of Divine Sovereignty. *Bib* 68: 153–177.

Bodi, D.
1991 *The Book of Ezekiel and the Poem of Erra.* OBO 104. Fribourg: Universitätsverlag; Göttingen: Vandenhoeck & Ruprecht.
2009 La révolte des travailleurs en Mésopotamie et dans la Bible et la résolution du conflit par un retour à l'état antérieur *andurārum* akkadien et *d^e^rôr* hébreu. Pp. 83–100 in *Centre et périphérie: Approches nouvelles des Orientalistes; Actes du colloque organisé par l'Institut du Proche-Orient Ancien du Collège de France, la Société Asiatique et le CNRS [UMR 7192], les 31 mai et 1er juin 2006.* Edited by J.-M. Durand and A. Jacquet. Paris: Maisonneuve.

Bottéro, J.
1966 Le "Dialogue pessimiste" et la Transcendance. *RTP* 99: 7–24.
1967–1968 Antiquités assyro-babyloniennes (Poème d'Atraḫasīs). *AEPHE* 89–122.

Bottéro, J. and Kramer, S. N.
1989 *Lorsque les dieux faisaient l'homme.* Paris: Gallimard.

Brinkman, J. A.
1980 Forced Laborers in the Middle Babylonian Period. *JCS* 32: 17–22.

Butler, S.
1998 *Mesopotamian Conceptions of Dreams and Dream Rituals.* AOAT 258. Münster: Ugarit-Verlag.

Cagni, L.
1969 *L'Epopea di Erra.* StSem 34. Rome: Istituto di Studi del Vicino Oriente.

Cancik-Kirschbaum, E.
2009 Reinigung und Vermischung: Eine altorientalische Vorstellung über die Natur des Menschen (Atramhasis I, 192–245). Pp. 141–150 in *Un/Reinheit: Konzepte und Praktiken im Kulturvergleich.* Edited by A. Malinar and M. Vöhler. Munich: Fink.

Cassin, E.
1968 *La splendeur divine : Introduction a l'etude de la mentalite mesopotamienne.* Civilisations et sociétés 8. La Haye: Mouton.

Cavigneaux, A.
1987 Notes sumérologiques. *ASJ* 9: 45–66.

Charpin, D.
1997 Manger un serment. Pp. 85–96 in *Jurer et maudire: Pratique politiques et usages juridiques du serment dans le Proche-Orient ancien; Actes de la table ronde, Paris 10–Nanterre, 5 octobre 1996*. Edited by F. Joannès and S. Lafont. Méditerranées 10–11. Paris: L'Harmattan.

Cohen, H. R.
1978 *Biblical Hapax Legomena in the Light of Akkadian and Ugaritic*. SBLDS 37. Missoula, MT: Scholars Press.

Cohen, M. E.
1988 *The Canonical Lamentations of Ancient Mesopotamia*. Potomac, MD: Capital Decisions.

Dossin, G.
1935 Prières aux "dieux de la nuit" (AO 6769). *RA* 32: 179–187.

Durand, J.-M.
1988 *Archives Epistolaires de Mari, Vol. 1*. ARM 26/1. Paris: Éditions Recherche sur les Civilisations.

Edzard, D. O.
1965 Māmītu. P. 95 in *Wörterbuch der Mythologie*. Edited by H. W. Haussig. Stuttgart: Klett.

Erman, A.
1927 *The Literature of the Ancient Egyptians*. London: Methuen.

Evans, G.
1963 The Incidence of Labour-Service at Mari. *RA* 57: 65–78.

Falkowitz, R. S.
1980 *The Sumerian Rhetoric Collections*. PhD. diss., University of Pennsylvania.

Farber, W.
2008 Die einleitende Episode des Erra-Epos. *AoF* 35: 262–267.

Fields, W. W.
1992 The Motif "Night as Danger" Associated with Three Biblical Destruction Narratives. Pp. 17–32 in *Sha'arei Talmon: Studies in the Bible, Qumran, and the Ancient Near East Presented to Shemaryahu Talmon*. Edited by M. Fishbane and E. Tov. Winona Lake, IN: Eisenbrauns.

Garelli, P.
1959 Asie occidentale ancienne. Pp. 50–104 in *Histoire générale du travail, vol. 1: Préhistoire et antiquité*. Edited by L.-H. Parias. Paris: Nouvelle librairie de France.

Grayson, A. K.
1975 *Assyrian and Babylonian Chronicles*. TCS 5. Locust Valley, NY: Augustin.

Horowitz, W.
2000 Astral Tablets in the Hermitage, Saint-Petersburg. *ZA* 90, 194–206.

Jacobsen, T.
1975 *The Treasures of Darkness: A History of Mesopotamian Religion*. New Haven: Yale University Press.

Kienast, B.
1965 *Igigū* und *Anunnakkū* nach der akkadischen Quellen. Pp. 141–158 in *Studies in Honor of Benno Landsberger on His Seventy-Fifth Birthday, April 21, 1965*. Edited by H. G. Güterbock and T. Jacobsen. AS 16. Chicago: University of Chicago Press.

Klein, J.
2011 A New Look at the Theological Background of the Mesopotamian and Biblical Flood Stories. Pp. 151–176 in *A Common Cultural Heritage: Studies on Mesopotamian and Biblical World in Honor of Barry L. Eichler*. Edited by G. Frame, E. Leichty, K. Sonik, J. H. Tigay, and S. Tinney. Bethesda, MD: CDL.

Köhler, L.
1916 Archäologisches: Nr. 11–15. *ZAW* 36: 21–28.

Kramer, S. N.
1989 *Myths of Enki, the Crafty God.* New York: Oxford University Press.

Kupper, J.-R.
1951 Notes lexicographiques. *RA* 45: 120–130.

Laessoe, J.
1956 The Atrahasis Epic: A Babylonian History of Mankind. *BO* 13: 90–102.

Lambert, W. G.
1968 Myth and Ritual as Conceived by the Babylonians. *JSS* 13: 104–112.
2013 *Babylonian Creation Myths.* MC 16. Winona Lake, IN: Eisenbrauns.

Lambert, W. G. and Millard, A. R.
1969 *Atra-ḫasīs, The Babylonian Story of the Flood (with the Sumerian Flood Story by M. Civil).* Oxford: Clarendon.

Lambert, W. G. and Parker, S. B.
1966 *Enūma eliš: The Babylonian Epic of Creation; The Cuneiform Text.* Oxford: Clarendon.

Livingstone, A.
1989 *Court Poetry and Literary Miscellanea.* SAA 3. Helsinki: Helsinki University Press.
1991 To Disturb the Dead: Taboo to Enmešarra. *NABU* 1991.1: 1.

Machinist, P.
1983 Rest and Violence in the Poem of Erra. *JAOS* 103: 221–226.

Michalowski, P.
1990 Presence at the Creation. Pp. 381–396 in *Lingering Over Words: Studies in Ancient Near Eastern Literature in Honor of William L. Moran.* Edited by T. Abusch, J. Huehnergard, and P. Steinkeller. HSS 37. Atlanta: Scholars Press.

Mrozek, A. and Votto, S.
1999 The Motif of the Sleeping Divinity. *Bib* 80: 415–419.

Niditch, S.
1982 The "Sodomite" Theme in Judges 19–20: Family, Community, and Social Disintegration. *CBQ* 44: 365–378.

Oppenheim, A. L.
1977 *Ancient Mesopotamia: Portrait of a Dead Civilization.* Rev. ed. Chicago: University of Chicago Press.

Oshima, T.
2014 "Let Us Sleep!" The Motif of Disturbing Resting Deities in the Cuneiform Texts. *Studia Mesopotamica* 1: 271–289.

Pettinato, G.
1968 Die Bestrafung des Menschengeschlechts dur die Sintflut: Die erste Tafel des Atramhasis-Epos eröffnet eine neue Einsicht in die Motivation dieser Strafe. *Or* 37: 165–200.

Picchioni, S. A.
1974 Principi di etica sociale nel poema di Atraḫasīs. *OrAnt* 13: 83–111.

Reisman, D.
1973 Iddin-Dagan's Sacred Marriage Hymn. *JCS* 25: 185–202.

Rendu Loisel, A.-C.
2010 *Bruit et émotion dans la literature akkadienne.* PhD dissertation, University of Geneva.

Roberts, J. J. M.
1971 Erra—Scorched Earth. *JCS* 24: 11–16.

Römer, W. H. P.
1965 *Sumerische "Königshymnen" der Isin-Zeit.* DMOA 13. Leiden: Brill.

Seux, M.-J.
1977 Review of *L'Epopea di Erra*, by L. Cagni. *OrAnt* 11: 72–74.

Shehata, D.
2001 *Annotierte Bibliographie zum altbabylonischen Atramhasīs-Mythos Inūma ilū awīlum*. GAAL 3. Göttingen: Seminar für Keilschriftforschung.

Sladek, W.
1974 *Inanna's Descent to the Netherworld.* PhD diss., Johns Hopkins University.

Smith, S.
1925 Miscellanea: (3) Nabonidus' Restoration of E-MAŠ-DA-RI. *RA* 22: 57–70.

Soden, W. von
1936 Schwer zugängliche russische Veröffentlichungen altbabylonischer Texte: 1. Ein Opferschaugebet bei Nacht. *ZA* 43: 305–308.
1966 Die Igigu-Götter in altbabylonischer Zeit. *Iraq* 28: 140–145.
1969 "Als die Götter (auch noch) Mensch waren" Einige Grundgedanken des altbabylonischen Atramḫasīs-Mythus. *Or* 38: 415–432.
1978 Die erste Tafel des altbabylonischen Atramḫasīs-Mythus. "Haupttext" und Parallelversionen. *ZA* 68: 50–94.
1979 Konflikte und ihre Bewältigung in babylonischen Schöpfungs- und Fluterzählungen: Mit einer Teil-Übersetzung des Atramḫasīs-Mythus. *MDOG* 111: 1–33.

Sprenger, A.
1862 *Das Leben und die Lehre des Moḥammad.* 3 vols. Berlin: Nikolai. https://books.google.fr/books?id=yJwPAAAAQAAJ.

Steinert, U.
2010 Der Schlaf im Lichte der altmesopotamischen Überlieferung. Pp. 237–285 in *Von Göttern und Menschen, Beiträge zu Literatur und Geschichte des Alten Orients: Festschrift für Brigitte Groneberg*. Edited by D. Shehata, F. Weiershäuser, and K. Zand. CM 41. Leiden: Brill.

Stephens, F. J.
1969 Sumero-Akkadian Hymns and Prayers. Pp. 383–391 in *Ancient Near Eastern Texts Relating to the Old Testament.* Edited by J. B. Pritchard. 3rd ed. with supplement. Princeton: Princeton University Press.

Stoebe, H.-J.
1973 *Das erste Buch Samuelis*. KAT 8.1. Gütersloh: Mohn.

Talon, P.
2005 *The Standard Babylonian Creation Myth Enūma eliš*. SAACT 4. Helsinki: Neo-Assyrian Text Corpus Project.

Thureau-Dangin, F.
1921 *Rituels accadiens*. Paris: Leroux.

Weippert, M.
1983 Slapende en ontwakende of stervende en herrijzende goden? *NedTT* 37: 279–289.
1984 Ecce non dormitabit neque dormiet qui custodit Israhel: Zur Erklärung von Psalm 121,4. Pp. 75–87 in *Lese-Zeichen für Annelies Findeiss zum 65. Geburtstag am 15 März 1984*. Edited by C. Burchard and G. Theissen. DBAT 3. Heidelberg: Diebner.

Wilcke, C.
1977 Die Anfänge der akkadischen Epen. *ZA* 67: 153–216.

CHAPTER 4

# Lorsque les généraux prêtent serment… : Quelques remarques sur l'usage du serment de loyauté (depuis la documentation d'Ur III jusqu'à l'époque néo-assyrienne)

Daniel Bonneterre

> Il (Moïse) prit le veau qu'ils avaient fabriqué, le brûla par le feu, le moulut en poudre fine, et en saupoudra la surface de l'eau qu'il fit boire aux Israélites (Ex. 32 20).

> Oaths are a divine judgment. The good and evil that they decide between amount to fortune and misfortune. Hence one speaks of eating and drinking one's oath. It either confirms or threatens one's very existence (Klinger 1987).

LES SERMENTS DE LOYAUTÉ constituent l'un des ressorts les plus puissants du système politique. Ils sont les garants de l'ordre en place. En Mésopotamie ils sont attestés par l'écriture, au premier millénaire, au second ainsi qu'au troisième, notamment à l'époque d'Agadé avec le roi Šarkališarri (2217–2193).[1] À chaque avènement et pour leur prise en fonction, les souverains font mettre par écrit des engagements jurés qui impliquent la sûreté de l'État. Dans cet article nous entendons présenter quelques réflexions entourant le serment, ses implications sociales et ses modalités. La mise en contexte d'un document de l'époque d'Ur III comptabilisant le combustible et les viandes pour un banquet spécial « Lorsque les généraux prêtent serment… » (Steinkeller : 2008) nous amène à réévaluer le rite, son aspect oral, et singulièrement l'ingestion des matières actives qui menacent l'organisme du jureur.

Avant d'aborder ce qui caractérise les serments de loyauté, nous devons brièvement clarifier quelques points essentiels. Le serment de loyauté des sujets à celui qui les dirige occupe dans le fonctionnement des systèmes étatiques un rôle déterminant. Il est le moyen le plus efficace, à la fois symbolique et rituel, pour assurer une mise en ordre des loyautés. Acte unilatéral (et même vertical pourrait-on ajouter), le serment intervient à des moments critiques pour contrôler et pour conjurer les forces du chaos. Il s'affronte en ce sens aux figures du désordre que sont incertitude et désobéissance, des figures qui peuvent être actives ou passives. Pour cela des rites divers (rites de cohésion ou rites d'intégration, épreuves initiatiques plus ou moins contraignantes, réjouissances collectives) traduisent par les gestes la nécessité d'intégrer chaque

*Note de l'auteur :* Je remercie Philippe Abrahami pour les observations précieuses qu'il m'a fait.

1. Pour la mention d'un serment prêté au roi Šarkališarri (2217–2193) incluant le déplacement des insignes royaux, voir la note de Foster (1986 : 50 n. 31).

individu dans le tissu social et politique. Malgré de multiples études consacrées au sujet (San Nicolò 1938 ; Verdier 1991 ; Lafont and Joannès 1996 ; Sandowicz 2012), le serment reste un acte complexe, encore mal défini, à la charnière du politique, du juridique, du religieux, du magique, un domaine suprationnel, un domaine qui met en jeu beaucoup plus que l'individu, comme l'a rappelé récemment le philosophe Giorgio Agamben (2011).

Il est de règle, pour les serments militaires, que des liens d'appartenance soient renforcés par des rituels d'initiation. Du coup, la prise de serment s'apparente à un rite initiatique avec toute sa dramaturgie. Les soldats vont rompre les liens sociaux antérieurs pour entrer grâce à des rites d'intégration sous l'autorité d'un chef. Les ethnologues ont souvent souligné la composante « ésotérique » de ces rituels d'initiation touchant en premier les jeunes hommes en âge de combattre, excluant femmes, enfants et vieillards, ainsi que les esclaves et les étrangers. Le regroupement prend alors corps autour de principes de secrets d'initiation et d'engagements jurés que l'on perçoit dans l'espace des mythes, des symboles et des rites, pour ne pas parler de sorcellerie (Balandier 1988: 41 ; 1984: 125). La procédure implique des dimensions surnaturelles, telle que l'invocation d'une divinité ou d'une instance morale supérieure, elle implique une disponibilité, dira-t-on, par exemple une voix de circonstance, un langage, des paroles mesurées, un engagement physique et corporel, une gestuelle, bref une panoplie de moyens complexes, quelquefois (mais pas toujours) explicites pour l'historien.

C'est dans cette perspective qu'il convient de placer la procédure du serment de loyauté (serment politique, ou serment promissoire [Lafont 1997]). Ce dernier a quelque chose d'unique et de sacré qui n'a que de lointains rapports avec le juridique, au sens contractuel (San Nicolò 1938). Le serment devient remise en ordre, ou plutôt il est le désordre momentanément réglé. C'est un acte fondateur renouvelé à chaque avènement du pouvoir. Promesse solennelle de fidélité et de dévouement au gouvernement, au régime. Le serment de fidélité (ou d'allégeance) comprend alors un rite oral, marqué par une ingestion d'aliments spécifiques censés travailler à l'intérieur du corps.[2] C'est pourquoi il est question de « manger la parole », ou encore de « manger le serment ».[3]

## Les modalités rituelles des serments de loyauté au premier millénaire

Dans le monde assyrien, dignitaires et fonctionnaires, ainsi que tous les membres importants de l'empire assyrien sont liés par de tels engagements jurés qui leur sont imposés (Marti 2010 ; Malbran-Labat 1982: 207) (*adê*). Le vassal qui manque à ses promesses s'expose, comme l'indiquent les malédictions lancées à son encontre,

2. En dehors des quelques aliments ordinaires, souvent d'une très grande banalité, ceux que l'organisme ingérait sans la moindre difficulté, les ingrédients d'une autre nature, valorisés rituellement, étaient ressentis comme potentiellement dangereux, et même chargés de poison. Le ventre des parjures et des traitres se trouvait l'espace de quelques heures dans une épreuve de type ordalique, rongé qu'il était par des forces obscures.

3. En Afrique on dit « manger la parole » ; en persan, « manger le serment », dans ce cas il est question de boisson soufrée destinée à accompagner la prestation de serment. Benveniste 1947 ; Koch-Piettre 2010.

non seulement à des sanctions sociales, des représailles en bonne et due forme, mais aussi à des sanctions divines (de type maladie) orchestrées par les puissances célestes garantes de la conformité de l'engagement. Les pièces décisives de ce dossier des *adê* ont été présentées par D. J Wiseman (1958), puis par S. Parpola et K. Watanabe (1988: 108–122). Ainsi, le serment que fait jurer le roi Assurbanipal, roi d'Assyrie, à ses serviteurs est-il de dénoncer sans détour toute parole mauvaise, toute parole défavorable, toute parole néfaste qui ne seraient ni convenables ni propices à Assurbanipal. Ces paroles ne sauraient être dissimulées, elles doivent obligatoirement être rapportées à Assurbanipal, le grand prince héritier, fils d'Assarhaddon. Les engagements jurés pour l'occasion ne sont pas simplement des paroles prononcées solennellement, ce sont des actes entourés de l'aura que procure la magie, celle des objets sacrés, celle des insignes divins, celle des actes exécutés à l'intérieur d'un lieu sacré, celle des gestes sacramentels et des manipulations mystérieuses autour de la nourriture assorties de malédictions à l'encontre des parjures :

« Vous ne ferez pas d'engagements jurés devant les dieux, lit-on dans le traité d'Assarhaddon, et vous ne vous engagerez pas les uns envers les autres en servant de la nourriture à table et en buvant à une coupe, en allumant du feu .. » (Wiseman 1958). Pareillement, dans les *Annales assyriennes*, les rites oraux rappellent à ceux qui pourraient les oublier les engagements pris (Borger 1996: 50). L'absorption d'aliments (et de matières non alimentaires) qui vont s'intégrer au corps du jureur pour exercer sur celui-ci une sorte de menace tant que la nourriture nourrissante reste dans le ventre du jureur : « Lorsque vous reviendrez dans vos cités que vous mangerez de la nourriture et oublierez ces engagements jurés, alors que l'eau que vous buvez maintenant, vous vous en rappellerez et vous respecterez ces engagements jurés que vous avez passés au sujet d'Assarhaddon » (*CAD* A/1: 131–134).

Il existe, ailleurs, d'autres exemples de manipulations rituelles impliquant l'ingestion de nourriture lors de la prise de serment :[4] « De même que le pain et le vin entrent dans les intestins, de même le serment qui entre liquide dans vos intestins ... ».[5] En analysant les procédures de prise de serment à l'époque néo-babylonienne, Małgorzata Sandowicz a également noté que les gestes ne se limitaient pas à jurer en touchant telle ou telle partie du corps, à main levée, face au soleil, ou à jurer la nuit en prenant à témoin les étoiles et les planètes, ou encore en donnant sa parole à l'intérieur d'un cercle magique de farine, mais consistaient aussi à « toucher » la carcasse du mouton sacrifié, pour être consommé (Sandowicz 2012: 100–101). De cette documentation du premier millénaire, il ressort de troublantes similitudes de forme et de fond avec les archives du second millénaire : textes hittites,[6] et celles de la Mésopotamie du Nord (Mari, Terqa, Chagar Bazar).

4. + Inscription sur un vase en argent ciselé dont on boit le contenu, Winckler 1894: 2:1 ; Luckenbill 1927 : 2:69–71.

5. Parpola and Watanabe 1988. L'Ancien Testament rapporte un rituel comparable d'absorption d'eau d'amertume et de malédiction composée d'un dixième d'*ephra* de farine d'orge et d'une poignée de terre prise sur le seuil du Temple. L'absorption de cette potion par la femme suspectée d'adultère avait pour but de laver les soupçons ou, au contraire, d'inculper celle-ci : « les eaux de malédiction, pénétrant en elle, lui seront amères : son ventre gonflera, son sexe se flétrira », Nm. V 15–28. Voir aussi Frymer-Kensky 1981.

6. Collins 2003. L'auteure note l'emploi spécifique des boyaux dans les pratiques de la magie.

## Les textes du second millénaire, archives de Mari

À l'image des engagements jurés assyriens, les serments à Mari (Durand 1991 ; 1997: 168–180 ; Charpin 2010 ; Lafont and Joannès 1996) s'imposent aux personnels du palais et tout spécialement à ceux qui occupent une position clé à l'intérieur de l'organisation du pouvoir. Ces serments de fidélité concernent en priorité la sécurité du roi et plus largement celle de son palais. Ces serments engagent aussi la loyauté et la probité du serviteur de l'État. L'un de ces protocoles (Charpin 2010), un serment prêté par les dieux, précise que toute action déloyale envers le roi régnant (en l'occurrence Zimri-Lim) doit être dénoncée au roi sans délai. Les devoirs qui incombent au serviteur sont ici définis explicitement. À l'instar des engagements assyriens, le serviteur de l'État ne peut garder le silence devant tout acte mauvais (tels que détournements des récompenses dues aux soldats méritants, il ne peut s'approprier une part du butin, ou privilège accordé). Il ne peut, non plus, accueillir des fugitifs recherchés par les autorités, ou encore utiliser des ouvriers pour faire, par exemple, rénover sa maison personnelle aux frais du palais. Voilà ce qui doit être dénoncé. En outre, ce serment ne saurait être sujet à la prescription : « Ce serment par les dieux prêté à Zimri-Lim tant que je vivrai ... (...) en tant que serviteur (*ša wardûtim*) que je lui prête de tout mon cœur ... Que ces dieux ... tous le tabou me fassent périr .... (...) qu'ils me maudissent pour toujours dans mon corps d'une mauvaise malédiction ... » Malgré l'état fragmentaire du document, on relève les caractéristiques essentielles du serment de loyauté ou d'allégeance : l'engagement est personnel, sacré, illimité, sincère, menaçant, et surtout garanti tout à la fois par les dieux, l'autorité royale et par l'action magique (de type ordalique) exercée sur le corps du jureur.

Plusieurs documents nous font savoir qu'avant de partir en campagne, les responsables militaires généraux, les scribes de l'état-major, les chefs de section, et les lieutenants devaient également prêter un tel serment au roi. Après avoir procédé à un recensement pour dénombrer les hommes disponibles, ceux qui étaient bons pour le service, on procédait à des engagements jurés au roi ainsi qu'aux dieux protecteurs. Selon toute vraisemblance, ces recrutements étaient plus ou moins forcés, dûment enregistrés par écrit, et donc n'étaient vraiment pas faits pour plaire à la population générale. Il fallait nécessairement offrir une compensation à la mobilisation. On procédait alors, comme c'est souvent le cas en pareille circonstance, à des réjouissances, à des distributions de vivres, et à la mise en place dans un climat festif d'un banquet en faveur des gens d'armes. De tels festins organisés pour la mobilisation de 3000 soldats nous sont connus par exemple à Chagar-Bazar (Talon et Hammade 1997: n° 19). Les raisons sont limpides : non seulement il fallait parer aux désertions, mais aussi s'assurer que les soldats méritants reçoivent leurs récompenses et qu'aucun officier ne s'avise de détourner leur part. Là encore, on avait recours à des rites oraux. Le serment d'allégeance, assimilé à un interdit alimentaire (*asakkum*) était physiquement placé dans la bouche du jureur « le serment par Samsi-Addad et Yasmah-Addad, j'ai placé dans ma bouche et dans celle du chef de section un serment par le roi ... etc. » (ARM II 13 [LAPO 17: 457]).

Gouverneurs et militaires, autant que devins, inspecteurs, et nombre d'autres catégories de professionnels prêtaient également serment, et engageaient un moment donné leur vie au service de leur maître, le roi (ARM XIII 147). Ces prestations de serment ne se déroulaient pas n'importe où, elles avaient lieu dans l'espace monumental de la porte principale du palais· Les archives de Mari font connaître une de ces procédures consistant à faire boire aux jureurs une potion faite d'eau et d'argile provenant justement de la porte sacrée (Durand 2008/2009; Charpin 2010). Ces archives font aussi connaître des modalités d'engagement juré « par les herbes du roi », une plante ingurgitée lors de la prise du serment qui allait magiquement se retourner pour empoisonner celui qui enfreignait son vœu. Après cette singulière cérémonie, la préparation était censée œuvrer à l'intérieur du corps humain. Celui-ci, en effet, ne s'imprégnait pas immédiatement des aliments ingurgités. On doit préciser que le ventre (celui des Anciens, pas celui des modernes), les intestins et la curieuse mécanique de digestion emplie de mystères insondables prenaient tout son temps pour assimiler *dangereusement* les aliments (Geller 1990; Charpin 1996). Le résultat était tangible. Plusieurs témoignages (notamment une lettre de Yasmah Addu[7]) portent à croire que ces serments étaient respectés et unanimement tenus. Quittons à présent Mari pour l'empire d'Ur III, et remontons encore quelques siècles.

## Un précurseur de l'époque d'Ur III

Toujours au sujet des supports magiques du serment, un texte administratif d'Ur III publié par Piotr Steinkeller dans les *Mélanges M. Sigrist* (2008) a retenu notre attention. Le texte appartient à la catégorie des documents de la vie pratique. Il nous informe indirectement de la réalité du serment des généraux à leur souverain. L'intérêt de cette tablette[8] est qu'elle cumule quatre types d'information: (1) l'enregistrement de combustibles pour les cuissons d'un banquet, (2) le banquet des généraux, et ses viandes particulières, (3) la prestation d'un serment de loyauté, (4) la date de l'enregistrement. Il s'agit d'un texte d'enregistrement de combustible en vue de procéder à la cuisson de viandes particulières. Il s'agit de beaux morceaux dûment listés (bœufs, porcs, moutons et volailles) et destinés à la table des généraux du roi Amar-Sin alors qu'ils lui prêtent serment dans la capitale.

1. *L'enregistrement des combustibles.* Ils sont destinés aux cuisiniers. Le scribe a donc consigné méticuleusement sur la tablette et à plusieurs reprises le terme SA GI, un terme que l'on traduit conventionnellement par canne de roseaux. L'emploi de cette plante comme combustible m'apparaît cependant paradoxal. Certes, le roseau est rapidement inflammable, peu coûteux, partout disponible et à peu de frais. Mais alors, dans ce cas, pour quelle raison tenir un registre détaillé des sorties ? On ne peut en réalité que s'étonner de l'emploi d'un tel combustible (même en grande quantité !) pour mener à bien la cuisson de gros morceaux de viande.[9] Sous son seul aspect technique, le roseau convient mal

7. Sur le texte ARM I 3 (+ LAPO 18 : 931), le manquement est compris comme une faute, une maladie contagieuse et morale : l'*assakku* des grands dieux Dagan et surtout le *dieu Itūr-Mēr* dieu des serments.

8. La tablette, initialement transcrite par Samuel Feigin dans les années 30 pour un collectionneur non identifié, a malheureusement depuis été perdue de vue ; elle n'a donc pas pu être collationnée par Steinkeller. Seule sa transcription nous est parvenue. Mis à part l'inconvénient de son origine incertaine, les renseignements sont suffisants pour rendre compte de l'ensemble.

9. Sur les divers emplois du roseau à brûler *qanû*, cf. CAD Q : 85–88.

à la cuisson, il fait de la fumée, produit des matières volatiles, des cendres (un peu comme du papier), mais pas de feu de cuisson (Gélard 2007). Il est notoirement impropre à la cuisson. On peut à la rigueur utiliser des ramures de palme pour cuire rapidement de minces galettes de pain, mais en aucun cas du roseau ordinaire. Les bois les plus recherchés pour le chauffage des fours sont normalement les bois blancs. Ils assurent une source d'énergie égale, plus stable et offrent l'avantage de produire de longues flammes, de faire du charbon et de cuire uniformément. C'est d'ailleurs ce que montrent les analyses anthracologiques faites par exemple sur les résidus des foyers sacrés d'Ébla : bois de câpriers, chênes blancs méditerranéens, frênes, ormes (Fiorentino et Caracuta 2010). Ces bois-énergie (comme ceux de construction) n'échappent aucunement à l'administration centrale.[10] L'État, depuis toujours et partout, encadre de façon autoritaire les prélèvements de bois de chauffe. Le texte en outre reflète le principe d'une sélection organisée : les bois sont comptés en fagots de façon claire, différenciée et systématique pour répondre à une réquisition (faite par le MAŠKIM).[11] Les combustibles (un bois, une espèce de saule ou peut-être une sorte de bambou comme ceux avec lesquels on faisait des barques, des meubles et de grandes maisons ?) ne sont pas indifférents, ils doivent être purs, et peut-être même aromatiques. Ils ont en effet à répondre à une cuisson précise : à feu vif ou bien lente, croustillante, au four ou bien au bain-marie. Or l'on sait que la cuisine mésopotamienne, pour être respectable, privilégie justement pour le ragoût ou le pot-au-feu, des plats qui requièrent une très longue cuisson, surtout pour la langue de bœuf et les tripes de bœuf (mentionnées dans les premières lignes).

2. *Le festin carné.* La quantité et la qualité du combustible n'est pas insignifiante, elle est à la hauteur de la cérémonie qui va suivre. Il s'agit de cuire les viandes de trois bœufs, des parties spécifiques, comme les langues et les tripes, il s'agit de cuire aussi deux porcs engraissés à l'orge, dix moutons gras, des agneaux, 77 perdrix et une bonne vingtaine d'autres petits volatiles. Toutes ces viandes sont le signe de fête, elles ne sauraient être apprêtées que pour une occasion exceptionnelle, certainement un festin donné à l'occasion de la prestation du serment.
3. *La prestation de serment.* Le document n'offre aucun détail sur la teneur de l'engagement juré. Son caractère officiel et cérémoniel ne fait cependant guère de doute (invocation du nom du roi, viandes issues vraisemblablement de sacrifices). De façon générale, le contexte festif et militaire correspond à ce que l'on sait des engagements jurés au souverain par ses officiers.
4. *La date de l'enregistrement.* Le texte est daté du 10^e^ mois de l'an Sept d'Amar-Sin, soit en 2040 selon la chronologie moyenne. Cette date est le moment où le roi envoie ses généraux se battre contre le Huhnuri (une région de l'Anšan/

10. On retrouve pareillement l'importance du bois, gros bois et petit bois, pour la cuisson des plats destinés au Grand Roi des Perses, dans le recueil des *Stratagèmes* de Polyen, cité par Briant (1996 : 299). Sur la provenance des bois : Cadelli 1994. Steinkeller 1987. Willcox 1991.

11. Sur le rôle du maškin voir Lafont 1997 : 43.

Kusistan[12]). Redoute-t-il la défection de ses officiers, s'inquiète-t-il des détournements ou bien pratique-t-il tout simplement une politique de grande prudence? Une chose est certaine, le roi fait organiser dans sa capitale, Ur, un festin carné en même temps qu'il fait prêter à ces hommes un serment de loyauté par le nom du roi.

## Le repas de viande, comme support du serment

Les pièces de viande évoquées dans ce texte ne se laissent pas réduire à de simples abats, quand bien même en ferait-on des morceaux gastronomiques. Les parties vitales que sont les rognons, le cœur, les poumons, la rate, les ris, la cervelle, la moelle, ne sont pas des viandes neutres, ni de simples organes des animaux de boucherie, ce sont des morceaux qui (même encore aujourd'hui) relèvent de ce que l'on appelle « la cuisine canaille », en ce qu'ils s'acoquinent avec les interdits. Ce sont des principes actifs toujours employés pour renforcer les pratiques de types magiques. Dans ce contexte leur présence n'a pas lieu de nous en étonner puisque l'on sait que la langue (et la salive) occupent une dimension qui tient à l'évidence.[13] La logique à l'œuvre vise à établir une sorte de correspondance « parlante », si l'on peut dire, à travers un serment matérialisé et rendu actif par l'absorption effective de la partie sensible de l'animal sacrifié.

Sur un plan physiologique, la langue de bœuf est un gros morceau qui atteint facilement les trois kilos. Elle est très épaisse et ne peut être cuite que comme un pot-au-feu (ou un court bouillon). Quant aux produits tripiers, tels les boyaux qui peuvent faire de la charcuterie, ils doivent être bien nettoyés, puis cuits à l'eau bouillante durant plusieurs heures ... dans les deux cas, on a besoin d'une cuisson très longue, et donc de combustibles en proportion.

Ce qui saute aux yeux dans ce texte ce n'est pas uniquement la grande variété des viandes (bœuf, porc, mouton, volailles), c'est la liste élaborée des fournitures de combustible, laissant entrevoir divers modes de cuisson : celle des ragoûts préparés au chaudron certainement, mais aussi celle des grillades, et peut-être même celle des tourtes « à la Bottéro ». Il est certes hasardeux d'en dire davantage, mais nous retrouvons dans l'assiette des militaires les espèces animales qui suivent la hiérarchie (du plus imposant au plus délicat). D'abord la chair bovine, c'est celle que l'on donne en priorité aux combattants, pour les rendre forts « comme un boeuf ». Donc des bœufs puissants et engraissés au grain au nombre de trois (ce sont eux qui requièrent les 120 fagots), des cochons également engraissés au nombre de deux (six fois moins de bois), une dizaine de moutons, et enfin septante-sept perdrix. La proportion de bois mise à la disposition du cuisinier pour cuire des viandes si variées laisse entendre un large éventail de plats.

12. Lafont 2009. Durant les neuf années du règne d'Amar Sin (c. 2046–2038 ou 1981–1973) qui succèdent à son père Šulgi, la guerre est sur différents fronts, et le roi est occupé par des campagnes militaires.

13. Langue et salive jouent dans les pratiques d'ensorcellement (et partant dans le folklore universel), un rôle assez significatif, Cf. Bottéro 1975 : 95–144.

## Conclusion

À ce stade nous pouvons établir plusieurs remarques. On connaissait depuis longtemps les serments de loyauté prêtés par les militaires néo-assyriens à leur souverain ainsi que ceux du second millénaire, issus de la riche documentation de Mari. On peut dorénavant ajouter à ce corpus un document administratif de l'époque d'Ur III et faire remonter au troisième millénaire l'antériorité de la pratique du serment de loyauté. L'intérêt majeur du document évoqué ne tient toutefois pas uniquement dans son caractère précurseur, il tient plutôt dans les informations indirectes (et précieuses) qu'il livre. Car, malgré son laconisme apparent, ce texte d'enregistrement fournit une mine d'informations appréciables concernant les préparatifs d'un festin au moment où les généraux prêtent serment.

Le document énumère les morceaux de viande qui seront à cuisiner et il privilégie deux pièces : les langues et les tripes. Ces deux pièces de viande, éminemment symboliques, sont destinées à la table des généraux et à nul autre. Elles ont mystérieusement partie liée avec le rituel de la prise de serment. L'ingestion de cette nourriture carnée (viandes spécifiques provenant de sacrifices) qui transite par le ventre du jureur, qui investit son corps, qui le tient lié (physiquement et magiquement), joue de toute évidence un rôle de gardien de mémoire.

La question du combustible qui est à la base de notre interrogation nous a permis, incidemment, d'ouvrir de nouvelles pistes de recherches. Comment en effet comprendre le terme de SA GI, sachant la nécessité absolue de disposer d'un combustible au pouvoir calorifique suffisant pour cuire les viandes et rendre efficace le rituel ? Comme le présente le texte, pour les besoins de la cérémonie, viandes et plantes combustibles doivent mutuellement se correspondre. L'ensemble est défini sans ambiguïté sur la tablette : « C'est lorsque les généraux prêtent serment ... » Pour les autorités, c'est une fête ; par contre pour ceux qui sont enrôlés de force, c'est une autre affaire ! Le désordre n'est pas pour aujourd'hui !

P200514. Trad. P. Steinkeller (2008)

| | | |
|---|---|---|
| 1. | 120 sa gi gud 3 ba-ra-šeg$_6$ | 120 bundles of reeds were used to cook 3 oxen; |
| 2. | ⌜8⌝ sa gi uzu-ma-la 2 ba-ra- šeg$_6$ | 8 bundles of reeds were used to cook 2 (ox) tongues (?); |
| 3. | [... sa gi] šag$_4$-gar$^!$ dùg gud 2 [ba] ra šeg$_6$ | [x bundles of reeds] were used to cook fine tripe of 2 oxen; |
| 4. | ⌜5+x Sa gi⌝ bar šáh niga 2 ba-ra šeg$_6$ | ⌜5+x bundles of reeds⌝ were used to cook 2 grain-fed pigs; |
| 5. | 50 sa gi udu-niga 10 ba-ra šeg$_6$ | 50 bundles of reeds were used to cook the sides of 10 grain-feed sheep; |
| 6. | 20 sa gi šáh niga [2] ba-ra šeg$_6$ | 20 bundles of reeds were used to cook [2] grain-fed pigs; |
| 7. | [x] sa gi sila$_4$ 10 ba-[ba-ra šeg$_6$] | [x] bundles of reeds were used to cook 10 lambs; |
| 8. | ⌜5⌝ sa gi dar$^{mušen}$ 77 ba-ra šeg$_6$ | ⌜5⌝ bundles of reeds were used to cook 77 partridges (?); |

| | |
|---|---|
| 9. 2 sa gi mušen tur 20 ba-ra-šeg₆ | 2 bundles of reeds were used to cook 20 small birds; |
| ud šagina-ne nam-érem in-kud-ša | (these reeds were spent) when the generals took the loyalty oath. Igi-Enlilaše, the requisitioner, Swore by the name of the king (to restitute the reeds?), Expanded at Ur. 10th month. Year Amar-Suen 7. |

## BIBLIOGRAPHIE


Agamben, G.
2011 *The Sacrament of Language. An Archaeology of the Oath.* Stanford: Stanford University Press.

Balandier, G.
1984 *Anthropologie politique.* 4e éd. Paris: Presses universitaires de France.
1988 *Le Désordre: Eloge du mouvement.* Paris: Fayard.

Benveniste, É.
1947 L'Expression du serment dans la Grèce ancienne. *RHR* 134: 81–94.

Borger, R.
1996 *Beiträge zum Inschriftenwerk Assurbanipals: Die Prismenklassen A, B, C = K, D, E, F, G, H, J und T sowie andere Inschriften.* Wiesbaden: Harrassowitz.

Bottéro, J.
1975 Antiquités assyro-babyloniennes. *AEPHE* 1975: 95–144.

Briant, P.
1996 *Histoire de l'empire perse de Cyrus à Alexandre.* Paris: Fayard.

Cadelli, D.
1994 Lieux boisés et bois coupés. Pp. 159–173 dans *Florilegium marianum II. Recueil d'études à la mémoire de Maurice Birot.* Dirigé D. Charpin et J.-M. Durand. Mémoire de NABU 3. Paris: Société pour l'étude du Proche-Orient ancien.

Charpin, D.
1996 Manger un serment. Pp. 85–96 dans *Jurer et maudire: Pratiques politiques et usages juridiques du serment dans le Proche-Orient ancien; Actes de la table ronde, Paris 10–Nanterre, 5 octobre 1996.* Dirigé par S. Lafont et F. Joannès. Méditerranées 10–11. Paris: L'Harmattan.
2010 Un nouveau « protocole de serment » de Mari. Pp. 49–75 dans *Opening the Tablet Box: Near Eastern Studies in Honor of Benjamin R. Foster.* Dirigé par S. Melville et A. Slotsky. CHANE 42. Leyde: Brill.

Collins, Billie J.
2003 The First Soldiers' Oath. *COS* 1.66:165–167.

Durand, J.-M.
1991 Précurseurs syriens aux protocoles néo-assyriens: Considérations sur la vie politique aux Bords-de-l'Euphrate. Pp. 13–71 dans *Marchands, diplomates et empereurs. Études sur la civilisation mésopotamienne offertes à Paul Garelli.* Dirigé par D. Charpin et F. Joannès. Paris: Recherche sur les Civilisations.
1997 *Documents épistolaires du palais de Mari.* LAPO 16. Paris: Cerf.
2008/2009 Résumé des cours, assyriologie *Annuaire du Collège de France.*

Fiorentino, G. et Caracuta, F.
2010 The Use of Plants in a Ritual Well at Ebla (Tell Mardikh)—Northwestern Syria. Pp. 307–320 dans *Proceedings of the 6th International Congress on the Archaeology of the Ancient Near East*. Dirigé par P. Matthiae, L. Nigro, et N. Marchetti. Wiesbaden, Harrassowitz.

Foster, B.
1986 Archives and Empire in Sargonic Mesopotamia. Pp. 46–52 dans *Cuneiform Archives and Libraries: Papers Read at the 30e Rencontre Assyriologique Internationale Leiden, 4–8 July 1983*. Dirigé par K. R. Veenhof. Istanbul: Nederlands Historisch-Archaeologisch Instituut.

Frymer-Kensky, T.
1981 Suprarational Legal Procedures in Elam and Nuzi. Pp. 129–130 dans *Studies on the Civilization and Culture of Nuzi and the Hurrians: In Honor of Ernest R. Lacheman on His Seventy-fifth Birthday*. SCCNH 1. Winona Lake, IN: Eisenbrauns.

Gélard, M.-L.
2007 Le roseau protecteur. *Technique et Culture* 48–49: 61–84.

Geller, M. J.
1990 Taboo in Mesopotamia: A Review Article. *JCS* 42: 105–117.

Klinger, E.
1987 Vows and Oaths. Pp. 301–305 dans vol. 15 de *The Encyclopedia of Religion*. Dirigé par M. Eliade. 16 vols. New York: Macmillan.

Koch-Piettre, R.
2010 Inscrire un serment en Grèce ancienne: Couper et verser. *Cahiers « Mondes anciens»* 1. https://journals.openedition.org/mondesanciens/112.

Lafont, B.
1997 Serments politiques et serments judiciaires à l'époque sumérienne: quelques données nouvelles. Pp. 31–48 dans *Jurer et maudire: pratiques politiques et usages juridiques du serment dans le Proche-Orient ancien; Actes de la table ronde, Paris 10–Nanterre, 5 octobre 1996*. Dirigé par S. Lafont et F. Joannès. Méditerranées 10–11. Paris: L'Harmattan.
2009 The Army of the Kings of Ur: The Textual Evidence. *Cuneiform Digital Library Journal* 5: 1–25. https://cdli.ucla.edu/files/publications/cdlj2009_005.pdf.

Lafont, S. et Joannès, F.
1996 *Jurer et maudire: Pratiques politiques et usages juridiques du serment dans le Proche-Orient ancien; Actes de la table ronde, Paris 10–Nanterre, 5 octobre 1996*. Méditerranées 10–11. Paris: L'Harmattan.

Luckenbill, D. D.
1927 *Ancient Records of Assyria and Babylonia*. 2 vols. Chicago: University of Chicago Press

Malbran-Labat, F.
1982 *L'Armée et l'organisation militaire de l'Assyrie d'après les lettres des Sargonides trouvées à Ninive*. HEO 19. Genève: Droz.

Marti, L.
2010 L'Empereur assyrien et ses devins. *JA* 298: 495–515.

Parpola, S. et Watanabe, K.
1988 *Neo-Assyrian Treaties and Loyalty Oaths*. SAA 2. Helsinki: Helsinki University Press.

Sandowicz, M.
2012 *Oaths and Curses: A Study in Neo-and Late Babylonian Legal Formulary*. AOAT 398. Münster: Ugarit-Verlag.

San Nicolò, M.
1938 Eid. *RlA* 2: 305–315.

Steinkeller, P.
1987 The Foresters of Umma: Toward a Definition of Ur III Labor. Pp. 73–115 dans *Labor in the Ancient Near East*. Dirigé par M. Powell. AOS 68. New Haven: American Oriental Society.
2008 Joys of Cooking in Ur III Babylonia. Pp. 185–192 dans *On the Third Dynasty of Ur: Studies in Honor of Marcel Sigrist*. Dirigé par P. Michalowski. Journal of Cuneiform Studies Supplemental Series 1. Boston: American Schools of Oriental Studies.

Talon, P. et Hammade, H.
1997 *Old Babylonian Texts from Chagar Bazar*. Brussels: Fondation Assyriologique Georges Dossin.

Verdier, R.
1991 *Le serment: Signes et fonctions*. Paris: Éditions du Centre national de la recherche scientifique.

Willcox, G.
1991 Exploitation des espèces ligneuses au Proche-Orient: Données anthracologiques. *Paléorient* 17: 117–126.

Winckler, H.
1894 *Sammlung von Keilschrifttexten II. Texten verschiedener Inhalts*. Leipzig: Pfeiffer.

Wiseman, D. J.
1958 *The Vassal-Treaties of Esarhaddon*. London: British School of Archaeology in Iraq.

CHAPTER 5

# Unjust Law: Royal Rhetoric or Social Reality?

Sophie Démare-Lafont

IT IS A COMMONLY ACCEPTED IDEA that law was introduced in human societies as a shield against revenge and retaliation, both expressions of disorder.[1] It is assumed that order depends on rigorous respect for the law issued by political authorities or local communities.[2] This is true up to a certain point, inasmuch as a legal rule usually meets the implicit requirement of justice, in other words when it does not contradict the notions of fairness, honesty, and rectitude.

But the assumption that the rule of law is necessarily and always just is far from self-evident. Examples of unjust laws are numerous nowadays, and lead to popular revolts when the brink of acceptance is reached. Law then reveals itself unable to maintain order. What brings peace and stability is basically justice. A rule of law is just a tool, a technical instrument framing the relationship between individuals or institutions. The purpose of the rule is to follow justice, namely the ethical and moral values that are supposed to underlie it. If not, law becomes nothing but a hollow sham or even worse, a means of oppression.

So, the notion of justice is subtle, subject to variation according to cultures and times, and mostly subjective. It has to do with equity, integrity, or probity, all behavioral qualities that are differently assessed depending on the individuals and the situations. In contrast, the rule of law is constant and uniformly enforceable each time the circumstances fit the case.

Thus, there is a tension between justice and law, the first being the goal while the second is the means (or at least one of the means).[3] The ideal rule of law should match technical effectiveness with just ends.

In the ancient Near East, these thoughts certainly applied despite the lack of any theoretical work of legal doctrine. The Mesopotamians developed a sense of justice that reflected a relativist conception. No human deed was just by itself, but only in comparison with an unjust one. Such use of opposite pairs aimed at creating a contrast

*Author's note:* I wish to thank the organizers of the RAI, especially my colleague K. De Graef, for doing me the honor of inviting me to give one of the keynote lectures.

1. This opinion is summarized in the following statement by Francis Bacon: "Revenge is a kind of wild justice; which the more man's nature runs to, the more ought law to weed it out." *Of Revenge*, *The Essays or Counsels, Civil and Moral*, 1625 (http://www.authorama.com/essays-of-francis-bacon-1.html).

2. One of the best modern examples is probably the law and order movement that developed by the middle of the 1960s in America, both as a social ideal and a political slogan. See Flamm 2005.

3. See, among others, Pound 1913.

in order to enhance each notion and emphasize the qualities of the virtuous individual versus the failures of his corrupted counterpart.

This rhetoric is a well-known stylistic device in Mesopotamian legal literature from Urukagina in the mid-third millennium on down to the Assyrian empire. Ur-Namma declares, for instance, in the prologue of his code: "I did not deliver the orphan to the rich. I did not deliver the widow to the mighty. I did not deliver the man with but one shekel to the man with one mina. I did not deliver the man with but one sheep to the man with one ox." (Ni 3191 iv 162–168 + Si. 277 ii 30–39: nu-síg lú níg-tuku-ra ba-ra-na-an-gar nu-mu-un-su lú á tuku-ra ba-ra-na-an-gar lú 1 gín-e lú 1 ma-na-ra ba-ra-na-an-gar lú 1 udu-e lú 1 gud-ra ba-ra-na-an-gar; trans. Roth 1997: 16).

Likewise, Hammurabi states in the epilogue of his code that he issued his "just jugdments" (*dīnāt mīšarim* xlvii 1) "in order that the mighty not wrong the weak (and) to provide just ways for the waif and the widow" (*dannum enšam ana la habālim ekūtam almattam šutēšurim*; xlvii 59–62; trans. Roth 1997: 133).

The two Akkadian keywords that are central to our topic and have been discussed at length are *kittum* and *mīšarum* (Cazelles 1973, 1987; Weinfeld 1992; Cancik-Kirschbaum 1999; Veenhof 2020). They occur mainly in the prologues and epilogues of the codes, and in numerous royal inscriptions. *Kittum* expresses the notion of firmness and stability, while *mīšarum* means literally what is straight. Both words are associated with the political power of the king in his mission of justice and apply above all to abuses of vulnerable persons and to dishonest officials as archetypes of iniquity and principal causes of disorder.

Wisdom literature and poetry resort to the same rhetoric. The Great Hymn to Šamaš, for instance, depicts how human behavior may please or annoy the god. It is significant that both attitudes are exemplified by the figures of the judge and the merchant, two essential characters of economic and social life. The roguish judge will go to jail while the careful one, who takes up the case of the weak for free, will have a long life.

> You show the roguish judge the (inside of) a jail, he who takes the fee but does not carry through, you make him bear the punishment. The one who receives no fee but takes up the case of the weak is pleasing to Šamaš, he will make long his life. The careful judge who gives just verdicts, controls the government, lives like a prince (Šamaš Hymn 97–102; Foster 2005: 631)

The fraudulent merchant will die prematurely and without heirs while the honest one will obtain wealth and posterity.

> He who commits fra[ud] as he hods the dry measure, who pays loans by the smaller standard, demands repayment by the extra standard, before his time, the people's curse will take effect on him, before his due, he will be called to account, he will bear the consequence (?). No heir will (there be) to take over his property, nor will (there be) kin to succeed to his estate. The honest merchant who pays loans by the [ex]tra (?) standard, thereby to make extra virtue,

> is pleasing to Šamaš, he will grant him extra life, he will make (his) family numerous, he will acquire wealth, [his] seed will be perpetual as the waters of a perpetual spring (Šamaš Hymn 112–122; Foster 2005: 632)

The message is clear and simple: powerful people should behave properly for fear of an immanent and unavoidable sanction. The deeds left unpunished by the human rule of law will not finally escape the omniscient divine justice.

These secular and religious compositions share the same lyrical tone to convey the perfect image of an idealized justice, be it divine or royal, that always prevails over evildoers and scoundrels (Edzard 1976).

A similar view is provided by the Babylonian Theodicy. In this refined debate between two friends on divine justice, the sufferer asserts that the world is ruled by injustice because acting properly toward his neighbor and his god does not prevent him from being oppressed, impoverished, and demoted. The answers of his optimistic friend all revolve around the contention that lies and falsehood are human and not divine features, hence the necessity to keep worshiping the gods and relying upon their inscrutable ways (Foster 2005, 914–922). Here, the just man is the one who accepts his fate and submits himself to the cosmic order, even if it results in misery and distress. For ultimately, the friend says, an earthly or heavenly authority will bring justice to the wronged man.[4] The king will redress the torts caused to the innocent, and the god will punish the concealed crook.

Injustice is thus acknowledged as an inevitable fact, a compulsive inclination of mankind. By contrast, justice appears as a precarious state that needs constant and precise means of preservation, one of which is the rule of law.

But what about unjust consequences that may accompany the normal enforcement of the law? I am not referring here to the obvious iniquities or abuses of power already mentioned: these are improper deeds that of course are not just but are not legal either.

What I want to investigate here are the situations where an injury is produced by legality itself. I shall concentrate on second-millennium documentation and mostly on the Old Babylonian period, which provides abundant and telling examples.

Sources on the subject can be distributed along three lines.

First, it sometimes happened that the implementation of a rule of law showed itself unjust in practice and led to drastic measures issued by the king. I shall begin with discussion of these cases.

Second, unjust affairs could be resolved by adjusting the problematic rule of law in order to make it more acceptable for reasons of either political benefit or general equity. This will be dealt with in the second part of this paper.

Third, there are situations in which injustice seemed fairly acceptable, at least to the political authorities, who tolerated legal discrimination and obviously reproachable practices. This will be the last part of the paper.

4. The figure of the "wronged man" is central in the Code of Hammurabi and has been the subject of various interpretations. See Démare-Lafont 2000; Roth 2002, with bibliography; and Graetz 2015.

## Correcting Unjust Law

The first example that comes to mind is connected with recurrent overindebtedness affecting massively large parts of the population during the second millennium. The only available remedy was the royal practice of debt cancellation.

The *mīšarum*-edicts and their Syrian and Assyrian *(an)durāru*-counterparts were typically measures of what is usually called social justice (see Weinfeld 1995; Westbrook 1995; Otto 1997; Charpin 2010: 83–96, with bibliography; Démare-Lafont 2019a). The loan contracts and sales of family houses that were the targets of these edicts were perfectly legal and unquestionable.[5] Yet the king pronounced them invalid in situations of deep economic crisis, when the pauperization of the middle classes prevented debtors from repaying their creditors and placed upon them a heavy financial burden. Therefore, the standard rule of law, according to which the creditor was entitled to recover his capital and the interest from the loan, became inadequate and even dangerous for public order: The insolvent debtor was unable to satisfy his creditor and exposed himself or his relatives to be seized and reduced to slavery, or to run away from his city to escape such a terrible fate, both outcomes that potentially threatened public peace and order. This justified the king's intrusion into private agreements, a rare initiative in Mesopotamian legal life, dictated by a kind of emergency. Even if some edicts were promulgated on happier occasions, such as the accession of a new king or a great victory (Charpin 2010: 91–94), they were primarily intended to reestablish justice against law.

It is remarkable that this purpose was obtained through a privilege, a derogation of the normal rules. This means that the assumed equality between the contracting parties was no longer actual (if it ever was). The right of the creditor to be paid off harmed the debtor because it involved consequences largely exceeding the initial stakes of the contract: giving away his wife or selling his house are too high a price to pay. Unscrupulous individuals certainly coveted the field or the workforce of borrowers and lent them grain or silver for the sole purpose of receiving their estate.[6] Of course, not all the creditors were rich and grasping, indifferent to the suffering of their debtors. One would expect, for instance, that the gods, often mentioned as money-lenders in Old Babylonian times, would agree to charitable loans only. Actually, the very fact that these contracts were included in the scope of the royal edicts shows that they were considered prejudicial as well.[7]

Basically, the mere enforcement of the creditor's right could end in a prejudice in a context of recurring overindebtedness, producing personal tragedies and economic disasters. Note that the legal principle in itself was not condemned by the king, who only reduced the pressure on some parts of the population until the next crisis. In this

5. Admittedly, sales of military land tenures should be considered illegal and were forbidden by the Code of Hammurabi. In fact, the primary reason for the debt cancellation edicts could have been the recovery of public land, given as pledge to the creditors or sold as if it was part of the soldier's estate (see Démare-Lafont, forthcoming). Kings would have extended this practice to licit contracts, in connection with recurring economic crises.

6. Steinkeller (2002: 114) assumes that such was the situation during the Ur III period.

7. Charpin (2005: 26–27) has shown that temple loans were often designed for profit making.

sense, justice appears as an interlude in an ocean of injustice. But we shall see later that even this small loophole could be bypassed.

Another illustration of the special dispensation of royal justice is provided by the power of mercy ([Démare-]Lafont 1999b: 31–37). Here again, the king made use of an arbitrary prerogative with limited scope and was considered able to undo a valid act, in this case a death sentence. This right to forgive is the corollary to his right to condemn and thus reflects the special nature of kingship. The decision relies solely on the king's good will and neither consent nor refusal requires justification. Immoral or biased reasons could motivate his choice to pardon or not. Besides, direct examples of royal mercy are few and we mostly hear about unforgivable acts. So the notion of justice seems questionable here, given the great deal of uncertainty that surrounds this royal activity.

In all these examples, strict observance of the rule of law would produce an unjust result, either for financial, political, or moral reasons. It is the task of royal justice to restore, at least temporarily, what has been disturbed by the normal course of the law.

## Adapting Unjust Law

So far, we have encountered royal intercessions that point to a case-by-case practice of justice, designed to redress what has been twisted by the rule of law.

Judges could act in the same manner, though on a lower level, in order to reduce the unjust impact of a rule of law.

See, for instance, this Old Babylonian letter that recalls a decision in a litigation concerning the return of the dowry after the death of a childless wife:

> Speak to Muhaddum: Thus say the judges of Babylon.
>
> May Šamaš and Marduk keep you in good health!
>
> Concerning the lawsuit of Ilšu-ibbišu, son of Warad-Sin, and Mattatum, we have seen their case, we have initiated proceedings against them according to the regulations of our lord (*ṣimdat bēlini*) and we have told to return to Mattatum all the dowry that Mattatum had given to her daughter and had brought into the house of Ilšu-ibbišu. We have despatched a soldier with her.
>
> Let them give all the valuables that are now to be seen (*mimma balṭam ša inanna innaṭṭalu*) (AbB 9 25; trans. Stol 1981: 17–19).

The letter contains the answer of the judges of Babylon to a local officer of Larsa, regarding a woman named Mattatum who gave her daughter in marriage to a certain Ilšu-ibbišu and granted her a dowry. After an unspecified span of time, the wife probably died without children, as Westbrook (1988: 92–93) assumed. In such a case, the complete dowry was to be given back to her family, in accordance with the provisions of the Code of Hammurabi (§163).[8] Veenhof (1997–2000: 73–74) argued convincingly

8. §163: "If a man marries a wife but she does not provide him with children, and that woman goes to her fate—if his father-in-law then returns to him the bridewealth that that man brought to his father-in-law's

that the "regulations of our lord" (*ṣimdat bēlini*) refer to the code itself, which means that, following the epistolary expression of the time, the "lord" here must be Hammurabi. An interesting feature of the document is that the case was first processed in Larsa, and then transferred to Babylon before coming back to Larsa for final enactment. This complicated procedure may reflect the status of the plaintiff, Mattatum, probably a citizen of Babylon who demanded the enforcement of the code against the local rules of Larsa, where her daughter probably lived. This option is another illustration of the subsidiarity of the law collections: written law was applicable only when someone (probably a Babylonian) asked for it explicitly (see [Démare-]Lafont 2000; and forthcoming). Here, the Babylonian provision favored Mattatum by imposing the return of the whole dowry, hence her request.

But the implementation of this rule was felt inequitable, judging by the last sentence of the letter, stating that Mattatum should receive only the available goods.[9] The Babylonian court thus reduced the requirement of the code to the available goods of the dowry, precluding the expendables that had already been used up. Veenhof (1997–2000: 73) considers that the final decision takes into account the point of view of Ilšu-ibbišu, because enforcing the basic rule, namely §163, would add unfairness to his sorrow. After having lost his wife, he would be compelled to repay the ordinary expenses of the couple. This is why he was liable only for the remaining assets.

Beyond this generous interpretation, there could be another, more pragmatic or even cynical reason for the clemency of the judges: What was at stake was less the pain of the widowed husband than the desire to pacify the relationship with a rebel city. It is well known that the conquest of this southern kingdom had been a challenging episode in the reign of Hammurabi, who eventually defeated the town in 1763 and tried to maintain a state of relative calm during the following years. It seems that this conquest implied, at least partially, the acceptance of Babylonian law as a sign of the victor's political domination (AbB 13 10; van Soldt 1994: 12–15; see the interpretation by Charpin 2000: 86). But here, as a gesture of conciliation, the judges of Babylon decided to soften the principle stated by the code. If this hypothesis is correct, we would have an example of incidental fairness, a kind of favoritism dictated by political reasons and not merely by justice.

There is however one field in which the court's indulgence is systematic, namely with regard to the first fault of a child toward his parents. The topic was studied by Cardascia (1988), who listed the legislative and contractual instances of this unformulated precept, according to which the first fault is excusable on the basis of a presumption of ignorance.

The most telling example comes from the Code of Hammurabi and deals with the disinheritance of a son:

> §168 If a man should decide to disinherit his son and declares to the judges, "I will disinherit my son," the judges shall investigate his case and if the son is

house, her husband will have no claim to that woman's dowry; her dowry belongs only to her father's house" (trans. Roth 1997: 112).

9. AbB 9 25: 18, *mimma balṭam ša inanna innaṭṭalu* "all the valuables that are now to be seen" (Stol 1981: 19); "everything which can be evaluated and can now (still) be spotted." (Veenhof 1997–2000: 73).

> not guilty of a grave offense deserving the penalty of disinheritance, the father may not disinherit his son.
> §169 If he should be guilty of a grave offense deserving the penalty of disinheritance by his father, they shall pardon him for his first one; if he should commit a grave offense a second time, the father may disinherit his son (trans. Roth 1997: 113).

The code states that when a man wishes to deprive one of his children of his share in the family estate, he should first declare his intention to the judges. Apparently, the decision of the father breaks social norms and oversteps the boundaries of usual parental authority.[10] Hearing the petition of the father, the court has to investigate the matter and if the son has committed no offense deserving such a penalty, the request of the father is to be rejected (§168). If they determine that there is just one serious misconduct, they shall forgive the son and only if a second grave offense has been committed is the father allowed to disinherit his child (§169). This solution relies on the idea that accountability for personal deeds requires full knowledge and understanding of their implications. The purpose of this two-step process is to advise the son solemnly after the first offense, in order to make him fully aware of what he did. He is deemed ignorant from the very notion of fault in its first commission. Therefore, he is merely warned of the wrongful nature of his act. The admonition is intended to help the son to mend his ways. But if he behaves improperly a second time, the lack of discernment cannot be postulated anymore and his father may disinherit him. The code assumes that punishing a child or a young man without any prior warning would be unfair. Enforcing the rule of law would thus lead to an injustice. Here, as in other instances of criminal law regarding children and teenagers, the level of personal liability is substantially reduced.[11] The mandatory leniency of the judges is a privilege of youth—and here again justice is a privilege.

Finally there are cases in which law created a legal imbalance that was not perceived as unjust by the Mesopotamians and this will be the third and last point.

## Allowing Unjust Law

These situations derive either from legal discrimination or unconscionable contracts.

Acts of legal discrimination appear as a corollary to the social inequalities that divided the Babylonian society. By assumption, they were not considered unjust.

The basic distinction between free persons and slaves has been the subject of many important studies showing all the nuances inside each category.[12] Despite the apparent antithetical nature of the two concepts of freedom and slavery in Mesopotamia, the boundaries between them were rather porous. An *awīlum* was not only a free man, he was also sometimes a citizen, a gentleman or even a member of the upper class

10. About the domestic jurisdiction of the father, see Démare-Lafont 2012.

11. See, e.g., in the realm of criminal law, the notion of rape which is diversely defined according to the age and status of the victim; Démare-Lafont 1999a: 133–171.

12. About Old Babylonian society, see Kraus 1973; Van De Mieroop 1999: 1–22; Von Dassow 2011: 214–217; and Démare-Lafont 2015, 2019b.

(*mār awilīm*), but he could become a *wardum*, at least temporarily, by reason of over-indebtedness or war. The *wardum* in turn was not always considered an object, and a high official could use this denomination as a sign of deference and respect toward the king.

Yet the antagonism of both statuses is highlighted in an Old Babylonian letter that raises the question of the primacy of law over justice:

> Speak to Šega-Enlila: Thus say Ili-iddinam, the town and the elders.
>
> May Šamaš grant you health for countless years!
>
> When the slave was caught inside the house, the town interrogated him and he only mentioned the son of Nur-Illabrat; he did not mention the son of the physician.
>
> And after he had been detained for four days and while they questioned him sharply he still only mentioned the son of Nur-Illabrat.
>
> Is it customary to extradit free citizens on the basis of what a slave says?
>
> When Ubarum went to Larsa because of his slave, he put the following question to his slave: "Who was with you?" <He answered>: "Only the son of Nur-Dingirmah was with me, the physician's son did not go (with us)."
>
> Now, question Ubarum [and if] he does not back off before you, he (= the physician's son) was indeed not mentioned in connection with the stolen barley. (. . .) (AbB 14 144; Veenhof 2005: 134–137).

A slave was caught in the act while robbing a house, and during his questioning, he gave the name of his partner (the son of Nur-illabrat) and exonerated another suspect (the son of the physician). This reiterated statement confronts the local judges with a complex issue: "Is it customary to extradit free citizens on the basis of what a slave says?" (lines 12–13 *ana pî wardim mār awīli ittanaddinu*).[13] In other words, should a free man be prosecuted on the sole word of a slave? It is unclear whether this is an ethical or legal dilemma, and apparently both aspects are at stake here. What causes a problem is not the fact that there is only one witness (actually the culprit) but that he is of a lower condition than the partner he denounces. In the accusatory system that prevailed in Mesopotamia, a formal accusation was obligatory to initiate the procedure. Implicitly, the text assumes that prosecution requires the action of a free citizen and this is probably the reason why Ubarum, the owner of the thief, is summoned and heard by a judge. This shrewdness was intended to help resolve the legal problem and consequently put an end to the unjust impunity of the partner by allowing the opening of a trial against him as well.

13. Thus with Veenhof 2005: 136. For another interpretation, see Wu 1995: "According to the testimony of the slave, the responsible person has been given up."

Another example of legal injustice is provided by some contractual clauses that explicitly circumvent the law in order to favor one party at the expense of the other. Such unconscionable contracts are attested mostly in the realm of debt cancellation and stem from the so-called peripheral cuneiform documentation from Syria and Cappadocia. Several contracts contain clauses by which the debtor renounces the benefit of a probably imminent edict.

For instance, in a Mari tablet, a couple borrows silver from a god and a goldsmith to be repaid one year later. Before the list of witnesses, a clause stipulates that "if an *andurārum*-edict is established, this silver will not be affected" (ARM 8 33: 13–14 KÙ-BABBAR *šu-ú ud-du-ra-ru-um, li-ša-ki-i*[*n*]*-ma ú-ul id-da-ra-ar*; see Durand 1982: 107 n. 1).

Another loan contract found at Mari but most likely written at Imar (A.2654; see Charpin 1990: 260–262; and Charpin and Ziegler 2003: 73–74), states that the silver borrowed by Halu-pu-Yama is *lā uddurarim* (line 2), "not affected by an *andurārum*-edict." As Charpin (1990: 263) rightly notes, the reference to the enthronement of the enigmatic Išar-Lim as king in the year-name indicates that the creditors anticipated an impending edict. Moreover, it is significant that the two lenders are the god Šamaš and the goddess Belet-matim, which means that the institution of the temple was eager to be repaid in any case. This is another reason to doubt the charitable nature of the temple loans.

Old Assyrian merchants sometimes resorted to the same practice by specifying in the contact that the debt should be paid off even in case of discharge by a royal edict (see examples in Balkan 1974).

The clause appears also in Terqa in sale contracts of fields, which are said *lā andurārim*, "not subject to an *andurārum*-edict."[14]

In all these cases, the debtors were probably compelled to accept the harsh conditions imposed by the creditors, if they wanted to obtain credit. Now, the question is: Were these immoral deeds legal? Actually, it seems that biased contracts were not prohibited. Appealing to the king to terminate them was certainly an option, but it is doubtful that it was ever implemented, if only because of the cost of such a procedure. In fact, in accordance with the common legal practices in Mesopotamia, the agreed dispositions of the parties served as legal rule between them, even if they disregarded royal provisions or local customs. A contractual clause could always go beyond (or below) the requirements of the law. For instance, some Neo-Babylonian marriage contracts threatened with death by iron dagger the wife seen—and not caught—with a man other than her husband, thus assimilating suspicion of adultery with the perpetrated crime, as observed by Westbrook.[15]

14. About the meaning of this clause, see Chavalas 1997.

15. The standard sentence is *i-na* $u_4$*-mu* [f]PN *it-ti* LÚ-NITA *šá-nam-ma am-ra-a-ta ina* GÍR AN-BAR *ta-ma-a-ta*, "Should [f]PN (wife) be seen with another man, she will die by the iron dagger" (Roth 1988: 186–187 and n. 3 for reference to the sources); Westbrook 1990: 562–563. A complementary explanation stresses that this provision always occurs along with heavy fines owed by the husband wishing to divorce. Both deterrent clauses aimed at preventing the parties from breaking the contract (Roth 1988: 205) and probably resulted from some bargaining between the two families: the poor wife who got married with no dowry was protected against repudiation almost for free, but she had to accept the harsh presumption placed on her (Wunsch 2003: 6–7). According to Waerzeggers 2020, the difference between the spouses is less economic than social.

In these matters, forced submission of a wife to her husband or of a debtor to his creditor is offensive to our modern minds and certainly aroused disapproval among many Mesopotamians. But as long as these situations were not denounced as unfair, again a purely speculative option, they remained valid because they were considered legal. Free will could thus produce lawful iniquity.

All the foregoing developments show that law does not by itself yield order. Justice is a much better candidate. The Babylonian experience is a good witness thereof, in that it reveals how the combination of the two complementary notions of law and justice allows balanced relationship within society. Oscillations of the pendulum in one direction or the other depended on what the social fabric felt was tolerable or not. In any event, civil tranquility would be impossible in a system based purely on automatic application of the law, without any consideration for morality. A world that bristles with law, and only law, would be either chaotic or despotic, definitely uncivilized. For, as Augustine put it, "justice removed, then what are kingdoms but great bands of robbers?" (*City of God* IV ix).

## BIBLIOGRAPHY


Balkan, K.

1974 Cancellation of Debts in Cappadocian Tablets from Kültepe. Pp. 29–41 in *Anatolian Studies Presented to Hans Gustav Güterbock on the Occasion of His 65th Birthday*. Edited by K. Bittel, Ph. H. J. Houwink ten Cate, and E. Reiner. PIHANS 35. Istanbul: Nederlands Historisch-Archaeologisch Instituut in het Nabije Oosten.

Cancik-Kirschbaum, E.

1999 'König der Gerechtigkeit'—Ein altorientalisches Paradigma zu Recht und Herrschaft. Pp. 52–68 in Torah—Nomos—Ius: Abendländischer Antinomismus und der Traum vom herrschaftsfreien Raum. Edited by G. Palmer, C. Nasse, and R. Haffke. Berlin: Vorwerk 8.

Cardascia, G.

1988 L'indulgence pour la première faute dans les droits du Proche-Orient ancient. Pp. 651–674 in *Estudios en homenaje al Profesor J. Iglesias*. Edited by J. Roset Esteve. Madrid: Seminario de Derecho Romano "Ursicino Alvarez."

Cazelles, H.

1973 De l'idéologie royale. *JANESCU* 5: 59–73.

1987 Aspiration à la justice dans le monde prébiblique. Pp. 371–387 in *Autour de l'Exode (études)*. Edited by H. Cazelles. SB. Paris: Lecoffre; Gabalda.

Charpin, D.

1990 *L'andurârum* à Mari. *MARI* 6: 253–270.

2000 Lettres et procès paléo-babyloniens. Pp. 69–111 in *Rendre la justice en Mésopotamie: Archives judiciaires du Proche-Orient ancient (IIIe–Ier millénaires avant J.-C.)*. Edited by F. Joannès. Saint-Denis: Presses Universitaires de Vincennes.

2005 Les dieux prêteurs dans le Proche-Orient amorrite (c. 2000–1600 av. J.-C.). *Topoi* 12/13: 13–34.

2010 *Writing, Law, and Kingship in Old Babylonian Mesopotamia*. Translated by J. M. Todd. Chicago: University of Chicago Press.

Charpin, D. and Ziegler, N.

2003 *Mari et le Proche-Orient à l'époque amorrite: Essai d'histoire politique*. FM 5. Paris: Société pour l'étude du Proche-Orient ancien.

Chavalas, M.
1997 *Naṣbum* in the Khana Contracts from Terqa. Pp. 179–188 in *Crossing Boundaries and Linking Horizons: Studies in Honor of Michael C. Astour.* Edited by D. G Young, M. W. Chavalas, and R. E. Averbeck. Bethesda, MD: CDL.

[Démare-]Lafont, S.
1999a *Femmes, droit et justice dans l'Antiquité orientale: Contribution à l'étude du droit pénal au Proche-Orient ancien.* OBO 165. Fribourg: Éditions Universitaires; Göttingen: Vandenhoeck & Ruprecht.
1999b Pardon légal et grâce royale dans les droits cunéiformes. Pp. 23–37 in *Le pardon.* Edited by J. Hoareau-Dodinau, X. Rousseaux, and P. Texier. Cahiers de l'Institut d'Anthropologie Juridique 3. Limoges: Presses Universitaires de Limoges.
2000 Codification et subsidiarité. Pp. 49–64 in *La codification des lois dans l'Antiquité: Actes du colloque de Strasbourg 27–29 novembre 1997.* Edited by E. Lévy. Travaux du Centre de Recherche sur le Proche-Orient et la Grèce antiques 16. Paris: de Boccard.
2012 La juridiction domestique au Proche-Orient ancien. Pp. 55–77 in *Histoires de famille: À la convergence du droit pénal et des liens de parenté: Actes du colloque international des 19–21 juin 2008, Faculté de droit de Montpellier.* Edited by L. Otis-Cour. Cahiers de l'Institut d'Anthropologie juridique 33. Limoges: Presses Universitaires de Limoges.
2015 Les inégalités sociales en Mésopotamie. Quelques précautions de vocabulaire. *Droit et cultures* 69: 75–87.
2019a L'endettement au Proche-Orient ancien au II<sup>e</sup> millénaire avant n.è. Pp. 245–256 in Liber amicorum*: Mélanges en l'honneur de Jean-Pierre Coriat.* Edited by E. Chevreau, C. M. Doria, and J. M. Rainer. Paris: Éditions Pantheon-Assas.
2019b Les discriminations juridiques au Proche-Orient ancien. Pp. 101–124 in *L'environnement méditerranéen: De l'Antiquité vécue à l'Antiquité réinventée.* Edited by J. Bouineau. Paris: L'Harmattan.
Forthcoming Law Collections and Legal Documents.

Durand, J.-M.
1982 Relectures d'ARM VIII. *MARI* 1: 91–135.

Edzard, D. O.
1976 "Soziale Reformen" im Zweistromland bis ca. 1600 v. Chr.: Realität oder literarischer Topos? Pp. 145–156 in *Wirtschaft und Gesellschaft im alten Vorderasien.* Edited by J. Harlatta and G. Komoróczy. Budapest: Akadémiai Kiadó.

Flamm, M. W.
2005 *Law and Order: Street Crime, Civil Unrest, and the Crisis of Liberalism in the 1960s.* Columbia Studies in Contemporary American History. New York: Columbia University Press.

Foster, B.
2005 *Before the Muses: An Anthology of Akkadian Literature.* 3rd ed. Bethesda, MD: CDL.

Graetz, S.
2015 To Whom Can a Wronged Person Turn for Help in the Old Babylonian Period? Pp. 237–260 in *Marbeh Ḥokmah: Studies in the Bible and the Ancient Near East in Loving Memory of Victor Avigdor Hurowitz.* Edited by S. Yona, E. L. Greenstein, M. I. Gruber, P. Machinist, and S. M. Paul. Winona Lake, IN: Eisenbrauns.

Jacquet, A.
2019 The *hubullum*-Debt in the Old Babylonian Period and Its Trace in the Loan Contract Documentation. Pp. 25-59 in *Debt in Ancient Mediterranean Societies: A Documentary Approach; Legal Documents in Ancient Societies VII,*

*Paris, August 27–29, 2015*. Edited by S. Démare-Lafont. Hautes Etudes orientales 56. Moyen et Proche-Orient 8. Geneva: Droz.

Kraus, F. R.
1973 *Vom mesopotamischen Menschen der altbabylonische Zeit und seiner Welt: Eine Reihe Vorlesungen*. MNAW.L 36.6. Amsterdam: North-Holland.

Otto, E.
1997 Programme der sozialen Gerechtigkeit. *ZABR* 3: 26–63.

Pound, R.
1913 Justice According to Law. *Columbia Law Review* 13: 696–713.

Roth, M.
1988 "She Will Die by the Iron Dagger": Adultery and Neo-Babylonian Marriage. *JESHO* 31: 186–206.
1997 *Law Collections from Mesopotamia and Asia Minor*. 2nd ed. WAW 6. Atlanta: Scholars Press.
2002 Hammurabi's Wronged Man. *JAOS* 122: 38–45.

Soldt, W. H. van.
1994 *Letters in the British Museum: Part 2*. AbB 13. Leiden: Brill.

Steinkeller, P.
2002 Money Lending Practices in Ur III Babylonia: The Issue of Economic Motivation. Pp. 109–137 in *Debt and Economic Renewal in the Ancient Near East: A Colloquium Held at Columbia University, November 1998*. Edited by M. Hudson and M. Van De Mieroop. International Scholars Conference on Ancient Near Eastern Economics 3. Bethesda, MD: CDL.

Stol, M.
1981 *Letters from Yale*. AbB 9. Leiden: Brill.

Van De Mieroop, M.
1999 *The Ancient Mesopotamian City*. Oxford: Oxford University Press.

Veenhof, K. R.
1997–2000 The Relation Between Royal Decrees and "Law Codes" of the Old Babylonian Period. *JEOL* 35–36: 49–83.
2005 *Letters in the Louvre*. AbB 14. Leiden: Brill.
2020 Justice and Equity in Babylonia. Pp. 15–25 in Law and Trade in Ancient Mesopotamia and Anatolia: Selected Papers by K. R. Veenhof. Edited by N. J. C. Kouwenberg. Leiden: Sidestone Press.

Von Dassow, E.
2011 Freedom in Ancient Near Eastern Societies. Pp. 205–224 in *The Oxford Handbook of Cuneiform Culture*. Edited by K. Radner and E. Robson. Oxford: Oxford University Press.

Waerzeggers, C.
2020 Changing Marriage Practices in Babylonia from the Late Assyrian Period to the Persian Period. *JANEH* 7 (2):101–31.

Weinfeld, M.
1992 "Justice and Righteousness": The Expression and Its Meaning. Pp. 228–246 in *Justice and Righteousness: Biblical Themes and Their Influence.* Edited by H. G. Reventlow and Y. Hoffman. JSOTSup 137. Sheffield: Sheffield Academic.
1995 *Social Justice in Ancient Israel and in the Ancient Near East*. Jerusalem: Magnes.

Westbrook, R.
1988 *Old Babylonian Marriage Law*. AfOB 23. Horn: Berger.
1990 Adultery in Ancient Near Eastern Law. *RB* 97: 542–580.
1995 Social Justice in the Ancient Near East. Pp. 149–163 in *Social Justice in the Ancient World*. Edited by K. D. Irani and M. Silver. Contributions in Political Science 354. London: Greenwood.

Wu, Y.
1995 *urruru* (D Stem of *arāru* B) "to Frighten" in TCL 18 90. *NABU* 1995.4: 85–87.

Wunsch, C.
2003 *Urkunden zum Ehe-, Vermögens- und Erbrecht aus verschiedenen neubabylonischen Archiven.* Babylonische Archive 2. Dresden: ISLET.

CHAPTER 6

# The Vocabulary of Rebellion in Neo-Assyrian Documents

Aline Distexhe

THIS PAPER ADDRESSES THE VOCABULARY of rebellion in Neo-Assyrian documents. Since it is generally assumed that certain terms are restricted to specific types of literature (Richardson 2010: 12), different kinds of documents have been considered in order to see if the same words are used therein and if they refer to the same social phenomenon. The corpus consists of the material published in the collection of the State Archives of Assyria (SAA), namely: the letters (SAA 1, 5, 10, 13, 15, 16, 17, 18, and 19), prophecies (SAA 9), treaties and loyalty oaths (SAA 2), the court poetry (SAA 3), oracular queries to the sun god (SAA 4), astrological reports (SAA 8), grants, decrees and gifts (SAA 12), the legal transactions (SAA 6 and 14) and the imperial administrative reports (SAA 7 and 11).[1]

Different terms meaning rebellion, revolt, insurrection, uprising, and so on, have been identified and their uses compared. This paper focuses on the most frequent items encountered: *sīḫu*, *bārtu*, and *nabalkattu* and the corresponding verbs *seḫû*, *bâru*, and *nabalkutu*. The nouns will be treated in one section, the verbs in another. Since *nakāru* is often mentioned in the immediate context of those items, the last section of this paper will deal with the root NKR in a noncomprehensive way.

Since the written sources were produced by those who held power, they mostly describe the phenomenon of rebellion as "a vile and pointless violation of order, damned from its inception" (Von Dassow 2010: ix). Rebels are seen as "the illegitimate and binary opposites to legitimate authorities" (Richardson 2010: xvii). In this respect, Mesopotamian sources would mention no "peasant revolts . . . , no workers' revolution, no enlightened overthrow of tyrannies . . . , nor insurrections of slaves and proletarians" (xvii). This will be investigated in Neo-Assyrian sources.

The aim is thus to determine the uses of the terms regarding the time and place but also the literary genre and the language register, and to distinguish different kinds of social phenomena designated by the words considered.

## Nouns for Revolt: *sīḫu*, *bārtu*, *nabalkattu*

The table shows the number of occurrences for each of the terms considered with the various English translations they receive in the SAA volumes. *Nabalkattu* is much

*Author's note:* This research was carried out as a part of a PhD dissertation under the supervision of Prof. Ph. Talon (ULB), funded by the FRS-FNRS. This paper owes much to the excellent publication edited by Richardson (2010), *Rebellions and Peripheries in the Cuneiform World.*

1. See the bibliography for full references for these volumes.

TABLE 6.1. Nouns for revolt and their translations in SAA volumes.

| | Letters | | Treaties | | Documents | | |
|---|---|---|---|---|---|---|---|
| *Sīḫu* | 6 | Revolt (2×)<br>Conspiracy (2×)<br>Rebellion (1×)<br>[Insur]gent (1×) | 7 | Rebellion (7×) | 52 | Insurrection (36×)<br>Uprising (8×)<br>Rebellion (3×)<br>Sedition (3×)<br>Revolt (2×) | 65 |
| *Bārtu* | 7 | Insurrection (2×)<br>Rebellion (4×)<br>Rebelled (1×) | 16 | Revolt (1×)<br>Insurrection (11×)<br>Rebellion (3×)<br>Revolted (1×) | 57 | Rebellion (50×)<br>Insurrection (1×)<br>Revolt (5×)<br>Uprising (1×) | 80 |
| *Nabalkattu* | 2 | Rebellion (1×)<br>[Uprising (1×)] | 1 | Revolt (1×) | 6 | Insurrection (1×)<br>Ladder (1×)<br>Retreat (1×)<br>Revolt (1×)<br>Revolution (2×) | 9 |

rarer than *sīḫu* and *bārtu*. In letters, all terms are surprisingly poorly attested. It does not mean that revolutions, or attempt at rebellions, or overthrow of the sovereign were rare. In treaties, which represent a much smaller corpus than letters, these words are proportionally overrepresented. The insistence found in treaties on prohibiting not only rebellion itself, but even the fact of talking or thinking about rebellion among the subjects of the empire tends to prove that on the contrary, such inclinations were very frequent.[2]

The *CAD* treats very briefly *sīḫu* (*CAD* S:240: rebellion, revolt; Mari, SB, NA, NB) and *bārtu* (*CAD* B:113: rebellion; from OB on; wr. syll. and ḪI.GAR).[3] *Nabalkattu* has a longer notice, "revolt" being its fifth sense (after 1. crossing, scaling, burglary, 2. ladder, ramp, 3. retreat, 4. change of mood, and before 6. part of a field left fallow, 7. excess, 8. revolution of a planet; from OA, OB on; *CAD* N/1:9). The translations found in the SAA collection do not shed more light on the distinction between the terms. Suffice it to say that when in treaties, *sīḫu bārtu* (the two terms being in asyndeton) is nearly always translated as "rebellion and insurrection," in oracular queries, the same sequence is generally translated by "insurrection and rebellion," "uprising and rebellion," or even "sedition and rebellion." This lack of coherence in the translations shows indeed that the exact respective meanings of the terms and their semantic oppositions are not yet precisely understood.[4]

2. Our understanding of the concepts of *rebellion, revolt, revolution* is affected by recent dramatic events like the American and French Revolutions or the more recent Russian and Chinese Revolutions (see Richardson 2010: xx–xxi and xx n.11). In order to avoid anachronism it has been chosen to use the term "rebellion" as a generic term to express every kind of uprising, upheaval, revolt, or even revolution that may have happened in the Neo-Assyrian Empire and that was important enough to have found its way into the written records. Such a stress on prohibiting rebellions in treaties may reflect what Richardson (2010: 11) described as "some nervousness on the part of the royal authority about the extent and precise nature of its ability to compel obedience."

3. The *CAD* gives *bartu* as the lemma with a short vowel, but the SAA volumes, followed here, normalize the form as *bārtu*.

4. In a structuralist perspective, it is assumed that a word is defined in opposition to others; a linguistic sign is what all others are not (see, e.g., Gaudin and Guespin 2000: 160; 168). The context of occurrence of a given

### *In Letters*

In letters from the eighth century BCE, *sīḫu* never appears—but perhaps it is randomly due to archaeological discoveries; *bārtu* is used to refer to popular insurrections as well as to palatial rebellions against the king.[5] In the seventh century BCE, *sīḫu* is the most frequent item, with both the meanings of popular uprising and political revolt against the sovereign.[6] It is interesting to note that the passages considered often mention the same persons: Šuma-iddin and Šarru-lu-dari both appear twice.

*Bārtu* still occurs in seventh-century letters, mainly with the verb *epēšu,* possibly in more literary contexts. Bel-ušezib, Esarhaddon's astrologer, uses *sīḫu* to refer to actual facts, historically dated and with personally named instigators (SAA 10: 112, see n. 6). He uses *bārtu*—the full expression is *ana* PN *bārtu epēšu,* "to rebel against someone"—when quoting astrological omens (SAA 10: 109, rev. 14).[7] Omens are scholarly texts written with lots of logograms—in authorial passages in letters, one never finds so many of these. Based on Bel-ušezib's letters, it might be proposed that *sīḫu* had become in the seventh century BCE the vernacular spontaneous Neo-Assyrian term, *bārtu* still appearing as a reminiscence of the vocabulary traditionally used in astrological omens. However the two other occurrences of *bārtu* are inconclusive in this perspective.[8]

In two letters of Babylonian origin, *sīḫu* is also associated with institutional, positively marked terms. In one of them, a "treaty of rebellion" ([*a*]-⸢*de*⸣-*e šá si-i-hi*)

---

word has to be taken into account since the syntagmatic axis can influence its meaning. Despite the inconsistencies, all the translations quoted in this paper come from the SAA volumes, unless otherwise mentioned.

5. For popular insurrections, see, e.g., SAA 5: 33, rev. 13 and rev. 15: *i—su-ri: bar-tu: me-me-*⸢*ni*⸣ [. . .] ⸢TA⸣ IGI: *bar-ti: pal-ha-ku.* "Some kind of an insurrection may occur; [. . .] I am afraid of an insurrection." Ša-Assur-dubbu, the writer, responsible for cutting timber in Urartu, fears troubles or even attacks by the local population probably tired of the presence of Assyrian soldiers; this does not look like a political will to overthrow the king, but rather a local attempt to get more independence. For palatial rebellions, see, e.g., SAA 1: 8, rev. 10: *bar-tu ina* UGU-*hi-ka e-pu-šú-ni la iš-li-ma šu-*[*x x x x x x x x x x x*]. "The one who [. . .] rebelled against you did not succeed." This well-preserved letter from Sargon II mentions a failed rebellion in Urartian territory, alluding to a political uprising against the king, organized by a precise individual. *Bārtu* also appears in SAA 15: 124, 9, in a passage too lacunar to be commented.

6. For popular uprising, see, e.g., SAA 13: 180, rev. 9–10: *ina pa-na-*⸢*at*⸣ (rev. 10') [*na-bal-kát-tu ù*] *si-ḫu ša* UN-MEŠ. "In the face of [an uprising and] revolt of the people [. . .]." This letter from Babylon written by Shuma-iddin alludes to a popular uprising, to troubles and insecurity in this town, and not to an overthrow of the sovereign. According to the edition *sīḫu* would be associated with *nabalkattu*, but the bases for such a restoration are not very strong since this association is not attested elsewhere in the corpus. For politcal revolt, see, e.g., SAA 16: 130, 6: This very lacunar administrative letter from Phoenicia and Transpotamia to Esarhaddon mentions Aduni-Ba'al and Šarru-lu-dari (the name is restored) in connection with an insurgent (*bēl-sīḫi*); SAA 10: 112, rev. 8: ⸢*si-i-ḫi*⸣ *ep-šú ina* IGI LUGAL ⸢*kap*?⸣*-du a-na pa-na-tu-uš-šú* (rev. 8). Bel-ušezib, Esarhaddon's astrologer, denunciates Šuma-iddin for taking part in a rebellion against the king that is "made and planned" in the palace (lit. "in the King's presence"). Šarru-lu-dari might have been induced to join the conspirator Šuma-iddin (*bēl-sīḫi*, rev. 13). Is it because nothing concrete has yet happened (the rebellion is only being planned) that SAA translates *sīḫu* and *bēl-sīḫi* by "conspiracy" and "conspirator" rather than by "rebellion" and "rebel"?

7. PN is used for "personal name." DUMU—LUGAL *šá ina* URU ZAG-MU *áš-bu* [*ana* AD-*šú* ḪI.GAR DÙ-*ma* AŠ.TE NU DIB]; "the son of the king who lives in a city on my border [will make a rebellion against his father, but will not seize the throne]."

8. They consist of SAA 16: 60, 8′ (*iq-ṭi-bu-u-ni ma-a* ⸢*bar-tu*⸣ *e-pu-*[*šu x x x x x x x x*]), where Nabu-reḫtu-usur tells the king people are not respecting the treaties and are making rebellion (*bārtu epēšu*) and of SAA 18: 201, 12 (ŠÀ-*ba-šú-nu* [*x x x*] ⸢*x*⸣*-ul ù bar-ta ma-al*), where the king is told by an anonymous informer that Belšunu and his family have "hearts full of rebellion."

is mentioned (SAA 18: 100, 4). If the term *adê* refers to an institutional Neo-Assyrian reality and designates political contracts between the crown and subjects or allies, oaths were also "imposed for the purpose of organizing rebellion" (Richardson 2010: 9): such oaths were, paradoxically, legally binding between the parties, but at the same time politically illegitimate. The expression *adê ša sīḫi* is indeed a nice oxymoron. The second letter (SAA 18: 36, rev. 2–rev. 5) mentions that "Bel-šuma-iškun had made an agreement with [someone]" (*rik-su it-*[*ti x x x x x x*] *ir-ta-ka-as*) in connection with a revolt (*si-hu a-na* ⌜UGU⌝ [*x x x x x*]). *Rikistu*-treaties were another kind of contract between crown and subjects/allies (Richardson 2010: 9). However in this lacunar text it is not clear if it is the rebels who made the agreement or the supporters of the king. Either way, the use of institutional vocabulary to describe rebellions is somewhat surprising; it is the exact opposite of the attempt to delegitimize the rebels that characterizes most mentions of rebellions. Unfortunately the historical context in which the "*adê* of rebellion" is sworn is not clear due to the lacunar state of the letter.

*Nabalkattu* appears only once in a letter from Akkullanu, in the apodosis of an astrological omen: "[If] Mars approaches Perseus, there will be a rebellion [BAL-*tum* GÁL-*ma*] in the Westland" (SAA 10: 100, 10).[9] The description of what is implied by the *nabalkattu* is terrible: "Brother will slay his brother; the palace of the ruler will be plundered; the treasure of the country will go over to another country; the emblem of the country will be cast down; the king of the world will be delivered by his gods to his enemy." When the same kind of prediction appears in an astrological report (SAA 8: 57, 7—see infra) with *bārtu*, the consequences implied are not described so precisely. Perhaps *nabalkattu* did imply greater upheavals than *bārtu* in the jargon of Neo-Assyrian scholars.

### *In Treaties*

Neo-Assyrian treaties (namely, the texts published in SAA 2) enounce the obligations of the people submitted to Assyrian kings and proffer maledictions in case they should not respect their engagement. It is prohibited to participate in a rebellion; moreover, it is compulsory to report it to the king if one hears of such an event. As already said, the insistence found in treaties on the interdiction to rebel and obligation to denounce rebels seems to indicate that such events were not rare.

*Bārtu* appears sixteen times while *sīḫu* only occurs seven times. The scarcity of occurrences of *sīḫu* in treaties perhaps confirms the impression gained from the letters that it was rather used for precise events, the protagonists of which were identified. It is not the case in treaties, where the speech is general, without any allusion to historical facts. *Nabalkattu* appears only once.

The syntagm "*sīḫu bārtu*," the two terms being in asyndeton, is frequent.[10] When mentioned, the person against whom the rebellion takes place is always expressed

9. Besides, *nabalkattu* had been—unconvincingly—restored in SAA 13: 180, rev. 10 (see n. 6 above); it is no more the case in SAA 18: 26 (= SAA 13: 180) where the lacuna before *sīḫu* is left empty.

10. The combination *sīḫu bārtu* is never encountered in letters. In *Esar*. 1 i 82, *sīḫi* is attested once with *bārtu* but the compound seems not yet lexicalized as it is in treaties and other documents, since the words are coordinated by *u*.

through "*ina* UGU PN." Four examples come from Esarhaddon's succession treaty (SAA 2: 6, 133; 2: 6, 166; 2: 6, 303; 2: 6, 498) and two passages from Zakutu's Treaty.[11] The first indicates that people must not talk of or give advice to rebel (*us-su-uk-tú* [*la de*]-⌜*iq**⌝-*tú mil-ku*! *la ṭa-a-bu šá si-ḫi bar-te* [. . .] [*ta-mal*]-⌜*lik**⌝-*a-ni ta-dáb-bu-ba-a-ni*; SAA 2: 8, 20); in the second case, someone who would hear words of (i.e., inciting to) rebellion ([*a-bu-tú la*] *de-iq-tú šá si-ḫi bar-te*) is asked to report it to the king and to his mother (SAA 2: 8, rev. 3). It is interesting to note that *milku ša sīḫi bārti* in the first case and *abūtu ša sīḫi bārte* in the second case are qualified negatively (*lā ṭābu, lā de'iqtu*). S. Richardson (2010: 4–6) has pointed out the "noise metaphor" as an important means to delegitimize the rebels on the part of the central authority. This could be exactly what is meant with these formulations: indeed words themselves are a great danger, and "it is critical for state authority to delegitimize [speakers who try to arrogate authority for themselves] rather than counter it because a proportional response by authority would shore up its categorical legitimacy" (5). Qualifying the words of the rebels as evil, or nonsense, is a step in that direction.

The person against whom the rebellion took place in the preceding examples was always the king. In the only case where *sīḫu* is used alone (i.e., without *bārtu*), the term is not used to refer to a rebellion against the legitimate king, but to incite loyal people to revolt against a usurper, who must be killed since he took the power illegitimately. This passage (SAA 2: 6, 245) is also the only case where the rebellion is *placed* (*šakānu*) and not *made* (*epēšu*).[12] According to Richardson (2010: 6–7), *sīḫu* comes from a translational movement verb, with the meaning of rising up and out of a lower stratum (*seḫû*), when *bâru* expresses a nontranslational motion, related to turbulence and confusion. Could *bārtu* and the confusion it implied not be appropriated to describe a legitimate revolt against a usurper?

*Bārtu* appears without *sīḫu* ten times in treaties, always either with the verb *epēšu* or with a derivate (*ēpišānu*). Three passages prohibit rebellious deeds and bad talk (*ep-šú bar-tu a-bu-tú la* DÙG.GA-*tú* (*la* $SIG_5$-*tú*); SAA 2: 6, 67; 107; 186). Two passages mention *bārtu* with *epēšu* in the sense of "to rebel against the king" (expressed through *ana* PN in SAA 2:6, 198 and through the suffix pronoun *-šu* in SAA 2: 6, 169). Five passages (SAA 2: 6, 136; 145; 147; 159; 254) mention "instigators of rebellion" (*ēpišānūte ša bārti*) who must be seized and killed.

More than once in treaties, *sīḫu bārtu* appears in the protasis when only *sīḫu* is found in the apodosis: "if anyone should speak to you of rebellion and insurrection, [. . .] you shall seize the perpetrators of insurrection" (SAA 2: 6, 133–136): *ēpišānūte ša bārti*, and never *ša sīḫi bārti*. It is somewhat surprising since in the annals of Esarhaddon (*Esar.* 1, i 82), *ēpiš sīḫi u bārti* is used.

11. SAA 2: 6, 133, "If one is told of a rebellion [*si-hu bar-tú*] intending to kill, assassinate, and destroy the crown prince [*šá* ⌜*du*⌝-[*a-ki*]-*šu ša-mut-ti-šu ḫul-lu-qi-šú*], he must stop the instigators of rebellion [*e-piš-a-nu-te šá bar-te*]." In the protasis the syntagm *sīḫu bārtu* appears but in the apodosis only *bārtu* is used. SAA 2: 6, 166, "A man who would besiege the king and rebel against him [*sīḫu bārtu ina* UGU-*ḫi* PN *epēšu*] must be defeated." SAA 2: 6, 303, "Someone who would rebel [*ina* UGU PN *sīḫu bārtu epēšu*] and seat himself on the throne must be killed." SAA 2: 6, 498 "The people submitted to the treaty must agree not to revolt against the king [*ina* UGU PN *sīḫu bārtu epēšu*]."

12. *Si-ḫu ina* UGU-*ḫi-šú la ta-šá-kan-a-ni.*

Esarhaddon's succession treaty often associates *abūtu lā ṭābtu* (*lā de'iqtu*) with *epšu bārtu.*[13] *Abūtu* receives the generic meaning of "thing" in the SAA translations ("anything which is not good [and proper]"). In the light of what has been said above about the will of the authorities to disqualify rebellious speeches, it is perhaps preferable to translate *abūtu la de'iqtu* by "offensive words" rather than "anything which is not good": indeed words themselves represent a great danger for the sovereign since they play an important part in the process of launching a rebellion.

*Nabalkattu*, in its only occurrence in treaties, also associates rebellious acts and words: *man-nu šá a-bu-tú la de-iq-tú* [*la*] ⌜*ṭa*⌝*-ab-tú ù na-bal-kàt-tu* [*ina*] ⌜UGU⌝ [. . .] ⌜*ta*⌝*-sa-*⌜*li*⌝*-a-ni te-ep-pa-šá-a-ni* (SAA 2: 8, 13). The *CAD* translates this passage as "whoever (among you) who makes up and spreads untruths and seditious lies about Assurbanipal" (*CAD* S, s.v. "salā'u," 97: "to cheat, lie, deceive"). SAA 2 reads "anyone (of you) who should [. . .] fabricate and carry out an ugly and evil thing or a revolt against your lord Assurbanipal, king of Assyria."[14] It is quite certain from the above-mentioned examples that "*ina* UGU" introduces the person against whom the rebellion is made, as translated in SAA 2. But it also seems best to translate *abūtu* by "word," as in *CAD*, and not "thing" (SAA 2), orality playing an important role in the process of rebellion. *Salā'u* is probably used to delegitimize the rebellious speech as a deceptive speech, *epēšu* to show that even words are effective and as punishable as acts themselves.[15] The actions and the words thus appear as two aspects defining a rebellion.

### *Other Documents*

In all other SAA volumes, *bārtu* appears fifty-seven times, *sīḫu* fifty-two, and *nabalkattu* only six times. *Sīḫu* and *bārtu* appear forty-one times together in asyndeton, among which thirty-eight examples come from the oracular queries. Indeed, one of the basic questions to the sun god is "will somebody make an insurrection and a rebellion" (*sīḫu bārtu epēšu*, fifteen times).[16] In this question, *epēšu* is always used; it is sometimes followed by forms of *epēšu* (Š stem), *dabābu* (G and Š stems), *qabû* (G and Š stems) and *mahāṣu* (Š stem). This follows the Mesopotamian habit of listing every possibility in order not to forget anything in a forecast. This question is also asked indirectly: "I ask you if somebody will make a rebellion against the king" (*sīḫu bārtu ana* UGU PN *epēšu*: fourteen times).[17] In those case, the basic question with *epēšu*

13. *Abūtu la de'iqtu* also appears with *sīḫu bārtu* (see SAA 2: 8, rev. 3 above) and with *nabalkattu* (see below).

14. Concerning the syntax, after *mannu ša,* one would expect a 3rd-person sg. verb, but all the verbal forms appear to stand in the 2nd pl. Parpola (1987b: 169) noted about lines 9–12, "This passage looks like an anacoluthon for *mannu ša ina libbi adê . . . iḫaṭṭūni. . . .* The unique construction in the following lines (*mannu ša* followed by a predicate in the second-person plural) likewise seems an anacoluthon for *mannu atta/attunu ša* and the like."

15. Another possible explanation would by that both objects appear in the beginning of the clause followed by the verbs, the first verb governing the first object and the second verb the second object, words being lied, falsely uttered, and acts being made.

16. SAA 4: 139, 23; 140, 7; 141, 3; 142, 20; 152, 9; 156, 7; 157, 1; 158, 4; 159, 6; 161, 5; 163, 6; 166, 5; 168, 6; 169, 3; 274, 5.

17. SAA 4: 139, rev. 10; 142, rev. 8; 152, rev. 4; 154, rev. 11; 155, rev. 7; 156, rev. 13; 157, rev. 7; 159, rev. 10; 164, rev. 6; 166, rev. 8; 169, rev. 6; 170, rev. 5; 171, rev. 4; 275, rev. 10.

can also be extended with G and Š stem forms of *epēšu, maḫāṣu, dabābu* but also with the expression *qātēšu ana lemutti ana libbi* PN *wabālu*. Another frequent question is: "Is the making of a rebellion against the king decreed and confirmed in a favorable case by the command of a God (Šamaš)" (*epeš sīḫi bārti ana* UGU PN *qabî kunni*: four times).[18] The compound *sīḫi bārti* also qualifies the people who are the subject of the oracular question: "Will they who plotted sedition and rebellion make rebellion [. . .]" (*ša ina* UGU *sīḫi bārti* [. . .]; once [SAA 4: 142, 13]). The four last cases consist of various or lacunar questions.[19]

It is worth noting that *qabû* is associated with rebellious speech in Neo-Assyrian oracular queries (in the basic question mentioned above), against Richardson (2010: 4 n. 18): "*qabû*, the most commonly used verb to denote speech, seems rarely if ever to have been used to describe illegitimate political speech." Indeed, elsewhere in Neo-Assyrian documents *qabû* is used with the meaning "to report (a rumor of rebellion or anything) to the king (or his mother)." But in five cases in appointment queries from the reign of Esarhaddon (SAA 4: 156, 7; 157, 1; 158, 4; 159, 6; 161, 5), *qabû* directly governs *sīḫu bārtu*. The G and Š stem forms (*i-qa-bi-i ú-šá-*[*qa*]-⌜*ba*⌝-[*a*]) are translated by "will he order it (i.e., the rebellion) or cause others to order it?" On the contrary, G and Š stem forms of *dabābu* (⌜*i*⌝*-da-bu-ub ú-šad-ba-ba*) are rendered by "will he plot it, or cause others to plot it."[20] The difference between *qabû* and *dabābu* in these sentences is not easy to establish and one hopes to find passages where only *qabû* occurs to try to determine its exact meaning when associated with illegitimate political speech.

*Sīḫu* and *bārtu* appear together, not in asyndeton but coordinated by *u* in an astrological prediction ([*ma-aṣ-ṣar-ti*] *šá ra-ma-ni-*⌜*šú*⌝ [*la—pa-an si-hi*] *u ba-ar-ti li-*⌜*iṣ*⌝*-*[*ṣur*]: "to guard oneself against uprising and rebellion"; SAA 8: 386, 11) and in two grants from Assur-etel-ilani who exempts Tab-sar-papahi (SAA 12: 35, 14) and a cohort commander (SAA 12: 36, 10) from taxes.[21] In both grants—mostly restored—the context is that of the revolt of Nabû-rehtu-usur.[22]

*Sīḫu* alone appears ten times. It is used twice in composition in the lexeme *bēl-sīḫi* meaning "insurgent" in extending the question: "will he make an insurrection and rebellion against the king *or will he make common cause with an insurgent*."[23] *Bēl-sīḫi* is a known lexeme (*CAD* S:241) but *bēl-bārti* is not lexically attested (*ša-barti*, meaning "rebel," is only attested in OB, *CAD* B:115). *Sīḫu* is really alone—not lexically conditioned—in two unassigned queries from the time of Assurbanipal (SAA 4: 321 and

18. SAA 4: 139, 24; 141, 5; 142, 22. In SAA 4: 143, 2, the formulation is more elaborate: *epeš sīḫi bārti ša* PN1 *ana* UGU PN2 *qabî kunni*.

19. *i-na si-ha* ḪI.GAR [. . .] URU.*a-mul i-*[*ṣab-ba-tu-ú*] (SAA 4: 63, 8); [*a-na*] UGU *si-hi* ḪI.GAR *šá* KA MÍ.⌜HUL⌝ [*x x x x x x x x*] [*i*]-⌜*dab*⌝-[*bu*]-*bu* (SAA 4: 166, rev. 10); *la-pa-an si-hi* [ḪI.GAR *x x x x x x x x x x x x x x x x x*] (SAA 4: 151, 5); *a-na* UGU *si-ha* [ḪI.GAR *i-na* UGU PN . . . *ip-pu-uš*] (SAA 4: 160, rev. 5).

20. The spellings given here are from SAA 4: 156.

21. In *Esar*. 1 i 82, *sīḫi u bārtu* is attested with the conjunctive *u* (see n. 10 above). *Sīḫu* is also attested in connection with *ešû* (*Esar.* 33, 1e4), a sequence absent from the letters. *Ešû* alone has not been looked for in letters.

22. This Nabû-rehtu-usur is a mystery. A man with this name ("a servant of the queen mother?", Luukko 2004: 229) is the writer of letters SAA 16: 59–61. Is it the same guy who is rebelling in Assur-etel-ilani's time?

23. SAA 4: 152, 10: *ú—lu it-ti* EN—⌜*si**⌝-[*ḫi o* KA-*šú i-šak-ka-a-na*]; SAA 4: 152, rev. 5: [*ú—lu*] ⌜KI*⌝ EN*—KIR KA-*šú* GAR-*nù*.

322) where it occurs six times.[24] Both queries seem less formulaic than others (no logograms are used except in the titles of the king) and only *sīḫu*—already characterized as vernacular—appears. Moreover—but is it significant?—both queries have apparently been written by a woman, allegedly Libbali-sarrat, the wife of Ashurbanipal (Frahm 2004, 45). She would not make use of the formulaic vocabulary familiar to scholars, but write her query in a more vernacular language, avoiding using *bārtu* and logograms.

It is not surprising in this respect that in pieces of court poetry written in vernacular Neo-Assyrian, *sīḫu* is used (SAA 3: 35, 16 and SAA 3: 39, 36) rather than *bārtu*.[25]

*Bārtu* appears without *sīḫu* in four badly broken oracular queries.[26] Four astrological reports mention that "there will be a rebellion" (*bārtu ibašši* / ḪI.GAR GÁL-*ši*).[27] In two cases, the Akkadian forms are written below the Sumerian words as glosses (see Talon 2003 for the function of such glosses). Two other reports (SAA 8: 245, 7; and 414, 3) mention that the son of a king living in "my border town"[28] will revolt against his father (*ana* AD-šú ḪI.GAR DÙ-*uš-ma*).[29] The usual expression *ana* PN *bārtu epēšu* is also found in SAA 8: 380, 2 where "a servant will make a rebellion against the house of his lord." Another report associates an important degree of violence with *bārtu*, since someone is killed (SAA 8: 535, 2: *ina* ḪI.GAR GAZ.MEŠ-*šú*). Finally, some passages in the reports are characterized by a lack of syntax, consisting of enumerations of elements: "for the king, rebellion, fall of the army" (*ana* LUGAL ḪI.GAR ŠUB-*tim* ERIM-*ni* [*x x*], SAA 8: 103, 11; see also SAA 8: 308, 3).

In short, *bārtu* generally appears in formulaic sentences in queries or astrological reports, texts written by learned men par excellence, as shown by the high number of logograms used. *Bārtu* is also often associated with violent events (fighting and killing); it could thus be a stronger, more negatively connoted term than *sīḫu* (see in this respect SAA 2: 6, 245 mentioned above, where *sīḫu* was used to refer to a legitimate insurrection).

*Nabalkattu* appears six times in the documents. This item is highly polysemous: in an unassigned query relating to Media (SAA 4: 43, 7) dated from the reign of Esarhaddon, the term is employed with the military meaning of ramp, having nothing to do with rebellion. In the context of the conquest of Egypt, the term also has a military meaning: "retreat" (SAA 4: 84, 12).[30] The word also appears in astrological reports to

24. SAA 4: 321, 2–5: *a-šá-ʾa-al-ka da-ba-bu an-ni-i ša si-hi ša a-na* $^{m}$*aš-šur*—DÙ—A MAN KUR—*aš-šur*.KI DUMU $^{m}$*aš-šur*—PAB—AŠ MAN KUR—*aš-ma iq-bu-u-ni ma-a si-hu ina* UGU-*ḫi-ka* ep-pu-šú qa-bi-i ku-nu-u*; SAA 4: 322, 2–rev. 3: [*a-šá*]-⌜*ʾa*⌝-*al-ka* TAv ŠÀ *da-ba-bi* [*an*]-*ni-i ša si-hi ša a-na* $^{m}$*aš-šur*—DÙ—A LUGAL KUR—aš-šur DUMU $^{m}$*aš-šur*—PAB—AŠ MAN KUR—*aš-šur-ma iq-bu-u-ni* ⌜*ma*⌝-*a si-hu ina* UGU-*hi-ka* ep-pu-šú* $^{m}$*aš-šur*—DÙ—A MAN KUR—aš-šur.KI i-bal-la-ṭa* ú-še-za-⌜ba*⌝ TAv ŠÀ *si-hi an-ni-i ina* UGU *ša si-hu ina* UGU-*hi*-⌜*šu*⌝ *e-pa-šú-u-ni iz-za-a*-⌜*za**⌝ *i-ma-qa-tu-u* [*x x x*].

25. SAA 3: 35, 16, *si-hu ú*-[x x *it-ta*]-⌜*bal**⌝-*kàt* ina qa*-⌜*ra*⌝-[*bu ina* ŠÀ-*bi up-pu-šu*]. The passage is very lacunar; a form of *nabalkutu* appears in the same line and there is a battle associated with the event. SAA 3: 39, 36, [*x x x x x*]-⌜*i*⌝-*šú si-hu ul ú-maš-ši.* The expression *sīḫu muššû* is lexicalized with the meaning: "distinguish, identify, find out a revolt" (*CAD* M/2, s.v. "*mussû*," 235); the passage is very lacunar.

26. SAA 4: 143, 1; 205, 5; 331, edge 1; 334, 8.

27. SAA 8: 25, 5; 57, 7; and 384, 13 mention of the place where the rebellion will occur; SAA 8: 45, 8 does not.

28. Rather than "the city on my border," as translated in SAA 8.

29. Both reports are very similar to a passage from SAA 10: 109, rev. 14, the above-mentioned letter from Bel-ušezib to Esarhaddon.

30. In *Esar*. 98, rev. 42, *nabalkattu* also means "military ladder."

announce a rebellion in very succinct formulations.[31] The text SAA 8: 400, 6 describes a rebellion in the Westland (*ina* KUR—MAR.TU.KI] *na-bal-kat-tum* ⸢GÁL⸣-[*ma*) as a terrible upheaval, in a passage close to SAA 10: 100, 10, the letter from Akkullanu quoted above, describing a *nabalkattu* rebellion—also occurring in the Westland—in very violent terms. The *nabalkattu*-rebellion thus seems even more terrible than the *bārtu*-revolt.

*Sīḫu, bārtu*, and *nabalkattu* only appear together in SAA 4: 154, 6: [*a-ma-tú la ṭa*]-*ab-tú la de-iq-tú a-mat le-mut-ti*[32] *šá si-ḫi bar-ti na-bal*-⸢*kat*⸣-[*ti o a*]-⸢*na*⸣ UGU $^{md}$*aš-šur*—ŠEŠ—SUM-*na* LUGAL KUR—*aš-šur*.KI TA ŠÀ-*bi-šú i-da-bu*-[*ub*]. The order in which the terms appear corroborate the idea of an increasing violence from the *sīḫu* to *nabalkattu.*

In brief, *bārtu,* used in nonscholarly letters in the eighth century to designate popular insurrections as well as political rebellions, is mainly restricted to learned, logographically written texts in the seventh century. *Nabalkattu* is the rarest and most formal word; it also qualifies the most violent revolts. *Sīḫu* is the vernacular word meaning "rebellion"—that would explain its absence in astrological reports. In treaties and oracular queries, the high proportion of attestations of *sīḫu bārtu* is worth noting, since this association never appears in letters. This compound looks like a catch-all term to describe all kinds of rebellious events in a vague way, fitting in well in the context of queries or treaties, but not in that—much more precise—of letters. Therefore, *sīḫu bārtu* maybe could be translated by "any rebellious deed," rather than "rebellion and insurrection." *Sīḫu*, in its only occurrence without *bārtu* in a treaty, qualifies a legitimate insurrection against a usurper—it is otherwise lexically conditioned, as in *bēl-sīḫi*; *bārtu* seems more heavily marked as a "bad, illegitimate" insurrection, a sense consistent with the etymology of the term. The distinction between the terms would then be located at two different levels: the language register and the intensity of the described phenomenon: *sīḫu* > *bārtu* > *nabalkattu*.

## Verbs for Revolt: *seḫû, bâru, nabalkutu*

If *nabalkattu*, as a noun, was very rare, the verb *nabalkutu* is far more frequent than *seḫû* and *bâru* in all the documents considered.

### *In Letters*

*Seḫû* (*CAD* S:208: to become troublesome, to become rebellious, to become disturbed; from OA, OB on) is very poorly attested: its only occurrence is partially restored (*is-se*-⸢*x*⸣; SAA 18: 113, rev. 15). In this letter Shumaya writes to the king that "everyone in this city (i.e., Zanaki) has become rebellious." The relevance of the restoration may be questioned since *seḫû* does not appear anywhere else in the corpus.[33] Similarly, *bâru*

31. SAA 8: 315,rev. 3; 495, rev. 1: "earthquake for revolt"; *ri-i-bu ana na-bal-kat-ti.*

32. Following Richardson (2010: 9), talking about "evil command" (*amat lemutti*) is a way to delegitimize the rebellious speech.

33. However, *seḫû* is used in *Esar.* 1 i 43.

TABLE 6.2. Verbs for revolt and their translations in SAA volumes.

| | Letters | | Treaties | | Other Documents | | |
|---|---|---|---|---|---|---|---|
| *seḫû* | 1 | To become rebellious | 0 | | 0 | | 1 |
| *bâru* | 1 | To rebel | 0 | | 3 | To revolt (2×)<br>To rebel (1×) | 4 |
| | 4 | | | | | | 61 |
| *nabalkutu* | 15 | To take (sb.) over (the mountains) (1×)<br>To come across (the moutain) (1×)<br>To overturn (2×)<br>To knock out (2×)<br>**Upheaval (1×)**<br>To turn upside down (2×)<br>**To rebel (2×)**<br>**To revolt (2×)**<br>To back out of (1×)<br>To back off (1×) | 7 | **To revolt (3×)**<br>To break away<br>To overturn<br>To turn over<br>**To overthrow** | 39 | **To revolt (3×)**<br>**To rebel (2×)**<br>To overturn (17×)<br>To cross (the frontier) (1×)<br>To transgress (4×)<br>To violate (1×)<br>To contravene (2×)<br>To break (a contract) (3×)<br>**To defect (3×)**<br>To redig<br>To change<br>To turn upside down | |

occurs only once in SAA 10: 362, 16: Mar-Issar reports an astrological prediction to Esarhaddon, using PN *bâru* in place of the much more frequent *ana* PN *bārtu epēšu*. This letter bears traces of an elevated language (*-ma* for coordinating two clauses, even if the Assyrian subjunctive in *–ni* also occurs); indeed, *bâru* is not a Neo-Assyrian vernacular term (*CAD* B, s.v. "*bâru* B," 130: to stir up a revolt; OB, Bogh., MB, SB).

*Nabalkutu*, by far the most frequent of the three verbs, appears fifteen times in letters, in the N and Š stem. It is also the most polysemous item.[34] In three eighth-century letters, the verb in the N stem, without any (at least preserved) complement, alludes to people refusing to obey the king's instructions, but certainly not planning a political organized insurrection against the king.[35] This is thus radically different from what was said above about the noun *nabalkattu*. In the seventh century however, things change: *nabalkutu* is associated with a battle in a letter from Nabû-sumu-lisir to Esarhaddon (SAA 18: 144, rev. 4): "[Whe]n they (i.e., the Qedarites) cam[e . . .], we i[nflicted] a [de]feat on them. And after they revolte[d (*ki-i ib-bal-ki-*⸢*tu*⸣-[*ú-ni*]), f]rom [those] days, [no] Qed[a]rites at [all have attacked] the city of the king, m[y] lord." The verb thus seems to acquire a stronger meaning, as the corresponding noun which, when attested, refers to a violent upheaval in the land. It is probably also the

34. See *CAD* N/1:11–20. In this corpus, *nabalkutu*, in the N and Š stem, has the meanings of: to cross (SAA 5: 137, 6), to make cross (SAA 1: 1, rev. 60 = SAA 19: 152, rev. 22), to overturn (SAA 1: 78, 7; 103, 13 and rev. 9), to change or cancel a decision (SAA 16: 32, rev. 10; SAA 16: 33, rev. 4; SAA 18: 181, rev. 18), to make someone change an opinion (SAA 5: 169, rev. 2). Those uses do not concern us so far.

35. SAA 1: 4, rev. 3: "[they did] not [do] any [work . . . (break of two lines) . . .] have rebelled ([*i-ta-b*] *al-*[*ki*]*-tu*)"; SAA 1: 172, rev. 35 (=SAA 19: 170): "The king my lord should know that they are *rebelling* (again this arrangement, while) we [. . .]"(*i-bal-*⸢*ku*⸣*-tu*); SAA 5: 200, rev. 11: "the king should send me a mule stable attendant to make him come forth and go with me. Otherwise, *he will (again) back off* [*i-bal-ka-ta*], fall away, keep alert grudgingly, and certainly not [go] with me". SAA translates "to back off": there is indeed an opposition between *uṣû / alaku* and *nabalkutu / maqatu*. But the translation "he will rebel" is possible, as in *CAD* N/1:14.

case in a letter from Illil-bani to Esarhaddon, concerning Elam and the fleeing of its king after a rebellion in the land of Arasi (SAA 18: 193, 10). If he flees, there must have been violence and danger. In the Š-stem, the causative meaning "to cause to rebel" also implies a violent event and important troubles: in SAA 10: 2, rev. 6, Nabu-zeru-lesir reports to Esarhaddon words of the substitute king, who denounced a conspiracy led by Sallaya "speaking about upheaval of the country" (*ina* UGU *šá-bal-ku-te ša ma-a-ti*). It is a rebellion planning to seize fortresses, with military implications.

### *In Treaties*

*Seḫû* and *bâru* do not occur at all in the preserved treaties. *Nabalkutu* appears seven times; three in the Š stem, in the maledictions at the end of Esarhaddon's succession treaty, with the meaning "to overturn, to turn upside down" (SAA 2: 6, 546; 574; 659); four in the N stem. The constructions attested are *nabalkutu* TA PN (SAA 2: 6, 175) and *ina* UGU-*hi* PN *nabalkutu* (SAA 2: 6, 186; 244; 310). The verb appears in lists of prescriptions, obligations, or interdictions imposed upon the people included in the treaty. It is interesting in these cases to look at the whole list in order to try to detect its inherent logic. Richardson (2010: 11–12) indicated that "care should also be taken to understand terms as deployed in specific narrative contexts, too: when, for instance, Aššurnaṣirpal II accuses some nation of 'rebelling', is it then different from a nation which, in the same annalistic account, serially 'rebels,' 'bands together,' *and* 'rises up . . . [to] wage war'?" Such lists (some parts of which have already been quoted above) will now be examined.

> SAA 2: 6, 180–187: "You shall not . . . set in your mind an unfavorable thought [*a-bu-tú la* DÙG.GA-*tú*] against Assurbanipal . . . ; you shall not revolt against him [*ina* UGU-*hi-šú ta-bal-kàt-a-ni*], nor make rebellion [*ep-šu bar-tu*], nor do anything to him which is not good [*a-bu-tu la* DÙG.GA-*tú te-pa-šá-niš-*[*u-ni*]]."

In this passage, there is a logical gradation, or climax, between the prohibitions. The first stage in the process of a rebellion is to have bad thoughts; then comes the rebellion, with the verb *nabalkutu*; only after that does the active phase take place, with *epšu bārtu epēšu*, the verb *epēšu* pointing to the active character. This last section associates "evil words," rather than "anything which is not good" (see above), with the active phase of rebellion.

> If either a bearded (courtier) or a eunuch puts Assurbanipal, the great crown prince designate, to death, and takes over the kingship of Assyria, you shall not make common cause with him [*is-si-šú ta-šá-kan-a-ni*] and become his servant [*a-na* LÚ.ARAD-*nu-ti-šú ta-tu-ra-a-ni*] but shall break away [*la ta-bal-kàt-a-ni*] and be hostile (to him) [*la ta-na-kir-a-ni*], alienate all lands from him [KUR. KUR *gab-bu is-si-šú la tu-šam-kar-a-ni*], instigate a rebellion against him [*si-hu ina* UGU-*hi-šú la ta-šá-kan-a-ni*], seize him [*la ta-ṣab-bat-a-ni-šú-u-ni*] and put him to death [*la ta-ṣab-bat-a-ni-šú-u-ni*]. (SAA 2: 6, 237–244)

The same gradation is discernable. The first action is the first and easier step, the last is the ideal, but hardest thing to do. One must: not support a usurper < not act as his servant < "break away" (revolt, *nabalkutu* in the sense of disobeying, as in eighth-century letters, hence the translation "break away" in SAA 2) < be hostile (*nakāru*) < make other countries hostile < organize an open rebellion (*sīḫu*), and finally, seize and kill him.

> If anyone makes rebellion or insurrection against Esarhaddon, king of Assyria and seats himself on the royal throne, you shall not rejoice over his kingship but shall seize him and put him to death. If you are unable to seize and put him to death, you shall not submit to his kingship [*a-na* LUGAL-*u-ti-šú ta-ma-gúr-a-ni*] nor swear an oath of servitude to him [*ta-me-tú ša* LÚ.ARAD-*nu-ti ta-tam-ma-a-ni-šú-u-ni*], but shall revolt against him [*ina* UGU-*hi-šu la ta-bal-kàt-a-ni*] and unreservedly do battle with him [*ina gam-mur-ti* ŠÀ-*bi-ku-nu qa-ra-a-bu is-si-šú la tu-pa-áš-a-ni*], make other lands inimical to him [KUR.KUR *šá-ni-a-te is-si-šú la tu-šam-kar-a-ni*], take plunder from him [*ḫu-ub-tu-šú la ta-ḫab-bat-a-ni-ni*], defeat him [*de-ek-tu-šú la ta-du-ka-a-ni*], destroy his name and his seed from the land [MU-*šú* NUMUN-*šú ina* KUR *la tu-ḫal-laq-a-ni*]. (SAA 2: 6, 302–310)

The best thing to do is to seize and kill the usurper. If this is impossible, the things to do are at least not to submit, and at best destroy the usurper and his seed. The intermediary stages are: not to serve < to revolt, disobey (*nabalkutu*) < do battle (*qarābu*) < make other lands hostile < plunder < defeat. Once again, *nabalkatu* is the stage just before the battle.

Such figures of climax seem to be a regular feature in Esarhaddon's succession treaty. It is written in the introduction of SAA 2, on treaty stipulations that "the order of the sections in no. 6 [i.e., Esarhaddon's treaty] reveals a well thought-out logical scheme systematically covering all possible forms of threats against the ruling house, starting from the definition of loyal conduct, and gradually proceeding to open rebellion and murder of the king" (Richardson 2010: xxxviii). It seems that not only are the sections logically arranged, but also the sequences of verbs inside each section. In such passages in treaties, *nabalkutu* does not imply the violence found in letters of the seventh century; it describes a stage coming before open rebellion and the associated battles, a meaning maybe more archaic, as in eighth-century letters.

### *In Other Documents*

There are three attestations of *bâru* in astrological reports: the construction is always PN1 PN2 *ibâr*(*u*) (versus PN1 *ana* PN2 *bārtu ippuš* in letters or queries).[36]

(*Ina* UGU-*hi* PN) *nabalkutu* means "to rebel against someone."[37] In SAA 3: 34, 23, fightings (*qa-ra-bu*) are associated with the revolt (*it-ta-bal-kàt*). SAA 4: 289, rev. 4,

36. SAA 8: 100, 7 (written ḪI.GAR, but a verb is needed there, rather than a noun *bārtu*); 241, 7; 438, 3.

37. SAA 4: 289, rev. 4; SAA 3: 34, 23; 35,16; SAA 8: 240, rev. 2 (if the restoration is correct, *nabalkutu* governs a direct object without any introducing preposition; [NUN KUR-*su*] BAL-*su*; see *CAD* N/1, s.v. "nabalkutu," 1c) 2', p. 14); SAA 3: 22, rev. 12 (there, the rebellion is against a treaty; *ina adê*); SAA 8: 8, rev. 2; 366, 2; 459, rev. 4 (in these three cases, SAA translates BAL-(*kat*)-*su* by "defect"; but the construction is exactly the same as in SAA 8: 240, rev. 2, where the translation says "revolt"); SAA 8: 535, 12 (the translation

an oracular query concerning the Šamaš-šumu-ukin war, asks: "When the Puqudean troops hear of this sortie of the king of Elam, will they rebel [*ib-ba-lak*-kit-ú*]? Will they turn hostile [*i-na-kìr*-ú*] to Assurbanipal?" As in treaties, *nabalkutu* is followed by a form of *nakāru*, which seems to bear stronger, more violent implications. It also means "to overturn" in oracular queries, in the depiction of extispicy (seventeen times)[38] and in a prophecy (SAA 9: 3, iv 19), "to cross (a frontier)" (SAA 4: 280, rev. 19), and "to transgress, contravene, break a contract" in the legal transactions of the royal court of Nineveh (ten times).[39]

## *Nakru/nakāru*

Since *nakāru* often occurs next to *nabalkutu*, the root NKR will be considered in this final section. The verb *nakāru* is very frequent, with many different meanings and in many different contexts, from "to become hostile, to be or become an enemy, to engage in hostilities, to be at war, to rebel against a ruler" to "to change" (*CAD* N/1:159–171).[40] It appears ten times in letters, eleven in treaties and twenty-three in other documents. Only the passages related to some kind of rebellion will be discussed briefly.

In letters from the eighth-century BCE, *issi* PN *nakāru* appears with the meaning "to be at war with/to revolt against" (SAA 5: 260, 7; SAA 5: 166, rev. 2; SAA 5: 113, 15).[41] In the last two cases, a battle (*qarābu*) is mentioned. In letters from the seventh century, *nakāru* with the suffix *-šu* (they will rebel *against* him) seems to allude to a refusal of the king's authority, a change of allegiance, but no mention is made as to whether there was a violent component or not (SAA 10: 112, 22).[42] Thus, if *nabalkutu* bears no violent implication in the eighth century and in treaties, but does in seventh-century BCE letters, it seems to be the opposite with *nakāru*: it would imply a violent activity in treaties and letters from the eighth century, but no longer in those from the seventh century BCE. Could both evolutions be somehow related? Indeed in treaties, the above-mentioned climax sequences show that *nakāru* (G stem) refers to more serious events than *nabalkutu*. In the D stem, the expression *ina šarrūti* (LUGAL-*ti*) *nukkuru*, "to abolish the rule of a king" (*CAD* N/1:168) is attested three times (SAA 2: 6, 55; 69; 128). Otherwise, the meanings of the D and Š stem are similar: "to make someone hostile to"/"to incite someone to rebel against someone else" (SAA 2: 6, 245; 312; 367). A passage where the verb occurs in the D stem is interesting, since it shows a sequence where actions are listed in the reverse order compared to the

"to rebel" seems plausible even in the absence of a complement; KUR BAL-*ma* is however translated by "the land will change" in SAA 8).

38. SAA 4: 35, rev. 3; 45, rev. 9; 59, rev. 3; 71, rev. 11; 213, rev. 3; 110, rev. 16; 266, rev. 10; 293, 4; 293, rev. 3; 308, 1; 310, 1; 310, 8; 311, 1; 313, 4; 320, 3; 320, rev. 5; 333, 1.

39. SAA 6: 174, rev. 5; 176, rev. 4; 289, rev. 4; 265, 9; SAA 14: 322, 7; 111, rev. 7; 331, 3; 125, 9; 472, 7; 196, rev. 7. The last occurrence of *nabalkutu*, in SAA 4: 333, 1, is obscure.

40. In the SAA translations, a single construction may be translated in different ways, whereas different constructions may receive the same translation.

41. The Š stem is also attested (SAA 18: 176, rev. 3): PN *šukkuru*: to incite PN to rebel.

42. In SAA 8: 376, 8, *nakāru* also governs a direct suffix object (*-šu*) without any introducing preposition.

passages quoted above. SAA 2: 6, 123–129 is an anticlimax, the list starting with the worst possible thing and ending with lesser crimes:[43] "You shall not do (anything) that is evil and improper [*la ṭa-ab-tú la de-iq-tú*] to Assurbanipal the great crown prince designate, whom Esarhaddon, king of Assyria, your lord, has ordered for you." What the evil and improper things are is specified in the following clauses: "you shall not seize him and put him to death [*ta-ṣa-ba-ta-šu-u-ni ta-du-ka-šú-u-ni*], nor hand him over to his enemy [*a-na* LÚ.KÚR-*šú ta-da-na-šu-u-ni*], nor oust him from the kingship of Assyria [*a-na* LUGAL-*u-te* KUR—*aš-šur tu-nak-*⌈*kar*⌉*-a-šú-u-ni*], nor sw[ear an oa]th to any other king or any other lord [*a-na* LUGAL *šá-nim-ma* EN *šá-nim-ma ma-*⌈*mit*⌉ [*ta-tam*]*-ma-ni*]."

Every time *nabalkutu* and *nakāru* appear in the same sentence, *nabalkutu* comes first, not only in treaties but also in oracular queries (SAA 4: 289, rev. 4, see above). *Itti* PN *nakāru* (SAA 4: 305, rev. 4; 41, rev. 5; 301, rev. 11; 41, 3;[44] 6) and *ana* PN *nakāru* SAA 8: 255, rev. 4; 212, 5 similarly mean "to rebel against someone." *Nakāru* also occurs without any complement (as in SAA 4: 305, rev. 5); there it probably simply means "to become hostile."

Finally, *nukurtu* (*CAD* N/2:328) once refers to the violent revolt—in fact, a civil war—of Šamaš-šumu-ukin (SAA 18: 187, 13).[45]

*Nakāru* and *nukurtu* seem to be the most violent of the terms investigated, implying battles, as can be deduced from the context (when the rebellion of Šamaš-šumu-ukin is so qualified), from the words occurring in the same sentences (*qarābu*), and from the climax figures in which *nakāru* always follows *nabalkutu*.

## General Conclusions

Lexicologists generally assume that three factors explain the choice made by a speaker between parasynonyms: diachrony, diatopy, and diastraty (i.e., the social background, the language register).[46] These factors are indeed relevant in the Neo-Assyrian material presented here. The time when the document was written determines the choice of the term used: In letters from the time of Sargon II, *sīḫu* never appears—however, the fortuity of archaeological discoveries may play important part in that state of affairs. *Bārtu* is the normal term for an insurrection in the eighth century, be it popular or planned by a would-be-king against the sovereign; both meanings will be taken over by *sīḫu* in letters from the seventh century BCE. For the verbs, *nabalkutu* seems

43. There is also an antithesis between this section and the following: you must not do (all the above-mentioned things); but if however somebody does these things, here is what to do (see also above, lines 130–137, then 138–146).

44. In SAA 4: 41, 3, the complement introduced by *itti* is a not a personal name but a geographical name (KUR.*aššur*).

45. Otherwise, *nukurtu* has the vague meaning of "hostilities" (in letters from the seventh century: SAA 10: 112, 21; SAA 18: 181, 10; and astrological reports: SAA 8: 100, rev. 4; 4, rev. 10; 35, 2; 36, 4; 212, rev. 6; 250, rev. 2; 300, edge 17; 336, 12; 341, 6; 444, 2; 490, 2; 490, 3; 255, 2; 295, 5; 359, 3; 502, 13). It also means "hostile message" in SAA 18: 138, 4 and in some astrological reports (SAA 8: 25, 7; 43, rev. 4; 111, 2; 168, 2; 177, 6; 320, rev. 2).

46. The language register is sometimes considered separately and called "diaphasic axis." This distinction is not relevant here.

to mean simply "to disobey" in eighth century letters and in treaties, but "to make a violent insurrection" in seventh-century letters—it is exactly the opposite for *nakāru*.

It is also clear that the type of document (letter, oracular query, astrological report, etc. ) has an impact on the forms used therein: *sīḫu* designates a rebellion in seventh-century letters, when *bārtu* becomes a formal term, used in stereotypical and formulaic contexts (astrological reports, constructions with *epēšu* or *ēpišānūte*). With regard to the language register, thus, *bārtu* is a learned word as opposed to *sīḫu,* the vernacular term. *Nabalkattu* is even more formal, used only by scholars—and yet, seldom—in specific contexts with the meaning of a "very serious rebellion" with terrible consequences. The astrological reports—a scholarly genre par excellence—are a good example: *sīḫu*, as a vernacular term, never appears; the normal term is *bārtu*, but in some (rarer) cases, *nabalkattu* also occurs, when the report alludes to more serious disorders.[47]

Consequently, the terms can be classified according to the intensity of the rebellious event referred to: *sīḫu* is less negatively connoted than *bārtu*, which qualifies a rebellion implying disorder and military or violent episodes, *nabalkattu* being even more tragic and implying a complete transformation of the order of things in the land.[48] Concerning the verbs, the distinction is between *nabalkutu* and *nakāru*. When together, the words always appear in ascending order (*sīḫu bārtu nabalkattu*; *nabalkutu nakāru*), creating a climax, a figure of speech often used in Neo-Assyrian documents.

All the passages considered refer to illegitimate insurrections (*sīḫu, bārtu, sīḫu bārtu, nabalkattu*) against the sovereign, with the exception of a sequence in Esarhaddon's succession treaty referring to a legitimate insurrection (*sīḫu*) against a usurper. Indeed, it is often said that in Mesopotamia rebels are described in a negative way as a threat to the social order, that rebellions are only aimed at taking power ("trading king for king," Richardson 2010: xvii). A large part of the documentation shows the attempt by the powers to delegitimize the discourse of the rebels, speech playing an important part in the outbreak of a rebellion. In official propaganda, revolts are also assimilated to crime, since *nabalkutu*, in legal texts, has the meaning of "to transgress a legal contract" (see Richardson 2000: 1–12 for the five metaphors describing rebellion in Akkadian sources).[49]

But a letter from Mar-Issar, Esarhaddon's agent in Babylonia (SAA 10: 348, rev. 10) offers a very different picture: "The citizens of Babylon, poor wretches who have got nothing, set up a wail and protested. (Whereupon) the commandant imprisoned (some) men from amongst them" (DUMU-MEŠ KÁ.DINGIR.RA.KI *muš-ke-e-nu-te ša me-me-e-ni-šu-nu la-áš-šú-u-ni ki-il-lu is-sa-ak-nu ib-ti-ki-i-ú*). This passage shows first that the lexemes to be considered are really varied and numerous: here, the *muškēnūtu* are revolting, and the verbs used are *(ik)kilu šakānu* and *bakû*. Second, and more important, this passage tends to show that a kind of workers' insurrection might have existed in Mesopotamia after all. *Muškēnu*, in Neo-Assyrian documents, alludes

47. In omens however, *sīḫu* is mentioned in *CAD* S, s.v. "sīḫu A," 240–241, with only two examples (Ach Ištar 4:32 and KAR 385 rev. 25 [SB *Ālu*]).

48. Inconsistencies in the translations in the *CAD* also imply a stronger meaning for *nabalkattu*: if *bārtu* is generally translated by "rebellion" in its entry, sub *nabalkattu*, when they co-occur, *nabalkattu* is translated by "revolt" or "revolution" and *bārtu* by "riots."

49. The metaphors are: noise and movement, children disobeying their parents, animals requiring control, breach of contract and crime, sin and perversion

to the lack of food or goods.[50] In this letter, it qualifies DUMU.MEŠ KÁ.DINGIR.RA.KI (i.e., the Babylonians) and it seems to have a sociological value: Mar-Issar talks about the poor people of Babylon who have nothing, almost as a social class. This single letter seems to reflect compassion on the part of the writer toward those poor people; their revolt appears legitimate and the "bad persona" is the commandant sending them to prison. Richardson (2010: xxi) considered that paradigms of individual freedom or socio-economic equality were anachronistic when studying ancient Mesopotamia. However, the first rebellion in Mesopotamian mythic history, the rebellion of the gods that led to the creation of men can be characterized in terms of economic exploitation, the gods going on strike because they are overburdened (in the words of Von Dassow 2010: ix). Would Mar-Issar's letter allude to such an insurrection of the poor, economically exploited class? Perhaps this is overinterpreting, but this passage shows that unexpected terms, such as *muškēnu*, have to be investigated if one hopes to identify references to another kind of rebellion, a socially motivated one in Akkadian sources. Indeed research on larger corpora and consideration of other lexemes (*baṭlu šakānu*, "to go on strike," *kapādu* "to plot," *dabābu ina* UGU PN "to plot," *mušamhiṣu* "troublemaker, instigator of rebellion," *mušadbibu* "instigator, one who misleads," etc.) is greatly needed. There is still a lot of work to do in this respect on the Neo-Assyrian material, but also more generally for all periods of Mesopotamian history.

## BIBLIOGRAPHY


Cole, S. W. and Machinist, P.
1998 *Letters from Assyrian and Babylonian Priests to Kings Esarhaddon and Assurbanipal*. SAA 13. Helsinki: Helsinki University Press.

Dietrich, M.
2003 *The Neo-Babylonian Correspondence of Sargon and Sennacherib*. SAA 17. Helsinki: Helsinki University Press.

Fales, F. M. and Postgate, J. N.
1992 *Imperial Administrative Records*, part 1: *Palace and Temple Administration*. SAA 7. Helsinki: Helsinki University Press.
1995 *Imperial Administrative Records*, part 2: *Provincial and Military Administration*. SAA 11. Helsinki: Helsinki University Press.

Frahm, E.
2004 Royal Hermeneutics: Observations on the Commentaries from Ashurbanipal's Libraries at Nineveh. *Iraq* 66: 45–50.

Fuchs, A. and Parpola, S.
2001 *The Correspondence of Sargon II*, part 3: *Letters from Babylonia and the Eastern Provinces*. SAA 15. Helsinki: Helsinki University Press.

Gaudin, F. and Guespin, L.
2000 *Initiation à la lexicologie française: De la néologie aux dictionnaires*. Brussels: de Boeck; Duculot.

Hunger, H.
1992 *Astrological Reports to Assyrian Kings*. SAA 8. Helsinki: Helsinki University Press.


50. This meaning can be deduced from a passage in Esarhaddon's succession treaty (SAA 2: 6, 220) where DUMU-*muškēnūti* are opposed to DUMU—SIG$_5$-MEŠ, and from SAA 10: 43, 15 (LUGAL NINDA-MEŠ *la ek-kal* LUGAL *muš-ke-e-nu*).

Kataja, L. and Whiting, R.
1995 *Grants, Decrees and Gifts of the Neo-Assyrian Period.* SAA 12. Helsinki: Helsinki University Press.

Kwasman, T. and Parpola, S.
1991 *Legal Transactions of the Royal Court of Nineveh,* part 1: *Tiglath-Pileser III Through Esarhaddon.* SAA 6. Helsinki: Helsinki University Press.

Lanfranchi, G. B. and Parpola, S.
1990 *The Correspondence of Sargon II,* part 2: *Letters from the Northern and Northeastern Provinces.* SAA 5. Helsinki: Helsinki University Press.

Livingstone, A.
1989 *Court Poetry and Literary Miscellanea.* SAA 3. Helsinki: Helsinki University Press.

Luukko, M.
2004. *Grammatical Variation in Neo-Assyrian.* State Archives of Assyria Studies 16. Helsinki: Neo-Assyrian Text Corpus Project
2013 *The Correspondence of Tiglath-pileser III and Sargon II from Calah/Nimrud.* SAA 19. Helsinki: Neo-Assyrian Text Corpus Project.

Luukko, M. and Van Buylaere, G.
2002 *The Political Correspondence of Esarhaddon.* SAA 16. Helsinki: Helsinki University Press.

Mattila, R.
2002 *Legal Transactions of the Royal Court of Nineveh,* part 2: *Assurbanipal through Sin-šarru-iškun.* SAA 14. Helsinki: Helsinki University Press.

Parpola, S.
1987a *The Correspondence of Sargon II,* part 1: *Letters from Assyria and the West.* SAA 1. Helsinki: Helsinki University Press.
1987b Neo-Assyrian Treaties from the Royal Archives of Nineveh. *JCS* 39: 161–189.
1993 *Letters from Assyrian and Babylonian Scholars.* SAA 10. Helsinki: Helsinki University Press.
1997 *Assyrian Prophecies.* SAA 9. Helsinki: Helsinki University Press.

Parpola, S. and Watanabe, K.
1988 *Neo-Assyrian Treaties and Loyalty Oaths.* SAA 2. Helsinki: Helsinki University Press.

Reynolds, F. S.
2003 *The Babylonian Correspondence of Esarhaddon and Letters to Assurbanipal and Sin-šarru-iškun from Northern and Central Babylonia.* SAA18. Helsinki: Helsinki University Press.

Richardson, S., ed.
2010 *Rebellions and Peripheries in the Cuneiform World.* AOS 91. New Haven: American Oriental Society.

Starr, I.
1990 *Queries to the Sungod: Divination and Politics in Sargonid Assyria.* SAA 4. Helsinki: Helsinki University Press.

Talon, P.
2003 The Use of Glosses in Neo-Assyrian Letters and Astrological Reports. Pp. 648–665 in *Semitic and Assyriological Studies: Presented to Pelio Fronzaroli by Pupils and Colleagues.* Edited by P. Marrassini. Wiesbaden: Harrassowitz.

Von Dassow, E.
2010 Preface. Pp. ix–xv in *Rebellions and Peripheries in the Cuneiform World.* Edited by S. Richardson. AOS 91. New Haven: American Oriental Society.

CHAPTER 7

# Legal Fiction in Emar and Ekalte: A Source of Order or Disorder in the Legal System?

Lena Fijałkowska

LEGAL FICTION IS DEFINED as an assumption that something is true even though in fact it is untrue (sometimes even blatantly so), made in order to alter how a legal rule operates; it is a device by which a legal rule or institution is diverted from its original purpose to accomplish indirectly some other object.[1] Such fiction, contrarily to a presumption, cannot be rebutted in court, and it is often criticized as making law too abstract and sometimes even absurd; especially in common law, numerous instances of legal fiction disappeared gradually, abolished by statutes. On the other hand, it is precisely statutes that in recent times have introduced many cases thereof into continental and European law. At present, in continental Europe creating legal fiction is mostly the privilege of the lawgiver, and sometimes also of courts of law. Moreover, it is usually forbidden to interpret such fiction extensively, that is to say, to apply it to situations that in the light of natural linguistic reading clearly fall outside its field of reference. In other words, leaving too much freedom to ordinary people is considered by the lawgiver dangerous for the stability of the legal system and therefore not allowed. Yet legal fiction still has a wide scope of application. It is often used simply for technical reasons, as in a German verdict according to which, as far as a law referring to the production of sweets was concerned, "Easter bunnies are Santa Clauses."[2] Another example comes from European Union law; according to the fruit jams directive, for the sake of legal commerce in the European Union a carrot is a fruit (Directive 2001/113/EC, Ann. III A1). The latter case has a much wider purpose than a mere technicality; should carrot stay a vegetable, Portugal would not be able to export its carrot jam. Other instances, such as fictitious serving of documents are created in order to facilitate the legal turnover.[3] Finally, a well-known and unambiguously positive example thereof is adoption, an institution whereby strangers

1. Garner 2009: 976. For a comparative analysis of select examples of legal fiction in Near Eastern and classical antiquity see Pfeifer 2013.

2. Fabricius 2011: 118. This sentence was pronounced by the court of the British Occupation Zone in Germany, which had to decide if the law allowing the production of chocolate Santa Clauses permitted, by the same token, also the production of Easter bunnies, which were not explicitly mentioned therein. There was no time for a new law before Easter, hence the verdict.

3. This institution exists in most legal systems. For instance, according to Polish Code of Administrative Procedure, a letter (containing, e.g., court or administrative documents) is deemed delivered if it was properly addressed, and an advice note was left at the addressee's residence twice within fourteen days (art. 44 KPA, DZ.U. 30/1960 poz. 168). Without such a regulation it would be hardly possible for courts and administrative organs to proceed against a person simply refusing to accept an official summons or another similar letter.

are treated as a child's biological parents, and biological parents as strangers in every sphere of the child's life. To sum up—using legal fiction means creating a kind of parallel legal reality, for legal-technical, social, economic, and many other purposes; however, today this creation is considered dangerous for the legal system if applied willfully by citizens and therefore it is reserved mostly to the lawgiver.

Now let us move from modern times to Late Bronze Age Syria. While studying legal documents from Emar and the roughly contemporary texts from Ekalte, it becomes immediately clear that not only was legal fiction very well known to their inhabitants, but it had a much wider scope of application than in modern times. The main differences concern, first of all, persons authorized to use this device, but also the way it worked and its purposes.

There was, however, an area when the way of applying it resembled the modern one, namely the law of sale; the clause *kī nikari*—"as a stranger," attested in a few real estate sales is a case in point.[4] It is contained in two categories of documents. In the first one, the parties are related, but the transaction is concluded "as with a stranger" (RE 51, TBR 56, Emar 120, all of Syro-Hittite style), whereas in the second one though there is no kinship between the parties, the buyer seems to have some right to the real estate due to his relationship to one of the previous owners.[5] It is therefore justified to assume, following Raymond Westbrook (2003: 686–687), that in case of a sale between parents, the seller was obliged to set a lower price, retaining the right of redemption as a result. The clause aims at avoiding those consequences by a fictitious suppression of kinship for the purpose of this particular transaction. In the second group, the kinship is fictitiously dissolved to avoid exercising his rights to the immovable by the buyer.[6] In both cases, legal fiction seems to work in quite a modern way, and the effects of its use are similar to the "arm length's principle" in real estate transactions in common law, according to which for a real estate sale to be qualified as a bona fide sale, i.e. a real one, the transaction must be conducted no differently than it would have been between strangers. Otherwise, it can be classified as gift by court, which might have unpleasant consequences especially as far as taxes are concerned (Garner 2009: 1635).

Numerous instances of legal fiction may be found in the realm of family and inheritance law. The most important institution fully based thereon, that is to say adoption, was known in Late Bronze Age Syria as well as all over the ancient Near East, and will be examined below. But first, it will be useful to analyze several expressions

4. For the law of sale in Emar see Di Filippo 2008: 419–456; Fijałkowska 2014: passim.

5. CM 13 12 (Syro-Hittite, a man redeems his brother's pledged house), ASJ 12 11 (Syro-Hittite, the expression is used in the part of the text relating the history of the sold house; the son of the first seller had bought it back from the buyer's sons "as a stranger." In the Syro-Hittite adoption-marriage document RE 25 the bride's father, who also adopts his son-in-law, states that he "freed" (*paṭāru*) the latter's slave with his family, acting "as a stranger." The clause occurs also in two Syrian contracts. In one of them (Emar 20) parties are somehow related to each other (the buyer is called "brother" of the seller's children, although they have different fathers), in the other one the relationship of the parties is not clear due to the mutilation of the tablet (ASJ 13 B). For the two scribal styles in Emar and the formularies of legal texts see Démare-Lafont 2010: passim. For tablet abbreviations, see bibliography at the end of this article. Unless otherwise noted, all translations follow the ones in the relevant text editions.

6. It is also possible that in this case the use of this expression is simply a way to inform that the buyer did not exercise such rights.

frequently occurring in testaments and adoption acts and constituting examples of obviously socially accepted and legally sanctioned use of fiction so as to protect family members or to divide inheritance according to the wishes of the testator.

The clearest example is the legal change (or rather extension) of woman's gender by means of testament. It was achieved by stating that the testator "made his daughter male and female."[7] The main purpose of this action seems to have been ensuring the continuity of the familial cult; in most cases, there were no sons in the family, and the now legally hermaphroditical daughter was to "invoke my gods and my dead" (RE 85).[8] This provision could also be conditional, in case of a childless death of the son (RE 23).[9] Another aim thereof was to ensure the continuity of the family line; it seems that if the daughter became "male and female," her children could be kept within her father's family (AO 5 13).[10] This intention was expressed with the statement "her children will be my children," which does not describe a real adoption, but rather introduces another legal fiction. The latter could be pushed further—apparently it was possible simply to legally turn one's daughter into a son, probably for the same purpose (TBR 72).[11] These examples show very well how this kind of fiction worked; it was intended to achieve only a specific purpose, and did not have any legal consequences outside this narrow area. Most importantly, the "male and female" or simply

7. See Westbrook 2001: passim. Similar provisions may be found at the same time on the other side of the ancient Near Eastern world, in Nuzi; see Grosz 1987a, 1987b; Paradise 1972.

8. RE 85: $^{f}$*A-ha-am-ma-du*$_4$ DUMU.MÍ-*ia* NU.GIG 13. *a-na* NITÁ *ù* MÍ *e-te-pu-us-*⸢*sí*⸣*-mi* 14. DINGIR.MEŠ-*ia ù e-ṭe*$_4$*-me-*⸢*e*⸣*-ia* 15. *li-ip-la-ah-mi ù* É-*ia* 16. *mim-mu-ia* HA.LA-*ia* 17. *ma-la ša a-bu-ia* 18. *id-di-na-am-mi* 19. *a-*⸢*na*⸣ $^{f}$*A-ha-am-ma-du*$_4$ 20. DUMU.MÍ-*ia at-ta-din-mi.* "Aha-madu, my daughter, the priestess *qadištu*, I made male and female, and my gods and my dead she shall invoke and all my inheritance part which my father gave me, I gave to Aha-madu."

9. RE 23: 11. *ù šum-ma* $^{m}$*Ip-qí-*$^{d}$KUR DUMU!-*ia* 12. *im-tù-ut ù* NUMUN.MEŠ NU.TUK 13. *a-nu-um-ma* $^{mf}$*A-ha-tu*$_4$ DAM-*ti-ia* 14. *a-na* MÍ *ù* NITA 15. *aš-ku-un-ši* 16. DINGIR.MEŠ-*ia ù me-te-ia* 17. *lu-ú tu*$_4$*-na-ab-b*[*i*] 18. *ù mi-im-mu-ia* 19. *lu-ú ti-il-qè*. "And if Ipqi-Dagan my son dies without progeny, now I made Ahatu, my wife, female and male, my gods and my ancestors she shall invoke and all that is mine she will take." This text is somewhat problematic, since it is the wife of the *de cuius* who is made "female and male," instead of the usual daughter. Beckman (1996) supposed that it could have depended on the age of the woman—an older woman would be able to become a patriarch, but not a younger one. However, another explanation is also possible—a scribal mistake. It is all the more probable since later in the same document we find the following statement: 20. *ù šum-ma* $^{m}$*Ip-qí-*$^{d}$KUR 21. *ù* $^{mf}$*A-ha-tu*$_4$ DUMU.MEŠ-*ia* 22. *i-mu-ta.* "And if Ipqi-Dagan *and Ahatu, my children* die" (emphasis added); it follows that Ahatu is the testator's daughter, and not his wife (although Beckman adds in the translation "and my [other] children," supposing an omission). Moreover, Ahatu is also appointed the only heir in the event of her brother's childless death, and should she in turn die without progeny, yet another heir is named, whereas in the only explicit case when the testator's wife becomes his unique heir, it is clearly said that there is no other one alive (ASJ 13 22: *a-wa-ra-ša mu*$_x$*-bá-li-la* NU.TUK). A similar provision is contained in only one other will, ASJ 13 30, where the wife is installed as unique heir conditionally, should the son not return from abroad; still, the same reservation about the lack of other inheritors is made. On the other hand, such an explanation was not necessary if the estate fell to the daughter, as is clear, for instance, from RE 85. To sum up: it is much more likely for Ahatu to have been the daughter, and not the wife of the testator. Another, this time clear, case of a conditional making of one's daughter "female and male" may be found in Semitica 46, 2, where such a provision pertains to both daughters of the testator in case of his son's childless death; they are supposed to continue the family cult and take care of their mother.

10. 11. [DUMU.MEŠ] *ša ul-la-du*$_4$ 12. [DUMU.MEŠ]-*ia*. "The children she will bear are my children." In another will (ASJ 13 25 = RA 1) after making his daughter female and male the patriarch calls her sons "my sons" (DUMU-*ia*), thus ensuring the continuity of the family line.

11. 3. $^{fd}$UTU-*la-i* DUMU.MÍ-*ia* GAL *a-na* DUMU.NITA 4. *e-te-púš-ši*. "My eldest daughter I made to a son." It is interesting to observe that in this provision the daughter's name is written with the female determinative, but later with the male one.

male daughter still remained a woman insofar that she could marry (a man), as in TBR 72, where the testator made his daughter a son and married her off in the same sentence. This way of using legal fiction might be compared to the modern construction of carrot as fruit—a carrot is a (legal) fruit only for certain, though important purposes, like jam production, and this change does not have consequences for the whole of its (legal as well as physical) existence as a vegetable. The only difference is that in Emar this effect was obtained by means of contract and not of statute or directive.

It was also feasible (and frequent) for a patriarch to turn, when needed, a lady of the estate into the lord thereof, appointing her "father and mother of the household."[12] This formula refers to another, widely attested instance of legal fiction, usually applied if the testator wanted to make sure that the position of his wife within the family would be well protected, and at the same time wished to postpone the division of the estate.[13] In order to achieve this goal a fiction was created that the patriarch still, in a way, lived in the person of his widow, who thus became not only the lady, but also the lord of the house. In several testaments this intention is expressed very clearly, the testator not only installing his wife as "father and mother of the household," but also stating that she is supposed to take his place within the estate.[14] In a few instances this status was bestowed upon the daughter instead of the wife, usually when the former is a priestess.[15] Finally, if the estate belonged to a woman (probably when she had been the sole heiress of her father), she could confer the status of "father of the household" upon her husband (Emar 30). Obviously it was not gained automatically due to marriage, which in turn did not deprive the matriarch of her position.[16] It seems therefore that legal fiction used to keep the estate undivided and the widow's fate secured worked in a similar way as making a daughter "male and female." It had legal consequences

12. A similar provision occurs in testaments from Nuzi, where the testator could convey his wife *abbūtu*—the paternal authority over the estate, as well as in Old Assyrian times. See Paradise 1972: 198–220; Zaccagnini 2003: 601; Michel 2000: passim.

13. For these purposes of the "father and mother" clause see Westbrook 2001: passim.

14. See, e.g., TBR 50: 6. . . . *a-nu-um-ma* 7. [mf]*A-hi-lìb-bi* DAM-*ia* 8. *a-bu u* AMA-*mu ša* É-*ia* 9. *ši-it-ma* É GAL A.ŠÀ GIŠ.KIRI$_6$.GEŠTIN 10. *bu-šu ba-ši-tu$_4$ ma-aš-ru* 11. *ša* É-*ia a-na* DAM-*ia* 12. *ad-din ki-ma!* SAG.DU-*ia* 13. *a-na* É-*ia aš-ku-un-ši*. "Now Ahi-libbi, my wife, is father and mother of my household. The main house, the field and the vineyard, goods, property, wealth of my house I gave to my wife. In my place over my household I put her." This does not mean, however, that the wife is the main or sole heir; it is clear from the remainder of the text that after her death, the estate will fall to the testator's children, unless they refuse to honor her, in which case she is allowed to give it to another relative of her husband on his father's side.

15. In Emar 31 a *harimtu*, in RE 57 and ASJ 13 23 a *qadištu*. The introduction to RE 57 seems to suggest that the testator had no wife, since he is said to have determined only the fate of his house and his daughter, who in turn had her own daughter and probably also sons. In ASJ 13 23 both the wife and daughter are named "father and mother" of the estate and are to be honored by the three sons of the *de cuius*. However, the indivisibility of the estate was to last only till the death of the wife, and afterward the four children, including the daughter, were allowed to divide it according to the testamentary provisions. Still, the sons were obliged to support (*wabālu*) their sister till her death. In other words, in case of the widow the purpose of the discussed provision was twofold—keeping the estate undivided and ensuring her support by the children, whereas as far as the daughter was concerned only ensuring support was aimed at. Finally, in Emar 31 the formula is slightly different: "fatherhood and mother" (*a-bu-ut-ti ù* AMA-*mi*) instead of the usual "father and mother," perhaps because the text is written in the presence of the king of Carchemish and possibly by one of his scribes (the end of the text is broken).

16. 3. É-*ia gáb-bá mím-mu-ia* 4. *a-na* [m]*Gu-l*[*a*] LÚ.*mu-ti-ia at-ta-din ù a-na a*-[*bu-ut-ti*] É-*ia* 5. *al-ta-kán-šu*. "My whole house, all that is mine I gave to Gula, my husband, and the fatherhood of my house I conferred upon him."

primarily within the family, giving the widow an authority she would not have otherwise (e.g., the right to disinherit an heir who would not honor her), and probably also improving her social standing. But even this status was not legally the same as that of a (real) patriarch, since in most cases the widow was not allowed to dispose of the estate she formally controlled, either *inter vivos* or by testament; usually the shares of the inheritors were already determined in the husband's will and could not be changed.[17] At the same time being (partly) a patriarch did not preclude a new marriage, although the latter usually resulted in the necessity to give up the widow's position and to leave the household. In other words, due to the fiction of becoming "father and mother of the household" a woman was usually made a half-patriarch, without the latter's full authority; probably to become a complete one, she would also have to become an heir to the whole estate, which seems to have been impossible if descendants or siblings of the testator were alive.

Numerous examples of very ingenious and sometimes also shocking use of legal fiction may be found in adoption documents. As previously mentioned, today a standard adoption creates two fictitious situations—that biological parents of the child and usually also the whole biological family thereof are strangers, and that a couple of biological strangers and their family are the child's family, with all the consequences. Most of this was not at all the case in Late Bronze Age Syria.[18] In the aforementioned case of a daughter made son and married off, not only is her husband adopted by the testator at the same time, but, should his wife die, he is also ordered to marry one of her sisters, who is his own adoptive sister too! Another case in point is a little dossier consisting of two texts. In the first one (TBR 41), Ikmu-Dagan makes his wife, Na'mi-sada, "father and mother" of his household and gives her control over his estate. Moreover, he makes his slave, Ipqi-Dagan, to be a son of his (the testator's) wife and his own eldest son. This is peculiar not only because the consent neither of the adopters nor of the adoptee seems necessary, and the fiction goes so far as to give the adoptee a stepmother and stepson for parents.[19] Thus, it becomes obvious that at least in this case, the familial relationship created legally is seen as something entirely dissociated from any biological reality; in Emar the Latin maxim *Adoptio naturam imitatur* is of no use. Let us just remind that a real relationship between a stepson and his stepmother would be deemed completely unacceptable and punished with death as adultery. On the top of it, this quasi-adopted son remains a slave, and will be free only upon the death of his so-called parents. The story goes further with the next text,

17. Westbrook (2001: 41) called the rights of the widow to her husband's estate "a purely nominal ownership." However, another qualification is possible—dower, i.e., life usufruct of the estate, without the possibility of disposing of it (unless the heirs did not honor the widow, in which case she could disinherit them and give their shares to other members of the testators family, who did support her. Still, she was never allowed to "give it to a stranger").

18. For a general analysis of adoptions in Emar see Bellotto 2009: passim.

19. 30. *a-nu-ma* $^{m}$*Ip-qí*-$^{d}$KUR ÌR-*ia* [*a-na*] DUMU-*ru-ut-ti* 31. *ša* $^{f}$*Na-a'-mi-ša-da* DAM-*ia* 32. ù $^{m}$IM-*ga-mil* DUMU-*ia* GAL-*šu at-ta-din-šu* 33. $u_4$-*mi*.MEŠ *ša* $^{f}$*Na-a'-mi-ša-da* DAM-*ia* 34. *ù* $^{m}$IM-*ga-mil* DUMU-*ia bal-ṭu* 35. $^{m}$*Ip-qí*-$^{d}$KUR *lip-làh-šu-nu-ti* 36. *ki-i-me-e i-pal-làh-šu-nu-ti* EGIR *ši-im-t*[*i-šu-nu*] 37. *ub-bal-šu-nu-ti a-na* $^{d}$UTU *za-ku*. "Now Ipqi-Dagan, my slave, I gave as son to Na'mi-sada, my wife, and Ba'al-gamil, my eldest son. As long as Na'mi-sada my wife and Ba'al-gamil my son live, Ipqi-Dagan will honor them. If he honors them, when their fate carries them he will be clear for god Shamash." It is obvious from the next text in this dossier, TBR 42, that Na'mi-sada is not the mother but the stepmother of the testator's children.

whereby the son of Ikmu-Dagan, Ba'al-gamil makes his stepmother into his mother and adopts his brothers as his sons.[20] As a result, he becomes the father of his mother's children. That the kind of incest normally leading to such a kinship would be severely punished, for example, by burning alive according to the Code Hammurabi (see §157 CH), does not seem to have bothered anyone. In the end, Ba'al-gamil has also to correct the inheritance order modified by all those adoptions, by naming his daughter as first heir of his biological son, to the detriment of his adopted sons who would otherwise precede her in the succession order by law.[21] Another document of this kind may be found in Ekalte (Ekalte 66). In this text one Zu-Anna adopts his brother as his son, and takes a slave of the latter for wife; their children are to be the children of both Zu-Anna and his brother-adopted-as-son. It is explicitly stated that both Zu-Anna, their biological father and Rasap-abu will be their fathers; again, no problem with such biological impossibility.[22] This somewhat problematic construction has its counterpart in a document from Emar featuring two women (TBR 28). The main protagonist is $^{f}$Ba'la-kimi, who installs her own mother as father and mother of her (Ba'la-kimi's) estate and explicitly states that as of now, her son Ribi-Dagan has two mothers to honor.[23]

Sometimes legal fiction was also used to correct the inheritance order within the family. Customary rules of succession appear to have allowed the eldest son to get a bigger share of the estate. However, the testator could change that, either fictitiously leveling out the age of all children ("there is no senior or junior between them"), or, equally fictitiously, correcting the seniority order ("PN is the senior brother, PN$_2$ is the junior brother"). Of course, the question arises if those are not simply technical terms, used to point out the scope of inheritance rights of individual heirs. However, in the Emar corpus there are instances of straightforward provisions pertaining to the inheritance order, as in the aforementioned Ikmu-Dagan story. In order to secure his daughter's interests, Ba'al-gamil simply states that "if my son dies, PN, my daughter, will succeed him." At the same time another man who wanted to install his daughter as a heir together with his sons, had to resort to legal fiction, naming her his second son, although it is clear from the text that in fact she was the eldest (but female) child (Emar

20. 2. *a-nu-ma* $^{f}$*Na-a'-mi-ša-da* DAM *a-bi-ia* 3. *a-na* AMA-*ia e-te-púš-ši-mi* $^{m}$*Tah-hu ù* $^{m}$*A-hi-ha-mi* 4.2 ŠEŠ.MEŠ-*ia a-na* DUMU-*ut-ti-ia e-te-púš-šu-nu-ti-mi* 5. *ù a-na* ŠEŠ-*ut-ti ša* $^{m}$*Hi-in-na-*$^{d}$IM DUMU-*ia* 6. *e-te-púš-šu-nu-ti*. "Now Na'mi-sada, my father's wife, I made to my mother, and Tahhu and Ahi-hami, my two brothers, I made my sons, and brothers of Hinna-Dagan, my son, I made them." This document has two other peculiarities. First, it is the only case of adoption to "motherhood" in the Emar corpus; second, for an unknown reason, making his brothers to his sons does not automatically result in them becoming brothers to the children of the adopter, hence a separate provision concerning their relationship to the biological son of the latter. For these texts see Bellotto 2009: 86–90.

21. 16. *šum-ma* $^{m}$*Hi-na-*$^{d}$IM BA.UG$_6$ $^{f}$*Aš-tar-si-ma-ti* 17. NIN-*šu* EGIR-*šu*. "If Himasi-Dagan dies, Ashtar-simati, his sister, will succeed him".

22. 1. $^{m}$*Zu-An-na* dumu $^{d}$IM-EN 2. $^{md}$GIR$_3$-*a-ba* ŠEŠ-*šu* 3. *a-na* DUMU-*šu iš-ku-un-šu* (. . .) 19. $^{f}$*Na-šu-sa-tum* 20. SAG.GEME$_2$ *ša* $^{d}$GIR$_3$-*a-bi* 21. DAM-*tum ša* $^{m}$*Zu-An-na* 22. DUMU.MEŠ *ša* $^{f}$*Na-šu-sa-tum* 23. *tu-la-dám* DUMU.MEŠ-*ru* 24. $^{md}$GIR$_3$-*a-bi* 25. *ù* DUMU.MEŠ *MZu-An-na*. "Zu-Anna son of Ba'al-be'lu made Rasap-abu, his brother, to his son. . . . Nasusatum, slave of Rasap-abu, will be Zu-Anna's wife. The children that Nasusatum will bear will be children of Rasap-abu and children of Zu-Anna."

23. 9. *a-nu-ma* $^{f}$*Ga-ni* AMA-*ia a-na a-bi ù* AMA 10. *ša* É-*ia al-ta-qì-ši* (. . .) 15. *ù a-nu-ma* $^{m}$*Ri-bi-*$^{d}$KUR 16. $^{f}$*Ga-ni ù* $^{f}$NIN-*ki-mi* 17. 2 AMA-*mi-šu li-ip-làh*. "Now Gani, my mother, as father and mother of my house I took. . . . And now Ribi-Dagan Gani and Ba'la-kimi, his two mothers, shall honor."

181).[24] Perhaps the reason for using different provisions to achieve a similar goal is that in the first case, the daughter was a biological child, and the "put aside" sons were in fact only adopted brothers of the testator. In the second instance, however, the boys were biological sons of the testator, hence to become an equal heir, placed as second and not last in the inheritance order, the daughter had to be fictitiously made a son.[25] In other words, though adoption did create a new legal situation and indeed turned the adoptee into the adopter's son, the biological kinship was still more, or at least equally important. This is a fundamental difference between the way the legal fiction on which adoption is based works in our legal systems and the way it used to work in Late Bronze Age Syria.

The conclusion suggests itself that in Emar and Ekalte legal fiction was a tool used willingly, widely, and often in ways very different from ours. The first difference consists in who was allowed to use it. Since the legal system was one of customary law, with very few, if any, statutes, it could not be the exclusive privilege of the lawgiver. Certainly it was at least to some extent regulated by the legal custom, but it becomes immediately obvious that much freedom was left to the participants of the legal turnover. The modern, merely technical use (the case of bunnies being Santas) does not seem to have been known, which is really surprising since this construction occurs mostly in statutes. The most widespread way in which legal fiction was applied can be compared to the one occurring in the European Union regulations (carrot as fruit)—a spotted use for a particular purpose, with no consequences in other legal areas (though, due to a different construction of the legal system, attested not in statutes but in everyday transactions). It is obvious in the case of the *kī nikari* clause or of the formulas correcting the inheritance order: both have results only for the sale and the particular inheritance case respectively. More complicated is the situation as far as adoptions and quasi-adoptions are concerned. Although the basic effect of adoption is the same as today—a fictitious parenthood relationship, much more freedom was granted the family head in changing the relations within the family, no matter what biological impossibilities those changes could create. At the same time, such innovations as changing one's daughter's gender (or extending it), or (legally) having children with one's mother, obviously worked only for some specific purposes as well, in contrast to the contemporary adoption, whose consequences are the same in relation to everybody and in every sphere of life of both the adopter and the adoptee. Making a daughter male, or proclaiming the adoption to sonship, motherhood, and so on seems to have been just the first step, followed by shaping the consequences thereof, again with a great deal of freedom. However, very often those consequences are left out of our texts, where probably only the basics were noted, and everybody knew what was to be achieved.

24. 4. $^{m}$*Ir-ib-*$^{d}$KUR DUMU-*ia* GAL $^{fd}$GÌR-DINGIR.MEŠ DUMU.‹MÍ›-*ia ša-nu-ú* 5. $^{m}$*A-bi-ka-pí* DUMU-*ia* TUR. "Irib-Dagan is my senior son, Rasap-ili is my second son, Abi-kapi is my youngest son."

25. The more-so that possibly the daughter was adopted, as the penalty clause seems to indicate:

14. *šum-ma* $^{fd}$GÌR-DINGIR.MEŠ *a-na pa-ni* ŠES.MEŠ-*ši ta-aq-*[*b*]*i* 15. *ú-ul* ŠEŠ.MEŠ-*ia at-tu-nu-mi* 16.TÚG-‹*ši*› *i-na* GIŠ.ŠÚ.A *li-iš-ku-un a-na m*[*ím*]*-mu-ia* 17. NU.TUK *a-šar* ŠÀ-‹*ši*› *li-il-li*[*k*]. "If Rasap-ili in front of her brothers says 'you are not my brothers,' she shall put her clothes on a stool and she shall go wherever she wishes." Such vocabulary is usually used in the penal clauses of adoption documents, when setting the penalty for a unilateral withdrawal from the contract and in other cases of relationships not based on biological kinship (e.g., in the aforementioned text TBR 41, when the penalty for the stepchildren denying their stepmother and vice versa is concerned).

To conclude, let us quote Morris Cohen, who wrote that "legal fiction is the mask that progress must wear to pass the faithful but blear-eyed watchers of our ancient legal treasures. But though legal fictions are useful in . . . mitigating or absorbing the shock of innovation, they work havoc in the form of intellectual confusion" (Cohen 1982: 126). However, this does not seem true for Late Bronze Age Syria. Although at first sight, especially family relationships in Emar and Ekalte created due to the use of legal fiction may seem to us a mess of biblical proportions, it appears that in fact the Syrians were quite adept in applying this legal tool. At the same time they knew the law well enough not to get discouraged by legal combinations, even the most tangled ones from our point of view. In other words, in this case havoc and intellectual confusion are only ours, as a result of our lack of full understanding of ancient legal reality.

Abbreviations used for the Emar and Ekalte texts:

| | |
|---|---|
| AO | Arnaud, D. La Syrie du moyen-Euphrate sous le protectorat hittite: contrats de droit privé. *AuOr* 5 (1987): 211–241. |
| ASJ | Tsukimoto, A. Akkadian Tablets in the Hirayama Collection, II. *ASJ* 13 (1991): 275–333. |
| CM 13 | Goodnick-Westenholz, J. *Cuneiform Inscriptions in the Collection of the Bible Lands Museum Jerusalem: The Emar Tablets*. CM 13. Groningen: Styx, 2000. |
| Ekalte | Mayer, W. *Tall Munbāqa—Ekalte—II: Die Texte*. WVDOG 102. Saarbrücken: Saarbrücker Druckerei & Verlag, 2001. |
| Emar | Arnaud, D. *Recherches au pays d'Aštata: Textes sumériens et accadiens*. Emar 6.3. Paris: Editions Recherche sur les Civilisations, 1986. |
| RE | Beckman, G. *Texts from the Vicinity of Emar in the Collection of Jonathan Rosen*. HANE/M 2. Padova: Sargon, 1996. |
| Semitica 46 | Arnaud, D. Mariage et remariage des femmes chez les Syriens du Moyen-Euphrate, à l'âge du Bronze récent d'après deux nouveaux documents. *Semitica* 46 (1996): 7–16. |
| TBR | Arnaud, D. *Textes syriens de l'âge du bronze récent*. AuOrSup 1. Barcelona: AUSA, 1991. |

## BIBLIOGRAPHY


Beckman, G.
1996 *Texts from the Vicinity of Emar in the Collection of Jonathan Rosen.* HANE/M 2. Padova: Sargon.

Bellotto, N.
2009 *Le adozioni a Emar*. HANE/M 9. Padova: S.A.R.G.O.N.

Cohen, M.
1982 *Law and the Social Order: Essays in Legal Philosophy*. 2nd ed. New Brunswick, NJ: Transaction Books.

Démare-Lafont, S.
2010 Eléments pour une diplomatique juridique des textes d'Emar. Pp. 43–84 in *Trois millénaires de formulaires juridiques.* Edited by S. Démare-Lafont and A. Lemaire. HEO 48. Genève: Droz.

Di Filippo, F.
2008 Gli atti di compravendita di Emar: Rapporto e conflitto tra due tradizioni giuridiche. Pp. 419–456 in *I diritti del mondo cuneiforme (Mesopotamia e regioni adiacenti, ca. 2500–500 a.C.)*. Edited by M. Liverani and C. Mora. Pavia: IUSS Press.

Fabricius, D.
2011 *Darwins angetretenes Erbe: Evolutionsbiologie auch für Nicht-Biologen.* Vol. 1 of *Kriminalwissenschaften: Grundlagen und Grundfragen*. Berlin: LIT.

Fijałkowska, L.
2014 *Le droit de la vente à Emar*. Philippika 64. Wiesbaden: Harrassowitz.

Garner, B. A., ed.
2009 *Black's Law Dictionary: Definitions of the Terms and Phrases of American and English Jurisprudence, Ancient and Modern*. 9th ed. St. Paul: West.

Grosz, K.
1987a On Some Aspects of the Adoption of Women in Nuzi. Pp. 131–152 in *Studies on the Civilization and Culture of Nuzi and the Hurrians*. Edited by D. Owen and M. Morrison. SCCNH 2. Winona Lake, IN: Eisenbrauns.
1987b Daughters Adopted as Sons at Nuzi and Emar. Pp. 81–85 in *La femme dans le Proche-Orient antique: Compte rendu de la 33e Rencontre Assyriologique Internationale (Paris, 7–10 Juillet 1986)*. Edited by J.-M. Durand. Paris: Editions Recherche sur les Civilisations.

Michel, C.
2000 A propos d'un testament paléo-assyrien: Une femme de marchand "père et mere" des capitaux. *RA* 94: 1–10.

Paradise, J. S.
1972 *Nuzi Inheritance Practices.* PhD diss., University of Pennsylvania.

Pfeifer, G.
2013 *Fortschritt auf Umwegen: Umgehung und Fiktion in Rechtsurkunden des Altertums*. Munich. PhD diss., Ludwig-Maximilians-Universität.

Westbrook, R.
2001 Social Justice and Creative Jurisprudence in Late Bronze Age Syria. *JESHO* 44: 22–43.
2003 Emar and Vicinity. Pp. 657–691 in vol. 1 of *A History of Ancient Near Eastern Law.* Edited by R. Westbrook. HdO 72. Leiden: Brill.

Zaccagnini, N.
2003 Nuzi. Pp. 565–617 in vol. 1 of *A History of Ancient Near Eastern Law*. Edited by R. Westbrook. HdO 72. Leiden: Brill.

CHAPTER 8

# What the "Man of One Mina" Wanted: Law and Commerce in the Ur III Period

Steven Garfinkle

THE KINGS OF EARLY MESOPOTAMIA are famed for producing royal inscriptions, such as the Laws of Hammurabi and the Laws of Ur-Namma that we have labeled "law codes." These texts open with grand statements about kingship and its divine foundation, but the focus of the body of these royal proclamations was on the regulation of commerce. Modern observers often regard these texts as evidence for the growth of the state sector and as proof of the desire of the crown to legitimize the extension of its authority.[1] The kingdom inaugurated by Ur-Namma is usually seen as an early example of this process.

The Third Dynasty of Ur is famous among Assyriologists for the substantial archives that survive from the last century of the third millennium BCE. The period also witnessed a proliferation in the drawing up of contracts and in the legal procedures developed to deal with them. Instead of documenting a tyrannical attempt to promote state power at the expense of the private sector, what the laws and other texts show is the need for state regulation of the economy to protect the accumulation of capital. My goal in this contribution is to show that the heads of households in southern Mesopotamia sought to draw the blanket of state protection over their transactions and thereby protect their commercial ventures and their accumulation of the means of production. The households that I am discussing were predominantly those that had access to property. These were relatively wealthy households of urban elites whose activities were well documented in the cuneiform record. During the Ur III period, these households increasingly connected themselves with state enterprise and the crown.

Let me start by briefly examining the beginning of the Laws of Ur-Namma.[2] After announcing the divine right of Ur-Namma to kingship and then highlighting his military prowess, the text turns to commercial matters. The king establishes standard weights and measures, and then he opens up and secures the rivers and roads for commerce. Following this we get one of the characteristic statements about justice in early Mesopotamia, "I did not deliver the orphan to the rich. I did not deliver the widow to the mighty. I did not deliver the man with but one shekel to the man with one mina. I did not deliver the man with but one sheep to the man with one ox. . . . I established justice in the land." (Roth 1997: 16–17)

1. For this view of the early law codes, see, e.g., Wells 2005: 185.
2. For the Laws of Ur-Namma, see Frayne 1997; Roth 1997; Civil 2011.

My intent here is not to revisit the role of texts like the Laws of Ur-Namma in the growth of legal traditions in early Mesopotamia, but rather to evaluate the role of the king's justice in state formation and the regulation of the economy. Texts like this are often read for their value as royal propaganda. And statements like the one quoted above buttress the common understanding of this era as one in which the crown asserted new, and authoritarian, control over the community. In this instance we see the king showing that his authority is so great that it can tame the interests of the "man of one mina." As an aside, let's be clear about one important point this particular passage raises. The king is articulating the protection of the elite from the super elite. In modern terms, he is shielding the 10 percent or 20 percent from the potential depredations of the 1 percent. The possession of even a shekel of silver worth of property was likely beyond the means of the mass of dependent laborers who formed the backbone of the communities of southern Mesopotamia.[3] But did the growth of the state in early Mesopotamia mean that the king was extending his coercive authority over a broader socio-political landscape? Or, was this more of a cooperative process in which the elite, and especially the men of one mina, sought out the protection of state regulation, and ultimately, the law?

As Laura Culbertson (2009: 152–156) noted, the Ur III kings championed legal centralism.[4] Certainly this is the gist of the prologue to Ur-Namma's laws. I will return below to the question of whether this centralism was achieved in practice; however, there is no doubt that the crown's allies in this endeavor were the commercial interests of the large noninstitutional households, the men of one mina. Examining the legal activities of these individuals takes us into the realm of what legal scholars of antiquity often call private law. Hans Neumann (2003) and Claus Wilcke (2007) wrote about this recently, and I would like to draw on both of their observations. Neumann pointed out that the advent of territorial states, or at least larger states, had a decisive impact on the development of private law. And by private law I mean here the regulation of transactions between individual households beyond the immediate view of the institutional economy.

At the same time, I agree with Wilcke's notion that the early territorial states, like the kingdom of Ur, were really composed of islands within larger territories.[5] These islands, as envisioned by Wilcke, were the urban centers connected to one another by roads and canals. The households, both individual and institutional, that controlled property and access to the means of production, were the social fabric of these islands. And here, I think that we can extend this metaphor of islands that I am borrowing from Wilcke. The households themselves were the islands within the territory of southern Mesopotamia. The larger state formation of early dynasts, like the Ur III kings, consisted of binding these islands in distant towns more closely to each other and to the

3. A mina was equivalent to sixty shekels, and in modern terms a mina equates to approximately half a kilo of silver. For a sense of scale, unskilled slaves could be purchased at that time for between one and three shekels, and even the price of a skilled slave only rarely exceeded ten shekels. Draft animals frequently cost less than ten shekels. These price conditions prevailed in an agrarian economy in which bottlenecks formed around the availability of labor and draft animals making them highly desired commodities.

4. Culbertson 2009: 152–156 also provides an examination of this concept in broader legal history and in the scholarship on early Mesopotamian law.

5. See Wilcke 2007: 16 where he also critiques the notion that the rise of territorial states had a decisive impact on the development of private law.

crown. To make this clear, we can use the terms recently employed by Seth Richardson (2012: 7–8) and note that the crown was in "political competition for constituencies." The households of wealthy urban professionals were essential clients for the newly forming regional state. Much of this was accomplished through the extension of state power over the economy through the law. Of course, as I stated above, this is usually understood as a coercive process by which the royal sector appropriated control. My basic contention here is that this was a process that not only favored entrepreneurial activity but one that was actively sought by the entrepreneurs who were the heads of many of these households.

This understanding of the process also places limits on the absolute authority of the state. The evidence gathered by Culbertson suggests that local judges and legal procedures retained significant function and authority in the Ur III period but operated alongside the growth of cadres of royal judges, *mashkim*, and royal messengers, all of whom played a growing role in the investigation and dispensation of justice, especially in places of crown primacy like Iri-sangrig, Puzrish-Dagan, and Nippur.[6] This fits in well with the model that I propose for the development of the Ur III state not as a grand centralizing experiment but rather as a movement in fits and starts in which the kings tried to assert their control over local social, political, and economic networks. Moreover, this works nicely with the metaphor that I borrowed earlier from Wilcke of seeing the Ur III state as a series of connected islands in southern Mesopotamia. Increasingly though, what bound these islands together were broader social networks under the protection of the legal authority of the king.

Culbertson (2009: 16) stated, "The dispute resolution system of the Ur III period was not a living, breathing instantiation of state power, but rather involved local, competitive forces among urban, provincial families of elites who sought to maintain and create power by way of local disputing traditions, many of which were likely to have predated the establishment of the Ur III state." At the same time, Manuel Molina (2013: 139) pointed out in his study of court officials that, "our texts show that the administration of justice in the Umma province was strongly pervaded by the influence of the royal administration. Military men, royal envoys and other royal representatives, commissioners in charge of the investigation, members of the local administrations, and peripatetic officials appointed by the Crown no doubt exercised their authority during the process." Moreover, in some well-documented cases the authority of these royal officials trumped that of governors and other provincial elites.[7]

What this suggests is an environment in which the kings of Ur were beginning to create statewide norms that took precedence over local courts and precedents. To return to my focus, this was clearly to the advantage of the commercial interests of individuals throughout the state who sought opportunity in the appearance of royal authority on a grander scale. I have chosen a couple of texts to illustrate the point I am making about entrepreneurial activity, the growth of royal authority, and the men

6. Wilcke 2007: 40 noted that *mashkim* was a function and not a profession. This is in line with the growth of responsibilities filled by elites in the Ur III state who often served in multiple capacities in addition to their hereditary professions. Their hereditary status was what permitted them to perform these extra roles on behalf of the growing state.

7. See Molina 2010: 210–211 for a case involving the governor of Umma and functionaries of the Garshana estate.

of one mina. One of the texts published by A. Leo Oppenheim from the collection of the New York Public Library was a loan between two merchants.[8] In this text Utul-Mama received 1 and 1/5 mana of silver from Ur-shaga and he pledged to weigh out the silver, along with 20 percent interest, in four months time. He then swore in the name of the king (mu lugal) that if he did not weigh it out at that time, then he would owe Ur-shaga twice the required amount. Seven men witnessed the transaction. Both of the principals were prominent merchants in their communities. Utul-Mama was active in SI.A-a's archive and Ur-shaga was active at Girsu-Lagash. The text comes from Nippur in the first year of Ibbi-Suen. Here we see this new notion of statewide community in action. Two men from different urban centers in southern Mesopotamia met in Nippur and exchanged an extraordinary sum, which was likely from a balanced account of the bala.

What I want to highlight in this text is the royal oath that was central to the transaction. Here we have two men who were clearly men of one mina. While merchants probably did not enjoy the same high social status as priests, governors, generals, and so on, they were prominent members of both their local communities and the new statewide community created by the kings of Ur. Merchants appear as significant participants in court cases (Molina 2013) and they were prominent in the lists of notables who dedicated animals at Puzrish-Dagan (Garfinkle 2013). These are exactly the type of individuals from whose depredations Ur-Namma claimed to be protecting more ordinary men of his kingdom. But it is a hallmark of their transactions that they sought the protections provided by royal oath.

In a second example, also from Nippur and published by David Owen (1982), a shabra was responsible for ensuring that a debt of one mana was settled with a merchant.[9] The shabra swore in the name of the king to return it and he sealed the envelope. The text noted that if he does not return it, then another individual will weigh out two mana of silver on his behalf. This third individual also swore an oath in the name of the king. The tablet ended with a list of four individuals identified as lú inim-ma-bi-me which we can translate as "these were the witnesses." The seal of the shabra was dedicated to the governor of Nippur whose servant he was (arad$_2$-zu). Here we find a prominent provincial official acting outside of the capacity of his office and swearing an oath in the king's name. Indeed both responsible parties swore separate royal oaths.

In their discussion of the legal environment of the Ur III state, Bertrand Lafont and Raymond Westbrook (2003: 197) defined the word lu$_2$ as "man, householder."

8. Oppenheim 1948 text P 1; also published by Sauren 1978 as text NYPL 370: 1 ma-na 12 gin$_2$ ku$_3$-babbar si-i$_3$-tum nig$_2$-kas$_7$-ak/ mash$_2$ 5 gin$_2$ 1 gin$_2$-ta/ ki ur-sa$_6$-ga-ta/ u$_2$-tul-ma-ma/ shu ba-ti/ iti shu-numun-a sag-she$_3$/ la$_2$-e-de$_3$/ tukum-bi nu-la$_2$/ 2-am$_3$ tab-be$_2$-de$_3$/ mu lugal i$_3$-pa$_3$/ 7 witnesses/ date.

9. Owen 1982: plate 98 (NATN 403): kishib 1 ma-na ku$_3$-babbar/ ad-da-a-ka/ ki shu-ni-an-nam-ka/ al-gal$_2$-la/ iti she-kin-ku$_5$ u$_4$ 15 zal-la tum$_3$-da/ mu lugal-bi in-pa$_3$/ tukum-bi nu-mu-de$_6$/ 2 ma-na ku$_3$-babbar/ la$_2$-a-da ur-d.da-mu-ke$_4$/ mu lugal-bi in-pa$_3$/ 4 witnesses/ lu$_2$ inim-ma-bi-me/ mu na-du$_3$-a mah ba-du$_3$/ kishib ad-da-a zi-re-dam/ date. Seal: [. . .]/ ensi$_2$/ nibru.ki/ shu-ni-[an-nam]/ sha[bra]/ dumu ur-[. . .]/ arad$_2$-[zu]. The Adda'a in this text was almost certainly a merchant with dealings in Nippur, see Garfinkle 2012: 131 and text 200. Shabra was a term used to identify the chief administrator of a household. The office was associated with both institutional households, like temples, and with large estates, like that at Garshana.

The term householder is very useful in the context of these agreements. The principals in NATN 403, along with the witnesses, were probably all men of one mina who headed individual households that controlled significant wealth. These householders appealed regularly to the king's authority for the maintenance of that property. The social and economic relationships among networks of households in early Mesopotamia likely imposed certain legal and commercial obligations on the heads of those households. Members of family firms and partnerships were expected to be available to witness the transactions of their associates. These two texts are good examples of commercial documents involving individuals who were administrators, notables, and merchants, and who engaged in entrepreneurial activity on behalf of their own interests. Texts like these also show us a view of royal activity that we do not often get from the large archives documenting the institutional economies of Umma and Girsu-Lagash in which we find scant evidence for the legal activities of the king and his court.[10]

Commercial documents, like sales and loans, recorded trade between households, as distinct from transactions that took place within households, and these texts were defined by the presence of oaths and witnesses. The oaths came in several forms and involved pledges to repay loans, pledges not to contest sales, and penalty clauses maintained through oaths if one of the transacting parties failed to fulfill their obligations. Penalty clauses were a key aspect of such texts throughout the history of the ancient Near East. This highlights how important it was for households to preserve their property and to preserve the advantages that they sought through commercial transactions. We have evidence for the force and the duration of such oaths. Proof of this can be found in the assignment of debts to the heirs of the original debtor. The Mesopotamian legal tradition is full of examples of wives and sons continuing to carry the debts of a household after the death of the head of that household.[11] The oaths often invoked both divine and royal authority, making the gods and the crown parties to the transaction. This was especially significant at times of state formation and growth in Mesopotamia.

The presence of witnesses was another key structural feature of commercial documents throughout Mesopotamian history. Witnesses were required precisely because the texts created or fulfilled commercial obligations. The witnesses stood as guarantors that the price had been carefully weighed and transferred or that the contracted amount of a loan had formally changed hands, and they were present for the oaths that bound the parties to the agreement. The witnesses were a crucial legal component of the texts. Ordinarily, the texts themselves could not alone create a legal obligation. It was the presence of the witnesses that ensured the protection of both parties in the event that the transactions were contested. Modern observers of the Ur III legal environment acknowledge the primacy of the testimony of witnesses and oaths versus the evidence provided by tablets (see Lafont and Westbrook 2003: 196; Culbertson 2009: 93); and as Samuel Greengus (1969: 513) noted long ago, "in ancient Mesopotamia

10. An exception to this is in the Iri-sangrig material published by Owen 2013a, 2013b. In these texts we find ample evidence for *mashkim* and other royal officials engaged in the administration of the law on behalf of the crown.

11. Westbrook 2003: 56–63 discusses the responsibilities of heirs. For an example from Ur III Nippur, see Garfinkle 2012: 130 and texts 159, 165, and 200.

written records were basically evidentiary in character rather than dispositive i.e. the documents (as do witnesses) serve only as an additional means of proving that a transaction had taken place but are not, in themselves, instruments of legal change." The loan and sale documents existed to protect the creditor or buyer by providing a record of the events and the witnesses to those events. The presence of the document was not enough to establish a claim; such a claim could only be demonstrated in conjunction with the witnesses, or, in the case of loans, perhaps with the additional proof of the seal impression of the debtor.

All of these practices were closely related to processes of state formation in Mesopotamia. Local and regional authorities within the urban centers enforced the oath clauses in our documents. These same officials provided the legal context for the examination of witnesses. Indeed, commercial documents could only proliferate in an environment of effective state regulation. The density of commercial documents in certain archives bears out these assumptions and shows the grave concerns for the protection of household property that attended the rise of the state in southern Mesopotamia. The archaeological provenience of the commercial documents also highlights these conclusions. These texts are most often found outside of the large administrative centers and concentrated among the archives of urban professionals such as merchants.

I have already highlighted the significance of the oaths in our texts. In the Ur III material, oaths were crucial to securing transactions. Debtors swore to repay their loans or be subject to substantial penalties. Sellers acknowledged the transfer of property. The growth in the use of oaths, and especially promissory oaths, was characteristic of the Ur III period in early Mesopotamia.[12] Lafont and Westbrook (2003: 209) noted, "A salient feature of the contracts of this period is the profligate use of the promissory oath. The standard form is in the name of the king (mu lugal)."[13] These authors highlighted the heavy use of promissory oaths, especially those in the name of the king, to secure the basic obligation of the transaction and identified this as an innovation of this era. What this attests to is the desire on the part of entrepreneurs and notables to seek state authority and regulation. The oath in the name of the king was usually reserved for promissory oaths in contracts (Lafont and Westbrook 2003: 194). In fact, this is a decisive element of contracts between households outside of the institutional economy. There are approximately 520 surviving attestations of this oath clause from the era of the Third Dynasty of Ur. Half of these come from Nippur, one of the very few sites in the Ur III kingdom in which the excavation of noninstitutional contexts took place. If we look at one of the most common references to witness lists we find a similar distribution. The phrase $lu_2$ inim-ma-bi-me, "these were

12. Culbertson (2009: 157) pointed out that, "While the Old Akkadian mu-lugal oaths could be sworn for specific promises, the Ur III oaths are far more generic, paired with any expression of intent or promise, and thus suggesting that the invocation of the king was a general expression that accompanied, and possibly required, a promissory act."

13. They also observed, "There is no ready explanation for this phenomenon . . ." I am arguing here that the explanation can be found in the growth of state regulation of commerce as a cooperative endeavor between the royal household and property owning households in the urban communities of the new territorial state" (213).

the witnesses (to the transaction)," is attested in approximately 360 Ur III texts, fully two-thirds of which come from Nippur.

The administrators who were doing the king's business within the institutional households of the state did not have cause to swear oaths in the carrying out of their official duties. In fact, the oath in the name of the king was characteristic of legal agreements between individual households, and the very presence of this clause implies a noninstitutional context for the creation of the document. This highlights the deep connection between the growth of commerce and the rise of effective state institutions. The entrepreneurs of this era actively sought royal protection for their endeavors. This process served to facilitate connections among the elites of the different cities of southern Mesopotamia and to bind those wealthy elites more closely to the king's household. There could be no commercial documents without the law, and therefore the growth of royal regulation and the crown's interest in justice was a necessity and a catalyst for the growth of commerce and, especially, for the interests of the men of one mina.

## BIBLIOGRAPHY

Civil, M.

2011 The Law Collection of Ur-Namma. Pp. 221–286 in *Cuneiform Royal Inscriptions and Related Texts in the Schøyen Collection.* Edited by A. R. George. Cornell University Studies in Assyriology and Sumerology 17. Bethesda, MD: CDL Press.

Culbertson, L. E.

2009 *Dispute Resolution in the Provincial Courts of the Third Dynasty of Ur.* PhD diss., University of Michigan.

Frayne, D.

1997 *The Ur III Period (2112–2004 BC)*. Royal Inscriptions of Mesopotamia. Early Periods 3/2. Toronto: University of Toronto Press.

Garfinkle, S. J.

2012 *Entrepreneurs and Enterprise in Early Mesopotamia: A Study of Three Archives from the Third Dynasty of Ur*. CUSAS 22. Bethesda, MD: CDL.

2013 The Third Dynasty of Ur and the Limits of State Power in Early Mesopotamia. Pp. 153–167 in *From the 21st Century B.C. to the 21st Century A.D.: Proceedings of the International Conference on Neo-Sumerian Studies Held in Madrid, 22–24 July, 2010*. Edited by S. J. Garfinkle and M. Molina. Winona Lake, IN: Eisenbrauns.

Greengus, S.

1969 The Old Babylonian Marriage Contract. *JAOS* 89: 505–532.

Lafont, B. and Westbrook, R.

2003 Neo-Sumerian Period (Ur III). Pp. 183–226 in vol. 1 of *A History of Ancient Near Eastern Law*. Edited by R. Westbrook. HdO 72. Leiden: Brill.

Molina, M.

2010 Court Records from Umma. Pp. 201–217 in *Why Should Someone Who Knows Something Conceal It? Cuneiform Studies in Honor of David I. Owen on His 70th Birthday*. Edited by A. Kleinerman and J. Sasson. Bethesda, MD: CDL.

2013 Court Officials at Umma in Ur III Times. *ZA* 103: 125–148.

Neumann, H.
2003 Recht im antiken Mesopotamien. Pp. 55–122 in *Die Rechtskulturen der Antike: Vom Alten Orient bis zum Römischen Reich*. Edited by U. Manthe. Munich: Beck.

Oppenheim, A. L.
1948 *Catalogue of the Cuneiform Tablets of the Wilberforce Eames Babylonian Collection in the New York Public Library: Tablets of the Time of the Third Dynasty of Ur*. AOS 32. New Haven: American Oriental Society.

Owen, D. I.
1982 *Neo-Sumerian Archival Texts Primarily from Nippur in the University Museum, the Oriental Institute, and the Iraq Museum*. Winona Lake, IN: Eisenbrauns.

2013a *Cuneiform Texts Primarily from Iri-Saĝrig/Al-Šarrākī and the History of the Ur III Period*, vol. 1: *Commentary and Indexes*. NISABA 15.1. Bethesda, MD: CDL.

2013b *Cuneiform Texts Primarily from Iri-Saĝrig/Al-Šarrākī and the History of the Ur III Period*, vol. 2: *Catalogue and Texts*. NISABA 15.2. Bethesda, MD: CDL.

Richardson, S.
2012 Early Mesopotamia: The Presumptive State. *Past and Present* 215: 3–49.

Roth, M. T.
1997 *Law Collections from Mesopotamia and Asia Minor*. 2nd ed. WAW 6. Atlanta: Scholars Press.

Sauren, H.
1978 *Les Tablettes cunéiformes de l'époque d'Ur des collections de la New York Public Library*. Louvain-la-Neuve: Université catholique de Louvain, Institut orientaliste.

Wells, B.
2005 2005 Law and Practice. Pp. 183–195 in *A Companion to the Ancient Near East*. Edited by D. C. Snell. Blackwell Companions to the Ancient World. Oxford: Blackwell.

Westbrook, R.
2003 The Character of Ancient Near Eastern Law. Pp. 1–90 in vol. 1 of *A History of Ancient Near Eastern Law*. Edited by R. Westbrook. HdO 72. Leiden: Brill.

Wilcke, C.
2007 *Early Ancient Near Eastern Law: A History of Beginnings; the Early Dynastic and Sargonic Periods*. Rev. ed. Winona Lake, IN: Eisenbrauns.

CHAPTER 9

# How Ancient Near Eastern Societies Regulated Life in the Community: Crucial Clues from Archaeology

Mònica Bouso and Anna Gómez-Bach

AS SOME SCHOLARS HAVE POINTED OUT, although the enormous amount of data provided by the cuneiform texts has given us a great deal of detailed information about certain aspects, we still have very little knowledge about the overall organization of Mesopotamian society (Stein 1994: 12). In this regard, the present contribution applies innovative theoretical and methodological approaches to archaeological evidence that can be very useful in complementing the textual data, while critically examining the historiography of the discipline itself.

First, then, this study will discuss a range of current interpretations for social organization and highlight problematic areas. Second, some methodological questions regarding the way to approach the subject will be underlined. Third, this paper will focus on reexamining what archaeology can really contribute to the understanding of the social structure in Ancient Near East, with an in-depth analysis of a number of selected and particularly clear examples of archaeological evidence. The aim is to integrate the material culture into research on social organization, in the hope that we may approach these issues from new directions. In order to provide a long-term perspective, specific case studies are included, ranging from the eighth to the third millennia BCE, and from the Middle Euphrates region to eastern Iraq, mainly the Jezireh and the central Mesopotamia areas (fig. 9.1). An attempt is made to underline the existence of different traditions in the early development of organizing communal life and to stress the diversity of these development trajectories in the various regions.

Specifically, we will discuss how public buildings, defensive walls, large structures with storehouses or silos, and the uniformity of certain ceramic vessels, among other elements, located in the *longue durée* landscape of the Ancient Near East, can help archaeologists understand how humans adapted to a sedentary lifestyle, and how this life was organized and regulated. Thus, using cases studies from several Near Eastern sites, we will examine some of the challenges that archaeology faces when attempting to understand the way in which people organized power relationships.

*Authors' note*: We would like to thank Dr. Walter Cruells for reading and commenting on a final draft of this paper. We are also grateful to Dr. Miquel Molist for allowing us to work on material from Tell Halula. We acknowledge the permission granted by the British Museum to include two photographs (fig. 9.4 and fig. 9.6). We are also indebted to W. G. E. Watson, who kindly corrected the English.

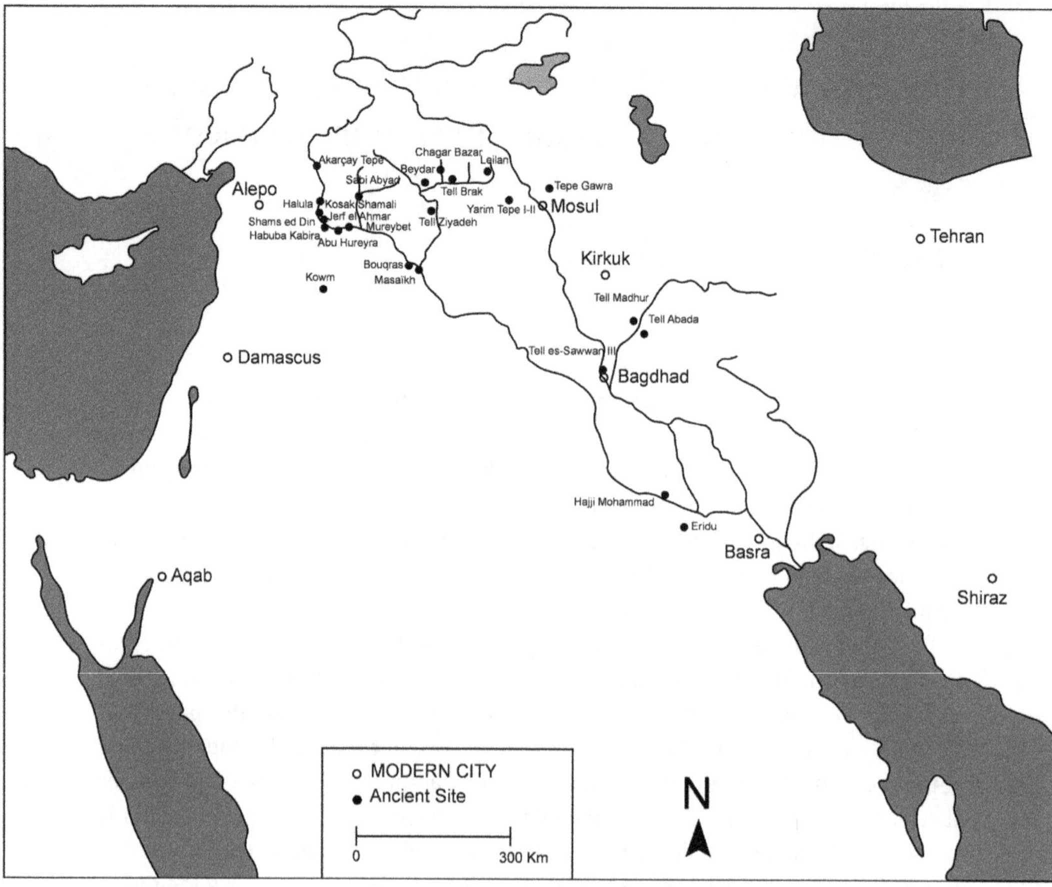


FIGURE 9.1 Map of the Near East showing sites mentioned in the text.

## Theoretical Considerations Regarding Social Structure

As far as the social structure is concerned, it has long been assumed that societies lived at subsistence level and were tribal in nature during the Neolithic period, and that eventually an egalitarian social structure was formed. G. Algaze and D. Fessler have pointed out that equal social status of this kind did not exist at all:

> To be sure, truly egalitarian societies have never existed. Every human group, no matter how simple, has natural elites that aspire to, and commonly achieve, some measure of power, wealth, and status in their lifetimes. By an "egalitarian" society we mean a society in which status and leadership are ephemeral, are based on personal achievement, and are shaped by individual factors such as intelligence, ambition, charisma, and luck. In short, an egalitarian society is one in which status is not inheritable and is not legitimized and reproduced through formal political or religious institutions. (2001: 9 n. 1)

In fact, they argue that the evolution of human societies exhibits a trend toward increasing complexity and hierarchical differentiation through time. They accept "the contention that resource abundance is a universally valid destabilizing force that helped drive the transition from egalitarian, mobile hunting and gathering groups to sedentary communities possessing some degree of internal social differentiation" (Algaze and Fessler 2001: 11).

In this context, the introduction of the concept of "social complexity" is understood as a way of identifying variability in a synchronic and diachronic way, identified by means of the archaeological data at all times. The Chalcolithic period would see the advent of a "chiefdom"-type elite authority built on a network of alliances, heredity, and the control of distribution channels for sought-after exotic materials, in short, the beginnings of social inequality. That is, the Chalcolithic would mark a shift from societies where all individuals had access to collective decisions toward "unequal" formulas characterized by delegations of authority that placed power in the hands of a few (Guilaine 2007: 6-7). Indeed, as Guilaine pointed out:

> L'anthropologie néo-évolutionniste anglo-saxonne avec sa déclinaison de niveaux de plus en plus hiérarchisés – bandes/tribus/chefferies/état – bute souvent sur la définition des chefferies : les cas de figure sont tels dans l'espace, le temps et le niveau de hiérarchisation que l'on finit par transformer le concept en une sorte de fourre-tout tant il est difficile de préciser comment s'articule le lien social. Si des auteurs européens voient déjà certaines cultures du Néolithique récent comme des chefferies héréditaires, d'autres considèrent les sociétés chalcolithiques comme encore « égalitaires » et estiment que le terme ne peut pas s'appliquer avant l'Age du Bronze. Evidemment, en Orient, le problème est différent car il se double ici, dès le IVe millénaire, de l'apparition de la ville, un marqueur qui dépasse largement le stade chalcolithique mais qui n'est pas pour autant le signe d'un véritable « état. » (2007: 6)

To sum up, traditional interpretations see increasing complexity leading to the appearance of a stratified society and state development. This model paints a picture of a hierarchical, territorial political and economic entity.

The awareness that, in fact, there was much more variation within ancient societies and fewer similarities between different types of settlement than had previously been acknowledged, together with the critique of any hierarchical structure, has led to new approaches to the topic (Ur 2004: 27–28). Therefore, in reaction to this model of social change, where societies move through a set of stages: from organized bands to tribes, to chiefdoms, and finally to the emergence of the state, C. L. Crumley (1995) has suggested reexamining the term "hierarchy." This entails the exploration of "heterarchy" and its relationship to "hierarchy," in order to apply it to the study of complex societies, as a new way of approaching aspects such as agency, conflict, and cooperation. Bearing in mind that not every social organization takes the form of a vertical hierarchy, the concept of heterarchy comes into play. It is defined as "the relation of elements to one another when they are unranked or when they possess the potential for being ranked in a number of different ways," and is understood as both a structure and a condition (3–4). This model takes into account the flexibility, both temporal and spatial, that the relationship between heterarchy and hierarchy can allow (4).

In addition, a new avenue of study is the application of complex adaptive systems. While these are most frequently used in the physical and natural sciences, an attempt is also made to use them in order to understand social systems. In this sense, this is the application of historical ecology: "they draw on a broad spectrum of evidence from the biological and physical sciences, ecology, and social sciences and humanities. As a whole, this information forms a picture of human environment relations over time in a particular geographic location" (Crumley 2007: 16). This is based on the concept of "a set of subsystems which are interrelated but without centralized control; a change in one aspect of one subsystem can result in changes in other connected subsystems and ultimately in dramatic and unpredictable global change" (Ur 2004: 33). In brief:

> The current theoretical paradigm in archaeology and elsewhere, which falsely assumes that the only form of complex order is hierarchy, no longer explains data collected in many parts of the world (Ehrenreich, Crumley, & Levy 1995). Complex systems theory and the concept of heterarchy can reinvigorate the interpretation of social systems and shed new light on the relationship between environmental change and societal collapse. (Crumley 2007: 26)

Taking into account the above-mentioned ideas and unlike traditional theories of hierarchical organizations that understood the different components of a society as a fixed formal structure, a fresh standpoint is proposed here. Social networks should be understood as a reflection of multiple relations (for which there is archaeological evidence) between the inhabitants within a given territory. Therefore, we suggest rejecting the simplistic sole perspective implied by elite-dominated regional centers in favor of more complex forms of organization, which can even include coexisting heterarchical and hierarchical relationships.[1]

Given the variety of organizational forms characteristic of these societies, we suggest that a less rigid analytical tool may be required and that the model can be best applied by exploring the interrelationships between different aspects of the given society, using archaeological data. Before analyzing the chosen aspects from the archaeological record, we must comment briefly on some methodological issues.

## Methodological Issues

The literary sources provide us with useful information on the economic structure of Near Eastern populations, but it is unequal in nature and are not transferable to all areas. Nonetheless, archaeology can certainly provide important data on this issue. Thus, one first research method that we would like to emphasize is to establish the technology used, the raw materials that are exploited, the species of animals hunted or

1. For instance, this approach has been taken by G. Philip (2001) regarding the Jordan region during the Early Bronze Age in that he "will treat Early Bronze Age Jordan as heterogeneous marked by multiple coexisting sources of power" (167).

domesticated, the vegetables cultivated, the storage systems used, and to some extent, some of the products imported.

However, we must recognize that our knowledge in this line of research is still very limited. Fundamentally, this may be because the considerable potential provided by archaeological research has been underused, and at many sites the faunal remains from historical periods have not been collected systematically. Even less attention has been paid to recovering and studying plant remains. In the same way, there has been no systematic analysis of residues in ceramic vessels on millstones to determine which products were either stored or prepared. Ultimately, not enough analysis of the archaeo-botanical data is carried out (palynological, carpological and phytolithic studies, and the analysis of microdebris).

An alternative way of approaching the issue archaeologically is by studying the administrative systems of the territory, which to some extent reflect the forms of social organization, their degree of socio-cultural development and, from a diachronic point of view, the process by which this has occurred. For example, the hierarchy of the population centers suggests a certain development of administrative structures. In most cases, scholars study the territory only in the vicinity of the site that is being investigated. Once again, sufficiently detailed regional studies are not available.

Third, the study of places where the control and acquisition of raw material are documented represents another line of research. It has been shown that, from the Prepottery Neolithic B period, objects such as seashells, turquoise, chalcedony and other gemstones, basalt, copper ores, or obsidian, were used as raw materials, or as prepared and finished products in circulation over long distances. First flint and then pottery also formed an important element of exchange. Other materials such as bitumen, salt, or oil, and other organic materials, are difficult to trace but were also probably used as essential items of exchange. Their presence in archaeological contexts varies, since they appear not only in burial sites but also in domestic locations and abandonment layers. These materials reveal the existence of extensive, established, and well-structured communication networks of intraregional exchange, with some of them being organized around a group manager who also acts as a dealer.

Fourth, another set of data should be discussed: It concerns the way in which material culture has often been studied separately, often without taking into account the degree of technological knowledge embedded in its production. Recent proposals have attempted to reformulate the parameters based on the analysis of technological complexity documented on both the diachronic and the synchronic levels (Roux 2013: 313). Until now, these have been set in a specific chronological sequence based on their presence in or absence from specific sites (fig. 9.2).

Other variables to consider, which can be studied using the archaeological record in order to track the organizational structure of these ancient societies, are funerary structures and anthropological evidence. Certainly, parameters such as the location of the tomb, the type of structure, and the type of deposition of the human remains, together with any grave goods indicate a certain way of understanding the relationship between the living and the dead. The importance of delimiting the space for the living and the dead must be emphasized, and the detailed study of their interaction will reveal the place for the dead in the society of the living and how this is transformed

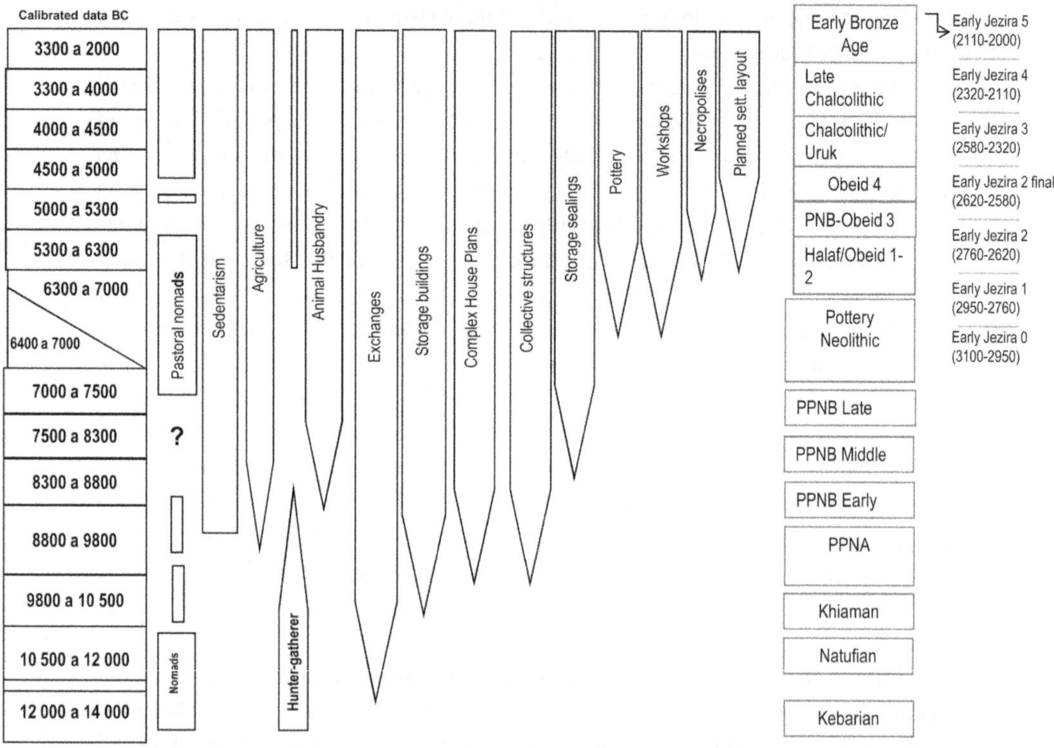


FIGURE 9.2. Table relating chronology and the main aspects dealt with in the text. Based in F. Hours, O. Aurenche, J. Cauvin, M. C. Cauvin, L. Copeland, and P. Sanlaville, 1994: *Atlas des sites du Proche Orient (14000-5700 BP)*. Travaux de la Maison de l'Orient Méditerranéen n.24. Lyon, p. 18, and Arcane new Jezireh periodization table in M. Lebeau, ed., *Associated Regional Chronologies for the Ancient Near East and the Eastern Mediterranean: Jezireh.* Turnhout, Brepols.

over time. Consequently these features reveal important aspects of social and cultural organization.

Last, another methodological issue involving the archaeological interpretation of data concerns terminology. Often a variety of terms, mainly related to architectural features such as "town," "city," or "village," are used in a vague and inaccurate way by researchers. The widely used concept of "public building" is particularly ambiguous, and in the same way, terms such as "unusual building" and "monumental" are also vaguely defined.

## Analysis of the Archaeological Data

Accordingly, considering all these aspects, it is now possible to set out and explain how the transition toward a more complex and interrelated society becomes visible in the material record. The focus will be on a few distinctive patterns, particularly: planned settlement layout, fortifications or encircling walls, complex house plans, storage buildings or structures, storage sealings, workshops, and the manufacture of pottery.

### *Planned Settlement Layout*

The first feature affecting the social aspects of a settlement is the way in which the population dealt with urban planning. Any planned settlement layout, as is well known, implies guidelines and previous organization, and therefore some form of town-planning consultation and control. The main aspects of this preparation include: the equitable distribution of housing space, working simultaneously to be able to take advantage of the party walls, enclosure of the collective area, and the delimitation of public spaces.

As P. de Miroschedji has pointed out, the close association between the appearance of metrology and the architectural planning should be noted: "It should be remembered (contra Arnold 1991: 10) that the introduction of metrology and architectural planning is independent from the invention of writing, as indicated by the Mesopotamian evidence which shows that units of measurements and grid planning were used since the beginning of the Ubaid period" (2001: 467 n. 3).

Archaeologically speaking, it is possible to observe the development of this process, although difficulties remain. From Prepottery Neolithic sites onward, the presence of organized and structured households has been considered complex enough to discuss whether a planned settlement layout exists in certain areas, such as the Middle Euphrates Valley, specifically at Jerf el Ahmar (Stordeur 1999) and at Tell Halula (Molist 1996; Molist and Vicente 2013: 38). Later, in the Halaf period, the accumulation of structures, such as those shown by the plan of Yarim Tepe I (northern Iraq) with several unicellular and multicellular rectangular and circular buildings dating from the sixth millennium (Merpert and Munchaev 1993a: 78, fig. 6.3), has been interpreted as a site with a regulated organization of settlement space. Another example is the fifth-millennium site plan of Tell Abada (Hamrin region) where an extensive area of the settlement was excavated (Jasim 1985; Pollock 2010: 97, fig. 7.2).

The process of planned settlement layout was already fully developed by the fourth millennium. An emblematic example is seen at the site of Habuba Kabira South, located on a narrow eastern edge of the lower Euphrates terrace, with evident signs of town planning. At its maximum extension the site covers about eighteen hectares, of which twenty thousand square meters of residential areas could be investigated. The excavations uncovered a symmetrical and balanced developed town plan: the perimeter wall with towers arranged at regular intervals and two access doors, internal distribution based on a main north-south axis, and several transversal paved streets with a drainage system, as well as a central walled district housing the cultural and administrative center. South of this there was an irrigated garden (Strommenger 1980: 33–35).

In the third millennium (ca. 2400) at Tell Beydar, ancient Nabada, (Jezireh) we find a clearly established planned layout. Built on several terraces and protected by two city walls and seven gates, the palaces and temples were located in the center of the upper town, surrounded by workshops and warehouses, while private quarters were located further toward the periphery. The acropolis gate controlled the access to the official sector installed on "Main Street," the city's main north-south oriented axis, equipped with a large stone canal system, running from the south gate of the upper city to the entrance of the palace (Lebeau and Suleiman 2014: 2–5; Quenet 2011: 24–26).

In short, all of these elements—the planned organization of space, the presence of a central axis, the distribution of the houses on *insulae*, and the rest, are indicators of social dynamics. Therefore they can provide evidence of how this community worked.

### *Fortifications/Encircling Walls, Water Supply Systems: Water Cisterns, Network of Irrigation Channels, and Similar Constructions*

In addition to urban planning, other features such as fortifications, encircling walls, and water system constructions imply collective activities. Certainly, these types of construction also require very large amounts of raw materials to build and maintain them, and additionally, they would have required considerable investment in time and labor. The presence of these elements (fortifications, encircling walls, etc.) could be interpreted in various ways. One interpretation may focus on the structure as a boundary, marking the limits of the village, and on its defensive function in a military context. Moreover, other interpretations emphasize the monumentality of these structures and see them as symbols of authority.

Archaeological excavations at Tell Halula (Middle Euphrates) have uncovered remains of an impressive stone wall some 1.2 meters wide and about eight meters high, dating to the eighth millennium. This structure has been interpreted as a large stone terrace wall, built as a collective construction and reused until Pottery Neolithic times (Molist and Faura 1996: 39–44; Molist 2008: 14).

Another example is the perimeter wall at Tell es-Sawwan III, located close to the Tigris River. This site, dating to the Samarran period, was settled during the seventh and sixth millennia. The excavations were able to recover early evidence of irrigation channels, and a building with twelve rooms, which may be a granary. The central part of the village contains a ditch, three meters deep, with a thick buttressed mud wall encircling an area of fifty by sixty meters. The enclosure wall fell out of use in level 3b–4 and was considered to be in use for only a short period of time (Yasin 1970: 6; Abu es-Soof 1968, 1971). This site was excavated by C. Breniquet, and subsequently reexamined (Breniquet 1991: 75; 1992).

As has already been mentioned, a significant fortified site is Habuba Kabira South (fourth millennium). The three-meter-wide city wall runs for more than six hundred meters in a straight line along the eastern part of the settlement and then turns toward the northeast where it continues in a straight line to the edge of the river terrace. The wall is reinforced with towers, nine from the north to the north gate and nine more between the two gates that provided access to the city. This fortification probably functioned as something more than a purely defensive structure, being a complex that housed administrators, storerooms, and other support facilities (Strommenger 1980: 35–36). The defensive wall was made of mud brick, requiring a massive expenditure of effort by the brick-making industry as well as those involved in its construction.

Excavations at the northern city gate of Tell Leilan, ancient Sheh'na (Jezireh), exposed a circumvallating city wall around the high mound dating to circa 2600, with the encircling wall extending for 3.7 kilometers and enclosing an area of ninety hectares (Ristvet 2007: 185–186). The seventy-five hectare lower town at Leilan was built at the same time. L. Ristvet (2007: 204–205) emphasizes the possibility of exploring the relationship between the construction of the fortification and the emergence of a distinct urban identity, since a clear separation between the city and the villages of its hinterland was established. As Ristvet has pointed out, the fortification's significance cannot be underestimated, bearing in mind the defensive and control functions of the city wall and gates:

> Neighborhoods were named after and defined by city gates, and the area just inside the gates was a public space used as a marketplace and court of law. The city wall and the city gate area served as locations where urban identities were constructed, where royal authority was delimited, and where power relationships were brokered in Mesopotamia. (2007: 184)

### *Complex House Plans*

The emerging complexity of the earliest sedentary societies in the Near East is also demonstrated by the increasing internal differentiation within sites. Complex house plans imply a highly developed architectural tradition that had its roots in the eighth millennium BCE, as the evidence unearthed in Tell Halula shows.

The house plans at Tell Halula exhibit a formal and regular spatial organization. The houses are built along an east-west axis, except on a few occasions where the geomorphology forced a change in the orientation. Each house has a limestone basement and mud-brick walls forming a rectangular plan with three to five rooms, and the entrance is south-facing. The internal divisions appear to show a standard pattern: a partially open area at the entrance where production and storage activities took place, back rooms where structures for storage and food production and a large number of tools have been recovered, and a central room. This large central room, with a surface area of between eighteen to twenty-two square meters, has certain main features, such as an oven and a hearth. There is also an area reserved for burials in the front part of the main room (Molist and Vicente 2013: 40; Anfruns and Molist 1996: 151; Guerrero et al. 2009: 379). The main production activities took place in the open spaces.

Another example is Sabi Abyad in the Balikh Valley where the village was destroyed by fire in about 6000 BCE. The so-called "burnt village" consists of a domiciliary area with a series of regular and rectangular structures, their dimensions ranging from between fifty and ninety square meters, and an extensive open area provided with fireplaces, ovens, and pits and interpreted as houses, granaries, and storehouses. Its buildings were usually divided into three rows, each of which consisted of a series of very small cubicles. As a consequence of fire, it was possible for archaeologists to recover rich material such as pottery, figurines, seals and stamp-seal impressions, lithic tools and obsidian implements, and similar items. The presence of some anthropological remains suggests the existence of burial rituals associated with a funeral house (Akkermans 1996; 2008: 643; Akkermans and Verhoeven 1995: 5–32; Verhoeven 1999: 25–44).

For the architectural plan in the Ubaid period, S. Kubba carried out a study on a number of Late Ubaid buildings and concluded that a standard unit of measurement of seventy two centimeters was used, the "Ubaid Cubit" (Kubba 1990: 47). The complexity of the design and construction of large buildings during this period can be seen in the site of Tell Madhhur (Hamrin). The excavations at Tell Madhhur (Hamrin) included the discovery, in level 2, of a well-preserved complex made up of several rooms. The freestanding building, dating from the fifth millennium (Late Ubaid period, Ubaid 4), is tripartite, and is composed of a cruciform central room extending the whole width of the house. Hence there is a well-conceived and well-executed domestic dwelling house plan (Roaf 1987: 426–428). Using the inventory of features and artifacts, S. Pollock (2010: 98, fig. 7.3) carried out an examination in order to distinguish the activities that would have taken place in the various rooms of the house. The results show that certain rooms were destined for storage, others for food preparation but not cooking, still others for both food preparation and cooking, and lastly, yet others for serving food.

The architecture of these large tripartite houses has been attributed to notable individuals who stood out from the mass of the village population, suggesting that the social organization probably lies in the preeminence of certain families or clans over the others (Huot 2007: 19).

Furthermore, P. Pfälzner has defined a type of house found in the Jezireh region in the third millennium BCE (specifically in the Early Jezireh III), the so-called "allotment house," which is characterized by its standardization both in terms of plot size and plan. Pfälzner (2012: 156) has interpreted this fact as a reflection of a centrally controlled town-planning and of the "egalitarian" structure of the urban society in this period.

### *Workshops*

This section focuses on the remains of workshops. It is assumed that the documentation of workshops implies specialized nonresidential craft activities. In this case, it is also possible to observe a development from craft workshops to another type that we could probably define as industrial.

Examples of craft activities, such as pottery manufacture, can be seen in the ceramic kiln of Yarim Tepe II (sixth millennium). The recent levels have yielded several structures that were built at the same time. In spite of the fact that their function is not clear, they have been defined as granaries. Contemporary with these structures there were further rectangular structures and several dwellings, including six *tholoi* and one structure consisting of a combustion chamber and an ash pit, together with the remains of a further oven sunk into the virgin soil. All this area had been interpreted as an industrial compound, with no more detailed information being available (Merpert and Munchaev 1993b: 139).

A further step is represented by the dome-shaped clay oven found at Tell Ziyadeh (Middle Khabur) dating to the fifth millennium, during the Halaf Ubaid transition period (Akkermans and Schwartz 2003: 171, fig. 5.9). This structure was found in phase A7, sector J and was interpreted as a circular kiln constructed of mud brick and double walled (two and half meters), with a vaulted roof having an air passage for ventilation. This structure is considered unique because it contained half-baked cooking pots (Buccellati, Buia, and Reimer 1991: 44). Another example comes from Tell Masaïkh (Middle Euphrates), where a craft area was located. Remains, possibly of kilns, as well as other materials were uncovered, such as lithic polishers, fragments of ochre, and a slow *tournette.* These were found in the open air and were interpreted as a pottery workshop (Robert 2010: 286).

In the Upper Euphrates, a pottery workshop from Kosak Shamali at post-Ubaid levels (levels five and six) has been recorded by the University of Tokyo and dated to 4400 BCE. The elaborate workshop highlights the growing social and economic complexity in these periods; in this context, the use of local clay from the Euphrates and Nahar Sarine sandbanks, which was shaped using a slow *tournette*. The surfaces of the vessels were smoothed using stone polishers, mainly river pebbles, ceramic scrapers and possibly horn. There was extensive evidence for the use of hematite and magnesium processed with grinding stones and blades. The painted motifs on the pots are mostly geometrical, although zoomorphic motifs such as birds are widely documented (Nishiaki and Matsutani 2001: 179–211).

Of considerable note is the industrial workshop, the "red libn building" (TW level 19), (ca. 4000 BCE) uncovered in area TW at Tell Brak (Jezireh), near the northern entrance to the ancient city. The building, consisting of massive red mud-brick walls and three floor levels, had several ovens and material in situ, including large quantities of raw materials (jasper, marble, serpentine and various diorites, bitumen, sheep/goat faunal remains, mollusks, etc.). Most of these had been brought there from considerable distances. In addition to deposits of numerous clay spindle whorls, a large collection of stamp sealings was also unearthed (Oates et al. 2007: 592, fig. 6).

Technology reached an exceptional level of development in the third millennium BCE. This can be seen at the Tell Beydar workshops, for instance in *Chantier* I, (EJ IIIb–a) and *Chantier* P (EJ IIIb) located in the northeastern and eastern part of the upper city respectively. Regarding the *Chantier* I, a whole sector, the northeastern part of the excavation area, was devoted during phase 2 (EJ IIIb) to specialized industrial activities to manufacture figurines and possibly also pottery production. Worth mentioning, among the different installations documented, are a basin for clay decantation, several kilns, and other workshop features including layers of ashes, slag, and assorted debris from the kiln area (Milano and Rova 2014: 93–95, fig. 12–13). Furthermore, in *Chantier* P, located in the eastern part of the upper city, the excavation uncovered a large public building (called the Eastern Palace) erected in level 5c and transformed into a metal workshop in level 5a–b (Pruβ 2011: 111). Specifically, in the previous large hall of the building, 16473, at least four metalworkers' kilns, which were in use at the same time, were installed. More evidence of the metal workshop, such as crucibles, was found in court 16425, among other rooms. It is interesting to note that door sealings were found in the workshop context. This fact, alongside the characteristics of the seal designs, allowed the excavators to indicate that the metal workshop was under control of the city's central administration (Pruβ 2011: 121–128, fig. 26).

### *Storage Buildings/Structures*

Storage buildings and structures that imply a use at the suprahousehold or communal level (i.e., large-scale storage) are discussed in this section. For storage on a large-scale, organization and planning are necessary, not only for the construction and location of the storage facilities, but also for the activities related to the collection and distribution of the products deposited in them. Therefore, the large storage structures indicate a collective management and the administration of agricultural reserves.

Early examples of storage systems begin to be documented from the Epipaleolithic times onward in the Levant (Kuijt and Finlayson 2009: 19069) and in the Euphrates Valley, such as at Abu Hureyra (Moore et al. 2000). In fact, the presence of collective storage system buildings can be found outside households and grouped in one part of the village throughout later Prehistory. Storage installations were identified at Mureybeth (Cauvin 1979; Ibañez 2008) and Jerf el-Ahmar (Stordeur 1999, 2006). These examples show complex agricultural practice and management, and the emergence of a collective consciousness. These elements acquire different forms, such as pit storage, excavated granaries on the floor, and granary buildings. The presence of charred grains in an isolated structure demonstrates that the structure was intended for storage. Their occurrence increased from Prepottery Neolithic B times onward in collective open spaces or in a private one such as at Tell Halula (Molist 1996, 2013). Of particular interest are grill-plan structures, for example, the adobe structures constructed with several parallel mud-brick walls with little separation between them, a type that brings to mind the Tigris high grill-plan structures that have been interpreted as grain drying surfaces.

Another type of storage structure has been found in ed-Din Tannira (Middle Euphrates), a site from the Halaf period. This is a silo, built of stone and mud brick, of which only the base is preserved, with an external diameter of 1.7 meters (Van der Stede 2010: 226; Seeden 1982: 93, fig.77).

Another outstanding feature unearthed in Tell Ziyadeh was a large building complex interpreted as a storage facility, dating to the early third millennium (EJ I–II). The complex consists of three units: a western grill-plan building, a central set of rooms, and an open area to the east (Hole 1999: 272, fig. 4; 273, fig. 5).

All this evidence, as has already been seen, suggests patterns of consumption well beyond any pattern typical of a family household.

### *Storage Sealings*

Due to the large amount of glyptic assemblages, in this section only a brief and selected inventory of seal impressions will be commented on for illustrative purposes (figs. 9.3 and 9.4). One of the most significant elements requiring social organization is the presence of storage sealings. As is known, these elements have an inherent association related to private property and also as a redistribution tool. Storage sealings acted as record-keeping devices before writing was invented. Indeed, the use of storage sealing implies an unequal distribution of goods, restricted access, and control devices.

It seems that the first examples of seal impressions on plaster, but also in clay, were found at Tell Bouqras, Tell Halula, and El-Kowm, dating from the seventh millennium. However, seal impressions on clay are abundant in the Halaf period (Akkermans and Duistermaat 1996: 18–19); for instance, those recorded at Chagar Bazar dating from the sixth millennium (Cruells et al. 2013: 474) and at Halula and Sabi Abyad, among others. The fire that affected the settlement of Sabi Abyad, around 5200 BCE (6000 cal BCE) made it possible to recover in situ hundreds of clay sealings pressed onto the fastening of containers or closing them. The sealings were associated with small and transportable containers, specifically: baskets, plaited mats, ceramic vessels, stone bowls, and leather bags. At least sixty-seven different stamp seals have been identified (Akkermans and Duistermaat 1996: 17–26).

FIGURE 9.3. Clay stamp seal from the excavations at Tell Halula, Late Neolithic circa 7400 BCE.

FIGURE 9.4. Seal and impression from the excavations at Brak, fourth millennium. Photo © Trustees of the British Museum, London.

By the Late Ubaid period, the use of seals to signify ownership or control had become a well-developed practice. Interestingly, a seal impression from Tepe Gawra (seal 993, phase XIA, level XI A/B, fifth millennium) shows human figures carrying bags (Rothman 2002: pls. 38 and 64).

According to J. Oates (Oates et al. 2007: 593), by the end of the fifth millennium the evidence implies a complex hierarchy of authority at Brak, as suggested by the discovery of sealings bearing impressions of more than one seal. This has allowed researchers to raise the possibility that there may have been two separate levels of administration or two equal but different types of official.

For the third millennium in the Jezireh region, A. McCarthy (2012: 217) has identified an indigenous northern Mesopotamian glyptic style (EJ III) developed throughout the shared complex administrative system of the region. Glyptic elements clearly functioned as part of the broader administrative system. Moreover, there are many ways in which seals were used, for example, as aids to memory referring to identity, embodiment, and power.

### *Manufacture of Pottery*

Further evidence for the emergence of socio-economic differentiation within the early sedentary societies of the Near East is provided by the increase in finishing techniques and the introduction of complex decoration in the manufacture of pottery. This is a gradual process that took place during the sixth and seventh millennia BCE. The presence

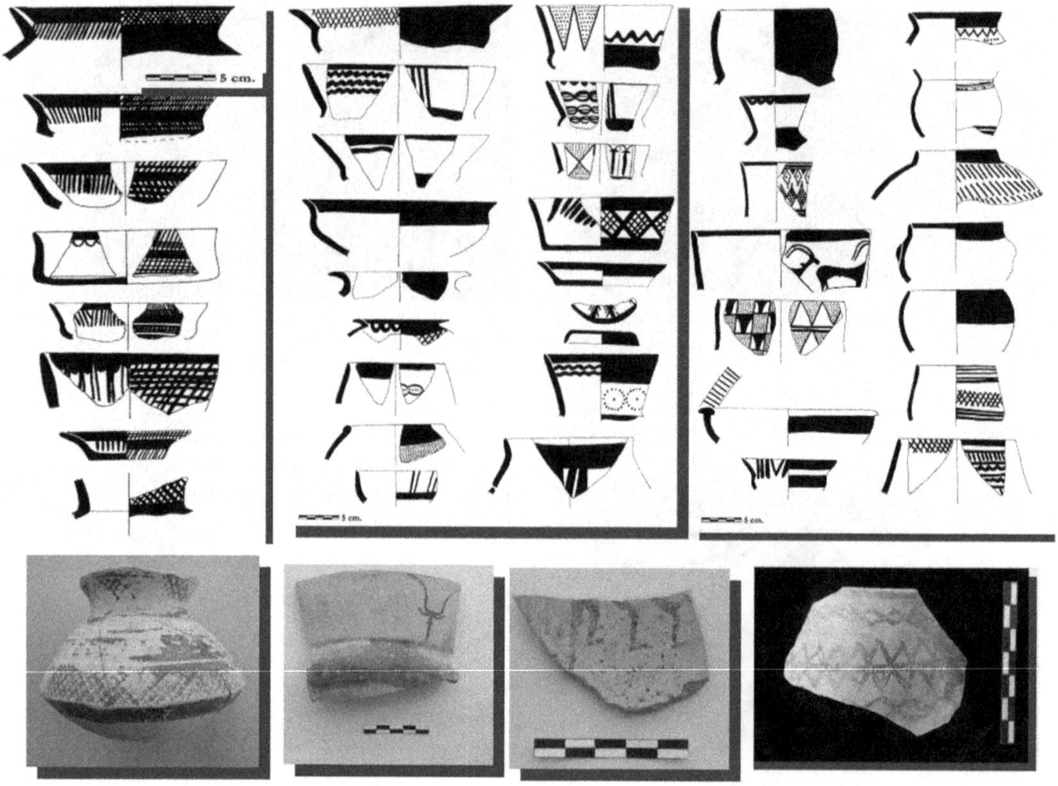


FIGURE 9.5. Examples of painted fine ware serving vessels (Early, Middle and Late Halaf) at Tell Halula, Gómez Bach 2011.

of painted pottery reinforces this process in both technological and social aspects. The manufacture of pottery can be seen as an indication of emulation and community identification. From the first pottery productions, the investment in time and raw materials seems to increase in specific vessels, and this has been viewed as evidence of reputation.

Around 6100 BCE, a new class of complex design configurations has also been associated with other material phenomena, such as basketry, clothes and textiles, wood, or even body painting. This activity has been linked to nomadism, cultural diffusion, or cultural affiliation with one group. Since pre-Halaf times the variability in pottery sets has been identified with processes of exchange, prestige, or emulation. Exhaustive pottery studies in recent fieldwork carried out at well-stratified sites such as Tell Sabi Abyad (Nieuwenhuyse 2008), Halula, Akarçay Tepe (Cruells 2005), or Chagar Bazar (Cruells 2006; Gómez Bach 2011), allow us to understand the complex nature of craft specialization in coarse or fine ware pottery and in all the steps of the *chaîne operatoire* (fig. 9.5)

The changes in material culture over time need to be related to social status, showing the introduction of new items of distinction among higher groups, and their filtering down to lower groups (Nieuwhenhuyse 2008: 220). Ubaid pottery studies also show an in-depth understanding of social aspects through a more technological point of view (Karsgaard 2010: 55). The main changes in pottery repertoires across

FIGURE 9.6. Bevelled rim bowl from the excavations at Nineveh. Photo © Trustees of the British Museum, London.

Mesopotamia have been described by several scholars. An increasing plainness of vessels and an increase in the proportion of closed forms would be related to homogeneous assemblages. Moreover, highly decorated forms decrease compared to simple monochrome motifs in the majority of archaeological sets from the fifth millennium BCE. This whole phenomenon has been described by D. Wengrow (2001: 168) as an "evolution of simplicity" and it persisted throughout the fourth millennium BCE.

Indeed, at the beginning of the fourth millennium a new kind of pottery style appeared throughout the whole Near East. The carefully decorated tableware of previous cultures was replaced by a coarse and undecorated pottery that seems purely utilitarian. The distinctive vessel of the period was the bevelled rim bowl (fig. 9.6). Due to its standardized characteristics this vessel is often interpreted as a container probably used for distributing rations (Bernbeck 1995; Pollock 2003: 27–32).

Later, in the mid to late part of the third millennium there was an increased specialization in the production of pottery. In general terms, the trend was toward standardization and functional specialization in the repertoire of shapes, accompanied by a decrease in decorated wares (Rova 2011: 57). Unfortunately, there are very few specific studies on pottery technology for this period, as E. Rova (2011: 50) has noted, specifically in relation to the Jezireh region. One example of this trend toward standardization can be seen in Tell Leilan, where at this time the Ninevite 5 tradition of ceramic decoration was finally abandoned in favor of new mass-produced forms. This change in production has been interpreted by the excavators as due to the authorities influencing or controlling the function of pottery (Ur 2004: 82). Pottery seems to have lost its important function as a symbolic identification of social groups, and came to acquire another role. Further research should be focused on identifying exchanges, transfers, and acculturation processes between these synchronic cultural groups.

## Concluding Remarks

This brief review of the evidence of social complexity is admittedly incomplete. It tends, however, to illustrate the major conclusions that are summarized here.

The manifestations of social complexity illuminated by the Near Eastern case studies discussed above has revealed how settlements gradually became planned, including their streets and buildings that were carefully designed, as well as impressive collective works, such as fortifications, along with nonresidential craft activity workshops. Certainly, we have seen clear examples of monumental and public architecture that can be linked to the imagery and symbolism of power. These constructions require, on the one hand, technical expertise and a very large workforce, and on the other, vast quantities of soil for mud bricks, copious amounts of water and straw, and the support of quite large areas of agricultural land.

Features such as specialization, advanced architectural planning on a large scale, concentration of food resources and their redistribution according to need and ability, long-term food storage, and interregional trade must have necessitated a complex bureaucratic system, and we have seen how the development of the administrative system became increasingly complex.

But how should all this evidence be interpreted? Taken together, these aspects required for their mobilization the recognition that such labor could be put to good use, and a cadre of administrative personnel who could direct them. As well as an indication of an organizational tradition that emphasized communal work complementing activities concerned with basic subsistence (agriculture and livestock), that created the opportunity for leaders to become managers. In addition, these leaders had to invest in providing canals, storage structures, and a series of facilities such as water reservoirs, as well as the organization to maintain and oversee all these installations to ensure that they worked efficiently. Indeed, a close connection between these activities and the development of administrative devices, such as memory tools (artificial memory objects) or glyptic elements, and the development of social organization, can be identified.

Consequently, all of these elements point to a social complexity indicative of regional politics. It is reasonable to suppose that the process was multifaceted, and would have combined individual leadership with diverse structures for group-based decision-making, such as the community elders. Yet it is not clear to what extent we should understand and explain this social complexity only from a material point of view. What seems necessary is to include in the analysis all these elements and their interrelations, since, for instance, fortified sites alone cannot be equated with any particular form of political organization.

By doing so, the analysis of all these elements will also contribute to refining our understanding of the evolution of complex societies, emphasizing their gradual and progressive development. This is particularly clear, as has already been seen, from the individual documentation of all these elements from the eighth and seventh millennia BCE, to reaching the high degree of developing and increasingly in the third millennium. As, for instance, the evidence at Tell Brak showed:

> Here our work has revealed monumental structures associated with organised craft activity, the manufacture of prestige goods, bureaucratic paraphernalia and evidence for the organisation and provisioning of labour beyond household

> levels, all dating from the late fifth and the early fourth millennia BC. (Oates et al. 2007: 587)

Nevertheless, a very important aspect should be kept in mind, which is the different pace of development of each community, partially determined by the intrinsic local characteristics, in addition to the differential archaeological records available to us. Such rhythms often escape a too-linear evolutionary explanation. At the same time, it is necessary to be aware of the complex dynamic social systems that change spatially, temporally, and cognitively, as well as their interrelationships.

In conclusion, all of these changes took place progressively and continually over the centuries and differed in degree and intensity from one area to another. Accordingly, strategies for maintaining livelihood were first organized, and then the urban way of life developed gradually, that is, authority was created gradually, depending on particular local conditions, and as a flexible and adaptive response to these circumstances. Given the available evidence, it seems impossible at this time to specify the kind of authority or the number of levels of political decision-making, since much more research remains to be undertaken. Nonetheless, the arguments presented here support the idea that a study of the socio-political structure of the Ancient Near East will have to take each of the elements discussed from reliable archaeological contexts into account in order to build up a comprehensive picture of past societies. We need to understand how each element interacts with, affects, and changes the others, and how these connections alter or reinforce existing patterns of economic, social, and political behavior.

This review of the evidence from north Mesopotamia presents an opportunity to devise an alternative framework for the study of the social organization by exploring the interrelationships between different aspects of the given society, by using archaeological data to investigate key dimensions of social organization

Lastly, we should insist on taking advantage of the use of archaeological tools, such as, for instance, the latest techniques of geophysical, topographic, and magnetic surveys in addition to aerial photography, in order to study synchronic and diachronic settlement patterns, site-by-site and region-by-region, so as to understand whether the settlements were part of a more complex network that controlled a territory and to observe social and environmental changes over time. By adopting improved excavation techniques, including fine sieving and flotation, or by studying site formation processes, we should be able to come up with the kind of information that will enable us to test the various hypotheses. Without resolving some of the major aspects concerning socio-economic organization, we will be unable to make further steps in our understanding of the intricate relationships between the different sectors that form part of these communities. Indeed, in our belief, a holistic and dialectical view with regard to past societies is needed, and that implies the practice of interdisciplinary research and recontextualising the textual evidence within the material and social picture.

## BIBLIOGRAPHY

Abu es-Soof, B.

1968 Tell es-Sawwan: Excavations of the Fourth Season (Spring 1967). *Sumer* 24: 3–15.

1971 Tell es-Sawwan: Fifth Season Excavations (Winter 1967, 1968). *Sumer* 27: 3–7.

Akkermans, P. M. M. G., ed.
1996 *Tell Sabi Abyad: The Late Neolithic Settelement.* PIHANS 76. Istanbul: Nederlands Historisch-Archaeologisch Instituut.

Akkermans, P. M. M. G.
2008 Burying the Dead in Late Neolithic Syria. Pp. 621–645 in *Proceedings of the 5th International Congress on the Archaeology of the Ancient Near East, Madrid, April 3–8 2006.* Edited by J. Cordoba, M. Molist, C. Pérez, I. Rubio, and S. Martínez. Madrid: Universidad Autónoma de Madrid.

Akkermans, P. M. M. G. and Duistermaat, K.
1996 Of Storage and Nomads: The Sealing from Late Neolithic Sabi Abyad, Syria. *Paléorient* 22.2: 17–44.

Akkermans, P. M. M. G. and Schwartz, G. M.
2003 *The Archaeology of Syria: From Complex Hunter-Gatherers to Early Urban Societies (ca. 16,000–300 BC).* Cambridge: Cambridge University Press.

Akkermans, P. M. M. G. and Verhoeven, M.
1995 An Image of Complexity: The Burnt Village at Late Neolithic Sabi Abyad, Syria. *AJA* 99: 5–32.

Algaze, G. and Fessler, D.
2001 A Reconsideration of the Origins of Human Settlement and Social Differentiation. Pp. 9–28 in *Studies in the Archaeology of Israel and Neighbouring Lands in Memory of Douglas L. Esse.* Edited by S. R. Wolff. SOAC 59. Chicago: Oriental Institute of the University of Chicago.

Anfruns, J. and Molist, M.
1996 Estructuras de enterramiento y prácticas funerarias. Pp. 151–160 in *Tell Halula (Siria): Un yacimiento neolítico del valle medio del Éufrates, campañas de 1991 y 1992.* Edited by M. Molist. Madrid: Instituto del Patrimonio Histórico Español.

Bernbeck, R.
1995 Lasting Alliances and Emerging Competition: Economic Developments in Early Mesopotamia. *Journal of Anthropological Archaeology* 14: 1–25.

Breniquet, C.
1991 Tell es-Sawwan: Realités et problemes. *Iraq* 53: 75–90.
1992 Rapport sur deux campagnes de fouilles à Tell es-Sawwan, 1988–1989. *Mesopotamia* 27: 5–30.

Buccellati, G., Buia, D., and Reimer, S.
1991 Tell Ziyada: The First Three Seasons of Excavations (1988–1990). *BCSMS* 21: 31–61.

Cauvin, J.
1979 Les fouilles de Mureybet (1971–1974) et leur signification pour les origines de la sédentarisation au Proche Orient. Pp. 19–48 in *Archaeological Reports from the Tabqa Dam Project-Euphrates Valley, Syria.* Edited by D. N. Freedman. AASOR 44. Cambridge: American Schools of Oriental Research.

Cruells, W.
2005 *Orígens i desenvolupament de la cultura Halaf a Siria.* PhD diss., Universitat Autònoma de Barcelona.
2006 La poterie. Pp. 25–80 in *Chagar Bazar (Syrie) I: Les sondages préhistoriques 1999–2001.* Edited by Ö. Tunca and A. M. Baghdo. Publications de la mission archéologique de l'Université de Liège en Syrie 1. Leuven: Peeters.

Cruells, W., Gómez, A., Bouso, M., Guerrero, E., Tornero, C., Buxó, R., Saña, M., Molist, M., Abd el-Meseih al Abdo, and Tunca, Ö.
2013 Chagar Bazar in North-Eastern Syria: Recent Work. Pp. 467–477 in *Interpreting the Late Neolithic of Upper Mesopotamia.* Edited by O. Nieuwenhuyse, P. Akkermans, R. Bernbeck, and J. Rogasch. Turnhout: Brepols.

Crumley, C. L.
1995 Heterarchy and the Analysis of Complex Societies. Pp. 1–5 in *Heterarchy and the Analysis of Complex Societies*. Edited by R. M. Ehrenreich, C. L. Crumley, and J. E. Levy. Archeological Papers of The American Anthropological Association 6. Arlington, VA: American Anthropological Association.
2007 Historical Ecology: Integrated Thinking at Multiple Temporal and Spatial Scales. Pp. 15–28 in *The World System and the Earth System: Global Socio-environmental Change and Sustainability Since the Neolithic*. Edited by A. Hornborg, and C. L. Crumley. Walnut Creek, CA: Left Coast Press.

Gómez Bach, A.
2011 *Caracterización del producto cerámico en las comunidades neolíticas de mediados del VI milenio cal BC: El valle del Éufrates y el valle del Khabur en el Halaf Final*. PhD diss., Universitat Autònoma de Barcelona.

Guerrero, E., Molist, M., Kuijt, I., and Anfruns, J.
2009 Seated Memory: New Insights into Near Eastern Neolithic Mortuary Variability from Tell Halula, Syria. *Current Anthropology* 50: 379–391.

Guilaine, J., ed.
2007 *Le Chalcolithique et la construction des inégalités: Proche et Moyen-Orient, Amérique, Afrique*. Paris: Errance.

Hole, F.
1999 Economic Implications of Possible Storage Structures at Tell Ziyadeh, NE Syria. *JFA* 26: 267–283.

Huot, J-L.
2007 De Oueili à Uruk: La Naissance des villes en Mésopotamie du sud. Pp. 11–30 in *Le Chalcolithique et la construction des inégalités: Proche et Moyen-Orient, Amérique, Afrique*. Edited by J. Guilaine. Paris: Errance.

Ibañez, J. J., ed.
2008 *Le site Néolithique de Tell Mureybet (Syrie du Nord): En hommage à Jacques Cauvin*. BARIS 1843. Oxford: Archaeopress.

Jasim, S. A.
1985 *The Ubaid Period in Iraq: Recent Excavations in the Hamrin Region*. 2 vols. BARIS 267. Oxford: Archaeopress.

Karsgaard, P.
2010 The Halaf-Ubaid Transition: A Transformation Without a Center? Pp. 51–68 in *Beyond Ubaid: Transformation and Integration in the Late Prehistoric Societies of the Middle East*. Edited by R. A. Carter and G. Philip. SAOC 63. Chicago: Oriental Institute of the University of Chicago.

Kubba, S.
1990 The Ubaid Period: Evidence of Architectural Planning and the Use of a Standard Unit of Measurement—The "Ubaid Cubit" in Mesopotamia. *Paléorient* 16: 45–55.

Kuijt, I. and Finlayson, B.
2009 Evidence for Food Storage and Predomestication Granaries 11,000 Years Ago in the Jordan Valley. *Proceedings of the National Academy of Sciences of the United States of America* 106: 10966–10970.

Lebeau, M. and Suleiman, A., ed.
2014 *Tell Beydar: The 2010 Season of Excavations and Architectural Restoration; A Preliminary Report*. Subartu 34. Turnhout: Brepols.

McCarthy, A.
2012 The End of Empire: Akkadian and Post-Akkadian Glyptic in the Jezirah; the Evidence from Tell Leilan in Context. Pp. 217–224 in *Seven Generations Since the Fall of Akkad*. Edited by H. Weiss. Studia Chaburensia 3. Wiesbaden: Harrassowitz.

Merpert, N. Y and Munchaev, R. M.
1993a Yarim Tepe I. Pp. 73–113 in *Early Stages in the Evolution of Mesopotamian Civilization: Soviet Excavations in Northern Iraq*. Edited by N. Yoffee and J. J. Clark. Tucson: University of Arizona Press.
1993b Yarim Tepe II. Pp. 128–162 in *Early Stages in the Evolution of Mesopotamian Civilization: Soviet Excavations in Northern Iraq*. Edited by N. Yoffee and J. J. Clark. Tucson: University of Arizona Press.

Milano, L. and Rova, E.
2014 Tell Beydar 2010: Fields I and R; Study of the Gyptic Material. Pp. 83–105 in *Tell Beydar: The 2010 Season of Excavations and Architectural Restoration; A Preliminary Report*. Edited by M. Lebeau and A. Suleiman. Subartu 34. Turnhout: Brepols.

Miroschedji, P. de,
2001 Notes on Early Bronze Age Metrology and the Birth of Architecture in Ancient Palestine. Pp. 465–491 in *Studies in the Archaeology of Israel and Neighbouring Lands in Memory of Douglas L. Esse*. Edited by S. R. Wolff. SOAC 59. Chicago: Oriental Institute of the University of Chicago.

Molist, M., ed.
1996 *Tell Halula (Siria): Un yacimiento neolítico del valle medio del Éufrates, campañas de 1991 y 1992*. Informes arqueológicos 4. Madrid: Ministerio de Educación y Cultura.
2008 *Tell Halula (Valle del Éufrates, Siria): Dos décadas de investigaciones arqueológicas.* Treballs d'Arqueologia del Pròxim Orient 2. Barcelona: Universitat Autònoma de Barcelona.
2013 *Tell Halula: Un poblado de los primeros agricultores en el valle del Éufrates, Siria*. 2 vols. Memoria Científica. Madrid: Ministerio de Educación, Cultura y Deporte.

Molist, M. and Faura, J. M.
1996 Estratigrafía y arquitectura. Pp. 17–44 in *Un yacimiento neolítico del valle medio del Éufrates, campañas de 1991 y 1992*. Edited by M. Molist. Informes arqueológicos 4. Madrid: Ministerio de Educación y Cultura.

Molist, M. and Vicente, O.
2013 Tell Halula 1995–2005: Análisis estratigráfico y arquitectónico de los diferentes horizontes históricos de Tell Halula. Pp. 31–86 in *Tell Halula: Un poblado de los primeros agricultores en el valle del Éufrates, Siria.* Edited by M. Molist. 2 vols. Memoria Científica. Madrid: Ministerio de Educación, Cultura y Deporte.

Moore, A. M. T., Hillman, G. C., Legge, A. J., and Huxtable, J.
2000 *Village on the Euphrates: From Foraging to Farming at Abu Hureyra.* Oxford: Oxford University Press.

Nieuwenhuyse, O.
2008 *Plain and Painted Pottery: The Rise of Neolithic Ceramic Styles on the Syrian and Northern Mesopotamian Plains*. Papers on Archaeology of the Leiden Museum of Antiquities 3. Turnhout: Brepols.

Nishiaki, Y. and Matsutani, T., ed.
2001 *Tell Kosak Shamali*, vol. 1: *The Archaeological Investigations on the Upper Euphrates, Syria: Chalcolithic Architecture and the Earlier Prehistoric Remains.* Tokyo: University Museum, The University of Tokyo.

Oates, J., McMahon, A., Karsgaard, P., Salam Al Quntar, and Ur, J. A.
2007 Early Mesopotamian Urbanism: A New View from the North. *Antiquity* 81: 585–600.

Pfälzner, P.
2012 Household Dynamics in Late Third Millennium Northern Mesopotamia. Pp. 145–162 in *Seven Generations Since the Fall of Akkad.* Edited by H. Weiss. Studia Chaburensia 3. Wiesbaden: Harrassowitz.

Philip, G.
2001 The Early Bronze I–III Ages. Pp. 163-232 in *The Archaeology of Jordan*. Edited by B. McDonald, R. Adams, and P. Bienkowski. Sheffield: Academic Press.

Pollock, S.
2003 Feasts, Funerals, and Fast Food in Early Mesopotamian Status. Pp. 17–38 in *The Archaeology and Politics of Food and Feasting in Early States and Empires*. Edited by T. L. Bray. New York: Kluwer; Plenum.
2010 Practices of Daily Life in Fifth-Millennium B.C. Iran and Mesopotamia. Pp. 93–112 in *Beyond Ubaid: Transformation and Integration in the Late Prehistoric Societies of the Middle East*. Edited by R. A. Carter and G. Philip. SAOC 63. Chicago: Oriental Institute of the University of Chicago.

Pruβ, A.
2011 Excavations in Field P in the Years 2004–2009. Pp. 111–175 in *Tell Beydar: The 2004/2–2009 Seasons of Excavations, the 2004/2–2009 Seasons of Architectural Restoration—A Preliminary Report*. Edited by M. Lebeau and A. Suleiman. Subartu 29. Turnhout: Brepols.

Quenet, P.
2011 Stratigraphy. Pp. 19–47 in *Associated Regional Chronologies for the Ancient Near East and the Eastern Mediterranean: Jezireh*. Edited by M. Lebeau. ARCANE 1. Turnhout: Brepols.

Ristvet, L.
2007 The Third Millennium City Wall at Tell Leilan, Syria: Identity, Authority, and Urbanism. Pp. 183–212 in *Power and Architecture: Monumental Public Architecture in the Bronze Age Near East and Aegean*. Edited by J. Bretschneider, J. Driessen, and K. van Lerberghe. OLA 156. Leuven: Peeters.

Roaf, M.
1987 The 'Ubaid Architecture of Tell Madhur. Pp. 425–435 in *Préhistoire de la Mésopotamie: La Mésopotamie préhistorique et l'exploration récente du djebel Hamrin; Colloque International du Centre National de la Recherche Scientifique 17–18–19 décembre 1984*. Edited by J.-L. Huot. Paris: Éditions du Centre de la Recherche Scientifique.

Robert, B.
2010 *Développement et disparition de la production céramique halafienne: Implications techniques et sociales à partir d'études de cas*. PhD diss., Université Lumière Lyon 2.

Rothman M. S.
2002 *Tepe Gawra: The Evolution of a Small Prehistoric Center in Northern Iraq*. University Museum Monograph 112. Philadelphia: University of Pennsylvania, Museum of Archaeology and Anthropology.

Roux, V.
2013 Spreading of Innovative Technical Traits and Cumulative Technical Evolution: Continuity or Discontinuity? *Journal of Archaeological Method and Theory* 20: 312–330.

Rova, E.
2011 Pottery. Pp. 49–127 in *Associated Regional Chronologies for the Ancient Near East and the Eastern Mediterranean: Jezireh*. Edited by M. Lebeau. ARCANE 1. Turnhout: Brepols.

Seeden, H.
1982 Ethnoarchaeological Reconstruction of Halafian Occupational Units at Shams ed-Din Tannira. *Berytus* 30: 55–96.

Stede, V. van der.
2010 *Les pratiques de stockage au Proche-Orient ancien: Du Natoufien à la première moitié du troisième millénaire avant notre ère*. OLA 190. Leuven: Peeters.

Stein, G.

1994 The Organizational Dynamics of Complexity in Greater Mesopotamia. Pp. 11–22 in *Chiefdoms and Early States in the Near East: The Organizational Dynamics of Complexity*. Edited by G. Stein and M. S. Rothman. Monographs in World Archaeology 18. Madison, WI: Prehistory Press.

Stordeur, D.

1999 Organisation de l'espace construit et organisation sociale dans le Néolithique de Jerf el Ahmar (Syrie, X–IX millénaire av.JC.). Pp. 131–149 in *Habitat et société: Actes des Rencontres 22–24 octobre 1998; XIXe rencontres internationales d'archéologie et d'histoire d'Antibes*. Edited by F. Braemer, S. Cleiziou, and A. Coudart. Antibes: APDCA.

2006 Les bâtiments collectifs des premiers Néolithiques de l'Euphrate: Création, standardisation et mémoires des formes architecturales. Pp. 19–31 in *Les espaces syro-mésopotamiens: Dimensions de l'expérience humaine au Proche-Orient ancien; Volume d'hommage offert à Jean-Claude Margueron*. Edited by P. Butterlin, M. Lebeau, J.-Y. Monchambert, J. L. Montero Fenollós, and B. Muller. Subartu 17. Turnhout: Brepols.

Strommenger, E.

1980 *Habuba Kabira Eine Stadt vor 5000 Jahren: Ausgrabungen der Deutschen Orient-Gesellschaft am Euphrat in Habuba Kabira, Syrien*. Mainz am Rheim: von Zabern.

Ur, J. A.

2004 *Urbanism and Society in the Third Millennium Upper Khabur Basin*. PhD diss., University of Chicago.

Verhoeven, M.

1999 *An Archaeological Ethnography of a Neolitic Community: Space, Place and Social Relations in the Burnt Village of Tel Sabi Abyad, Syria*. PIHANS 83. Istanbul: Nederlands Historisch-Archaeological Instituut.

Wengrow, D.

2001 The Evolution of Simplicity: Aesthetic Labour and Social Change in the Neolithic Near East. *World Archaeology* 33: 168–188.

Yasin, W.

1970 Excavation at Tell es-Sawwan: The Sixth Season (1969). *Sumer* 26: 3–20.

CHAPTER 10

# A Variationist Approach to Orthographic and Phonological Peculiarities of the Language in the Laws of Hammurabi

Rodrigo Hernáiz

THE LANGUAGE IN THE PROLOGUE and the epilogue of the Code of Hammurabi belongs to a different register than the one of the corpus of laws and it is regarded as a literary work. This paper will focus, however, on the language in the corpus of laws, and will ask what kind of register it actually conveys.

Although the laws in the Code of Hammurabi and the letters from the royal palace are normally grouped together in a common *Kanzleisprache* (von Soden 1931: 163), I will try to show that the text of the laws shows significant differences at times, not only with Old Babylonian literary inscriptions like the prologue and epilogue of the Code of Hammurabi, but also partly with the Old Babylonian language of the letters sent by King Hammurabi himself. Interestingly, many of these differences seem to concentrate in particular parts of the corpus of laws.

The object of the present study is the behavior of sibilants in the text of the laws. Old Babylonian sibilants present a particularly interesting linguistic phenomenon: we find a variety of signs to render them and, most importantly, some of them seem to undergo a phonological change from Old Akkadian to Middle Babylonian. The different stages of this change were established by Sommerfeld in *GAG*, presenting a development from *affricate* (a conjunction of two phonetic traits: *stop* plus *fricative*) through a process of *deaffrication* (loss of the *stop* component) towards a complete *fricative* sound (§§30, 35–36).

Some canonical Old Babylonian texts including the language of the Laws of Hammurabi—as it is normally presented—belong to some sort of intermediate stage where basically:

- *affricates* are written with Z-signs (ZA, ZI, ZU) and occur in word-initial position and double consonants.
- *fricatives* are written with S-signs (SA, SI, SU) and occur in the other cases.

As for any linguistic change, we expect to see different rhythms and locations in the process, which was also anticipated by W. Sommerfeld: "regionale und orthographische Verschiedenheiten sind wahrscheinlich" (cited in *GAG* §30).

*Author's note:* This paper was written in the frame of the FPI predoctoral research grant BES-2009-013834 of the Spanish Ministry of Economy, related to the FFI2008-05004-C02-01 project. I would like to gratefully thank Prof. J. Sanmartín and Dr. M. Worthington for their valuable comments on an earlier version of the paper. Prof. W. Sommerfeld also shared most generously not only ideas but also texts and bibliographical material that made this paper possible. Of course, any remaining inadequacies or mistakes are my own responsibility.

*Language variation and change* is a branch of linguistics that deals with language change and sociolinguistic questions through quantitative and qualitative analysis of data, focusing on variables and considering not only internal linguistic factors but also external linguistic conditionings.[1] I will apply this variationist perspective to contrast the CV-signs used to render the (conventionally interpreted as) sibilant phoneme /s/ in the laws of the Code of Hammurabi with the surrounding sociolinguistic reality of the time; I will call this variable (s, z).[2]

Some significant samples of Old Babylonian texts—especially letters—are presented in the first part of the survey in order to determine the range of diversity of the variable (s, z) in the contemporary linguistic environment of the Code of Hammurabi. In the second part I will deal with the exceptions to the deaffrication *rule* in the proper laws of the Code of Hammurabi.

In parallel, I will also compare different ways to render the so-called emphatic sibilant in the signs ṢI (ZÍ) and ṢÍ (ZI): variable (ṣi, ṣí).

Finally, I will conclude that some of the exceptional spellings in the Laws of Hammurabi are difficult to understand as the result of purely internal linguistic constrains or stylistic shifts, but rather respond to sociolinguistic parameters.

## The Variables (s, z) and (ṣi, ṣí) in Contemporary Old Babylonian Texts

To answer the question of whether the written evidence suggests a more or less standard rendering of sibilants already in Old Babylonian at the time of Hammurabi, I present two different types of texts that show that the situation was in fact not uniform; first, a group of Old Babylonian royal inscriptions representing an elevated or literary register: Hammurabi`s inscriptions, the stela of Dadusha and a cone inscription from Larsa dated to the reign of Warad-Sîn; and second, a corpus of letters, closer in nature to a vernacular Old Babylonian register.[3]

Tables 10.1 to 10.3 show a number of orthographic exceptions to the rule of use of Z- or S-signs for sibilants.[4] Moreover, the exceptions are different from one group to another; in the inscription from Larsa they consist of Z-signs for expected fricative

1. For an example of a variationist quantitative approach applied to Akkadian texts see Worthington 2010.

2. The variable (s, z) represents the grammatically independent different orthographies—either S-signs (SA, SI, SU) or Z-signs (ZA, ZI, ZU)—used to render the sibilant phoneme /s/ and its allophones, conventionally transliterated by the pairs sa-sà, si-sí, su-sú as described in the already mentioned section of *GAG* §30.

3. For the inscriptions, see Frayne 1990. There is little information about the date of these copies but it is generally accepted that they are OB (see Gelb's [1948: 267] comments on the OB clay-nails shape characteristics). The Neo-Babylonian copy of a Hammurabi's royal inscription in Frayne 1990 has not been included here. For the stela of Dadusha, see Ismaïl and Cavigneaux 2003. Notice on the two nonstandard forms with SÚ, that no SU sign appears in the text. See also n. 9 below. For a contrast to *qí-ís-**sú***, see *i-qí-si̲-im* ("he gave to her") on an inscription from Ipiq-Adad II (RIME E4.5.14.3:10). The term "contemporary" for these texts is understood in a broad sense. According to Charpin (2004: 386–390) the conventional reign dates would be: Hammurabi (1792–1750), Dadusha (?–1779), Warad-Sîn (1834–1823). The table is taken from Frayne 1990, 267–268.

4. The difficult *re-ši*-ZU/SU-*nu* (RIME E4.3.6.2:44) is not included here nor in Streck 2006.

TABLE 10.1. Instances of variables (s, z) and (ṣi, ṣí) in Hammurabi's Royal Inscriptions (RIME 4: E4.3.6.2; 6; 7; 12; and 17).

| Standard use of variable (s, z) | Nonstandard | Variable (ṣi, ṣí) |
|---|---|---|
| *as-**sú**-úḫ* (NSH) | *ip-pa-al-**sa₆**-ni* (PLS) | ***ṣi**-ra-tim* |
| *ṣe-er-ra-**sí**-na* (2×) (*ṣerratum*) | ***sa₆**-ap-ḫa-tim* (*saphum*) | ***ṣi**-a-tim* (3×) |
| *ù-um-mi-**sú*** ('MD) | | ***ṣi**-it* |
| *ka-ra-as-**su*** (Š+Š: *karašum*) | | ***ṣi**-ra-am* |
| *e-pu-ús-**su**-um* (Š+Š: 'PŠ)[a] | | |

[a] Frayne 1990: 349:46. For the expected S-sign in the context of a contact between two /š/ see A. Westenholz 2006: 253 n.4; and Streck 2011: §44. All the items are extracted from Frayne's edition. Notice, however, that a few exemplars of the cones also present variants. E.g: inscription E4.3.6.12: *e-pu-ús-**sú**-um* (ex.1) and *ú-um-mi-**su*** (ex. 2).

TABLE 10.2. Instances of variables (s, z) and (ṣi, ṣí) in CV sibilant signs on the Stele of Dadusha.

| Standard use variable (s, z) | Nonstandard | Variable (ṣi, ṣí) | |
|---|---|---|---|
| *ú-pa-as-**sà**-**sú*** (PSS) | ***sa**-pa-nim* (SPN) | *ṣi-a-tim* | ***ṣ**[**í**-t]i-ša* |
| *ša-as-**sú**-ri-šu* (*šassūrum*) | ***si**-ih-pí-im* (*sihpu*) | | ***ṣí**-ri-iš* |
| *aṭ-ru-us-**sú**-um-ma* (ṬRD) | *ka-ab-**sú**-šu* (KBS) | | ***ṣí**-ri-im* |
| *ša-al-la-as-**sú**-nu* (*šallatum*) | *qí-is-**sú*** (Š+Š: Q'Š) | | *ma-ar-**ṣí**-iš* |
| *ma-as-**sú*** (*mātum*) | | | |
| *qá-qá-as-**sú*** (*qaqqadum*) | | | |
| *ša-al-la-as-**sú*** (*šallatum*) | | | |
| *er-ṣe-**sú*** (*erṣetum*) | | | |
| *pur-gul-lu-**sú*** (*purkullūtu*) | | | |
| *uš-zi-is-**sú*** ('ZZ) | | | |

TABLE 10.3. Instances of variables (s, z) and (ṣi, ṣí) in an inscription dated to the reign of Warad-Sîn of Larsa (RIME E4.2.13a.2).

| Standard use of variable (s, z) | Nonstandard | Variable (ṣi, ṣí) |
|---|---|---|
| *i-na-**sà**-ḫu-u* (NSH) | *pi-**sà**-an-na-šu* (*pisannum*) | *ṣi-a-at* |
| ***sí**-ip-pi-šu* (*sippum*) | *pa-ar-**sú**-ú* (PRS) | |
| *li-is-**sú**-uḫ* (NSH) | *a-**sú**-ur-ra-šu* (*asurrûm*) | |
| GIŠ.IG-***sú*** (*daltum*) | | |

sibilants, whereas the stela from Eshnunna presents nonstandard S-signs in word-initials, although Z-signs for expected S-signs also occur. We also notice that Dadusha's stela issues ṢÍ more frequently than not, sometimes in clear contrast to the royal inscriptions from Hammurabi (***ṣí**-ri-im* vs. *ṣi-ra-am*).[5] Can a merely grammatical, phonological, or stylistic explanation account for these alternations? Is it just a random use of orthographic alternatives? We will return to these questions later.

5. For clarity purposes I will refer in this paper to signs ṢI and ṢÍ, for the signs ZÍ and ZI respectively.

I will now compare these preliminary observations on the sibilants in Old Babylonian inscriptions with the orthographic characteristics of some contemporary letters; namely, the corpus of letters from Hammurabi in the collection Altbabylonische Briefe (AbB; theoretically the most similar to the laws of the CH), the letters from Lu-Ninurta (Hammurabi's highest official, active in Babylon), the letters from Silli-Shamash from Larsa (an employee by the important merchant Balmunamhe) and a group of selected letters from the Diyala region published by A. Goetze (1958a) in *Sumer* 14.[6] It is, in sum, a sample of letters from different locations (Babylon, Larsa, Diyala) and social ranks:[7]

1. Letters from Hammurabi (AbB):
   1.1. SÀ/SA signs: twenty-six occurrences; no nonexpected orthographies; (0 percent variation).[8]
   1.2. SÍ/SI signs: twenty-seven occurrences; no nonexpected orthographies; (0 percent variation).
   1.3. SÚ/SU signs:[9] fifty-two items; three nonexpected: *ú-**sú**-úh-šu-nu-ti* (5.136), *ip-ru-**sú**-ma* (4.40) and *li-ik-ki-**sú**-ma*(13.23); two damaged signs;[10] (6 percent exceptions).[11]
   1.4. S-signs in contact between Š from root, plus Š from suffix: six occurrences; one nonexpected: *tu-še-ep-pé-es-**sú**-nu-ti* (5, 136); (16.6 percent exceptions).[12]
   1.5. ṢI: twenty-three occurrences (most of them forms of *ṣibtum* [ten times] and *ṣimdatum* [five times]).
   1.6. ṢÍ: No occurrences (apart from a difficult *m*[*u*]-*ṣ*[*í(?)*] (13.15)).
2. Letters from Lu-Ninurta (AbB):
   2.1. SÀ/SA signs: two occurrences; no nonexpected orthographies (0 percent variation).
   2.2. SÍ/SI signs: six occurrences; two nonexpected orthographies: ***si**-ki-il-tim* (4.111); ***si**-it-ti* (9.200); one sign difficult to read;[13] (40 percent exceptions).

6. Letters from Hammurabi directed to Mari are not included in this survey since they show interesting differences from the rest of the letters sent by Hammurabi. AbB letters will be referred directly by the AbB volume number.

7. I have not considered PNs in this paper as they often present traditional orthographies. See A. Westenholz 2006: 258.

8. By "nonexpected" I refer to the deviances from the OB pattern for sibilants previously explained.

9. On the reliability of the differentiation of signs ZU and SU in some OB cases see A. Westenholz 2006: 253 n.4 and 258: "the ancient scribes, or quite often the modern copyists and editors of the texts do not distinguish adequately between the very similar signs SU and ZU."

10. The sign ZU or SU in *li-is*-ZU/SU-*ni-ik-ku-nu-ši-im* (9.190) (see Streck 2006: 240 n.71) and *ka-am*-Z[U]/S[U]-*ú* (2.59) (after LIH II.75) cannot be safely distinguished.

11. For clarity of the presentation, I include in this list all the S-signs or Z-signs resulting from contact between dental or sibilant (except Š, see below) plus personal suffixes in the same group as the other Z- or S-signs.

12. Streck 2006: 239 n. 62 "The signs are damaged but in the copy of J.A. Knudtzon, BA 4 p. 99 they look more like -EZ-ZU- than -EZ-SU-". See also A. Westenholz 2006: 253 n.4.

13. UH-*ta-na*-AZ-*s*[*i*](?) (4.58. See note 58b in Kraus 1968 [AbB 4]).

2.3. SÚ/SU signs: fifteen occurrences (all cases of sibilant/dental + suffix); one unusual form: *ṣa-bi-it-**sú*** (4.120), which still uses SÚ. (0 percent).
2.4. S-signs in Š+Š contact: one occurrence; no nonexpected orthographies; (0 percent).
2.5. ṢI: eleven occurrences/ṢÍ: two occurrences: *ṣí-tim* (4.111) and *tu-še-eṣ-ṣí* (4.111).

3. Letters from Silli-Shamash (AbB):
   3.1. SÀ/SA signs: six occurrences (all of them ZA); one nonexpected: *na-**sà**-hi-im* (10.193); (16.6 percent variation).
   3.2. SÍ/SI/SÉ/SE signs: four occurrences (all of them ZI); no nonexpected (0 percent).
   3.3. SÚ/SU signs: five occurrences (all of them ZU); three nonexpected orthographies: *ip-ru-**sú**-ni-im-ma* (10.177), *er-**sú*** (14.58), *er-**sú**-ú* (14.60); (60 percent exceptions).
   3.4. ṢI: one occurrence: *ṣi-bi* (14.64)/ṢÍ: nine occurrences.
4. Letters from Harmal in *Sumer* 14 (Goetze 1958a):
   4.1. Almost all occurrences are S-signs (thirty-nine times) with one exception in ***sí**-la-tu-ka* (letter 12). Used for every phonological environment: É-***su***, ***si**-ma-at*, and so on.
   4.2. ṢI: No occurrences/ṢÍ: ten occurrences.

The roughly contemporary samples taken from royal inscriptions and letters suggest that the Old Babylonian language at the time of Hammurabi was orthographically and linguistically not uniform. The exceptions make it difficult to establish a standard general orthography for the variants of the survey. However, some patterns seem to emerge. The letters present more exceptions to the canonical representation of sibilants in the peripheral texts from the Diyala and Larsa in a way that coincides to some extent with the type of exceptional cases already seen in the royal inscriptions: Virtually exclusive use of Z-signs (no matter what the phonetic environment) in the examples from Larsa, and main use of S-signs in the Diyala region. This points to the existence of tendencies of varying strength toward different systems for the analyzed variables.

This unevenness has been already observed in several Assyriological studies, initiated by Goetze (1958b), who established a northern and southern Babylonian spelling division for sibilants, and notably Sommerfeld (2006: 371), who demonstrated with multiple examples the *Dialektunterschiede* in Old Babylonian sibilants from the Diyala region and encouraged the study of general variation and "die real existierende akkadische Sprache."

Yet the picture shown here does not intend to be a rigid and well-established division. Modern dialectology shows that the limits between variants can certainly be diffuse and many factors can play an important role: geography, nature of the text (e.g., the difference between the Diyala letters and the inscription of Dadusha), and social status, among others.

The scattered data presented above represent only a sample of contemporary yet dissimilar features of the variable (s, z) on the background frame of a linguistic change that took place between the third and second millennium BCE. The synchronic

TABLE 10.4. Example of contrasting variants (ṣi, ṣí) in Old Babylonian letter exercises.

| | | |
|---|---|---|
| Letter *o)* Sippar[a]<br>***ṣí-bi-ti*** ×2 **[*šu*]-*ṣí*** ***ka-ar-ṣí-ka*** | Letter *m)* unknown<br>(copy of *n)*?)<br>*ṣi-bi-tim* ***šu-ṣí-i*** | Letter *t)* unknown<br>(Larsa?)<br>*ṣi-bi-tim* ×2 *šu-ṣi-a-am* |
| Letter *p)* Sippar<br>*šu-ṣi-a-am* ***kar-ṣí-ka*** | Letter *n)* Kish<br>*ṣi-bi-tim* [x-x]-*i-ma*(?) | |
| Letter *q)* Sippar<br>***šu-ṣí-a-am*** | Letter *r)* Kish[b]<br>*ṣi-bi-tim* **[*š*]*u-ú-ṣí*** | |
| Letter *s)* Ur<br>***ṣí-bi-tim*** ***šu-ṣí-i*** | | |

[a] It is "ein normaler Brief" according to Kraus 1959, and the model for the school exercises *m)* and *n)*.

[b] Kraus: 1959: 28: "sich äusserlich nicht von einem normalen Briefe unterscheidet."

variables realize tendencies in a spectrum of spellings with more than one system involved, either due to orthographic traditions, or, most likely, to dialectal linguistic realities. Other texts are therefore expected to convey some degree of mixture, since variation also exists at individual levels. However, the study of quantitative parameters of relative frequency in different samples may reveal significative variational patterns.

According to this view, internal phonological or grammatical factors alone do not seem to account for all the distributional routes of variable (s, z). Can we say the same about the variable (ṣi, ṣí)?

A series of copying-letters scribal exercises reveal that even Old Babylonian scribes in their education did not follow one standard but several patterns to render the variable (ṣi, ṣí).[14]

We can observe evident differences in the distribution of the variable (ṣi, ṣí), which clearly speaks against any type of general prescriptivism on the orthography at that time and endorses the idea that sociolinguistic realities lay behind the divergence of the variable: with cases of exclusive use of ṢI (letter *t)*), exclusive use of ṢÍ (letters *o)* and *s)*), as well as an intermediate mixed system ṢI-ṢÍ (*ṣi-bi-tim*, ***šu-ṣí-i***). Although admittedly, the evidence presented here is way too scarce to draw any general conclusions, the examples in table 10.4 also match the quantitative observation that the writing of ṢI is more frequent than ṢÍ in the realization of the phonic segment {ṣi-bV} in the whole corpus of letters from Altbabylonische Briefe (where ṢI is used 201 times for 37 times of ṢÍ).[15] Obviously, rough numbers alone do not account for

14. Taken from Kraus 1959, 26–29. The letters show features and contents that led Kraus to interpret them as copying exercises. These were found in different places (Sippar, Ur, Kish, Larsa?). If rightly understood as school exercises they might have been written in the same place where they were found. They all dated back to OB, but unfortunately no further information about any chronological distinction between them is available, so we cannot exclude a chronological factor as related to the variation. Moreover, the letters differ in other details as well, e.g., the greeting formula in the three texts from Sippar present: *o)* (d)UTU *li-ba-al-li-iṭ-ka*; *q)* (d)UTU *ú* (d)MARDUK *li-ba-al-li-ṭú-ka*; *p)* (d)UTU *ù* (d)MARDUK *aš-šu-mi-ia da-ri-iš* $u_4$*-mi ša-pí-ri li-ba-al-li-ṭú*. These formulations can reflect different chronologies (Sallaberger 1999).

Letters *m)*, *n)* and *o)* were grouped together by Kraus for their similar content; Kraus also found similarities between letter *o)* and letters *p)* and *q)*. Finally *r)*, *s)* and *t)* were included in another group because of their content and partially identical forms.

15. Mainly for the substantives *ṣibittum*, *ṣibtum*, and *ṣibûtum*.

TABLE 10.5. AbB letters with the cluster {ṣi-bV} written with ṢÍ that also present other occurrences of the variable (ṣi, ṣí).

| | | |
|---|---|---|
| ***ṣí**-bu-sú-nu* | ***ṣí**-ir-ma-šu-[n]u-[š]i* | 2.91 |
| ***ṣí**-bu-tam* | *ú-še-**ṣí**-ma* | 2.136 |
| ***ṣí**-bi-it* | *[it-t]a-**ṣí**-i* | 2.143 |
| ***ṣí**-bi-it* | *ma-ha-**ṣí**-im, ta-ra-**ṣí**-im, ma-ha-**ṣí*** | 3.55 |
| ***ṣí**-bi-tim* (×2) | *ka-ar-**ṣí**-ka, [šu]-**ṣí*** | 5.234[a] |
| ***ṣí**-bu-su* | *i-ta-**ṣí*** | 9.184 |
| ***ṣ[í]**-bu-ti-ia/ṣi-bu-ti* | *ṣi-im-da-at* | 9.6 |
| ***ṣí**-bi-it/ṣi-bu-ti* | | 12.58 |

[a] Letter *o)* in Kraus 1959.

a general preference in Old Babylonian for one or the other option if we do not take into account the asymmetry of the data gathered in Altbabylonische Briefe, which inevitably comprehends an unbalanced number of texts belonging to some particular periods, individuals, or geographical areas.

However, we can obtain relevant information if we study the implicational conclusions of the use of both signs. As we saw in the scribal examples of table 10.4 on the substantive *ṣibittum* and the verb *šuṣûm*, the former is written with ṢÍ only in the group that also writes the latter with ṢÍ. Accordingly, the thirty-seven cases of the phonic segment {ṣi-bV} written with ṢÍ in Altbabylonische Briefe show that same preference for ṢÍ in almost all the other items.[16]

Only the last two letters also present ṢI, but interestingly it is also in the segment {ṣi-bV}.[17]

Not surprisingly we also find in Altbabylonische Briefe a series of letters with ṢI in the cluster {ṣi-bV} but ṢÍ in other cases (see table 10.6). This mixed group is of great interest for variationist research because it shows that the distribution of its variation can tell us something about the lexical or phonological background of the written evidence. It suggests that some orthographic alternations are not just the result of random fluctuations but might have phonetic or phonological grounds. The implicational tendency, according to which some letters present ṢÍ in several cases and ṢI in the phonic segment {ṣi-bV}, but that there are not full examples of the opposite (letters with exclusively ṢÍ in the cluster {ṣi-bV} and ṢI elsewhere) can be an indication of the existence in that phonic segment of a distinguishing feature: an allophone, a lexical property, the result of a mixed text, a linguistic change in progress, or similar.

Finally, there is a group of sixteen Altbabylonische Briefe letters where not only the cluster {ṣi-bV} but also every other item of the variable (ṣi, ṣí) is written exclusively with the ṢI-sign (twenty-two items in total). They include, among other forms, *ú-uṣ-ṣi* (1.3; 9.161) which differs with *ú-uṣ-**ṣí*** (6.64) from table 10.6.

16. PNs like DN-*na-ṣi-ir* or the like are not included in the paper. See supra n. 7.

17. From the microsociolinguistic point of view it is interesting to remark that the sender of the last letter (12.51) was a businessman whose letters also included the forms: *a-ta-**ṣí*** (9.51), *tu-ši-**ṣí**, tu-ši-**ṣí**-ma* (9.53), *at-ta-**ṣí*** (twice: 9.54 and 9.57), *nu-**ṣí*** (9.55). There are no instances of ṢI attested in his letters apart from the occurrence shown in table 10.5, which reinforces the idea of a lexical or phonologic background acting on the different orthography of items like *ṣi-bu-ti* in the utterances of certain individuals or dialects in OB.

TABLE 10.6. AbB letters with the cluster {ṣi-bV} written with ṢI but also containing ṢÍ elsewhere.

| | |
|---|---|
| *ṣi-bu-tam* / ***ṣí-il-pa-at-ni*** | 3.52 |
| *ṣi-bu-tam* / ***uš-ta-ṣí-a-kum*** / *uš-ta-ṣ*]*i-a-kum*[a] | 6.62 |
| *ṣi-bu-ti-ia* / ***i-ṣí*** (×3) | 7.73 |
| *ṣi-bi-tim* / **[*š*]*u-ú-ṣí*** | 5.80[b] |
| *ṣi-bi-ṭe₄-mi-im* / ***ni-ka-ṣí*** | 6.8 |
| *ṣi-bu-tam* / ***ú-uṣ-ṣí*** | 6.64 |
| *ṣi-bu-tam* / **[*l*]*u-še₂₀-ṣí-i-šu*** | 8.156 |
| *ṣi*(!)(AD)-*bu-u*[*t*]-*k*[*a(?)* / ***hal-ṣí*** | 8.44 |
| *ṣi-bi-tim* / ***šu-ṣí-i*** | 10.89[c] |
| *ṣi-bu-ti* / ***ṣí-bi-it*** | 12.58[d] |

[a] Very doubtful reading. Frankena 1974: 6: 62 n. 62.b: "Nach dem Zusammenhang ergänzt."
[b] Letter *r)* in Kraus 1959.
[c] Letter *m)* in Kraus 1959.
[d] Already seen in table 10.5.

Regarding the variable (ṣi, ṣí), we have then acknowledged the existence of at least three groups of letters according to the relative frequency and the distribution of the variable in a given phonic segment ({ṣi-bV}). Under this variationist perspective, we can better examine other cases of the variable (ṣi, ṣí), like the variation shown in a group of selected items of the Code of Hammurabi compared to the Altbabylonische Briefe letters of those contemporary individuals that we analyzed before.

Table 10.7 presents variation among letters sent by well-known individuals, contemporary to Hammurabi (and therefore to the CH). Any attempt to develop a general, merely grammatical or phonological explanation to give account for such a complicated variation (in nonliterary and nearly contemporary late OB texts) would be almost impossible, or would have to admit severe exceptions. Meanwhile, sociolinguistic factors—like the diversity shown before—can help clarify the picture, with some individuals falling more or less into some of the paradigmatic categories.

Finally, and before examining the laws of the Code of Hammurabi, it is meaningful to draw attention to the importance of the distributional patterns in a given corpus.

Letters from an individual are normally written in different times, to different addressees, under different pragmatic, physical, or geographical circumstances, and

TABLE 10.7. Correlated forms regarding the variable (ṣi, ṣí) in CH and in groups of AbB letters sent by contemporary individuals.

| Lu-Ninurta | Silli-Shamash | Hammurabi | CH[a] |
|---|---|---|---|
| ***ṣí-tim*** | | *ṣi-tim, ṣi-i-tim* | |
| *ṣi-bi-it* | *ṣi-bi* | *ṣi-bi-is-sú* | *ṣi-ba-a-at* |
| ***tu-še-eṣ-ṣí*** | ***ú-še-eṣ-ṣí-a-am*** | | |
| *ú-še-ṣi* | ***tu-ši-e-ṣí*** | *tu-še-ṣi* | *ú-še-ṣi-ma* (×2) |
| | ***uš-te-e-ṣí*** (×2) | *tu-uš-te-ṣi* | ***uš-te-ṣí, uš-te-ṣí-a-am*** |

[a] Occurrences in the corpus of laws of the stele of the Louvre. The prologue and epilogue are not part of the research.

perhaps by different scribes. There are too many variables for us to control for, and also an epigraphic study of the tablets is often difficult and sometimes impossible.

Nevertheless, a distributional survey of the features can shed light on the reasons for the existence of the variables. Let's have a look at the exceptions to the sibilant pattern in the letters of Hammurabi and his official Lu-Ninurta:

Hammurabi: From a total of more than 150 letters published in Altbabylonische Briefe, only four nonexpected orthographies were found in the variables under study.[18] Interestingly, two of them: *ú-**sú**-úh-šu-nu-ti*[19] and *tu-še-ep-pé-es-**sú**-nu-ti*[20] belong to the same letter (5.136). Unfortunately the tablet is not available anymore, so the question of whether it was an epigraphic lack of distinction between ZU and SU cannot be solved. It is also interesting to notice that we deal here with two exceptions opposed to the deaffrication process cline, portraying a conservative feature rather than an innovative one. A third exception occurs in letter 4.40 where two different forms coexist: the expected *ip-ru-su-ma* and again, a conservative *ip-ru-**sú**-ma*. What stands out in this letter has to do with other orthographic conventions. Here we find the only two occurrences (in the whole corpus of AbB letters sent by Hammurabi) where the phonetic complement to the Sumerogram A.ŠÀ is written with an L-sign: A.ŠÀ-***lim*** and A.ŠÀ-***li***, which contrasts with more than a hundred occurrences of A.ŠÀ-*um*, *-im*, *-i*, *-ia* or *-am*.[21] In summary, it results from the distributional survey that three out of four exceptions show some special degree of peculiarity compared to the rest of the letters.

Lu-Ninurta: In the survey shown before, we found two exceptions to the pattern for the variable (s, z), and also a curious distribution of the variable (ṣi, ṣí): eleven tokens with ṢI for only two with ṢÍ. Again, we notice that one of the first two exceptions, si-*ki-il-tim*, is found in letter 4.111, exactly the same letter that shows the only two attestations for ṢÍ: ***ṣí**-tim* and *tu-še-eṣ-**ṣí***.[22] The use in the same letter of northern forms, also differs from the southern features in the majority of the letters sent by Lu-Ninurta. Again, it seems that some variables and orthographic exceptions tend to be grouped together in specific letters.

## The Distribution of the Variables in the Laws of the Code of Hammurabi

After a general approach to some variationist methodological questions applied to Old Babylonian, I will first present the variables in the laws of the Code of Hammurabi

18. The form *is-sa-an-qú-ni-ik-kum* (5.135) is not included after being collated as *is-**sà**-an-qú-ni-ik-kum*. S. Streck 2006: 223.

19. Z-sign used for a simple intervocalic sibilant.

20. For the contact of Š+Š see Streck 2011: 20, §44: "/š/ in Kontakt mit anlautendem /š/ der Pronominalsuffixe wird meist S, seltener Z geschrieben." See also in other letters from Hammurabi: *e-ri-is-su* (13.7) or *e-te-er-ri-is-su-ma* (13.27).

21. Notice also that the orthographic pattern in Hammurabi's letters in this case is directly opposite to Lu-Ninurta's, where *-lum*, *-lim*, *-li*, *-lam* and *-el* (typical southern OB) are used ninety-four times to complement A.ŠÀ for only ten times *-am*, *-im* or *-um*.

22. The other exception, ***si**-it-ti* (9.200) might belong to a different type of phonological process: a variation on some lexical items between /s/ and /š/. Von Soden *AHw*, s.v. "šittum," hints: "*šittum, sittum:* a) südbab: *si-it-ti*." A grammatical or phonological cause for the variation is, of course, not discarded. Cf. other forms with ṢI in Lu-Ninurta's letters: *ú-še-ṣi* (4.125), *ṣi-bu-ut* (4. 69), *ṣi-im-da-at* (4.56), etc.

and I will then question if all the exceptions to the variable (s, z) can be conditioned by particular phonological or lexical constraints, and whether an examination of the distribution of the exceptions can point to any kind of underlying pattern.

As is well known, the corpus of laws generally follows the Old Babylonian affricate/fricative distributional pattern explained in *GAG* §30. However, Sommerfeld 2006 crucially proved that the Code of Hammurabi is a rather heterogeneous text with an extensive group of orthographic differences and phonological variables. Dialectal differences in Old Babylonian were also explained.[23]

That same year A. Westenholz (2006: 258–260 [appendix]) offered a group of examples ("merely illustrative") that evidence some dialectal variation in the use of signs for sibilants in Old Babylonian.

On the other hand, the latest state-of-the-art study on Old Babylonian sibilants is M. P. Streck 2006, a thorough study of occurrences covering the Code of Hammurabi, letters and inscriptions of Hammurabi, and the letters of the governors of Qaṭṭunan. The other variable of our concern, (ṣi, ṣí), has been analyzed by L. Kogan 2004, who presents a distributional analysis of the signs ZI and ZÍ in the Code of Hammurabi. However, and despite the number of grammatical or phonological factors taken into account in the last two studies, the question of the irregular distribution of the variables remains unclear (Streck 2006: 225, 240; Kogan 2004: 19). Both studies examine the bulk of attestations basing their analysis on the assumption of the existence of a general standard Old Babylonian linguistic system (Mari and other peripheral regions excluded) and do not consider the pragmatic and sociolinguistic diversity that—as suggested before—operates in Old Babylonian. Correspondingly, the texts are thought to display a "relatively uniform corpus," (Streck 2006: 215) and even the items belonging to the literary parts of the Code of Hammurabi are only secondarily mentioned as potentially significant for explaining the distribution of the variables.[24]

In the present study I will focus exclusively on the variation in the text of the laws of the Code of Hammurabi, disregarding the prologue and the epilogue since they convey a different register and therefore could alter the initially expected uniformity of the corpus of laws.[25]

According to this, I draw out the following orthographic (or phonological) variants:[26]

1. SÀ/SA signs: thirty-five occurrences; four exceptions to the deaffrication rule, all of them use of the Z-sign for expected SA: *i-**sà**-ak-ki-il*, *ú-**sà**-ah-ha-mu-ši*, *ú-**sà**-ap-pa-ah* (twice); (11.4 percent exceptions).[27]
2. SÍ/SI/SI$_{20}$ signs: eleven occurrences; two exceptions (both use of ZÍ): ***si$_{20}$**-im-ma-am*; (18.2 percent exceptions).[28]

23. See Sommerfeld 2006: 371–374 for a view of the sibilants in OB texts from the Diyala region.

24. Kogan (2004: 20) acknowledges, however, that most of the exceptions to his hypothesis occur in the literary parts of the CH and also ponders the possibility of conflation of orthographic traditions in the CH.

25. Unless otherwise indicated, I will refer to the CH text from the version preserved in the stele of the Louvre in Paris.

26. Excluded from §§1, 2, and 3 are the Z- or S-signs resulting from contact between dental or sibilant plus suffix. They are presented separately in §§4 and 5.

27. Cf. other forms from the CH laws like *i-<u>sa</u>-ad-dar-ma* (twice) or *ú-<u>sa</u>-ar-ri-ir-ma*. See Streck 2006 for a commented list of all the occurrences and their locations.

28. Cf. five occurrences in CH laws of *sí-im-ma-am*.

3. SÚ/SU signs: twenty-one occurrences; one exception SU for expected Z-sign in ***su**-ni-ša*; two cases with no clear reading; (5.2 percent of exceptions).[29]
4. Signs resulting from contact between a dental or sibilant (apart from Š) + Š from a suffix: ninety-three occurrences; one orthographic exception: *mu-**sa₆***; (1.1 percent).[30]
5. Š (from a root) + Š from a suffix: two occurrences; one exception, use of ZA for an expected SA: *er-re-**sà***; (50 percent exceptions).[31]
6. ṢI: nine occurrences
7. ṢÍ: fourteen occurrences
8. A less frequent sign present in the corpus of laws to render sibilants is ZÍ for the (conventionally transliterated) forms /zi/ and /ze/. ZÍ is used three times (all for the form ***zí**-it-tam*) whereas ZI is used twenty-three times (including ***zi**-it-tim* or ***zi**-it-ti-ša* [twice]). For /ze/, ZÍ appears four times (e.g., *i-**zé**-er-ma*) against three times ZI (including also the form *i-ze-er-ma*).[32]

In comparison with the letters sent by Hammurabi shown in §2.2, the variants in the laws of the Code of Hammurabi bear important peculiarities:

1. The laws in the Code of Hammurabi present more variation for the variable (s, z) than the corpus of letters from the king himself in Altbabylonische Briefe. Although the alternation of CV Z-signs and S-signs to render the alleged affricate/fricative allophones of /s/ is generally followed (always in the case of contact of a dental or sibilant and a suffixal /š/), there are exceptions to this rule:[33]

Only the use of the variants SÚ or SU seems to behave differently from the rest, presenting more unexpected spellings in the letters than in the laws. However, we must keep in mind that these two signs have a very similar shape, and therefore are considered a less safe determinant for variation (A. Westenholz, 2006: 258), especially in the cursive script of the Old Babylonian letters.[34]

It is remarkable that even though letters are generally supposed to be a better source for evidence in variationist linguistics (they often show fewer conventions than public texts and therefore they tend to make use of different features more specific to the vernacular language), the laws have a wider range of orthographic variation.

2. In the corpus of laws there is a balanced number of occurrences of signs ṢI (nine times) and ṢÍ (fourteen).[35] The letters sent by Hammurabi in Altbabylonische Briefe,

29. For SU for expected Z-sign, cf. *sú-ni-ša* (twice) and *sú-un* (twice) in other parts of the CH laws. For ZU?-*qá-am*, see Streck 2006: 219 n.17. For *it-tar-ka*-ZU?-*ma*, Borger 2006: I:24: "*sú(? su?)*."

30. Cf. *mu-sà* (18 times). For the interpretation of SA₆ as "an archaic member of the Z-sign," see Streck 2006: 224.

31. The other form is *er-re-**su**-ma*.

32. Although in the Old Babylonian record ZI is overwhelmingly more frequent than ZÍ to render /zi/, it is not so unusual to find ZÍ for /ze/, e.g., *zé-eh-pí*.

33. Cases of contact of a dental or sibilant and a suffixal /š/ are not included in the table.

34. If we follow A. Westenholz's principle and do not consider the SÚ/SU variable cell, the different occurrences of nonstandard orthographies in the CH and in Hammurabi letters are also statistically significant (p=0.02).

35. Kogan (2004) pointed to the fact that the variation between the two signs could be related not only to consonantal features but also to a vocalic difference.

TABLE 10.8. Relative frequency of nonstandard orthographies of the variable (s, z) in Hammurabi's letters and in CH.

| | Hammurabi's letters | | | CH | | |
|---|---|---|---|---|---|---|
| | **Total (N)** | **Nonstandard** | **Percent** | **Total (N)** | **Nonstandard** | **Percent** |
| /$^{t}$sa/, /sa/ | 26 | 0 | 0% | 35 | 4 | 11% |
| /$^{t}$si/, /si/ | 27 | 0 | 0% | 11 | 2 | 18% |
| /$^{t}$su/, /su/ | 23 | 3 | 13% | 21 | 1 | 5% |
| /sV/>/š+š/ | 6 | 1 | 17% | 2 | 1 | 50% |
| Total | 82 | 4 | 5% | 69 | 8 | 12% |

however, consistently use only the sign ṢI (twenty-three times). A purely quantitative analysis cannot establish formal differences since most of the twenty-three tokens in the letters belong to the same word types, but it is noteworthy to compare similar forms like those shown in table 10.7 supra.[36]

3. All in all, there is an important difference in the range of orthographic variation for sibilants between the corpus of letters sent by Hammurabi and the corpus of laws of the Code of Hammurabi, even though they allegedly belong to the same type of linguistic register (unlike the prologue and the epilogue). The gap is even more significant when we take into account the fact that the letters form a necessarily uneven corpus, since they were written in diverse chronological, pragmatic, or geographical conditions (or by different hands).

If we took the corpus of laws of the Code of Hammurabi as a uniform and standardized text, the exceptions to the variable (s, z) observed before could be seen as conditioned by internal Old Babylonian phonological or lexical constraints. Streck (2006: 224) shows some possible examples of this in a few loanwords or in the root SDR, the attestations of which consistently present S-signs at word-initial position.

Can all the exceptions to the variables in the Code of Hammurabi be the result of general Old Babylonian phonetic or phonological constraints? In some cases, such as for the unexpected spelling ***si***$_{20}$*-im-ma-am* (XIX rev. 21), we find the exact lexical counterpart elsewhere in the laws, written with the expected Z-sign *sí-im-ma-am* (XVIII rev. 7, 56, 75; XIX rev. 30; XXVIII rev. 57), which suggests that a consistent lexico-phonological distinction would not explain the different orthographic choice here.[37] For the exceptions *ú-**sà**-ap-pa-ah* (VII rev. 41; VIII rev. 8), *ú-**sà**-ah-ha-mu-ši* (XIII rev. 18), and *i-**sà**-ak-ki-il* (VII rev. 40) we do not have identical counterparts in the Code of Hammurabi, so a certain constraint could not, in principle, be discarded. Some Old Babylonian letters in Altbabylonische Briefe show similar (although not identical) phonological items, with the expected S-sign: *ú-sa-ap-pí-ih* (7.187), but also with the exceptional Z-sign: *ú-**sà**-a[p-p]a-hu-ma* (9.20). The latter is the phonetically most similar form to the Code of Hammurabi *ú-**sà**-ap-pa-ah* (in AbB) and admittedly behaves

36. Esp. the forms of *ṣimdum*, *ṣimdatum*, or *ṣibtum*: *ṣi-im-da-tim* (5×), *ṣi-im-dam*, *ṣi-im-dam-ma*, *ṣi-bi-it* (4×), *ṣi-bi-is-sú-nu* (3×), *ṣi-bi-is-sú*, *ṣi-bi-it-ni*.

37. In some cases even the phonic context of the form is identical: *ù lu* ANŠE ***si***$_{20}$*-im-ma-am kab-tam* (XIX rev. 20–21); *ù lu* ANŠE ***sí**-im-ma-am kab-tam* (XIX rev. 29–30).

like the two exceptions in the Code of Hammurabi. This similarity seems to be relevant from a purely intralinguistic grammatical view, but taking into account sociolinguistic factors, we find that the sender, Shamash-hazir, writing letters to a certain Belshunu, uses almost exclusively Z-signs for /s/ in his letters, even in occurrences where S-signs would have been expected, like in *i-ip-ru-**sà**-[a]m* (9.137). He cannot therefore be considered a paradigmatic member of the group of individuals who used spellings according to the deaffrication rule. His letters seem rather to belong to a group where the Z-sign/S-sign interchange is not consistently distinguished and Z-signs are favored for most instances of /s/.[38] Not surprisingly, the opposite case is also possible and other occurrences of expected spellings of the variable (s, z) in the Code of Hammurabi can be compared to irregular spellings in the Old Babylonian letters. For example, *ú-<u>sa</u>-an-ni-iq-ma* (XXI rev. 59), finds a counterpart in a letter by Silli-Shamash from Larsa: *ú-**sà**-an-ni-qá-am-ma* (10.193). Previously, it was shown that the letters from Silli-Shamash in Altbabylonische Briefe present only the Z-sign variant. For more cases of Z-signs for intervocalic /s/ in texts from Larsa and Kutalla, see A. Westenholz 2006: 259.

In summary, the fact that the linguistic situation in Old Babylonian at the time of the Code of Hammurabi is not completely uniform prevents us from inferring generalizations on phonological or grammatical constraints applicable to every occurrence of unexpected orthographies in different Old Babylonian texts. If there were such constraints for the five exceptions to the use of SÀ or SA in the laws of the Code of Hammurabi, it would be necessary to refine the search for the sociolinguistic or dialectal parameters responsible for the uneven distribution of its variables among the diverse array of Old Babylonian texts.

The second issue that deserves consideration is the distribution of nonstandard occurrences of the variables. Some significant peculiarities have already been shown for the Altbabylonische Briefe letters sent by Hammurabi and Lu-Ninurta, where some particular letters bore more unexpected spellings in relation to the rest of the letters of the individual corpus. Can an examination of the distribution of the exceptions in the Code of Hammurabi also show any kind of pattern? Kogan (2004: 19), in his analysis of the distribution of ZI and ZÍ signs proposed that some segments of the Code of Hammurabi are particularly salient in as much as they gather the attestations for exceptional usage of the ṢI sign, attributing it to a consistent use in these portions of the Code of Hammurabi of "the 'Standard Babylonian' orthographic system."

The idea of a Standard Babylonian orthography is difficult to maintain after examining Old Babylonian school letters and official letters (supra). However, the orthographic heterogeneity of the Code of Hammurabi (Sommerfeld 2006) and the acknowledgment of the chronological, stylistic, and geographic variety of the Old Babylonian language suggest that an irregular distribution of the variants could convey significant information.

For the present study I have chosen to isolate the parts of the Code of Hammurabi laws where we find the sign SÀ for the expected sign SA.[39] They are presented in

38. Maybe also rendering a phonological distinction.

39. This is only a representative sample of a salient combination of different variants in particular parts of the laws. Other unusual orthographic peculiarities such as the sign $SI_{20}$ are not present in table 10.9. See Sommerfeld 2006.

TABLE 10.9. Laws in CH in which the five cases of SÀ instead of the expected SA occurred, and content-related laws 142 and 179 with their relevant orthographic features.

| **§ 141** | **§ 142 (aforegoing to 143)** | **§143** |
|---|---|---|
| ***i-sà-ak-ki-il*** (for SA)<br>***ú-sà-ap-pa-ah*** (for SA)<br>***e-zé-eb-ša***<br>***e-zé-eb-ša***<br>*i-iz-**zi**-ib-ši*<br>***sí**-ki-il-tam* | ***mu-sa₆***<br>***wa-ṣí-ma***<br>*i-ze-er-ma* | ***ú-sà-ap-pa-ah*** (for SA)<br>***wa-ṣí-a-at***<br>***bi**-sà* (syllabic for É) |
| **§ 172** | **§ 178** | **§179 (related to 178)** |
| ***ú-sà-ah-ha-mu-ši*** (for SA)<br>***zí-it-tam***<br>***uṣ-ṣí***<br>***šu-ṣí-im***<br>*i-pár-ra-**su**-ma*<br>*i-iz-**zi**-ib* | ***e-re-sà*** (for SA ([š+š]))[a]<br>***ú-ša-am-ṣí-ši***<br>***ì-kal***<br>*i-na-ad-di-nu-**šim**-ma*<br>***zi**-it-ti-ša* | ***uš-tam-ṣí-ši*** |

[a] This is also the only exception of a Z-sign for a contact [š+š] found by A. Westenholz 2006 on his OB survey.

table 10.9 under the law number where they occur (plus two coadjacent and related laws: §§142 and 179).[40] The table also shows every other occurrence in said laws of CV-signs of the variable (s, z) and (ṣi, ṣí), as well as other relevant orthographic singularities with special attention given to the use of signs ZI and ZÍ to render /zi/.

The five exceptional usages of SÀ for the variable (s, z) are concentrated in a rather small and specific part of the laws.[41] Moreover, they knit together a large percentage of exceptional or less frequent spellings in the whole corpus of laws, including:

1. One of the three occurrences of sign ZÍ to render /zi/: ***zí-it-tam***.[42] The other two cases occur in nearby laws §137 and §180, out of the range of this chart but related to §§141 and 178 respectively. (Its counterpart, ZI for /zi/, occurs twenty times in the laws).
2. Two of a total of four instances of sign ZÍ rendering /zé/ (*e-**zé**-eb-ša*). The other two cases are in §137 (which also has the unusual ***zí**-it-tam*) and §193. The counterpart sign ZI for /ze/ is only used three times in the laws, including §142, in the table.[43]

40. Unexpected or less frequent spellings and occurrences of ṢÍ are in bold. The division of the text in laws to show the variables that they include is conventional and serves the purpose of helping to visualize the distributional patterns. It does not necessary imply that there exists a rigid orthographic or linguistic boundary.

41. On the other hand, the five laws of the table are not orthographically homogeneous and also employ expected spellings. E.g., law 172 alternates a Z-sign and a S-sign for simple intervocalic sibilants (*ú-**sà**-ah-ha-mu-ši* but *i-pár-ra-**su**-ma*).

42. Alternating in the same group we find in §178 ***zi**-it-ti-ša*.

43. Admittedly, it is difficult in this case to assign the label "unexpected" to ZÉ since it is not uncommon in OB texts.

3. The only use in the whole corpus of a verb *prima alef* in present tense without a double sign for the initial cluster {i-iC-}: ***ì-kal*** (recalling an older spelling tradition) against more than twenty examples throughout the text of forms like *i-ip-pa-al*, *i-ik-ka-al*, *i-il-la-ak*, and so on. It also presents the only syllabic use of the sign Ì.
4. The only syllabic writing ***bi-sà*** against nine logographic É plus phonetic complement.
5. The only use of $SA_6$ throughout the corpus of laws.[44]
6. One of four uses of the sign ŠIM in the laws, for eighty times *ši-im*, including the same law.
7. Finally they present a constant use of emphatic ṢÍ, six times (out of a total of fourteen in the whole group of laws) with no occurrence of ṢI (which occurs nine times in the laws, mainly at word-initial position).

Regarding the last observation, the use of only one of the signs from the variable (ṣi, ṣí) in this section of the laws, it could of course be due exclusively to phonological or lexical reasons.[45] It is also important to underline the fact that other parts of the laws show S-signs for intervocalic /s/ and also ṢÍ: §16: *ši-**si**-it*; *uš-te-**ṣí**-a-am* (VIII.44; 46). Strict clear-cut divisions that set apart well-defined segments do not seem to exist in the corpus of laws, but rather some sections present a greater density of differences in the choice of a nonexpected variants compared to the rest of the laws or to the letters of King Hammurabi.

Moreover, the distribution of the variants in other Old Babylonian copies of the laws differ crucially from those on the stele. In the laws from duplicate *r)* we find a contrast in the forms *ú-**ṣí**-a-am-ma* and *ú-ṣi-a-am* (both rendered in the stele with ṢÍ (V.62; VI.2).[46] This shows that Old Babylonian duplicates, although showing some degree of variation as well, are not restricted by exactly the same rules as the laws on the stele when rendering the variables.[47] The inclination to consider these duplicates as copies affected to a certain extent by extralinguistic factors (such as some sort of contrast between the model from where the copy was written and the linguistic or orthographic background of the copyist) can also be applied to the text on the stele in the Louvre. Obviously, the pragmatic function of the text on the stele is different from that of the larger Old Babylonian duplicates, and subsequently an aesthetic or stylistic element can also be taken into consideration. However, the stylistic variability

44. It is also highly infrequent in OB letters, although it is attested in royal inscriptions, see table 10.1, and also in the prologue of the CH.

45. Notice that the four cases in the laws of the phonic segment {ṣi-bV} are consistently written with the sign ṢI.

46. For *r)*, see Borger 2006: 4 for references to all the duplicates of the CH and their designations, which I follow here. See also Oelsner 2012 for a complete and updated account of the duplicates of the CH. For the contrasting forms, see Borger 2006: 11. See also comments on the difficulties of *r)* in Borger 2006: 4. Finkelstein (1967) does not show this deviation. In general, OB duplicates of the laws of Hammurabi substitute ṢÍ signs for ṢI signs: tablet *r)*: *ú-ṣi-a-am-ma* (§3), *u-še-ṣi-ma* (§44); tablet *S)*: *ma-ha-ṣi-im* (§116), *wa-ṣ[i-ma]* (§142). Evidence for the opposite, change from ṢI to ṢÍ, has not been attested in the major OB tablets *r)* and *S)*.

47. Many other spelling and morpho-phonological differences also exist between the laws on the stele and on OB duplicates.

of orthographies in the stele would not explain why it affects signs that surely had a phonetic/phonological distinctive trait, like the signs SÀ and SA, which clearly emerge according to a determined pattern. Also, the uneven distribution of exceptions to the variables of this study, or the extraordinary exceptional use of some archaic features like the form *ì-kal* (§178) cast doubts on a plausible conscious attempt by the scribe(s) to use the variation with a consistent stylistic purpose.[48] Furthermore, other texts of a public nature like the contemporary royal inscriptions shown before show some degree of dialectal influence in their use of sibilants, like the preference for Z-signs in Larsa (table 10.3), which resembles the same preference in groups of letters like those sent by Silli-Shamash, or the use of word-initial S-signs in Dadusha's inscription (table 10.2), clearly similar to other texts from the Diyala valley (Sommerfeld 2006: 371–374).[49] The variability in the Code of Hammurabi mirrors the productive differences of diatopic, diachronic, or diastratic nature in the broad spectrum of the Old Babylonian language.

## Conclusions

The Old Babylonian language at the time of Hammurabi was not uniform. This general statement, valid for any language at any given time becomes observable at least in the case of graphical representation of sibilants in Old Babylonian, which probably rendered different phonetic realities. Subsequently, different types of texts, particularly scribal and official letters, corroborate the idea that the time of Hammurabi did not witness a rigid orthographic prescriptivism for Old Babylonian. Hence, any attempts to draw general grammatical rules for such a variation need to take into account the sociolinguistic and chronological determinants of specific samples. The two variables introduced here (s, z) and (ṣi, ṣí) can be the subject of variationist research for Old Babylonian from which we can expect more than one system of representation accomplished under different determinants, including geographical, chronological, or social factors, in a complex process toward a Middle Babylonian stage where fricative S-signs and ṢI signs are more frequent in the written evidence.[50]

Even though the language of the Code of Hammurabi generally follows the orthographic patterns for sibilants stated in *GAG* §30, a careful study of all the cases reveals an underlying internal variation that does not match either quantitatively nor qualitatively other relevant corpora, more particularly the letters sent from the royal palace by King Hammurabi in Altbabylonische Briefe.[51] The laws show a higher degree of

48. It also does not explain the contemporary variability across texts, like the forms of the scribal exercises of table 10.4.

49. For Silli-Shamash, see also A. Westenholz 2006: 259, 5. On his survey the "inconvenient dated evidence" for a single intervocalic /s/ NOT written with an expected S-sign: *i-ZI-ig-šu*, *i-ZA-hu-ra-ak-kum*, and *i-Z[A-k]i-bu-šu*, come from Kutalla and Larsa at the time of Rim-Sin for the first two cases, and Lagaba for the last one, the reading of which is "not certain." These forms curiously resemble the four exceptional uses of SÀ in the laws of the CH shown in table 10.9.

50. Notice however that the written evidence from MB is sparser and less representative of the different areas than that of the OB texts.

51. The relevance of the comparison between these two corpora is justified since they are supposed to bear a similar register, see *GAG* §2d: "das Ergebnis einer bewussten Sprachreform ist die

variation and more occurrences of infrequent spellings from nonliterary Old Babylonian texts. They also present different types of exceptions, the more important being those where Z-signs occur, in opposition to the late Old Babylonian tendency to increase the use of S-signs.[52] The results of the variationist approach show that the corpus of letters from Hammurabi, consisting of 187 different texts (which contain approximately 8700 complete word tokens of about 2200 word types) present less variation than the single, although large, text of the laws, less spontaneous and more carefully written on a monumental stele (with approximately 5500 word tokens of around 1200 word types).[53]

The distributional patterns of the variants in the Code of Hammurabi compared to the distributional patterns in the corpus of letters suggest that the lack of uniformity in the laws cannot only be explained with grammatical or stylistic constraints. The variants could be motivated by social and linguistic correlation parameters, such as different time, sources, geographies, or registers underlying the final completion of the texts on the stele.[54]

Along this line Sommerfeld (pers. comm.) and Kogan (2004: 20) have hinted at a sort of source criticism for the Code of Hammurabi. On a different historical and content-driven view, D. Charpin 2003 and M. Van de Mieroop 2005 coincide in the analysis that

> the Code of Hammurabi belongs to a tradition of similar, older texts, from which it borrowed a great deal. It also resulted from the king's judicial activities. "Traditional" cases and those judged by the king were systematized with the aim of giving the code the appearance of an exhaustive collection. (Charpin 2010: 72)

> For certain of his laws clear antecedents exist. . . . When Hammurabi's code was written, the authors thus based themselves partly on these older texts. Since Hammurabi's code was longer, however, they needed to formulate new cases, and probably used various means to do so. . . . It seems also that actual verdicts by the king lay at the basis of new clauses. (Van De Mieroop 2005: 109)

In summary, the variationist perspective in the study of the orthography of two variables, (s, z) and (ṣi, ṣí), encounters in the Code of Hammurabi a quantitatively reduced sample size. However, even though the limitations of a statistical comparison

Verwaltungssprache Hammurabis (1728–1686), die uns in seinen Gesetzen und den Briefen seiner Kanzlei bezeugt ist."

52. See examples for this in A. Westenholz 2006: 259 n.4, 206 n.7.

53. Word token count is according to the conventions for Akkadian words in transcriptions. This account is general and does not exclude the occurrences of PNs or GNs, far more numerous in the letters and not studied in the present survey.

54. According to Hernández Campoy and Almeida (2005: 86) it is not unusual in historical-sociolinguistic studies to deal with documents which either present: "artificial internal variation—with many fragments written in different dialects—since the text bears a mixture of the original dialect and that of the scribe or scribes" or "(motivated), given the continuing evolution of language, merely by the time of writing" (my translation). For the concept of *Mischsprache* in composite texts see Laing 1989. Notice that other OB copies of the CH (like *r)*) do present a clearer mixing of linguistic features in the writing of variable (ṣi, ṣí), but also in other variables like the presence or absence of mimation or initial /w/.

between such different corpora could not dismiss categorically a merely random fluctuation of the variants; their occurrences and distribution plus several other orthographic peculiarities of the text differ convincingly from a selected group of Old Babylonian texts, including the Altbabylonische Briefe letters sent by King Hammurabi himself. The case of the orthography of sibilants (s, z) is particularly relevant since they represent a phonetic/phonological change that was happening in Old Babylonian. A further study of a wider spectrum and quantity of texts, contemporary with the Code of Hammurabi, would be expected to reinforce the present conclusions according to which said variables, present in the Code of Hammurabi, behave in a different way in texts from different areas and times, and therefore are neither just free variables nor altogether grammatically motivated, but are also contextually or socio-historically significant.

## BIBLIOGRAPHY

Borger, R.
2006 *Babylonisch-assyrische Lesestücke*. 3rd ed. AnOr 54. Rome: Pontifical Biblical Institute.

Charpin, D.
2003 *Hammu-rabi de Babylone*. Paris: Presses Universitaires de France.
2004 Histoire politique du Proche-Orient amorrite (2005–1595). Pp. 25–480 in *Mesopotamien: Die altbabylonische Zeit*. By D. Charpin, D. O. Edzard, and M. Stol. OBO 160.4. Fribourg: Academic Press; Göttingen: Vandenhoeck & Ruprecht.
2008 *Lire et écrire à Babylone*. Paris: Presses Universitaires de France.
2010 *Writing, Law, and Kingship in Old Babylonian Mesopotamia*. Translated by J. M. Todd. Chicago: University of Chicago Press.

Finkelstein, J. J.
1967 A Late Old Babylonian Copy of the Laws of Hammurapi. *JCS* 21: 39–48.

Frankena, R.
1974 *Briefe aus dem Berliner Museum*. AbB 6. Leiden: Brill.

Frayne, D.
1990 *Old Babylonian Period (2003–1595 BC)*. RIME 4. Toronto: University of Toronto Press.

Gelb, I. J.
1948 A New Clay-Nail of Hammurabi. *JNES* 7: 267–271.

Goetze, A.
1958a Fifty Old-Babylonian Letters from Harmal. *Sumer* 14: 3–78.
1958b The Sibilants of Old Babylonian. *RA* 52: 137–149.

Hernández Campoy, J. M. and Almeida, M.
2005 *Metodología de la investigación sociolingüística*. Estudios de lengua inglesa 12. Málaga, Comares.

Hurowitz, V. A.
2011 What Was Codex Hammurabi, and What Did It Become? *Maarav* 18: 89–100.

Ismaïl, B. H. and Cavigneaux, A.
2003 Dādušas Siegesstele IM 95200 aus Ešnunna: Die Inschrift. *BaM* 34: 129–156.

Kogan, L.
2004 ZI and ṢI in Codex Hammurāpi (with an Appendix on the Laws of Eshnunna). *Babel und Bibel* 1: 13–22.

Kraus, F. R.
1959 Briefschreibübungen im Altbabylonischen Schulunterricht. *JEOL* 16: 16–39.

Laing, M.
1989 Dialectal Analysis and Linguistically Composite Texts in Middle English. Pp. 150–169 in *Middle English Dialectology: Essays on Some Principles and Problems.* Edited by A. McIntosh, M. L. Samuels, and M. Laing. Aberdeen: Aberdeen University Press.

Oelsner, J.
2012 Zur Einteilung des Kodex Hammu-rāpi im Altertum. *ZABR* 18: 79–125.

Sallaberger, W.
1999 *"Wenn Du mein Bruder bist . . ." Interaktion und Textgestaltung in altbabylonischen Alltagsbriefen.* CM 16. Groningen: Styx.

Soden, W. von
1931 Der hymnisch-epische Dialekt des Akkadischen. *ZA* 40–41: 163–227.

Sommerfeld, W.
2006 Varianten in der Keilschrift-Orthographie und die historische Phonologie des Akkadischen. Pp. 359–376 in *Šapal tibnim mû illakū: Studies Presented to Joaquín Sanmartín on the Occasion of His 65th Birthday.* Edited by G. del Olmo Lete, L. Feliu, and A. Millet Albà. AuOrSup 22. Sabadell: AUSA.

Streck, M. P.
2006 Sibilants in the Old Babylonian Texts of Hammurapi and of the Governors in Qaṭṭunān. Pp. 215–251 in *The Akkadian Language in Its Semitic Context: Studies in the Akkadian of the Third and Second Millennium BC.* Edited by G. Deutscher and N. J. C. Kouwenberg. PIHANS 106. Leiden: Nederlands instituut voor het Nabije Oosten.
2011 *Altbabylonisches Lehrbuch.* PLO 23. Wiesbaden: Harrassowitz.

Van De Mieroop M.
2005 *King Hammurabi of Babylon: A Biography.* Oxford: Blackwell.

Westenholz, A.
2006 Do Not Trust the Assyriologists! (Some Remarks on the Transliteration and Normalization of Old Babylonian Akkadian). Pp. 252–260 in *The Akkadian Language in Its Semitic Context: Studies in the Akkadian of the Third and Second Millennium BC.* Edited by G. Deutscher and N. J. C. Kouwenberg. PIHANS 106. Leiden: Nederlands instituut voor het Nabije Oosten.

Worthington, M. J. V.
2010 *i-ba-aš-šu-ú* vs. *i-ba-aš-šu* from Old to Neo-Babylonian. Pp. 661–706 in *Language in the Ancient Near East.* Edited by L. Kogan, N. Koslova, S. Loesov, and S. Tishchenko. Babel und Bibel 4.2. Winona Lake, IN: Eisenbrauns.

CHAPTER 11

# "For Each Runaway Assyrian Fugitive, Let Me Replace Him One Hundred-Fold": Fugitives/ Runaways in the Neo-Assyrian Empire

Krzysztof Hipp

THIS PAPER AIMS TO PRESENT one aspect of what we regard as disorder, a form of anarchy affecting any socio-political structure, that for thousands of years has characterized the relations between some individuals at the one extreme and the authority at the other, namely various motivated escapes from the existing social environment, this time of the Neo-Assyrian Empire. I was stimulated to take up this topic because of my research interests comprising, among others, contacts between Urartu and Assyria and smaller political entities sandwiched between the rival empires. They seem to have been a safe haven for fugitives. This has not been subject to a thorough analysis in the broader context of the whole empire.[1]

At the beginning, I would like to emphasize that in terms of genre the relevant sources concerning fugitives are varied, but not numerous. Additionally, due to their fragmentary state of preservation we are not able to draw far-reaching conclusions or generalizations. Frequently we have only a small piece of information about a given event without a more detailed context. In many cases it is impossible to answer such basic questions as to who the fugitive was, where he came from, or to where he fled. But above all, what motives made him run away and whether he succeeded in this risky enterprise.

As far as the relevant sources are concerned, we have in total over 120 documents at our disposal that contain some information, sometimes only a short and inconclusive piece, about fugitives.[2] Of that number 70 are of particular importance and interest to us, because the event is set in a broader context. Of course, the most extensive and important group comprises the royal correspondence from the time of the Sargonids, whose addressee was usually the king himself. Less numerous, but also significant, are the interstate treaties, administrative records, and Esarhaddon's Letter to the God describing the campaign against the land of Šubria in 673 BCE.

*Author's Note:* The title is a quotation from Esarhaddon's Letter to the God. Translation by Leichty 2011, RINAP 4.33 tablet 2 obv. i:16.

1. The problem of runaways in the Neo-Assyrian Empire was outlined by Lanfranchi (1997: 85–86 and n. 33).

2. Full bibliographical information for all SAA volumes is given in the bibliography. SAA 1: 8, 23, 30, 35, 128, 171, 179, 183, 194, 195, 197, 223, 235, 240, 244, 245, 246; SAA 2: 1, 2, 6, 9; SAA 5: 11, 32, 34, 35, 36, 48, 52, 53, 54, 79, 100, 121, 128, 227, 228, 245; SAA 7: 112; SAA 8: 456; SAA 10: 111, 160; SAA 11: 159, 162, 163, 169, 203, 207; SAA 13: 20, 33, 107, 171, 178; SAA 15: 1, 43, 53, 54, 62, 74, 75, 91, 101, 147, 150, 151, 169, 184, 216, 232, 243, 244, 255, 285, 292, 294, 300, 315; SAA 16: 34, 122, 136, 148, 186; SAA 17: 89, 99, 132, 148, 149; SAA 18: 6, 7, 24, 39, 61, 65, 72, 84, 124, 125, 148, 170, 176, 180, 183, 184, 185, 194, 198; SAA 19: 31, 40, 44, 45, 48, 93, 126, 183, 186, 188.

If we take a closer look at the geography of escapes, it seems that this social phenomenon was more common in the northern and eastern provinces than in the west, which may be due to two reasons. One is a general predominance of the records from the former regions, and the other—a close proximity of the inaccessible terrain of the Taurus and Zagros Mountains, where Assyrian control was limited or simply did not exist. A good example here is the, already mentioned, land of Šubria, a buffer statelet.[3] Due to its location and, as T. Dezsö (2006: 37–38) and later K. Radner (2012: 263) convincingly pointed out, due to its religious sanctuary, it willingly accepted fugitives both from Assyria and Urartu, granting land, gardens, and houses to them (SAA 5: 52, rev. 2–rev. 6).[4] This country was a safe haven to "robbers, thieves, or those who had sinned, those who had shed blood, [. . . offi]cials, governors, overseers, leaders, (and) soldiers" (RINAP 4.33.ii.1–ii.3). It is obvious that fugitives always attempt to seek shelter in the countries that can protect them from their persecutors and where they can feel beyond the reach of justice and punishment. Therefore, the northern rival of Assyria, Urartu and the Mannean provinces, were popular destinations for runaways. Aside from the escapes to the neighboring countries, fugitives ran away within the Assyrian Empire, for example, from one province to another.

It is also interesting to investigate the escapes in the opposite direction, from another country to Assyria. This problem will be dealt with in due course.

Individuals or small groups of a few people were those who primarily decided to run away. This modus operandi is understandable. A sudden disappearance of one or two people may have gone unnoticed for a longer period of time, and consequently the chances of a successful escape increased considerably. But there are exceptions to this rule. For example, Ša-Aššūr-dubbu , governor of the province of Tušḫan, informs the king about the escape of 40 soldiers to Šubria (SAA 5: 35), and from the letter of Aššūr-bēlu-da"in in SAA 5: 79 we learn about a wave of escapes that swept across the province of Ḫalzi-atbāri. He reports to the king that 380 fugitives have been captured and probably several dozen are still on the run. Unfortunately, we do not know the underlying causes of these events.

Although Marduk of Borsippa writes to the king that "N[o] one who sins against the lord of kings [e]scapes." (SAA 18: 176, rev. 10–rev. 11; trans. Reynolds 2003), only part of the document relates that the escapes failed and the sinners were captured. However, if they did succeed, a number of steps were taken. An investigation was being conducted; an interrogation was underway (SAA 1: 194), and consequently a manhunt started.[5] The fugitive's place of residence was searched and the area where he came from was checked (SAA 1: 245).[6] We know that in some cases the searching party was despatched to the dangerous hostile territories of the land of Šubria, where they were exposed to attacks and ambushes (SAA 5: 32).

Who were the fugitives in terms of their social background? They were people from various strata. In the sources the most numerous group comprises those from the

3. A key destination for runaways: SAA 5: 32, 34, 35, 52, 53, 54; SAA 19: 186.

4. The letter from Aššūr-dūr-pānīja, governor of Til-Barsip, to Sargon II.

5. The context of SAA 1: 194 is uncertain but it seems that Sargon is asked to investigate the matter of some missing cavalrymen from the royal corps stationed in Ḫarrān.

6. In SAA 1: 245 a man is wanted by the king. His hometown was checked and the fugitive's brother was questioned.

lowest stratum—servants/slaves and deportees from the newly subdued lands. Their motives are rarely known. Probably, the main reason was unbearable living conditions or too heavy *ilku* burdens. In the letter SAA 1: 183 an unknown official writes to Sargon that the *ilku* burdens have made many people of Carchemish flee to Arpad. And the deportees from Tabal, due to a shortage of provisions (inter alia homes and livestock), escaped from the province of Parsua to Mannea (SAA 15: 54, Nabû- rēmanni's letter). Escapes of highly qualified artisans were a particularly heavy loss because it was not easy to find replacements, for example, carpenters from Ṣūpat in letter SAA 1: 179.

Army deserters quite frequently appear in the sources. They were mainly from cavalry units. Besides ordinary soldiers we can also encounter high-ranking officers among runaways. For example, a commander-of-fifty of the Gurrean troops from Mēturna, who wanted to avoid being prosecuted for murdering the mayor of the city, escaped with fifteen fellow accomplices through Šubria to Urartu (SAA 5: 53).

Avoidance of prosecution for criminal offences was the main reason for escapes and they concern all social groups of the empire (from slaves, through soldiers, to state officials). The crimes include theft (e.g., the case of Ilu-pīja-uṣur, a shepherd and cohort commander, described in SAA 1: 235), fencing involving a Tabalean who sold stolen goods to Babylon (SAA 18: 170), smuggling (the crime committed by the Kummean runaways according to SAA 5: 100), negligence (in SAA 13: 107, where ten village managers escaped and did not appear for the review by Nādinu, an inspector of the Nabû temple in Kalhu). Finally, the sources inform us about the escapes of the people accused of murder (e.g., letters SAA 13: 171; SAA 19: 40).[7] Those various criminals, despite going into hiding, still posed a real threat to the inhabitants, because "They do not fear [the king]. They rove about like runaways." This quotation is from SAA 13: 20 (rev. 3–rev. 4; trans. Cole and Machinist 1998) about the shepherds who turned into criminals. When it was possible they formed bigger groups attacking the local residents (SAA 19: 188).[8] In SAA 5: 227 and 228 Šamaš-bēlu-uṣur, the governor of the province of Arzūḫina informs Sargon about the bandits prowling in the area.[9] The problem must have been serious, since in order to ensure the safety of the residents, troops were dispatched.

It is obvious that, as I mentioned, safe and preferable areas for fugitives were inaccessible places beyond the reach of law, such as mountainous regions. Esarhaddon in the Letter to the Gods (RINAP 4.33.obv.i.36) writes about the royal city of Upūmu in Šubria as one that "is situated like a cloud atop a mighty mountain." And Taklāk-ana-Bēl informs Sargon (SAA 1: 240) about the insubordination of the residents of the city of Lapsia, who had fled onto the top of a nearby mountain before the officer (major domo) was dispatched to them. Aside from the mountains, fugitives may have found shelter in the Mesopotamian marshes such as in the land of Bīt-Amukāni,

7. SAA 13: 171, Killers on the run somewhere in Babylon; SAA 19: 40, captives from Til-Barsip. (rev. 2–rev. 8) "The men are criminals; they will get up run a[way. They are] be[nt on ] killing" (trans. Luukko 2012).

8. SAA 19: 188, "Six criminals terrorizing the town of Nasḫur-Bēl." These were runaway servants of different officials.

9. SAA 5: 227, the menservants of the chief confectioner were attacked by criminals in Babiti. The perpetrators were not captured. The king is also informed that bandits from Arrapḫa and of the domain of the palace herald joined forces and were raiding Arzūḫina. SAA 5: 228, four criminals (two from Arrapha and two from Arzūḫina) were captured.

home to thirty indomitable families, the so-called marsh dwellers; SAA 18: 185 (rev. 8–rev. 14) written by Nabû-ušallim of Bīt-Dakkūri (appointed by Esarhaddon) tells of the helplessness of the authorities toward this group: "As long as they live in Bīt-Amukāni, their brothers will not be subdued and they will not do the work of the king, my lord."

An escape beyond the borders of the empire was a crime not only against the authority, but also against the gods themselves (SAA 16: 122).[10] If captured, traitors could expect severe punishment. Esarhaddon cracked down on the fugitives captured in Šubria in a cruel way: "I cut off [th]eir [hands] (and) removed their noses, eyes, (and) ears" (RINAP 4.33.rev. iii.24'). But was this way of handling fugitives normal or was it dictated by a specific political situation?

No Neo-Assyrian codices have survived (Radner 2003, 883), but it seems that the law concerning fugitives, slaves in particular, did not differ considerably from those that we know from Mesopotamia from other periods, especially from the second millennium BCE. Escape was a crime against the existing social order, therefore punishment must have been severe enough to discourage others to attempt to flee. Yet, as D. C. Snell (2001: 85) has rightly pointed out in his book *Flight and Freedom in the Ancient Near East*, "The interesting thing about the legal material is that it did not usually deal with the punishment of the escaping slaves." In the Code of Hammurabi (Meek 2011: 157) the death penalty is meted out to those who help fugitives run away and to those who hide them (e.g., §§15 and 16).[11] Much less restrictive in this respect is the code of Lipit-Ištar of Isin (Steele 1948: 437–438), which requires an exchange of slaves or the compensation of fifteen shekels of silver, if there were no slaves (§§12 and 13 respectively).[12]

We have a few Neo-Assyrian letters that tell us about lending a helping hand to runaways: SAA 1: 23; SAA 18: 6; and SAA 19: 186. From the first one we learn that a certain Balṭi-iqbi maintains the fugitives. He is to return them to his son and immediately to appear before the king. In the second letter, Mār-bīti-ibni, a citizen of Der, helps fifteen fugitives. And the last document reports that a certain village mayor made it possible for two slaves, whose owner was the governor of the province of Tillê, to flee to the city of Upūmu in Šubria. We do not know what sort of punishment those who actively supported fugitives faced, and those who helped to capture them may have expected to be rewarded (the CH §17).[13] The letter SAA 17: 148, dated to the reign of Sargon II, says that Kīnâ of Nēmed-Laguda will get, as a reward, one of

10. SAA 16: 122, Unassigned letter. "(7–8) Who [angers] the gods? He who [defects] from [his own country] to the enemy country, [commits] a crime which the go[ds . . .]" (trans. Lukko and Van Buylaere 2002).

11. §15. "If a seignior has helped either a male slave of the state or female slave of the state or a male slave of a private citizen or a female slave of a private citizen to escape through the city-gate, he shall be put to death. §16. If a seignior has harbored in his house either a fugitive male or female slave belonging to the state or to a private citizen and has not brought him forth at the summons of the police, that householder shall be put to death." (trans. Meek 2011).

12. §12. "If a slave-girl or slave of a man has fled into the heart of the city and it has been confirmed that he (or she) dwelt in the house of (another) man for one month, he shall give slave for slave. §13. If he has no slave, he shall pay fifteen shekels of silver" (trans. Steele 1948).

13. §17. "If a seignior caught a fugitive male or female slave in the open and has taken him to his owner, the owner of the slave shall pay him two shekels of silver" (trans. Meek 2011: 157)

the animals—a horse, a donkey, or a sheep—if he captures Ḫazā-il, possibly a sheikh of Gambūlu.

In order to prevent escapes to the neighboring countries Assyrians signed interstate treaties. Let us quote L. L. Orlin (2007: 89) here: "The treaty thus represents the strongest assertion of the desire and the ability to perform promises that are guaranteed by solemn oaths to the gods and protected by the threat of invocation of curses."

The treaty obliged both parties to extradite fugitives. A good example is the fifteenth-century treaty struck between Idrimi from Alalakh and Pilliya of Kizzuwatna (Reiner 2011: 210). This document regulated all aspects of extradition.

The problem of obligation of extradition, in the first millennium, has been discussed by S. Parpola (2003: 1063) in the chapter "International Law In The First Millennium" in the volume *History of Ancient Near Eastern Law*. Surviving Neo-Assyrian treaties contain some information concerning how to treat runaways. In the treaty between Šamšī-Adad V and Marduk-zākir-šumi I (SAA 2: 1, obv. 13'–obv. 14') we read: "The king (of Assyria) shall indicate to him (Marduk-zākir-šumi) the fugitives [who] fled [from Assyria to Babylonia]," and in another one between Matī-il and Aššūr-nērārī V (SAA 2: 2, obv. iii 19'–obv. iii 23') the king of Arpad "shall not conceal (or) protect (any) chariot-[figh]ter or cavalryman [. . .], nor send him to another country." (trans. Parpola and Watanabe 1988)

During the rebellion of Šamaš-šumu-ukīn, Assurbanipal signed a treaty with a group of Babylonians (SAA 2: 9), according to which any opponents of the Assyrian king were to be captured and sent back to Assyria. Although the treaty does not mention the political fugitives from Assyria, it seems that they may have belonged to the conspirators. Unfortunately, two other international treaties have not been preserved, but we know that they existed and dealt with the extradition of fugitives. Esarhaddon signed such a treaty with Rusa II. After the Šubrian campaign all Urartian defectors were to be returned to the northern neighbor of Assyria (RINAP 4.33.iii.28'–iii.34'). Somewhere between 673 and 669 Assyria signed a peace treaty with Elam. In SAA 18: 7 either Šamaš-šumu-ukīn or Assurbanipal orders Šulmu-bēli-lašme to return, at once, the fugitive named Iasar with his family. The above treaty changed their status. From that time on, they were king's servants and any delay in their extradition may have had negative consequences in the relations between those two powers. This letter is also evidence of the fact that those fugitives who found asylum may never have felt safe and secure. They had to reckon with rapid political changes, which dramatically affected their status. In Esarhaddon's Succession Treaty (SAA 2: 6), a loyalty oath, which was to protect Assurbanipal's life from the threats of a potential rebellion, one can find two passages relating fugitives or an escape itself. On the one hand, the person bound by the oath was obliged to capture and kill the conspirators, but if they managed to run away, the obligation was to hunt the fugitives down until they are slain.[14] On the other hand, if the person learned about the conspiracy and was detained by the rebels, the treaty ordered the detainee to run away and appear before Assurbanipal.[15]

Finally, I would like to take a closer look at the problem of escapes to Assyria. The Assyrian Empire supported fugitives fleeing to Assyria for asylum from hostile

14. SAA 2: 6, 130–146 §12 Action against those suborning treason.
15. SAA 2: 6, 173–179 §15 Obligation to escape from rebels.

countries. They were even encouraged to do that. A good example is SAA 15: 184, in which Marduk-šarru-uṣur writes to the king about a possible acquisition of the runaways from Bīt-Zerî.[16] Deserters especially were a valuable source of information for Assyrian intelligence operating along the borders and inside the hostile territory (thoroughly analyzed by Dubovský 2006). What is more, the fugitive may have come from or represented a higher stratum of the society, for example, the fugitive Urartian governor (SAA 1: 8) or a eunuch of Aššūr-lē'i, ruler of Karalla staying with Nabû-ḫamātū'a, deputy of the province of Māzamua (SAA 5: 218).[17] At a later time, such fugitives might be useful in any political action either giving an opportunity for interference into domestic affairs of the neighboring country (creating and supporting the opposition, etc.), or even for a direct military intervention. The Assyrian king instructed his officials how to proceed with new fugitives from such countries as Urartu, Mannea, Media, or Ḫubuškia. SAA 16: 148 contains a list of the investigation procedures for the fugitives coming to the border forts.[18] Much emphasis is placed on the preparation of an accurate interrogation report. A great number of desertions had an impact on the evaluation of the political situation inside the hostile country and, as a result, may have led to a military intervention against the Assyrian enemy. In SAA 10: 111 (rev. 13–rev. 18) Bēl-ušēzib, a well-known astrologer of Esarhaddon, advises the ruler to conduct a campaign against Mannea, because "Deserters outnumber fighting men among the enemy—therein lies your advantage. At the entry of the whole army, let patrols make sorties, capture their men in the open country and question them; if the Indareans are keeping away from them, the army can invade and throw itself against the cities." (trans. Parpola 1993).

To sum up, due to the limited sources at our disposal, we are not able to assess the scale of escapes within the Assyrian Empire and to the neighboring countries. However, because there were attempts to counteract them (inter alia, by checking the number of newly arriving deportees as in SAA 1: 195 and by keeping a record of the escapes, e.g., a list of fugitives from the province of Šimu [SAA 11: 163]), it seems that fighting this social phenomenon was a priority.[19] An additional argument for the importance of this problem can be gleaned from the fact that higher-ranking officials dealt with it and directly reported the matters to the king. Such a well-functioning machine, which the Neo-Assyrian state was, could not afford in the long run to accept actions that disrupted the internal order of this multiethnic empire and, what is important, in many cases could also have undermined its economic base. Any conclusions from the above presented material must be taken cautiously and the application of the principle *pars pro toto* can be only a partial solution to the problem.

16. Edge 1–edge 4: "'Let us send them tokens through a Babylonian.' Perhaps the gods of the king my lord will make it (happen) and they will desert. I shall then send him to the king, my lord" (trans. Fuchs and Parpola 2001). See also Dubovský 2006: 176–179.

17. SAA 1: 8 is a fragment of an interesting correspondence between Sargon II and the Urartian king.

18. Esarhaddon writes to Aššūr-ušallim, an Assyria's royal envoy: rev. 9–rev. 17: "Let one [. . .] scribe . . . [who] guards [. . .]s write it down from his dictation, let it be sealed with the cross-shaped (stamp) seal, and let Aḫu-dūr-enši, the cohort commander of the crown prince, quickly bring it to me by express delivery."

19. SAA 1: 195 is a review of deportees made by Nabû-pāšir, governor of the province of Ḫarrān, during the reign of Sargon II. SAA 11: 163, a badly preserved list, consists of fugitive names and the towns from which they came.

**BIBLIOGRAPHY**


Cole, S. W. and Machinist, P.
1998 *Letters from Assyrian and Babylonian Priests to Kings Esarhaddon and Assurbanipal.* SAA 13. Helsinki: Helsinki University Press.

Dezsö, T.
2006 Šubria and the Assyrian Empire. *AArH* 46: 33–38.

Dietrich, M.
2003 *The Babylonian Correspondence of Sargon and Sennacherib.* SAA 17. Helsinki: Helsinki University Press.

Dubovský, P.
2006 *Hezekiah and the Assyrian Spies: Reconstruction of the Neo-Assyrian Intelligence Services and Its Significance for 2 Kings 18–19.* BibOr 49. Rome: Pontifical Biblical Institute.

Fales, F. M. and Postgate, J. N.
1992 *Imperial Administrative Records*, part. 1: *Palace and Temple Administration.* SAA 7. Helsinki: Helsinki University Press.
1995 *Imperial Administrative Records*, part 2: *Provincial and Military Administration.* SAA 11. Helsinki: Helsinki University Press.

Fuchs, A. and Parpola, S.
2001 *The Correspondence of Sargon II*, part 3: *Letters from Babylonia and the Eastern Provinces.* SAA 15. Helsinki: Helsinki University Press.

Hunger, H.
1992 *Astrological Reports to Assyrian Kings.* SAA 8. Helsinki: Helsinki University Press.

Lanfranchi, G. B.
1997 Consensus to Empire: Some Aspects of Sargon II's Foreign Policy. Pp. 81–87 in *Assyrien im Wandel der Zeiten: XXXIXe Rencontre assyriologique internationale, Heidelberg 6.–10. Juli 1992.* Edited by H. Waetzoldt and H. Hauptmann. HSAO 6. Heidelberg: Heidelberger Orientverlag.

Lanfranchi, G. B. and Parpola, S.
1990 *The Correspondence of Sargon II*, part 2: *Letters from the Northern and Northeastern Provinces.* SAA 5. Helsinki: Helsinki University Press.

Leichty, E.
2011 *The Royal Inscriptions of Esarhaddon, King of Assyria (680–669 BC).* RINAP 4. Winona Lake, IN: Eisenbrauns.

Luukko, M.
2012 *The Correspondence of Tiglath-pileser III and Sargon II from Calah/Nimrud.* SAA 19. Helsinki: Neo-Assyrian Text Corpus Project.

Luukko, M. and Van Buylaere, G.
2002 *The Political Correspondence of Esarhaddon.* SAA 16. Helsinki: Helsinki University Press.

Meek, T. J.
2011 The Code of Hammurabi. Pp. 155–178 in *The Ancient Near East: An Anthology of Texts and Pictures.* Edited by J. B. Pritchard. Foreword by D. E. Fleming. Princeton: Princeton University Press.

Orlin, L. L.
2007 *Life and Thought in the Ancient Near East.* Ann Arbor: University of Michigan Press.

Parpola, S.
1987 *The Correspondence of Sargon II*, part 1: *Letters from Assyria and the West.* SAA 1. Helsinki: Helsinki University Press.
1993 *Letters from Assyrian and Babylonian Scholars.* SAA 10. Helsinki: Helsinki University Press.

2003 International Law in the First Millennium. Pp. 1047–1066 in vol. 2 of *A History of Ancient Near Eastern Law*. Edited by R. Westbrook. 2 vols. HdO 72. Leiden: Brill.

Parpola, S. and Watanabe, K.

1988 *Neo-Assyrian Treaties and Loyalty Oaths*. SAA 2. Helsinki: Helsinki University Press.

Radner, K.

2003 Neo-Assyrian Period. Pp. 883–910 in vol. 2 of *A History of Ancient Near Eastern Law*. Edited by R. Westbrook. 2 vols. HdO 72. Leiden: Brill.

2012 Between a Rock and a Hard Place: Muṣaṣir, Kumme, Ukku and Šubria: The Buffer States Between Assyria and Urartu. Pp. 243–264 in *Biainili-Urartu: Proceedings of the Symposium Held in Munich, 12–14. October 2007*. Edited by S. Kroll, C. Gruber, U. Hellwag, M. Roaf, and P. Zimansky. Acta Iranica 51. Leuven: Peeters.

Reiner, E.

2011 Akkadian Treaties from Syria and Assyria: Treaty Between Idrimi and Pilliya. P. 210 in *The Ancient Near East: An Anthology of Texts and Pictures*. Edited by J. B. Pritchard. Foreword by D. E. Fleming. Princeton: Princeton University Press.

Reynolds, F.

2003 *The Babylonian Correspondence of Esarhaddon and Letters to Assurbanipal and Sin-šarru-iškun from Northern and Central Babylonia*. SAA 18. Helsinki: Helsinki University Press.

Snell, D. C.

2001 *Flight and Freedom in the Ancient Near East*. CHANE 8. Leiden: Brill.

Steele, F. R.

1948 The Code of Lipit-Ishtar. *AJA* 52: 425–450.

CHAPTER 12

# Perfections of Justice? Measure for Measure Aspirations in Biblical and Cuneiform Sources

Sandra Jacobs

THE QUEST FOR PERFECT JUSTICE remains a tantalizing ideal, the absence of which is most acute for victims of crime, particularly for those harmed or injured by a serial offender. While it is rarely possible to provide an equitable punishment that reflects the full depth and impact of an offense, our sense of justice is compromised no less in contemporary society, where the conviction of a life sentence does not preclude a killer's future, long-term, release. Such realities underline the ancient Mesopotamian belief that perfect justice was ultimately divine, and where *kittum u mīšarum,* "truth and justice," (Roth 1997: 81) was achieved by reproducing the heavenly order on earth. In this context "judgement was thus a transposition of divine practices into the human sphere," in which the underlying notions of stability (*kittum* from *kânum*, "to be stable, or solid,") and precision (*mīšarum* from *ešērum*, "to be right, straight,") were integral to the mankind's continuity (Démare-Lafont 2011: 335). Accordingly conditions in the natural environment were presumed to echo those in the cosmic arena, in which divine retribution played a crucial role.

The aspiration for judicial precision was inextricably linked to the near-instinctive desire to achieve a notional equivalence between a crime and its punishment, where the tailoring of a sanction to correspond to the sin was variously recommended in ancient sources. While such processes have a complex textual history, appearing invariably stereotypical in their demands for physical retaliation, as in the case of *ius talionis*, (Jackson 1973: 273–304; Cardascia 1979: 169–183; Westbrook 1986: 52–69; Houtman 1996: 381–397; Davis 2005; Levine 2008: 187–203; Rothkamm 2011; Jacobs 2014: 68–189), this paper will instead explore the nonbodily specific demands for retaliatory measures, where the correspondence between the nature of the crime and its subsequent punishment is expressly desired. In the context of the traditions preserved in the Hebrew Bible and in early rabbinic sources this process has been designated as reflective talion (Jacobs 2014: 127–134), and may be differentiated from the mode of instrumental talion, which describes a punitive injury of the body part responsible for carrying out, or initiating, the crime (Shemesh 2005; Jacobs 2010).

The core belief, that there was an intrinsic link between a negative act and its consequence for the perpetrator (Blenkinsopp 1995; Haase 1997; Ego 2007), no doubt encouraged by the conviction that a just allocation of punishment would correspond proportionally to the nature and extent of the crime committed, rather as the psalmist (7:17) explains: "his mischief will recoil upon his own head; his lawlessness will come down upon his skull," and similarly, Eccl 10:8: "He who digs a pit will fall into it; he who breaches a stone fence will be bitten by a snake."[1] This rationale is recalled in the postflood experience of Utnapishtim, who explains to Gilgamesh that once he and his wife returned to dry land, they provided the appropriate thanksgiving offerings to the gods, who descended like flies. Once sated, Ea proceeds to rebuke Enlil: "You sage of the gods, you hero. How could you lack counsel and cause the deluge? On him who commits a sin, inflict his crime! On him who commits a wrong, inflict [his] wrongdoing! Slack off, lest it be snapped! Pull taut, lest it become [slack!]." (George 2003: 715) Ea's criticism of Enlil (in effectively wiping out mankind entirely with a flood) presumes that even the gods ought to be bound by talionic convention: "on him who commits a sin, inflict his crime." A more ideal allocation of divine justice is recommended, as Ea then suggests that less widespread human destruction would have been a more responsible option: "Instead of the deluge you caused, lion could arise to diminish the people . . . wolf could arise to diminish the people . . . famine could happen to slaughter the land . . . Erra could arise to slaughter the land." (lines 189–195; George 2003: 714–717). Here the desire for the gods to distribute punishment more equitably and restrict it to sinners exclusively is presented as a more sensitive and intelligent option for the gods.

Unlike these entirely destructive consequences, the earlier attestation of such sentiments was also configured in positive terms, where the following advice appears in the corpus of Sumerian proverbs: "Let kindness be repaid to him who repays kindness," (Alster 1997: 1:216), and later in bilingual Akkadian-Sumerian forms: "May kindness be repaid to him who does a kindness. May Ḫunma grant favour to him of whom favour is predicated." (Lambert 1960: 264). In this same vein, "he who insults is insulted; he who sneers, is sneered at" (Alster 1997: 1:92), where Bendt Alster (1997: 2:384) explains "a person is treated according to his behaviour," and thus: "let revenge be taken on one who takes revenge" (2:431). Nor were such expressions restricted to anecdotal or literary conventions, but were notionally present in a number of Babylonian, Assyrian, and biblical Hebrew laws. While it is reasonably clear that the scribes responsible for the laws in the Covenant Code (Exod 20:19–23:33) did have access to the provisions from Hammurabi's laws, there is no need to assume that this collection was "directly, primarily and throughout dependant on the Laws of Hammurabi" (Wright 2009: 3), given the diversity of legal elements witnessed in the parallel biblical traditions. In terms of the tailoring of a punishment to correspond to its crime, there are four cases in the Babylonian laws where this process is implied:

1. CH §1: If a man accuses another man and charges him with homicide but cannot bring proof against him, his accuser shall be killed. (Roth 1997: 81)

   This is in distinct contrast to the right of the blood avenger (variously the *bēl napšāti*, or in biblical tradition, the גאל הדם, or "blood redeemer") to slay the killer after a homicide was committed (Barmash 2005: 27, 50–52). Codex Hammurabi §1 is, however, paralleled in the Deuteronomic revision of the talionic formulation: "If the man who testified is a false witness, if he has testified falsely against his fellow, you shall do to him as he schemed to do to his fellow. Thus you will sweep out evil from your midst; others will hear and

1. Unless otherwise noted all biblical translations are from NJPS.

be afraid, and such evil things will not be done again in your midst. Nor must you show pity: life for life, eye for eye, tooth for tooth, hand for hand, foot for foot" Deut 19:18b–24, and exemplified in meticulous relief in the book of Susanna (Jackson 1976: 37–54). Alternatively, the book of Esther, "a tale reminiscent of the Arabian nights," (Dalley 2007: 195) describes how the archvillain Haman was hung on the gallows he had built originally for Mordechai the Jew and states: "With the promulgation of this decree, let the evil plot, which he devised against the Jews recoil on his own head" (Esth 9:25). Admittedly here the charges brought to the king's attention were presented as acts of civil disobedience (Esth 3:3–5; 8), rather than homicide.

2. CH §229: If a builder constructs a house for a man but does not make his work sound, and the house that he constructs collapses and causes the death of the householder, that builder shall be killed. (Roth 1997: 125).

   In terms of professional damages, the relevant innertextual parallel listing the injuries caused by a negligent physician, constitutes an example of instrumental talion, in which the offending organ is punished, where Codex Hammurabi §218 states: If a physician performs major surgery with a bronze lancet upon an *awīlu* and thus causes the *awīlu*'s death, or opens the *awīlu*'s temple with a bronze lancet and thus blinds the *awīlu*'s eye, they shall cut off his hand, (Roth 1997: 123). In both cases, compensation, that is, a sum of money paid to the family of the victim to satisfy the wrong or injury inflicted would have been an available option (Roth 1987: 351).

3. CH §230: If it should cause the death of a son of the householder, they shall kill a son of that builder. (Roth 1997: 125).

   Here the equivalence between the status of the victim and the substitute provided is identical, unlike Codex Hammurabi §210: "If that woman should die, they shall kill his daughter," and also Codex Hammurabi §44a "If anyone makes a man fall into a fire, so that he dies, he shall give a son in return" (Roth 1997: 223). As in the Codex Hammurabi §229, "probably the son or daughter, as the case might be, was seldom put to death as talion could be avoided by compensation, and a sum of money would be offered and accepted if the builder had no son" (Driver and Miles 1952: 426). In the memories of the biblical scribes, divine retribution was less accommodating. This evokes the actions of the pharaoh who decreed that "every boy that is born you shall throw into the Nile" (Exod 1:22), and was punished concomitantly: "In the middle of the night the Lord struck down all the first-born in the land of Egypt, from the first born of Pharaoh who sat on the throne to the first born of the captive who was in the dungeon and all the first born of the cattle" (Exod 12:29).

4. CH §231: If he shall cause the death of a slave of the householder, he shall give to the householder a slave of comparable value for the slave (Roth 1997: 125).

   In this case, the phrase: "a slave of comparable value for the slave," *wardam kīma wardim*, offers a further example of live, human substitution, where the association between the formulation נפש תחת נפש "a life for a life" in Exod 21:23 and its Middle Assyrian precursor in *kīmu ša libbiša napšate umalla* (MAL A50, lines 69, 73, 81, A52 line 91 [Driver and Miles 1935]) as "he pays (on the principle of) a life (for a life), does not denote the killing of the assailant's slave, (Jacobs 2012: 241–253). This, too, would need not preclude compensation, even though live, human substitution has been specified, as similarly with the injury caused by the negligent physician (CH §219): "If a physician performs major surgery with a bronze lancet upon a slave of a commoner and thus causes the slave's death [*wardam kīma wardim iriab*] he shall replace the slave with a slave of comparable value," (Roth 1997: 123).

Although vicarious punishments remain conspicuously absent in the main legal collections of the Hebrew Bible—the Covenant Code (Exod 20:22–23:19), the Holiness Code (Lev 17–26), Priestly Law (Lev 12:2–8; Num 27:8–11; 30:4–17; 36:7–12), and the Deuteronomic Code (Deut 12–26)—the need to co-ordinate a punishment with its crime is encapsulated in the talionic formulation in Exod 21:22–25; Lev 24:18–20; and Deut 19:21. Bernard Jackson (2006) identifies two separate linguistic formulations which qualify the principle (*ius talionis*) in the Covenant Code as follows: "When men fight and one of them pushes a pregnant woman and a miscarriage results, but no [other] damage ensues, the one responsible shall be fined, according as the woman's husband may exact from him: the payment to be based on reckoning. But if [other] damage ensues, the penalty shall be life for life, eye for eye, tooth for tooth, hand for hand, foot for foot, burn for burn, wound for wound, bruise for bruise." (Exod 21:22–25).[2]

In this well-known נפש תחת נפש "life for life," עין תחת עין "eye for eye," axiom, the formulation is characterized by the use of the preposition תחת (*taḥat*), meaning "in place of." Elsewhere in biblical syntax, תחת (*taḥat*) appears either as an adverbial accusative, or a preposition, and is variously translated as "underneath, below, instead of" (BDB: 1065). To all intents and purposes, the preposition תחת (*taḥat*) functions here virtually identically to the *aššum* clause in cuneiform law (Roth 2001; Jacobs 2014: 96–99). In relation to its use in the Covenant Code, Jackson (2006: 166) maintains that its use in Exod 21:23–25 "has precisely the quantitatively limiting effect," that is, only one life, organ, or limb, was specified to correspond to the precise life, organ or limb of the injured victim, down to the very burn, bruise, or other (unspecified) wound.

This is clearly differentiated from its less-well-known accompaniment, the כאשר (*ka'asher*) formulation of talion, observed also in the above passage, where Exod 21:22 כאשר ישית עליו בעל האשה "according as the woman's husband may exact from him," where the conjunction כאשר (*ka'asher*) meaning "according as, as, when, or according to that which" (BDB: 455), is an amalgamation of the substantive כי (*ki*), meaning "the like of, as" (BDB: 453), and the relative particle אשר meaning "which, as to which" (BDB: 81). This formulation is indicative of "*qualitatively* equivalent retribution," (Jackson 2006: 197 [emphasis original]), where it determines the amount of compensation required for the loss of life of an unborn child in the Covenant Code (Jacobs 2014: 86–94).

Other examples of "*qualitatively* equivalent retribution," which utilize this כאשר (*ka'asher*) conjunction are present also in narrative sources, where, for example, Judg 1:6–7 states: "Adoni-bezek fled, but they pursued him and captured him; and they cut

2. In the above NJPS translation, the word "other" has been placed in brackets, as it is not present in the Hebrew of Exod 21:22d, where ולא יהיה אסון is witnessed in the MT.

off his thumbs and his big toes. And Adoni-bezek said, 'Seventy kings, with thumbs and big toes cut off, used to pick up scraps under my table; as I have done so God has requited me.'" Here the phrase כאשר עשיתי כן שלם־לי אלהים "as I have done so God has requited me," acknowledges the "*qualitatively* equivalent retribution," while further emphasizing the role of divine justice in this process. In addition, the characterization of Samson (in his role as military leader and in the aftermath of his uncontrollable rage), is equally informative, as this reported conversation in Judg 15:10–11 indicates: "They [the Philistines] said: 'We have come to take Samson prisoner [לעשות לו כאשר עשה לנו] and to do to him as he has done to us.' Thereupon three thousand men of Judah went down to the cave of the rock of Etam, and they said to Samson, 'You knew the Philistines rule over us; why have you done this to us?' He replied, [כאשר עשו לי כן עשיתי להם] 'as they did to me, so I did to them.'" More poignantly, the book of Judges records how Jephtah's daughter tells her father: עשה לי כאשר יצא מפיך "do to me as you have vowed," (Judg 11:36), prior to her sacrifice. These narrative exemplars recall the use of the כאשר (*ka'asher*) formulation of talion in legal pentateuchal sources, as follows:

| | | |
|---|---|---|
| Exod 21:22 | As the woman's husband | כאשר ישית עליו |
| | may exact from him | בעל האשה |
| Lev 24:19 | As he has done so | כאשר עשה |
| | shall it be done to him | כן יעשה לו |
| Lev 24:20 | The injury he inflicted on another, | כאשר יתן מום באדם |
| | shall be inflicted on him. | כן יתן בו |
| Deut 19:19 | You shall do to him | ועשיתם לו |
| | as he schemed to do to his fellow | כאשר זמם לעשות לאחיו |
| Num 14:28 | I will do to you | כאשר דברתם באזני |
| | just as you have urged me | כן אעשה להם |
| Num 15:14 | As you do, | כאשר תעשו |
| | so shall it be done | כן יעשה |
| Num 33:56 | So that I will do to you | והיה כאשר דמיתי לעשות להם |
| | what I planned to do to them | אעשה לכם |

And in prophetic sources:

| | | |
|---|---|---|
| Obad 1:15 | As you did, so it shall be done to you; | כאשר עשיתה יעשה לך |
| | Your conduct shall be requited | גמלך ישוב בראשך |
| Jer 50:15 | Take vengeance on her, | הנקמו בה |
| | Do to her as she has done | כאשר עשיתה עשו־בה |
| Ezek 12:11 | As I have done, | כאשר עשיתיכן יעשה להם |
| | So it shall be done to them | |
| Ezek 16:59 | I will deal with you | ועשיתי[ועשית] אותך |
| | As you have dealt. | כאשר עשית |
| Lam 1:22 | And deal with them | ועולל למו |
| | As You have dealt with me. | כאשר עוללת לי |

Although never directly articulated formally in Babylonian law, such expressions of idealized justice appear unequivocally in the Middle Assyrian law code. In this context, both the comparable provisions in the Covenant Code (Exod 21:22–25) and in MAL A50 (Driver and Miles 1935), deal with the injuries sustained by a pregnant woman in a brawl, where the Assyrian provides the following rationale:

| | | |
|---|---|---|
| Line 65 | DAM *ša-a* LÚ] *ša* DAM-*at* LÚ | The wife of the man] who [caused] the (other) married woman |
| Line 66 | *ša-*[*a* ŠÀ$^{bi}$-*ša ú-ša-ad-di*]-*ú-ni* | [to lose] the fruit of [her womb] |
| Line 67 | *ki-*[*i- ša-a e-pu*]-*šu-ši-ni* | shall be treated as [he has] he treated her |
| Line 68 | e-*pu-*[*šu-šu ki-mu-ú ša*]-*a lib-bi-ša* | for the fruit] of her womb, he pays |
| Line 69 | *nap-ša-a-te u-ma-al-la.* | (on the principle of) a life (for a life) |

In this context, it is accepted that the expression, *kī ša ēpušūšini eppušūšu* "and they shall treat him as he treated her" (MAL A50, line 67 [Driver and Miles 1935: 418–419]), is a general introductory principle that underlies the subsequent terms of the law (1935: 112–113). Accordingly the attacker's own wife was to incur the same injury as her husband has inflicted, based on the (unstated) presumption first, that the assailant had a wife, and second, that she was also pregnant. Meir Malul's (2010: 205) Hebrew translation is the most apposite in this instance: כפי שעשה לה כן יעשו לו, where he documents the relevant variants in Deuteronomic tradition. The Assyrian tablet continues to itemize the penalty for fatal injuries to the woman, providing gender-determined consequences for the loss of her unborn child: In the event that the injured wife dies, the assailant is to lose his life, *a'īla idukkū*, (LÚ *i-du-uk-ku,* "the man shall be put to death," MAL A50, line 71 [Driver and Miles 1935: 418–419]). a verdict that could technically be converted to compensation. Likewise, in the event of the loss of a male child—and where the husband of the injured wife has no son and heir—again, "the striker shall be put to death," *māḫiṣāna idukkū* (MAL A50, line 79 [Driver and Miles 1935: 418–419]). However, if the unborn child was female: *kīmū ša libbiša napšāte umalla*, "the assailant pays on the principle of a life [for a life]," (MAL A50, line 81 [Driver and Miles 1935: 419]), and interestingly תחת ילדיה נפשות ימלא (Malul 2010: 205). In this context the formal requirement is for the assailant to replace the dead girl with a live daughter (either of his own, or that of a slave), and if not, then to offer compensation for this loss, where it is by no means apparent that the assailant's own daughter was to be vicariously killed. (Houtman 1996: 381–397; 2000: 166; Jackson 1973: 293; 2006: 211; Jacobs 2012: 248–253; 2014: 104–106).

Yet while the Akkadian relative particles *kî/kīma* functions similarly in purpose and meaning to the biblical כאשר/כי (*ki/ka'asher*) conjunction in the talionic formulation, the Akkadian, *kî*, ("like, in the manner of, as, according to, instead of," *CAD* K:322–325), is not restricted to designating "*qualitatively* equivalent retribution," (Jackson 2006: 197). In this sequence its quantitative role is evident in MAL A52, lines 89–90, where the law addresses an assault upon a prostitute, which results in the loss of her unborn child. Here punishment of the assailant is provided: *miḫṣī ki miḫṣī išakkanušu* "blow by blow shall be laid upon him," (*mi-iḫ-ṣi ki-i mi-iḫ-ṣi i-ša-ak-ku-ú-nu-uš* [Driver and Miles 1935: 420–421], represented in modern Hebrew as מכה תחת מכה [Malul 2010, 206]). That "this suggests a distinction between punishment of a private nature by talion or otherwise, and that of a public nature inflicted with an instrument officially prescribed for the purpose, i.e. 'rods' (Ass. *iṣḫaṭṭē*)" (Driver and Miles 1935: 363) remains unconfirmed. More importantly, the use of *kīma,* as both a preposition, yet also a subordinating conjunction (See *CAD* K:367–369; and Richardson 2008: 232–233), indicates the terminological flexibility in the Akkadian provisions, where its conversational use is informative: *pištam kīma pištim aqbīšm*, "I returned insult for insult," (*kîma, CAD* K:367).

While there is no evidence that biblical scribes had access to the Middle Assyrian law code (nor to any of the fragments from Tablet A found at Nimrud), and no direct cultural trajectories can be reconstructed between the two societies (Morrow 2013: 183–190) it may well be that these aspirational expressions are entirely random and coincidental. However, like the elements of Gilgamesh within Homer's *Iliad* and *Odyssey*, it may be more appropriate to view these "as much more distant relatives" (George 2003: 57), whose earlier, tenuous relationship is both long-buried and irretrievable. Within the Hebrew Bible the process of reflective talion sharply articulated the demand for an equivalence between a crime and its punishment in all its major genres, where there appears to be no formal borrowing from the terminology of Hammurabi's laws. Although this does little to further our knowledge of the "diversity of enforceable rules," (Démare-Lafont 1994: 118), let alone the "subsidiarity," of statutory national law (Démare-Lafont 2013: 58–59) in Near Eastern antiquity, this discussion nonetheless illuminates the widespread desire to achieve the instinctive human desire for precision perfect, or measure for measure, justice.

## BIBLIOGRAPHY

Alster, B.

1997 *The Proverbs of Ancient Sumer: The World's Earliest Proverb Collection.* 2 vols. Bethesda, MD: CDL.

Barmash, P.

2005 *Homicide in the Biblical World.* Cambridge: Cambridge University Press.

Blenkinsopp, J.

1995 *Wisdom and Law in the Old Testament: The Ordering of Life in Israel and Early Judaism.* Oxford: Oxford University Press.

Cardascia, G.

1979 La place du talion dans l'histoire du droit penal à la lumière des droit du Proche-Orient ancient. Pp. 169–183 in *Melanges offerts à Jean Dauvilliers.* Toulouse: Centre d'histoire juridique méridionale.

Dalley, S.

2007 *Esther's Revenge at Susa: From Sennacherib to Ahasuerus.* Oxford: Oxford University Press.

Davis, J. F.

2005 *Lex Talionis in Early Judaism and the Exhortation of Jesus in Matthew 5.38–42.* JSNTSup 281. London: T&T Clark.

Démare-Lafont, S.

1994 Ancient Near Eastern Laws: Continuity and Pluralism. Pp. 91–118 in *Theory and Method in Biblical and Cuneiform Law: Revision, Interpolation and Development.* Edited by B. Levinson. JSOTSup 181. Sheffield: Sheffield Academic.

2011 Judicial Decision-Making: Judges and Arbitrators. Pp. 335–357 in *The Oxford Handbook of Cuneiform Culture.* Edited by K. Radner and E. Robson. Oxford: Oxford University Press.

2013 From the Banks of the Seine to the Bay of Chesapeake: Crossglances on Ancient Near Eastern Law. *Maarav* 18: 55–61.

Driver, G. R. and Miles, J. C.

1935 *The Assyrian Laws: Edited with Translation and Commentary*. Oxford: Clarendon.

1952 *The Babylonian Laws*, vol. 1: *Legal Commentary*. Oxford: Clarendon.

Ego, B.

2007 God's Justice: The "Measure for Measure" Principle in 2 Maccabees. Pp. 141–154 in *The Books of the Maccabees: History, Theology, Ideology; Papers on the Second International Conference on the Deuterocanonical Books, Pápa, Hungary, 9–11 June, 2005*. Edited by G. G. Xeravits and J. Zsengellér. JSJSup 118. Leiden: Brill.

George, A. R.

2003 *The Babylonian Gilgamesh Epic: Introduction, Critical Edition and Cuneiform Texts*. 2 vols. Oxford: Oxford University Press.

Haase, R.

1997 Talion und spiegelnde Strafe in den keilschriftlichen Rechtscorpora. *ZABR* 3: 195–201.

Houtman, C.

1996 Eine Schwangere Frau Als Opfer Eines Handgemenges (Exodus 21:22–25): Ein Fall von Stellvertretender Talion im Bundesbuch? Pp. 381–397 in *Studies in the Book of Exodus: Redaction—Reception—Interpretation*. Edited by M. Vervenne. BETL 126. Leuven: Peeters.

2000 *Exodus*, vol. 3: *Chapters 20–40*. HCOT. Leuven: Peeters.

Jackson, B. S.

1973 The Problem of Exodus XXI 22–25 (Ius Talionis). *VT* 37: 273–304.

1976 Susanna and the Singular History of Singular Witnesses. Pp. 37–54 in *Essays in Honour of Ben Beinart: Jura legesque antiquiores necnon recentiores*. Edited by W. de Vos and B. Beinart. Cape Town: Juta.

2006 *Wisdom Laws: A Study of the Mishpatim of Exodus 12:1–22:16*. Oxford: Oxford University Press.

Jacobs, S.

2010 Instrumental Talion in Deuteronomic Law. *ZABR* 16: 263–278.

2012 נפש תחת נפש A Life for a Life and Napšate Umalla. Pp. 241–253 in *The Ancient Near East in the 12th–10th Centuries BCE: Culture and History; Proceedings of the International Conference Held at Haifa University, 02–05 May 2010*. Edited by G. Galil, A. Gilboa, A. M. Maeir, and D. Khan. AOAT 392. Münster: Ugarit-Verlag.

2014 *The Body as Object: Physical Disfigurement in Biblical Law*. LHBOTS 582. London: Bloomsbury.

Lambert, W. G.

1960 *Babylonian Wisdom Literature*. Oxford: Clarendon.

Levine, B. A.

2008 Scripture's Account: Lex Talionis. Pp. 187–203 in *Torah Revealed, Torah Fulfilled: Scriptural Laws in Formative Judaism and Early Christianity*. Edited by J. Neusner, B. D. Chilton, B. A. Levine. London: T&T Clark.

Malul, M.

2010 *Law Collections from the Ancient Near East*. Haifa: Pardes. [Hebrew]

Morrow, W.

2013 Tribute from Judah and the Transmission of Assyrian Propaganda. Pp. 183–192 in *"My Spirit at Rest in the North Country" (Zechariah 6.8): Collected Communications to the XXth Congress of the International Organization for the Study of the Old Testament, Helsinki 2010*. Edited by H. M. Niemann and M. Augustin. BEATAJ 57. Frankfurt am Main: Lang.

Richardson, M. E. J.
2008 *A Comprehensive Grammar to Hammurabi's Stele*. Gorgias Handbooks 8. Piscataway, NJ: Gorgias Press.

Roth, M. T.
1987 Homicide in the Neo-Assyrian Period. Pp. 351–365 in *Language, Literature, and History: Philological and Historical Studies Presented to Erica Reiner.* Edited by F. Rochberg-Halton. AOS 67. New Haven: American Oriental Society.
1997 *Law Collections from Mesopotamia and Asia Minor*. 2nd ed. WAW 6. Atlanta: Scholars Press.
2001 The Because Clause: Punishment Rationalization In Mesopotamian Laws. Pp. 407–412 in *Veenhof Anniversary Volume: Studies Presented To Klaas R. Veenhof on the Occasion of His Sixty-Fifth Birthday.* Edited by W. H. van Soldt, J. G. Dercksen, N. J. C. Kouwenberg, and T. J. H. Krispijn. PIHANS 89. Leiden: Nederlands Instituut voor het Nabije Oosten.

Rothkamm, J.
2011 *Talio esto: Recherches sur les origines de la formule 'œil pour œil, dent pour dent' dans les droits du Proche-Orient ancien, et sur son devenir dans le monde gréco-romain.* BZAW 426. Berlin: de Gruyter.

Shemesh, Y.
2005 Punishment of the Offending Organ in Biblical Literature. *VT* 55: 343–365.

Westbrook, R.
1986 Lex Talionis and Exodus 21:22–25. *RB* 93: 52–69.

Wright, D.
2009 *Inventing God's Law: How the Covenant Code of the Bible Used and Revised the Laws of Hammurabi*. Oxford: Oxford University Press.

CHAPTER 13

# Putting Some Order in Ur III Letter-Orders

Daniele Umberto Lampasona

LETTER-ORDERS ARE A PECULIAR KIND of administrative texts utilized in several Mesopotamian cities. Even if not reaching the overabundance of other categories such as receipts or delivery texts, their presence is well attested throughout the entire Mesopotamian history: the first documents clearly definable as letter-orders date back to the Pre-Sargonic times (e.g., NBC 5823, VAT 4845, and AO 12186), and this kind of administrative text proved to be so useful and versatile that they were still in use two millennia later, during the Hellenistic domination (McEwan 1981: 150–151).

During the Ur III period, the time period of this paper, the usage of these documents increased significantly, and the number of found letter-orders pertaining to this age reaches about seven hundred exemplars. Almost half of these documents have been published by E. Sollberger (1966), in the only monograph up to now entirely devoted to the letter-orders of this period; the successive book of P. Michalowski (1993), in fact, contains letters coming from different periods and pertaining to different genres. Since the appearance of Sollberger's study, many documents have been discovered and labeled as letter-orders, sometimes erroneously; the most recent article about the subject was presented by P. Notizia and A. Di Ludovico (2012), while the last publication of a large collection of documents was produced more than ten years ago by M. Molina (1999–2000).

In my PhD dissertation (Lampasona 2012) I gathered and translated all the Ur III letter-orders published hitherto; all the texts have been entered in a particular scheme in order to enhance correlations, tendencies, patterns, and anomalies, and finally precise data about the content and the distribution of this documentary type are available. After a small introduction to the genre and to its textual analysis, this paper will concentrate on the exposition of the statistical results pertinent to distribution, verbs, products, dates, and seals contained in the texts. At the end there will be a small appendix about prosopographical possibilities offered by letter-orders.

## What It Is, and What It Is Not: A "Letter-Order"

At present, the BDTNS database contains 717 documents under the tag of letter-order; several of these, actually, are texts only similar to letter-orders, but belonging to different categories, mostly letters or reports.[1] The label "letter-order" was introduced

1. The database is available at http://bdts.filol.csic.es.

more than sixty years ago by A. L. Oppenheim (1948, referred to texts H 24, H 35 and I 43), but without any further definition. The locution, nevertheless, seems already quite explicit, having the basic meaning of "a letter requesting the fulfillment of an order." The denomination stresses, therefore, two distinct elements, the letter and the order: in the writing the epistolary nature comes off in the typical introduction "Say to. . . ." while the jussive or volitive content is in the presence of a task assigned to the receiver ("Do . . ." or "May he do . . .").

Carefully following this definition, we have to expunge from the corpus several texts, even from Sollberger's publication.[2] Most of the times this is due to the lack of an order, as in TCS 1 50: "Say to Da'aĝu and Ur-Lamma: '*Šū-Kūbum*, to whom the great chancellor has given a field of 0.1.0 because he had no subsistence, has taken me as commissary.'" Even if this text starts with the typical address "Say to PN," there is no trace of a request, thus the document should not be considered a letter-order; it seems more suitable to the category of reports, since it was meant to inform the receiver about something, but without asking for an action.

Letter-orders have also been confused with other kinds of documents, like royal letters (see Michalowski 2011). The main difference between the two genres consists in the use of verbs: while in the letter-orders the most common form is the third-person singular ("May he do"), in other letters the sender addresses the receiver directly, using the first- and second-person singular. Classic letters, moreover, usually contain a longer informative part and some greeting formulas.

Having excluded standard letters, reports, and other kinds of documents, the number of Ur III letter-orders should, therefore, be lowered to 581.

Surely the definition of letter-order can also be intended subjectively: in his book about Neo-Babylonian letter-orders, for example, J. MacGinnis (1995: 16) says that "the basis for identification of a text as a letter-order is the occurrence of the characteristic phrase 'send' or 'give.'" If we would apply the same rule to Ur III letter-orders, almost half of the documents would be considered not pertaining to the corpus, since orders also concerned many other activities, such as watering fields or transferring materials.

## The Ideal Letter-Order

The gathering of all the published letter-orders has allowed an evaluation of the documents as a whole, the first attempt so far to find regular patterns through both a linguistic-grammatical analysis and a socio-economic one.

Thanks to the comparison of a large number of documents, in fact, it has been possible to reconstruct the ideal structure of the genre; unfortunately, one can only outline a theoretical model, since we have not yet found a single letter-order containing all the different sections of the text. Table 13.1 represents an example of an ideal letter-order:[3]

The great majority of these documents is quite short (about ten lines), and contains only one verbal form (the order), excluding the introductory formulas; their language

2. The first five examples are TCS 1 14, 50, 81, 83, 144.
3. For the translation of the verbs see below.

TABLE 13.1. Hypothetical example of a complete letter-order.

| Text | Section | Sub-section |
|---|---|---|
| "This is what $PN_1$ said: | Heading | Sender |
| 'After you will have said to $PN_2$: | | Receiver |
| "I received the barley of $PN_3$", | Body | Informative part 1 |
| may he release $PN_3$. | | Order |
| I will bring him his barley. | | Informative part 2 |
| Let him receive his tablet.' | Conclusion | Exhortation |
| Year: the temple of Šara was built. | | Date |
| Seal of $PN_1$." | | Mention of the seal |

is nearly always Sumerian, and in the few Akkadian texts we find many Sumerograms. The structure presents three principal sections, the heading, the body, and the conclusion. Each one of these three major parts can be subdivided in more specific subsections: sender and receiver; informative parts and order; exhortation, date and the mention of the sealing. A bit external to the textual analysis is the actual sealing, while literally external is the envelope that contained the letter, found in just a small minority of the cases. Among all these elements, the only one strictly necessary to qualify a text as a letter-order is the order; all other information is nonessential, and even if the mention of the receiver is missing, we can reasonably suppose that the sender had said his name to the messenger or that he had written it on the envelope, making its repetition on the tablet superfluous. The order, instead, could not be communicated orally, since the receiver would have asked for proof to perform the task.

The name of the sender is always followed by the form NA-BE$_2$-A, that can be analyzed as NA.I$_3$.B.E.A.AM$_3$: NA is the modal prefix utilized with affirmative meaning (Thomsen 1984: 195; Edzard 2003: 19); I$_3$ is the conjugation prefix; B is the accusative inanimate class pronominal prefix; E is the singular *marû* verbal root of the verb DUG$_4$; A is the nominalizing suffix; and AM$_3$ is the enclitic copula. The form should be translated as "This is what PN said," but it is often expressed by scholars with "So says PN." The few letters in Akkadian presenting the name of the sender use the simple form *um-ma* PN, "Thus (says) PN."

After the name of the receiver we find the most common verb of the corpus, usually written U$_3$-NA-A-DUG$_4$; the form can be parsed as U.I$_3$.NA.E.DUG$_4$: U is the modal prefix; I$_3$ is the conjugation prefix; NA is the third-person singular dative prefix; E is the second-person singular subject pronominal prefix (which turned into A because of vowel harmony); and DUG$_4$ is the *hamṭu* verbal root. The modal prefix U has a prospective value (Thomsen 1984: 208–211; Edzard 2003: 121–123; Gragg 1973: 131–134; Wilcke 2010: 58–59; contra Kaneva 2000: 524–530), and it is usually linked to a subsequent imperative, in the form "do [prospective] and then do [imperative]." The absence of verbs conjugated in the imperative mood in the letter-orders led the scholars to translate the form as a plain "tell PN," canceling any prospective value of the prefix. However, if it is true that the main verb of these documents is not in the imperative, but in the precative, it is also true that the two moods are semantically comparable, as both are oriented toward the execution of a task. Thus, the original value of the prefix U can be maintained and the form can be translated as "after you will have said to PN." Letters in Akkadian use the form *qi-bi₂-ma*, second-person masculine singular of the imperative G of the verb *qabûm*, to which the marker of direct speech *–ma* is attached. It is worth stressing that both $U_3$-NA-A-$DUG_4$ and *qi-bi₂-ma* are directed to the messenger, and not to the addressee: these messages were said aloud, and not read by the receiver.

The second main section usually begins with an informative part, where the reasons behind the request from the sender are explained. In the rare cases when there is a similar subsection also after the order, it can contain the consequences of performing the task (a compensation if it is carried out, or a menace if it is not) or other information related to the administration of the order, like who is responsible for its completion. This informative part is of great importance for the socio-economic reconstruction, because it contains data about people and actions involved in the documents, notions not obtainable otherwise. From a linguistic point of view, moreover, since the verb $U_3$-NA-A-$DUG_4$ refers to the messenger, this informative part represents a sort of direct speech, the only part of the letter that was actually read aloud by the delegate of the sender.

Orders are expressed in the precative mood, as seen above. The most common task is, by far, "to give," written usually $HE_2$-NA-AB-$ŠUM_2$-MU; the form can be explained as $HE_2$.$I_3$.NA.B.$ŠUM_2$.E: $HE_2$ is the modal prefix utilized with precative value; $I_3$ is the conjugation prefix; NA is the third-person singular dative prefix; B is the accusative inanimate class pronominal prefix; and $ŠUM_2$.E is the verbal root, followed by the *marû* indicator (that turned into U because of vowel harmony). Almost all the orders in these documents present a similar form and are analyzable in the same way; the rare cases of the imperative mood in Sumerian are due to the Akkadian influence: all the letter-orders in Akkadian, in fact, use the imperative to express the tasks. The widespread use of the precative mood makes "may he give" a preferable translation in comparison with "let him give," which is more suitable for an imperative. Letter-orders, therefore, should actually be called "letter-requests."

After the order (and a second informative part), the writer could insert an exhortation, a short sentence that had the purpose of strengthening the content of the order and avoiding complications. The most common exhortation is "May he not contest," followed by "It is an emergency" and "Quickly!" Quite interesting are the few sentences that play on the receiver's feelings, as "Who is like my brother?" or "Who is like my mother?" Since it is unlikely that a subordinate used similar phrases toward a superior, and it would be useless for a superior to talk about his authority toward a subordinate, the presence of similar exhortations lets us understand that letter-orders were usually exchanged between officials of the same level or in unofficial contexts.

The last part of the text contained, although not as often as we would like, the date and the mention of the seal, accompanied by the actual sealing.

Only seventeen of the found texts were still accompanied by an envelope. Even if Sollberger (1969: 3) assumed that "every letter, or at least every unsealed or unaddressed letter, had one [envelope]," the small quantity of finds makes it unlikely; nevertheless, we can suppose that envelopes were much more common, although there are no clues on their actual usage and quantity.

## Geographical Distribution

Letter-orders have been found in eleven different cities, defining an area almost corresponding with the local idea of the land of Sumer, whose most northern city is here represented by Nippur. Among the principal Sumerian cities that are absent from the corpus are Adab, Larsa, and Isin, where, in general, few Ur III texts have been discovered, and Irisagrig, whose texts have been studied for only a short time. Instead of them, cities quite far from the Sumerian heartland like Eshnunna, Mari ,and Susa are attested, even if with only a small number of documents. Other big southern centers, like Uruk, Garshana, Shuruppag, and Ur, contribute some to the corpus, some with only one text, while the three principal cities are Girsu, Umma, and Nippur, also the three locations where the most Ur III textual production has been found.

The geographical distribution of the letter-orders is shown in graph 13.1, and it appears immediately evident how many of these documents were recovered in Umma and Girsu; almost three quarters of the texts come from these two cities alone.

## The Orders

In the 581 letter-orders there are 106 different verbs used as command. A simple division tells us that every verb should be attested more than five times, but the tasks appear in a widely uneven distribution: the great majority of the verbs, in fact, are

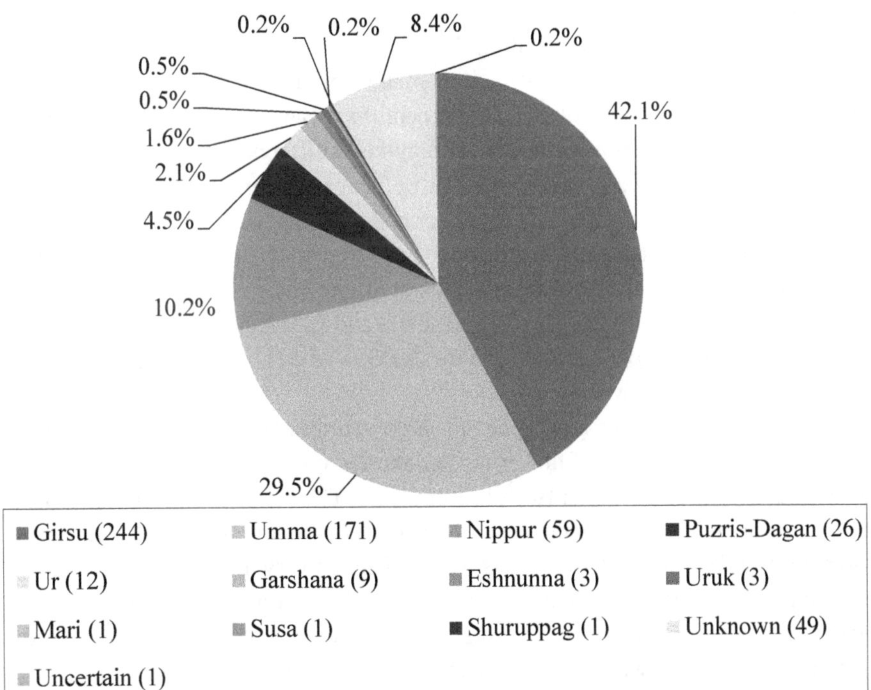


GRAPH 13.1. Geographic provenience of the letter-orders.

used only once or twice, while there is a small number of verbs repeated more than ten times, up to almost four hundred recurrences. All these actions can be divided in nine different categories, depending on their semantic sphere.

The most important group contains verbs of a commercial nature, although we should not talk about exchanges, but more about unidirectional goods movements. This group collects 20 different verbs, attested 491 times, that is, 65.4 percent of all the orders; it appears clear that the main aim of these documents was to move wares and people. As already said, ŠUM$_2$ ("to give") is the most frequent order in the whole corpus, with 389 attestations, representing—alone—51.8 percent of all the requests. Among the other verbs of this group there are TUM$_{2/3}$ ("to bring"), GE$_4$ ("to send"), GAR ("to place"), ŠU ŠUM$_2$ ("to entrust"), and ŠU TEG$_4$ ("to accept").

The second most numerous group collects verbs related to a detentive ambit, for both people and goods. The actions pertaining to this sphere are only six, but they are attested eighty-four different times, mostly thanks to the great diffusion of the verbs ŠU BAR ("to release") and DU$_3$ ("to keep in custody," always used in the negative form), which were intended as antonyms.

The following two groups are linked to the previous two: The first one is composed of verbs related to the financial world (fifty-six attestations), the second one by actions pertaining to the juridical sphere (twenty appearances). The financial group is separated from the commercial one because in its verbs there is an accentuated focus on the economic nature of the actions, as demonstrated by the most common forms: ZIG$_3$ ("to issue, to expend"), LA$_2$ ("to pay"), and SA$_{10}$ ("to buy"). In the same way, juridical verbs, although they could lead to release or keep a person in custody, are tightly bound to processes, with actions like SI SA$_2$ ("to arbitrate"), MU/ZI PAD$_3$ ("to make swear"), EN$_{3/6}$ TAR ("to pose questions," so "to investigate") or INIM DI DUG$_4$ ("to hold court proceedings").

The tasks of these administrative documents could also refer to administrative practices themselves: verbs like GIN ("to confirm"), SAR ("to write"), and KIŠIB RAH$_2$ ("to affix the seal") are attested twenty-eight different times. This group contains sixteen different verbs, but only a few of them appear more than once.

Letter-orders were used as well to ask for manual labor; a cluster of verbs pertains specifically to the agricultural world, albeit their twenty-one attestations seem really few in comparison with the extreme diffusion of the tasks assigned. The two most frequent actions required are URU$_4$ ("to sow") and A DE ("to irrigate"), but in the corpus we also find more specific activities as ĜIŠ RAH$_2$ ("to thrash [the grain]") or ĜIŠ UR$_3$ ("to harrow").

Orders requiring other kinds of work are even less common, with just fifteen appearances. All the verbs of this group are attested only once, except GUB ("to be available"), which appears in two different texts. The actions here considered can be very different, going from the naval world (GID$_2$, "to tow") to handicrafts (ZAL, "to melt"), and show that letter-orders were utilized in very dissimilar spheres.

Another small assemblage of orders contains the four attestations of movement verbs; the low number of similar tasks is no wonder, since it is quite rare to order somebody to go somewhere without specifying any other action to perform.

All the remaining verbs ("to open," "to eat," "to touch," etc.) are too different to form a precise subdivision and belong to the last group.

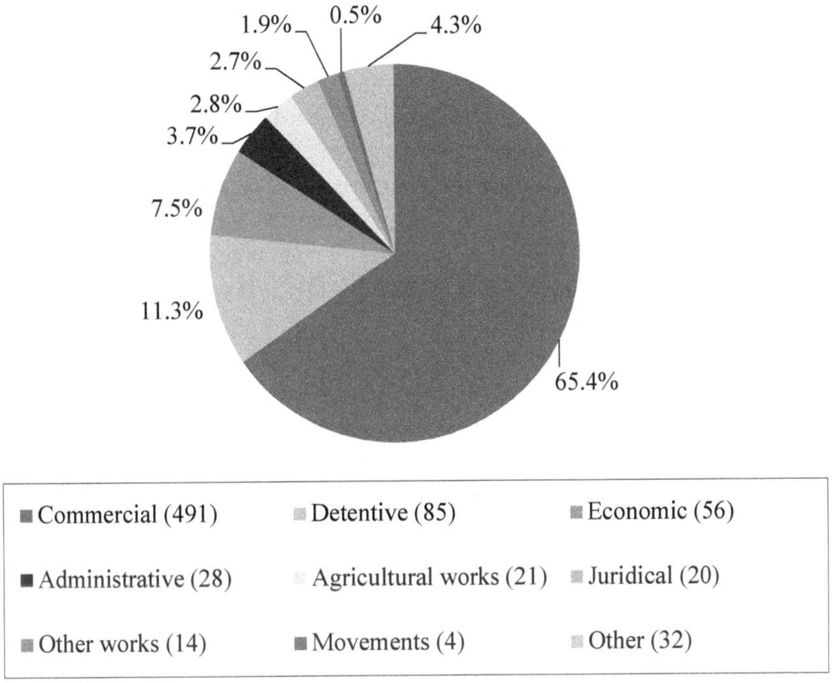


GRAPH 13.2. Tasks subdivision in the letter-orders.

The presence of these groups in the corpus is shown in graph 13.2. From the graph it appears even clearer that the principal function of letter-orders was an administrative-commercial one: they regarded mainly movements of goods, but these were not trades (since there is no trace of prices or compensations), but requests or assignments.

## The Products

Since most of the documents concern good exchanges, letter-orders offer a favorable view on Sumerian products administration; the various wares traded can be subdivided in fourteen different categories, showing a highly differentiated usage of these texts.

As easily predictable, cereals and semiprocessed goods are the most important category: the importance of barley and other grains in the Mesopotamian economy is reflected also in the letter-orders, with 224 different attestations. Barley alone appears in one of its variants in 184 texts, meaning that one in three letter-orders regarded this cereal. Without any doubt, the wide diffusion of barley in these documents is also due to its use as a ration and value measure, but letter-orders do not usually tell us when it was disbursed for an alimentary and when for an economic employment.[4] Besides barley, letter-orders report wheat, emmer, and cereal seeds. To this group also belong semiprocessed cereals, such as bran, semolina, and various types of flour.

4. Much clearer in this sense are the five texts talking about "interest-bearing barley" and "interest on barley."

Goods properly destined to be eaten form the second group, which contains thirty-two different elements. Dates ($ZU_2$-LUM) are the most attested food, and with apples ($^{ĜIŠ}$HAŠHUR), figs (PEŠ), and others contribute to make fruit the principal alimentary genre. Cereals were also elaborated and requested as bread or beer; the beverage appears in seven distinct varieties, to which one must add the beer bread (KAŠ NINDA). Equally attested are dairy products, whose main representative is clarified butter ($I_3$-NUN); all these goods were requested in small amounts, most probably because of the perishable nature of the products. Letter-orders contain tasks related also to spices, such as sesame (ĜIŠ-$I_3$) or salt (MUN), and vegetables, for example, lentils ($GU_2$-TUR-TUR).

The third group, also numbering thirty-two elements, contains animals; clearly the final use of them was an alimentary one, but since many of them were (or could have been) requested for cultic practices, they are treated here as a separate section. The most attested animals are ovines, with fourteen different typologies, while caprines are found in only three kinds. The simple ox (GUD) is the animal variety that appears the most, with fifteen attestations, and with it we can find four other sorts of bovine. Equines, that is, donkeys, are cited rarely, albeit they appear in five varieties in only four texts. Also in four letters there are requests for fish, always presented as roasted ($KU_6$ $ŠEĜ_6$).

Less attested are textiles, with twenty-five different occurrences. Most of them still do not have a precise identification, and their nature as cloth is clear only through the presence of the determinative $TUG_2$ and from the fact that they were requested in cardinal numbers, without any unit of measure. The most common textile is wool (SIKI), appearing in ten letters; wool came from ovines and caprines, and was measured by its weight. Wool and fabrics appear also as rations, alone or together with barley supplies.

Utilized in alimentary, cultural, textile, and cosmetic ambits, oily substances appear thirty-two different times. Sesame oil ($I_3$-ĜIŠ) is the most common product, being requested in twelve letters; it was always disbursed in small quantities and a couple of times also as ration. Between the other oily substances we can find two qualities of bitumen, one measured by its weight ($ESIR_2$-$HAD_2$, "dried bitumen"), and the other by its volume ($ESIR_2$-$E_2$-A "house$^?$ bitumen").

Well attested were plants without an alimentary use, appearing fifty-three different times. In the greatest number of cases the related orders concern reeds (GI), since they were used for many diverse activities; reeds were distributed by their weight or by the number of bundles, depending on their variety and on their usage. The other plants are almost all hardly identifiable, and, again, we are helped only by the determinative $U_2$ and by the requests made by bundle numbers.

Trees occupy a different category, since they were requested for their wood, measured by pieces or by weight. Willow ($^{ĜIŠ}$MA-NU) is the most attested tree with six occurrences, followed by date palm ($^{ĜIŠ}$ĜIŠNIMBAR) and pine ($^{ĜIŠ}U_3$-$SUH_5$). Wood was usually ordered in low quantities (under 10 pieces), but there are three cases where the amount of timber is much higher, up to 180 pieces of pinewood. In addition to dates and wood, date palms also occur in letter-orders with palm fiber (MANGAGA), measured by weight and involved in making ropes, and palm midrib ($^{ĜIŠ}ZE_2$-NA), measured by quantity.

The fervent naval activity of Sumerian world is also confirmed in the letter-orders, where nautical products are cited twenty-one different times. Although wood and reeds were certainly utilized in the boat construction process, the elements of this group have a clear naval purpose, while reeds and wood could also have been utilized for fire or to carve other kinds of objects. Boats are named in only three texts, but more attested are the various elements useful to build them, like planks, boards, junctions, and oars, of which we can find several varieties.

Letter-orders also contain trades of valuable objects, like metals and precious stones. Silver, which had premonetary functions, appears on eleven texts, and in two of them it is specified that it had to be delivered in exchange for some material, giving us interesting value equivalences.[5] Together with silver, although way less frequently mentioned, copper and red gold also appear in the letters. Only in one text are lapis lazuli and rare stones requested.

The following group is the most generic one, comprising all the objects that could not be better classified, and therefore it is a very diverse section, with twenty-nine different products. The most frequent elements in this subdivision are containers, used for different purposes and made of different materials (reeds, clay, skin, bronze). Other products can be associated because of their common raw materials (wooden nails, straw mats), but most of them are simply utensils or finished products, like soap, bronze combs, or mortars.

Letter-orders also dealt with the agricultural world, hosting several orders related to fields, orchards, and agricultural instruments. The simple field (A-ŠAG$_4$ or A-ŠAG4AŠAG) is attested twenty-one different times, mostly in texts ordering a change of property or of management; occasionally the documents, to better identify the field, present the name of the owner or other interesting topographical information, like canal denominations or the names of the surrounding fields.

A small minority of the orders have as their object an economic term, referring more to a concept than to a tangible reality. Excluding the rations, already catalogued under their respective compositions, this group comprises eleven elements, among which are rent, assignment, interest, and pay; their quantities are never specified, testifying that the receivers of the letters already knew the amounts involved.

Parallel to the economic terms are the administrative terms, attested in the same quantity (twenty-four times). In most of the occasions, orders pertaining with this group are related to tablets administration, using words such as documents, writings, dispositions, and other synonyms.

The last category of products contains workers, considered a sort of ware and demanded, delivered, and sent just like barley or bundles of reeds. Workers are requested forty-one different times, mostly through a generic denomination, ĜURUŠ, sometimes accompanied by a qualification, as tower, gardener, or oxen driver; other unspecialized manpower was provided by the dependent workers (ERIN$_2$) and the rented workers (LU$_2$ HUĜ-ĜA$_2$). Some other workers appear to be more qualified, especially if working in the agricultural ambit or in the nautical world; we can, thus, find duatar-gardeners (DU$_3$-A-TAR), fatteners (KURUŠDA), and towers

5. In ITT 2 02751 one shekel of silver is equivalent to one GUR of barley; in YOS 4 140 one and a half shekels of silver are the pay for every IKU of field worked.

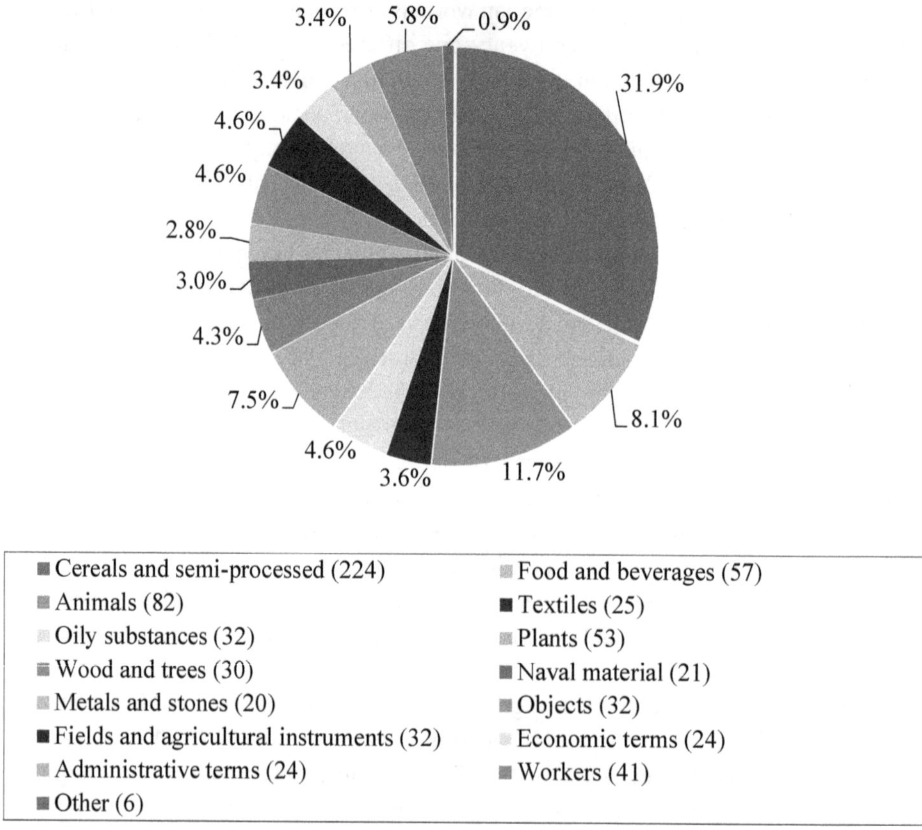


GRAPH 13.3. Products subdivision in the letter-orders.

(MA$_2$-GIDx). It seems quite plausible that the main difference between a "tower" and a "worker tower" resided in the ability of the employee: the first title better suits a professional tower, while the second to a generic worker, used as a tower just occasionally.

A small number of other terms appears untranslatable or not readable.

The various attestations of the products are summarized in graph 13.3. Connecting this graph to the preceding one we can assert that the most common use of the letter-orders was to request and exchange cereals, especially barley.

## Chronological Distribution

Unfortunately, only a small quantity of letter-orders bears a chronological indication: the sixty-seven texts where a date is present are equal to 11.5 percent of the corpus. Almost all of these report the year name (twenty-nine documents) or the year with the month name (twenty-eight), but there are some cases where only the month is indicated (nine), and one (CUSAS 3 1039) where even the day is specified.

These letters are distributed over almost forty years, from Š 32/V (TCS 1 358) to IS 7/XII (UET 3 220), and are unevenly divided: while several years are not covered by any document, there are others where we can find up to four or five texts. The reign

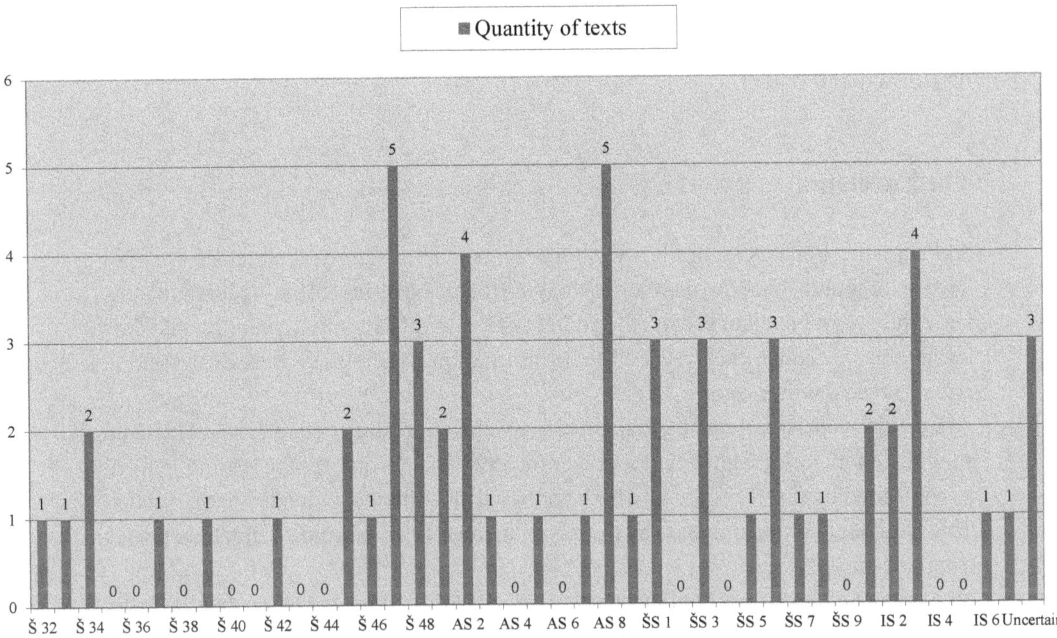


GRAPH 13.4. Chronological distribution of the dated letter-orders.

of Shulgi, unsurprisingly, supplies the greatest share of texts (eighteen, 31 percent of the dated documents), while from the times of Ibbi-Sîn come only ten letters. But comparing the number of letter-orders with the number of years of reign (considering only the period between the first and the last dated document), we can see how the best ratio comes from the reign of Shu-Suen, with one and three quarters texts per year, followed by Amar-Suen, with one and a half texts per year.

## The Sealings

More common than writing the date was affixing the seal. In the whole corpus there are 190 sealed letters (one third of the amount), presenting a total of 116 different sealings. Many of them appear only once, while the two most common belong to Aradĝu, "scribe, son of Ur-niĝar, chief cattle administrator," and to Lukalla, "scribe, son of Ur-E'e, chief cattle administrator," with 10 exemplars each.[6]

Both the classical typologies of seal appear in the letter-orders, with a higher prevalence of personal seals (129 texts) over dedicatory seals (43). The first kind presents, in its complete form, the name of the owner and his title, followed by the name of the father and his title. In the second one the focus is on a person of a higher status, with the owner consecrating the seal to him.

In rare cases, the presence of the seal is also mentioned in the text, with the sentence "Seal of PN." While in other kinds of documents, like receipts, this phrase can

6. In the corpus we find two more sealings of Aradĝu, but their legend is slightly different.

be understood as “PN received (the aforementioned material),” in the letter-orders this wording always corresponds with the actual seal impressed, which most probably belonged to the sender.

## The Envelopes

Although there is a close similarity of these texts to letters, only seventeen envelopes have been found. The low number of these artifacts, nevertheless, is understandable, since they were meant to protect the content of the text from indiscreet eyes, and they became useless once they reached their destination, where they were destroyed in order to read the message.

Even in such a restricted a group there are some interesting peculiarities. The main subdivision includes eight envelopes completely blank except for the sealing, which, as confirmed by text TCS 1 279, where the two data coincide, belonged to the sender. This kind of envelope only comes from Nippur, and no other kind of envelope comes from this city.

A couple of envelopes contain an answer to the original letter, stating that the order has been actually accomplished (*JCS* 24 133 and OLP 15 56), while another document records on the envelope the same text that was on the letter (TCS 1 053). The envelope connected to text *JCS* 28 168 6 contains only the words “Ur-Bilgamesh in Ur”: most probably, this document traveled to Ur from another city, proving that letter-orders were used not only in local exchanges, but also in wider ones.

## Tendencies

The aforementioned statistical records can give us several pieces of information about verbs, products, and seal practices, but these data, if taken separately, can be of little help in reconstructing the social and economic history of the twenty-first century BCE. The investigation of the single sections, nevertheless, is a step necessary for a deeper analysis, obtained through the comparison of the different pieces of information, in order to discover tendencies and patterns that would have not been possible to discover by examining just a small group of texts or focusing only on a single characteristic. All the preceding sections, therefore, have been analyzed both individually and globally, in particular connecting the data about the content of the text with their geographical and chronological distribution.

Considering the text composition, the principal variation from the standard is represented by the letters coming from Puzris-Dagan, which never mention the name of the sender, and also quite often do not indicate the receiver; it seems plausible that in this city senders regularly used reliable messengers and provided them orally the name of the receiver.

Relating the orders with their geographical origin it is possible to notice how some cities look specialized in peculiar ambits, differing from the general distribution of the tasks seen in graph 13.2. In Nippur, for example, letter-orders were written more in association with detentive uses (15.7 percent instead of 11.3 percent), while in Umma there was a higher diffusion of commercial letter-orders (76.1 percent instead of 65.4 percent). Girsu, the city with the most findings, has a higher rate of documents dealing with economic (11.9 percent instead of 7.4 percent), administrative (4.9 percent instead of 3.7 percent), and agricultural tasks (4.3 percent instead of 2.8 percent). Reversing the comparison, some actions seem deeply connected with precise cities, in particular with Girsu, source of the 56.5 percent of the detentive orders, 66.7 percent of the agricultural tasks, and 69.6 percent of the economic assignments.

The products distribution confirms our previous knowledge about two Sumerian cities. Letter-orders dealing with animals, in fact, come for the most part from Puzris-Dagan, the sorting center of Sumerian cattle, while many of the documents containing requests of reeds and herbs come from Umma, a town where naval manufacture was a primary activity.

It looks peculiar that dates, generally quite uncommon in these texts, are even more rare in letters dealing with juridical and detentive issues, matters where a chronological indication would seem of some importance; it is possible that these letter-orders did not have legal value, but only referred to other documents, perceived as more official, of which they were the fulfillment. More than half of the letter-orders provided with a date come from Umma (thirty-eight of sixty-seven), and the percentage of dated letters in this city reaches 22.2 percent, in spite of a general mean of 11.5 percent.

In a similar way, almost the half of the sealed letter-orders (42.6 percent) come from Umma, while only 18.6 percent come from Girsu, in spite of the higher number of texts found in this city. Reversing the analysis, 47.9 percent of the documents from Umma and 52.5 percent of the ones from Nippur contain a sealing, whereas only 14.3 percent of the letters from Girsu do so.

As mentioned previously, one peculiar kind of envelope, containing only the sealing, is deeply linked to Nippur: we have found these exemplars only in Nippur, and this is the only kind of envelope from Nippur. Even though the number found is not large, this strict correlation lets us reasonably assume that the next time a similar envelope is found, it can be associated with the same city.

Commercial letter-orders, although present in a greater quantity, and so, theoretically nearer to the medium value, show a higher percentage of dates and sealings, letting us conclude that these documents were considered more important than the others. The principal aim of letter-orders, then, appears to be the administration of product exchanges, especially barley, not only because these texts were the majority, but also because they were written with more care.

In conclusion, although composing an administrative corpus much smaller than the one formed by receipts or messenger texts, letter-orders have proven to be an interesting and prolific textual typology, which could help us to better reconstruct the Ur III world thanks to their extreme variety supported by a strong internal coherence.

## Appendix: The Prosopographical Reconstruction

A peculiar area where the letter-orders corpus shows its potential is the reconstruction of personal identities. It is manifest how an exact identification of the people appearing in the texts could help historical research, primarily because Ur III studies still lack, for various reasons, a complete research on prosopography like the one available for Neo-Assyrian times (Radner 1998, 1999; Baker 2000, 2001, 2002, 2011). The only two considerable works on this subject are either more dedicated to providing an onomastic catalogue (Limet 1968), or primarily focused on other kinds of analysis (Hilgert 2002).

In the whole letter-order corpus 791 different personal names are found, attested 1699 times. A cross-analysis of the various data of the texts allows the possibility of recognizing if two or more attestations referred to the same person, thus identifying some precise personalities. The possession of the same (or very similar) seal, obviously, is the best proof of correspondence, but we can also find important clues in the same geographical provenance, in the performing of similar activities, and in relationships with the same people. The last two points, in particular, involve letter-orders, since the corpus has proven to be coherent in place, time, and content, and the informative parts of the texts often contain this kind of information.

The most attested personage in the corpus is the famous Ur-niĝar of Umma, head of the most influential family of the city. Even though he is mentioned in twenty different letter-orders, Ur-niĝar appears, usually with the title of chief cattle administrator, but only in the seals of some his sons, like Ayakalla, Aradĝu and Lukalla; Ur-Lisi and Ur-E'e, although being his sons, seal letter-orders without citing their patronymic, showing a different relationship with the father.[7]

Another example of the prosopographical potential of the letter-orders is presented by one Lu-Ninĝirsu, who appears in ten letters, again only as a patronymic in the seals of his three sons. These seals belong to subsequent periods, and the patronymic bears different professions; from this we can infer that he started his career as an animal fattener and later (before šs 1) he became the shepherd of the *nakabtum*. Utilizing just letter-orders, and not even texts where Lu-Ninĝirsu is actively participating or being mentioned by someone, it is possible to reconstruct his career, his family, and the development of both.

Other various minor identifications can assist in reconstructing the place of origin of the tablets, the period of time they belong to, or other information. The seal of message YOS 4 143 has been partially reconstructed with the help of texts MVN 3 226 and Aleppo 047; the seal on letter CST 531 has been identified thanks to the presence on the document of Lu-kitus-lu, attested with Aradĝu in text Aleppo 075. Once the Bazi mentioned in missives *BiOr* 26 379 and *AuOr* 17 31 was identified as the same person, it was possible to locate the first epistle as also coming from the city of Girsu; the same is true for texts TCS 1 106 and TCS 1 114, where the same seal occurred on both, but whose provenience (Umma) was known only from the first one.

The letter-orders corpus, therefore, proves to be of great help in the reconstruction of personal identities, thanks to its coherence and its variety, and consisting, furthermore, of a limited number of texts. Every successful identification, moreover, serves as a reference point for recognizing other people mentioned in the texts, creating a sort of concentric network where every discovery provides support for the previous ones and allows for other identifications. If, for example, we would find some attestations of a certain Ur-Nanše and we managed to identify him with certainty, we would establish a fulcrum in our reconstruction; it would then be possible to apply the information we have about

7. The name "Ur-niĝar" occurs nineteen other times in the corpus, but refers to other people.

him and his texts (date, city, activities) to the people with whom he has connections, completing their personal profiles. Each one of these individuals, who represent a first circle around the fulcrum, will have relationships with other people, and the data pertinent to this second circle will influence the first one, reflecting, furthermore, on the original center of the network, Ur-Nanše himself. As shown, every new person whose identity is established with certainty helps the reconstruction of all the others, directly or through several degrees of separation. This concentric model is a mere simplification of the interpersonal connections, in reality much more interrelated, but it represents a first attempt through which we can understand the composition of Sumerian society.

## BIBLIOGRAPHY


Baker, H. D.

2000 *The Prosopography of the Neo-Assyrian Empire*, vol. 2, part 1: *H–K*. Helsinki: Neo-Assyrian Text Corpus Project.

2001 *The Prosopography of the Neo-Assyrian Empire*, vol. 2, part 2: *L–N*. Helsinki: Neo-Assyrian Text Corpus Project.

2002 *The Prosopography of the Neo-Assyrian Empire*, vol. 3, part 1: *P–Ṣ*. Helsinki: Neo-Assyrian Text Corpus Project.

2011 *The Prosopography of the Neo-Assyrian Empire*, vol. 3, part 2: *Š–Z*. Helsinki: Neo-Assyrian Text Corpus Project.

Edzard, D. O.

2003 *Sumerian Grammar*. HdO 71. Leiden: Brill.

Gragg, G.

1973 A Class of "When" Clauses in Sumerian. *JNES* 32: 125–134.

Hilgert, M.

2002 *Akkadisch in der Ur III Zeit*. Imgula 5. Münster: Rhema.

Kaneva, I. T.

2000 Parataxe und Hypotaxe im Sumerischen: Die Rolle der Modalpräfixe. Pp. 521–537 in *Studi sul Vicino Oriente Antico dedicati alla memoria di Luigi Cagni*. Edited by S. Graziani. Napoli: Istituto universitario orientale.

Lampasona, D. U.

2012 *Le letter-Orders del periodo Ur III*. PhD diss., University of Naples "L'Orientale."

Limet, H.

1968 *L'anthroponymie sumérienne dans les documents de la 3e dynastie d'Ur*. Paris: Belles Lettres.

MacGinnis, J.

1995 *Letter Orders from Sippar and the Administration of the Ebabbara in the Late-Babylonian Period*. Poznań: Bonami.

McEwan, G. J. P.

1981 *Priest and Temple in Hellenistic Babylonia*. FAOS 4. Wiesbaden: Steiner.

Michalowski, P.

1993 *Letters from Early Mesopotamia*. WAW 3. Atlanta: Scholars Press.

2011 *The Royal Correspondence of the Kings of Ur: An Epistolary History of an Ancient Mesopotamian Kingdom*. MC 15. Winona Lake, IN: Eisenbrauns.

Molina, M.

1999–2000 Neo-Sumerian Letter-orders in the British Museum I. *AuOr* 17–18: 215–228.

Notizia, P. and Di Ludovico, A.

2012 A New Ur III Letter-Order from the Semitic Museum at Harvard University. *CDLB* 2012.3: 1–6.

Oppenheim, A. L.
1948 *Catalogue of the Cuneiform Tablets of the Wilberforce Eames Babylonian Collection in the New York Public Library: Tablets of the Time of the Third Dynasty of Ur*. AOS 32. New Haven: American Oriental Society.

Radner, K.
1998 *The Prosopography of the Neo-Assyrian Empire*, vol. 1, part 1: *A*. Helsinki: Neo-Assyrian Text Corpus Project.
1999 *The Prosopography of the Neo-Assyrian Empire*, vol. 1, part 2: *B–G*. Helsinki: Neo-Assyrian Text Corpus Project.

Sollberger, E.
1966 *The Business and Administrative Correspondence Under the Kings of Ur*. TCS 1. Locust Valley, NY: Augustin.

Thomsen, M. L.
1984 *The Sumerian Language: An Introduction to Its History and Grammatical Structure*. Mesopotamia 10. Copenhagen: Akademisk Forlag.

Wilcke, C.
2010 Sumerian: What We Know and What We Want to Know. Pp. 5–76 in vol. 1 of *Language in the Ancient Near East: Proceedings of the 53e Rencontre Assyriologique Internationale*. Edited by L. Kogan, N. Koslova, S. Loesov, and S. Tishchenko. 2 vols. Babel und Bibel 4. Orientalia et Classica 30. Winona Lake, IN: Eisenbrauns.

CHAPTER 14

# Luminous Oils and Waters of Wisdom: Shedding New Light on Oil Divination

Alex Loktionov and Christoph Schmidhuber

THE CRUCIAL POSITION DIVINATION HELD in Mesopotamian religion and society, as well as beyond the Babylonian and Assyrian heartlands, has long been acknowledged and has justly received scholarly attention since the early days of Assyriology (e.g., Klauber 1913; Zimmern 1901). Much progress has been made in the contextual study of divinatory theory and practice (e.g., Koch 2010; Rochberg 2007), although mainly focusing on extispicy and celestial divination, leaving aside the smaller, but considerable corpora relating to other types of divination. Oil divination is one such example. This paper attempts to elucidate its potential to contribute to current discussions concerning divination with insights from both the field itself but also other relevant Assyriological themes.

## Previous Research

To date, most of the work on oil divination has been carried out by G. Pettinato (1966) in his *Die Ölwahrsagung bei den Babyloniern*. Apart from producing a composite text based on several manuscripts, mostly assigned to the Old Babylonian Period and partially to the Middle Babylonian Period, he also provided a valuable introduction contextualizing the omens themselves with reference to other sources attested for oil divination, with the *Ritualtafeln für die Wahrsager* (Zimmern 1901) serving as a key source. A considerable proportion of this argument falls back on Pettinato's double volume, which remains the main reference work in this field.

## Oil Divination in Mesopotamian Cultural History

Sources outside the omen corpus testify to the considerable value attached to oil divination at least from the Old Babylonian period onward. In the ancient Mesopotamian cultural memory, oil divination, just like extispicy, is traced back to the antediluvian king Enmeduranki of Sippar and ultimately to the gods Shamash and Adad. This idea can be seen in certain Kuyunjik texts:

> *šamnu ina mê naṭālu niṣirti* $^{d}$*Anim* $^{d}$*Ellil u* $^{d}$*Ea ušabrûšu*
> they showed him (Enmeduranki) how to observe oil on water; a mystery of Anu, Enlil, and Ea. (Lambert 1967: 132: 17)

And also:

> *mār* [lú]*bārê šamni zēru dārû pir'i Enmeduranki šar Sippari*[ki]
> An expert in oil, of abiding descent, offspring of Enmeduranki, King of Sippar. (Lambert 1967: 132: 22–23)

Emphasizing the ancient (or even divine) roots of oil divination would likely have contributed to the formation of a scholarly identity among its practitioners. It can therefore be claimed that at least in theory oil divination was highly valued, perhaps even at a level comparable to extispicy.

The type of decisions for which the method was employed remains somewhat unclear. There is relatively little evidence for oil divination pertaining to royal decision-making. Indeed, one incantation states that oil could be brought by poor women seeking the verdict of Shamash (Polonsky 2000: 98), which might be seen as an indication of oil divination as being of fairly low status. However, this is not necessarily the case, as it could merely indicate a broader presence of the method across multiple social strata, or may conceivably even allude to an offering outside a divinatory context. However, occasional references can be found in royal contexts, such as this inscription by Sargon II:

> *ina mākalti bārûti īpulannima*
> He answered me in the bowl of divination. (Campbell-Thompson and Hamilton 1932: 103)

And this one by Esarhaddon:

> *ina mākalti bārûti têrēti tukulti iššaknunim*
> In the *mākaltu*-bowl of the diviners trustworthy oracles were set for me. (Borger 1956: 19)

Having underlined the important role oil divination played as a means to read signs from the gods, we can look at the observations in our practical reconstructions of the performance of oil divination alongside further thoughts on various aspects of the written evidence.

## The Practical Dimension

It must be emphasized that the practicals were not designed to objectively recreate oil divination exactly as it was originally performed. There is no conclusive information on what containers were used, the type of oil is unclear, and so is the way the pouring was carried out: Was it in an interrupted or continuous motion, what were the volumes poured, and what was the height for the oil to fall through before making impact? Rather, the aim was simply to engage with the changing materialities of oil and water when the two come into contact, to get some general idea of which outcomes were viable, which variables were important, and whether or not these are duly reflected in the omen corpus.

FIGURE 14.1. Single mass of oil after first stage of experiment: oil on water.

FIGURE 14.2. Multiple masses of oil, of varying shapes and sizes, after second stage of experiment: water over oil on water.

The method followed Pettinato's implicit suggestion that first oil was poured on water and subsequently more water was poured atop the oil already in the bowl. The key observation was that the first pouring—oil on water, consistently resulted in a single mass forming near the center of the vessel (fig. 14.1). This lack of variation is highly significant, contrasting with thirty different ominous outcomes for this stage attested just in Pettinato's *Hauptmanuskript*. Many of these pertained to more than one mass of oil being present; for instance:

> *Šamnum ana ṣīt* [d]*Šamšim ipṭurma 7 tutturū ūṣûni manzāz kūbi ana mākālim*
> (When) the oil spreads out toward the sunrise and seven patches go out: position of a foetus for feeding. (Pettinato 1966: 2:15)

This proved quite impossible to achieve. Of course, the discrepancy may be associated purely with methodological inconsistencies, in particular the height from which oil was poured, but even so the difference between one oil mass and seven is quite large, and therefore it is tempting to assume genuine discrepancy between hypothetical outcomes listed and feasible outcomes attained.

At the same time, the anticipated high levels of variation were duly visible during the second stage (fig. 14.2), when additional water divided up the initial oil mass into surface patterns that were different each time. For example:

> *7 šulmu manzāz malkim*
> 7 bubbles—position of the Prince (demon). (Pettinato 1966: 2:22)

In view of the aforementioned experiments, this is quite realistic, even acknowledging methodological flaws. Overall, it therefore seems sufficiently clear that the two stages of pouring would have yielded different results, even if modern inadequacies mean one cannot be certain what these were. The variety of outcomes increased rapidly from the first to the second stage, but this is not at all reflected in the corpus, which lists similar ranges of possibilities for both stages. This implies that the first part purposefully included very unlikely or indeed impossible protases. This is of course seen in other, more extensive omen compendia. One example from *Šumma izbu* will suffice, although there are many more:

> *Šumma laḫru nēša ulidma pāni kalbi šakin* [d]*Nergal ikkal*
> If a ewe gives birth to a lion and it has the face of a dog—Nergal will consume. (de Zorzi 2011: 62)

Needless to say, this is biologically impossible, but purely hypothetical omens like this must have existed for a reason. In all probability, they aimed to ensure that all bases were covered; creating an impression of great thoroughness where answers are available even if the impossible manifests itself. The same may be true of oil omina: indeed, in view of the usual lack of variability after the first step, the chance of any other sign occurring at this point would perhaps have been seen as especially ominous. It would also have serious implications for the whole outcome of the query, including the subsequent step that built on the initial observation. The hypothetical omens may be a remedy for this—attempts to predict the unpredictable, so that even the impossible could be interpreted if the need arose.

By contrast, the omens pertaining to the second step reach the other extreme: instead of there being too many, at first sight there seem far too few. Judging from the experiments, the number of distinguishable combinations should essentially be unlimited, but only thirty-two outcomes are recorded as protases. Thus, the second stage omens necessitated a highly critical approach to the materiality of the results, with the diviner needing to fit potentially infinite outcomes into finite and highly restricted interpretations, which could then be linked to an apodosis. This would provide vast scope for subjectivity based on individual perceptions of phenomena that failed to clearly match any protasis.

## Multiple Variables: Size, Shape, Wind, and Light

Moreover, the large number of variables brought out in the protases adds further diversity to an already highly subjective process. Obvious ones include the number and position of oil bubbles, both in relation to one another, to compass points, and to relative directions. For instance:

> *Šamnum šulmam iddima ana šumēl šamnim ishuramma šumēl šamnim iṣbat wāšib maḫrika awātika uštenēṣṣi*
> The oil emitted a bubble and it lingered on the left of the oil, and seized the left (side) of the oil, the one who dwells by your side will keep dismissing your words. (Pettinato 1966: 2:21)

The role of wind likewise cannot be discounted, sometimes leading to the movement of oil bubbles to positions very different from where they were on the point of impact. Based on the experiments, this seems like a feasible process. Particular significance is attached to omens featuring movement toward cardinal points. Here is an example:

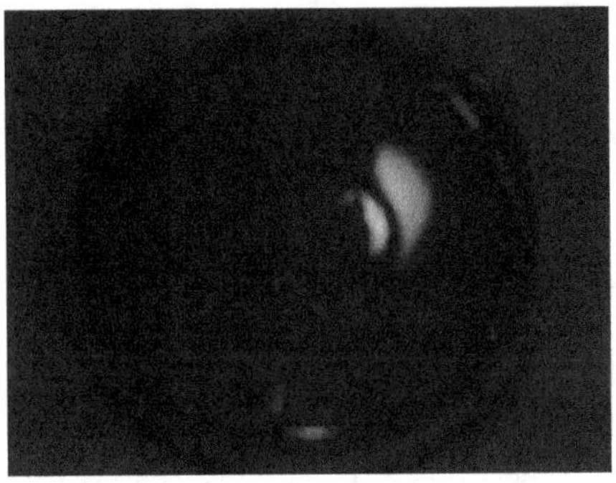

FIGURE 14.3. Greater prominence of luminous sheen (shininess) on the oil surface in conditions of low light intensity.

> *Šamnum ana erēb Šamšim ipṭur lummun libbim*
> The oil spread out toward the sunset (west): grief. (Pettinato 1966: 2:24)

Furthermore, additional trials carried out at low light intensity (fig.14.3) highlighted the immense significance of the impact of light on the perceived nature of the bubbles. The shininess of the oil was altered most of all, as the images demonstrate. Interestingly, reexamining the written record with respect to light, it is noteworthy that the ritual significance of the sun goes beyond its cosmological signifier Shamash, divine judge and oracle, but also emphasizes pure nonembodied light, that is, the materiality of the sun as itself. Several sources emphasize the sunrise as the exact point of time at which judgment is provided, an issue that was expertly addressed at the 44th Rencontre (Polonsky 2000). Specifically for divination, there is considerable evidence for the relationship between light and a truthful answer, as indicated both in the ritual tablets (Zimmern 1901), as well as in the formulaic disregard-clauses in Neo-Assyrian divination queries (Starr 1990):

> *ina šērim lām Šamši napāḫi bārû egubba irammuk*
> Shall the extispicer clean (his hands) in the holy water vessel at dawn before sunrise. (Zimmern 1901: 112–123: line 3)

> *aradka pulpul ina Šamši šatturi nīqe liqqi // erēna liššima ana maḫār Šamši lizziz*
> "Your slave, this and that, may offer a sacrifice in the early morning hour, he may raise the cedar staff and stand in front of Shamash." (Zimmern 1901: 100–101: lines 69–70)

> [*ezib ša dīn ūmi annî kī ṭābû*] *kī ḫaṭû ūmu saḫpu šamû izan*[*nun*]
> [Disregard the (formulation) of today's case, be it good], be it faulty, (and that) the day is overcast and it is ra[ining]. (Starr 1990: 26: line 3')

On top of that, at least one source suggests that good light conditions were crucial to the choice of the place of extispicy, again emphasizing the role of light in the act of divination:

> *ūlā ṣābū lā ṭâb ana šaqîm // ina libbi ūrim šá bīt ilim ina kallâmāri // niklu memēni lu nakla // ina pān iṣṣūri ina pān memēni aḫullâ // [ina] muḫḫi ūrim ša bīt ᵈMarduk ša šarrum bēli iqbûni // [ina] libbi ṭâb ana epāše ulûlu ṭâb // u ūmu šanû ana bārûti ṭâbma // ina pitti linnepiš*
>
> Alternatively, if it is not good to let the men go to the roof of the temple at dawn, some expedient must be formed on account of the bird (and) anything beyond it. [Co]ncerning the roof of the temple of Marduk about which the king, my lord, spoke, it is good to perform (the ritual) there. Elul (VI) is a good month; and the 2nd day is suitable for extispicy. Let it be performed accordingly. (Parpola 1993: 183, lines 1–8′)

Ancient concern about wind and light thus underlines the importance of the weather, built environment, and the time of day on the act of oil divination. In particular, they emphasize the duality of the sun and sunlight as both a metaphor, namely Shamash and justice, and a physical reality. In a wider context, this is no new concept—it may, for example, be worth drawing parallels to Egyptian Atenist dualities in the Amarna period (e.g., Sandman 1938: 90–96).

## Inherent Subjectivities of Perception and Interpretation

These last two variables, wind and light, highlight the crucial role of *looking* at different points in time during the divination. This is perhaps an issue where the oil divination methodology differs most strikingly with many other divinatory techniques reliant on a static medium, like a *šumma izbu* foetus or an extispicy liver. The water surface never stays the same, and the time of observation would clearly be instrumental in the outcome. Whether this point varied from practitioner to practitioner or was objectively agreed on is unfortunately not preserved in existing records.

Building on this inherent subjectivity of interpretation, one can see how oil divination could be especially useful for generating the divine legitimacy needed to endorse predetermined actions. With highly ambiguous results probably never exactly matching any particular prescribed omen, and the extra temporal dimension perhaps allowing the omen to be taken at whatever point the bubble pattern was most suitable, it is likely that an experienced diviner could implicitly render the outcomes favorable. Oil divination can therefore be seen as a way of purposefully transferring agency from an individual intent on committing a particular action, to a supernatural entity (in this case Shamash) providing a firm and unquestionable endorsement. Such a framework has already been suggested for Neo-Assyrian extispicy (Koch 2010: 54), but it seems that it is equally if not more applicable to oil divination, with its greater range of variables and increased scope for ambiguity. Furthermore, the extra step of matching up the constantly changing surface pattern with the fixed protases in the corpus was likely associated with a complex and selective learning process that is as yet poorly understood but was clearly an element within the *bārûtu* tradition. Employing Koch's (2010: 50) theory of mind mechanism, one can go as far as saying that oil diviners may have effectively created a variable and ambiguous disembodied consciousness materialized in the oil and water, and representing the will of a higher deity. Coupled with their own status as professionals possessing specialized esoteric knowledge, this could have been a highly effective way of legitimizing predetermined actions.

## The Wider Context of Oil Divination: Parallels with Extispicy?

Of course, oil divination did not develop in isolation and its place in a wider divinatory framework is certainly worthy of further research. Extispicy has already been mentioned in passing at various points, and it certainly seems to have some interesting parallels with oil divination. That should be the subject of another paper, so just one more connection will be discussed. This relates to the term *šulmu*, which is used in both divinatory corpora—in oil omens, it is thought to mean "bubble," but it also denotes an important aspect of liver morphology alongside its usage as the abstract noun "well being." Some examples can illustrate this:

> 7 *šulmū manzāz malkim*
> 7 bubbles—position of the Prince (demon). (Pettinato 1966: 2:22)

And in extispicy:

> ... *dannatum šakin šulmu imittam u šumēlam* [*šak*]*in* ...
> ... The "Strength" is present. The "Well-Being"(?) is present (Starr 1990: 20 line 14')

What is to be made of this unusual vocabulary link and the similar ways of employing light in both divination types is not altogether clear. As has been shown, the omina in Pettinato's *Hauptmanuskript* indicate that the procedure was carried out at sunrise. The disregard clause quoted earlier shows that this was also the case with extispicy, with light intensity clearly affecting the method. In such a context it is of course unsurprising that both methods also share a link to Shamash as the ultimate source of the verdicts that they, quite physically, elucidate.

## Conclusion

Overall, the various strands of research presented here are but preliminary bases for further investigation, highlighting the potential contribution of oil divination to wider divinatory debate, and reevaluating extant primary material in the light of ideas triggered by engaging with subjective experience of the ancient ritual, however imperfect the attempt. The highly ambiguous nature of omen interpretation, alongside the vital role of light as a divine and physical concept, likely generated an interesting interplay of theory and practice drawing on both cosmological and mundane experience.

**BIBLIOGRAPHY**


Borger, R.
1956 *Die Inschriften Asarhaddons Königs von Assyrien*. AfOB 9. Graz: Self-published.

Campbell-Thompson, R. and Hamilton, R. W.
1932 *The British Museum Excavations on the Temple of Ishtar at Nineveh, 1930–31*. Annals of Archaeology and Anthropology 19. Liverpool: University Press.

Klauber, E. G.
1913 *Politisch-religiöse Texte aus der Sargonidenzeit*. Leipzig: Pfeiffer.

Koch, U.
2010 Three Strikes and You're Out! A View on Cognitive Theory and the First-Millennium Extispicy Ritual. Pp. 43–60 in *Divination and Interpretation of Signs in the Ancient World*. Edited by A. Annus. OIS 6. Chicago: Oriental Institute of the University of Chicago.

Lambert, W. G.
1967 Enmeduranki and Related Matters. *JCS* 21: 126–138.

Leichty, E.
1970 *The Omen Series Šumma Izbu*. TCS 4. Locust Valley, NY: Augustin.

Parpola, S.
1993 *Letters from Assyrian and Babylonian Scholars*. SAA 10. Helsinki: Helsinki University Press.

Pettinato, G.
1966 *Die Ölwahrsagung bei den Babyloniern*. 2 vols. Rome: Instituto di Studi del Vicino Oriente, Università di Roma.

Polonsky, J.
2000 Ki-$^{d}$Utu-è-a: Where Destiny Is Determined? Pp. 89–100 in *Landscapes: Territories, Frontiers and Horizons in the Ancient Near East; Papers Presented to the XLIV Rencontre Assyriologique Internationale, Venezia, 7–11 July 1997*, part 3: *Landscape in Ideology, Religion, Literature and Art*. Edited by L. Milano, S. de Martino, F. M. Fales, and G. B. Lanfranchi. 3 vols. HANE/M 3. Padova: Sargon.

Rochberg, F.
2007 *The Heavenly Writing: Divination, Horoscopy and Astronomy in Mesopotamian Culture*. Cambridge: Cambridge University Press.

Sandman, M. A. J.
1938 *Texts from the Time of Akhenaten*. Bibliotheca Aegyptiaca 8. Brussels: Edition de la Fondation égyptologique Reine Elisabeth.

Starr, I.
1990 *Queries to the Sungod: Divination and Politics in Sargonid Assyria*. SAA 4. Helsinki: Helsinki University Press.

Zimmern, H.
1901 *Beitrage zur Kenntnis der babylonischen Religion*. Leipzig: Hinrichs.

Zorzi, N. de.
2011 The Omen Series Šumma Izbu: Internal Structure and Hermeneutic Strategies. *Kaskal* 8: 43–75.

CHAPTER 15

# (Mis)Translating Gender: The Scribes Couldn't Have Been Competent, They Didn't Go to Yale

Kathleen McCaffrey

GENDER THEORY, a methodology that encompasses both feminist and queer theory and the closely related study of power and ethnicity, has become a standard tool of analysis in the humanities over the past twenty years, yet it is still at best erratically used in Assyriology.[1] Apart from a handful of contributors with exposure to gender theory through broader studies in archaeology, art history, classics, or theology, most recent gender-themed research within ancient Near Eastern Studies displays little or no awareness of gender theory, and the only nonnormative gender status as yet widely entertained in ancient Near Eastern Studies is a postulated "third gender" of hermaphrodites and men unable to have sex with women (Asher-Greve 1997a: 438; Gabbay 2008; Nissinen 2010: 76).[2] Accepting philological assurances about the orthodoxy of gender roles in early history, few gender theorists have delved into the arcane languages and literatures of the ancient Near East. On the other side, the heavy use of jargon, labels that sometimes seem politicized, and theoretical frameworks (e.g., Foucault) that are predicated on European history and thus difficult to extrapolate to non-Western cultures have given philologists the impression that gender theory has little practical application to the ancient Near East.[3]

The merger of Assyriology and theoretical gender studies has the potential to revitalize both endeavors. Assyriology offers a nearly pristine data set that encompasses half of recorded history, bearing directly on modern controversies about sexuality and religion, while gender theory promises to illuminate the primary Near Eastern data in unexpected ways. Nonetheless one must begin by acknowledging that the old expediency of partnering across disciplines without mutual cross training has been unproductive. Gender theorists cannot work at remove from the original texts because texts translated by area specialists have already been interpreted with unexamined assumptions. Assyriologists cannot apply extraneous gender theory without understanding how that theory was derived and where it is likely to fall short in explaining ancient data.

1. For aversion to gender theory in Assyriology see Michalowski 1990: 381; 1996: 192–193; Asher-Greve 1997b: 223; 1998; 2000a: 126; 2000b: 5; Liverani 2000: 331; Ferrara 2002: 134.

2. Those with exposure to gender theory are, e.g., Guinan 1997; Van De Mieroop 1999: ch. 5, "Gender and Mesopotamian History"; Bahrani 2000, 2001; Chapman 2004; Ackerman 2005; Assante 2007b, 2009; Nissinen 2010; Stökl 2013.

3. For the inappropriateness of applying Foucault to ancient history see Halperin 2002: ch. 1; Chapman 2004: 5 n. 14.

Contradicting the common sense that sex and gender are biologically determined, the most basic insight of gender theory is that categories and concepts of sex/gender are culturally variable. Terms such as "homosexual" and "transvestite" and even "prostitute," "hermaphrodite," and "eunuch" refer to concepts that are culturally specific to the Western tradition. Ethnographic studies have revealed that non-Western informants often have no equivalent categories and find the terms so incomprehensible that they do not know how to answer or respond with puzzled inquiries about the researcher's own culture.[4] Neither anatomical sex nor choice of sex object tend to be the foremost determinants of gender identity in some ancient or non-Western cultures (Ringrose 1996: 95; Nanda 2000: 2, 17, 44; Halperin 2002: 37–38; Towle and Morgan 2002: 472–473). Instead of two anatomically defined categories, behavioral taxonomies include additional or alternate gender statuses that vary from one culture to the next, ranging from religio-political offices with gender aspects to institutionalized gender categories defined by considerations of behavior, age, and/or social status. Gender variant statuses are also more likely to be transient than anatomically defined gender categories, with some individuals opting or aging in/out over a lifetime.[5]

Prior to the development of gender theory deduced from cross-cultural comparisons, travelers and ethnographers coming from the West were often bewildered to encounter foreigners in unfamiliar gender roles, designated by terms that were difficult to map to their own vocabularies. Struggling to make sense of the unfamiliar categories, they misidentified gender variants as transsexuals, eunuchs, transvestites, homosexuals, prostitutes, or hermaphrodites, applying their own labels interchangeably or fretting over the poor fit with their own terminology (Hill 1935; Devereux 1937; Wikan 1982: 148, 172; Herdt 1994: 23–24, 64; Roscoe 1994: 329–331; Horswell 1997; Murray 1997b: 250–252, 254 n. 21; Nanda 2000: 18). The same smorgasbord can be seen in Assyriological translations of Sumerian and Akkadian gender-related terms (table 15.1).

Problems of translation have also manifested in more subtle ways. The tendency of many texts to designate some individuals (especially the goddess Ishtar and women who seem ordinary in other respects) with irregular grammar is most evident in Akkadian due to the lack of grammatical gender in Sumerian and Hittite. Texts from various regions and periods display the occasional inflection or suffixed pronoun (especially *-šu/-ša* "his/her" and *-ka/-ki* "your [m.]/your [f.]" and *-šu/-ši* "he/she [acc.]") that conflicts with apparent sex. For well over a century, students of Akkadian have been told to overlook this type of inconsistency. For instance, the earliest Akkadian

4. E.g., when asked by anthropologists to provide information about homosexuals in their societies, nineteenth-century Melanesians and Native American informants could not understand the question (Kessler and McKenna 1978: 36; Roscoe 1998: 122). Among many examples from the Middle East, Wikan 1982: 148, 170 cites miscommunications with her Sohari informants about the nature of the Omani *xanith* and *bitxannith*; Necef 1992: 73 comments that Turks have difficulty explaining *ibneler* to Europeans; Thesiger 1964: 125 observes the absence of female prostitution and unfamiliarity with the idea of homosexuality in Marsh Arab society; the anthropologist Westphal-Hellbusch 1997: 234 reports on her inability to elicit information from Marsh Arabs about an older cross-dressed man who was being treated affably.

5. Hill 1935: 273; Thesiger 1964: 131; Wikan 1982: 174–175; Besnier 1996: 311; Murray 1997c: 211; 1997a: 257; Westphal-Hellbusch 1997: 237–238; Nanda 2000: 59. Unawareness of this aspect of gender variance can be seen in Assyriological arguments that presume that biological parenthood is incompatible with gender variant status, e.g., evaluations of the *assinnu* (Stökl 2012: 58).

TABLE 15.1. Assyriological translations of Sumerian and Akkadian gender-related terms.

| | |
|---|---|
| UR-SAL/*assinnu* | Jastrow (1917: 239) eunuch; *CAD* (A/2:341–342) cultic personnel; Sladek (1974: 40) heterosexually impotent being; Reiner (1985: 42) either a eunuch, homosexual or, most likely, a transvestite actor; Roscoe (1996) homosexual; Worthington (2012: 205) male cultic prostitute; Stökl (2012: 61) cult official of Ishtar; Zsolnay (2013: 98-99) strong-man cultic warrior |
| KAR-KID/*ḫarimtu* | *CAD* (Ḫ:101) prostitute; Westenholz (1989: 262) one who is outside the culturally defined bounds of controlled sexuality; Assante (1998: 10, 86) single independent woman who resides outside a patriarchal household; Cooper (2006b: 13) commercial prostitute; Roth (2006: 24) private prostitute; Silver (2006: 658) cultic prostitute |
| KURGARRA/*kurgarrû* | Kramer (1963: 491) sexless creature; *CAD* (K:557) actor, cultic performer; Cooper (1983: 259) certainly a homosexual, possibly a eunuch; Nissinen (2010: 76) in common with the *assinnu*, a third gender or nongender of men with mixed evidence of castration |
| SAĜ-UR-SAĜ/? | Bullough (1971: 192) eunuch; Reisman (1973: 187) male homosexual; Leick (1994: 158) hermaphrodite; Westenholz (2007: 338) costumed asexual or hermaphroditic personnel; ePSD (2014) cultic performer |

grammar instructs students to disregard masculine verbs that reference the warrior goddess Ishtar, while the most recent grammar states that Mesopotamian scribes did not always distinguish masculine and feminine pronouns (Sayce 1872: 66, 118; Huehnergard 2000: 598). The presupposition that runs through the secondary literature is that the modern Assyriologist is better trained and more careful than Mesopotamian scribes who continually blundered with grammatical gender.[6] The slight theoretical toolkit of intuitive philology provides no check on the mind-set that "we should not let manuscripts bully us into accepting their readings when we have good reason to believe that ours are better" (Worthington 2012: 299) or standard of comparison for evaluating mismatches sprinkled across tens of thousands of texts. Emendations of irregular gender introduced at the point of transcription are also seldom footnoted, rendering the normalization process invisible to most readers.

Turning a spotlight in particular on the unfeminine referencing of members of the *ḫarimtu* category, this study proposes that the habitual normalization of Akkadian texts is blurring gender statuses that are foreign to Western gender logic, particularly forms of ancient female variance. Assyriology promises to be especially important for understanding the range of female experience in the past for, while gender studies has come a long way in correcting false first impressions about male gender variants, it has made less progress in detecting and analyzing female variance. One would expect the female gender identity to be as variable and complex as the male, yet most

6. Lacheman 1973: 100; Foster 1987: 35 n. 68; George 2003: 299, 440; Stökl 2009: 96–98; Worthington 2012: 109. For gender normalization of Sumerian irregularities (NIN in masculine names, $^{d}$INANA.NITA "male Inanna" at Mari, the GALA's effeminate speech) see Selz 2000: 32; Heimpel 2002; Cooper 2006a: 44.

studies have focused on men, conceptualizing gender variant identities as shifts from male to variant male status while allotting a single reproductive function to women.

In trying to account for why historical gender variance has seemed to be a male phenomenon, it has been suggested that female variance may have gone missing from the historical record because patriarchal societies constrained its expression, making manifestations individual and private (Morris 1994: 25; Nanda 2000: 7–8). This explanation falls short because evidence has been accumulating that observers are often oblivious to nonconformist female behavior that is right in front of them. Even when female variance exists side by side with male variance and even when it is characterized by cross-dressing and unfeminine behaviors, the female gender variant tends to go unnoticed or is misconstrued as a prostitute.[7] The lack of salience is due to several factors. Experimental psychologists have demonstrated that the ingrained bias of Western observers to see mixed or ambiguous cues as masculine effectively obliterates the female presence.[8] Female gender variance is also overlooked because it has a cultural and historical dynamic of its own that is not a derivation or reversal of male variance (Nanda 2000: 7). Female gender variance does sometimes correlate with sexual orientation, but the defining characteristic that distinguishes female transgenderance from effeminacy is that a socially masculine status enables a woman of any preference to be personally autonomous and to participate in public life.

Gender theory invites us to reassess the *ḫarimtu* controversy with new questions and a larger data set. This study builds on J. Assante's (1998, 2003, 2007a, 2007b, 2009) thesis that the gist of the term *ḫarimtu* was not sexual and that it referenced an independent woman who belonged to a distinct legal category. Presuming that any reference to sexual activity supports the traditional translation, Assante's critics have focused on key passages that allude to sex, passing lightly over citations that seem out of character.[9] The incompatible references, however, are in line with a pattern observed by gender theorists in other specialties. Lacking a defined role for socially masculine women in the Western tradition, Westerners have tended to overlook or misconstrue female gender variance in non-Western cultures, perceiving female personal autonomy and fraternization with men (the point of greatest tension) as the loose conduct of a common prostitute. The Mesopotamian *ḫarimtu* (defined by her residence

7. Blackwell 1984; Morris 1994: 31; Grémaux 1996; Dickemann 1997; Blackwood 1998; Gilchrist 2000; cf. Walls 2001: 1–92; and Nissinen 1998: 19–36 for the similar overlooking of female variance by queer theorists. Ackerman 2005: 138–148 stands apart in recognizing the liminality and agency of various female characters in the Gilgamesh Epic.

8. E.g., Western observers commonly infer masculinity when no visible sex is present, sex-typing stuffed animals, cartoon characters, and babies as male. See Kessler and McKenna 1978, ch. 6: "Toward A Theory of Gender," 143–169.

9. Rubio 2001: 409; Marsman 2003: 419. See the negative reviews of Cooper 2006b: 20 §12; Roth, 2006; also Silver 2006: 658 and Cooper 2013: 51 who resurrect the old notion of temple prostitution. Steele 2007: 303–305 n.17 offers a measured defense of Assante's interpretation. *Ḫarimtu* is equated with SAL LUGAL 'female ruler' in *Malku* = *šarru* (Kilmer, 1963), and this type of woman often surfaces in royal or religious contexts where one does not expect a common whore. *Ḫarimtu*s perform funerary rites in Gilgamesh VI 16 and at Ebla (Pasquali 2015: 98); they perform unidentified rites under the aegis of the head of the lamentation specialty at Sippar Ammānun (Gallery 1980: 334–336; Tanret and Lerberghe 1993: 441). Hittite texts reference *ḫarimtu*s running with a weapon near a cult image, attending sheep sacrifices (probably divinatory) in front of the king, and in a royal lineage (Yigit 2008: 76–78). Other incongruities include references that associate the *ḫarimtu* with barrenness (Foster 1987: 38); purity (KI-SIKIL KAR-KID, Assante 1998: 51); and music (Shehata 2009: 103).

outside a male-headed household and her disrespectful, talkative, and assertive nature) fits the pattern of gender-crossing women who were initially mistaken for prostitutes by European observers (e.g., the Thai *thom*, the Balkan sworn virgin, and Aztec noblewomen) (Arvey 1988: 190; Morris 1994: 31; Grémaux 1996: 269). The same confusion can be seen in the unfounded accusations that were levied at European women who moved beyond the confines of normative femininity while residing in the Middle East, for instance Isabella Eberhardt and Gertrude Bell. Although Eberhardt and Bell cross-dressed and lived public lives in several Middle Eastern countries without antagonizing Arab observers, contemporary Europeans regarded their gender-crossing behavior as proof that they were scandalously promiscuous or sexually deviant (Kobak 1988: 100; Wallach 1996: 197).

## Irregular Gender in Gilgamesh I–II

In the context of an ancient Mesopotamian literature that is very often characterized by plots and motivations that seem obscure to modern readers, the *ḫarimtu* Shamhat has appeared to be a familiar figure, the whore with a heart of gold practicing the world's oldest profession. We recognize the woman who seduces Enkidu in the first tablet of the Gilgamesh Epic as a stock character, and we take for granted that Mesopotamians viewed her in the same light. M. Nissinen (2010: 74), for example, has remarked that the prostitute Shamhat is probably the only character in the Gilgamesh Epic whose sexual role would have been considered normal by the original audience.

Perceptions that seem self-apparent can be tested with a gender-bending exercise that reverses the sex of Enkidu and Shamhat. Replacing the hairy man on the steppe, Enkidat (generated by adding the feminine *–at* suffix) is a naked wild *woman* with long unbound hair, running wild with the beasts. The topsy-turvy seducer is a lothario named Shamhu. The story remains the same up to the point when the hunter enlists Shamhu's assistance. "Go, Shamhu," he urges, "Show no fear! Bare your manly pecs . . . expose your full monty!"[10] Shamhu is eager to comply. Shedding his clothing, he piques Enkidat's curiosity and lures her closer. Upon seducing her, he persuades her to follow him to the great city, supplying her with clothing, food, and drink along the way.

The substitution sheds light on a thought process that is normally submerged, namely, the subtext of inference that frames how we perceive the interaction between Shamhat and Enkidu. The chain of inference begins with the conviction that Shamhat's behavior is unnatural. Her lack of modesty looks like the brazen behavior of a prostitute, indicating that she is motivated by lucre rather than lust. The reader thus concludes that the hunter is the active agent and Shamhat is "a female body for hire who silently obeys her employer's directions" (Walls 2001: 21). Let us consider, however, how the substitution of a male seducer alters expectations. It somehow does not seem quite so intuitively self-apparent that a young man bursting with *kuzbu* "sex appeal" who exposes his body without shame and pursues nonmarital sex with an inexperienced woman can only be a prostitute acting under someone else's direction.

10. The phrase 'full monty' (from a 1997 British film by that name) refers to a male body that is entirely naked and displayed in a titillating manner to a female audience.

Even if an older man has pointed out the naked woman and urged the young man to have a go at her, most of us would reason that a young woman who runs around naked in the wilderness is asking for trouble, and the young man who wants to get to know her probably has something in mind other than a paycheck. The double standard in how we evaluate the same set of circumstances is based on the perception that sexually opportunistic behavior is natural for one sex but not for the other.

The thought experiment demonstrates that an invisible condition underlies the chain of logic that Shamhat is a prostitute, namely, the presumption of social femininity. The conviction that physical sex always determines social gender frames how the cultural outsider evaluates the same set of facts, inspiring inferences that may not be in the original.[11] Connotations of prostitution are read into Shamhat's behavior that would require corroboration if the protagonist were male, and different conclusions are reached about her motivation. The eye of the cultural outsider glides over the Mesopotamian man who leads the way or provides for a woman; he is behaving according to expectation because Mesopotamian law required a man to provide for individuals under his authority (MAL §45–46, Roth 1997: 170–171). In contrast, the reversal of the expected power dynamic between a man and a woman demands explanation, and the normalization that springs to mind is that the woman's agency is limited and situationally appropriate because it is nurturing.

In fact, Shamhat's behavior is aggressive rather than maternal. *She* initiates the sexual encounter with Enkidu, throwing off her clothes without shame and fearlessly approaching a big, hairy *lullû amēlu* "savage man," described as so *šaggāšû* "murderous" that even the experienced hunter has feared to approach (I 129, 178–179). After the seduction, Shamhat stands over Enkidu, while he sits quietly at her feet in the subservient posture of a woman (I 203). Assertive body language is again seen in the positioning of Shamhat in front of Enkidu. Instead of walking alongside Enkidu during their journey to Uruk, Shamhat takes him by the hand, *panī-šu illak* "walking in front of him" (Boğazköy a 7) or *ireddē-šu* "leading him" (Penn 73; MS bb 36). Similar control is indicated in the Schøyen fragment, in which Enkidu thanks and blesses the *ḫarimtu* after they arrive in Uruk "because *you led me* to Uruk" (1 4–5 [emphasis added]).

Shamhat's boldness and her body language would have been salient to a Mesopotamian audience, not only because it contradicted the shy female norm, but because the act of walking in front was laden with gender connotations in the ancient Near East. It was customary for friends to walk hand in hand; for example, Gilgamesh and Enkidu stroll hand in hand while walking within the city of Uruk (III 19), while the Assyrian king's ceremonial parade holding a cult image by the hand proclaimed to the populace that their king was the god's friend and equal. When a power differential placed one person under the authority of another, the dominant person walked in front, as seen in ancient Near Eastern idioms for walking behind or following that signify coming under someone's authority (Wilcke 1987: 83–84) or in the praise directed to the goddess Inanna in line 127 of the Inninsagurra Hymn: "You are great! No one passes in front of you!"[12]

11. E.g., George's (2003: 549) translation of Shamhat's *dīdū* in I 188 (a type of loincloth worn by both sexes) as "skirts" encourages the reader to imagine Shamhat in feminine clothing.

12. Positional dominance can be relative and temporary. Individuals who act as intercessors walk in front of the person they are escorting, occupying the symbolic middle ground between the person who is

## Grammatical Gender in Gilgamesh I–II

The interpretation that Shamhat "civilizes" Enkidu has crowded out other explanations, influencing us to perceive a contrast with the story of the unmanning of Samson (a wild hairy man who like Enkidu lived in the wilderness, knew no beer, and killed a lion) (Judg 13:7–14:6; Mobley 1997: 230–233; Dick 2006: 256). Perceiving Shamhat as passive and benevolent, we have paid little attention to her unfeminine speech and associated grammatical irregularities. Shamhat orders Enkidu about with forceful imperatives: "Come! Get up! Eat! Drink! (Penn: 56, 59, 96, 98; MSS B, P: I 209), and her actions are described with less common Š and D-stem verbs that specify her personal agency (*šūkulum, šaqûm, lubbušum, šuršûm* "to feed, give drink, provide with clothing, cause to acquire") rather than G-stem verbs that lack connotations of causality. Shamhat's agency is further marked by irregular grammatical referencing, invisible in translation, that indicates that Shamhat has taken sexual advantage of Enkidu, leaving him weak, defiled, and humiliated.[13]

Although the original text is always translated with normative grammar, most copies of the first two tablets of the Gilgamesh Epic reference Shamhat at least once with irregular grammatical gender. The corpus (setting aside fragments that do not reference Shamhat) consists of two Old Babylonian tablets that are unprovenanced but perhaps from Larsa (George 2003: 167) (MSS Penn, Schøyen, ca. eighteenth century); a Middle Babylonian recension from a temple library in the Hittite capital (MS Boğazköy, ca. fourteenth century); three Neo-Assyrian copies from the royal library at Nineveh (MSS B, F, P, seventh century); and three Late Babylonian copies from the sixth century or later found in private houses (MSS x, Babylon; h, unprovenanced but probably from Babylon or Borsippa; bb, Uruk).

The most remarked upon gender irregularity is a simile attested in three far-flung manuscripts: MSS Penn (I 167), Boğazköy (a 7), and bb (II 36). In setting out for the city of Uruk, the *ḫarimtu* Shamhat is described as walking in front of Enkidu *kīma ilim* "like a (male) god" or *kīma ilī* "like (male) gods." The presence of this gender anomaly in widely dispersed manuscripts has bothered Assyriologists for decades. Reasoning that it made more sense for the ideogram to be "mother" or "child" rather than DINGIR "god," mid-twentieth-century Assyriologists tried to attribute the incongruity to poor orthography until the discovery of the Boğazköy tablet, bearing the phonetic complement *-lim* after the DINGIR sign, forced the uncomfortable conclusion that the sign was what it appeared to be.

Since it is suspicious to find an anomaly of this magnitude in unrelated manuscripts, one would expect that it would have invited scrutiny of other examples of irregular

being escorted and a party at the other end. The different protocols can be seen in the variable positioning of Shamhat and Enkidu. Acting as an intercessor, Shamhat walks in front of Enkidu en route to Uruk, but they trade places upon reaching Uruk (OB Penn 175–77). Similarly, Enkidu walks beside Gilgamesh while inside the city but moves to the front on the journey to the Cedar Forest (MS BB III 6).

13. References to Enkidu becoming "wise" and "like a god" (Gilgamesh I 202, 207, 214) upon having sexual intercourse with Shamhat have been misinterpreted as positive remarks about becoming human. They more likely reference special abilities that compensate for the loss of reproductive virility or femininity. As seen in the praising of wise Ninsun in tablets I–II, wisdom in the context of the Gilgamesh Epic refers to the ability to prophesy or interpret dreams. Gender variants are god-like, acting as intercessors and mediating between realms, because they are inherently liminal.

grammatical gender associated with Shamhat. The secondary literature demonstrates that Assyriologists have instead treated the simile as a lone exception, brushing it aside with one normalization strategy after another.[14] The lack of attention given to the irregular gender referencing of Shamhat's genitals is a case in point. Shamhat's *ūru* "vulva" is mentioned in two places (I 181, 189, with no manuscript preserving both lines). Line 181 of MS P from Nineveh exhibits the expected *ūr-ki* "your (f.) vulva," but MS F from the same library has the second-person masculine singular genitive *ūr-ka* "your (m.) vulva." A similar third-person disagreement occurs in line 189: MS B from Nineveh reads *ūr–ša* "her vulva" and MS x from Babylon *ūr–šu* "his vulva."[15] Without a theoretical framework to account for grammar unaligned with sex, the irregular pronouns have looked insignificant; for example, when I showed this referencing to a respected Assyriologist, he had trouble grasping why it might be significant, remarking, "But of course they're errors . . . you can't castrate a woman!"

The supposition that pronouns and other grammatical inflections are reliable indicators of biological sex is not supported by the cross-cultural evidence. Societies that recognize more than two gender categories vary in how they reference nonnormative statuses. Names, verbs, and pronouns can align with either anatomical sex or social gender/sexuality.[16] Social practice can also be mixed, with irregular grammar applied to only one sex or predominating in self-referencing or in speech directed to gender variant individuals rather than in third-party discourses about them.[17] Variable gender referencing of the same individual can mark a temporal or hierarchical distinction, acknowledging a previous or temporary status, but inconsistency is also seen in

14. The simile was initially corrected to "like a mother" or "like a little child." In arguing that he had personally verified that "like a male god" was visible on the tablet, Renger (1972: 190) observed that the phrase recalled a scene especially common in Old Babylonian glyptic, a divine intercessor leading a supplicant by the hand toward a deity. Although the reading "like a god" was reconfirmed by the Boğazköy tablet, Renger's confirmation was rejected due to perceptions of gender incongruity: Bailey (1976: 438) "but wouldn't the more natural interpretation be that 'like a god' refers to Enkidu"; George (2003: 167) "the introducing deities in such presentations are always goddesses"; Foster (2005: 61) "one expects comparisons of men to gods in order to exalt their status and attributes, but not women with gods." Such comments reveal that the wellspring of George's current proposal (that the only plausible subject is the "magnificent figure, almost god-like" of Enkidu) is the conviction that the gender content is *unnatural* when the line is read in the usual manner. Gender theory allows for a different resolution of the grammatical and visual discrepancies. The simile likens the *ḫarimtu* Shamhat to an intercessor deity because she performs the "in-between" function of guiding Enkidu to Uruk. The intercessor deities depicted on cylinder seals are public females who are socially rather than biologically masculine, making them especially suited for liminal functions. They do not cross-dress (in common with royal women) due to the greater salience of their divine rank, although in a few instances intercessor masculinity is marked in the visual record by the addition of a beard to the female costume (e.g., see seal of Ur-DUN išib-[d]Ningirsu, Westenholz 2012: 259, fig. 12.5).

15. Shamhat is also referenced with masculine possessive pronouns in other contexts. The pronouns that reference her *dīdū* "loincloth" in line 188 are lost in the breaks of MSS P and F, but MSS B and x display the earlier contrast: "her loincloth" vs. "*his* loincloth." Feminine pronouns reference Shamhat's *kuzbu* "sex appeal" in all Nineveh manuscripts (*-ki* or *-ša* twice each in B and F, four times in P), and even once in the *kuzub–ki* of MS x I 181, but a masculine pronoun again crops up in the *kuzub-šu* in MS x I 189.

16. Pronoun examples from the Middle East: Iraqi *mustarjil* (sex/gender unaligned), Thesiger 1964: 165; Omani *xanith* (aligned), Wikan 1982: 175; Turkish *ibne* and *köçek* (unaligned), Janssen 1992: 87; Jewish Iraqi *dhakar binta* (unaligned), Sofer 1992: 106, 111.

17. For *hijra, travesti* examples see Herdt 1991: 200; Kulick 1997: 579; females only in Hindi, Hall 2001: 146.

societies that lack a fixed procedure, with pronoun usage not only varying from one person to the next but even within the speech of a single individual.[18]

The argument can be made that the unaligned possessive pronouns are all errors, but translators have not put forward evidence that this is the case or footnoted their corrected translations. Methodological considerations, including the rule of thumb in textual criticism that the more difficult or more embarrassing reading is more likely to be older, invite us to reconsider whether the masculine pronouns are scribal errors. It has seemed natural to privilege MS B because the grammar in that manuscript is uniformly aligned with sex, but MS x (with the largest number of gender deviations) is a manuscript at far remove that is acknowledged to preserve a better copy when judged on other criteria.[19] The fact that MSS P and F occasionally match MS x requires the tall coincidence that copyists at Nineveh and Babylon, working in entirely different scribal circles centuries apart, blundered in ways that do not come naturally to speakers who equate sex and gender, altering second- and third-person pronouns to mislabel Shamhat's vulva as masculine.

It is easier to imagine the process in reverse. If unaligned pronouns referenced an alternate gender status within Babylonia (employed either when a speaker wanted to clarify or emphasize a gender distinction or reflecting usual linguistic practice), transmission in places or periods with different linguistic customs would have created tension around references such as "*his* vulva." Since the Gilgamesh Epic was not a sacred text that scribes felt impelled to copy word for word, but a more loosely transmitted text (Young 2007: 180), copyists had motive and leeway to normalize the text with pronouns that flowed naturally from their own internalized perspectives, introducing alignment where it did not originally exist, ranging from the unfailingly regularized grammar in MS B to the less systematically corrected MSS P and F.[20]

The common Akkadian verb for sex is *niāku(m)*, a verb that takes a direct object and that carries explicit connotation of active agency or penetration. A *nā'ikānu* "one who does *niāku*" is an inserter, not an insertee; for example, despite their very different agencies, the deliberately promiscuous wife and the young rape victim are both *nīkta* (the accusative object of the act of *niāku*) in Middle Assyrian laws.[21] Since the Akkadian word for sex has strong connotations of positionality and male agency, one would expect a *ḫarimtu* to be a *nīkta*, the sex object of her client, were she really an ordinary prostitute. But that is not the case. An OB thesaurus groups the *ḫarimtu* with *waṣītum* "she who goes out" and *naiāktu* "she who does *niāku*," implying that a

18. E.g., Grémaux (1996: 256) remarks in a case study of an anatomically female gender variant from Montenegro, "Talking about Mikas, my informants alternately used 'he' and 'she' as was also observed by Gusic when Mikas was still alive." For other examples of variable grammatical gender referencing, see Hall 2001: 154, 156.

19. All Nineveh manuscripts transpose I 186–87 in contrast to MS x, indicating that the latter is more likely to preserve the original text in this portion of the epic (George 2003: 430). MS B also combines I 195–96 and substitutes different verbs in I 199–200 than other manuscripts.

20. The explanation that the MS x copyist mechanically substituted *–šu* for *–ši* and *–ka* for *–ki* due to sound shifts in later Akkadian overlooks the fact that MS x does distinguish Shamhat with feminine pronouns when there is need to clarify who is doing what to whom, e.g., "he will see *you* (f.)" in I 183.

21. For the connotations of *niāku* in general see Ackerman 2005: 77; MAL §23 and §55; Roth 1997: 161, 175.

*ḫarimtu* woman did not follow purdah (seclusion and veiling) and was the active agent in her sexual liaisons (Lambert 1992: 139).

The verb *niāku* is nowhere used to describe intercourse between Enkidu and Shamhat. Line I 194 in the Nineveh manuscripts reads *Enkidu tebī-ma Šamḫat irḫi* "Enkidu was erect and inseminated Shamhat," but MS x I 194 from Babylonia comes to a clear stop with *tebī-ma* "Enkidu was erect." The verb that describes sex between Enkidu and Shamhat in OB Penn II 46 (also the couple's second encounter in MSS B, F, h I 300) is *urtammū,* a Dt stem of *râmu* "to love" that indicates passive or reciprocal behavior.[22] While verbs that reference loving and achieving erection attest to Enkidu's physical capacity for sex, they do not establish that he is the active partner.[23]

Although Assyriologists have marveled at Enkidu's stamina in his initial union with Shamhat, perceiving a "super-human" male sexual response (Walls 2001: 25), the wording of the sex scene calls into question whether Enkidu is in the upper position of control. The statement in I 183 that Enkidu will approach Shamhat upon seeing her open vulva has imprinted generations of scholars with the mental image of Shamhat lying on the ground with her legs spread apart. Transfixed by Shamhat's thighs, Assyriologists have paid little attention to depictions of Near Eastern goddesses standing upright while exposing their vulvas.[24] The latter provide reason to question the traditional inference that Shamhat is supine (which is not actually stated) and are a better fit with other indications that Shamhat is upright, luring Enkidu to recline on a garment saturated with her physical sex (designated with the f. *-ki* even in MS x).[25]

Pronoun irregularities also call into question who is positioned on top during Enkidu's seduction, a critical factor in assessing agency. The collection of sex omens translated by Ann Guinan (1997: 465) opens with the warning that a man will incur harm if he allows a woman to take the upper position during intercourse, indicating the importance of position in Mesopotamian active/passive gender logic: "If a man, a woman mounts him, that woman will take his vigor; for one month he will not have a personal god" (omen 1). It is thus significant that two independent sources, MS P from Nineveh and MS x from Babylon, position Shamhat on top of Enkidu in line I 191: *eli-šu iṣlal* "s/he lay on top of *him*."[26] Pronouns are again irregular in another allusion to sexual activity that is indicative of agency and position. Manuscript x I 186 reads: "let your [m. *-ka,* referencing Shamhat] love stroke *over him*" (*eli ṣērī-šu*) in contrast

22. The translation "the two of them made love" (Kovacs 1989: 12; George 2003: 174–177, 557; cf. CAD R:145 "the two of them caressed each other") captures the implicit lack of active male agency implied by this verbal inflection.

23. In I 192 Shamhat "does the action/work of a woman" to her sex object, the *lullâ* (acc.) "savage man." George's translation, that Shamhat "treats" Enkidu, carries a shade of meaning not indicated in the original Akkadian, that Shamhat acts to please Enkidu. The phrase can be interpreted quite differently as indicating that Shamhat is the active agent "doing sex" to a more passive partner.

24. Upright winged goddesses exposing their vulvas are depicted on a fourteenth–thirteenth-century gypsum vessel from Tomb 45 at Assur and in a relief from the Ishtar-Shauska temple at Nuzi; Ornan 2005: 233, fig. 23.

25. Shamhat's subsequent actions indicate that she is upright because it does not make sense for her to hop up to spread her clothing on the ground (I 184, 191) after the lovemaking has already begun. The rationale for spreading her garment would have been to create an enticing place for Enkidu to recline, positioning Shamhat in the upper position of control.

26. MSS B and P in I 184 read *eli-ki liṣlal* "he will lie upon you (f.)" while the line is broken in MSS F and x. MS B also has the feminine *-ša* in I 191 "he lay upon *her*" while MS F is again broken.

to the *eli ṣērī-ki* "over *you* (f.)" in MSS P and B I 186. Line I 193 displays the same grammatical gender divide: "stroked *over him*" (MS x) vs. "stroked *over her*" (MS B), with MSS P and F not preserving the line.[27]

## Legal/Economic Documents

Assyriologists who have not been exposed to gender theory commonly assume that names are trustworthy indicators of sex.[28] Examples of unaligned grammatical gender are plentiful in the scattered translations of Mesopotamian wills, contracts, receipts, and letters, but, lacking explanation for such anomalies, it has been usual for translators to normalize or ignore irregularities of this kind, treating the variations as outliers or orthographic variations without semantic value. Grammatical gender irregularities more often concern females than males and are especially frequent in the referencing of public women. In the mid-second millennium BCE, personal names in the ancient Near East began to be prefixed with gender determinatives, the vertical DIŠ sign (indicated in transcription as /$^{\mathrm{I}}$/ or /$^{\mathrm{m}}$/) for a male and the pubic triangle SAL or MUNUS (/$^{\mathrm{f}}$/) for a female. Significant numbers of feminine names with /$^{\mathrm{m}}$/ or dual /$^{\mathrm{mf}}$/ determinatives have come to light in archives from Nippur, Babylon, Nuzi, Nimrud, and Ur, particularly in matronyms used by sons.[29] J. A. Brinkman has demonstrated that women who are referenced in this manner in the Kassite era act as independent agents in legal contexts, very likely because they are heads of household. P. Abrahami's review of texts in the archive of Tulpun-naya at Nuzi identifies eight texts that reference women with the dual /$^{\mathrm{mf}}$/ determinative in contexts where they act under their own authority.

Legal and business texts from Nuzi and Emar provide clear examples of masculine grammar marking the social status of biological females who are public women, while associated texts designate women who are under their own authority as *ḫarimtus*. The name of the king's twin sister at Emar is marked with a masculine determinative, and the name of the NIN.DINGIR priestess ($^{\mathrm{m}}$Iba DUMU Ili-Abi) from the same city is composed of a masculine determinative, a patronym, and a common man's name.[30]

27. Line I 186 is misplaced in all Nineveh texts. The double masculine pronouns (*he* was stroking *him* referencing a man and a woman) are likely to have been extremely confusing, inviting scribes to amend the text according to Assyrian norms. Note also that the repetition of the same verbs and phraseology in MS x I 186, 193 and I 271, 284 draws an explicit parallel between Shamhat's actions and the manner in which Gilgamesh makes love to Enkidu.

28. Assyriological assertions that Mesopotamian kings were all men or that this or that prophet or cultic performer is male or female are grounded on the presumption that a name proves the sex of its bearer; see, e.g., Stol 1991: 191; Cooper 2006b: 18; Stökl 2009: 97–98; Suter 2012: 201; Cooper 2013: 50; cf. the greater sophistication of Northwest Semiticists, Moore 2014.

29. For Kassite examples from Nippur and Babylon, see Brinkman 2007; Neo-Assyrian examples from Nimrud, Meier 1991: 541 n. 7; two Kassite patronyms with feminine determinatives from Ur, Gurney 1983: 56, 76. For examples of double m.-f. determinatives in the archive of Tulpun-naya from Nuzi, see Abrahami 2011: 2.

30. Fleming 1992: 84 comments "the name Iī-abī is used consistently for males at Emar" and "should not be the name for the female nin.dingir of $^{\mathrm{d}}$IM;" see Pruzsinszky 2003: 614 for the king's twin sister. Such examples indicate that in this era especially high social rank conferred an honorary masculinity that exempted a woman from purdah.

In contrast to the conventional gender referencing of daughters in marriage contracts from Nuzi, wills that concern daughters adopted as "sons" reference the daughter-sons with masculine nouns and pronouns, while a will from Emar calls a daughter-son a *ḫarimtu* (Lacheman 1973: 100; Roth 2006: 32). The Middle Assyrian Assur M 8 archive (eighty lists of barley rations provided to construction workers) records several *ḫarimtus* of working age who are heads of households.[31] A sealed contract from Nuzi records the freeing of Utubalti, a woman who had been dedicated to Ishtar as a security pledge *ana ḫarimūtu* "for *ḫarimtu*-ship." Assyriologists have clashed over whether the contract proves cultic prostitution, but no one has taken into consideration that Utubalti is designated with a third-person masculine singular pronoun (l. 6: *umteššir-šu* "I/he released *him*"), marking her as masculine while serving at the temple.[32]

## Grammatical Gender Irregularity in Ritual and Prophecy

Nearly two dozen individuals are named as performing "*ḫarimtu* rituals" in receipts that come from an archive that belonged to Ur-Utu, the head of the lamentation profession at Sippar Ammanun.[33] Although some scholars cite these texts as evidence that temple income was derived from sexual activities, presuming that a ritual performed by a *ḫarimtu* must involve prostitution, the irregular referencing of the performers does not support that conclusion.[34] Unlike Mesopotamian matriarchs designated with the /$^{mf}$/ determinative, whose social masculinity was supported by the intersectionality of age or rank, the individuals compensated for *ḫarimtu* rituals are referenced with masculine determinatives and masculine names.[35] The mismatch between the *ḫarimtus*' sex and their names points to a highly inverted social masculinity (probably including full or partial cross-dressing), performed by women in emulation of the *cross-dressed martial goddess* Ishtar-Annunitum.[36] The degree of inversion indicates

31. Llop 2014: 450, n. 38. No *ḫarimtu* has a husband in the Assur archive although some have children, indicating that women of *ḫarimtu* status were sometimes widowed or divorced.

32. SMN 1670. Assyriologists who see the *ḫarimtu* as a prostitute argue that the text proves that a girl was given to the temple explicitly for prostitution. Critics contend that it only indicates that Utubalti did not live under the authority of a male relative. See Wilhelm 1990: 523; Stol 1995: 183 n. 4; Silver 2006: 640; cf. Assante 1998: 61.

33. For Sippar texts that reference *ḫarimtus* see Gallery 1980; Lerberghe 1982: 282; Lerberghe and Voet 1991: 92; Tanret and Lerberghe 1993: 91–98. The sex/gender identity of a second group of personnel in the Ur-Utu archive who perform *rēdûtum* "soldier/follower" rituals remains unclear since the performers are referenced with dual m-f determinatives and most bear names (e.g., Elmesum, Qistum, Risatum) that are gender neutral; however the association with a weapon again points to f. sex / m. gender variance of overlapping or more specialized/limited character.

34. Those arguing for sexual activities are Cooper 2006b: 18; Silver 2006: 655–658; Cooper 2013: 50. In contrast, the translators of the Ur-Utu archive (Tanret and Lerberghe 1993: 441) are more restrained, commenting, "there is, in our texts, not the slightest evidence of a sexual nature of these rites;" see also Shehata 2009: 101–103 who argues that the linkage between *ḫarimtus* and ritual/musical activities associated with the lamentation profession is inconsistent with ordinary prostitution.

35. Van Lerberghe 1982: 282 comments that "it is remarkable that in these texts *harimūtum* is always preceded by the male determinative 'lu' and is followed by the name of a man."

36. The fact that no individual performs a *ḫarimtu* ritual more than once in the Ur-Utu archive and that performers are selected by the hand of Ishtar-Annunitum points to a rite of incorporation into the lamentation profession. The *ḫarimtu* and soldier rituals performed at Sippar Ammanun recall rituals in earlier

a more strongly differentiated social masculinity, accentuated by the need to secure a gender identity unsupported by sex, age, or rank.[37] Recalling the Boğazköy text that mentions a *ḫarimtu* running with a dagger in a ritual context, a receipt from the Ur-Utu archive (CT 48 45) that records payment for a bronze axe manufactured for both *ḫarimtu* and soldier rites fits comfortably with the idea that the *ḫarimtu* rituals at Sippar Ammanun were warrior-like rather than sexual.[38] The masculine referencing of *ḫarimtu*s in the Ur-Utu archive is also consistent with the more general use of *ḫarimtu* as an occupational patronym written with the /m/ determinative.[39]

I. Zsolnay and J. Stökl have questioned Simo Parpola's contention that prophecy was associated with irregular gender in Mesopotamia, proposing instead that indications of gender variance in the two corpora that mention oracles (thirty-seven letters from Mari/Ešnunna and eleven tablets from Nineveh) are better explained as coincidence or scribal error.[40] The association between irregular gender referencing and non-normative gender proposed in this study does not support the suggestion that scribal error is the most likely explanation for the irregularly referenced prophets in the Assyrian Ishtar prophecies. In further support, it should be noted that four individuals who interpret dreams or prophesy in the Gilgamesh Epic are also associated with irregular gender. Enkidu's gender variance is indicated by the well-known pun that implies that he is an *assinnu*, and he acts as a seer in this text, interpreting dreams and prophesying the fates of Huwawa and Shamhat. The "gardener" Ishullanu prophesies a wretched future for himself and is referenced in MS A from Nineveh and MS a from Assur with

---

sources performed by the *kurgarrû* and SAĜ.UR.SAĜ in honor of Ishtar-Annunitum. The different nomenclature in the Ur-Utu archive can be explained as slippage between specific and general labels for the same thing. Ishtar-Annunitum's devotees would usually have been designated by the titles of their offices, but overlap between the cultic offices associated with the goddess and the special gender status of everyone in those roles enabled speakers to substitute a more general label. Similar slippage can be observed in the variable referencing of the GALA/*kalû* cultic office and the socially feminine *assinnu* gender status. Ishtar-Annunitum's martial *kurgarrû* and SAĜ.UR.SAĜ functionaries can thus be understood as biologically female, a subset of the socially masculine *ḫarimtu* gender category.

37. In contrast to the social prominence of women designated with double determinatives, the patronyms borne by individuals who perform *ḫarimtu* rituals indicate that these individuals came from a lower social stratum (Tanret and Lerberghe 1993: 443).

38. Interpretations that *ḫarimtu*-rituals were sex acts in the service of the temple (Silver 2008; Cooper 2003: 51) ignore the association with weaponry. CT 48 45 reads "14 shekels of silver for a battle-axe for *ḫarimtu*-type/soldier-type [*harimūtum rēdûtum*] rites of the goddess Annunitum." The battle-axe suggests that at least some rituals performed by *ḫarimtu*s in various cultic capacities were martial cultic dances, perhaps involving superficial ritual lancing, which would be consistent with the bloodletting mentioned in rites performed by *kurgarrû*.

39. For the *ḫarimtu* patronym written with a masculine determinative see Brinkman 2006: 32 n. 60.

40. An interpretation put forward by Parpola 1997: IL-L; also Teppo 2008: 82; criticized by Zsolnay 2013; and Stökl 2009, 2012, 2013. Stökl proposes that grammatical gender incongruities in the Assyrian Ishtar prophecies are scribal errors or reference something other than gender. E.g., Stökl (2009: 96–97) states that he personally inspected SAA 9 1.4 and verified a masculine gentilic paired with DUMU.MUNUS "daughter" in the prophet's name in line 40, but he rejects the implication of gender ambiguity remarking, "It is easier to assume a scribal error." He accounts for SAA 9 1.1 in the same manner, "The easiest explanation for the female gender determinative in front of an obviously male name is, in my view, scribal error." Stökl (2012: 121–123) argues that two ambiguously referenced prophets are "simply female"; a third masculine name with a feminine determinative is more likely to be scribal error "than cross-gender dress and/or behavior." Stökl (2013: 78) is more cautious in his 2013 publication, but he still makes light of grammatical gender discrepancies.

the second-person feminine pronoun *-ki* in a particularly incongruous context (VI 68: *kiššūta-ki* "your [f.] power/authority").

The presumption that Shamhat is a prostitute has distracted us from noticing the similar social profiles of Shamhat and Ninsun, the "nurturing" queen mother of Uruk.[41] In common with Shamhat, Ninsun does not have a husband, residing in her own Egalmah rather than in a male-headed household, and, like Shamhat, the great *šarratum* interprets dreams and speaks in the high (masculine) Akkadian style. Although it has not been evident in translations that again privilege MS B over other testimonies, three tablets from Nineveh and two from Babylonia reference Ninsun with masculine grammar.

Ninsun is referenced in Tablet I with both the masculine genitive suffix DUMU-*šu* "his (Ninsun's) son" (MSS P and h I 259, h I 286) and the masculine independent dative pronoun *ana šāšū-ma ana* AMA-*šu* "to *him* (Ninsun), to his mother" (MS h I 294). Tablet III manuscripts exhibit similar irregularities. Distressed by her son's impending departure, Ninsun cleanses herself seven times in an elaborate purification ceremony, dons special garments and a crown, and climbs to the temple roof to present an incense offering to the rising sun, a rite of intercession to a more powerful deity. A partially broken line (III 42) situates *ḫarimtu*s within Ninsun's temple in the presence of the purified queen. Prior to this event, MSS M and BB from Nineveh reference Ninsun with feminine pronouns, but *both* Neo-Assyrian manuscripts switch to the masculine pronoun when describing Ninsun's rooftop prayer, stating that Ninsun lifts *idī-šu* "*his* arms" in prayer to the sun god (III 45). Since pronouns in copies from Babylonia usually align with gender, the pronouns in the Tablet III manuscripts from Babylon and Uruk are also likely to have been masculine, although their fragmentary state preserves only one example: DUMU-*šu* "*his* (Ninsun's) son" in MS c from Uruk (III 35).

## Conclusion

Gender theory is most useful for alerting philologists as to where they are likely to go wrong in translating the gender-related content of a non-Western culture. The intuition that gender irregularity implies sexual or genital abnormality pressures translators to force foreign gender terms into their own ill-fitting conceptual slots or to engage in translation gymnastics to deny that gender incongruity is present.[42] Otherwise competent scholars thus become inured to poor translation practices, routinely correcting unaligned grammar without notation believing the errors to be obvious and translating content according to what feels natural rather than sticking to what is on the tablets.

In addition to checking the pitfalls of common sense (that gender categories are biological givens and that genitalia/gender are aligned except when genital impairment is present), gender theory offers a corrective to the propensity to fixate on male variance while overlooking the female. Unless a translator has been sensitized by *both* feminist and queer theory, attention will be riveted on the *assinnu*s at Mari, while

41. E.g., "Ninsun . . . is all that a mother should be: caring, nurturing" (Harris 2000: 121).

42. See the gender normalization of a royal seal at Ur: McCaffrey 2008: 203–207.

the servant girl and the upper class women who also prophesy look "average" and "unassuming."[43] Fully inverted *ḫarimtu*s will also go unnoticed because women with masculine names can only be distinguished from anatomical males when texts specifically mention their *ḫarimtu* status, and the strangeness of such references makes them look like outliers. Gender theory thus offers a new approach toward reconstructing the roles of both male and female gender variants, bringing *ḫarimtu*s and their professional cultic activities as seers, intercessors, and martial dancers out of the shadows.

## BIBLIOGRAPHY

Abrahami, P.
2011 "Masculine and Feminine Personal Determinatives Before Women's Names at Nuzi: A Gender Indicator of Social or Economic Independence?" *CDLB* 2011: 1. https://cdli.ucla.edu/pubs/cdlb/2011/cdlb2011_001.html.

Ackerman, S.
2005 *When Heroes Love: The Ambiguity of Eros in the Stories of Gilgamesh and David.* Gender, Theory, and Religion. New York: Columbia University Press.

Arvey, M.
1988 Women of Ill-Repute in the Florentine Codex. Pp. 179–204 in *The Role of Gender in Pre-Columbian Art and Architecture.* Edited by V. Miller. Lanham, MD: University Press of America.

Asher-Greve, J. M.
1997a The Essential Body: Mesopotamian Conceptions of the Gendered Body. *Gender and History* 9: 432–461.
1997b Feminist Research and Ancient Mesopotamia: Problems and Prospects. Pp. 218–237 in *A Feminist Companion to Reading the Bible: Approaches, Methods and Strategies.* Edited by A. Brenner and C. R. Fontaine. FCB 11. Sheffield: Sheffield Academic.
1998 From Thales to Foucault . . . and Back to Sumer. Pp. 29–40 in *Intellectual Life of the Ancient Near East: Papers Presented at the 43rd Recontre Assyriologique Internationale (Prague July 1–5, 1996).* Edited by J. Prosecký. Prague: Academy of Sciences of the Czech Republic.
2000a Review of *Sex and Eroticism in Mesopotamian Literature,* by Gwendolyn Leick. *NIN* 1: 125–127.
2000b Stepping into the Maelstrom: Women, Gender and Ancient Near Eastern Scholarship. *NIN* 1: 1–22.

43. Zsolnay 2013: 82. Recent Assyriological arguments that the *assinnu* is not defined by gender variance demonstrate how the propensity to overlook female variance distorts evaluations. Pointing to the feminine form *assinnatu* on the *Malku* = *šarru* list, Stökl (2012: 59) asks, "If the assinnu were emasculated men, what is an assinnatu, who in that text is equated to entum ('high priestess')?" Stökl questions whether *assinnus* were castrated but overlooks parallel female variance. Presuming that the high priestess must be an ordinary woman, Stökl concludes that *assinnu* and *assinnatu* designate male and female cultic functionaries without the implication of gender variance. Zsolnay's (2013) interpretation of the *assinnu* as a cultic heroic warrior is based on the same logic. Zsolnay infers that *assinnu* and SAĜ.UR.SAĜ are synonyms because they are adjacent in lexical list *lu₂* = ŠA 184. This leads her to conclude that the *assinnu* was manly because effeminacy is inconsistent with being a martial cultic official. Zsolnay assumes that Ishtar's functionaries are all biologically male, overlooking that the cult of a martial goddess provides an inherent prototype for a female martial functionary. The explanation that *assinnu* and SAĜ.UR.SAĜ functionaries were complementary gender inverts who often worked together in the service of Ishtar provides a logical rationale for the *lu₂* = ŠA pairing, in keeping with the overall evidence that the *assinnu* was not virile.

Assante, J.
1998 Kar.kid/*ḫarimtu*, Prostitute or Single Woman? A Reconsideration of the Evidence. *UF* 30: 5–96.
2003 From Whores to Hierodules: The Historiographic Invention of Mesopotamian Female Sex Professionals. Pp. 13–47 in *Ancient Art and Its Historiography*. Edited by A. A. Donohue and M. D. Fullerton. Cambridge: Cambridge University Press.
2007a The Lead Inlays of Tukulti-Ninurta I: Pornography as Imperial Strategy. Pp. 369–407 in *Ancient Near Eastern Art in Context: Studies in Honor of Irene J. Winter*. Edited by J. Cheng and M. H. Feldman. CHANE 26. Leiden: Brill.
2007b What Makes a "Prostitute" a Prostitute? Modern Definitions and Ancient Meanings. *Historiae* 4: 117–132.
2009 Bad Girls and Kinky Boys? The Modern Prostituting of Ishtar, Her Clergy and Her Cults. Pp. 23–54 in *Tempelprostitution im Altertum: Fakten und Fiktionen*. Edited by M. Lindner. Oikumene 6. Berlin: Antike.

Bahrani, Z.
2000 The Extraterrestrial Orient: Colonizing Mesopotamia in Space and Time. Pp. 5–10 in *Landscapes: Territories, Frontiers and Horizons in the Ancient Near East; Papers Presented to the XLIV Rencontre Assyriologique Internationale Venezia 7–11 July 1997*, part 3: *Landscape in Ideology, Religion, Literature and Art.* Edited by L. Milano, S. de Martino, F. M. Fales, and G. B. Lanfranchi. HANE/M 3. Padova: Sargon.
2001 *Women of Babylon: Gender and Representation in Mesopotamia.* London: Routledge.

Bailey, J. A.
1976 Male, Female and the Pursuit of Immortality in the Gilgamesh Epic. *La Parola del Passato* 17: 433–457.

Besnier, N.
1996 Polynesian Gender Liminality Through Time and Space. Pp. 285–328 in *Third Sex, Third Gender: Beyond Sexual Dimorphism in Culture and History*. Edited by G. Herdt. New York: Zone Books.

Blackwell, E.
1984 Sexuality and Gender in Certain Native American Tribes: The Case of Cross-Gender Females. *Signs: the Journal of Women in Culture and Society* 10: 27–42.

Blackwood, E.
1998 *Tombois* in West Sumatra: Deconstructing Masculinity and Erotic Desire. *Cultural Anthropology* 13: 492–521.

Brinkman, J. A.
2006 The Use of Occupation Names as Patronymns in the Kassite Period: A Forerunner of Neo-Babylonian Ancestral Names? Pp. 23–43 in *If a Man Builds a Joyful House: Assyriological Studies in Honor of Erle Verdun Leichty*. Edited by A. K. Guinan, M. d. J. Ellis, A. J. Ferrara, S. M. Freedman, T. Rutz, L. Sassmannshausenn, S. Tinney, and M. W. Waters. CM 31. Leiden: Brill.
2007 Masculine or Feminine? The Case of Conflicting Gender Determinatives for Middle Babylonian Personal Names. Pp. 1–10 in *Studies Presented to Robert D. Biggs, June 4, 2004: From the Workshop of the Chicago Assyrian Dictionary*, vol. 2. Edited by M. T. Roth, W. Farber, M. W. Stolper, and P. von Bechtolshei. AS 27. Chicago: Oriental Institute of the University of Chicago.

Bullough, V. L.
1971 Attitudes Toward Deviant Sex in Ancient Mesopotamia. *Journal of Sex Research* 7: 184–203.

Chapman, C. R.
2004 *The Gendered Language of Warfare in the Israelite-Assyrian Encounter.* HSM 62. Winona Lake, IN: Eisenbrauns.

Cooper, J. S.
1983 *The Curse of Agade.* Baltimore: Johns Hopkins University Press.
2006a Genre, Gender, and the Sumerian Lamentation. *JCS* 58: 39–47.
2006b Prostitution. *RlA* 11:13–21.
2013 Sex and the Temple. Pp. 49–57 in *Tempel im Alten Orient: 7. Internationales Colloquium der Deutschen Orient-Gesellschaft 11.–13. Oktober 2009, München.* Edited by K. Kaniuth, A. Löhnert, J. L. Miller, A. Otto, M. Roaf, and Walther Sallaberger. Wiesbaden: Harrassowitz.

Devereux, G.
1937 Institutionalized Homosexuality of the Mohave Indians. *Human Biology* 9: 498–527.

Dick, M. B.
2006 The Neo-Assyrian Royal Lion Hunt and Yahweh's Answer to Job. *JBL* 125: 243–270.

Dickemann, M.
1997 The Balkan Sworn Virgin: A Cross-Gendered Female Role. Pp. 197–203 in *Islamic Homosexualities: Culture, History, and Literature.* Edited by D. E. Murray and W. Roscoe. New York: New York University Press.

Ferrara, A. J.
2002 Review of *Love Songs in Sumerian Literature: Critical Edition of the Dumuzi-Inanna Songs,* by Y. Sefati. *JNES* 61: 131–134.

Fleming, D. E.
1992 *The Installation of Baal's High Priestess at Emar.* HSS 42. Atlanta: Scholars Press.

Foster, B. R.
1987 Gilgamesh: Sex, Love and the Ascent of Knowledge. Pp. 21–42 in *Love and Death in the Ancient Near East: Essays in Honor of Marvin H. Pope.* Edited by J. H. Marks and R. M. Good. Guilford, CT: Four Quarters.
2005 A New Edition of the Epic of Gilgamesh. *JAOS* 125: 59–66.

Gabbay, U.
2008 The Akkadian Word for "Third Gender": The *kalû* (gala) Once Again. Pp. 49–56 in *Proceedings of the 51st Rencontre Assyriologique Internationale Held at the Oriental Institute of the University of Chicago, July 18–22, 2005.* Edited by R. D. Biggs, J. Myers, and M. T. Roth. SAOC 62. Chicago: Oriental Institute of the University of Chicago.

Gallery, M. L.
1980 Service Obligations of the *kezertu*-Women. *Or* 49: 333–338.

George, A. R.
2003 *The Babylonian Gilgamesh Epic: Introduction, Critical Edition, and Cuneiform Texts.* 2 vols. Oxford: Oxford University Press.

Gilchrist, R.
2000 Unsexing the Body: The Interior Sexuality of Medieval Religious Women. Pp. 89–103 in *Archaeologies of Sexuality.* Edited by R. A. Schmidt and B. L. Voss. London: Routledge.

Grémaux, R.
1996 Woman Becomes Man in the Balkans. Pp. 241–281 in *Third Sex, Third Gender: Beyond Sexual Dimorphism in Culture and History.* Edited by G. Herdt. New York: Zone Books.

Guinan, A. K.
1997 Auguries of Hegemony: The Sex Omens of Mesopotamia. *Gender and History* 9: 462–479.

Gurney, O. R.
1983 *The Middle Babylonian Legal and Economic Texts from Ur.* London: British School of Archaeology in Iraq.

Hall, K.
2001 "Unnatural" Gender in Hindi. Pp. 133–162 in *The Linguistic Representation of Women and Men*. Vol. 2 of *Gender Across Languages*. Edited by M. Hellinger and H. Bussmann. 4 vols. Philadelphia: John Benjamins.

Halperin, D. M.
2002 *How to Do the History of Homosexuality.* Chicago: University of Chicago Press.

Harris, R.
2000 *Gender and Aging in Mesopotamia: The Gilgamesh Epic and Other Ancient Literature.* Norman: University of Oklahoma Press.

Heimpel, W. J.
2002 The Lady of Girsu. Pp. 155–160 in *Riches Hidden in Secret Places: Ancient Near Eastern Studies in Memory of Thorkild Jacobsen*. Edited by T. Abusch. Winona Lake, IN: Eisenbrauns.

Herdt, G.
1991 Review of *Neither Man nor Woman: The Hijras of India*, by Serena Nanda. *American Anthropologist* 93/1: 199–200.
1994 *Third Sex, Third Gender: Beyond Sexual Dimorphism in Culture and History.* New York: Zone Books.

Hill, W. W.
1935 The Status of the Hermaphrodite and Transvestite in Navaho Culture. *American Anthropologist* 37: 273–279.

Horswell, M. J.
1997 *Third Gender, Tropes of Sexuality and Transculturation in Colonial Andean Historiography*. PhD diss., University of Maryland.

Huehnergard, J.
2000 *A Grammar of Akkadian.* HSS 45. Winona Lake, IN: Eisenbrauns.

Janssen, T.
1992 Transvestites and Transsexuals in Turkey. Pp. 83–91 in *Sexuality and Eroticism Among Males in Moslem Societies*. Edited by A. Schmitt and J. Sofer. New York: Haworth.

Jastrow, M., Jr.
1917 Descent of the Goddess Ishtar to the Netherworld. Pp. 235–241 in *The Sacred Books and Early Literature of the East*, vol. 1: *Babylonia and Assyria.* Edited by C. F. Horne. New York: Parke, Austin, and Lipscomb.

Kessler, S. J. and McKenna, W.
1978 *Gender: An Ethnomethodological Approach.* Chicago: University of Chicago Press.

Kilmer, A. D.
1963 The First Tablet of "*malku* = *šarru*" Together with Its Explicit Version. *JAOS* 83: 421–446.

Kobak, A.
1988 *Isabelle: The Life of Isabelle Eberhardt.* London: Chatto & Windus.

Kovacs, M. G.
1989 *The Epic of Gilgamesh.* Stanford: Stanford University Press.

Kramer, S. N.
1963 Cuneiform Studies and the History of Literature: The Sumerian Sacred Marriage Texts. *Proceedings of the American Philosophical Society* 107: 485–527.

Kulick, D.
1997 The Gender of Brazilian Transgendered Prostitutes. *American Anthropologist* 99: 574–585.

Lacheman, E. R.
1973 Real Estate Adoption by Women in the Tablets from URU Nuzi. Pp. 99–100 in *Orient and Occident: Essays Presented to Cyrus H. Gordon on the Occasion of His Sixty-Fifth Birthday*. Edited by H. A. Hoffner Jr. AOAT 22. Kevelaer: Butzon & Bercker; Neukirchen-Vluyn: Neukirchener Verlag.

Lambert, W. G.
1992 Prostitution. Pp. 127–157 in *Aussenseiter und Randgruppen: Beitrage zu einer Sozialgeschichte des Alten Orients*. Edited by V. Haas. Xenia 32. Konstanz: Universitätsverlag Konstanz.

Leick, G.
1994 *Sex and Eroticism in Mesopotamian Literature*. London: Routledge.

Lerberghe, K. van
1982 New Data from the Archives Found in the House of Ur-Utu at Tell ed-Der. Pp. 280–283 in *Vorträge gehalten auf der 28. Rencontre assyriologique internationale in Wien, 6.–10. Juli 1981*. Edited by H. Hirsch and H. Hunger. AfOB 19. Horn: Berger.

Lerberghe, K. van and G. Voet
1991 *Sippar-Amnānum: The Ur-Utu Archive*. MHET 1. Ghent: University of Ghent.

Liverani, M.
2000 Review of *Cuneiform Texts and the Writing of History*, by Marc van de Mieroop. *Or* 69: 330–332.

Llop, J.
2014 The Families in the Middle Assyrian Administrative Texts from the "Big Silos" of Assur (Assur M 8). Pp. 443–455 in *La famille dans le Proche-Orient ancient réalités, symbolismes, et images: Proceedings of the 55th Rencontre Assyriologique Internationale at Paris 6–9 July 2009*. Edited by L. Marti. Winona Lake, IN: Eisenbrauns.

Marsman, H. J.
2003 *Women in Ugarit and Israel: Their Social and Religious Position in the Context of the Ancient Near East*. OTS 49. Leiden: Brill.

McCaffrey, K.
2008 The Female Kings of Ur. Pp. 173–215 in *Gender Through Time in the Ancient Near East*. Edited by D. Bolger. Gender and Archaeology 17. Lanham, MD: AltaMira.

Meier, S. A.
1991 Women and Communication in the Ancient Near East. *JAOS* 111: 540–547.

Michalowski, P.
1990 Presence at the Creation. Pp. 381–396 in *Lingering Over Words: Studies in Ancient Near Eastern Literature in Honor of William L. Moran*. Edited by T. Abusch, J. Huehnergard, and P. Steinkeller. HSS 37. Atlanta: Scholars Press.
1996 Sailing to Babylon, Reading the Dark Side of the Moon. Pp. 177–193 in *The Study of the Ancient Near East in the Twenty-First Century: The William Foxwell Albright Centennial Conference*. Edited by J. Cooper and G. Schwartz. Winona Lake, IN: Eisenbrauns.

Mobley, G.
1997 The Wild Man in the Bible and the Ancient Near East. *JBL* 116: 217–233.

Moore, J.
2014 Scribal Culture in the Ancient Near East. *Oxford Biblical Studies Online*. http://www.oxfordbiblicalstudies.com/resource/scribal.xhtml.

Morris, R.
1994 Three Sexes and Four Sexualities: Redressing the Discourses on Gender and Sexuality in Contemporary Thailand. *Positions* 2: 15–43.

Murray, S. O.

1997a Male Actresses in Islamic Parts of Indonesia and the Southern Philippines. Pp. 256–261 in *Islamic Homosexualities: Culture, History, and Literature*. Edited by S. O. Murray and W. Roscoe. New York: New York University Press.

1997b The Sohari *Khanith*. Pp. 244–255 in *Islamic Homosexualities: Culture, History, and Literature*. Edited by S. O. Murray and W. Roscoe. New York: New York University Press.

1997c Some Nineteen-Century Reports of Islamic Homsexualities. Pp. 204–221 in *Islamic Homosexualities: Culture, History, and Literature*. Edited by S. O. Murray and W. Roscoe. New York: New York University Press.

Nanda, S.

2000 *Gender Diversity: Crosscultural Variations*. Prospect Heights, IL: Waveland.

Necef, M. Ü.

1992 Turkey on the Brink of Modernity: A Guide for Scandinavian Gays. Pp. 71–75 in *Sexuality and Eroticism Among Males in Moslem Societies*. Edited by A. Schmitt and J. Sofer. New York: Haworth.

Nissinen, M.

1998 *Homoeroticism in the Biblical World: A Historical Perspective*. Translated by K. Stjerna. Minneapolis: Fortress.

2010 Are There Homosexuals in Mesopotamian Literature? *JAOS* 130: 73–77.

Ornan, T.

2005 *The Triumph of the Symbol: Pictorial Representation of Deities in Mesopotamia and the Biblical Image Ban*. OBO 213. Fribourg: Academic Press Fribourg; Göttingen: Vandenhoeck & Ruprecht.

Parpola, S.

1997 *Assyrian Prophecies*. SAA 9. Helsinki: Helsinki University Press.

Pasquali, J.

2015 Éblaïte za-ni-tum, “prostituée.” *NABU* 2015.3: 94–98.

Pruzsinszky, R.

2003 *Die Personennamen der Texte aus Emar*. SCCNH 13. Bethesda, MD: CDL.

Reiner, E.

1985 *Your Thwarts in Pieces: Your Mooring Rope Cut; Poetry from Babylonia and Assyria*. Michigan Studies in the Humanities 5. Ann Arbor: University of Michigan.

Reisman, D.

1973 Iddin-Dagan’s Sacred Marriage Hymn. *JCS* 25: 185–202.

Renger, J.

1972 Note brève 14: Gilg. P ii 32 (PBS 10.3). *RA* 66: 190.

Ringrose, K. M.

1996 Living in the Shadows: Eunuchs and Gender in Byzantium. Pp. 85–109 in *Third Sex, Third Gender: Beyond Sexual Dimorphism in Culture and History*. Edited by G. Herdt. New York: Zone Books.

Roscoe, W.

1994 How to Become a Berdache: Toward a Unified Analysis of Gender Diversity. Pp. 329–372 in *Third Sex, Third Gender: Beyond Sexual Dimorphism in Culture and History*. Edited by G. Herdt. New York: Zone Books.

1996 Priests of the Goddess: Gender Transgression in Ancient Religion. *HR* 35: 195–230.

1998 *Changing Ones: Third and Fourth Genders in Native North America*. New York: St. Martin’s Press.

Roth, M. T.

1997 *Law Collections from Mesopotamia and Asia Minor*. 2nd ed. WAW 6. Atlanta: Scholars Press.

2006 Marriage, Divorce, and the Prostitute in Ancient Mesopotamia. Pp. 21–39 in *Prostitutes and Courtesans in the Ancient World*. Edited by C. A. Faraone and L. K. McClure. Wisconsin Studies in Classics. Madison: University of Wisconsin Press.

Rubio, G.
2001 Review of *Babylonischer Liebesgarten: Erotik und Sexualität im Alten Orient*, by V. Haas. *WZKM* 91: 408–411.

Sayce, A. H.
1872 *An Assyrian Grammar for Comparative Purposes*. London: Trübner.

Selz, G. J.
2000 Five Divine Ladies: Thoughts on Inana(k), Ištar, In(n)in(a), Annunītum, and Anat, and the Origin of the Title "Queen of Heaven." *NIN* 1: 29–62.

Shehata, D.
2009 *Musiker und die vokales Repertoire: Untersuchungen zu Inhalt und Organisation von Musikerberufen und Liedgattungen in altbabylonischer Zeit*. Göttingen: Universitätsverlag Göttingen.

Silver, M.
2006 Temple/Sacred Prostitution in Ancient Mesopotamia Revisited: Religion in the Economy. *UF* 38: 631–663.

Sladek, W. R.
1974 *Inanna's Descent to the Netherworld*. PhD diss., Johns Hopkins University.

Sofer, J.
1992 Testimonies from the Holy Land: Israeli and Palestinian Men Talk About Their Sexual Encounters. Pp. 105–11 in *Sexuality and Eroticism Among Males in Moslem Societies*. Edited by A. Schmitt and J. Sofer. New York: Haworth Press.

Steele, L. D.
2007 Women and Gender in Babylonia. Pp. 299–316 in *The Babylonian World*. Edited by G. Leick. New York: Routledge.

Stökl, J.
2009 Ištar's Women, YHWH's Men? A Curious Gender-Bias in Neo-Assyrian and Biblical Prophecy. *ZAW* 121: 87–100.
2012 *Prophecy in the Ancient Near East: A Philological and Sociological Comparison*. CHANE 56. Leiden: Brill.
2013 Gender "Ambiguity" in Ancient Near Eastern Prophecy? A Reassessment of the Data Behind a Popular Theory. Pp. 59–79 in *Prophets Male and Female: Gender and Prophecy in the Hebrew Bible, the Eastern Mediterranean, and the Ancient Near East*. Edited by S. Carvalho and J. Stökl. AIL 15. Atlanta: Society of Biblical Literature.

Stol, M.
1991 Old Babylonian Personal Names. *SEL* 8: 191–212.
1995 Women in Mesopotamia. *JESHO* 38: 123–144.

Suter, C. E.
2012 Kings and Queens: Representation and Reality. Pp. 201–226 in *The Sumerian World*. Edited by H. E. W. Crawford. London: Routledge.

Tanret, M. and van Lerberghe, K.
1993 Rituals and Profits in the Ur-Utu Archive. Pp. 435–449 in *Ritual and Sacrifice in the Ancient Near East: Proceedings of the International Conference Organized by the Katholieke Universiteit Leuven from the 17th to the 20th of April 1991*. Edited by J. Quaegebeur. OLA 55. Louvain: Peeters.

Teppo, S.
2008 Sacred Marriage and the Devotees of Ištar. Pp. 75–92 in *Sacred Marriages: The Divine-Human Sexual Metaphor from Sumer to Early Christianity*. Edited by M. Nissinen and R. Uro. Winona Lake, IN: Eisenbrauns.

Thesiger, W.
1964 *The Marsh Arabs*. London: Longmans.
Towle, E. B. and Morgan, L. M.
2002 Romancing the Transgender Native: Rethinking the Use of the "Third Gender" Concept. *GLQ* 8: 469–497.
Van De Mieroop, M.
1999 *Cuneiform Texts and the Writing of History*. London: Routledge.
Wallach, J.
1996 *Desert Queen: The Extraordinary Life of Gertrude Bell; Adventurer, Adviser to Kings, Ally of Lawrence of Arabia.* New York: Anchor Books.
Walls, N. H.
2001 *Desire, Discord and Death: Approaches to Ancient Near Eastern Myth.* ASOR Books 8. Boston: American Schools of Oriental Research.
Westenholz, J. G.
1989 Tamar, Qĕdēšā, Qadištu, and Sacred Prostitution in Mesopotamia. *HTR* 82: 245–266.
2007 Inanna and Ishtar: The Dimorphic Venus Goddesses. Pp. 332–347 in *The Babylonian World.* Edited by G. Leick. New York: Routledge.
2012 In the Service of the Gods: The Ministering Clergy. Pp. 246–274 in *The Sumerian World.* Edited by H. E. W. Crawford. London: Routledge.
Westphal-Hellbusch, S.
1997 Institutionalized Gender-Crossing in Southern Iraq. Pp. 233–243 in *Islamic Homosexualities: Culture, History, and Literature*. Edited by S. O. Murray and W. Roscoe. New York: New York University Press.
Wikan, U.
1982 *Behind the Veil in Arabia: Women in Oman.* Chicago: University of Chicago Press.
Wilcke, C.
1987 A Riding Tooth: Metaphor, Metonymy and Synecdoche, Quick and Frozen in Everyday Language. Pp 77–102 in *Figurative Language in the Ancient Near East.* Edited by M. Mindlin, M. J. Geller and J. E. Wansbrough. London: School of Oriental and African Studies.
Wilhelm, G.
1990 Marginalien zu Herodot Klio 199. Pp. 505–524 in *Lingering over Words: Studies in Ancient Near Eastern Literature in Honor of William L. Moran.* Edited by T. Abusch, J. Huehnergard, and P. Steinkeller. HSS 37. Atlanta: Scholars Press.
Worthington, M.
2012 *Principles of Akkadian Textual Criticism.* SANER 1. Berlin: de Gruyter.
Yiğit, T.
2008 Study of the MUNUS(.MEŠ)KAR.KID in the Hittite Cuneiform Texts. *Or* 77: 75–78.
Young, I. M.
2007 Textual Stability in Gilgamesh and the Dead Sea Scrolls. Pp. 173–184 in *Gilgameš and the World of Assyria: Proceedings of the Conference Held at the Mandelbaum House, The University of Sydney, 21–23 July 2004.* Edited by J. Azize and N. Weeks. ANESSup 21. Leuven: Peeters.
Zsolnay, I.
2013 The Misconstrued Role of the Assinnu in Ancient Near Eastern Prophecy. Pp. 81–99 in *Prophets Male and Female: Gender and Prophecy in the Hebrew Bible, the Eastern Mediterranean, and the Ancient Near East.* Edited by J. Stökl and C. L. Carvalho. AIL 15. Atlanta: Society of Biblical Literature.

CHAPTER 16

# Rétablir l'ordre par la mort dans les textes législatifs du début du IIe millénaire av. J.-C.

Virginie Muller

LE DÉBUT DU IIÈME MILLÉNAIRE AV. J.-C. connaît une relative abondance de textes législatifs cunéiformes puisqu'il a fourni le code de Lipit-Ištar (CLI) rédigé en sumérien, les lois d'Ešnunna (LE) et enfin le célèbre code d'Hammu-rabi (CH), tous deux rédigés en akkadien.[1] À la lecture des différents articles de ces textes, se dégage l'image de sociétés où les individus sont définis soit par leur appartenance à une catégorie de personne soit par leur activité professionnelle ou leur fonction. Les textes mentionnent trois catégories : les *awīlum*/LU₂,[2] les *muškēnum*/MAŠ.EN.GAG[3] et les esclaves (*wardum*/IR₃-*amtum*/GEME₂).[4] Les documents législatifs peuvent aussi faire référence aux individus selon leur lien de dépendance avec ces catégories : « épouse de (*aššat*) », « fils de (*mār*) » ou « fille de (*mārat*) ».[5] Les membres des sociétés mésopotamiennes se définissent également par les différents métiers ou fonctions spécifiques qu'ils exercent, comme par exemple les marchands ou les religieuses.

L'appartenance à l'un de ces groupes donne à l'individu un statut, d'où découle sa place dans la société et son rang sur l'échelle sociale. Ce statut implique des prérogatives et des obligations spécifiques, ainsi qu'une différence de traitement et de considération, comme le montre, entre autres, la gradation des peines sanctionnant un même crime établie par les textes législatifs suivant le statut de la victime. C'est le cas, par exemple, de la punition pour la fausse-couche provoquée suite à des coups : on trouve une différenciation des châtiments à la fois pour la perte du fœtus mais aussi pour l'éventuel décès de la femme enceinte. C'est ainsi que la compensation pour la mort du fœtus d'une esclave est, suivant les codes de lois, de 5 ou de 2 sicles d'argent, montant moins important que celui pour le fœtus d'une fille d'*awīlum*, à savoir entre 20 et 10 sicles d'argent.[6] De même, si la femme décède suite aux coups qui ont provoqué la fausse-couche, la punition du coupable sera différente : soit la peine capitale dans le cas d'une fille d'*awīlum*, soit une simple indemnité financière dans le cas d'une

1. Pour la présentation, l'édition et la bibliographie antérieure relatives à ces textes, cf. Roth (1997). Concernant le débat sur la valeur législative réelle ou non de ces lois, l'article le plus complet est celui de Renger (1994) ; pour une mise à jour, cf. Démare-Lafont (2000), Westbrook (2000) et Roth (2000).

2. À noter que le terme *awīlum* peut désigner simplement « quelqu'un », mais peut aussi désigner des individus appartenant à des groupes différents lorsqu'il est mis en parallèle avec un autre statut, cf. Kraus (1973), ainsi que Westbrook (2006, 147s) notamment pour les différentes traductions possibles.

3. Pour ces catégories, cf. Von Dassow (2014).

4. Cette distinction est bien marquée dans le code d'Hammu-rabi, ainsi que dans les lois d'Ešnunna, mais la mention des *muškēnum* n'est pas systématique dans les autres corpus législatifs.

5. Pour la relation de dépendance des *mār*/*mārat awīlum*/*muškēnum*, cf. Roth (2013).

6. Respectivement dans CLI f et CH 213, ainsi que dans CLI e et CH 209.

esclave.[7] On retrouve cette hiérarchie des peines dans de nombreux autres articles des codes de lois, pour des crimes plus ou moins graves.[8]

Ces sociétés proche-orientales sont donc organisées hiérarchiquement autour de différents groupes inégalitaires, dont la mobilité sociale est faible et ses mouvements codifiés.[9] La cellule domestique, avec à sa tête généralement le père ou le mari, constitue la base sur laquelle repose cette structure. La place d'un individu dans l'échelle sociale détermine à la fois ses droits et devoirs, mais aussi son traitement d'un point de vue juridique.

À partir de ce postulat, quatre fautes mentionnées dans le corpus législatif paléo-babylonien seront analysées : la remise en cause du statut d'esclave, certaines conduites des religieuses, l'adultère de la femme et enfin les relations sexuelles entre personnes apparentées. L'objectif de cette étude est de montrer que ces fautes portent toutes atteinte à l'organisation de la société et que leur répression exige alors un procédé d'exécution spécifique de la peine de mort.

## Présentation et analyse des cas

### *La remise en cause du statut d'esclave*

L'esclave, qu'il soit permanent ou temporaire,[10] est une personne propriété d'une autre, son maître, qui est alors le seul à disposer de certains droits à son encontre. Cependant le code d'Hammu-rabi documente des fraudes commises par un tiers relatives au statut servile. La première est l'aide aux fuyards, comme dans ces deux paragraphes : « Si quelqu'un a fait sortir par la grande porte (de la ville) ou bien un esclave du palais, ou bien une esclave du palais, ou bien un esclave de *muškēnum*, ou bien une esclave de *muškēnum*, il sera tué »,[11] et : « Si quelqu'un a abrité dans sa maison ou bien un esclave, ou bien une esclave fugitifs appartenant au palais ou bien à un *muškēnum*, et s'il ne l'a pas fait sortir à l'appel du crieur, ce maître de maison sera tué ».[12] Quel que soit son propriétaire, du plus haut placé, le palais, au plus bas, le *muškēnum*, la disparition d'un esclave était annoncée par le héraut de la ville. Ainsi toute la population en était informée et devait se mobiliser au cas où elle rencontrerait le ou la fugitive.[13] Lui apporter son aide, en l'abritant ou en lui faisant franchir la porte de la ville, était un moyen de favoriser son évasion et donc de remettre en cause son statut servile. Dans

7. Respectivement dans CLI e et CH 210, ainsi que dans CH 214. Pour la fausse-couche, cf. également Démare-Lafont (1999, 345s).

8. Cf. par exemple Van Den Driessche (1980, 21s).

9. Bien que l'impression d'une société figée transparaisse dans les codes de lois, les documents de la pratique présentent en fait une multitude de situations, cf. par exemple Westbrook (2003, 376s).

10. Pour une définition et une analyse détaillée des différents types d'esclaves présents au Proche-Orient ancien, cf. Westbrook (1995).

11. CH 15 : *šum-ma a-wi-lum lu* $IR_3$ $E_2$.GAL *lu* $GEME_2$ $E_2$.GAL *lu* $IR_3$ MAŠ.EN.GAG *lu* $GEME_2$ MAŠ.EN.GAG $KA_2$.GAL *uš-te- ṣi*$_2$ *id-da-ak.*

12. CH 16 : *šum-ma a-wi-lum lu* $IR_3$ *lu* $GEME_2$ *hal-qa*$_2$*-am ša* $E_2$.GAL *u*$_3$ *lu* MAŠ.EN.GAG *i-na bi-ti-šu ir-ta-qi*$_2$*-ma a-na ši-si-it na-gi-ri-im la uš-te-ši*$_2$*-a-am be-el* $E_2$ *šu-u*$_2$ *id-da-ak.*

13. Cette coopération des autres citoyens pouvait même être récompensée par le maître de l'esclave fugitif, comme dans CH 17 qui mentionne une rétribution de 2 sicles d'argent.

le second article, il s'agit bien d'une aide à la fuite puisque les codes documentent dans d'autres paragraphes le vol ou la rétention d'un esclave.[14]

L'atteinte au statut servile peut également se faire par un affranchissement abusif, réalisé par une autre personne que son propriétaire : « Si quelqu'un a dupé un barbier et (s')il a rasé la mèche d'un esclave qui n'est pas à lui, cet homme (= celui qui a présenté l'esclave au barbier) on le tuera et devant sa porte on l'exposera ».[15] À l'époque paléo-babylonienne, les esclaves portaient l'*abbuttum,* une coiffure particulière dont la nature exacte est discutée, permettant d'identifier leur statut au premier coup d'œil.[16] Sa coupe, symbolique et décidée uniquement par son propriétaire légal, signifiait l'affranchissement de l'esclave.[17]

Il s'agit à chaque fois d'atteintes à l'autorité et non pas aux biens matériels du maître. Ces crimes semblent plus graves et entraînent la peine capitale, alors que la perte d'un esclave suite à sa mort, même donnée intentionnellement, était généralement réglée par une simple compensation financière.[18] Le fait d'avoir aidé à changer le statut de l'esclave constitue, en plus d'un affront à l'autorité du propriétaire, un cas d'infraction au système structuré des groupes sociaux mis en place par la communauté, puisque le contrevenant s'octroie lui-même le pouvoir de modifier illégalement la place d'un de ses membres.

### *La conduite des religieuses*

Une autre faute concerne les religieuses : « Si une religieuse-*nadītum* ou une prêtresse-*entum* qui ne séjourne pas dans le *gâgu* a ouvert un cabaret ou y est entrée pour (boire) de la bière, cette femme on la brûlera ».[19] La religieuse-*nadītum* et la prêtresse-*entum* jouent un rôle important dans la vie religieuse, elles sont donc censées avoir une conduite irréprochable et suivre les obligations inhérentes à leur office.[20] Ce paragraphe du code d'Hammu-rabi a suscité plusieurs interprétations, notamment en ce qui concerne la nature du crime qui y est mentionné : le cabaret a parfois été compris comme un lieu à mauvaise réputation, utilisé notamment pour la prostitution, ce qui rend leur entrée interdite aux religieuses. Le crime des contrevenantes serait alors une faute sexuelle, une atteinte aux mœurs. S. Maul a proposé une autre interprétation : la taverne, la bière, etc. seraient revêtus d'un aspect magique, où le patient pourrait déposer son impureté. L'interdit qui vise ces religieuses serait alors de nature

14. Notamment dans CLI 12 où celui qui a gardé dans sa maison un esclave fugitif pendant un mois doit compenser un esclave pour un esclave, ainsi que dans CH 7 et CH 19 où ceux qui sont pris en possession d'un esclave volé sont mis à mort.

15. CH 227 : *šum-ma a-wi-lum* ŠU.I *i-da-aṣ-ma ab-bu-ti* $IR_3$ *la še-e-em ug-da-al-li-ib a-wi-lam šu-a-ti i-du-uk-ku-šu-ma i-na* $KA_2$-*šu i-ha-al-la-lu-šu.*

16. Sur ce terme, cf. Westbrook (1995, 1667), avec la bibliographie antérieure.

17. Cf. par exemple le contrat d'adoption TIM 4 15.

18. Ce cas de figure est présent dans de nombreux articles et lors de circonstances variées : par exemple, dans LE 24 (le décès causé par le créancier d'un esclave mis en gage entraîne une compensation), dans CH 214 (qui sanctionne par une amende la mort d'une esclave enceinte) ou encore dans CH 219 (où le médecin doit compenser un esclave équivalent à celui qui est mort lors d'une intervention chirurgicale).

19. CH 110 : *š[u]m-ma* LUKUR NIN.DINGIR *ša i-na* $GA_2$.$GI_4$.A *la wa-aš-ba-at* $E_2$.KURUN.NA *ip-te-te* $u_3$ *lu a-na* KAŠ *a-na* $E_2$.KURUN.NA *i-te-ru-ub a-wi-il-tam šu-a-ti i-qal-lu-*$u_2$*-ši.* Pour une analyse détaillée de ce paragraphe (protagonistes, châtiment . . .), cf. Roth (1999).

20. Pour une synthèse récente sur les religieuses, cf. Barberon (2012).

magique, puisque ces femmes doivent préserver un état de pureté rituelle : entrer dans la taverne pourrait les souiller et les rendre impropres à leur charge (Maul 1992, 395s). Enfin, selon M. T. Roth, ce paragraphe punirait un délit économique : ces femmes concurrenceraient les cabaretières professionnelles-*sābītum.*[21]

Quelle que soit l'interprétation retenue, les religieuses ne devaient pas entrer dans un cabaret, lieu jugé comme incompatible avec leur fonction, et dans le cas contraire, il s'agit d'une transgression aux obligations liées à leur charge, imposées par la communauté dans laquelle elles évoluent.[22] Ce paragraphe dénote donc l'autorité qu'exerce la société sur les servantes du culte, puisque leur rôle a une dimension communautaire.

### *L'adultère de la femme*

Un autre crime portant atteinte à la structure de la société et impliquant une femme est l'adultère de l'épouse, présent dans de nombreuses dispositions des textes législatifs (cf. Démare-Lafont 1999, 29–91). Le code d'Ešnunna ne le cite qu'une seule fois : « Si, à ce jour, il conclut un contrat et une cérémonie-*kirrum* avec son père et sa mère, et l'épouse (est son) épouse (légitime). Le jour où elle sera prise dans le giron d'un autre homme, elle mourra, elle ne vivra pas ».[23] Le code d'Hammu-rabi est plus prolifique et contient plusieurs paragraphes sur ce thème, avec différents cas de figure plus ou moins détaillés. Le plus simple est le paragraphe 129 qui énonce : « Si l'épouse d'un homme a été surprise couchant avec un autre mâle, on les liera et on les jettera à l'eau. Si le maître de l'épouse fait grâce à sa femme, alors le roi graciera (aussi) son serviteur ».[24] Deux autres paragraphes détaillent des situations particulières qui peuvent pousser la femme à l'adultère. Le premier concerne la conduite de l'épouse en cas d'absence prolongée du mari : si elle a de quoi survivre dans sa maison, elle n'est pas autorisée à fréquenter un autre homme, et si c'est le cas, elle sera alors traitée comme une femme adultère, c'est-à-dire « convaincue et jetée à l'eau ».[25] Dans le second exemple, la femme qui rejette son mari et qui est sorteuse, c'est-à-dire qui va à la rencontre d'occasion d'adultère, sera également jetée à l'eau.[26] Quant au paragraphe 153 du code d'Hammu-rabi, il présente un cas d'adultère aggravé puisqu'il a conduit

21. Roth (1999, 453s). Cette interprétation a cependant été critiquée : aucun article connu ne traite de la « concurrence déloyale », et la mort sur le bûcher semble être une peine excessive pour une simple faute économique.

22. Les textes de la pratique documentent cependant qu'une *nadītum* pouvait posséder un cabaret, cf. Lion (2011–2012, 397).

23. LE 28 : *šum-ma* U$_4$.BI *ri-ik-sa-tim u*$_3$ *kir-ra-am a-na a-bi-ša u*$_3$ *um-mi-ša iš-ku-un-na i-hu-us-si* DAM *u*$_4$*-um i-na su-un* LU$_2$ [*iş*]- *ş*[*a-a*]*b-ba-tu i-ma-at u*$_2$*-ul i-ba-al-lu-*[*uţ*].

24. CH 129 : *šum-ma aš-ša-at a-wi-lim it-ti zi-ka-ri-im ša-ni-im i-na i-tu-lim it-ta-aş-bat i-ka-su*$_2$*-nu-ti-ma a-na me-e i-na-ad-du-u*$_2$*-šu-nu-ti šum-ma be-el aš-ša-tim aš-ša-su*$_2$ *u*$_2$*-ba-la-aţ u*$_3$ *šar-ru-um* IR$_3$*-su*$_2$ *u*$_2$*-ba-la-aţ*.

25. CH 133 : « Si un homme est capturé et (s')il y a de quoi manger dans sa maison, son [épouse tien] dra [sa maison et surveillera] son corps ; [dans la maison d'un autr]e elle [n'en]trera [pas]. [Si] cette femme n'a pas sur[veillé] son corps et est entrée dans la maison d'un autre, cette femme on la convaincra et on la jettera à l'eau » (*šum-ma a-wi-lum iš-ša-li-il-ma i-na* E$_2$*-šu ša a-ka-a-lim* [*i*]*-ba-aš-ši* [*aš*]*-ša-su*$_2$ [*a-di mu?*]*-sa*$_3$ [*şa-ab-t*]*u?* [*pa-gar*$_2$*-š*]*a* [*i-na-şa-a*]*r* [*a-na* E$_2$ *ša-ni-i*]*m* [*u*$_2$*-ul i-ir-*]*ru-ub š*[*um*]*-ma* MI$_2$ *ši-i* [*pa*]*-g*[*a*]*r*$_2$*-ša la iş-şur-ma a-na* E$_2$ *ša-ni-im i-te-ru-ub* MI$_2$ *šu-a-ti u*$_2$*-ka-an-nu-ši-ma a-na me-e i-na-ad-du-u*$_2$*-ši*).

26. CH 142–143 : « Si une femme a rejeté son mari et a dit : « Tu ne m'étreindras plus », son cas sera décidé dans son quartier. Si elle ne prend pas garde à soi et est sorteuse, dilapide (le bien de) sa maison, dénigre son mari, cette femme on la jettera à l'eau » (*šum-ma* MI$_2$ *mu-sa*$_3$ *i-ze-er-ma u*$_2$*-ul ta-ah-ha-za-an-ni*

au meurtre du conjoint : « Si l'épouse d'un homme, à cause d'un autre mâle, a fait tuer son mari, cette femme on l'empalera ».[27]

L'adultère doit être considéré comme une double atteinte. Il porte préjudice à l'autorité du mari sur son épouse, en remettant en cause sa prédominance en tant que chef de famille. Mais il entraîne aussi une rupture des liens matrimoniaux sur lesquels reposent la cellule domestique, en bafouant les prérogatives maritales (une femme mariée se devait d'avoir des relations sexuelles uniquement avec son époux). C'est donc le statut « marié » de la femme, et pas seulement l'offense elle-même, qui dicte ici la peine de mort.[28] Du point de vue de l'amant, celui-ci usurpe les prérogatives du mari, c'est pourquoi il est lui aussi mis à mort.[29] Le paragraphe CH 153 comporte également une autre dimension : la femme complice, voire instigatrice, du meurtre de son époux a trahit la confiance familiale.[30]

### *Les relations sexuelles entre personnes apparentées*

La dernière faute analysée concerne l'inceste qui désigne le commerce charnel entres des parents, qu'ils soient ascendants, descendants ou collatéraux.[31] Le code d'Hammurabi est le seul recueil à le documenter au II^ème^ millénaire av. J.-C., au travers de cinq cas,[32] dont deux prescrivent la peine capitale : « Si un homme a choisi une fiancée pour son fils et (si) son fils l'a connue sexuellement, (si) lui-même, par la suite, s'est couché sur son sein et (si) on l'a surpris, cet homme on le ligotera (et) on le jettera à l'eau »,[33] et « Si un homme, après son père, s'est couché sur le sein de sa mère, on les brûlera tous les deux ».[34]

---

*iq-ta-bi wa-ar-ka-sa$_3$ i-na ba-ab-ti-ša ip-pa-ar-ra-as$_2$-ma šum-ma a na-aṣ-ra-at-ma wa-ṣi$_2$-a-at bi-sa$_3$ u$_2$-sa$_3$-ap-pa-ah mu-sa$_3$ u$_2$-ša-am-ṭa* MI$_2$ *šu-a-ti a-na me-e i-na-ad-du-u$_2$-ši).*

27. CH 153 : *šum-ma aš-ša-at a-wi-lim aš-šum zi-ka-ri-im ša-ni-im mu-sa$_3$ uš-di-ik* MI$_2$ *šu-a-ti i-na ga-ši-ši-im i-ša-ak-ka-nu-ši.*

28. LE 28 prend bien soin de spécifier clairement le statut de la femme mariée notamment en mentionnant les deux actes constitutifs du mariage, le contrat et la cérémonie. Pour une étude plus détaillée du rôle du statut de la femme lors d'un adultère, cf. Démare-Lafont (1999, 44–62). C'est également le cas lors de viols, qui est plus une atteinte à l'honneur du chef de famille qu'à la victime, cf. l'étude consacrée aux délits mettant en cause les liens conjugaux de Szlechter (1985, 70–82 et 89–94).

29. Cependant, cela n'est le cas que lorsqu'il connaît le statut matrimonial de la femme. Par exemple, dans le paragraphe 7 du code un peu plus ancien d'Ur-Nammu, l'homme séduit par une femme mariée est laissé libre, tandis que la séductrice est mise à mort. Les lois médio-assyriennes, à une époque plus récente, montrent également l'importance de cette connaissance du statut de la femme, notamment dans le paragraphe 13A où l'homme averti, et bien que ce soit elle qui soit venu à sa rencontre, est mis à mort.

30. Voir également le compte-rendu de procès 2 N-T 54, édité dans Jacobsen (1959), qui mentionne l'empalement des meurtriers d'un homme, ainsi que de son épouse qui en avait été informée.

31. Pour une vue d'ensemble, incluant les cas d'inceste mentionnés dans les lois hittites et dans la Bible, cf. Démare-Lafont (1999, 173–235).

32. Les trois autres cas sont : CH 154 qui mentionne l'inceste d'un homme avec sa fille et entraîne le bannissement du père. CH 156 qui présente un homme couchant avec sa belle-fille, mais contrairement au CH 155 celle-ci est « sexuellement inconnue » de son fiancé, et entraîne une compensation financière. Enfin CH 158 qui traite de l'inceste d'un homme avec sa belle-mère après le décès de son père et qui indique qu'il sera chassé de la maison et exclu de l'héritage.

33. CH 155 : *šum-ma a-wi-lum a-na* DUMU-*šu* E$_2$.GI$_4$.A *i-hi-ir-ma* DUMU-*šu il-ma-si$_2$ šu-u$_2$ wa-ar-ka-nu-um-ma i-na su$_2$-ni-ša it-ta-ti-il-ma iṣ-ṣa-ab-tu-šu a-wi-lam šu-a-ti i-ka-su$_2$-šu-ma a-na me-e i-na-ad-du-u$_2$-ši*$^!$.

34. CH 157 : *šum-ma a-wi-lum wa-ar-ki a-bi-šu i-na su$_2$-un um-mi-šu it-ta-ti-il ki-la-li-šu-nu i-qal-lu-šu-nu-ti.*

Les cas d'inceste les plus graves, outre leur caractère immoral et d'atteinte aux mœurs, sont donc ceux qui impliquent des femmes qui ont le statut d'épouse, même après la mort de leur mari. On retrouve ici la même importance pour le statut légitime de la femme que dans les cas d'adultère.

## La peine de mort : Essai d'interprétation des modalités d'exécution spécifiques

Les quatre fautes analysées ci-dessus se règlent toujours par la mort du coupable, formulée de manière « simple », c'est-à-dire sans précision ni détail. On trouve donc dans les lois d'Ešnunna la tournure *imat ul iballuṭ*, tandis que le code d'Hammu-rabi emploie le verbe *dakûm* sous deux formes : *iddâk* et *iddukū* (CH 227), la première étant la manière la plus courante d'énoncer la peine de mort.[35]

Cependant, dans plusieurs des cas présents, le code d'Hammu-rabi prescrit également des sanctions moins courantes qu'on retrouve peu dans les autres recueils de lois de cette époque.[36] La plus fréquente est la noyade (*ana mê nadûm* ; CH 129, 133, 142–143 et 155),[37] toujours appliquée pour des femmes adultères,[38] mais aussi pour l'amant de celle-ci, ainsi que dans certains cas d'hommes incestueux (CH 155). Le supplice par le feu (*qalûm* ; CH 110 et 157) était également présent dans des cas en lien avec les mœurs.[39] Enfin le supplice du pal (*ina gašīšim šakānum* ; CH 153) était beaucoup plus rare (il n'en existe que quelques attestations, que ce soit dans les textes législatifs ou dans les documents de la pratique[40]) punissant la femme adultère instigatrice du meurtre de son mari. Il s'agit d'un châtiment particulièrement grave puisqu'il prive le condamné de sépulture, condition *sine qua non* pour que son esprit ne soit pas tourmenté. Enfin, la peine capitale pouvait parfois être accompagnée d'une sanction supplémentaire, à savoir l'exposition du corps du fautif dans un lieu public (*halālum* ; CH 227, pour le coupable d'un affranchissement abusif). Tout comme le supplice du pal, cette sanction avait un caractère exemplaire et dissuasif, permettant ainsi de prévenir d'éventuelles autres fautes de ce type.

Dans le code d'Hammu-rabi, sur les 282 lois conservées, 32 prescrivent la peine de mort, la majorité concernant des vols ou des homicides par négligence. Sur ces 32 lois, seulement 11 énoncent des peines de mort aux modalités spécifiques et sévères.[41]

35. Ces tournures et leurs implications ont déjà été largement discutées par le passé, cf. Szlechter (1962, 174s) et Westbrook (1997).

36. Pour un aperçu d'ensemble de la peine de mort dans les textes législatifs, cf. Szlechter (1962).

37. Pour les différents cas de noyade en général, cf. San Nicolò (1938). La noyade est également prescrite dans certains contrats de mariage de la même époque, à l'encontre de la femme demandant le divorce, cf. les textes réunis en appendix dans Westbrook (1988).

38. Cependant, la peine capitale pour la femme infidèle est la sanction prescrite dans le cas du flagrant délit ou en présence de preuves, comme on le voit avec l'emploi du verbe *kanûm* dans CH 133. L'accusation d'adultère n'entraîne pas forcément la mort dans les autres situations : comme dans CH 131 où elle doit prêter serment, ou dans CH 132 où elle doit subir l'ordalie par le fleuve pour se disculper.

39. Sur la peine de mort par le feu, cf. Démare-Lafont (2005).

40. Pour l'empalement en général, cf. Fuchs (2003–2005).

41. Au total, sont prescrites dans le code d'Hammu-rabi : 3 morts par le feu (dont CH 25 qui punit immédiatement le voleur profitant d'un incendie), 5 noyades (dont CH 108 pour la cabaretière malhonnête), 1 empalement et 2 expositions publiques du corps du fautif (dont CH 21 suite à l'effraction d'une maison) ; pour une vue d'ensemble cf. le tableau 2, "Dramatic Executions in the Law of Hammurabi", dans Roth (1999, 464).

On peut donc se demander si ce choix ne serait pas motivé par l'aspect global de ces crimes, la remise en cause de la structure de la société, et justifierait alors d'être sévèrement réprimé dans les codes de lois. Certes le choix spécifique de l'emploi de la noyade ou du feu a pu être interprété du point de vue du genre du fautif (la noyade est par exemple employée en majorité pour punir des femmes) ou de la nature de l'offense (le caractère immoral de l'inceste, par exemple, nécessiterait une purification par l'eau ou le feu). Cependant ces crimes ont tous un point commun : une relation de hiérarchie entre les différents protagonistes (maître-esclave, religieuse-communauté, époux-épouse), l'offenseur étant celui qui a normalement des obligations envers l'offensé. Ces liens constituent la structure de la société, ce qui peut expliquer que leur non-respect entraîne une répression rigoureuse et marquante.

## Synthèse

Les quatre crimes étudiés à partir des textes législatifs ont mis en évidence plusieurs fautes commises par différents membres de la communauté, mais qui ont toutes trait à l'organisation de la société, que ce soit des infractions aux contraintes liées au statut de l'esclave ou de la religieuse, ou des atteintes dans le cadre domestique (usurpation de l'autorité du maître sur son esclave ou de celle du mari sur sa femme). Le chef de maisonnée est le garant de l'ordre domestique et détient la place la plus élevée dans le microcosme de la vie quotidienne. Il est donc important de rétablir cette autorité. Mais dans une société où la communauté prime sur l'individu, l'Etat intervient alors, au moyen des lois,[42] dans des crimes domestiques relevant normalement du chef de famille, puisque la remise en cause de l'ordre familial remet en cause, par sa base, toute la structure de la société.

Tout acte transgressant cette organisation est donc considéré comme particulièrement grave et se trouve réprimé dans les textes législatifs au moyen de la peine de mort. Mais celle-ci est cependant très souvent exprimée par des modalités d'exécution spécifiques. La finalité de ces peines particulières et rares est de servir d'exemple à l'ensemble de la société et de dissuader le reste de la communauté de commettre ces fautes, et ainsi de préserver sa stabilité. La mort du fauteur de troubles permet un retour à la normale (rétablissement de l'autorité du maître/époux, élimination de la souillure religieuse), permettant ainsi de transformer le désordre en ordre.

### BIBLIOGRAPHIE

Barberon, L.

2012 *Les religieuses et le culte de Marduk dans le royaume de Babylone.* NABU 14. Archibab 1. Paris: Société pour l'étude du Proche-Orient.

Démare-Lafont, S.

1999 *Femmes, droits et justice dans l'antiquité orientale : Contribution à l'étude du droit pénal au Proche-Orient ancien.* OBO 165. Fribourg: Academic Press; Göttingen: Vandenhoeck & Ruprecht.

42. Il faut cependant nuancer l'image donnée par le corpus législatif: les textes de la pratique documentent des situations beaucoup plus complexes et parfois différentes.

2000 Codification et subsidiarité dans les droits du Proche-Orient ancien. Pp. 49–64 in *La codification des lois dans l'Antiquité : Actes du colloque de Strasbourg, 27–29 novembre 1997*. Édité par E. Lévy. Travaux du Centre de recherche sur le Proche-Orient et la Grèce antiques 16. Paris: De Boccard.

2005 La peine du feu dans les droits cunéiformes. *Ktèma* 30: 107–121.

Fuchs, A.

2003–2005 Pfählen. *RlA* 10:438–439.

Jacobsen, T.

1959 An Ancient Mesopotamian Trial for Homicide. *Studia Biblica e Orientalia* 3 (= *Analecta Biblica el Orientalia* 12): 130–150.

Kraus, F. R.

1973 *Vom mesopotamischen Menschen der altbabylonischen Zeit und seiner Welt*. Mededeelingen der Koninklijke Nederlandsche Akademie van Wetenschappen, Afd. Letterkunde 36/6. Amsterdam: Noord-Hollandsche Uitgeversmaatschappij.

Lion, B.

2011–2012 Les cabarets à l'époque paléo-babylonienne. *Cahier des thèmes transversaux Arscan Thème* 11: 393–400.

Maul, S. M.

1992 Der Kneipenbesuch als Heilverfahren. Pp. 389–396 in *La circulation des biens, des personnes et des idées dans le Proche-Orient ancien. Actes de la XXXVIIIe Rencontre Assyriologique Internationale (Paris, 8–10 juillet 1991)*. Édité par D. Charpin et F. Joannès. Paris: Editions Recherche sur les Civilisations.

Renger, J.

1994 Noch einmal: Was war der ‹Kodex› Hammurapi—ein erlassenes Gesetz oder ein Rechtsbuch? Pp. 27–59 in *Rechtskodifizierung und soziale Normen im interkulturellen Vergleich*. Édité par H.-J. Gehrke. ScriptOralia: Reihe A, altertumswissenschaftliche Reihe15. Tübingen: Narr.

Roth, M. T.

1997 *Law Collections from Mesopotamia and Asia Minor*. Deuxième édition. Atlanta: Scholars Press.

1999 The Priestess and the Tavern: LH §110. Pp. 445–464 in *Munuscula Mesopotamica, Festschrift für Johannes Renger*. Édité par B. Böck, E. Cancik-Kirschbaum et T. Richter. AOAT 267. Münster: Ugarit-Verlag.

2000 The Law Collection of King Hammurabi: Toward an Understanding of Codification and Text. Pp. 9–31 in *La codification des lois dans l'Antiquité : Actes du colloque de Strasbourg, 27–29 novembre 1997*. Édité par E. Lévy. Travaux du Centre de recherche sur le Proche-Orient et la Grèce antiques 16. Paris: De Boccard.

2013 On *mār awīlim* in the Old Babylonian Law Collections. *JNES* 72: 267–272.

San Nicolò, M.

1938 Ertränken. *RlA* 2:472.

Szlechter, E.

1962 La peine capitale en droit babylonien. Pp. 146–178 in vol. 4 of *Studi in onore di Emilio Betti*. 5 vols. Milan: Giuffrè.

1985 Délits mettant en cause les liens conjugaux et familiaux en droits sumérien et babylonien. *Revue internationale des Droits de l'Antiquité* 32: 69–95.

Van Den Driessche, J.

1980 La peine de mort et les châtiments corporels dans le Code Hammurabi. *Akkadica* 19: 1–37.

Von Dassow, E.

2014 *Awīlum* and *muškēnum* in the Age of Hammurabi. Pp. 291–308 in *La famille dans le Proche-Orient ancien : Réalités, symbolismes et images; Proceedings of the 55e Rencontre Assyriologique Internationale, Paris.* Édité par L. Marti. Winona Lake, IN: Eisenbrauns.

Westbrook, R.

1988 *Old Babylonian Marriage Law.* AfOB 23. Horn: Berger.

1995 Slave and Master in Ancient Near Eastern Law. *Chicago-Kent Law Review* 70: 1631–1676.

1997 A Matter of Life and Death. *JANES* 25: 61–70.

2000 Codification and Canonization. Pp. 33–47 in *La codification des lois dans l'Antiquité : Actes du colloque de Strasbourg, 27–29 novembre 1997.* Édité par E. Lévy. Travaux du Centre de recherche sur le Proche-Orient et la Grèce antiques 16. Paris: De Boccard.

2003 *A History of Ancient Near Eastern Law.* 2 vols. HdO 72. Leiden: Brill.

2006 Reflections on the Law of Homicide in the Ancient World. *Maarav* 13: 143–147, 152–173.

CHAPTER 17

# To Be Guilty at Nuzi

Paola Negri Scafa

AMONG THE DIFFERENT ASPECTS that order, disorder, and their relationships can assume, in this work a very specific field has been chosen: the moment in which judges in Nuzi pass judgment.[1]

Guilty or not guilty: with one of these expressions a process can usually end; and usually the purpose of a process is to establish if not the truth, at least the innocence or the guilt of the defendant.

Moreover, the process is an extremely important moment in the life of a community, because it is the tool by which it is possible to again establish a violated social order beyond any rhetoric. This also applies to the kingdom of Arrapḫa, of which Nuzi is an administrative center of considerable importance. As it happens in other contexts, so also in the Nuzi texts where processes are registered, the goal is basically to record the guilt or innocence of the people who have appeared before the courts, thus restoring the social order.

What happens through court procedures provides some evidence to reconstruct rules and law in use in that small kingdom, albeit in an indirect way. In fact, the kingdom of Arrapḫa belongs to those historical contexts for which collections of laws have not been found; only references to edicts are known, as the well-known *šūdūtu* clause, mentioned in many texts, demonstrates. It is also possible to mention at least two edicts that refer to other topics. The first is AASOR XVI 51, according to which it is forbidden that palatine officials prostitute their daughters, thus limiting parental authority, and the second is HSS XV 1, an edict containing administrative provisions issued by the king and addressed to the *ḫazannu* of another town of the kingdom, Tainsuḫwe. For the rest, it is possible to reconstruct the rules, laws, or customs only indirectly through the many documents, such as contracts or wills, in which the existing law finds its practical application.

This, obviously, also applies to lawsuits. The last comprehensive study of this topic dates from the 1960s when Roy Hayden (1962) made a careful analysis of the documentation in his dissertation. In the last thirty years, much work has been done in the publication of texts and documents of Nuzi and many significant studies on the law of the ancient Near East have been carried out. It does not seem out of place, then, to reconsider this topic.

1. Nuzi, Nuzians or Nuzi corpus are terms commonly used to include the people or documents that were found not only in Nuzi (Yorghan Tepe), but also in the tablets coming from Al-Ilāni (Kirkuk) and Tell al-Faḫḫar.

Court and legal documents of Nuzi come mostly from private archives: only small sets of documents come from the palace. Contracts, lawsuits, and legal documents found in the palace often seem to belong to the private archive of an eminent person. Perhaps only the few texts related to the Kussi-ḫarpe trials can be considered public documents, because they record depositions against an official.[2] And they were probably stored by public authorities just because of their public nature. Unfortunately the judgments are missing, those documents being only deposition records, and for this reason they will not be discussed here.

The actions mentioned in the texts that will be discussed here fall in today's categories of trials and lawsuits: they include a formal examination of evidence in court by a group of judges and claims of complaints made in court by somebody.

Nevertheless, it must be remembered that the Nuzi documents that are usually defined as trials and lawsuits cannot be considered like records in court. They are rather the reports in which the essential moments of the case are recorded, sometimes briefly annotated, sometimes with more details. The texts in question are structured according to a well-established pattern: an opening formula, followed by the statements of the plaintiff and of the defendant, with the plaintiff generally occupying the first place. Other details of the facts are also presented to the court, sometimes briefly, sometimes meticulously; this section of the texts is usually devoted to the search for evidence: witnesses are called in and questioned and occasionally an intervention by officials sent by the court to investigate is mentioned. A key aspect emerges from these statements: the search for evidence may also involve the use of extrarational procedures, such as oaths and ordeal, which are used quite frequently, even in the presence of witnesses. Then, the final part occurs, in which, typically, the penalty is imposed, usually on the defendant.

The courts of the kingdom of Arrapḫa may discuss cases that can be considered either civil law actions, such as lawsuits related to real estate or breach of contracts, and criminal law actions, such as torts, damages, or violations and damage to the person and the property.

In the present essay some processes related to criminal law, and in particular those related to the category that can be defined as larceny, will be discussed, in practice that means offenses such as theft, misappropriation, burglary, cases concerning movable property, such as objects or animals; litigations concerning real estate will not be taken into account at this stage.

In analyzing these lawsuits, particular attention will be paid to the financial aspect in order to establish the relationship between the economic value of stolen property and the penalties. It is not easy because the results of the trial are not always known, either because the texts are fragmentary (as is common in Assyriology) or because the sentence is not reported. In any case, what is of interest here is not the reconstruction of the procedures, but the possibility of analyzing the different parts of the texts, the final one included, where the economic aspects of the penalties are recorded. In this way it will be possible to bring the concept of punishment according to the Nuzi legal mentality into sharper focus.

2. Kussi-ḫarpe was a *ḫazunnu* who is quoted in the scarce date formulae of Nuzi (JEN 13, 31,46, 23, 252, 257, 455, 587, 591, 693, 806, 916). See Negri Scafa 2008.

## Larceny

The articulated series of crimes against property that can be labeled larceny corresponds to approximately 30 percent of the documented lawsuits.

The most common crimes against property, which became the most widely discussed cases in the courts, concern:

- burglary
- misappropriation and loss of animals
- theft aggravated by breach of confidence, including theft of barley and breaking a tablet
- theft aggravated by trespassing
- theft by night
- theft of barley for fattening sheep
- theft of copper
- theft of grain
- theft of large animals
- theft of small animals
- theft of straw and breaking of seals
- theft of wood
- trespassing

It is possible to give some partial details about the most frequently stolen goods: among the animals the most common are cows and oxen, horses, kids, sheep, and pigs; among the objects are parts of a chariot and shoes.

## Analysis of the Documents

It is not possible to analyze in detail all the documents in our possession, but some considerations on the available texts can provide interesting details.

Preliminarily, it must be remembered that to study the texts from Nuzi, it is necessary to analyze documents organized according to the records of family archives, from those consisting of hundreds of texts, such as the archives of the great family of Teḫip-tilla and of Šilwa-teššup, to the small family archives found in the dwellings of the city. Chronological details are very scanty in the texts; there is no dating system that allows us to reconstruct the chronological succession of the documents. Therefore, in order to arrange the documents chronologically, modern scholars find a remedy for the lack of date formulas by applying other systems, mainly through prosopography. The texts taken into consideration in the present work will be analyzed with the help of prosopography.

## Theft of Animals

Turning to the court documents, the first group concerns misappropriation, namely a type of crime in which the perpetrator of the theft is a person who is trusted to take care of the good. In the texts taken into account, some subgroups can be recognized:

### *Misappropriation and Loss of Animals*

1. This category is well represented in the archive of Teḫip-tilla son of Puḫi-šenni by Teḫip-tilla himself (the second generation of the family) and includes his relationships with a family of herdsmen, two generations of which worked for him: Taia s. Ward–aḫḫêšu and his son Beliia.

   These herdsmen are not always up to the trust: in JEN 341 Taia s. Ward-aḫḫêšu affirms that an ox has been injured by another ox; requested of witnesses, he admits he has no witness and therefore is condemned. Nevertheless Taia s. Ward-aḫḫêšu seems to have been a reliable person whom Teḫip-tilla could trust: in one case (JEN 6) he has acted as a witness, and in another contract (JEN 596) again he seems to act in the interest of Teḫip-tilla.

   The behavior of the son of Taia, Beliia, also seems in general to be beyond reproach: he also works as a herdsman for Teḫip-tilla, but nevertheless in two cases (JEN 326 and JEN 353) he is in the unpleasant position of defendant. In fact, in JEN 326 Beliia is charged with having skinned three oxen or rather, he has been taken *in flagrante* by the witnesses: therefore the judges send him to the gods. Beliia does not agree and Teḫip-tilla wins the case; and then the judges fine Beliia three oxen. The situation in JEN 353, where the defendant Beliia is charged with having skinned two oxen, is more complex; he attempts to charge the butcher Ar-teia, but Ar-teia denies the charge. In this case also the judges require a suprarational procedure, sending Beliia to the gods: Beliia does not agree and Teḫip-tilla again wins the case. In this case also the judges fine the defendant with the same number of animals involved in the case.
2. Enna-mati, son of Teḫip-tilla, belongs to the third generation of the family and is involved in many lawsuits that are predominantly related to previous contracts entered into by his father. Those lawsuits are mostly connected to real estate.

   However, Enna-mati also faces trials referring to theft of movable property, specifically of animals. In one case (JEN 360) two brothers, Kuari and Kanizza sons of Qišt-Erra, who seem to be trusted persons, have acted without Enna-mati's permission (*ba-lu-ja-ma*) appropriating the flesh of a dead horse and consuming it. Accused, the two brothers in turn accused Ṭab-arrapḫe, but they are contradicted by witnesses. Finally, the judges require a suprarational procedure, sending the two brothers to the gods: they do not agree and Enna-mati wins the case. The judges fine the defendants with a horse, the same type of animal involved in the case.
3. Misappropriation and loss of animals also occurs in the fourth generation of the archive of Teḫip-tilla s. Puḫi-šenni. In the documents of the grandsons of Teḫip-tilla (JEN 335), Tur-šenni son of Enna-mati acts on behalf of his brother Takku, entrusting a cow of his brother to Šimika-atal s. Šeḫli-tilla. But Šimika-atal injures and kills the cow. Tur-šenni charges Šimika-atal with the death of the cow on behalf of his brother, the defendant admits his guilt, and is punished with a fine of a cow.

So far, we have observed that the fines imposed on defendants are in practice the recovery of the animal lost in a 1:1 ratio between the lost good and the imposed penalty, apparently without any mark-up against the culprits. This does not change through the generations.

### *Misappropriation and Breach of Confidence*

In consideration of what is said above, the excessive imbalance between good lost and punishment imposed in JEN 349, where a lawsuit is discussed between Enna-mati and Ilimiia, is striking. Iliimia has not paid a compensation of an ox: After eight years of waiting, Enna-mati appeals to the judges and his claim is recognized. The judges fine Ilimiia one ox and two hundred sheep. Rather than the misappropriation of an ox by Ilimia, the real argument seems to be the nonpayment of the compensation promised by Ilimiia himself to Enna-mati. It is possible that the heavy penalty of one ox and two hundred sheep—precisely in a ratio 1:27—has been imposed by the judges to punish the nonpayment, thus a ratio of 1:1 plus a supplementary fine (so the ratio becomes 1:27.6).

Thus the breach of confidence usually concerns people who have close relations with each other and belong to the same social sphere. Nevertheless, there are cases of theft carried out by people outside the circle of the robbed persons, but who had forms of responsibility for the stolen goods. These cases can also be considered breach of confidence.

An interesting case is that of JEN 358, where Nupanani is charged with the theft of parts of a chariot of Enna-mati: his responsibilty is greater because he may have been on guard duty when parts of the chariot were stolen. The value of the stolen parts is not known, however, the penalty imposed on Nupanani is quite high: two oxen, two asses, and twenty sheep.

### *Aggravating Circumstances*

The breaking of a seal or of a tablet appears to be an important aggravating circumstance.

For example, in the case narrated in JEN 342, Urḫiia is accused of stealing the contents of a barn after breaking the seal; the fine is to return the entire contents of the barn plus one ox: a 1:1 ratio plus an extra penalty for breaking the seal.

Similarly, in JEN 381, where some barley of [f]Matteia is stolen, in addition to restoring the goods, the two defendants are sentenced to pay one ox as a fine for the breaking of a tablet presented during the trial. So in this case also, the ratio is 1:1 plus an extra penalty for breaking an important document.

The fact that a theft occurs at night also seems to be an aggravating circumstance in a lawsuit. A useful reference may be offered by three cases: the first is EN 9/1 437 where a theft by night of two *šaššuku* trees belonging to Ḫismi-teššup is recorded; the theft is further aggravated by trespassing, so the defendant Ḫui-tilla is sentenced to pay two MA.NA of silver, the equivalent of four oxen, four asses, and forty sheep.

A second text recording a theft by night is HSS IX 141, where ten *imēru* of barley and a tree of Šilwa-teššup mar sarri were stolen by night by Ullunzi. Arik-kauli, the gardener of Šilwa-teššup, goes in court and testifies against Ullunzi, who is fined of two oxen, two asses, and twenty sheep.

In EN 9/1 405, Akip-tašenni seizes three men stealing one bundle of barley and other goods from the palace; each of the three men is ordered to pay two oxen, two asses and twenty sheep.

### *Thefts of Large Animals*

Moving on to the thefts related to animals, some variety can be observed in the penalties. Aggravating circumstances are not recognizable.

For example, in JEN 334, each of the two defendants was sentenced to pay two horses for the theft of a horse of Teḫip-tilla: therefore a ratio of 1:4 or better a ratio of 1:2 for each defendant.

This sentence seems to be confirmed by the sentence in another lawsuit where the defendant, accused of stealing an ox, is ordered to pay two good oxen. The ratio is 1:2 in this case also.

In EN 9/417, there is further confirmation of this orientation to punish each defendant as if they were the only culprit. There also the penalty is multiplied by the number of convicted defendants: in that fragmentary lawsuit Naḫiia charges three men, Paia, Ennamati, and Ḫašip-tilla, with the theft of an ox: each of the defendants is fined two oxen: therefore we again have a ratio of 1:2, multiplied by three, the number of the defendants.

### *Thefts of Small Animals*

Theft of small animals is fairly common as well, and it is impossible to analyze all the cases in detail, but the examples cited below are representative. A comparison between thefts of small animals and large animals can be a point of interest.

At first glance, the situation is different in comparison to the theft of large animals. For a theft (JEN 343) of two kids of Teḫip-tilla, Bêl-abi is ordered to pay twenty-four goats. Therefore, JEN 343 records a ratio of 1:12.

The ratio recorded in JEN 672 is greater: Kel-teššup son of Ḫutiia claims that Šaḫluia has stolen his sheep. The defendant is sentenced to pay twenty-four sheep, a ratio of 1:24, double that of the former case, perhaps because he attempted to lead the judges astray asserting that the sheep was born in his house.

Again a ratio 1:12 is conveyed in the sentence of the judges in JEN 347 where the defendant Ar-šimika is ordered to repay Teḫip-tilla with twelve sheep for the theft of a sheep from the sheepfold. This case is interesting because of procedural reasons: Ar-šimika appeals to the king, who sat in Karana in those days. The king condemns him to pay one ox.

## A Short "Off the Subject": The Animals

A brief digression as we make some observations concerning animals. The subject of animals is interesting because of their economic importance. Most of the documentation (Cross 1937) concerns sheep and cattle (Morrison 1981), while a more sparse documentation refers to pigs.[3] Donkeys and horses are also mentioned; the latter were used mainly in the military.[4] The existence of a *sūqu ša usandû* the "street of the fowl-

3. Studies on pigs are very scarce: the most exhaustive is Lion 2009.

4. See Zaccagnini 1978. Horses are often recorded in texts related to the highest social class of the *rākib narkabti*.

ers," refers to a profession related to animals. There are cases in which the animals are regarded in a premonetary function, the equivalent of the silver. Because of their economic importance, it is normal that they are the center of many economic and business activities.[5] Texts related to animals are numerous: often in lists of small cattle the animals are recorded with great accuracy, sometimes including color and physical characteristics.

Because of their monetary function it is natural that they were often subject to theft. This is also shown by the number of the trials related to livestock in the Nuzi corpus: 44.8 percent.

In addition to being the object of theft, animals and livestock are often listed in the penalties imposed by the judges: in this case, the preferred animals are sheep, cattle, or donkeys, apart from the cases in which the stolen animal is replaced by an identical one.

## Theft of Other Goods: Burglary

The goods that can be stolen are numerous; with the theft of wood being considered particularly serious. In addition to what has been said above about the theft of trees at night, there are two cases of particular interest.

One is HSS IX 12, where the theft of wood is recorded: Paia son of Ḫanatu, the defendant, involves another person, Turar-teššup, supporting his statements with the presence of witnesses; the plaintiff is Ḫutiia, a representative for Shilwa-tessup, who wins the lawsuit. But it is Turar-teššup who is condemned to pay thirty-three yokes and one ox; this means a ratio of 1:33 plus the value of the ox, which is the equivalent of ten shekels of silver.

HSS XIII 422 also belongs to the archive of Šilwa-teššup: the plaintiff is Aḫ-illika and the defendant is again Paia son of Ḫanatu: the matter of the lawsuit is a theft of wood, which has been burned. Both the litigants swear and make their declarations, both are sent to the *ḫuršân* ordeal. The judges cannot decide and the decision will be taken by the king.

These two texts are very interesting from a procedural point of view: in HSS XIII 422 the *ḫuršân* procedure is quoted, while the procedure quoted in IX 12 is the *našû ilāni*. The two procedures are different because of the difference in the nature of the cases: in the first case Paia has burned the stolen wood: there is no more evidence and for this reason the judges decide for the ordeal after the oaths of both the plaintiff and the defendant. In HSS IX 12 witnesses are called. The presence of witnesses seems to be determinant in the choice of the procedures: If there are no witnesses the parties often reinforce their positions with oaths and the judges can send the cases to the *ḫuršan*. It is usually the plaintiff who brings witnesses, especially if, as in criminal law, the burden of the proof is on the defendant, this being the way by which he can corroborate his counterclaim.

5. In Nuzi two documents of exceptional interest have been found that offer important procedural suggestions on the management of cattle: see Abusch 1981.

In the lawsuits of Nuzi the *ḫuršan* procedure is widely used, both in the cases involving real estate, and in cases of the theft of animals; being a supernatural procedure it does not provide for direct economic actions, but anyone who refuses to undergo the procedure loses the case and suffers financial damage.[6]

Also interesting is a case of burglary: in JEN 125 Kel-teššup swears that his house has been robbed; as the culprit is unknown, it is the whole community that must restore the damage. The defendants also swear that they are not guilty. Unfortunately the results of the trial are not given; it would be interesting to know whether the whole community has been fined and to what extent. In any case, the interest of this text is the fact that a community is considered responsible when the culprit is unknown; this is a Mesopotamian tradition that is shared by the Hurrian people of the kingdom of Arrapḫa.

## Trials Series

When some trials are linked by the presence of the same plaintiff and the same defendant, one wonders if they are to be considered forms of appeal before a hierarchically higher court, or simply an attempt of a plaintiff or of a defendant to search for a more favorable court.

Only the analysis of the groups of texts can clarify the nature of the cases, whether they should be considered forms of appeal before a hierarchically higher court, or if they should be considered simply parts of linked trials.

The best-known case series of Nuzi is related to Kušši-ḫarpe, the mayor of the city: this series is quoted here only for the sake of information; the lack of judgment makes it impossible to compare the crimes with the penalties, and therefore it is not consistent with the present work. Actually Kušši-ḫarpe is an unusual character: his name appears in some of the few date formulas in Nuzi, and he is known from nineteen legal texts found in the palace. This series of documents is somewhat special because they are not real processes, but collective tablets, summarizing statements of various people involved in the crimes committed by the shameless official. Consequently only parts of the lawsuits are recorded: among the mentioned crimes, theft of objects and livestock, embezzlement, and misappropriation are listed. On some of the tablets the seals of people known elsewhere as judges are recorded; because of the different names and the different mentioned scribes, it is possible to conclude that all those documents record various legal actions distributed over a certain period of time. Even though these texts lack the judgments, it is probable to assume that things did not turn well for Kušši-ḫarpe.

In any case, there are some texts that are closely connected to each other.

Two small group of lawsuits are more in line with the lawsuits discussed here: one concerns EN 9/1 431 and 425, the other group includes EN 9/1 424, EN 9/1 432, EN 9/1 443, and EN 443 9/1 448.

6. The text JEN 659 + SMN 1651 offers the evidence of the *ḫuršan* procedure in the court: see Wilhelm 1995, with bibliography.

The text EN 9/1 431 is a memorandum of a lawsuit on a failed payment of a horse: Utḫap-tae son of Zike charges Ḫutiia son of Kalmaš-šura; in EN 9/1 425 the problem is resolved, because Utḫap-tae recovers the thirty shekels of silver from Ḫutiia. This small set shows that often a case was not solved by a single event, but required more hearings and more questioning, each of which contributed to the general solution of the matter.

The other small set, consisting of EN 9/1 424, EN 9/1 432, EN 9/1 443, and EN 9/1 448 is more useful in analyzing the problem of the appeal. The action moves through two generations of plaintiffs against the same defendant (Negri Scafa 2005). Everything starts in EN 9/1 443, a badly damaged tablet, with a trial between Taḫirišti son of Ipsa-ḫalu and Arik-kanari son of Šalim-puti about a flock of sheep.

The trial continues into the next generation between the son of Taḫiristi, Uzimpalitu, and Arik-kanari son of Shalim-puti. The matter of the trial is a flock of 180 sheep. The parties meet three times, once before the judges of Kumri (EN 9/1 448), another time in a trial where also a brother of Uzimpalitu testifies (EN 9/1 424), and finally before the king (EN 9/1 432). In all the trials, which always concern the flock of 180 sheep, Arik-kanari is condemned. It is difficult to decide if the second trial is an appeal before a hierarchically higher court, or is only an attempt of Arik-kanari to better negotiate his own situation before a different court. Certainly the discussion before the king implies an appeal before the highest authority: in this case the whole situation, starting from the first trial, is similar to the modern appeals courts, hierarchically higher than the courts.

## Conclusions

To conclude this overview it could be useful to reconsider briefly the penalties imposed: the decisions of the Nuzi judges are varied and it is not easy to discern a standard or unifying criteria. In the cases of theft of large animals, it is not uncommon for a 1:2 ratio between the stolen property and the penalty to be imposed, while for the theft of small animals the ratio can range from 1:12 to 1:24. In some cases, the penalty seems to be a simple compensation; it happens, for example, in situations of misappropriation. The only unifying criterium seems to be the imposing of fines for this class of crimes, sometimes very heavy, but not other kinds of penalties.

In this, it is important to mention that the situation of Nuzi is not too different from similar situations in Mesopotamia. However, elements such as the breaking of a seal or a tablet are aggravating circumstances and therefore require a further penalty; after all the written documents constitute a warranty and it is important to safeguard them.

There are also very heavy penalties, which would suggest a situation of aggravating circumstances, such as trespassing or extrajudicial elements that can influence the trial, as in the case of JEN 349, where a lack of compensation that lasted for eight years is punished with the additional penalty of two hundred sheep.

And finally, were guilty people able to pay their fines? Certainly they had problems, as a pair of texts, JEN 358 and JEN 466, demonstrate.

As seen before, JEN 358 is a lawsuit where Nupanani is charged with the theft of wooden parts of a chariot: Nupanani may have been on guard duty when parts of the chariot were stolen and this can explain the very punitive fine: two oxen (equal to

TABLE 17.1. Relations between crimes and penalties: a recapitulative table.

| Crime | Penalty |
|---|---|
| Burglary | Unknown (but the community could be involved) |
| Misappropriation and loss of animals | Ratio 1:1 |
| | 1:1 + 200 sheep |
| Theft aggravated by breach of confidence | Parts of the chariot stolen or 2 oxen, 2 asses, and 20 sheep (the value of the stolen parts is unknown) |
| Theft by night aggravated by trespassing | Two *šaššuku* trees or 2 MA.NA silver (= 4 oxen, 4 asses, 40 sheep). |
| Theft by night | Ten *imēru* of barley and a tree or 2 oxen, 2 asses, and 20 sheep. |
| | Bundle of barley and other goods from the palace or 2 oxen, 2 asses, and 20 sheep |
| Theft of barley and breaking of tablet | Ratio 1:1 + an extra penalty |
| Theft of large animals | Ratio 1:2 (for each defendant) |
| Theft of small animals | Ratio 1:12 |
| | Ratio 1:24 |
| Theft of straw and breaking of seals | Ratio 1:1 + an extra penalty |
| Theft of wood | Ratio of 1:33 + the value of the ox = 10 shekels silver |

20 shekels), two asses (equal to 13.34 shekels), and twenty sheep (equal to 26.66 shekels), for total value of sixty shekels, namely one MA.NA silver. However, Nupanani obtained a mitigation of this sentence, which another text (the ṬUPPI TAMGURTI JEN 466) demonstrates: there Nupanani acknowledges that he must give a mina of silver to Enna-mati as a fine after a lawsuit, but manages to pay cheaper fine, a Nullu slave. And this can open new prospects in this field.

In any case, he again establishes the order: *quod erat in votis*.

## BIBLIOGRAPHY

Abusch, T.
1981 Notes on a Pair of Matching Texts: A Shepherd's Bulla and an Owner's Receipt. Pp. 1–9 in *Studies on the Civilization and Culture of Nuzi and the Hurrians in Honor of Ernest R. Lacheman on His Seventy-fifth Birthday, April 29, 1981*. Edited by D. I. Owen and M. A. Morrison. SCCNH 1. Winona Lake, IN: Eisenbrauns.

Cross, D.
1937 *Movable Property in the Nuzi Documents*. AOS 10. New Haven: American Oriental Society.

Hayden, R. E.
1962 *Court Procedure at Nuzi*. PhD diss., Brandeis University.

Lion, B.
2009 Les porcs à Nuzi. Pp. 259–286 in *General Studies and Excavations at Nuzi 11/2*. SCCNH 18. Bethesda, MD: CDL.

Morrison, M.
1981 Evidence for Herdsmen and Animal Husbandry in the Nuzi Documents. Pp. 257–296 in *Studies on the Civilization and Culture of Nuzi and the*

*Hurrians in Honor of Ernest R. Lacheman on His Seventy-fifth Birthday, April 29, 1981.* Edited by D. I. Owen and M. A. Morrison. SCCNH 1. Winona Lake, IN: Eisenbrauns.

Negri Scafa, P.

2005 Documents from the Buildings North of the Nuzi Temple: The "Signed" Texts from Square C. Pp. 133–160 in *General Studies and Excavations at Nuzi 11/1.* Edited by D. I. Owen and G. Wilhelm. SCCNH 15. Bethesda, MD: CDL.

2008 The Scribes of Nuzi: the Date Formulae and Their Use in the Nuzi Texts. Pp. 119–126 in *Proceedings of the 51st Rencontre Assyriologique Internationale, Held at the Oriental Institute of the University of Chicago, July 18–22, 2005.* Edited by R. D. Biggs, J. Myers, and M. T. Roth. SAOC 62. Chicago: Oriental Institute of the University of Chicago.

Wilhelm, G.

1995 Ein neuer Text zum Ordal in Nuzi (JEN 659 + SMN 1651). Pp. 71–74 in *General Studies and Excavations at Nuzi 9/3.* Edited by E. R. Lacheman and D. I. Owen. SCCNH 5. Winona Lake, IN: Eisenbrauns.

Zaccagnini, C.

1978 Pferde und Streitwagen in Nuzi. *Jahresbericht des Instituts für Vorgeschichte der Universität Frankfurt am Main* 1977: 21–38.

CHAPTER 18

# Fremde Götter—eigene Götter: Zu den neuassyrischen Götterbeschreibungen

Reettakaisa Sofia Salo

„JED[ER SCHW]ÖRE BEI AŠŠUR, dem Vater der Götter, dem Herrn der Länder! [. . .] Dito bei allen Göttern von Assyrien! Dito bei allen Göttern von Sumer und Akkade! Dito bei allen Göttern der Länder! Dito bei allen Göttern des Himmels und der Unterwelt! Dito bei allen Göttern vom Land und Gebiet von jedem Einzelnen!"[1] Dieser Auszug aus dem Thronfolgevertrag Asarhaddons ist außerordentlich: Er erwähnt sowohl assyrische Götter als auch Götter aus anderen Ländern und Regionen. Was die letzteren betrifft, wird unter ihnen noch weiter differenziert. Dies ist ungewöhnlich, denn im Allgemeinen muss festgestellt werden, dass die neuassyrischen Königsinschriften trotz ihres beachtlichen Umfangs nur sehr wenige Erwähnungen der „fremden Götter" enthalten.

Mit den „fremden Göttern" werden im Folgenden solche Götter bezeichnet, die in Assyrien offensichtlich nicht verehrt oder aus einem sonstigen Grund mit einem anderen Volk in Verbindung gebracht wurden. Folgendem Aufsatz liegen zwei Kriterien zu Grunde, anhand derer die Götter bestimmt wurden, die in diesem Zusammenhang als „fremd" bezeichnet werden. Erstens sind die Pronominalsuffixe zu nennen: „Sein Gott" oder „ihr Gott" ist sehr unwahrscheinlich gleichzeitig als ein Gott des assyrischen Königs oder seines Reichspantheons zu verstehen. Zweitens spielen die Ortsnamen hierbei eine Rolle, denn sie geben einen eindeutigen Hinweis darauf, dass die erwähnten Götter und Göttinnen mit einem anderen Land oder einer anderen Nation aus assyrischer Perspektive in Verbindung gebracht worden sind. Im Folgenden wird der Frage nachgegangen, in welchen Zusammenhängen und wie über diese fremden Götter gesprochen wird. Diese Erwähnungen werden mit den expliziten Nennungen der assyrischen Götter verglichen.

Bei der Suche nach Belegen, in denen Götter ausdrücklich mit Assyrien kombiniert werden, stellt sich zunächst die Frage, ob in den Quellen der Begriff als Bezeichnung für die Stadt Assur oder das Land Assyrien verwendet wird. Im Folgenden sind keine allgemeinen Götterauflistungen berücksichtigt worden, sondern nur jene Belegstellen, in denen das Adjektiv „assyrisch" auftaucht. Von diesen Fällen können die Gottesbezeichnungen „assyrische Ištar", „assyrische Ninlil" und „assyrischer Enlil" unberücksichtigt bleiben, denn es ist davon auszugehen, dass es sich hierbei um eine

1. $^{d}$*aš-šur* AD DINGIR.MEŠ EN KUR.KUR *ti-t[am-ma-a]* [. . .] DINGIR.MEŠ KUR-*aš-šur* (DÙ-*šú-nu* MIN) DINGIR.MEŠ KUR-*šu-me-ri u* URI.KI DÙ-*šú-nu* MIN DINGIR.MEŠ KUR.KUR DÙ-*šu-nu* MIN DINGIR.MEŠ *šá* AN-*e u* KI.TIM DÙ-*šú-nu* MIN [DINGIR].MEŠ KUR-šu[!] *na-gi-šu* DÙ-*šú-nu* MIN (SAA 2 6,25.38–40A/B).

Differenzierung der Kultorte—also um die Stadt Assur—handelt, nicht um das Land. In anderen Fällen muss man den Kontext zur Erarbeitung heranziehen.

Der Aufsatz ist nach den Textgattungen gegliedert worden: Es werden zuerst Beispiele aus den Vertragstexten und danach aus den Feldzugsberichten besprochen. Die Erwähnungen der babylonischen Götter sind weitestgehend außer Acht gelassen worden, da sie bei dieser Fragestellung eine besondere Gruppe bilden würden. Ihre Wahrnehmung müsste wegen der zentralen kulturellen Rolle Babylons für den gesamten antiken Vorderen Orient und der sich ständig verändernden politischen Situation stark diachron betrachtet werden. Weiterhin werden die Götter der Hauptstadt, des Kernlandes und der Peripherie von Babylonien sehr unterschiedlich dargestellt.

## Vertragstexte

Die neuassyrischen *adê*-Verträge beziehen die Götter der beiden Seiten als Treuegaranten und Eidgötter ein. Hierbei werden insbesondere die fremden Götter oft mit Ortsnamen determiniert, weswegen die Verträge für diese Fragestellung eine zentrale Quellengattung bilden. Die bislang bekannten neuassyrischen Staatsverträge sind von Parpola und Watanabe in der Reihe *State Archives of Assyria* (1988) gesammelt publiziert worden: Die Ausführungen dieses Unterkapitels folgen vorwiegend diesem Band.[2]

### *SAA 2 2*

Der Vertrag zwischen Assurnirari V. (754–745) und Mati'ilu (aram. Mati'-'el), dem König von Arpad in Bit Agusi (SAA 2 2), enthält eine Auflistung der Götter, bei denen die Vertragspartner vereidigt worden sind (VI,6–27). Nach einer gemischten Auflistung assyrischer und babylonischer Götter werden vermutlich die Götter von Mati'ilu eingeführt. Dies geschieht ohne irgendeine zusammenfassende Überleitung, wobei eine gewisse Ambiguität bestehen bleibt und man zunächst klären muss, welcher Seite die Götter, die teilweise mit einem Ortsnamen versehen sind, zuzuordnen sind.

| SAA 2 2,VI,17–26 | |
|---|---|
| $^{d}$IM šá URU *kur-ba-ìl* KI.MIN | „Dito bei Adad von Kurba'il! |
| $^{d}$IM *šá* URU *ḫal-la-ba* KI.MIN | Dito bei Hadad von Aleppo! |
| $^{d}$IGI.DU *a-lik maḫ-ri* KI.MIN | Dito bei $^{d}$IGI.DU, der vorangeht! |
| $^{d}$7.BI *qar-du-ti* KI.MIN | Dito bei den heldenhaften Šibitti! |
| $^{d}$[*d*]*a*-⸢*gan*⸣ o! UR[U *m*]*u*?-*ṣur-u-na* KI.MIN | Dito bei Dagān von Muṣuruna![3] |
| $^{d}$*m*[*i-il-qar-tu* $^{d}$*ia-s*]*u-mu-na* KI.MIN | Dito bei M[elqart und Esh]mun! |
| $^{d}$*k*⸢*ù*⸣!-*b*[*a-ba* $^{d}$*kar-*]*ḫu-ḫa* KI.MIN | Dito bei Kub[aba und Kar]huha! |
| $^{d}$IM $^{d}$[X] ⸢$^{d!}$*ra*!-*ma*!-*nu*!⸣ | Dito bei Hadad, [...] und Rammān |
| *ša* UR[U *di-maš-qa* KI.MIN] | von [Damaskus]! |
| $^{d}$ZA-[*x x x x x x x x*] | [Dito bei] ZA[...]" |

2. Zu der Diskussion über die allgemeine Bedeutung der *adê*-Verträge s. zuletzt Lauinger 2013 (insbes. 99f.114f [Lit.]).

3. Mit Lipiński 2000 (286.613) gegen SAA 2 2,VI,21 (vgl. aber die Diskussion i. d. Anm. z. St.).

Adad von Kurbaʾil, der wegen des Ortsnamens hier noch definitiv zu den assyrischen Göttern zu zählen ist (Schwemer 2001, 595f), bildet eine Art Überleitung zu den aramäischen Göttern: Adad spielte nämlich auch in den aramäischen Panthea eine wichtige Rolle (s. z. B. Niehr 2010: 212.215). Danach wird Hadad von Aleppo erwähnt: Dieser Wettergott war als Adad im Neuassyrischen Reich allgemein bekannt und empfing unter diesem Namen schon unter Salmanassar III. (858–824) Opfer von den Assyrern.[4] Hier sollte Hadad aber wohl zu den Göttern Matiʾilus gezählt werden: Er wird als Eidgott evtl. auch in den aramäischsprachigen Sefire-Verträgen Matiʾilus erwähnt, die keinerlei direkte Verbindung zu den Neuassyrern haben.[5] Hadad von Aleppo hatte insgesamt eine große überregionale Bedeutung und ist in direkter Kontinuität zum Addu-Kult in Aleppo zu sehen (Niehr 2010: 250f). Weiterhin gehörte Aleppo zu dieser Zeit nicht zum assyrischen Gebiet (Radner 2006: 58).

Bei den Göttern $^{d}$IGI.DU[6] und den Šibitti kann es sich wieder genauso gut um in Assyrien oder in beiden Reichen verehrte Götter handeln: Die Šibitti (= das Siebengestirn, die Pleiaden) kommen oft u.a. in den neuassyrischen Feldzugsberichten vor; aber sie sind auch in den Sefire-Verträgen als eine Schwurgottheit von Arpad belegt (KAI 222,11; vgl. auch Niehr 2010: 246). Bei $^{d}$IGI.DU ist die Auslegung von der Entscheidung über die Lesung abhängig. Ebenso ist auch der Gott Dagān/Dagon seit Langem ein bekannter Gott in Assyrien (vgl. insbes. Feliu 2003). Hier wird er dennoch mit dem Ortsnamen Muṣuruna (= die Märsche) spezifiziert, wobei Muṣuruna für „the territory of northern Ḥiğaz and Negev“ steht und deswegen keiner der Vertragsparteien wirklich gut zuzuordnen ist. Das Gebiet scheint dennoch bis zu den Philistäerstädten gereicht zu haben und Dagān von Muṣuruna ist dadurch als ein philistäischer Gott zu interpretieren (Lipiński 2000: 613). Aus diesem Grund und weil Dagān auch als phönizischer Erntegott bekannt war, sollte er in diesem Zusammenhang wohl zu den Göttern des Matiʾilu gezählt werden.

Melqart, Eshmun, Kubaba, Karhuha, Hadad von NN und Rammān von Damaskus führen die sehr internationale Götterliste weiter. Melqart war der königliche Haupt- und Schutzgott von Tyros, der wegen der regen phönizischen Handelsbeziehungen im Mittelmeerraum allgemein bekannt war, aber dennoch seine Verbindung zu Phönizien und vor allem Tyros behielt (Bonnet 2010: 56f.67–70). Melqart wurde auch in den aramäischen Königreichen verehrt, was durch eine Votivinschrift des Königs Barhadad[7] aus Breğ, 7 km nördlich von Aleppo, bestätigt wird (KAI 201; vgl. auch Niehr 2010: 247). Der phönizische Gott Ešmun ist seinerseits besonders bedeutend in den sidonischen Königsinschriften aus der Achämenidenzeit, aber er wird schon im 2. Jt. v.

4. S. z. B. RIMA 2, 102.2,II,87.

5. KAI 222,10 ist bei der Auflistung der Götter Matiʾilus fragmentarisch. Nach der Lücke sind die Buchstaben [. . .]*lb* (= [A]leppo) überliefert. Wegen der Bekanntheit des Hadad-Kultes in Aleppo scheint mir die Lesung sicher zu sein. Vgl. dazu die Übersetzung von Fitzmyer (1995: 43). Die Schwurgottliste des Vertragspartners aus KTK (= Kitikka?) ist dafür sehr assyrisiert (Niehr 2010: 263–265).

Anders Schwemer 2001 (595): Seines Erachtens wurde hier „der überregional bekannte Adad von Ḫalab [. . .] in die Reihe der assyrischen Götter aufgenommen“.

6. Das Theonym Palil als Lesung von $^{d}$IGI.DU ist nicht gesichert, aber in den neuassyrischen Texten kann man das Sumerogramm nicht direkt als Nergal lesen, da er oft im gleichen Text schon mit einer anderen Schreibung vorkommt. So auch hier, s. SAA 2 2,12: $^{d}$U.GUR = Nergal. S. zu den verschiedenen Möglichkeiten Krebernik 2004.

7. Es handelt sich entweder um Barhadad I. (ca. 900 v. Chr.) oder Barhadad II. (ca. 880–843 v. Chr.).

Chr. in den die phönizische Küste thematisierenden Texten erwähnt (Bonnet 2010: 71). Die Göttin Kubaba ist bekannt vor allem aus ins 2. Jt. v. Chr. zu datierenden Texten aus Karkemisch und Ugarit; im 1. Jt. wird sie in mehreren aramäischen Inschriften erwähnt, z. B. als Gattin von Rakkabʾel, dem Dynastiegott von Samʾal (Hawkins 1983; Niehr 2010: 276). Karhuha, der Gott der Jagdtiere, war Paredros von Kubaba in Karkemisch (Haas 2011: 192.224). Was die Zeile VI,24 betrifft, stellt sich die Frage, ob mit Hadad und Rammān doch nicht der gleiche Gott gemeint sind, denn der Wettergott Hadad von Damaskus ist häufig mit dem Epitheton *rammān* (= „Donnerer") belegt. Die beiden können dennoch auch getrennt betrachtet werden, vor allem da die Zeilen VI,24f fragmentarisch erhalten und die Lesungen deswegen unklar sind.[8]

Nach diesen Göttern bricht der Vertrag leider ab: Vom letzten Gottesnamen ist nur das erste Zeichen erhalten, was keine eindeutige Identifikation ermöglicht. Im Kontext der aramäischen Götter könnte man vorsichtig vermuten, dass an dieser Stelle der aramäische Mondgott Śahr erwähnt wurde. Śahr ist nicht in den Texten aus Aleppo, aber im Gebiet von Bit Agusi in Neirab, südöstlich von Aleppo, belegt (Niehr 2010: 253f).

## *SAA 2 3*

Die Inschrift Ninive A von Asarhaddon (681–669) bezieht sich auf den Thronfolgevertrag Sanheribs (705–681) und berichtet über die Vereidigung.[9]

| RINAP 4 1,I,17–19 | |
|---|---|
| *ma-ḫar* ᵈ*aš-šur* ᵈ30 ᵈUTU ᵈAG ᵈAMAR.UTU DINGIR.MEŠ KUR *aš-šur*ᴷᴵ DINGIR.MEŠ *a-ši-bu-te* AN-*e u* KI-*tim áš-šú na-ṣar ri-du-ti-ia zi-kir-šú-un kab-tu ú-šá-az-ki-ir-šu-nu-ti* | „Vor Aššur, Sîn, Šamaš, Nabû, Marduk, den Göttern von Assyrien, den Göttern, die im Himmel und in der Unterwelt wohnen, ließ er [= Sanherib, RSS] sie ihren ernsten Eid wegen des Beschützens meiner Thronfolge schwören" |

Ein Teil dieses Thronfolgevertrags ist fragmentarisch erhalten (SAA 2 3).[10] Die überlieferten Stücke enthalten zwei Götterauflistungen, die zwar die assyrischen Götter nicht explizit erwähnen, dafür werden aber in diesen Auflistungen die Formulierung „Götter des *akītu*-Hauses" (= DINGIR.MEŠ *šá* É.*á-ki-it*) erwähnt: In SAA 2 3, Rs. 8′ ist die Formulierung eindeutig, aber in einem fragmentarischen Kontext

8. Rammān, eine Hadad-Gestalt und das Oberhaupt des Lokalpantheons von Damaskus, wird auch in der Hebräischen Bibel erwähnt: s. den damaszenischen Königsnamen Tabrimmon in 1Kön 15,8 und den Tempel des Rinnom in 2Kön 5,18. Die beiden Belege befinden sich im Kontext der Aramäerkönige. Sach 12,11 unterstützt die Gleichstellung von Hadad und Rammān: „An jenem Tag wird in Jerusalem die Trauer groß sein, wie die Trauer um Hadad-Rimmon in der Ebene von Megiddo." S. zu Rammān auch Niehr (2010: 311f) und Schwemer (2001: 623f).

9. Vgl. auch RINAP 4, 5,I,10′–15′.

10. Der Name Asarhaddons ist im überlieferten Teil des Vertrags leider nicht erhalten. Dass es sich um Asarhaddon als einen von der üblichen Thronfolgepraxis abweichenden Nachfolger von Sanherib handeln muss, ergibt sich aus der Inschrift Ninive A (RINAP 4 1,I,8–19; s. dazu auch SAA 2, XXVIII).

erhalten; die vorangehenden Zeilen enthalten eine Götterauflistung. „Götter des *akītu*-Hauses" werden analog in den Zeilen Vs.11′ und Rs.5′ ergänzt.[11] Die Prozessionsgötter des assyrischen *akītu*-Festes sind, wie Pongratz-Leisten (1994: 116.127f) gezeigt hat, klassische Götter des assyrischen Pantheons: Erwähnt bzw. ergänzt werden auf der Vorderseite des Nachfolgevertrags von Sanherib [Aššur, Mullissu, Šerua], Sîn, Nikkal, Šamaš, Nu[r, Anu, Antu, Enlil, Adad, Š]ala, Kippat-mati, [Ištar des Himmels, Ištar von Ninive], Ištar von [Arbela, die assyrische Ištar, Zababa, Ba]bu, Ninurta und Nusku. Die Rückseite erwähnt anstelle von Ninurta und Nusku die Reihe Ea, Belet-ili, Kakka und Nergal. Die Auswahl der Götter sollte mit dem Bau des *akītu*-hauses in der Regierungszeit Sanheribs zusammenhängen.

Die Auflistung bei der Asarhaddon-Inschrift fügt hinzu noch Marduk und Nabû, was sicherlich mit der Babylon-freundlichen Politik dieses Königs zusammenhängt, andererseits ist die Abkürzung der Götterliste erstens gattungsbedingt und zweitens dadurch, dass es sich um eine Bezugnahme handelt, zu erklären.

### *SAA 2 5*

Der Vertrag Asarhaddons mit Baal, dem König von Tyrus (SAA 2 5) enthält unter den Vertragsflüchen u.a. diesen übergreifenden Fluch:

| SAA 2 5,IV,8′f | |
|---|---|
| DINGIR.MEŠ GAL.MEŠ *šá* AN-*e ù* KI-*tim* DINGIR.MEŠ KUR *aš-šur*KI DINGIR.MEŠ KUR.URI.KI DINGIR. MEŠ *e-bir*-ÍD *ar-rat la nap-šú-ri li-ru-*⌜*ku*⌝*-nu* | „Die großen Götter des Himmels und der Unterwelt, die Götter Assyriens, die Götter von Akkad und die Götter von Ebirnāri mögen euch mit einem unlösbaren Fluch fluchen!" |

Der Fluch kommt in einem für die zwischenstaatlichen Staatsverträge typischen Kontext vor: Eine Auswahl der Götter der beiden Vertragsparteien ist berücksichtigt, hier findet man zusätzlich als ein weiteres internationales Element noch die Götter von Akkad, wobei erneut auf die Babylon-Politik Asarhaddons hinzuweisen ist. Der internationale Charakter des Vertrags macht die Differenzierung nötig. In diesem Zusammenhang ist es wieder interessant zu sehen, dass die Götter teilweise gemischt vorkommen: Manche der vor diesem allgemeinen Fluch erwähnten Götter sind als assyrisch zu verstehen, andere sind ihrerseits definitiv Götter der Tyrer. Der Vertrag ist leider am Anfang der Kolumne IV abgebrochen und die Fluchliste dadurch nicht vollständig: Die ersten erhaltenen Götternamen sind Ištar [von Arbela], Gula und die Sibitti. Die ersten beiden Göttinnen kann man einigermaßen sicher den assyrischen Göttern zuzuordnen;[12] danach folgt ein Fluch von Bethel und Anat-Bethel:

11. Die Ergänzungen sind überzeugend wegen der weiteren Listen der Götter des *akītu*-Hauses. S. zur vollen Diskussion Parpola (1987: 163f.178–180).

12. Die unterschiedlichen Ištar-Gestalten der verschiedenen Kultorte hatten in Assyrien eine zentrale Rolle inne und die Göttinnen des ähnlichen Typus (Krieg, Sexualität) wurden in Phönizien unter anderen Namen verehrt. Die Heilgöttin Gula war sowohl in Babylonien als auch in Assyrien beliebt; sie war auch mit vielen anderen Heilgöttinnen, u.a. der sumerischen Ninisinna gleichgesetzt worden (Hutter 1996: 48).

| SAA 2 5,IV,6′f | |
|---|---|
| $^{d}$*ba-a-a-ti*-DINGIR.MEŠ $^{d}$*a-na-ti-ba-*⸢*a*⸣-[*a-ti*-DINGI]R.MEŠ *ina* ŠU.2. UR.MAH *a-ki-*⸢*li*⸣ [*lim-nu-u-k*]*u-nu* | „Mögen Bethel und Anat-Bethel euch in die Pranken eines fressenden Löwen [ausliefern]!“ |

Bethel ist ein ursprünglich syrischer Gott, der auch in verschiedenen aus zwei Götternamen zusammengestellten Namen erwähnt wird, z. B. unter dem hier erwähnten Namen von Anat-Bethel,[13] die sein Paredros war. Zusätzlich zu diesem Vertrag Asarhaddons gibt es Belege in den aramäischen Texten aus Elephantine sowie im Papyrus Amherst 63, der trotz der demotischen Schrift vor allem aramäische Traditionen aufweist (Koenen 2006; Kottsieper 1988: insbes. 217–224; Niehr 2010: 248). Hierbei stellt sich wegen ihrer Stellung in diesem Vertrag die Frage, ob Bethel und Anat-Bethel zu den assyrischen Göttern gezählt werden sollten. Dies wäre auf jeden Fall möglich; wenigstens hat ihre Erwähnung eine Brückenfunktion, die in den zusammenfassenden folgenden Zeilen noch deutlicher ist.

Nach der allgemeinen Erwähnung verschiedener Göttergruppen in IV,8′f (s.o.) folgen zweifelsohne die Flüche durch die tyrischen Götter. Für den ersten Fluch in IV,10′–13′ sind die verschiedenen Baal-Manifestationen Baʿalšamem, Baʿal Malage und Baʿal Ṣaphon zuständig:

| SAA 2 5,IV,10′–13′ | |
|---|---|
| $^{d}$*ba-al-sa-me-me* $^{d}$*ba-al-ma-la-ge-e* $^{d}$*ba-al-ṣa-pu-nu* TU15 *lem-nu ina* GIŠ. MÁ.MEŠ-*ku-nu lu-šat-ba* GIŠ.*mar-kas-ši-na lip-ṭu-ur* GIŠ.*tar-kul-la-ši-na li-is-su-hu e-du-u dan-nu ina* [*tam-t*]*im li-ṭa-bi-ši-na šam-ru a-gu-u e-li-ku-nu li-l*[*i-a*] | „Baʿalšamem, Baʿal Malage und Baʿal Ṣaphon mögen einen bösen Wind gegen eure Schiffe heben, ihre Seile mögen auftrennen, ihr Ankerpfahl möge ausreißen, eine starke Welle möge sie ins Meer senken, eine wütende Wasserflut möge sich gegen euch erheben!“ |

Der Inhalt des Fluches spielt auf den Wettergottcharakter der Götter an: Die Verfluchten sollen beim Segeln vom bösen Wind getroffen werden und dadurch Schiffsbrüche erleiden. Die Charakterisierung der tyrischen Götter entspricht also den Vorstellungen der Verehrer dieser Götter, die verschiedene Manifestationen des im tyrischen Pantheon wichtigen Gottes Baʿal sind. Baʿal Malage ist von diesen drei am schlechtesten zu greifen, denn der Name ist nur hier belegt.[14] Was den Baʿal Ṣaphon betrifft, handelt es sich hierbei um eine besonders aus den ugaritischen Quellen

13. Anat, die eine zentrale Funktion im ugaritischen Ba'al-Zyklus hat, spielte in Phönizien keine große Rolle (Bonnet 2010: 85f).

14. Die Bedeutung von Malage bleibt umstritten: Man hat u.a. Ableitungen von *mlḥ* (= „Seemann“) bzw. *malga* (= „Hafen“) vorgeschlagen und eine mögliche Verbindung zu Zeus Meilíchios besprochen (Bunnens 1992). Ohne weitere Belege bleibt die Bedeutung unklar, wobei die an sich in diesem Kontext gut vorstellbaren Ableitungsvorschläge aus dem maritimen Bereich vielleicht doch zu stark davon abhängig sind, dass man eine besondere Seefahrerreligion in Tyros postuliert hat, die sich—gegen Bonnet (2010: 56; vgl. auch 76)—m.E. nicht beweisen lässt.

bekannte Baʿal-Manifestation, die ihren Namen dem Berg Ṣaphon verdankt.[15] Baʿal Ṣaphon war ein allgemein bekannter westsemitischer Wettergott, der vor allem wegen seines Sieges über den Meeresgott Yammu in den ugaritischen Mythen zu einem Seefahrtsgott erklärt werden kann (Lipiński 1995: 244.247), aber meines Erachtens dennoch besser als ein allgemein verehrter und starker Schutzgott interpretiert werden sollte, der nicht in jedem Zusammenhang etwas mit Seefahrt zu tun haben muss.[16] Der Himmelsgott Baʿalšamem war ein ursprünglich aramäischer Wettergott, der oft als Schutzgott aramäischer Könige vorkommt und auch in Phönizien häufig verehrt wurde (Bonnet 2010: 65; Niehr 2010: 294f.298). Dass ein allgemein bekannter Gewittergott für einen solchen Fluch zuständig ist, überrascht nicht. Niehr 2003 (44) hat diese drei Götter als „transregionale Wettergötter [. . .] des Küstenstreifens des östlichen Mittelmeeres" bezeichnet.

Zu bemerken ist, dass der Fluch nicht nur durch die tyrischen Götter vollzogen wird, sondern auch vorwiegend gegen das Volk von Tyrus gerichtet ist. Die Stadt und ihre Wirtschaft waren von ihrer Flotte nicht zu trennen und ihre Außenwahrnehmung war schon in der Antike stark mit der Seefahrt verbunden. Für Assyrien waren Schiffe nicht von zentraler Bedeutung, auch wenn das Neuassyrische Reich zeitweise über eine Flotte verfügte. Am ehesten bedienten sich die Assyrer der phönizischen Schiffe (Bass 2006: 1429f).

Der zweite tyrische Fluch durch Melqart und Ešmun verheißt beim Vertragsbruch Zerstörung des Landes, Deportation seiner Einwohner und eine allgemeine Armut:

SAA 2 5,IV,14′–17′

$^{d}$*mi-il-qar-tu* $^{d}$*ia-su-mu-nu* KUR-*ku-nu a-na ha-p*[*e*!]-⸢*e*!⸣ UN.MEŠ-*ku-nu a-na šá-la-li li-di-nu* TA* KUR-*ku-nu* [*lis-su-h*]*u*!-⸢*ku*!-*nu*!⸣ ŠUKU.MEŠ *ina pi-i-ku-nu ku-zip-pi*! *ina la-ni-ku-nu* Ì.MEŠ *ina pa-šá-ši-ku-nu lu-ḫal-li-qu*

„Melqart und Ešmun mögen euer Land zur Zerstörung und eure Leute zur Deportation preisgeben! Aus eurem Land [mögen] sie euch [ausreißen]! Das Essen aus eurem Mund, die Gewänder von euren Gestalten und das Öl für eure Salbung mögen sie zum Verschwinden bringen!"

Melqart, „König der Stadt", war der Schutzgott von Tyros und stark mit dem phönizischen Königtum verbunden. Die Verehrung von Melqart war im Mittelmeerraum durch die phönizischen Handelsverbindungen weit verbreitet und sie stellte ein wichtiges Identifikationsmerkmal in der tyrischen Diaspora dar. Zusätzlich zum Königtum

15. Der Berg kann entweder mit Ǧebel el-Aqra identifiziert oder als „altererbter kanaanäischer Funktionsbegriff" verschiedener Berge (und unterschiedlicher Götter) verstanden werden. Vgl. Kottsieper 1997: 415f.

16. Vgl. z. B. Bordreuil 1986: 82–86, der u.a. Baʿal Ṣaphon auf einem ins 6. Jh. v. Chr. datierten Amulett aus Tyros direkt als einen Schutzgott der Seemänner interpretiert. Meines Erachtens weist in der Inschrift nichts darauf hin, sondern es handelt sich um einen sehr allgemein gehaltenen Text, der um den Segen von Baʿal Ṣaphon und Baʿal Hammon bittet: *lbʿlḥmn wlbʿlṣpn kybrknn* („À Baal Ḥamon et à Baal Ṣaphon pour qu'ils me bénissent vraiment"; ebd., 83) Die beiden Götter können am einfachsten als Schutzgötter des Amuletträgers interpretiert werden—egal ob er eine Schifffahrt plante oder nicht.

hatte Melqart einen Jenseitsbezug (Bonnet 2010: 67–70). Der sidonische Stadtgott Ešmun wurde einerseits außerhalb von Sidon und in der hellenistischen Zeit vor allem als Heilgott verehrt, andererseits hatte er starke dynastische Bezüge, was insbesondere im Königsepitheton „Priester von Ešmun" sichtbar ist. Melqart und Ešmun werden in den phönizischen Quellen oft zusammen erwähnt, was jeweils mit einer Vereinigung von Tyros und Sidon zu tun haben sollte (Bonnet 2010: 54–56).

Die Flüche haben einen direkten Bezug zu Melqart und Ešmun als die Haupt- und Schutzgötter von Tyros und Sidon. Der Untergang von Tyros würde bedeuten, dass ihre Götter versagt haben oder dass sie im Sinne einer „divine abandonment" ihre Bewohner ohne Schutz gelassen hätten. Der dynastische Charakter der beiden Götter entspricht also gut den Fluchinhalten. Was Ešmun betrifft, kann zusätzlich festgehalten werden, dass sein Name von *šmn*, dem Wort für Öl, abgeleitet ist (Lipiński 1995: 155), was sowohl mit seinen therapeutischen Eigenschaften als auch mit der Salbung beim Thronaufstieg der Könige in Verbindung zu sehen ist. Der zweite Aspekt hat seine direkte Entsprechung im abschließenden Teil des zweiten Fluchs.

Der dritte und letzte Fluch ist der Göttin Astarte, die in Tyros mit Melqart ein königliches Paar bildete, aber in Sidon auch als Paredros von Ešmun bekannt ist, zugeschrieben worden:

| SAA 2 5,IV,18′f | |
|---|---|
| $^{d}$*as-tar-tú ina ta-ḫa-zi dan-ni* GIŠ.BAN-[*ku-nu li-*(*iš*)*-bir ina šap*]*-l*[*a* LÚ*.KÚR*-ku-nu*] *li-še-ši-ib-ku-nu* LÚ*.KÚR *a-ḫu-u li-za-i-za mim-*[*mu-ku-nu*] | „Astarte möge euren Bogen in der Mitte des Kampfes brechen und euch zu den Füßen eurer Feinde kriechen lassen, möge ein fremder Feind euer Eigentum aufteilen!" |

Astarte war in Phönizien die weibliche Gottheit schlechthin und spielte in den Panthea verschiedener Städte eine zentrale Rolle. Sie kombinierte die beiden Aspekte des Krieges und der Sexualität und ist dadurch mit der mesopotamischen Ištar vergleichbar (Bonnet 2010: 78–81). Dieser kriegerische Fluch passt also mit den üblichen Astarte-Vorstellungen zusammen, kann aber nicht von einem Ištar-Fluch unterschieden werden. Die Motive Brechen des Bogens, Kriechen zu den Füßen der Feinden und Plündern kommen genauso in neuassyrischen Ištar-Flüchen vor: vgl. z. B. SAA 2 4, Rs. 20f; SAA 2 9, Rs. 24'f (beide nur fragmentarisch erhalten).

### *SAA 2 6*

Der Thronfolgevertrag Asarhaddons hat am Anfang des Textes zwei Götterauflistungen, bei denen nach einer längeren Liste von Namen allgemeinere Formulierungen vorkommen. Die Zeilen 16–20 listen die Götter auf, die bei der Schließung dieses Vertrags als göttliche Zeugen fungierten,[17] danach folgt:

17. Himmelskörper: Jupiter, Venus, Saturn, Merkur, Mars, Sirius; weitere Götter: Aššur, Anu, Enlil, Ea, Sîn, Šamaš, Adad, Marduk, Nabû, Nusku, Uraš, Nergal, Mullissu, Šerua, Belet-ili, Ištar von Ninive, Ištar von Arbela. Auf diese Götter der Versammlung wird noch in der Zeile 373 Bezug genommen: DINGIR.MEŠ *ša pu-uh-ri*. Vgl. auch Z. 397–400.

SAA 2 6,21–23

DINGIR.MEŠ *a-ši-bu-ti* AN-*e* KI.TIM
DINGIR.MEŠ KUR *aš-šur* DINGIR.
MEŠ KUR *šu-me-ri u* [UR]I.[K]I
DINGIR.MEŠ KUR.KUR DÙ-*šú-nu*

„die Götter die im Himmel und in
der Unterwelt wohnen, die Götter
von Assyrien, die Götter von Sumer
und Akkad, alle Götter aller Länder"

In den Zeilen 25–40 ist zunächst die Forderung zum Eid bei verschiedenen assyrischen und babylonischen Göttern zu finden. Danach werden Zuordnungen zu verschiedenen Städten, Ländern und Regionen erwähnt, wobei zuerst die konkreten Namen Assyrien, Sumer und Akkad vorkommen, danach die schon in der Einleitung erwähnten allgemeineren Formulierungen, von denen in diesem Zusammenhang nur noch eine hervorzuheben ist: „Dito bei allen Göttern vom Land und Gebiet von jedem Einzelnen!" ([DINGIR].MEŠ KUR-*šu*[!] *na-gi-šu* DÙ-*šú-nu* MIN).[18] Das Auftreten der assyrischen Götter in diesem Vertrag geschieht in den Auflistungen immer an erster Stelle: So bei den Göttern (25–30) und danach auch bei den Göttern der einzelnen Städte (31–37) und denen der verschiedenen Länder bzw. Gebiete (38–40). Sie werden von den anderen differenziert, um erstens die Stellung über den anderen Göttern und ihre Rolle für die Herrschaftslegitimation darzustellen, andererseits muss die Definition „von Assyrien" wegen der anderen erwähnten Göttergruppen vorhanden sein.

Die Vertragsflüche in SAA 2 6,466–471 sind ihrerseits interessant, denn sie erwähnen die Götter Aramiš, Anat-Bethel, Kubaba und evtl. auch Bethel (vgl. SAA 2 5,IV,6′).[19] Leider ist der Aramiš-Fluch nur fragmentarisch erhalten.

SAA 2 6,466–471

[[d]]*a-ra-miš* EN *im*[?] *x* [*x x x x x x x x*
*x*]-*ku-n*[*u x x x x x x x x x x x*]-*tu* [[d]*ba-a-*
*a-ti*-DINGIR.MEŠ [d]*a-na-t*]*i-ba-a-a-ti-*
DINGIR.[MEŠ] *ina* ŠU.2. UR.M[AH
*a-ki-li*] *lim-nu-ku-nu* [d]*kù*-KÁ [d]I[5 *ša*
URU].*gar-ga-miš ri-im-ṭu dan-nu ina*
ŠÀ-*ku-nu liš-kun* [KÀŠ].MEŠ-*ku-nu*
*ki-ma ti*!-*ki ana kaq-qar lit-ta-tuk*!

„[Möge] Aramiš, Herr von [. . .]
euc[h . . .]! Mögen [Bethel und Anat]-
Bethel euch in die Pranken eines [fressenden] Löw[en] ausliefern! Möge
Kubaba, Göt[tin von] Karkemisch eine
schwere Krankheit in euch setzen!
Möge euer [Urin] wie Regentropfen
auf den Erdboden tropfen!"

Ein neues Exemplar des Thronfolgevertrags von Asarhaddon ist in Tell Tayinat (ant. Unqi; Hauptstadt von Kullania) 2009 gefunden worden (Lauinger 2012: 90). Seine Präambel ist leider nicht erhalten, aber der Text enthält einen kompletten Aramiš-Fluch. Das erste Zeichen nach dem Zeichen EN scheint in den beiden Versionen unterschiedlich zu sein: Sollten die beiden Aramiš-Flüche tatsächlich unterschiedlich gewesen sein, wäre das als ein weiteres Beispiel für den Vergleich interessant, da die beiden

18. SAA 2 6,40. Vgl. zu einer Zuordnung verschiedener Götter zu bestimmten Gebieten Dtn 32,8 in den Versionen von 4Q Dtn[q], 4Q Dtn[j] und LXX. S. zu der neueren Diskussion über die Lesungen Himbaza 2002 und Joosten 2007 (beide mit Lit.).

19. Streck 1998 (183f) hat in Bezug auf die Fluchfolge von SAA 2 6 darauf hingewiesen, dass im Kontext der geographisch benachbarten Götter spätestens ab dem Aramiš-Fluch die westlichen Götter auf die mesopotamischen Götter folgen.

Versionen sonst vorwiegend identisch sind. Vor dem Bethel- und Anat-Bethel-Fluch stehen in der Tell Tayinat-Version zusätzlich noch zwei weitere Flüche:

T VI,44–47
$^{d}$*a-ra-miš* EN URU KUR SI EN URU KUR ⸢*az-a-i*?⸣ A.MEŠ SIG$_{7}$.MEŠ *li-mal-li-*⸢*ku-nu*⸣ $^{d}$IM $^{d}$«DIŠ»*ša-la šá* $^{uru}$*kur-ba-ìl si-*⸢*iḫ-lu*⸣ UZU.MEŠ ⸢*la* DÙG.GA⸣ *ina* ⸢*zu*⸣*-mur* KUR-*ku-*[*n*]*u li-šab-ši* $^{d}$*šar-rat-a-am-qár-*⸢*ru-u-na*⸣ TA ŠÀ-*ku-*[*n*]*u li-šá-ḫi-ḫa tul-t*[*u*]

„Möge Aramiš, Herr von der Stadt und dem Land Qarnê, Herr von der Stadt und dem Land von Aza'i, euch mit grünem Wasser füllen! Mögen Adad und Šāla von Kurba'il stechenden Schmerz des Fleisches und nichts Gutes für den Körper eures Landes entstehen lassen! Möge Šarrat-Ekron einen Wurm aus eurem Inneren ausspeien lassen!"

Aramiš wird in diesem Text mit der Stadt Qarnê, die südlich von Damaskus lag, in Verbindung gebracht. Wegen der Aramiš-Elemente in Personennamen ist es vorgeschlagen worden, dass der Gott als das Haupt eines Lokalpantheons agierte, aber da er ansonsten fast nur über Personennamen bekannt ist, kann der Fluch nicht mit seinen üblichen Eigenschaften verglichen werden (Lauinger 2012: 119). Die ursprünglich syrischen Götter Bethel und Anat-Bethel sind hier für einen identischen Fluch wie in SAA 2 5,IV,6′ f (s.o.) zuständig. Was Kubaba betrifft, erhalten die beiden Exemplare einen eher allgemein gehaltenen Krankheitsfluch, aber ihre Stellung als Hauptgöttin von Karkemisch scheint in beiden Versionen vorausgesetzt zu sein. Bemerkenswert ist weiterhin, dass T VI,50 nicht nur die Göttin Kubaba, sondern auch ihren Paredros Karhuha erwähnt: $^{d}$*ku-bába* $^{d}$*kar-ḫu-ḫa šá* $^{uru}$*gar-*⸢*ga*⸣*-miš*. Dies kann mit den Vertragspartnern aus Unqi zusammenhängen, aber es darf nicht vergessen werden, dass Karhuha auch in SAA 2 2 unter den aramäischen Göttern erwähnt wurde und in Assyrien also wenigstens namentlich bekannt war.

Der Fluch mit Adad und Šāla bildet eine Brücke zwischen den beiden Vertragspartnern, denn Adad und sein Paredros Šāla waren häufig in den aramäischen Panthea prominent (vgl. Niehr 2010: 212.215f.225–229), aber der Bezug zu Kurba'il ist eher assyrisch zu verstehen. Die beiden Götter gehörten zusätzlich zu den Göttern der assyrischen *akītu*-Prozession (s.o.). In den aramäischen Kulten war Adad ein Wettergott, der zusätzlich eine Rolle im Rechtswesen spielte, aber die aramäischen Belege kommen auch oft in assyro-aramäischen Bilinguen vor und können also nicht getrennt von assyrischen Vorstellungen betrachtet werden. Šarrat-Ekron ist identisch mit der aus der Ekron-Inschrift bekannten Göttin Ptgyh, deren Eigenschaften leider unbekannt sind. Ptgyh sollte aber keine ursprünglich semitische Göttin sein (Gitin, Dothan und Naveh 1997: 10–12; Lauinger 2012: 119). Ihre Erwähnung sollte also mit den Vertragspartnern aus Tell Tayinat zusammenhängen und als ein Beispiel einer Modifikation des Vertragstextes wegen der verschiedenen Vertragspartner verstanden werden.[20]

20. Vgl. Lauinger 2012: 119 (mit Lit.) zu Fragmenten aus Nimrud, die möglicherweise zusätzliche Flüche an gleicher Stelle enthalten haben.

### *SAA 2 9 und SAA 2 10*

Die zwei erhaltenen Verträge Assurbanipals (669–627) sind jeweils mit nur einem Vertragspartner geschlossen worden, was auch die Götterdarstellung beeinflusst. Der Vertrag mit den babylonischen Verbündeten nennt die Götter der beiden Vertragspartner ziemlich neutral nebeneinander (SAA 2 9, Rs. 2′): [DINGIR.MEŠ *š*]*á* KUR *aš-šur*$^{KI}$ *u* KUR UR[I$^{KI}$] = [die Götter v]on Assyrien und Babylon[ien].[21] Dies überrascht gerade in Bezug auf die babylonischen Götter nicht. Aššur wird hierbei „Vater der Götter" (AD DINGIR.MEŠ) genannt und wird als erster Gott direkt vor Marduk namentlich erwähnt, was seine Machtposition unterstreicht. Marduk trägt dennoch das Epitheton „König der Götter" (LUGAL DINGIR.MEŠ) und wird also keineswegs als unwichtig empfunden. Die Götterliste hat also keinen polemischen Charakter. Zarpanitu wird in der Zeile Rs. 21′ erwähnt; Mullissu kommt in den erhaltenen Teilen des Vertrags gar nicht vor.

Der leider nur in Fragmenten erhaltene Vertrag Assurbanipals mit dem nordarabischen Stamm Qedar nennt die Götter von Qedar nur neben den assyrischen Göttern als Zeugen der Vertragsschließung, wobei keiner namentlich genannt wird: [(IGI) DINGIR.MEŠ KUR]-*aš-šur* DINGIR.MEŠ KUR *qi-id*-[*ri* DÙ-*šú-nu*] = „[vor allen Göttern von] Assyrien und Göttern von Qed[ar]" (SAA 2 10,2′). Die qedaritischen Götter spielen als Vertragsgötter des Vertragspartners eine Rolle, die aber vermutlich untergeordnet ist, wie es der politischen Lage Qedars entspricht.

### *Zwischenergebnis*

Die Erwähnungen der fremden Götter in den Vertragstexten dienen vor allem der Einhaltung des Vertrags. Hierbei werden die Götter der beiden Vertragsparteien erwähnt, um die beiden Seiten fester an den Vertrag zu binden. Eine Differenzierung der Götter ist teilweise vorhanden, aber keineswegs eindeutig: Eventuell sind die erwähnten Götter u.a. auch ausgesucht worden, da sowohl die Assyrer als auch ihr Vertragspartner mit ihnen vertraut waren oder mit ihnen etwas verbinden konnten. Bei den Flüchen scheinen die Assyrer einerseits solche ausgesucht zu haben, die mit den Vorstellungen der Verehrer der jeweils zuständigen Götter im Einklang waren, was besonders deutlich beim Vertrag mit Baal von Tyrus (SAA 2 5) zum Ausdruck kommt. Andererseits konnten hierbei Texte benutzt werden, die mit einer ähnlichen assyrischen Gottheit auch in Verwendung waren, so z. B. bei Astarte und Ištar. Die eher summarischen Erwähnungen der Götter des Vertragspartners und ihre Unterordnung im Vergleich zu den eigenen Göttern haben nahe Parallelen in der hethitischen Praxis (Schwemer 2008: 139).

Die zwei Versionen des Thronfolgevertrags von Asarhaddon aus Nimrud und Tel Tayinat haben gezeigt, dass von einem Vertrag verschiedene Versionen angefertigt werden konnten. Die Unterschiede sind dabei nicht sehr groß und dienen

21. Vgl. auch die vorgeschlagene Übersetzung von SAA 2 9,1′f.: „[Wir schwören bei Aššur, Šerua,] Belet-[ili . . .] allen [Göttern von Assyrien und Babylonien und allen] großen Göttern [des Himmels und der Unterwelt]."

ausschließlich der Sicherung des Vertrages dadurch, dass die (wichtigsten) Götter des Vertragspartners zu den Fluchgöttern hinzugefügt worden sind.

Die assyrischen Götter werden eher selten explizit erwähnt. Im innerassyrischen Kontext dient dies der Vollständigkeit und den religionspolitischen Interessen der einzelnen Könige, vgl. z. B. die unterschiedlichen Götterlisten im Thronfolgevertrag Sanheribs und in der späteren Bezugnahme darauf in der Asarhaddon-Inschrift Ninive A. In internationalen Verträgen kommen sie als Gegensatz zu den fremden Göttern vor. In diesen Fällen werden die assyrischen Götter immer zuerst bei den geographisch definierten Göttergruppen, an der prominentesten Stelle, erwähnt, um ihre höhere Machtposition zu betonen.

## Feldzugsberichte

In den Feldzugsberichten der neuassyrischen Könige kommen Götter der anderen Völker ziemlich selten vor und die wenigen Belege sind eher kurz und uninformativ. Es gibt drei längere Feldzugsberichte mit genaueren Beschreibungen der urartäischen, arabischen und elamischen Götter. Der Inhalt der anderen Belege wird anschließend in einem kurzen Überblick skizziert.

### *Urartäische Götter*

Sehr interessant für diese Fragestellung sind die verschiedenen Berichte über den 8. Feldzug Sargons II. (722–705) im Jahr 714 in Bezug auf die Eroberung und Plünderung der urartäischen Stadt Muṣaṣir, die als Sitz des Gottes Ḫaldi ($^{\text{URU}}$*Mu-ṣa-ṣir šu-bat* $^{\text{d}}$*Ḫal-di-a*) genannt wird (Ann. 153; vgl. auch Gottesbrief IV,336).[22] Die längste Version des Berichts ist im Gottesbrief Sargons II. zu finden (IV,336–414): Es wird deutlich, dass Ḫaldi als der Dynastiegott sowohl von Urzana von Muṣaṣir als auch von Rusa (= Ursā) von Urartu zu verstehen ist und dass Ḫaldi eine zentrale Rolle in der Legitimation des urartäischen Königtums spielte. Dies zeigt sich in der Beschreibung der urartäischen Thronbesteigungszeremonien mit den dazugehörigen Geschenken, Opfern und Insignien (IV,338–342). Weiterhin trägt Ḫaldi im Gottesbrief IV,347 das Epitheton „Zuflucht von Urartu" (= *tu-kul-ti* $^{\text{KUR}}$*ur-ar-ṭi*).[23] Bagbartu wird nur als seine Gattin erwähnt.[24]

Muṣaṣir war Ḫaldis Sitz und Kultzentrum, dessen überregionale Bedeutung auch durch die große Menge des geplünderten Gutes deutlich wird: Nach der Auflistung der Beute aus dem Palast folgt die Beschreibung dessen, was aus dem Tempel mitgenommen wurde (IV,368–407). Da Ḫaldi und Bagbartu verschleppt wurden und ihr

22. Die Annalen- und Prunkinschriftbelege beziehen sich in diesem Unterkapitel auf Fuchs 1994; der Gottesbrief Sargons II. wird nach Mayer 2013 zitiert.

23. Dies lässt sich auch durch urartäische Inschriften bestätigen; von der Diktion her sind sie aber den assyrischen Inschriften sehr ähnlich (Salvini 1995: 185). Der kriegerische Aspekt von Ḫaldi kommt in den Inschriften Sargons II. nicht zum Ausdruck.

24. Auf Urartäisch: 'Aruba(i)ni bzw. Uarubani (Salvini 1995: 187). Zusätzlich zu Ḫaldi und Bagbartu werden keine weiteren Götter genannt. Unerwähnt bleiben z. B. die zwei anderen Götter der obersten Göttertrias, der Wettergott Teišeba und der Sonnengott Šiuini (ebd., 183). Dies überrascht wegen des starken Muṣaṣir-Bezugs aber nicht sonderlich.

aufgelistetes Eigentum ohne Kultstatuen keinen Zweck haben würde, ist es meines Erachtens klar, dass die beiden eine Kultstatue hatten. Unter den sonstigen Schätzen werden einige Kultgegenstände erwähnt: eine goldene Harfe für die Durchführung des Kultes der Bagbartu; reich dekorierte Kleider und Schmuck der beiden Götter, das Bett von Ḫaldi, zwei mit Steinen dekorierte Tragealtärchen sowie Becken, die die Könige von Urartu mit Opferwein zu füllen pflegten, um vor Ḫaldi Opfer durchzuführen (IV,368.377.385–388.391.397f).[25] In diesem eher wirtschaftlich geprägten Kontext der Beuteauflistung ist durchaus zu bemerken, dass die Assyrer wenigstens über grundlegende Kenntnisse über den urartäischen Kult verfügten, denn bei manchen Gegenständen wird erwähnt, dass sie im Kult eine Rolle spielten. Besonders interessant ist die Erwähnung der urartäischen Könige in Bezug auf die Weinopfer, denn diese Libationen sind archäologisch nachweisbar (Salvini 1995: 188).

Kürzere Versionen in Bezug auf Ḫaldi und Bagbartu finden sich in den Annalen und der Prunkschrift aus Khorsabad (Ann. 160f; Prunk 76): Nach der Auflistung der Beute aus dem Ḫaldi-Tempel—laut den Angaben u.a. über 160 Talente Silber samt einem Stier, einer Kuh und einem Kalb aus Bronze—wird berichtet, dass auch die Götter Ḫaldi und Bagbartu, die beide als Götter von Urzana weiter definiert werden, zu dieser Beute zählen und mit ihrem Eigentum in den Tempel Aššurs gebracht wurden. Sowohl die Annalen als auch die Prunkinschrift Sargons II. berichten über den Selbstmord des Ursā von Urartu, aber nur die Prunkinschrift erwähnt ausdrücklich, dass er den Selbstmord begeht, nachdem er von der Deportation seines Gottes Ḫaldi unterrichtet wurde.[26]

Im Zentrum des neuassyrischen Interesses stehen schließlich in diesem Fall wirtschaftliche und machtpolitische Fragen. Die Plünderung der Stadt Muṣaṣir bekommt den großen Stellenwert vermutlich wegen der jahrelangen Probleme mit Urartu und den eine Schaukelpolitik praktizierenden Randgebieten: Die bergigen, schwer erreichbaren Gebiete von Urartu und Muṣaṣir waren nach Tiglatpileser III. von den assyrischen Armeen nicht betreten worden. Weiterhin war Muṣaṣir einerseits das Kultzentrum eines größeren Gebietes: Das Heiligtum lag im Zagrosgebirge außerhalb des urartäischen Territoriums (Salvini 1995: 183). Andererseits war Muṣaṣir ein zentraler Kultort diverser Dynastien—beides waren zentrale Auslöser der größer angelegten Tempelplünderungen und der sog. Godnappings in der neuassyrischen Zeit (Berlejung 2002: 199).[27] Die Ausführlichkeit des Berichtes im Gottesbrief ist sicherlich auch der verwendeten Gattung zu verdanken, die mehr Raum für kommentierte Auflistungen lässt.[28] Die Annalentexte sind wesentlich kürzer, auch wenn Ḫaldi auch in ihnen eine Rolle spielt, vor allem bei der Beute. Die Prunkinschrift erwähnt zusätzlich, dass der

25. Über die Dekorationen des Tempels berichten noch die mitgeschleppten, mit Götterdarstellungen dekorierten Schlösser und Schlüssel des Tores, das als der Schmuck des Heiligtums galt (IV,367–407).

26. Der Tod Rusas folgte laut dem Gottesbrief der Nachricht über die Deportation der Urartäer nach Urartu (IV,410–413), wobei das Schwert als Selbstmordwaffe nicht erwähnt wird.

27. Hierbei handelt es sich z. B. um die Dynastiegötter der jeweiligen Herrscher (Spieckermann 1982: 350f).

28. Die Genauigkeit könnte auch damit zusammenhängen, dass alles doch nicht zugunsten von Aššur und Assyrien geplündert wurde und hier eine Rechtfertigung zu sehen ist (vgl. Z. IV,405–407). Mayer 2013: 72 weist in diesem Zusammenhang auf „Sargons eigenes Unbehagen wegen seines Vorgehens" hin. Sargon mag in diesem Text eine geschönte Version der Ereignisse abliefern, aber m.E. kann dies dennoch nicht so interpretiert werden, dass die Plünderung nicht beabsichtigt oder dass das ganze Eigentum zurückgegeben

urartäische König nach dem Godnapping Selbstmord begeht. Deutlich ist die Machtdemonstration, die auch als Abschreckung für andere Gebiete dienen sollte.

### *Arabische Götter*

Die zweite etwas ausführlicher dargestellte Gruppe der fremden Götter sind die arabischen Götter. In der neuassyrischen Zeit werden sie erstmalig mit ihren Thronen sowie der militärischen Ausrüstung und den Stäben der Göttinnen in den Inschriften Tiglatpilesers III. (745–727) erwähnt (RINAP 1, Tiglatpileser III., 42,9′–22′; 48,24′f).[29]

Die arabischen Götter kommen dann wieder in den Inschriften über die Araberfeldzüge Sanheribs (705–681) kurz vor, da er nach dem Sieg über die Königin Teʾelḫunu u.a. auch ihre Götter plünderte (RINAP 3/1 35,5″).[30] Dies wird in den Inschriften von Asarhaddon bestätigt.[31] Die Feldzugsberichte Asarhaddons thematisieren ihrerseits die Rückgabe dieser Götter, nachdem der König Hazael (842–810) mit reichlichem Tribut zu Asarhaddon gekommen war und darum gebeten hatte (RINAP 4 1,IV,1–24).[32] Interessant ist, dass Asarhaddon die Götterstatuen vor der Rückgabe restaurieren ließ, wenn auch nicht ohne ein eigenes Interesse: Die Statuen wurden nicht nur aufpoliert, sondern erhielten auch eine Inschrift, die vor allem die Macht Aššurs über diese Götter thematisierte und gleichzeitig als eine Prestigeinschrift des Königs funktionierte. Die arabischen Götter werden namentlich genannt: Es handelt sich um die Götter Atar-samayin, Dāya, Nuḫāya, Ruldāwu, Abirillu und Atar-qurumâ ($^{d}$*a-tar-sa-ma-a-a-in* $^{d}$*da-a-a* $^{d}$*nu-ḫa-a-a* $^{d}$*ru-ul-da-a-a-ú* $^{d}$*a-bi-ri-il-lu* $^{d}$*a-tar-qu-ru-ma-a*; RINAP 4 1,IV,10–12). Abgeschlossen wird die Auflistung mit der zusammenfassenden Aussage „Götter der Araber" (DINGIR.MEŠ *šá* LÚ.*a-ri-bi*).

Alle diese Götter sind mit der Ausnahme von Abirillu auch durch andere Quellen bekannt: Atar-samayin ist eine in assyrischen Quellen übliche aramäische Schreibform des Namens einer auch aus anderen Quellen bekannten Göttin ʿAṯtar des Himmels, die mit der südarabischen Oase Duma verbunden war und in manchen Quellen als Sonnengöttin vorkommt (Knauf 1985: 79.82f; Weippert 1973: 44f, Fn. 24). Dāya ist ansonsten nur aus sabäischen Personennamen bekannt. Mit Nuḫaya und Ruldāwu sind die arabischen Götter Ruḍā und Nuhā gemeint: Der erste ist möglicherweise ein Mondgott; der zweite definitiv ein Sonnengott. Atar-qurumâ ist wahrscheinlich eine Manifestation von Atar-samayin. (Knauf 1985: 84–86).[33]

---

worden wäre. In den Quellen ist nur davon die Rede, dass Ḫaldi (und eben nicht sein Besitz!) nach Muṣaṣir zurückgebracht wird (gegen Mayer 2013: 72f).

29. S. auch die kürzere Version in RINAP 1, Tiglatpileser III., 49,18.

30. S. dazu auch Frahm 1997: 131.133.

31. RINAP 4 1,IV,3–5; 2,II,48–50; 4,II′,4′–9′; 6,III′,1′–4′. Die Inschriften Asarhaddons nennen Teʾelḫunu nicht namentlich, sondern reden über *apkallatu*: Dies ist ein Titel, den die assyrischen Schreiber als einen Personennamen verstanden haben und es handelt sich also um die gleiche Königin (RINAP 3/1, S. 232, Anm. z. Z. 53′[Lit.]).

32. Vgl. auch RINAP 4 6,III′,1′–10′ und 97,7–14a. Kürzere Versionen—u.a. ohne die Auflistung der Götternamen—erwähnen die Restauration der Statuen sowie die Inschrift. S. RINAP 4 2,II, 46–62; 3,III,1′–5′ und 4,II′,2′–14′.

33. Götterstatuen, die mit einer Aššur-Inschrift versehen werden, sind bei Asarhaddon auch in Bezug auf die Götter von Laialê, dem König der Stadt Iadiʾ zu finden (RINAP 4 2,III,24–36; 3,III,25′–32′). Die kürzeren Varianten über den Feldzug in das Land Bāzu erwähnen die Episode mit den Göttern von Laialê gar nicht.

Dass die Götter der in der Zeit politisch eher irrelevanten Araber einen so großen Stellenwert bekommen, hängt möglicherweise mit dem Bild Asarhaddons zusammen, das er sich damit schuf, dass er die Götterstatuen zurückgab. Dies hat auch eine Bedeutung als Machtdemonstration, wie auch die Begegnung mit den eher exotischen Arabern im Allgemeinen. Die arabischen Götter sollten außerhalb von Arabien und—nach der Plünderung—außerhalb von Ninive eher unbekannt gewesen sein, wobei diese Fremdheit zu der Namensnennung auch seinen Teil beigetragen haben kann. Die Situation dauert dennoch nicht lange an, denn schon unter dem Nachfolger Hazaels werden die Götter wieder nach Assyrien verschleppt.

Die arabischen Götter werden auch noch in den Inschriften Assurbanipals thematisiert. Es wird erzählt, dass Jautaʾ, der die Statue von Atar-samayin zurückbekommen hatte (BIWA B,VII,93–98; C,IX,90′–95′; S. 113.243), aufständisch wurde und dass die Flüche der Vertragsgötter ihn trafen, wobei nur die assyrischen bzw. babylonischen Götter aufgelistet werden:

BIWA B,VIII,27–30 (S. 114.244)

| | |
|---|---|
| *ar-ra-a-ti ma-la ina a-de-šú-un šaṭ-ru ina pi-it-ti i-ši-mu-šú-nu-ti* AN.ŠÁR $^{d}$30 $^{d}$UTU $^{d}$EN *u* $^{d}$AG $^{d}$15 *šá* NINAKI $^{d}$15 *šá* URUARBA.IL DINGIR.MEŠ GAL.MEŠ EN.MEŠ-*ia* | „Die Flüche, alles was in ihrem Vertrag geschrieben war, verhängten dementsprechend über sie Aššur, Sîn, Šamaš, Bel, Nabû, Ištar von Ninive und Ištar von Arbela, die großen Götter, meine Herren“ |

Die längere Version des Feldzugsberichtes im Prisma A hat eine abweichende Beschreibung der Flüche (BIWA A,IX,53–74; S. 67f.248): Es wird ausdrücklich auf die Vergleichsflüche des Vertragseides Bezug genommen. Interessant ist auch, dass die Folgen eines Vertragsbruchs auch durch eine „Araber-Perspektive“ dargestellt werden:

BIWA A,IX,68–74 (S. 67f.248)

| | |
|---|---|
| UN.MEŠ KUR *a-ri-bi* DIŠ-*en a-na* DIŠ-*en iš-ta-ʾa-lu*$_4$ *a-ḫa-meš um-ma ina* UGU *mi-né-e ki-i ep-še-e-tú an-ni-tú* ḪUL-*tú im-ḫu-ru* $^{KUR}$*a-ru-bu um-ma áš-šu a-de-e* GAL.MEŠ *ša* AN:ŠAR *la ni-iṣ-ṣu-ru ni-iḫ-ṭu-ú ina* MUN mAN.ŠAR.DÙ.A LUGAL *na-ram* ŠÀ-*bi* $^{d}$*en*$^{!}$-*líl* | „Die Einwohner Arabiens fragten einander gegenseitig folgendermaßen: Woran liegt es, dass Arabien eine solche schlimme Behandlung erfährt? (Die Antwort lautete) folgendermaßen: Weil wir den feierlichen Vertrag bei Assur missachtet und gegen die Wohltat Assurbanipals, des Herzenslieblings Enlils, gesündigt haben!“ |

Die arabischen Götter oder ihre Verschleppung kommen in diesem längeren Bericht dennoch wesentlich kürzer zur Sprache: Es wird nur eine Götterdeportation bis nach Damaskus kurz erwähnt (BIWA A,IX,3–8, S. 65.247).

Besonders interessant ist noch ein an eine arabische Göttin gerichteter Votivtext Assurbanipals (K 3405), deren Name leider nicht erhalten ist. Am ehesten ist an Atar-samayin zu denken, so auch Cogan 1974 (19f).[34] Assurbanipal widmet der Göttin ein Sternemblem, weil sie ihm den Sieg über den arabischen König (!) Jauta' gegeben hat. Der Text weist zusätzlich darauf hin, dass schon Sanherib mit der Unterstützung dieser Göttin die Araber besiegen konnte und dass Asarhaddon die Götterstatuen an Hazael zurückgegeben hatte (Cogan 1974: 15–21). Dies ist ein einzigartiges Beispiel dafür, dass die assyrischen Könige nicht nur in den Annalen mit den ganz fremden Göttern argumentierten, sondern dass diese Götter auch in der Praxis von ihnen wenigstens in irgendeiner Weise verehrt wurden.

### *Elamische Götter*

Der ausführlichste Bericht, in dem die fremden Götter eine Rolle spielen, ist in den Inschriften Assurbanipals über seine Feldzüge gegen Elam überliefert (BIWA A,V,63–VII,81; F,IV,17–VI,21; T,IV,36–V,32; S. 49–61.167f.239–243). Die umfassende Schilderung der Eroberung von Susa 646 v. Chr. enthält eine Vielzahl von religiösen Motiven. Erstens wird Susa schon grundsätzlich als das wichtigste Kultzentrum Elams dargestellt:

BIWA A,V,128f; F,IV,69f (S. 52.241)

| | |
|---|---|
| $^{\text{URU}}$*šu-šá-an ma-ḫa-zu* GAL-*ú mu-šab* DINGIR.MEŠ-*šú-un a-šar pi-riš-ti-šú-un* | „Susa, die große Kultstadt, Wohnsitz ihrer Götter, Stätte ihres [= der Götter, RSS] Geheimnisses“ |

Im gleichen Zusammenhang wird der Tempelturm dieser Stadt genauer beschrieben, alles im Anklang an das übliche Aussehen der elamischen Tempel (BIWA A,VI,27–29; F,V,19–21; S. 53.241; Koch 2006, 1964). Die folgende Schilderung des elamischen Hauptgottes Inšušinak lautet:

BIWA A,VI,30–32; F,V,21–23 (S. 53.241)

| | |
|---|---|
| $^{\text{d}}$MÙŠ.ŠÉŠ DINGIR *pi-riš-ti-šú-un ša áš-bu ina pu-uz-ra-a-ti ša mam-ma-an la im-ma-ru ep-šet* DINGIR-*ti-šú* | „Inšušinak, ihr geheimnisvoller Gott, der im Verborgenen wohnt, dessen göttliches Wirken niemand sieht“ |

Die Darstellung Inšušinaks als ein geheimnisvoller Gott passt weiterhin mit der Schilderung seiner Kultstadt zusammen und weist darauf hin, dass die Schreiber dieser Inschrift wenigstens irgendeinen Überblick über den Kultbetrieb in Susa hatten. Inšušinaks Name, „Herr von Susa“ hängt mit seiner Kultstadt zusammen und der Gott hatte viele verschiedene Funktionen, aber in diesem assyrischen Bericht kommt seine Ähnlichkeit mit dem Unterweltsgott Nergal am stärksten zum Ausdruck. Inšušinak

34. Cogan argumentiert wegen der Zeile Rs. 6 ($^{\text{d}}$*iš-tar be-el-tu šá-qu-tu* = Ištar, erhabene Herrin) und des astralen Geschenks, dass die Assyrer Atar-samayin als eine Ištar-Manifestation verehrten. Dies ist zwar möglich, aber meines Erachtens nicht ganz so eindeutig: Erstens spricht die Inschrift über die arabische Göttin ansonsten nur in der 3. Person und zweitens kommen nach der Nennung von Ištar noch Aššur und Mullissu vor. Es ist also gut möglich, dass die (rein assyrische) Ištar-Figur wegen der Kriegsereignisse erwähnt wird: In solchen Fällen kommt Ištar oft ohne ein Toponym vor.

verkörperte in Elam eben alle Aufgaben des mesopotamischen Brüderpaares Ninurta und Nergal; weiterhin hatte er u.a. eine dynastische Funktion inne (Koch 2011: 64–67).

Es folgt eine Liste sämtlicher Götter und Göttinnen (BIWA A,VI,33–43; F,V,23–31; S. 53f.241), die aus Susa verschleppt wurden, zusammen mit ihrem Schmuck, ihrem Eigentum, ihren Geräten sowie ihrem Kultpersonal *sangugē* und *puḫlalē*. Diese beiden Begriffe sind laut Borger elamische Berufsbezeichnungen und würden ihrerseits auch für außerordentlich gute Kenntnisse über die elamische Religion sprechen (BIWA A,VI,46; F,V,33; S. 54.241). Von den erwähnten Göttern und Göttinnen (Šumudu, Lagamaru, Partikira, Ammankasibar, Uduran, Sapag/k, Ragiba, Sungursarā, Karsa, Kirsamas, Šudānu, Ajapag/ksina, Bilala, Panintimri, Silagarā, Nab/psā, Nabirtu und Kindakarb/pu) sind die meisten als akkadische Wiedergaben von aus elamischen Inschriften bekannten Götternamen zu verstehen.[35] Nur der Gott Sapag/k wird weiterdefiniert (BIWA A,VI,36f; S. 53.241): „deren Gottheit die Könige von Elam ständig verehrten" (*ša* LUGAL.MEŠ KUR ELAM.MA$^{KI}$ *ip-tal-la-ḫu* DINGIR-*us-su-un*). Bei der Beschreibung der Zerstörung ist es interessant, dass den Göttern und Göttinnen das gleiche Schicksal wie den Tempel trifft: Sie werden von Asarhaddon zu den Phantomen[36] gerechnet (DINGIR.MEŠ-*šú u* $^{d}$15.MEŠ-*šú am-na-a a-na za-qí-qí*; BIWA A,VI,64; F,V,43; S. 55.241).

Die verborgenen Aspekte des elamischen Kultes kommen am Schluss dieses Berichts zum dritten Mal zum Ausdruck: Es wird erzählt, wie die Kampftruppen Assurbanipals in die verborgenen Wälder, in die sonst keine Fremden gehen durften, eingedrungen sind und den verbotenen Bereich angeschaut und verbrannt haben. Diese „heiligen Wälder" mit ihren heiligen, mit Altären ausgestatteten Bezirken waren häufig und kommen in den elamischen Texten oft vor. Deutlich wird, dass die Elamer einen Ahnenkult mit den verstorbenen Königen praktiziert haben, denn die Grabstätten werden durch die Assyrer zerstört und die Gebeine werden nach Assyrien verschleppt, wo ihnen die Totenopfer und Wasserspenden versagt werden (BIWA A,VI,65–75; F,V,44–54; S. 55.241; vgl. auch Koch 2011: 40.75–79).

Um die Wiederaufnahme des Kultes zu verhindern, wurde Erde von Susa, Madaktu und Ḫaltemaš eingesammelt und nach Assyrien gebracht. Die totale Zerstörung Elams inkl. der Zerstreuung von Salz und Kresse wird mit einer Beauftragung durch die Göttin Nanâ legitimiert: Sie habe Assurbanipal berufen, um sie zurück nach Uruk zu bringen (BIWA A,VI,96–122; F,V,66–VI,10; S. 56–58.242). Deutlich wird wieder, dass die assyrischen Könige sich genauso gut von den fremden Göttern angesprochen

35. Von diesen Göttern sind viele auch aus den elamischen Texten bekannt. Šumudu ist die neuassyrische Schreibung des elamischen Gottes Simut; Lagamaru bzw. Lagamal steht für den ursprünglich akkadischen Gott Lagamar (*lā gamaru* = Keine Gnade); Partikira für die Göttin Parti (ursprünglich Mašti) mit der Ergänzung *-kira*, wohl für ki-ri (elamisch für Göttin). Bei Ammankasibar handelt es sich um einen ansonsten unbekannten Gott—der erste Teil des Namens könnte für den Gott Humban stehen. Mit Uduran könnte der kämpferische Gott Hutran gemeint sein—dann mit einer Lesung $^{d}$*ḫu-tú-ra-an*—, was aber nicht zwingend ist. Kirsamas ist eine Fehlschreibung für Kirmas, die übliche neuassyrische Namensform für die elamische Kirwäs. Šudānu ist evtl. der elamische Šidu. Bilala steht für die Göttin Belala, die evtl. eine astrale Gottheit war. Panintimri sollte eine Verschreibung für den Gott Pinengir sein; mit Silagarā ist evtl. Silir gemeint (mit dem Epitheton „thronend"). Der Gott Nabirtu sollte der elamische Mondgott Napir sein, wobei in einer feminisierten Form (Hinz und Koch 1987; Koch 2006: 1959–1964).

Sapag/k, Ragiba, Karsa, Ajapag/ksina, Napsā und Kindakarbu sind nur aus den neuassyrischen Quellen bzw. diesem Text bekannt.

36. S. zur Übersetzung von *za-qí-qí* CAD Z, 58–60, s.v. *zaqīqu*.

fühlen konnten.[37] Die assyrischen Götter werden bei diesem Feldzugsbericht einerseits als Unterstützer und Helfer beim Kampf erwähnt, andererseits sind die Götter Assurbanipals mit ihren Kultstätten die Empfänger der Beute.

Die Ausführlichkeit der Beschreibung der Zerstörung sollte zunächst mit den langjährigen Problemen Assurbanipals mit den Elamern zusammenhängen. Da mit diesem Feldzug, der nicht nur der Abschreckung, sondern der Zerstörung Susas diente, endlich Ruhe für eine etwas längere Zeitperiode geschaffen wurde, bekam er entsprechend einen größeren Stellenwert in den Inschriften. Andererseits spielte dabei die Kooperation Elams mit dem aufständischen Bruder Šamaš-šum-ukīn, der ca. 650 auf dem Thron in Babylon saß, eine große Rolle. Die Zerstörung von Susa ist der einzige Fall der kompletten Zerstörung eines Heiligtums in der neuassyrischen Zeit (Berlejung 2002: 198f). Im Allgemeinen kann festgestellt werden, dass die Hinweise auf die elamische Religion im Großen und Ganzen richtig sind, vor allem was den Gott Inšušinak betrifft. Die Beschreibung des Kultes ist bemerkenswert akkurat und viele der aufgelisteten Göttern auch aus den elamischen Texten bekannt.

### *Andere Erwähnungen*

Was die anderen Erwähnungen der fremden Götter in den Feldzugsberichten betrifft, können sie ziemlich kurz zusammengefasst werden.

In den meisten Fällen handelt es sich bei den relativ kurzen Notizen um Bemerkungen der Verschleppung der Götter. In den allermeisten Fällen gibt es eine kurze Notiz als einen Teil einer längeren Beuteauflistung: „Ich schleppte seine Götter aus seiner Stadt ab" (*i-na* ŠÀ URU-*šu* [...] DINGIR.MEŠ-*ni-šu* [...] *áš-lu-*⌜*la*⌝) bzw. „Ich schleppte ihre Götter ab" (DINGIR.MEŠ-*šú-nu áš-lu-la*; RIMA 3, Salmanassar III., 1,IV,17.21.33f.).[38] Die üblichsten Zusatzdefinitionen der Götter sind in diesen Zusammenhängen die Possessivsuffixe in 3. Person Singular und Plural, die sich auf die besiegten Herrscher oder die eroberten Gebiete beziehen und dadurch den machtpolitischen Zweck dieser Erwähnungen verdeutlichen.[39] An der nächsten Stelle kommen geographische Notizen, z. B. eine Zielangabe: „Ich schleppte Ianzû [...] zusammen mit seinen Göttern [...] ab in meine Stadt Assur" (ᵐ*ia-an-zu-ú* [...] *a-di* DINGIR.MEŠ-*ni-šú* [...] *a-na* URU-*ia aš-šur ub-la*; RIMA 3, Salmanassar III., 40,III,1f). Es wird ansonsten gelegentlich nur erwähnt, dass die Götter mit ihrem Eigentum verschleppt wurden. Das Godnapping führte bei den Hethitern oft zur Erweiterung des Pantheons, was in Assyrien meistens nicht der Fall gewesen zu sein scheint (Schwemer 2008: 140).

In seltenen Fällen wird die Unterordnung der fremden Götter Aššur gegenüber auch durch verschiedene religiöse Motive verdeutlicht. In den Texten von Assurdan II. (934–912) und Adadnirari II. (911–891) wird explizit erwähnt, dass die Götterstatuen Geschenke für Aššur sind: „Ich schenkte ihre Götter als Geschenke für Aššur,

37. Vgl. dazu auch K 1364 u.a. (Cogan 1974, 14 mit Lit.) und die Darstellungen der Zerstörung Babylons und der Berufung zu dieser Aufgabe durch Marduk.

38. Zu der Formelhaftigkeit und der Vokabel der Notizen s. schon Cogan 1974, 22f.

39. Als eine Variante kann noch DINGIR.MEŠ É AD-*šú* [...] *as-su-ḫa-am-ma* (= „Ich entfernte die Götter des Hauses seines Vaters mit Gewalt") in den Inschriften Sanheribs in Bezug auf Ashkelon erwähnt werden (RINAP 3/1 4,39 u. pass.).

meinen Herrn“ (DINGIR.MEŠ-*ni-šu-nu ki-i qi-š*[*u*]-*te a-na aš-šur* EN-*ia*; RIMA 3, Assurdan II., 1,58; Adadnirari II., 1,16). Deutlich ist dennoch, dass die verschleppten Götterstatuen in Assyrien keine besondere Behandlung bekamen: Sie werden unter der restlichen Beute aufgelistet und scheinen in den meisten Fällen einfach irgendwo abgestellt worden zu sein (Cogan 1974: 26–30). Hiermit hängt auch die Notwendigkeit des Aufpolierens der arabischen Götterstatuen bei ihrer Rückgabe zusammen.[40] Hierbei sollte noch das Motiv „divine abandonment“ erwähnt werden, womit die Assyrer ihren Erfolg begründeten. So steht z. B. in den Sanherib-Inschriften vom Judi Dagh in einer sehr einfachen Form: „Ihre Götter verließen sie“ (DINGIR.MEŠ-*šu-un i-zi-bu-šu-nu-ti-ma*; OIP 2, 64,22–24).[41]

Die neuassyrischen Königsinschriften erwähnen „die großen Götter von Assyrien“ außerhalb der Verträge nur sporadisch.

In der Sargonidenzeit häufen sich die Belege, in denen gewisse (große) Götter und Göttinnen stärker mit dem Land Assyrien verbunden werden. Dies könnte zusätzlich zu der besseren Quellenlage damit zusammenhängen, dass sich die Sargonidenkönige wesentlich mehr mit Babylon und den babylonischen Göttern beschäftigten als ihre Vorgänger und dadurch die Betonung der assyrischen Götter im Gegensatz zu den Babylonischen wichtiger wurde. Typisch sind die Formeln „die großen Götter, die Assyrien bewohnen“ (DINGIR.MEŠ GAL.MEŠ *a-ši-bu-ut* KUR *aš-šur*$^{\text{KI}}$; Fuchs 1994: Stier 98 u. pass.) und „die Götter und Göttinnen, die Assyrien bewohnen“ (DINGIR.MEŠ *u* $^{\text{d}}$IŠ.TAR.MEŠ *a ši-bu-ut* KUR *aš-šur*$^{\text{KI}}$; Fuchs 1994: Prunk 176 u. pass.). Oft finden sich diese Erwähnungen bei den Bauinschriften, z. B. in denen von Dūr-Šarrukīn. Hierbei geht es um die neue Hauptstadt, die in Verbindung zum ganzen Land dargestellt werden muss: Die Anwesenheit der assyrischen Götter kann sowohl als eine religiöse Legitimation von Dūr-Šarrukīn als auch als eine Absicherung der Stadt durch den strahlenden Blick Aššurs verstanden werden. Dass die politische Hauptstadt kein explizit religiöses Zentrum ist, kommt neben der bleibenden Bedeutung von Assur als Kultort darin zum Ausdruck, dass die Götter und Göttinnen nach den Eröffnungsfeierlichkeiten in ihre Städte zurückkehren (Fuchs 1994: Prunk 167–177 u. pass.).[42] Ähnliches ist in den Ninive-Inschriften Sanheribs und Asarhaddons zu beobachten.

Die früheren Erwähnungen sind meistens mit einem ausländischen Kontext zu erklären. Es kann sich darum handeln, dass die Inschrift in einer entfernten Gegend aufgestellt wurde und mit ausländischen Adressaten zu rechnen war. S. z. B. die Steleninschrift Adadniraris III. (810–783), die am Orontes in der Nähe der Stadt Antakya in der Südtürkei gefunden worden ist (RIMA 3 203). Die Stele gehört in den Zusammenhang mit dem Syrien-Feldzug 796 v. Chr. (vgl. Veenhof 2001: 242). Weiterhin scheint

40. Die anderen, keine weiteren Informationen enthaltenden Belege der Godnappings sind:

Tiglatpileser III.: RINAP 1 47,19.21; 48,16′.
Sargon II.: Fuchs 1994: Prunk 105–107.
Sanherib: RINAP 3/1, Sanherib, 16,III,26–30; 17,II,87–91; 18,II,1″–5″; 22,II,60–64; 23,II,57–61; 29,I′,1′f.
Asarhaddon: RINAP 4 1,IV,71f; 2,III,22f; 3,III,22′–24′; 4,II,34′–36′; 103,11f.

41. Vgl. zu den Judi-Dagh-Inschriften Frahm 1997: T 116–121, 151.

42. Die Türschwelleninschrift des Palastes L in Dur-Scharrukin bringt die Götter nicht nur mit Assyrien, sondern auch mit der Stadt in Verbindung (SL, 4–6).

es wahrscheinlich, dass hiermit die Macht Assyriens und dadurch die Wirkung der Drohung der gelegentlich aufgelisteten Flüche durch die assyrischen Götter unterstrichen wurde: Das größte Reich hatte auch die stärksten Götter auf seiner Seite. Um die assyrische Macht geht es auch in den Fällen, wenn die assyrischen Könige Statuen „im Tempel seiner Götter", also im Tempel des besiegten Herrschers, errichten lassen. Der politische Kontext und die Unterordnung der lokalen Götter unter Assyrien sind der Hintergrund für die explizite Erwähnung der fremden Götter.

Einige Sanherib-Inschriften bezeichnen den König als einen, „der das Verehren der Götter des Himmels und der Götter Assyriens besonders gut kennt" (*pa-làḫ* DINGIR. MEŠ *šá* AN-*e ù* DINGIR.MEŠ KUR *aš-šur*[KI] *ra-biš mu-du-u;* RINAP 3/1, Sanherib, 11,5; 12,5f; 13,4f; vgl. auch VA 8254 [s. dazu RINAP 3/1, Einl. zur Inschrift 11 [Lit.]). Deutlich ist meines Erachtens, dass diese Erwähnungen der assyrischen Götter ohne eine Ausländerperspektive dem Ruf Sanheribs als erfolgreicher Versorger des Kultbetriebes im gesamten Assyrien dienen sollen.

## Schlussfolgerungen

Im Allgemeinen ist daran festzuhalten, dass die Assyrer die sogenannten fremden Götter grundsätzlich ernst genommen und an ihrer Göttlichkeit nicht gezweifelt haben, was schon in den eingesetzten Determinativen deutlich ist. Klar ist jedoch, dass die Rangordnung der Götter für sie eindeutig war. In der göttlichen Rangordnung hatte Aššur in Bezug auf die anderen Götter immer die oberste Position.

Die fremden Götter werden insgesamt sehr sporadisch erwähnt. Die besprochenen drei Fälle aus den Feldzugsberichten haben gezeigt, dass, wenn die fremden Götter beschrieben werden, dieses auch mehr oder minder richtig gemacht wird. Deutlich ist, dass alle Aspekte und Funktionen der Götter nicht zur Sprache kommen und dass die Namen nicht immer korrekt wiedergegeben werden. Die Berichte über die elamischen und urartäischen Götter enthalten dennoch auch—soweit wir es überprüfen können—richtige Informationen über den Kultbetrieb und die Tempelbauten. Entweder haben sie diese grundlegenden Kenntnisse über die religiösen Verhältnisse von mehreren Gebieten gehabt und sie nur in diesen politisch besonders bedeutenden Fällen ausgeschrieben oder sie haben sich in eben diesen Fällen darum bemüht, Material für den Bericht zu sammeln. Wegen der großen Menge der Deportierten war dies auch nicht besonders schwer. Außerhalb dieser drei Fälle wird dennoch kaum etwas gesagt und wenn, dann meistens in den Beutelisten.

Zusammenfassend kann man also sagen, dass die Assyrer keineswegs daran interessiert waren, religiöse Themen in den offiziellen, nicht-kultischen Texten zu thematisieren. Dies sieht man auch daran, dass die kürzeren Versionen und Zusammenfassungen über die Ereignisse eines bestimmten Feldzugs die Erwähnungen der Götter oft gnadenlos kürzen oder sogar ausfallen lassen, auch wenn andere Einzelheiten—zum Beispiel eine ausführliche Beuteliste—noch im Bericht dabei wären.

Die Differenzierung zwischen den eigenen und den fremden Göttern ist im Rahmen der Vertragstexte vorhanden, aber keineswegs eindeutig. Die beiden Göttergruppen kommen vor, aber eine genaue Zuordnung scheint die Assyrer nicht interessiert zu haben. Vielleicht wurden die ambivalenten Götter auch mit Absicht ausgesucht, damit die beiden Vertragspartner mit möglichst vielen Göttern etwas anzufangen wussten. Die Hauptsache war schließlich, dass der Vertrag von dem Vertragspartner eingehalten wurde. In den Verträgen und Feldzugsberichten dienen die Erwähnungen der eigenen und der fremden Götter vorwiegend der Betonung der Macht der assyrischen Götter und des assyrischen Königs.

## LITERATUR


Bass, G. F.
2006 Sea and River Craft in the Ancient Near East. *CANE* 3:1421–1431.

Berlejung, A.
2002 Notlösungen—Altorientalische Nachrichten über den Tempelkult in Nachkriegszeiten. Pp. 196–230 in *Kein Land für sich allein. Studien zum Kulturkontakt in Kanaan, Israel/Palästina und Ebirnâri für Manfred Weippert zum 65. Geburtstag*. Herausgegeben von U. Hübner und E. A. Knauf. OBO 186. Freiburg: Universitätsverlag; Göttingen: Vandenhoeck & Ruprecht.

Bonnet, C.
2010 Die Religion der Phönizier und Punier. Pp. 11–185 in *Religionen in der Umwelt des Alten Testaments II. Phönizier, Punier, Aramäer*. Herausgegeben von C. Bonnet und H. Niehr. KStTh 4.2. Stuttgart: Kohlhammer.

Bordreuil, P.
1986 Attestations inédites de Melqart, Baal Ḥamon et Baal Ṣapon à Tyr (Nouveaux documents religieux phéniciens II). Pp. 77–86 in *Religio Phoenicia. Acta Colloquii Namurcensis habiti diebus 14 et 15 mensis Decembris anni 1984*. Herausgegeben von C. Bonnet, E. Lipiński und P. Marchetti. Studia Phoenicia 4. Collection d'études classiques 1. Namur: Société des études classiques.

Borger, R.
1996 *Beiträge zum Inschriftenwerk Assurbanipals. Die Prismenklassen A, B, C = K, D, E, F, G, H, J und T sowie andere Inschriften. Mit einem Beitrag von Andreas Fuchs*. Wiesbaden: Harrassowitz.

Bunnens, G.
1992 Baal Malagê. P. 59 in *Dictionnaire de la Civilisation Phénicienne et Punique*. Herausgegeben von E. Lipiński. Turnhout: Brepols.

Cogan, M.
1974 *Imperialism and Religion: Assyria, Judah and Israel in the 8th and 7th Centuries B.C.* SBLMS 19. Missoula, MT: Scholars Press.

Feliu, L.
2003 *The God Dagan in Bronze Age Syria*. CHANE 19. Leiden: Brill.

Fitzmyer, J. A.
1995 *The Aramaic Inscriptions of Sefire*. Rev. ed. BibOr 19. Rome: Potificio Istituto Biblico.

Frahm, E.
1997 *Einleitung in die Sanherib-Inschriften*. AfOB 26. Wien: Berger.

Fuchs, A.
1994 *Die Inschriften Sargons II. aus Khorsabad*. Göttingen: Cuvillier.

Gitin, S., Dothan, T. and Naveh, J.,
1996 *Assyrian Rulers of the Early First Millennium BC II (858–745 BC)*. RIMA 3. Toronto: Toronto University Press.

1997 A Royal Dedicatory Inscription from Ekron. *IEJ* 47: 1–16.

Grayson, A. K. und Novotny, J.
2012 *The Royal Inscriptions of Sennacherib, King of Assyria (704–681 BC), Part 1*. RINAP 3.1. Winona Lake, IN: Eisenbrauns.

Haas, V.
2011 Hethiter. Pp. 145–291 in *Religionen des Alten Orients 1. Hethiter und Iran*. Herausgegeben von V. Haas und H. Koch. GAT 1/1. Göttingen: Vandenhoeck & Ruprecht.

Hawkins, J. D.
1983 Kubaba. A. Philologisch. *RlA* 6: 257–261.

Himbaza, I.
2002 Dt 32,8, une correction tardive des scribes. Essai d'interprétation et de datation. *Bib* 83: 527–548.

Hinz, W. und Koch, H.
1987 *Elamisches Wörterbuch*. 2 bd. Archäologische Mitteilungen aus Iran Ergänzungsband 17. Berlin: Reimer.

Hutter, M.
1996 *Religionen in der Umwelt des Alten Testaments I. Babylonier, Syrer, Perser*. KStTh 4.1. Stuttgart: Kohlhammer.

Joosten, J
2007 A Note on the Text of Deuteronomy XXXII 8. *VT* 57: 548–555.

Knauf, E. A.
1985 *Ismael. Untersuchungen zur Geschichte Palästinas u. Nordarabiens im 1. Jahrtausend v. Chr*. ADPV 9. Wiesbaden: Harrassowitz.

Koch, H.
2006 Theology and Worship in Elam and Achaemenid Iran. *CANE* 3:1959–1969.
2011 Iran. Pp. 19–144 in *Religionen des Alten Orients 1. Hethiter und Iran*. Herausgegeben von V. Haas und H. Koch. GAT 1/1. Göttingen: Vandenhoeck & Ruprecht.

Koenen, K.
2006 Bethel [Gott]. In: Das Wissenschaftliche Bibellexikon im Internet (www.wibilex.de), 2008 (Zugriffsdatum: 08.03.2014), (http://www.bibelwissenschaft.de/stichwort/15104/).

Kottsieper, I.
1988 Anmerkungen zu Pap. Amherst 63. I: 12,11–19. Eine aramäische Version von Ps 20. *ZAW* 100: 217–244.
1997 Anmerkungen zu Pap. Amherst 63. Teil II–V. *UF* 29: 385–434.

Krebernik, M.
2004 dPALIL(IGI.DU). *RlA* 10: 281.

Lauinger, J.
2012 Esarhaddon's Succession Treaty at Tell Tayinat. Text and Commentary. *JCS* 64: 87–123.
2013 The Neo-Assyrien *adê*: Treaty, Oath, or Something Else? *ZABR* 19: 99–115.

Leichty, E.
2011 *The Royal Inscriptions of Esarhaddon, King of Assyria (680–669 BC)*. RINAP 4. Winona Lake, IN: Eisenbrauns.

Lipiński, E.
1995 *Dieux et déesses de l'univers phénicien et punique*. Studia Phoenicia 14. OLA 64. Leuven: Peeters.
2000 *The Aramaeans: Their Ancient History, Culture, Religion*. OLA 100. Leuven: Peeters.

Luckenbill, D. D.
1924 *The Annals of Sennacherib*. OIP 2. Chicago: The Oriental Institute of the University of Chicago.

Mayer, W.
2013 *Assyrien und Urarṭu I. Der Achte Feldzug Sargons II. im Jahr 714 v. Chr.* AOAT 395.1. Münster: Ugarit-Verlag.

Niehr, H.
2003 *Ba'alšamem. Studien zu Herkunft, Geschichte und Rezeptionsgeschichte eines phönizischen Gottes.* Studia Phoenicia 17. OLA 123. Leuven: Peeters.
2010 Religion in den Königreichen der Aramäer Syriens. Pp. 187–324 in *Religionen in der Umwelt des Alten Testaments II. Phönizier, Punier, Aramäer.* Herausgegeben von C. Bonnet und H. Niehr. KStTh 4.2. Stuttgart: Kohlhammer.

Parpola, S.
1987 Neo-Assyrian Treaties from the Royal Archives of Nineveh. *JCS* 39: 161–189.

Parpola, S. und Watanabe, K.
1988 *Neo-Assyrian Treaties and Loyalty Oaths.* SAA 2. Helsinki: Helsinki University Press.

Pongratz-Leisten, B.
1994 *Ina šulmi īrub. Die kulttopographische und ideologische Programmatik der akītu-Prozession in Babylonien und Assyrien im 1. Jahrtausend v. Chr.* BaF 16. Mainz am Rhein: von Zabern.

Radner, K.
2006 Provinz. C. Assyrien. *RlA* 11: 42–68.

Salvini, M.
1995 *Geschichte und Kultur der Urartäer.* Darmstadt: Wissenschaftliche Buchgesellschaft.

Schwemer, D.
2001 *Die Wettergottgestalten Mesopotamiens und Nordsyriens im Zeitalter der Keilschriftkulturen. Materialien und Studien nach den schriftlichen Quellen.* Wiesbaden: Harrassowitz.
2008 Fremde Götter in Ḫatti. Die hethitische Religion im Spannungsfeld von Synkretismus und Abgrenzung. Pp. 137–157 in *Ḫattuša-Boğazköy: das Hethiterreich im Spannungsfeld des Alten Orients: 6. Internationales Colloquium der Deutschen Orient-Gesellschaft, 22.-24. März 2006, Würzburg.* Herausgegeben von G. Wilhelm. Wiesbaden: Harrassowitz.

Spieckermann, H.
1982 *Juda unter Assur in der Sargonidenzeit.* FRLANT 129. Göttingen: Vandenhoeck & Ruprecht.

Streck, M. P.
1998 Die Flüche im Sukzessionsvertrag Asarhaddons. *ZABR* 4: 165–191.

Veenhof, K. R.
2001 *Geschichte des Alten Orients bis zur Zeit Alexanders des Großen.* GAT 11. Göttingen: Vandenhoeck & Rupert.

Weippert, M.
1973 Die Kämpfe des assyrischen Königs Assurbanipal gegen die Araber. Redaktionskritische Untersuchung des Berichts in Prisma A. *WO* 7: 39–85.

CHAPTER 19

# "Not Even Her Own Jewelry": Marital Property in the Middle Assyrian Laws

JoAnn Scurlock

IN THE CLASSIC AGE OF ASSYRIOLOGY, ancient Mesopotamian law was interpreted through the lens of Roman law, early Germanic law, and English common law.[1] With many more documents now at our disposal, it is time for a major reassessment of this classic legacy. Several of the Middle Assyrian laws regulating marriage have long puzzled and/or horrified Assyriologists. Conventional wisdom, as epitomized in G. R. Driver's and J. C. Miles' treatment of these laws, has it that Assyrian women were of such low status that they were not even capable of the ownership of the few baubles given them by their husbands. Because a view is conventional, however, it does not follow that it is wisdom. In fact, the idea that a husband retained ownership of any gifts given to the bride and the notion that a husband could help himself to his wife's property according to his whim are based, in my humble opinion, on the most profound misunderstanding of these Assyrian laws of marriage.

That a married woman should lose all her property to her husband, all of which would be forfeited on divorce, and have no right to own even her own clothing and jewelry seemed plausible to Driver and Miles since that had been the law of England, their "we," until the late nineteenth century.[2] They were aware that a woman's dowry in Babylonia and Assyria did not, at any point in the marriage, automatically become the husband's property (Driver and Miles 1935: 205–211). But apparently on the other side of the coin, there was MAL A 35, which seemed to be describing a situation in which a widow was losing all her property (including what was left of her *širku*-dowry) and, as Driver and Miles (1935: 221) note, potentially any property that belonged to her under her own right to her husband:

> "If a widow enters a man's house, whatever (and) as much as she brings with her, all of it, belongs to her husband. But if he enters to the woman, whatever

*Author's note:* I would like to dedicate this article to my father, Dr. John E. Scurlock (1920–2009), Professor of Constitutional and Comparative Law at the University of Missouri at Kansas City.

1. UN = laws of Ur-Namma; LI = laws of Lipit-Ishtar; CE = laws of Eshnunna; CH = laws of Hammurabi of Babylon; MAL = Middle Assyrian laws; NBL = Neo-Babylonian laws; the Alamannic Laws and Pactus Legis Alamannorum are cited from Rivers 1977; Rothair's Edicts and the Laws of Liutprand and Aistulf are cited from Drew 1973; Gulathing is cited from Larson 1935. The Skeltana Riucht is cited from Fairbanks 1939; the Laws of Aethelberht are cited from Whitelock 1979; the Burgundian Code is cited from Drew 1949.

2. English divorces required grounds, so this would be comparable to a divorce for adultery or other fault in the wife. As they point out, this stripping of a woman's jewelry may be a "shock to modern ideas of decency and justice" but it was part of the common law of England (Driver and Miles 1935: 200).

(and) as much as he brings with him, all of it, belongs to the woman." (MAL A 35)

Unfortunately for the English common law analogy, the second half of the law will, by this interpretation, have made a man marrying a widow lose his property to her, something completely unimaginable in England. So Driver and Miles were willing to allow for English common law for widows, having them lose their property to their husbands on remarriage.[3] The other half of the law could, however, not possibly, be referring to the contrary situation.

In other words, the second half of MAL A 35 had to refer, not to the widow that it specifies, but to mistresses in general, and not to the man's property, although that is what the law says, but to the few baubles that her lover had given her.[4] By contrast, again, according to Driver and Miles, any gifts given by the groom to his bride remained his property and could be taken back at any time.[5] So, allegedly, Assyrian married women had fewer rights vis-à-vis their husbands than did their husband's mistresses. Taking into account MAL A 40, which does not allow illegally veiled prostitutes to have the jewelry given them by their customers confiscated, the legal status of a married woman in Assyria would have been lower than that of a prostitute.

But that was the case in English law, as reflected in the doctrine of coverture by which man and wife were considered to be legally one person and, as was snidely commented: "That one person was the man."[6] Incredibly, this doctrine was supposed to be reflection of the "fact" that: "So great a favorite is the female sex of the laws of England!" (Blackstone 1765: 445). Not surprisingly, then, the appalling lack of rights being fathered off onto Assyrian women in general and Assyrian widows in particular was not greatly bothersome to Driver and Miles.

Although unlike Driver and Miles, modern scholars have not grown up in the shadow of coverture, their view of the Middle Assyrian laws has not progressed much beyond them. Things are only somewhat better in Babylonia, where the long shadow of P. Koschaker and A. van Praag still falls across the field. On careful examination, it appears that the crux of the problem with our classical legacy is that it was based on an anthropological approach that allowed what was, in places, hilariously misinterpreted early Germanic and Roman law to act as a Procrustean bed to the ancient source material. Beginning over again from scratch produces a radically different perspective on women's rights (or lack thereof) in Babylonia and Assyria.

We, in our modern Western society, tend to think in terms of equality or inequality of rights. However, when dealing with parties that are, in fact, unequal, justice is hardly served by pretending a nonexistent parity. So, for example, eastern European

3. Driver and Miles (1935: 220–222). They do not attempt to explain why a widow with no male relatives to go to bat for her should receive less protection from the law than a first-time bride.

4. Driver and Miles (1935: 220–222). This is followed in Cardascia (1969: 182–184). Saporetti (1979: 17–20) avoids the entire problem by defining the widow as a woman *sui juris* due to lack of potential guardians in the form of her own or her former husband's male relatives. In systems of *manus* (or *mundium*), however, a woman can never be out of guardianship no matter what. She may, in these systems, be allowed to choose her guardian, but she still has one. For an explicit statement on this subject, see Rothair's Edict 204.

5. Driver and Miles (1935: 193–198, 198–205, 215). So also S. Lafont (2003: 541) following Cardascia (1969: 69).

6. For a full discussion, see Dogget (1992: 34–61).

immigrants with marginal command of English were by no means equal to the Chicago meat packing plants that employed them. Justice then, requires a certain amount of paternalism on the part of lawmakers or, to put it in ancient terms, the purpose of the law was to "protect the poor and the weak from oppression by the rich and powerful."

To put it differently, ancient Mesopotamia was inclined to justice rather than equality before the law when both desiderata could not be satisfied. This bias applies particularly to women because, in most societies, including our own, men and women are by no means equal in terms of potential earning power and, therefore, treating them as equals would, in many circumstances, actually be unjust.

Societies generally divide into those in which women are regarded as useless parasites and those in which women are a valued addition to the family. The classical legacy described bride-price marriage as "Kaufehe" and took it as reflecting a primitive level of civilization and/or mistreatment of women.[7] In fact, bride price is attested in the most advanced civilizations, such as the silk-producing regions of China, and reflects a high rather than a low cultural valuation placed on women. Something you want, you are willing to pay for (bride price); if it is junk, you pay somebody to take it off your hands (dowry).

By that measurement, Babylonia and Assyria rate light years above classical Athens (a dowry system with fully developed attitudes on the subject of women as parasites) but yet still fall short of Islamic law (a bride-price system). In other words, the laws of marriage in ancient Mesopotamia generally reflect neither a dowry system nor a bride-price system but one in which contributions to the new household are supposed to be made on both sides of the aisle. The payments incidental to a normal marriage, as given in the laws of Hammurabi (with Assyrian equivalents) are listed in table 19.1.

To the amazement and confusion of many, Hammurabi's laws (CH) and the Middle Assyrian laws (MAL) seem to be on one system and actual contracts and the so-called Neo-Babylonian laws (NBL) on another—not in terms of who gives what to whom but on the terms used to describe two of the payments.[8] The CH's and MAL's terms for the dowry and the husband's gift to support the bride after his death are reversed in the NBL and all contracts on the ground from all periods with one exception, and that is a Larsa marriage contract that uses the Sumerogram for *šeriktu* for the dowry (YOS 8.152, *apud CAD* A/3:103b). Since we are considering primarily the contents of the laws themselves, we shall simplify matters and avoid endless confusion by consistently using CH and MAL terminology even when referring to evidence drawn from the NBL and from contracts on the ground. So, henceforth we will be speaking of *biblu* or *zubullu*-bridal presents, *terḫatu*-bride-price, *šeriktu* or *širku*-dowry and *nudunnû*-widow's dower.[9]

7. For a discussion, see Driver and Miles (1935: 142–173); Westbrook (1988: 59–60); Kienast (2014: 73–83).

8. For a discussion of this problem, see Westbrook (1988: 24–28). Neo-Babylonian laws follow the convention of contracts because they are actually exercises used to train scribes who are going to have to write contracts.

9. *Pace* Roth (1989: 7–8), a dowry is not, in any culture on earth, including Roman law, a payment made to the husband by the bride or her agent acting on her behalf. Such payments may occur, but they are never classed as "dowry."

TABLE 19.1. Normal marriage chart 1: marriage payments.

| Payment | Giver | Recipient | Purpose |
|---|---|---|---|
| *biblu/zubullu* | Groom | Bride's father | The wedding feast/insurance of good faith on both sides |
| *terḫatu* | Groom | Bride's father | Equals the silver portion of the *biblu*; insurance of good faith; compensation for children (often passed on to the bride)[a] |
| *šeriktu/širku* | Bride's father | Bride | Her support; counterbalance to the *terḫatu* and *nudunnû* |
| *nudunnû* | Groom | Bride | Her support after his death |

[a] With Oelsner, Wells, and Wunsch (2003: 934) and *pace* Roth (1989: 11), the *biblu* is not some strange custom foreign to Babylonia introduced in the Neo-Babylonian period from Egypt or Persia. A portion of the groom's payments was taken up by the provisions for the wedding feast, the bride's responsibility in our culture. These perishables generally did not, for obvious reasons, have to be refunded after the wedding feast had been celebrated, which allows us to understand that UN §15; LI §29; CE §25; and CH §§160–161 are from before and CE §18 is from after this celebration.

Of these, the only really problematic payment is the *terḫatu*-bride-price. Assyriologists have tied themselves into knots trying to explain what the purpose of this could be, and have veered between the Skylla of "Kaufehe" and the Charybdis of denying any connection whatsoever between *terḫatu* and bride price.[10] Lost in the shuffle is the obvious fact, denied by both dictionaries, that etymologically *terḫatu* is from *reḫû*. Given the hair-raising custom of betrothal by act of intercourse with girls as young as three years old described by Maimonides, a desire to dissociate the term from anything to do with sexual intercourse is quite understandable.[11]

However, *reḫû* is not the usual word for sexual congress (*nâku*) but means specifically "to impregnate." Thus, a *terḫatu* would not be a "payment for right of intercourse" but a "payment for the right to impregnate." The simplest explanation is that, if a *terḫatu* was not paid, any children produced by the couple would belong to their mother (and her family) rather the man and his family. This is, essentially the difference, from the man's point of view, between prostitution, in which he pays for the right of sexual intercourse but has no claim on the prostitute's children, and marriage, which is engaged in precisely with a view to producing children.

This understanding of *terḫatu* brings CH §175 back into line with CT 48 53 (Westbrook 1988: 66–68), without a need for a law as literature or social status distinctions or Romanesque-turns-of-law explanations. If the slave himself paid the *terḫatu* (as in CH §175), then they were his children. If, however, the slave's master paid the *terḫatu* (as in CT 48 53) (Westbrook 1988: 123), all present and future children of the bride will have belonged to him, as stipulated in the document. Similarly, if a *qadištu* paid the *terḫatu* for a woman for her husband as in CT 48 57 (Westbrook 1982: 1:178) the children will legally have belonged to her and not to her spouse.

10. For a discussion, see Driver and Miles (1935: 142–173); Westbrook (1988: 59–60).

11. Code of Maimonides 4: *The Book of Women* (I. Klein 1972: III.11). The custom of extremely young child marriages may have been designed to allow crypto-Jews to decline marriage offers from neighboring Muslims without rendering themselves suspect in the process. A reply of, "So sorry, but she is already married" will have revealed nothing about the real reason for the refusal.

Since this was the sale of a woman's fertility and not the woman herself, it is hardly surprising that, in Babylonian marriage contracts, the amount of *terḫatu* is less than the going rate for slave girls.[12] Similarly a widow is less likely to produce lots (more) children than a newly minted bride and consequently should have gotten a smaller payment for her fertility, and indeed she does. Finally, given this reason for the payment, it is hardly surprising to see it so frequently returned to the new wife by her father as a sort of indirect dowry.

These arrangements were doubtless the norm for Assyria, although one would hardly know it from the Middle Assyrian laws. But, in ancient Near Eastern legal writings generally, no words are wasted on the obvious. This interpretation of *terḫatu* readily explains by what right the father-in-law can, in Assyria, exercise the levirate (MAL A 30, 33, 43). By the payment of *terḫatu*, he has bought his daughter-in-law's children, and can, therefore, do whatever it takes to produce them. If it is obvious that this is not going to happen before the marriage is consummated, the *terḫatu* has to be refunded, as specified in MAL A 43. Conversely, if a man has made his payments and his wife dies and his father-in-law refuses him a substitute in the form of one of his wife's sisters, he is entitled to his money back (MAL A 31). Moving forward in time, the part of the *mahr* (usually ten dirhems) that is to be paid up front under Islamic law by the husband to his wife is what entitles him to keep the children in case of divorce.

If marital payments were essentially identical, it does not necessarily follow that the position of women in society was identical in Assyria and Babylonia. It was in theory possible, but in practice unusual, for women to inherit property in any period in Babylonia. What this meant was that a woman went from being supported by her father or brothers to being supported by her husband and, consequently, the typical locus of residence for a married couple was in the husband's house.

Given that the husband, under these circumstances, was contributing more to the marriage than his wife, it was only fair that he should have had more rights in the marriage than she. Therefore, as in classical Athens where women were actually legally incapable of ownership of any substantial property, we might expect the husband to have a unilateral right of divorce. What this means is not only that a wife does not have to consent in order to be divorced but that a wife may not divorce her husband or, to put it differently, the husband has a unilateral right not to be divorced against his will.

This is what one might expect and, indeed, both the laws and private contracts directly reflect the differing rights of husband and wife under Babylonian law (*pace* Westbrook 1988: 79–83; 2003b: 389). In Hammurabi's laws, Babylonian husbands are said to "leave" (*ezēbu*) their wives, but the Babylonian wife is invariably said to "hate" (*zêru*) her husband.[13] The difference in language is not, as has been argued, a matter of rhetoric but of right. The hating party wants a divorce, the leaving party does not need to ask for one. And the hatred was not going to do the wife a great deal of good. Under Hammurabi's laws, a husband could not be forced to divorce his wife, even by the court, if he did not wish to do so.[14]

12. For some figures, see Driver and Miles (1935: 145). For the full range of attested bride prices, see Stol (2012: 131–167).

13. This is noted in Westbrook (1988: 22–23); see also CT 6 26a, *apud* Westbrook (1988: 117). He, however, insists that this is mere rhetoric and of no consequence.

14. The bad wife of CH §141 may be divorced or not divorced at the husband's discretion.

This did not, however, mean that a Babylonian wife without a right of divorce did not have some means of ridding herself of an abusive husband. On the contrary, as in classical Athens and later Islamic law, the wife was, at least in theory, allowed to appeal to the court for dissolution of her marriage.[15] Unlike a divorce, dissolution requires grounds, which may, in Islamic law, be no more than incompatibility. So too in Hammurabi's laws with the exception that an unhappy spouse literally risked her life by appealing to the court for assistance in this matter.[16] This places Babylonian law at a disadvantage not only with respect to Islamic law, as might be expected, but to that of classical Athens, where the wife could be prevented by her husband from applying to the court for a divorce but, as we know from model legal cases, was in no real danger of being killed even if caught in flagrante with another man.

Old Babylonian private contracts generally declined to take advantage of this remedy, such as it was, that allowed a woman safely to "hate" her husband. Instead, the penalty for a wife's hatred, fault or no fault, was death by drowning, as specified in the law for fault cases.[17] Alternatively, the wife might be thrown from a tower.[18] This is final proof, if further proof were needed, that the Babylonian husband had a unilateral right of divorce. It is not really freedom of speech unless you have freedom after the speech, and you cannot be said to have a right to divorce if you risk death by public execution in attempting to exercise it.

Forcing a man to support a wife whom he hates is hardly fair, but it is in nobody's interest to allow a husband to dump his bride as soon as he has gotten what he wanted either, so measures were taken both to discourage divorce and to ensure that the wife was, in fact, supported, both during and after her marriage. The principle is clearest in cases where the law really did not wish the husband to be divorcing his wife. Cases of the sort appear already in the laws of Lipit-Ishtar. A man wishes to jettison a wife in favor of a prostitute who has caught his fancy and against whom the wife has obtained an injunction to prevent his visiting her (LI §30). The law cannot prevent the husband from divorcing his wife but it does make him pay a divorce penalty and prevent him from marrying his mistress. The code of Eshnuna does everything in its power to prevent the divorce of a wife with children, stripping the husband of every shred of personal property, including the house.

Hammurabi's laws, as indeed do all the Babylonian legal codes, penalize the divorcing husband monetarily. They do not, however, allow themselves to actually forbid divorce except under the most extreme of circumstances, as in the case of the wife with *li'bu* (CH §148). The latter term, as we know from later medical texts, refers

15. With Driver and Miles (1952: 291–292, 299–303); and *pace* Westbrook (1988: 45–46, 81–82, 93; 2003b: 387), CH §§142–143 are not referring to an inchoate marriage, as if that would make any difference.

16. *Pace* Groneberg (1989), "binding and throwing into the water" is a reference to execution by drowning and not a reference to the water ordeal as CH §§108–110 and CH §129 make abundantly clear. A woman undergoing an ordeal "throws herself into the holy river" as in CH §132.

17. CT 48.50, *apud* Westbrook (1988: 122); CT 48 51, *apud* Westbrook (1988: 122–123); CT 48.55, *apud* Westbrook (1988: 123); BAP 89, *apud* Westbrook (1988: 127); BAP 90, *apud* Westbrook (1988: 127–128); PBS 8.2 252, *apud* Westbrook (1988: 129); PRAK I B 17, *apud* Westbrook (1988: 129–130); TIM 4 46, *apud* Westbrook (1988: 131); TIM 4 47, *apud* Westbrook (1988: 131); TLB 1 229, *apud* Westbrook (1988: 132); YOS 12 371, *apud* Westbrook (1988: 137).

18. CT 6 26a, *apud* Westbrook (1988: 117); CT 48.52, *apud* Westbrook (1988: 123); CT 48 56, *apud* Westbrook (1988: 124); VAS 8 4–5, *apud* Westbrook (1988: 134).

TABLE 19.2. Normal marriage chart 2: fate of marriage payments on divorce initiated by husband.

| Payment | Status |
|---|---|
| *terḫatu* | If turned over to the wife by her father, the *terḫatu* leaves with her (CH §138), otherwise divorce money instead (CH §§139–140, cf. §156); if she has been behaving badly, this is forfeit/does not need to be paid (CH §141) |
| *šeriktu/širku* | Refunded to the wife (CH §§137–138, cf. §156) |

to a specific type of fever (Scurlock and Andersen 2005: 29–32, 814]). Of the modern diseases that would present with the type of fever in question most would either have killed the patient or have responded to treatment within too short a time to have generated such a law. The sole exception is secondary syphilis. Such a wife was not going to produce children to support her; neither was she going to find another husband. So the law allowed the husband the right to set his sick wife aside in a separate house and to take another wife as an alternative to letting him divorce her.[19] If she was the one who wanted the divorce, however, the husband could send her away without having to pay the usual divorce penalty.

Penalizing the husband for divorcing his wife and allowing the wife to apply to the court for dissolution resulted in a potentially awkward situation. Insofar as women were allowed to terminate their marriages in Babylonia, they got considerably less than what they would have gotten if the husband had divorced them, all else being equal (no children involved); see tables 19.2 and 19.3 for a detailed listing.

This was more than fair, since whichever party wanted the termination of the marriage was forced to compensate the other for the rupture. And, no matter what happened, Hammurabi's laws attempted to ensure that a wife would have at least her dowry at the end of the day. Hammurabi law §141 does not give a Babylonian husband the right to help himself to his wife's dowry for bad behavior that does not explicitly include adultery or the theft that is conventionally read into the law by puzzled commentators (*pace* Westbrook 1988: 76–77; 2003a: 388). Even RS 17 159, which is a divorce of a wife on grounds of adultery, allows her to take her dowry with her when she leaves (Márquez Rowe 2003: 726). Certainly, there would be no greater penalty for simply "scattering" one's household and "belittling" one's husband.

Alalakh contracts envision the exact situation of CH §141 in the divorcing husband whose wife "pulls at his nose" (Márquez Rowe 2003: 709–710) and, although she loses the bride price, she gets to keep the dowry. We may understand from this last parallel that the bad bride of CH §141 has been doing what she could to annoy her husband into divorcing her with the obvious motive of collecting the extra payment due by a divorcing husband. The law punishes this rather underhanded tactic by giving the wife the divorce settlement to which she would have been entitled had she been the one to initiate proceedings (namely just her dowry) and/or by denying her the divorce altogether, at the husband's discretion. This also explains what is going on with CH §142–143.

19. Rothair's Edict 180 is hardly so charitable, allowing a man to dump a betrothed who has become leprous, mad, or blind in both eyes on the grounds that her illness must result from her "weighty sins."

TABLE 19.3. Normal marriage chart 3: fate of marriage payments on divorce initiated by wife.

| **Payment** | **Status** |
|---|---|
| *terḫatu* | If turned over to the wife by her father, forfeited and in any case no divorce money (CH §142) |
| *šeriktu/širku* | Taken with her by the wife (CH §§142, 149)[a] |

[a] Apparently this was also the case at Ugarit (Márquez Rowe 2003: 726–727).

The bad wife who ends up getting drowned has been trying to get a divorce payment by annoying her husband as in CH §141, and only when that tactic has failed has she appealed to the court. Driver and Miles (1952: 299–303) suggest that her refusal of conjugal rights also strengthens the presumption that her activities outside the house were of a sexual nature.

In practice, as we know from a lone Neo-Babylonian contract from Susa, the bride could, by prior agreement with her father or brothers, be allowed to buy her way out of the marriage by leaving her dowry behind her.[20] Provisions in Old Babylonian contracts that allow women to divorce their husbands on penalty of losing what are sometimes substantial amounts of property and/or their children point to similar possibilities for the earlier period.[21]

The absence of a right to divorce and the perils of appealing to a Babylonian court for dissolution will probably have meant that the most common way of solving marital problems in Hammurabi's Babylonia will have been for the unhappy wife to persuade her husband to let her go, usually by surrendering all or part of her dowry to him. Thus, it is not surprising to find wives (usually a widow with children and some property to bargain with) being allowed, by stipulation, to divorce husbands. This particular arrangement is also found in Islamic law.

Such was the usual situation in Babylonia. But suppose that the prospective wife was actually in a much stronger financial position than her prospective husband and, since women were legally capable of owning property, there is no reason this could not have happened. Fairness would then dictate that the husband, being now the weaker party, would be the one in a disadvantaged position and in need of such protection as the law cared to offer.

Indeed, a number of otherwise completely anomalous documents from the Old Babylonian period suggest that there were, in fact, situations in which husband and wife essentially changed places. So, for example, as we saw above, the Babylonian

20. Roth (1989: no. 34). Roth translates: "she will forfeit(?) her entire dowry in favor of Harri-menna, and thereby she will relinquish her means of support(?)." What the text says is: "she leaves her entire dowry at the disposal of Sharri-menna and thus she thwarts [*parāku*] the back of his neck." The latter expression is a bit odd, but no odder than the English expression "fire his ass," which is a rude colloquialism with intensive power for "to fire(!)." *Parāku* is used of breaking agreements, and in this case, the unhappy bride will have well and truly broken her relationship to Sharri-menna by the simple fact of leaving her dowry behind her when she leaves. The contract from Susa is the only known Neo-Babylonian contract that contemplates a wife divorcing her husband (Oelsner, Wells, and Wunsch 2003: 935).

21. ARN 37, *apud* Westbrook (1988: 112); BIN 7 173, *apud* Westbrook (1988: 116); PBS 8/2 155, *apud* Westbrook (1988: 128–129); cf. VAS 18 114, *apud* Westbrook (1988: 136) (she loses her daughter).

husband had the unilateral right to divorce his wife subject to the payment of divorce money. However, Greengus, Ischali 25 (*apud* Westbrook 1988: 126; see Westbrook 1988: 69) records a court settlement in which a woman is ordered to pay (divorce) money to her husband's father. Not only is it the wife and not the husband who pays, but the wife's hem is cut without any action being taken by the husband, and the final clause forbids the wife from remarrying her husband by uttering the formula: "You are my husband."[22] In Islamic law, a husband who divorces his wife may not remarry her unless she has been married to someone else in the meantime, so we are contemplating an exact reversal of what will have been the normal situation in Babylonia.

Again, in Babylonia, the couple resided in the husband's house, and the husband was able to oust his wife from it without having to pay any divorce money if she was the one who was at fault. However, in ITT II 2, 3547, the wife is said to be still living in her father's house, her husband is said to have mistreated her and she is separating herself from her marriage to him (NAM.DAM.NI.TA TÚG IB.DA.AN.UR) without having to pay a shekel.[23]

Once again, in Babylonia an unhappy wife might be prevented from terminating her marriage and/or be reduced to buying her way out of it by private stipulation. However, in CT 48 61, it is the husband who, in daring to attempt to divorce his slave wife is to be enslaved himself by the woman's mistress into whose house he has apparently entered.[24] Finally, in BE 6/2 40 and 47 ((*apud* Westbrook 1988: 114–115), a Babylonian husband is allowed to buy his way out of an unhappy marriage by refunding the *terḫatu*-bride-price that had been given to him by his wife on entry and by paying what is still called "divorce-money," although it functions more like an unhappy wife's dowry.

But what about Assyria? In so far as conventional wisdom will allow that, in one of the two cultures, a husband could divorce his wife and the wife only appeal to have her marriage dissolved, and in the other, both husband and wife had the right of divorce, prior prejudice insists that Babylonia must be the culture in which women have "real" rights and Assyria the one in which they do not.[25] However, as with so many other issues involving Assyria and Babylonia or Assur and Marduk, the sides of the debate may be perfectly drawn, but the assignment of sides is reversed from the actual situation on the ground.

In Assyria, women had the right to divorce their husbands, and this is reflected in contracts on the ground where the usual practice was for both parties to pay equal amounts on divorce.[26] This was possible in Assyria because of another difference

22. Insistence on referring to these as inchoate marriages, and correspondingly failing to apply the lessons that may be learned from them by taking the situation described as the exact reverse of normal makes nonsense of Westbrook (1988: 48–50), who argues for the absence of any *verba solemna* in Babylonian marriage (48–50). If you bound the hem to marry and cut the hem to divorce and you said, "You are not my wife" to divorce, you will certainly have said, "You are my wife" to marry. Note that the *verba solemna* were subsequently recognized in Westbrook (2003b: 387) (cf. Oelsner, Wells, and Wunsch 2003: 935) without, however, correcting misconceptions on the subject of inchoate marriage.

23. ITT II 2 3547: 22–23. See Koschaker (1924: 210–212).

24. *Apud* Westbrook (1988: 124–125). See Westbrook (1988: 79).

25. This is particularly clearly spelled out in Cardascia (1969: 67).

26. Kienast (2014: 81–83); S. Lafont (2003: 536). *Pace* Saporetti (1979: 7, 14–15), there is no reason other than prior prejudice to regard this situation as exceptional. All that is exceptional is that the bride's

between Assyria and Babylonia on the subject of women's rights. In Hammurabi's Babylonia, women were, in principle, only entitled to a dowry, which, with the exception of virgin priestesses, rarely included any substantial property.[27] In Assyria, by contrast, as we know from actual documents, women could (and did) receive inheritance shares equal to those of their brothers (S. Lafont 2003: 544; Saporetti 1979: 11–12; *pace* Driver and Miles 1935: 190, 238–239). Women could also inherit equal shares at Emar (Westbrook 2003a: 679–680), which had similarly equal rights of divorce subject to equal monetary penalties for both parties to a marriage (Westbrook 2003a: 670).

As in Babylonia (CH §§151–152 is very clear on this point), each party of an Assyrian married couple was, unless stipulated otherwise, responsible for the others' debts.[28] In Assyria, and not in Babylonia, this mutual responsibility was understood as "reverencing [*palāḫu*]" one another, as close to the idea of companionate marriage as you are likely to find anywhere in the world before modern times.[29]

What the system of equal payments amounted to was that, whoever initiated the divorce, the husband got back the *terḫatu*-bride-price, which in Assyria, as elsewhere generally, will have been turned over to the wife by her father, and did not have to give a *nudunnû*-widow's dower.[30] The wife, for her part got to keep her *širku*-dowry, making for a no-fault divorce and absolute equality between the spouses. This was the situation in Elephantine, whose military colony included refugees from the former Assyrian Empire. Whoever initiated the divorce, and women could do this, the bride price (*mohar*) that had been returned to the bride was forfeit, and the bride got to take her dowry with her when she left (Porten 2003: 863–881).

To put it differently, if the Assyrian wife wanted to leave with her *širku*-dowry, she had to refund her ex-husband the *terḫatu*-bride-price and forfeit the *nudunnû*-widow's dower. Conversely, if the husband wanted to get rid of her, he could pocket the *terḫatu*-bride-price and keep the *nudunnû*-widow's dower, but he had to refund his ex-wife her *širku*-dowry before he expelled her from his house. To avoid endless arguments about the amount due for either of these items, surviving contracts simply specify an amount of money to be paid by whoever institutes the divorce.[31] This could reflect the value of payments made by both parties at the marriage, or be set

parents have taken the precaution of making sure, by contract, that their daughter does not end up buying her way out of the marriage by agreeing to part with her dowry. This was already true in the Old Assyrian period (Veenhof 2003: 451; Kienast 2014: 81) and continued to be true in the Neo-Assyrian period (Radner 2003: 896). *Pace* Cardascia (1969: 67) and Radner (2003: 894), there is no reason other than prior prejudice to regard this situation as exceptional. It is remarkable that contract evidence for rights of divorce is only "exceptional" when the contracting parties are Assyrian.

27. Westbrook (2003b: 395). This seems to have been the situation also at Ugarit (Márquez Rowe 2003: 730) and in the Neo-Babylonian period (Oelsner, Wells, and Wunsch 2003: 940).

28. It is otherwise stipulated in Neo-Assyrian marriage contracts CTN 2 no. 247 rev. 11′–13′ and ND 2316 7–13 (Parker 1954: 40).

29. Quotation from Röllig (1969–1970: 129–130). See *CAD* P, s.v. "*palāḫu*," 5g, which, of course, carefully distances the Assyrian examples from the meaning of the word in other contexts. Note also the phrase: "like a bride whom they love" in MAL A 46 miscited (as 4B) in Saporetti (1974: 4). Of course, this is taken as "exceptional."

30. With Cardascia (1969: 194–195) and *pace* S. Lafont (2003: 536). This is reflected in the fact that, in MAL A 29, the *širku*-dowry is separately listed from "whatever she has brought from the house of her father" and that, in MAL A 38, the divorcing husband's *terḫātu* is cleared "for the woman."

31. That these payments are equal shows, if there were any doubt on this score, that the presents given by the two Assyrian families were intended to offset one another.

at a lesser or greater amount as desired to make it easier or harder for the marriage to be terminated. Where only small amounts of money were involved it would not have been necessary to go to the expense of having made a written copy of the verbal contract which is presumably why we have so few marriage contracts from Assyria.

Assyrian law will have had less of a problem than Babylonian with wifely maneuvering, since a wife could freely divorce her husband, and would receive the same amount whoever initiated the divorce. This is certainly equality, but it is not necessarily justice, since one party or the other might actually be at fault in a divorce. Old Assyrian marriage contracts attempt to address this situation by adding to the usual penalties on divorce by either party a payment for *šillatu* (cursing/slander) by the wife and, conversely, for "mistreatment" by the husband (Veenhof 2003: 454). The infamous "wife beating" statute (MAL A 59) defines what constitutes mistreatment by laying down what, exactly, a husband could do to his wife by way of domestic discipline without having "done anything actionable [*arnu*]." Anything in excess of this standard, as we know from these Old Assyrian contracts, will have resulted in compensation paid by the husband to the wife, a similar solution to that of Islamic law for the same problem.[32]

The wife may also have been able to get a court-ordered dissolution of the marriage as in Babylonia. This is suggested by the parallel between MAL A 59 (wife beating) and MAL A 44, which involves a pledge. Both laws set standards for the amount of abuse to be tolerated in the relationship, and it is the same standard. A pledge who was mistreated in excess of this standard would surely have been able to obtain a court-ordered release. This would be the equivalent of a wife being allowed to leave her husband's house with her *terḫatu*-bride-price and *širku*-dowry (the value of the debt that was being forfeited by the mistreating creditor). The Assyrian husband could potentially have had recourse to the courts for wifely slander as well, although one can imagine the fingers pointed behind his back if he did so.

In any case, even if the Assyrian husband was the one to initiate the divorce, he needed to do no more than disentangle and refund the dowry and/or pay the amount to which he had agreed on his contract. If he wanted there to be no unpleasantness on this subject, he could give her a gift above and beyond this amount, but Assyrian law, unlike Babylonian, did not require him to do so. It is for this reason that MAL A 37 states that the divorcing husband does not have to give divorce money to his wife: "If a man leaves his wife, if he wishes, he may give her something. (If) he does not wish to give her something, she may go out empty." (MAL A 37).[33]

32. On this subject, early Germanic law held similar views: "No man shall strike his wife at the table or at an ale feast; if he strikes her in the sight of assembled men, he shall pay her such an atonement as he could demand in his own case; and the same the second time and the third time, [if he repeats the offense]. Olaf: After that she has the right to leave him, taking with her the husband's gift and property set aside to balance the marriage portion." (Norwegian Laws, Gulathing, 54)

33. Cardascia (1969: 67) interprets this as meaning that the Assyrian husband has an absolute right of divorce, as opposed to the Babylonian conditional one, meaning that he did not have to pay divorce money (cf. also Saporetti 1979: 10). In fact, legal systems that give the husband a right of divorce by simple declaration also make him pay for the privilege—otherwise there would be very few, if any, married couples. So, e.g., the "freely" divorcing Muslim husband is required to pay his ex-wife her *mahr*, to surrender any property that she brought with her or that he has deeded to her in the course of the marriage, and to continue to support her during her three-month waiting period. In the hill country of Pakistan, it is the custom of a

By stipulation, as we again know from an actual Neo-Assyrian contract, it was possible to have the best of both worlds and go by Assyrian rules allowing free divorce for both parties and Babylonian rules that made the husband pay extra if he was the one who wanted the divorce:[34] "If F 'hates' M, [it, i.e., the dowry] ⌜returns⌝ (to F); if M 'hates' F, he doubles it and gives (it to F)."[35]

With MAL A 37 we are, as usual, betrayed by the expressionistic minimalism of the laws. It would have been obvious that the dowry went out with the woman, since this was not, in any sense, in the husband's gift, so why bother to mention it?[36] For the duration of the marriage, the Assyrian husband and his brothers not only did not own, but could not lay claim to, the wife's *širku*-dowry, the *terḫatu*-bride-price returned to by her father, or the *nudunnû*-widow's dower provided her by his father when she entered his house, with one apparent exception: "If a woman has entered her husband's house, her *širku* and whatever she has brought from the house of her father and/or what her father-in-law gave her when she entered is cleared for her children; the children of her father-in-law may not claim (it). But if her husband *i-pu-ag-ši*, he may give (it) to whichever of his children he pleases." (MAL A 29)

The first half of this law is perfectly clear: a woman's dowry, her returned bride price, and her widow's dower, or other gifts from her father and father-in-law are held in trust for her children. Conventional wisdom, however, generally interprets MAL A 29 to mean that the husband has the right to help himself to his wife's property according to his whim. The understanding is that the reservation of marital property

man to put all of his property in his wife's name in order to avoid having his brothers claim it back after his death, leaving his children penniless. Here, if a man attempted to exercise his right to a divorce, he would be, as we were told by our friend Imran, "screwed."

34. This was the exact situation at Alalakh, namely Assyrian equal rights of divorce and Babylonian extra payment by the divorcing husband (Márquez Rowe 2003: 709–710). The Neo-Assyrian contract in question involves a mother-in-law who is a *šakintu*. These women were generally the daughters or other female relatives of tributary kings, so it is possible that this *šakintu*, whose name is "servant of Ashtarte," was keen to ensure for her daughter the same sort of right of termination of marriage that was customary in her ancestral home.

35. Postgate (1976: no. 14) restoring [*ta-tu*]-*ra-ma* in line 48. *Pace* Radner (2003: 896), the *šakintu*'s daughter is not going to lose her dowry if she wants a divorce. The most curious variant, which may reflect Egyptian rather than Assyrian law since all parties seem to be Egyptians, is TIM 11 14 in which a woman is purchased for marriage from her father/brother for a half-mina of silver. The woman is to be supported during the husband's lifetime by being given the income (from a prebend) of Ishtar of Arbela for herself and her children. This part of the agreement, at least, sounds like creeping Egyptian custom since, in Assyrian law, gifts by a husband to a wife were intended to support her after his death and would never have been valid only for his lifetime. Similarly Egyptian-sounding is the striking informality of the divorce section of the document (Manning 2003: 836–837). A broken clause provides for the wife paying to be able to freely leave his house to the tune of a broken amount of refined silver, presumably the half mina that was her bride-price equivalent. Since she is to enjoy her income for her husband's lifetime, she will not lose her dowry equivalent, so the two parties will have divided the conjugal property (the silver plus the prebendary income) equally between them. The converse situation, in which the husband initiates the divorce, ought to come out the same way under Assyrian law, with the ex-wife refunding the bride-price equivalent and then being allowed to keep her dowry equivalent, for her lifetime this time, and with possibility of passing it on to her children. Instead, the wife is to pay ten shekels to her husband as her "departure money," only a third of the original "purchase price." Again, this would appear to be an Egyptian custom, which required the wife to refund half of the conjugal property if she divorced him and required the husband to pay a supplemental amount if he was the one to initiate the divorce (Manning 2003: 836–837). In this case, the supplemental payment will have been twenty shekels, leaving only ten shekels to be refunded.

36. On this point, see also S. Lafont (2003: 542) following Cardascia (1969: 192).

for the wife and her children of the first half of the law only applies if the husband does not exercise the right allegedly given him by the second half of the law to deprive his wife of her possessions by force (and violence).[37]

G. Cardascia, who interprets MAL A 37 as reflecting the husband's absolute right to a divorce, understands the last sentence in MAL A 29 to refer to the husband's further privilege that, if he found fault with his wife, he could "drive her out," helping himself to her dowry into the bargain.[38] This is quite impossible. The Middle Assyrian laws lay out in great detail what can (and cannot) happen to a wife who has offended her husband in any conceivable way, including general annoyance, and appropriation of her dowry figures nowhere among the possible sanctions; Roman law is irrelevant to the issue at hand (*pace* Cardascia 1969: 163). In the late Republic, the husband could indeed retain part of his adulterous wife's dowry. However, the object of this retention was not to punish her but to support her children, who stayed with him at divorce.[39] This means that the adulterous Roman wife's children got her dowry even in this situation, whereas the Assyrian wife's children are allegedly being deprived in MAL A 29.

Driver and Miles (1935: 211) suggested alternative is that the husband "survives" his wife. This is invoking once again the English common law rules of coverture. The suggestion is effectively nullified by LI §24; CH §§162, 167, 171, 173–174; and NBL §13. By these laws, marital property goes to the wife's children, and not the husband's children if he does indeed survive her.

Translations of the passage have always tiptoed around the fact that, in the final clause, the object of the verb *puāgu* is feminine singular, and therefore refers to the woman. When applied to persons, *puāgu* means: "to kidnap or abduct."[40] So, a correct translation of MAL A 29 would read: "If a woman has entered her husband's house, her *širku* and whatever she has brought from the house of her father and/or whatever her father-in-law gave her when she entered is cleared for her children; the children of her father-in-law may not claim (it). But if her husband abducted her, he may give (it) to whichever of his children he pleases." (MAL A 29)

Marriage by capture is a phenomenon of all societies in which arranged marriages are the norm (Scurlock 2006: 61–103). Because parental consent is not, in this case, necessary; indeed, the usual context is when the boy has not been allowed to marry the girl of his dreams, there is a certain amount of romanticism attached to this custom. Late Roman law was very fierce in punishing all parties to such marriages. Nonetheless, it was the custom for a Roman groom to pretend to abduct the bride so as to ensure, by a form of love magic, that the couple would be happy together. In most societies, the problem of irregular unions is handled by a post facto legitimation of the

37. S. Lafont (2003: 542), citing also Postgate, Saporetti, Cardascia, Borger, and Roth. Ebeling and Driver and Miles part company with the rest of conventional wisdom on this issue (see Cardascia 1969: 161–163 for discussion).

38. Cardascia (1969: 67, 70, 161–164, 191–192). Similarly Cuq (1922: 47; 1929: 435–436), Saporetti (1979: 11–12). For a discussion, see Driver and Miles (1935: 210–211).

39. The ration was one-sixth of the dowry for each child up to three meaning that, under no circumstances did he keep more than half of the dowry (Nicholas 1962: 88).

40. In other words, it refers to people being brought forcibly in, quite the opposite of the "driving away" of Cardascia's translation. Even accepting the mistranslation still does not yield divorce for cause; there is nothing in "driving away" that speaks either of a divorce or wifely misconduct, and special pleading (Cardascia 1969: 70, 163) will not make it so.

situation whereby the parties are eventually married, often after one or more children have been born.

Even so, this is not quite a normal marriage, and usually has consequences for the parties involved. So, in rural Turkey, such marriages do not require the usual presents to be exchanged.[41] This was clearly not the case in Assyria, but there were consequences for the children of the union, and it is they, and not the wife, who are the ones who are potentially losing property in this law. "But if her husband abducted her, he may give (her property) to whichever of his children he pleases (after she dies)" (MAL A 29). In a normal situation in which there was more than one wife, each child would have had a right to inherit from his/her mother. "If a woman has entered her husband's house, her *širku* and whatever she has brought from the house of her father and/or whatever her father-in-law gave her when she entered is cleared for **her** children" (MAL A 29 [emphasis added]).

As for why the children of the irregular union have lost this right, it is to be remembered that the parents were unmarried when one or more of the children was conceived. This means that they preceded the marital gifts and were not, therefore, entitled to benefit from them. Note that nothing said that they could not inherit their mother's property, but they were not entitled to do so.

The situation with the woman's jewelry in MAL A 25–26, and MAL A 38 is a bit more complex.

> If a woman is still living in her father's house and her husband is dead, the brothers of her husband are undivided, and she has no children, the undivided brothers of her husband may take whatever jewelry her husband put on her that has not gotten lost. Whatever remains they shall make the gods pass by, prove (it) and take (it). They shall not be subjected to the water ordeal or an oath. If a woman is still living in her father's house and her husband is dead, whatever jewelry her husband put on her, if there are children by her husband, they may take (it). If there are no children by her husband, she herself may take (it). (MAL A 25–26)

> If a woman is still living in her father's house and her husband has left her, he may take the jewelry that he himself put on her; he may not claim the *terḫatu* that he brought. It is cleared for the woman. (MAL A 38)

As usual, the conventional interpretation of these laws is that Assyrian rulings on this subject reflect the retention of ownership by the husband of any gifts given to the wife.[42] However, it is an odd sort of ownership indeed since the woman is somehow not responsible for the loss of what is allegedly her husband's property (Cardascia 1969: 69).

41. "By *kız kaçırma*, a man avoids costly bridewealth gifts to the woman and her family, and the woman's family avoid the expenses of a village wedding, which are considerable." For full details, see Starr (1978: 186–189 [no. 24]).

42. So, e.g., Driver and Miles (1935: 193–205); Cardascia (1969: 69, 152–158, 192–196); Saporetti (1979: 11–12); S. Lafont (2003: 541–542). Saporetti (1979: 11–12) uses this to "prove" that Assyrian women had no property rights. More subtly, Cuq (1922: 47–48; 1929: 436) regards these gifts as revocable.

Also to be noticed is that the laws are very specific that the jewelry that is being taken away are items given to the wife by the now deceased husband, not items she bought herself or that were given her by her father, and the husband's brothers have to prove that the jewelry is theirs and cannot simply take whatever the wife has with her. Under English law of coverture, a married woman could own nothing, not even her dresses and jewelry, and that regardless of their ultimate origin, so there should have been no fuss about proving anything.

The key, I believe, is to recognize that, in these (and other Middle Assyrian laws) a married woman, with children and a deceased husband no less, is still living in her father's house. This is not, to put it mildly, the normal situation, as envisaged in Hammurabi's laws, in which the husband continues to live in his father's house and his wife moves in with him.

P. Koschaker and É. Cuq took this striking difference in the location of the wife after marriage seriously, dividing Assyrian marriage into two types. The normal marriage where the wife went to her husband's house seemed to Cuq (1922: 47–49; 1929: 435–438) to resemble an ancient Roman marriage with *manus* (wife is under husband's absolute control). The other type, he compared to Roman marriages without *manus* (wife remains under her father's absolute control). Koschaker (1933: 84–87) made a similar division, but was thinking more in terms of the Muntehe of early Germanic law, which he understood, incorrectly, as having as its "most important consequence" that the husband had an exclusive right of divorce.[43] In fact, there was no such thing in early Germanic law as a marriage in which the husband did not purchase his wife's *mundium*.[44] These people being Christian, there was also no such thing as divorce. What you could get was a separation (living apart with no right of remarriage as long as the ex-spouse lived). Taking separation as a calque for divorce still does not save Koschaker's model since, in early Germanic law, marriages could end in separation by right of the wife where separation was free.[45] Gifts given to the wife by the husband would be forfeited but, if she had grounds, she could take these also with her when she left.[46] On the other side of the coin, the husband had to pay extra if he was the one

43. See Westbrook (1995: 425–426), who summarizes Koschaker's opinions drawn from forty years-worth of articles on the subject.

44. When a woman marries, her guardianship is purchased by her husband (Alamannic Laws, L.2, LIII.2; Rothair's Edict, 165, 183, 187–188, 190, 200, 214–216; Liutprand, 14.VIII, 30.I, 57.IIII, 114.XI, 126.X, 127.XI; Skeltana Riucht, VIII, IX, X; Norwegian Laws, Gulathing, 25, 27; note Aistulf, 15.VI).

45. "If she wishes to depart freely, let her take what she legally obtained. Let the bedding be equally divided" (Pactus Legis Alamannorum, XXXIV.3).

46. "The gift that is given to a woman shall remain her lawful property, no matter how the marriage is terminated. Olaf: The husband shall [by payment of mund] acquire [control of] all the goods that come with a maiden, but for every ora an ora shall be given [by him] in return. But of a widow's property [he acquires] one-half. This balancing of mund and marriage portion shall remain in force in all cases except two: if the wife dies without children or if she leaves [her husband] without cause. Both: No man shall strike his wife at the table or at an ale feast; if he strikes her in the sight of assembled men, he shall pay her such an atonement as he could demand in his own case; and the same the second time and the third time, [if he repeats the offense]. Olaf: After that she has the right to leave him, taking with her the husband's gift and property set aside to balance the marriage portion. And if a man wishes to separate from his wife, let him announce the termination of the marriage so [distinctly] that each one can hear the other's voice, and let him have witnesses present" (Norwegian Laws, Gulathing, 54).

to initiate the separation.[47] If there were children and the wife took them, she got half of the joint property. If he kept them, she still got an heir's share in his estate.[48]

The spectacular exception to these rules of free separation is the Burgundian Code, where the wife attempting this was "drowned in mire."[49] Not that this helps Koschaker's model a great deal since the best that the husband could achieve by way of separation under these laws was to forfeit all his property. That is unless he successfully accused his wife of adultery, witchcraft, or violation of graves, in which case he not only got a separation but could get her punished into the bargain.[50] If she was executed, he could even remarry, making this a real divorce. A rash of laws slapping husbands on the wrist for falsely accusing their wives of these three crimes suggest that, in Burgundy, this was the preferred method for husbands to get rid of burdensome wives.

Koschaker's contrasting *muntfreie Ehe*, which he saw in the women continuing to reside in their father's houses, was supposed not to involve the payment of a *terḫatu*, an easily falsifiable statement. Marriage by purchase seemed an abhorrent concept, at least in application to Hammurabi, and Koschaker's categories, even as he defined them, did not really work out well. Current conventional wisdom, therefore, has it that there was only one type of marriage in Assyria, namely the one that was essentially equivalent to a Roman marriage *cum manu*.[51] This, of course, presupposes that all the references in the laws to a woman living in her father's house are simply "exceptional."[52]

It is also specified in a number of laws that the woman is living in her husband's house. Was this, too, "exceptional"? For Driver and Miles, yes, since it allowed them to use MAL A 28 and MAL A 35, which envisage a widow moving into a man's house (without benefit of marriage) or, more precisely, it allowed them to use the first half of MAL A 35 to support their coverture for widows theory. So what is impolitely referred to in America as "shacking up" is, according to Driver and Miles, the normal

47. "If a husband dismisses his wife, let him compensate her with 40 solidi, and have no [more] authority over her guardianship [*mundium*], and return all things to her that she legally obtained. If he keeps anything, let this woman have the authority over the property and let him pay 12 solidi. Concerning anything as small as a fibula [*nastula*, brooch], which is legally hers, let the husband swear or return it." (Pactus Legis Alamannorum, XXXV.1–3)

48. "If she wishes to go away with the children, she is to have half the goods" (Aethelberht, 79). "If the husband wishes to keep [the children], [she is to have the same share] as a child" (Aethelberht, 80).

49. "If any woman leaves (puts aside) her husband to whom she is legally married, let her be smothered in mire" (Burgundian Code, XXXIV.1).

50. "If anyone wishes to put away his wife without cause, let him give her another payment such as he gave for her marriage price and let the amount of the fine be 12 solidi. If by chance a man wishes to put away his wife, and is able to prove any of these three crimes against her, that is, adultery, witchcraft, or violation of graves, let him have full right to put her away: and let the judge pronounce the sentence of the law against her, just as should be done with criminals. But if she admits none of these three crimes, let no man be permitted to put away his wife for any other crime. But if he chooses, he may go away from the home, leaving all household property behind, and his wife with their children may possess the property of her husband" (Burgundian Code, XXXIV.2–4).

51. See Cardascia (1979: 63–64). For a complete discussion of this issue, see Driver and Miles (1935: 134–173).

52. Driver and Miles (1935: 138); similarly Saporetti (1979: 8). Saporetti (1979: 8–9) manages to find no less than nine types of marriage in Assyria, none of which have anything to do with the woman's continuing residence in her father's house.

Assyrian marriage and all other formulations, whether the woman is said to be living in her father's house, or entering/living in that of her husband refer to "exceptional" situations.[53]

Some scholars take references to a woman living in her father's house as an "inchoate marriage."[54] However, there is nothing inchoate about a marriage that has produced children and whose survivor is called a widow.[55] Others simply insist that, in this alleged *manus*-marriage analogue in which the woman is completely under her husband's control, she could nonetheless continue to reside in her father's house for her entire life.[56]

This is simply impossible. A woman who was actually completely under the authority of her husband, as the patrician Roman in a *manus* marriage, could not make loans and purchase property on her own account, as Assyrian women are attested doing.[57] Neither could she spend more than three nights a year away from her husband's bed, no matter with whom she was staying, without destroying her husband's *manus*.[58]

That is by no means all that is wrong with the Roman model. Roman patrician marriages with *manus* could not end in divorce. Even in marriages without *manus*,

53. Driver and Miles (1935: 138–142, 190). It is hard to convey the utter confusion of an argument that manages to describe the exact type of marriage among modern Arabs and ancient Greeks, a type whose existence in Assyria it consistently denies, and has as its trump card the alleged absence of any such custom of *errēbu*-marriage in Babylonia. Even if true, this would hardly be relevant to the Assyrian case.

54. So, e.g., Driver and Miles (1935: 139, 159, 173–186); Westbrook (1988: 21, 27, 34–38, 49). This incorrect assumption has made a bit of a mess of arguments on the subject of *nudunnû* (Driver and Miles 1935: 198–205; Westbrook 1988: 24–28). Even more puzzling is the idea that the wife getting a court-ordered annulment in CH §142 is "inchoately married" and still living in her father's house (Westbrook 1988: 45–46, 81–82, 93), although the law is very clear that she is being allowed to return to her father's house which she must have left for this clause to make any sense. For more discussion, see Driver and Miles (1952: 299–303).

55. This is the situation contemplated in MAL A 33.

56. Radner (2003: 895) ("total control" by the husband of the wife); similarly Cardascia, (1969: 63); S. Lafont (2003: 533). What Radner ignores are numerous documents from the Neo-Assyrian period in which palace women buy tracts of real estate and slaves and make loans to other women or unrelated men, all with no hint that authorization of any kind was required before they could do this (Kwasman and Parpola 1991: nos. 81–99, 247–256; Mattila 2002: nos. 8–14, 174–177). For continuing to reside in her father's house, see Driver and Miles (1935: 204); Cardascia (1969: 63–64, 168–169); S. Lafont (2003: 536). In the last case, this is one of a series of misapplications of comparative material. Anyone who has the right to alienate his land by outright sale is not a "feudal tenant" (S. Lafont 2003: 524) and the difference between a "patrician" and a "plebian" is not that the latter were an "intermediate class of semi-free persons" (534). There were, in any case, no patricians or plebians in Assyria (*pace* Driver and Miles 1935: 15–17, 181–182 and passim) and if there had been, there would be two types of marriage, the patrician *manus* marriage and the plebian non-*manus* marriage, a possibility that Driver and Miles (1935: 134–173) hotly deny.

57. S. Lafont (2003: 533). Cardascia (1969: 70–71) recognizes this as a problem and has to insist that the women in these contracts are unmarried. This would make sense if the Assyrian women were supposed to be under English law, where adult women had rights to property when single adults but lost them when they "became one person" with their husbands, only to regain them again after they were widowed. Cardascia's (1969: 63) Roman-reconstructed Assyrian women went from the *manus* of their fathers to the *manus* of their fathers-in-law and eventually husbands. Under no circumstances, married or unmarried would they ever have been able engage in contracts on their own authority. So the model fails, or would if hard evidence from contracts were allowed to contradict it.

58. Cuq (1922: 49; 1929: 437) was well aware of this, and was able to use MAL A 24, which specifies that a woman living in her husband's house is not to spend more than three or four nights away from home without consequences to follow in support of his *manus* marriage thesis. Unfortunately for this connection, the consequences of sojourning are mutilation of the runaway wife and the woman who seems to be orchestrating her escape, punishments of a sort to suggest that potential adultery and not mere absence from the domicile was the actual concern of the law.

a husband could only divorce his wife after the death of his father. As if to add insult to injury, so long as that father lived, a husband could be forced to divorce his wife whether he wished to or not. Late Roman law muddied the waters still further by not allowing a husband to forgive his adulterous wife, prosecuting him as a pimp if he dared to do so. Instead, there was a mandatory divorce, and the bad wife was then to be relegated to an island for life. On the other side of the coin, the right of the husband to kill his adulterous wife whom he has caught in flagrante and without a prior trial, corresponds to no marital right of a Roman husband with, or without, *manus*.

If it does not look like a duck, does not quack like a duck, and cannot swim, it is not a duck, bird though it might be. We need to abandon once and for all the completely inappropriate application of a peculiarly Roman institution that has no analogues outside of Rome, as the Romans themselves noted.[59] We are not to be confused by the fact that a number of features of late Roman law are strikingly close to that of Mesopotamia. So, for example, in the later empire, there appears something called the *donatio ante nuptias* which sounds suspiciously like a *nudunnû* (Nicholas 1962: 89–90). The fact that it is in direct contradistinction to a basic principle of Roman law forbidding gifts between husband and wife, as well as the lateness of its appearance on the scene, point strongly to influence on Roman law of the law of conquered populations, particularly in the eastern part of the empire.[60]

There were indeed two types of marriage in ancient Mesopotamia generally (not just in Assyria), as well as in Egypt and among the Hittites. In Assyria as revealed in the Middle Assyrian laws, there was an apparently more common type of marriage in which the woman moved in with her husband, and a second type in which the husband moved in with his wife. As for why this needed to happen, there were certain situations in which the normal arrangement would not have been appropriate. If a man had no sons, it was possible to make a daughter one's heir. To avoid extinguishing the family line, a man could then be found willing to become part of the bride's family and to move into her father's house. We even have a term (*errēbūtu*) to describe this situation.[61]

We may readily understand what implications this change of location might have had for the newly married couple by taking up an old suggestion of Benno Landsberger (1968: 59, with other possibilities) after K. Balkan (1948: 147–152, summarized by Friedrich 1959: 96; cf. Gordon 1981: 155) that the odd marriage was equivalent to the Turkish custom of *içgüveylik*. This is a very old custom indeed in what is now Turkey, and is laid out in some detail in the Hittite laws and myths, which are more or less contemporary with the Middle Assyrian laws.

59. "There are few Roman institutions which differ so fundamentally from their modern counterparts as marriage." (Nicholas 1962: 80).

60. This will have been from Syria rather than Egypt, since it is intended to support the wife after his death and not for the duration of the marriage.

61. This custom is attested at Nuzi in the form of adoption contracts in which a man is adopted for marriage into his wife's family (Gordon 1981: 155–160; Zacagnini 2003: 589). A similar practice appears at Emar (Westbrook 2003a: 668–669). The relevance of *errēbu*-marriage for the Middle Babylonian period in Babylonia has been suggested by Gurney (1983: 136–138) and Slanski (2003: 502). The Neo-Babylonian period shows no evidence for *errēbu*-marriages. A curious pattern of naming children after both sets of grandparents might suggest that a compromise had been worked out in which the couple resided in the husband's house but the children produced by the union were divided between the two families, some being part of (and receiving dowries or inheritances from) one of the families and the rest from the other.

The Hittites called this an *antiyant* marriage and the way they handled the situation was to simply treat the husband who moved in as a sort of wife. Similar customs may be located in the early laws (UN §15; LI §29) and, as we have seen, in the odd Old Babylonian document (see above), although the details are much more sketchily presented by comparison with a wealth of information in Hammurabi's laws about women who moved in with their husbands.[62]

Assyrian law has much more to say about the *errēbu*-marriage situation but less clarity on the subject of the normal marriage. Indeed here, as in other places, one gets the impression, noted already by Driver and Miles (1935: 15), that Hammurabi's laws were the default rulings for Assyrian law, which might account for the fact that the largest number of copies of these laws were actually made in the Neo-Assyrian period.

There is also a distinct possibility that such marriages were more common in Assyria than in Babylonia. This follows naturally from differences in women's rights between the two neighbors. We may note that, in urbane and philosophically rich Athens, women were under guardianship and had no property rights. In order to obtain a dissolution of their marriages, they had to take refuge with the court and hope that their husband did not, like Alcibiades, prevent them from making their case by carrying them bodily back home again. The locus of the marriage was the husband's house and this was, in the case of women with no brothers, a close relative (usually an uncle) whom she was forced to marry. Militaristic Sparta, by contrast, was the closest that ancient Greece came to freedom for women as well as men. Particularly shocking to Aristotle, otherwise a great admirer of Sparta, was the fact that Spartan women were allowed to inherit property. The locus of marriage was, according to our accounts, the woman's house to which the husband (or one of his mess mates) paid only occasional visits. These are extreme examples, to be sure, and do not really convey either Assyrian or Babylonian custom. They do, however, demonstrate the close correlation between enhanced rights for women and the chances of a married couple living in the bride's family house.

If the Hittite model had been followed in this anomalous situation, what would have happened is that the man would essentially have become a wife with all the normal payments and obligations reversed.[63] This is apparently, as we have seen, precisely what happened in Babylonia. The exact reversal of husbandly and wifely roles explains why no special provisions exist in Hammurabi's laws. As with medical texts, masculine nouns do not necessarily imply masculine gender. If it was the woman who was now the husband and the man the wife, the law could simply be applied as written.

In Assyria, however, a marriage was understood as a balanced bundle of rights and duties in which both parties were entitled to children, the woman to support, and the man to obedience. In principle, having the man move in with the woman should have meant that he was entitled to support and she to obedience. That is indeed what seems to have happened with widows exercising their right to do as they pleased without

62. *Pace* B. Lafont and Westbrook (2003: 202–203), these are not references to the groom coming into his father-in-law's house to celebrate the wedding. The wedding feast has, at this point, not yet taken place and will not do so for some time yet. See above.

63. At Emar, the divorced adopted son-in-law was the one who had to leave the house, apparently with children in tow (Westbrook 2003a: 670–671). A sort of male levirate seems also to have been a possibility (Westbrook 2003a: 671).

worrying about the formalities of marriage, producing that dramatic shift in property ownership of parties to a relationship depending on the location of the conjugal household that gave Driver and Miles such grief: "If a widow enters a man's house, whatever (and) as much as she brings with her, all of it, belongs to her husband. But if he enters to the woman, whatever (and) as much as he brings with him, all of it, belongs to the woman." (MAL A 35)

This ruling was probably, as much as anything, a practical measure since, without benefit of contract, it would have been extremely difficult to determine who, exactly, had owned what before the couple began to live together.[64] To avoid endless lawsuits, it was simplest to rule in favor of the party in whose house the couple happened to be living. MAL A 35 also reveals what might be termed the default setting of Assyrian law. And that default is not that the man gets the woman's property on any possible pretext but the quite contrary proposition that, no matter what happens, there is to be absolute equality between the sexes before the law.

It would seem that, in Assyria, (sexual) freedom was indeed "just another word for nothing left to lose." This was, however, never intended to be a permanent arrangement. Even widows exercising their right to what we might term "living in sin" had only two years of complete freedom before they were subject to what we now call common law marriage (MAL A 34). At this point, normal marriage rules will have applied, requiring wifely obedience and husbandly support. The widow-now-wife-again will then have been able to receive gifts from her lover-now-husband and/or to claim part of her new husband's property to support her after his death.

And, on the other side of the coin, Assyrians apparently balked at the idea of a kept man except as a default setting for irregular relationships. Or, to put it differently, they did not wish to encourage men to evade their obligation to support their wives simply because they had married up in the social hierarchy and moved in with her parents. In Babylonia, this sort of thing was a very rare problem; in Assyria this may have been common enough for the problem of what is colloquially referred to in America as "gold-digging" to become apparent.

That a woman would be bossing a man about was not the problem, as may readily be seen by Assyrian acceptance of the custom of levirate marriage (MAL A 43). Levirate marriage has a bad reputation but it has been argued, with justice, that the intent is not merely to ensure the continuation of the male line but also to provide the woman with children and thus to ensure her support.[65] The result of the practice will also have

64. On this point, see also Cuq (1922: 48; 1929: 439).

65. For levirate marriage having a bad reputation, see, e.g., Cardascia (1969: 63, 66–67, 166–68). Driver and Miles (1935: 139, 181–185, 240–250); Saporetti (1979: 5, 8–9, 15–16). All seem to think that the levirate is automatic in patriarchal systems and/or part of the Roman system of *manus*. Neither is the case. There is no form of paternal control/*patria potestas* that will allow a woman's husband's father to exercise the levirate on a man's daughter before or after the marriage. The closest that this can come is the rule in early Germanic law that guardianship of a married woman passes to her husband's relatives when the husband dies, unless they refuse to allow her to remarry or otherwise mistreat her, in which case it reverts to her relatives (Rothair's Edict, 182–183, see also 195). Marriage to the widow's husband's brothers was not an option in this case, being expressly forbidden by church incest laws. Neither was the levirate practiced in Rome, and it is relatively rare worldwide. Even in the Jewish diaspora, the dead man's brother's duty involves only intercourse with the widow; marriage is not required. The claim that sons automatically inherit their father's wives among "other races" and that this is somehow relevant to "*patria potestas* in Assyria" (Driver and Miles 1935: 182) is unusually revealing of the underlying prejudices that haunt the study of

often led to a situation in which the wife was older than her husband, in extreme cases, even raising him from childhood. So likely is this to produce a husband completely dominated by his wife that marriage of mature women to much younger men were expressly forbidden in early Christian ("barbarian") law codes.[66] The custom of levirate marriage also treats the wife as the valuable member of the family with potential husbands merely expendable cogs of which one was as good as another.

The husband's continuing duty to support despite his having entered into his father-in-law's house may readily be seen by comparing the abandonment situation with both types of marriage. So, MAL A 36 (*errēbu*) and MAL A 45 (normal) prescribe essentially the same solution for this problem, with the only difference being the amount of time the wife is required to wait before remarrying and the involvement of the authorities in the normal marriage, where the woman, having moved into her husband's house and not been given her *nudunnû* up front, had no independent means of support.

This principle of continuing duty to support produced a situation in Assyria in which the entering husband, despite the fact that he is moving in with his wife, still has to give a *terḫatu*-bride-price and provide a *nudunnû*-widow's dower as he would have done if she had moved in with him.[67] Although these payments come from the same parties as their homophonous counterparts in a normal marriage, their function in the *errēbu*-marriage will have been quite different. So long as the marriage lasted, the marital property will probably have been managed by the party in whose house the couple was residing. Catastrophes aside, the problem of legal ownership will only

Semitic civilizations ("other races" = Hebrews and Arabs specifically [239–240]). It joins such comments as "marriage by purchase . . . implies a low level of civilization [154] . . . the Sumerians had passed the stage of marriage by purchase . . . among the Semites, however, marriage was a genuine marriage by purchase" (218). The issue of support for the woman with children is particularly clear in MAL A 33 where the levirate is given as an alternative to the widow being supported by her children.

66. "A most vain and grasping suasion and perversion has appeared in these times which seem to us, in conjunction with the rest of our judges, to be illegal: women, adult and mature in age, have joined themselves in union with small boys who are under the legal age and claim them as their legitimate husbands." (Liutprand 129.XIII).

67. Consequently, the levirate intended to ensure the bride's support after her husband's death still applies (MAL A 30, 33). In this situation, the children will actually belong to the bride's family and not the groom's, so we are talking about the father-in-law fulfilling a duty rather than exercising a privilege. MAL A 30 envisages a very complex situation in which a man, having already married one son into another family is just on the verge of marrying another son in the same direction when the first son dies. By the rules of leviriate (MAL A 33), the father of the sons may find another son for his son's widow, and MAL A 31 allows him to substitute the live son for the dead one in the already completed marriage. If he does, so, he will forfeit the *terḫatu*-bride-price he has given for the second marriage, since he has broken off one engagement to make another, but he may still chose this as a preferable alternative to losing yet another marriageable son to his daughter-in-law or having to provide her with the *nudunnû* that will be due if he does find another husband for her. If, on the other hand, the father of the daughters wants to cancel the second marriage, he is the one to break the engagement, and in that case, the father of the sons may chose whether he wants to go with the levirate option or get his money back. The father of the sons will, of course, still have to provide a *nudunnû* to his ex-daughter-in-law even if he exercises the refund option. What will be different is that the two families will no longer be tied to one another. The father of the surviving son will also have to find him another wife if he opts to have his money back, meaning the payment of yet another set of bridal presents to another family. But if the father of the sons and the father of the daughters have become hostile over this, it might be better to extract oneself and move on. The law does not presume to make this decision for the father of the sons; he may weigh his options and take whichever of them he prefers. With Driver and Miles (1935: 174–175) and *pace* Cuq (1922: 50–51; 1929: 439, Cardascia (1969: 166–168), and Saporetti (1979: 5, 8) there is no question of the still-living son getting to marry both women over the objections of his wives' father.

have arisen when the marriage terminated due to divorce or the death of the husband. At this point, even though he paid it, the entering husband's *terḫatu*-bride-price should behave as if this *terḫatu*-bride-price had been given to his father and then turned over to him. Conversely, even though he is the one who gave it and not the one who got it, his *nudunnû*-widow's dower should be treated legally like a wife's *širku*-dowry.

In this situation, the *nudunnû*-widow's dower will largely have consisted of edibles, slaves, and the customary gifts of jewelry on the birth of children, particularly sons.[68] In a sense, of course, this *nudunnû* was the entering husband's dowry since he brought it with him from his father's house as his contribution to the household. Therefore, whenever in a normal marriage the woman (or her family) would get her *širku*-dowry, the entering husband (or his family) should get his *nudunnû*-widow's dower, and that includes any jewelry he may have given his wife.[69]

So, in case of divorce without children, the exact mirror image of a normal Assyrian marriage dissolving should appear, namely that whoever divorces whom, the husband should get refunded his *nudunnû*-widow's dower and the wife should get to keep the *terḫatu*-bride-price. Or, to put it differently, it was now the entering husband who, if he wanted to depart taking with him with his *širku*-dowry equivalent (the *nudunnû*/jewelry), had to leave the *terḫatu*-bride-price with his exwife and, conversely if the wife wanted to get rid of him, she could pocket the *terḫatu*-bride-price, but had to refund her exhusband his *širku*-dowry equivalent (the *nudunnû*/jewelry) before she expelled him from her house. And this is exactly the pattern reflected in MAL A 27 and 38.

> "If a woman is still living in her father's house (and) her husband has been coming in, (and the marriage breaks up), whatever *nudunnû* her husband gave her, he himself may take, but he may not claim what belongs to her father's house." (MAL A 27)

> "If a woman is still living in her father's house and her husband has left her, he may take the jewelry which he himself put on her; he may not claim the *terḫatu* which he brought. It is cleared for the woman." (MAL A 38)

The effect is, of course, to retain the similar penalties to be paid by either party initiating the divorce typical of a normal Assyrian marriage contract. Assyrian law also hastened to clarify that a woman was liable for her husband's debts, regardless of whose house the couple happened to be living in: "If a woman is still living in her father' house and her *nudunnû* has been given her, whether she has been taken to the house of her father-in-law or not, she is responsible for the debts, fines, and compensation payments of her husband." (MAL A 32)[70]

68. The widow's dower at Emar is actually called a *tudittu* (Westbrook 2003a: 680–681). This was either a "pectoral" (*CAD* D:168–170) or a "toggle-pin" (Klein 1983: 255–284) or a "necklace with counterweights" (Maxwell-Hyslop 1971: 154–156). For a discussion, see Farber (1987: 96–99). Whatever it was exactly, it was some sort of jewelry and the term is being used, at Emar, to describe the husband's gift to his wife to support her after his death.

69. This was simply dismissed out of hand as "impossible" by Driver and Miles (1935: 155).

70. The formulation is somewhat clumsy, but the intent is clear—a wife is responsible for her husband's debts whether she enters his house or he enters hers. *Pace* Driver and Miles, (1935: 140), we are talking about living somewhere and not just popping in for a visit every now and again. S. Lafont (2003: 541), following

TABLE 19.4. Normal marriage chart 4: fate of marriage payments on death of wife with children.

| Payment | Status |
|---|---|
| *terḫatu* | Stays with bride's family unless it has been returned to the bride in which case it goes to her children (MAL A 29) |
| *šeriktu/širku* | Stays with groom's family (CH §162); goes to her children (LI §24; CH §§162, 167, 171, 173–174; NBL §13; MAL A 29); if he dies, she keeps this (CH §§171–172, 176; NBL§ 13) and gets the *nudunnû* if there is one (CH §171; cf. §§150, 172; NBL §13) or an heir's share in the estate if there isn't (CH §172; cf. §176) and gets to live in the house as long as she wishes (CH §§171–172; MAL A 46); the *nudunnû* goes to his children if she has others (CH §172; cf. §150) |

Similarly, when the entering husband died leaving behind children, the situation should be similar to what happened when, in a normal marriage, a wife died leaving children; see table 19.4.

So, if the entering husband dies, the jewelry that he gave his wife should, like the *širku*-dowry of the entering wife, be cleared for **his** children and that is exactly the ruling of MAL A 26: "If a woman is still living in her father's house and her husband is dead, whatever jewelry her husband put on her, if there are children by her husband, they may take (it)." (MAL A 26)

Where trouble arises in interfacing the reversed situations of husband and wife with the husband's continuing duty to support is when the entering husband dies without children. Again, in principle, his situation ought to be that of an entering wife who dies without children; see table 19.5.

If the husband is the one to enter, the *nudunnû*-widow's dower is essentially the husband's *širku*-dowry. By reversed rules, then, the entering husband's *širku*-dowry analogue ought to go back to his family. However, the entering husband's jewelry is not just a *širku*-dowry analogue but also a *nudunnû*-widow's dower, and the purpose of a normal *nudunnû*-widow's dower is to support a woman if her husband dies, which is exactly what has happened. What is more, by Assyrian law, as we know from MAL A 29, if the woman enters her husband's house and has children, even if she was given her *nudunnû*-widow's dower by her father-in-law (the family property being undivided), nobody, not even the sons of her father-in-law (her husband's brothers) have a claim on this *nudunnû*-widow's dower. "If a woman has entered her husband's house, her *širku* and whatever she has brought from the house of her father and/or what her father-in-law gave her when she entered is cleared for her children; the children of her father-in-law may not claim (it)." (MAL A 29)

Cardascia (1969: 69, 174–177), argues that the *nudunnû* belonged to the husband for the duration of the marriage on the basis of this law, which is interpreted as the husband's creditors being able to seize it "even if it had been deposited outside the matrimonial home, in the house of the bride's father." Quite apart from the silliness about deposit outside the matrimonial home, the reason that a husband's creditors could seize the *nudunnû* was not that this was the husband's property but that the wife was liable for her husband's debts, and the wording of the law leaves no doubt whatsoever on this score.

TABLE 19.5. Normal marriage chart 5: fate of marriage payments on death of wife without children.

| Payment | Status |
|---|---|
| *biblu*/zbl | Does not return regardless of who dies (CE §18; MAL A 31, 42–43) |
| *terḫatu* | Returns to groom's family regardless of who dies (CE §§17–18; CH §§163–164) |
| *šeriktu*/*širku* | Returns to bride's family (CH §§163–164; NBL §10); if husband dies, she gets the *nudunnû* if there is one (NBL §12) plus her *šeriktu* or a share in her husband's estate (NBL §12) |

But this is the case of an entering husband, and there are no children, so what the jurists do in this case is to split the difference. If the brothers are divided (MAL A 26), the jewelry behaves like a *nudunnû*-widow's dower and stays with the wife and their children, if any: "If a woman is still living in her father's house and her husband is dead, whatever jewelry her husband put on her, if there are children by her husband, they may take (it). If there are no children by her husband, she herself may take (it)." (MAL A 26)

However, if the brothers are undivided (MAL A 25), the jewelry is actually part of the husband's father's estate so it counts as *širku*-dowry and returns to the groom's family. Assyrian law generally attempted to avoid endless arguments by confining refunds to the remaining bits of what was brought, excluding "corn or sheep or anything edible."[71] Applying these rules to MAL A 25, the jewelry or, more precisely, that part of the jewelry that has not disappeared in the meantime, should go to the deceased husbands' brothers, and so it does: "If a woman is still living in her father's house and her husband is dead, the brothers of her husband are undivided, and she has no children, the undivided brothers of her husband may take whatever jewelry her husband put on her that has not gotten lost. Whatever remains they shall make the gods pass by, prove (it) and take (it). They shall not be subjected to the water ordeal or an oath." (MAL A 25)

So, the jewelry in MAL A 25–26 and 38, that is, jewelry provided by an entering husband to his wife is not just the normal *nudunnû*-widow's dower but also functions as a sort of male *širku*-dowry, producing the patterns of retention and loss reflected in the laws.

In conclusion, when properly analyzed, Assyrian laws do not represent a situation in which women are essentially the property of their husbands. What is more, in terms of rights, the status of women in late second millennium Assyria actually compares quite favorably with that of Hammurabi's Babylon.[72] This is perhaps not so surprising given that in the Old Assyrian period wives regularly ran the family business in Assur while their husbands lived in Anatolia. With the development of empire, many of the

71. As specified in MAL A 30–31. Cf. YOS 2 25, *apud* Westbrook (1988: 136–137), where the soldiers are to recover of the marital property "anything that is now to be seen."

72. I would not go so far as to say that: "In Old Babylonia the status of the wife was in essence that of a chattel" (Skaist 1963: 168). However, I would concur that: "In other regions of the Near East for which we have documents the status of the wife was legally much higher. The husband could divorce her, and she could divorce him. He could not marry a second wife except in certain circumstances. Were it not for the fact that here, too, the wife is the object of the marriage agreement, one might say that the two were legally equal to each other" (Skaist 1963: 168–169).

menfolk will have spent a good deal of the year off fighting in some distant campaign, once again leaving women in charge at home. Is it then, so surprising that, like Spartan women, who were proverbial for their freedom by comparison with their Athenian sisters, Assyrian women also fared better than Babylonian? Or could it be that the female sex was a greater favorite of the laws of Assyria than the law of England?

## BIBLIOGRAPHY


Balkan, K.

1948 Eti hukukunda içgüveylik (Die Stellung des eingeheirateten Schwiegersohnes in das Haus der Schwiegereltern eintritt). *Ankara Üniversitesi Dil ve Tarih-Coğrafya Fakultesi Dergisi* 6: 147–152.

Blackstone, Sir W.

1765 (1902) *Commentaries on the Laws of England.* Edited by William Draper Lewis. 4 vols. Philadelphia: Welsh.

Cardascia, G.

1969 *Les Lois Assyriennes.* LAPO 2. Paris: Cerf.

Cuq, É .

1922 Un recueil des lois Assyriennes. *RA* 19: 44–65.

1929 *Études sur le droit Babylonien, les lois Assyriennes et les lois Hittites.* Paris: Geuthner.

Dogget, M. E.

1992 *Marriage, Wife-Beating, and the Law in Victorian England.* London: Weidenfeld & Nicolson.

Drew, K. F.

1949 *The Burgundian Code: Book of Constitutions or Law of Gundobad; Additional Enactments.* Philadelphia: University of Pennsylvania Press.

1973 *The Lombard Laws.* Philadelphia: University of Pennsylvania Press.

Driver, G. R. and Miles, J. C.

1935 *The Assyrian Laws: Edited with Translation and Commentary.* Oxford: Clarendon.

1952 *The Babylonian Laws,* vol. 1: *Legal Commentary.* Oxford: Clarendon.

Fairbanks, S.

1939 *The Old West Frisian Skeltana Riucht.* Cambridge: Harvard University Press.

Farber, W.

1987 Tamarisken-Fibeln-Skolopender: Zur philologischen Deutungder "Reiseszene" auf neuassyrischen Lamaštu-Amuletten. Pp. 85–105 in *Language, Literature and History: Philological and Historical Studies Presented to Erica Reiner.* Edited by F. Rochberg-Halton. AOS 67. New Haven: American Oriental Society.

Friedrich, J.

1959 *Die hethitischen Gesetze.* DMOA 7. Leiden: Brill.

Gordon, C. H.

1981 *Erēbu* Marriage. Pp. 155–160 in *Studies on the Civilization and Culture of Nuzi and the Hurrians in Honor of Ernest R. Lacheman.* Edited by M. A. Morrison and D. A. Owen. SCCNH 1. Winona Lake, IN: Eisenbrauns.

Groneberg, B.

1989 Dimtu. *NABU* 1989.3: 52.

Gurney, O. R.

1983 *Middle Babylonian Legal and Economic Texts from Ur.* London: British School of Archaeology in Iraq.

Kienast, B.
2014 Zum altassyrischen Eherecht. Pp. 73–83 in *He Has Opened Nisaba's House of Learning: Studies in Honor of Åke Waldemar Sjöberg*. Edited by L. Sassmannshausen. CM 46. Leiden: Brill.

Klein, H.
1983 Tudittum. *ZA* 73: 255–284.

Klein, I.
1972 *Code of Maimonides*, vol. 4: *The Book of Women*. YJS 19. New Haven: Yale University Press.

Koschaker, P.
1924 Beiträge zum altbabylonischen Recht. *ZA* 35: 192–212.
1933 Fratriarchat, Hausgemeinshaft und Mutterrecht in Keilschriftrechten. *ZA* 41: 1–89.

Kwasman, T. and Parpola, S.
1991 *Legal Transactions of the Royal Court of Nineveh*, part 1: *Tiglath-Pileser III Through Esarhaddon*. SAA 6. Helsinki: Helsinki University Press.

Lafont, B. and Westbrook, R.
2003 Mesopotamia: Neo-Sumerian Period (Ur III). Pp. 183–226 in vol. 1 of *A History of Ancient Near Eastern Law*. Edited by R. Westbrook. 2 vols. HdO 72. Leiden: Brill.

Lafont, S.
2003 Mesopotamia: Middle Assyrian Period. Pp. 521–563 in vol. 1 of *A History of Ancient Near Eastern Law*. Edited by R. Westbrook. 2 vols. HdO 72. Leiden: Brill.

Landsberger, B.
1968 Jungfräulichkeit: Ein Beitrag zum Thema "Beilager und Eheschliessung" (mit einem Anhang: Neue Lesungen und Deutungen im Gesetzbuch von Ešnunna). Pp. 41–105 in vol. 2 of *Symbolae Iuridicae et Historicae Martino David Dedicatae*. Edited by J. A. Ankum, R. Feenstra, and W. F. Leemans. 2 vols. Leiden: Brill.

Larson, L. M.
1935 *The Earliest Norwegian Laws, Being the Gulathing Law and the Frostathing Law*. Records of Civilization, Sources, and Studies 20. New York: Columbia University Press.

Manning, J.
2003 Egypt: Demotic Law. Pp. 819–862 in *A History of Ancient Near Eastern Law*. Edited by R. Westbrook. 2 vols. HdO 72. Leiden: Brill.

Márquez Rowe, I.
2003 Anatolia and the Levant: Alalakh, Ugarit, and Canaan. Pp. 693–743 in vol. 1 of *A History of Ancient Near Eastern Law*. Edited by R. Westbrook. 2 vols. HdO 72. Leiden: Brill.

Mattila, R.
2002 *Legal Transactions of the Royal Court of Nineveh*, part 2: *Assurbanipal Through Sin-šarru-iškun*. SAA 14. Helsinki: Helsinki University Press.

Maxwell-Hyslop, K. M.
1971 *Western Asiatic Jewelry, c. 3000–612 BC*. London: Methuen.

Nicholas, B.
1962 *An Introduction to Roman Law*. Clarendon Law Series. Oxford: Clarendon.

Oelsner, J., Wells, B., and Wunsch, C.
2003 Mesopotamia: Neo-Babylonian Period. Pp. 911–974 in vol 2 of *A History of Ancient Near Eastern Law*. Edited by R. Westbrook. 2 vols. HdO 72. Leiden: Brill.

Parker, B.
1954 The Nimrud Tablets, 1952—Business Documents. *Iraq* 16: 29–58.

Porten, B.
2003 Egypt: Elephantine. Pp. 863–882 in vol. 2 of *A History of Ancient Near Eastern Law*. Edited by R. Westbrook. 2 vols. HdO 72. Leiden: Brill.

Postgate, J. N.
1976 *Fifty Neo-Assyrian Legal Documents*. Warminster: Aris & Phillips.

Radner, K.
2003 Mesopotamia: Neo-Assyrian Period. Pp. 883–910 in vol. 2 of *A History of Ancient Near Eastern Law*. Edited by R. Westbrook. 2 vols. HdO 72. Leiden: Brill.

Rivers, T.
1977 *Laws of the Alamans and Bavarians*. Philadelphia: University of Pennsylvania Press.

Röllig, W.
1969–1970 Review of *Old Babylonian Contracts and Juridical Texts*, by J. van Dijk. *WO* 5: 129–130.

Roth, M.
1989 *Babylonian Marriage Agreements 7th–3rd BC.* AOAT 222. Kevelaer: Butzon & Bercker; Neukirchen-Vluyn: Neukirchener Verlag.

Saporetti, C.
1979 *The Status of Women in the Middle Assyrian Period.* Introduction and translation by Beatrice Boltze-Jordan. Monographs on the Ancient Near East 2.1. Malibu, CA: Undena.

Scurlock, J. A.
2006 But Was She Raped: A Verdict Through Comparison. *NIN* 4: 61–103.

Scurlock, J. A. and Andersen, B.
2005 *Diagnoses in Assyrian and Babylonian Medicine: Ancient Sources, Translations, and Modern Medical Analyses.* Urbana: University of Illinois Press.

Skaist, A.
1963 *Studies in Ancient Mesopotamian Family Law Pertaining to Marriage and Divorce*. PhD diss., University of Pennsylvania.

Slanski, K.
2003 Mesopotamia: Middle Babylonian Period. Pp. 485–520 in vol. 1 of *A History of Ancient Near Eastern Law*. Edited by R. Westbrook. 2 vols. HdO 72. Leiden: Brill.

Starr, J.
1978 *Dispute and Settlement in Rural Turkey: An Ethnography of Law.* Social, Economic, and Political Studies of the Middle East 23. Leiden: Brill.

Stol, M.
2012 Payment of the Old Babylonian Brideprice. Pp. 131–167 in *Looking at the Ancient Near East and the Bible Through the Same Eyes: Minha LeAhron: A Tribute to Aaron Skaist*. Edited by K. Abraham and J. Fleishman. Bethesda, MD: CDL.

Veenhof, K.
2003 Mesopotamia: Old Assyrian Law. Pp. 431–483 in vol. 1 of *A History of Ancient Near Eastern Law*. Edited by R. Westbrook. 2 vols. HdO 72. Leiden: Brill.

Westbrook, R.
1982 *Old Babylonian Marriage Law*. 2 vols. PhD dissertation, Yale University.
1988 *Old Babylonian Marriage Law.* AfOB 23. Horn: Berger.
1995 Muntehe. *RlA* 8:425–426.
2003a Anatolia and the Levant: Emar and Vicinity. Pp. 657–691 in vol. 1 of *A History of Ancient Near Eastern Law*. Edited by R. Westbrook. 2 vols. HdO 72. Leiden: Brill.

2003b Mesopotamia: Old Babylonian Period. Pp. 361–430 in vol. 1 of *A History of Ancient Near Eastern Law*. Edited by R. Westbrook. 2 vols. HdO 72. Leiden: Brill.

Whitelock, D.
1979 *English Historical Documents I c. 500–1042*. 2nd ed. London: Methuen.

Zacagnini, C.
2003 Mesopotamia: Nuzi. Pp. 565–617 in vol. 1 of *A History of Ancient Near Eastern Law*. Edited by R. Westbrook. 2 vols. HdO 72. Leiden: Brill.

CHAPTER 20

# Disorder and Its Agents: The Akkadian Epic of Anzû Revisited

Dahlia Shehata

A PRIME EXAMPLE for the dynamics of order and disorder taking place within the frame of a mythological narration is the Babylonian creation epic Enūma Eliš (Lambert 2013; Talon 2005). Its central theme is the battle between two opponents: The god Marduk on one side, an outstanding divine hero, and the goddess and monster Tiamat on the other side threatening her own divine offspring. It is a divine battle in its most traditional sense—a fight delivering cosmological power. Both Marduk and Tiamat represent opposing cosmic principles; they are personifications of the creative and destructive powers, of order and of disorder.

Cosmic struggles between order and disorder envisioned in so-called *Chaosmythen* are well known from many cultures from all over the world throughout most epochs of human history.[1] Frequent topics bound to them are the world's creation, the legitimization of authority, and, lastly, the manifestation and ritual renewal of the existing world order.

As was shown by others (Lambert 1986), the Enūma Eliš strongly relies in its structure and setting on the Akkadian Anzû Epic, which in contrast to the Enūma Eliš is already known from second millennium manuscripts.[2] Apart from the basic fight between a god and a monster, both also end with the exaltation of the hero after victory and thus close with the proclamation of the hero's many names. Their first purpose is thus the legitimization of authority. Still, the Enūma Eliš goes even further. There, the supreme god Marduk not only takes over divine kingship, but also emerges in the role of the world's creator.

Such an outstanding presentation is not at all the case for Ninurta in the Anzû-Epic. In fact, reviewing the chain of narration, even the distinction between order and disorder and its representatives is not that definite and leaves room for varying perceptions.

The leading topic of the Ghent Rencontre 2013 is an occasion to revisit the Anzû-Epic's protagonists and their literary presentation regarding the differentiation of order and disorder.

## The Anzû Myth and Its Contents

The text of the Akkadian Anzû Epic, identified from altogether twenty-two cuneiform manuscripts is handed down in three versions (see table 20.1).[3]

1. See Annus 2002 for ancient Near Eastern examples.
2. For the latest editions of the Anzû Epic, see Vogelzang (1988); and Annus (2001).
3. In addition to the already known and published manuscripts enumerated in Annus (2001: xxxv–xxxviii) there are further two identified manuscripts from Assur preserving parts of the first tablet of the

TABLE 20.1. The three versions of the Anzû Epic and their sources.

| Version | Date | Recension | Sources' provenance |
|---|---|---|---|
| (1) Standard Babylonian | ninth–sixth cent. BCE | Standardized three-tablet version | Nineveh, Tarbīṣu, Kinalua?, Borsippa?, Ḫuzirīna, Assur, Sippar, Amnānum? |
| (2) Old Babylonian | late second mill. BCE | 4 tablets only II–III preserved | Susa |
| (3) Neo-Assyrian Sultantepe version | eighth–seventh cent. BCE | 1 tablet | Ḫuzirīna |

Most of the known manuscripts hand down a canonical Standard Babylonian version, which is the text I will mainly refer to in this article. The Old Babylonian version from Susa, though much shorter, builds the basis for the elongated Standard Babylonian three-tablet version.[4] Lastly, the archive of Sultantepe preserves an independent and very short Neo-Assyrian version with about seventy-four lines that apart from the main plot shows no parallels to any other known version (Vogelzang 1988: 19–23, 119–132).

Apart from all Akkadian sources for the myth about Anzû, there is the interesting but difficult text known after its modern title Ninurta and the Turtle or Ninurta's Pride and Punishment that has survived on several Old Babylonian fragments from Nippur and Ur.[5] The story's main plot is similar to the Akkadian Anzû Epic though the protagonists are Ninurta and an Anzû chick (amar $^{an}$IM.DUGUD/MI$^{mušen}$).[6] However, since the text contains passages unknown from any of the Akkadian versions, it is frequently used to reconstruct lost parts of the Akkadian Anzû-story.

The plot of the text (see table 20.2) deals with the theft of the tablet of destinies by the giant eagle-like Anzû. The tablet of destinies was initially held by Enlil. As demonstrated within the story, this tablet gives to its holder ultimate power and supreme control over the world's destinies. The choice of a god capable of regaining the tablet of destinies and accomplishing the less desirable part of the job, which is to defeat evil Anzû, falls on the son of the betrayed, Ninurta. After an initial failure, Ninurta finally manages to capture and destroy powerful Anzû. At this point the text is broken for approximately fifty lines. At the end of the third and last tablet, which is again well preserved, he is celebrated and praised as the outstanding hero and king of the gods who has restored divine order.

SB version (pers. comm. Prof. S. M. Maul, Heidelberg), two fragments from Nineveh as well as one fragment from Sultantepe that preserve parts of SB III. A new edition of the epic with all its versions is in preparation.

4. According to the preserved tablets II and III we may reconstruct around 320 lines for the OB Version in contrast to 540 lines of the SB Version; see further Vogelzang (1988: 190–201) for a comparison of both versions.

5. *ETCSL* 1.6.3; the latest edition is presented by Alster (2006); a new edition integrating the hitherto unpublished Nippur-tablet CBS 15085+15007(+)8319 is in preparation.

6. Alster (2006: 18) translates "Young Anzu."

TABLE 20.2. The plot of the Anzû Epic.

| | |
|---|---|
| Tablet I | Prologue and introduction |
| | Riverbeds, sky, and springs without water |
| | Discovery and appointment of Anzû |
| | In the temple |
| | Stealing of the tablet of destinies |
| | Request of three candidates and Ninurta's choice |
| Tablet II | In the mountains |
| | First fight and Ninurta's failure |
| | Sharur's/Adad's errand |
| TabletIII | Second fight and Anzû's defeat |
| | *broken* |
| | Ninurta's refusal |
| | and rehabilitation *(broken)* |
| | Epilogue: [In the temple] |

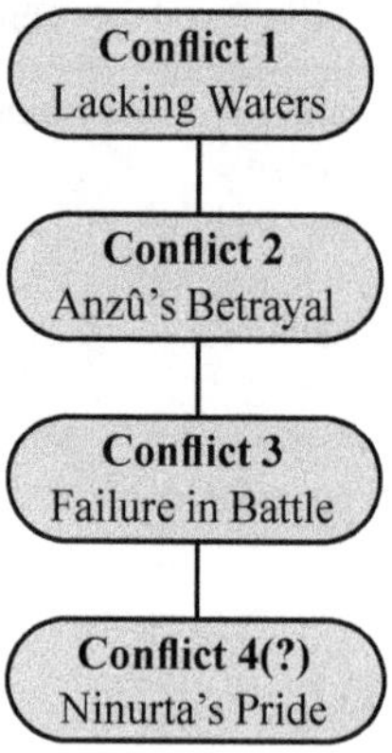


The outline of the story's dynamics is built on several emerging conflicts, which is a common feature for Akkadian epic literature.[7] In our case, these conflicts are connected to each other in a causal chain with every resolved conflict bearing the nucleus for the next one:

1. The story begins with the description of a world that lacks all waters. They are absent from springs, from riverbeds, and even from heaven (SB I 17–20).[8] This primordial situation is resolved by bringing Anzû into Enlil's temple. From that moment on, the water flows into the chief god's bath and into the whole world.[9]

   Even though it does not fully deserve to be designated a conflict, this situation initiates the story's dynamics on two levels. First, it introduces the myth's cosmological topic, which is water in its different manifestations. Second, it presents to us the first interference in the world's destinies, which is of course undertaken by the god Enlil. It was he who—following Ea's advice—chose a new designation for Anzû and brought him into his own temple. As is well known, this decision already bears a disharmony, which is the impetus for the whole story's dynamics.
2. The second conflict is the tablet's theft.
3. The third conflict is rather subordinate. The "hero's failure" is a standard narrative feature increasing tension at the story's climax. Here, it additionally points to Ninurta's incapability of overcoming evil Anzû all by himself. Final victory needs Ea's preeminent wisdom. This is a remarkable difference from the Enūma Eliš, where Marduk acts totally self-dependent from the very beginning.

7. The best examples are the Enūma Eliš and Atraḫasīs (Lambert and Millard 1969).

8. Although review and collation of the tablets in preparation for a new edition has led to a new line numbering for SB tablet I of the Anzû-Epic, in this article the line quotations are given according to Annus (2001).

9. Though the text does not explicitly point to this connection, most authors interpret the pure waters in Enlil's bath (SB I 65, 79) as resulting from Anzû's new presence in the temple; see Vogelzang (1988: 135); and Annus (2001, x).

4. The fourth conflict is reconstructed on the basis of the Sumerian poem Ninurta and the Turtle.[10] There, Ninurta seeks to get a hold of the tablet of destinies desiring absolute power for himself.[11] Since he is not entitled to such powers, Ea overwhelms him with the help of a turtle and holds him back in a black hole in the abzu. Though the end of the main tablet UET 6/1 2 is broken, we may still reconstruct that only because of the request of his mother is the hero finally released (Alster 2006: 29–30). A similar scenario might be reconstructed for the Akkadian Anzû Epic since SB tablet III preserves in line 73. ⌜DUB⌝ NAM.MEŠ *la u*$_2$*-t*[*ar*$^?$ x x x x x (x x x)].[12] This sentence is followed by a gap of approximately thirty-five lines that must have contained some important development of the narrative. Interestingly, its length is comparable to the chapter containing Anzû's betrayal on SB tablet I 65–91.

## The Protagonists

Following the entrance of the protagonists in the text, I will start my reflections with Anzû. In contrast to his latest behavior in the myth paralleled in Neo-Assyrian and later iconography (fig. 20.1), he was not always "evil," Akkadian *lemnu*.[13] The text itself introduces Anzû in two passages, once in an extended report made by the Igigū-gods to their sovereign Enlil (SB I 25–41), and another time in an explanatory consultant speech of Ea again directed to Enlil (SB 49–54). Here I cite parts of the Igigū report:

SB Anzû I 25–29
On Sharshar, the high mountain . . .
in the bosom of the Anun[na-gods *of the mountain*$^?$]
[. . .] had born [*flying*$^?$] Anzû.
A saw are his win[gs . . . ]
[His m]outh [ . . . ][14]

SB Anzû I 35–41
At [his] roa[r . . .
The southwind . . .
The heavy [north]wind$^?$ . . .

10. Wiggermann (1982: 421–422) followed by Vogelzang (1988: 139); differently Annus (2001: xiii) "The textual evidence is not sufficient for claiming that Ninurta is not eager to return the tablet"; see discussion in Shehata 2017, 183–87.

11. UET 6/1 2 obv. 6–7(/SLTN 41 rev. 1) [x x (x)-n]a-ke$_4$ a-nir im-ĝa$_2$-ĝa$_2$; ge$_{24}$-e me-bi šu-ĝu$_{10}$-uš l[i-b]i$_2$-kur$_9$ nam-⌜en-bi⌝ nu-ak-e "The [ ] of [ ] grumbled annoyed: 'And me? These *me* have not come into my hand; Thus I won't exercise their lordship'"; see also Kramer (1984: 232) and Alster (2006: 16, 18).

12. Coll. 2009; see also Vogelzang (1988: 70) against Saggs (1986: 24) [*tu*]*p-šīmāti*$^{MEŠ}$*-ma u*$_2$-⌜x⌝ and Annus (2001: 27) [DUB] NAM.TAR.MEŠ-*ma u*$_2$ [*x x x x x x x*].

13. Several passages in the Anzû Epic SB II 21, 117, 140; III 20, 36, 62, 116; see also K3476 (Livingstone 2007: 122–123) 7 next to Asakku; for images see in general Braun-Holzinger (1998–2001: 524).

14 Coll. March 2014 with new readings for SB I 28. [*š*]*a*$_2$*-aš*$_2$*-ša*$_2$-⌜*ru ap*⌝*-r*[*a-šu*$_{(2)}$ *x x x x x x x (x)*] and 29. [*pi*]-⌜*i*⌝-*š*[*u x x x x x x x x x x (x)*].

FIGURE 20.1. Neo-Assyrian cylinder seal showing Ninurta fighting Anzû; drawing by the author according to Porada (1948: No. 689).

The mass [*of the* . . .
Thunderstorms . . .
They clash . . .
The four winds . . . [15]

According to the epic, the Anzû bird is a child of the mountain. Begotten by mountain and sweet underground water-gods he clearly represents a chtonic character.[16] On the other hand, Anzû is a winged figure, he is *mupparšu* "flying," thus his sphere of action is the sky where he controls storms and winds, and probably also the movement of clouds.[17] Thanks to the Anzû bird, who takes a new position at Enlil's temple leaving behind his original homeland, the waters begin to flow throughout the formerly dry lands.

Another famous passage often referred to in this connotation since it explicitly refers to Anzû as lord of flowing waters is given in the Sumerian Epic of Lugalbanda. Here also Anzû was appointed to his position by Enlil:

Epic of Lugalbanda lines 99–102
(Anzud): "I am the prince who decides the destiny of rolling rivers.
I keep on the strait and narrow path the righteous who follow Enlil's counsel.
My father Enlil brought me here.
He let me bar the entrance to the mountains as if with a great door."[18]

15. SB I 35. [*a*]-*na rig-m*[*i-šu$_2$ x x x x x x x (x)*] 36. ⸢$^{\text{TUMU}}$⸣ulu$_3$$^{lu}$ [*x x x x x x x x (x)*] 37. *kaš-šu* ⸢$^{\text{TUMU}}$⸣.[*x x x x x x x (x)*] 38. *gi-ip-šu* [*x x x x x x x (x)*] 39. *a-šam-ša$_2$-a-tum-m*[*a*' *x x x x x x x (x)*] 40. *in-nen-du*-⸢*u$_2$*⸣-[*ma*? *x x x x x x (x)*] 41. tumu *er-bet-ti i*[*š-x x x x x x x (x)*].

16. Similarly Wilcke (2007: 13).

17. A review of Anzû's connection to rain and winds taking into account the different interpretations of his name in logographic writing MI$^{\text{MUŠEN}}$ / AN.MI$^{\text{MUŠEN}}$ (ED II-IIIa), AN.IM/NI$_2$.MI$^{\text{MUŠEN}}$ (ED IIIb), and AN.IM.DUGUD$^{\text{MUŠEN}}$ (Ur III and later) is presented by Zand (2010).

18. Translation after Black (1998: 59); see further *ETCSL* 8.8.2; and Wilcke (1969: 100–103).

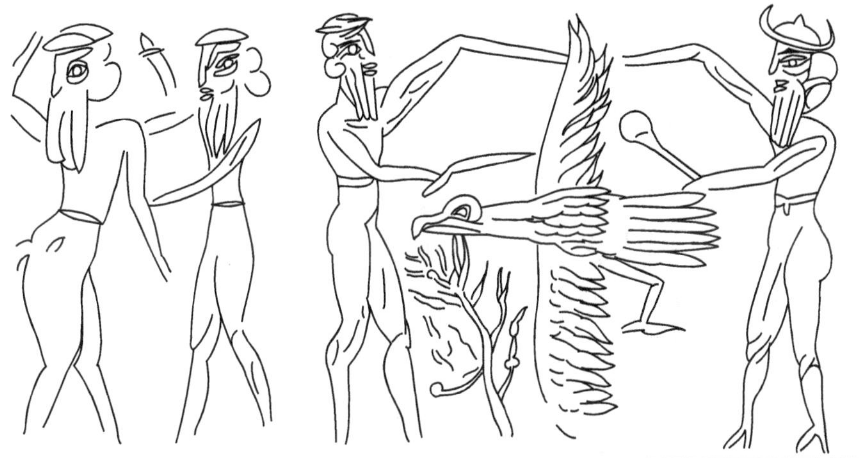

FIGURE. 20.2. Old Akkadian cylinder seal, Tell Asmar; drawing by the author according to the photograph in Boehmer (1965: Tafel XXVIII 334).

The positive and obviously productive aspect of the Anzû bird predominates in third and early second millennia evidence. In these epochs, he was imagined as the well-known lion-headed giant bird serving as an apotropaic figure at gates and on amulettes.[19]

This lion-headed Anzû bird was in the first instance a good character, a protective and assisting spirit standing by Ninĝirsu, and also kings and other kinds of human heroes.[20] The emphasis on these characteristics as well as the enormous strength, farsightedness, and speed, are traceable in texts until the Isin-period.[21]

By the early Old Akkadian period we find a seemingly independent mythological account from images that feature a giant bird-of-prey fighting two gods in the mountain (fig. 20.2). This obviously hostile bird figure is only known from several Old Akkadian cylinder seals.[22] They show the bird by a mountain, sometimes next to a tree, being attacked by two armed gods using mace and dagger. On a well-worked Old Akkadian cylinder seal from Kish (fig. 20.3), the leading god carries a bow and is depicted in a typical posture of threatening the enemy, though with his foot put on the mountain's top.

This posture is comparable to many images either referring to kings or gods in similar positions dating from Old Akkadian times on until the very end of the cuneiform tradition in Mesopotamia. In the case of our myth's protagonists it recalls two literary passages chronologically separated by about one thousand years. The first is from the Sumerian Ninurta and the Turtle while the second is from the *Göttertypentext*:

19. E.g., the famous relief from the entrance of the Ninḫursaĝa-temple in Tell el-ʿUbayd (ca. 2600 BCE) or as part of an amulette in Aruz (2003: 231–232:158c); most images of the lion-headed eagle are gathered in Fuhr-Jaeppelt 1972.

20. Anzû as symbol and assistant of Ninĝirsu is increasingly represented within the Lagash dynasties with examples from the stele of vultures as well as from the Gudea cylinders.

21. See elaboration in Lugalbanda and the Anzud-Bird, lines 111–219, esp. 185–190 (*ETCSL* 1.8.2.2); other references in Šulgi *A* 42–45 (*ETCSL* 2.4.2.0) or Lipit-Ištar *A* 7–8 (*ETCSL* 2.5.5.1).

22. Examples in Boehmer (1969: No. 323–325, 334–336).

FIGURE 20.3. Right part of an Old Akkadian cylinder seal, Kish (ca. 2250 BCE); drawing by the author according to the photograph in Boehmer (1965: Tafel XXVII 324).

Ninurta and the Turtle (UET 6/1, 2 obv. 17–18)
(Enki to Ninurta): "As for the bird which your mighty weapon has captured, from now to eternity you will keep your foot set upon its neck."[23]

mušen ⸢$^{ĝiš}$tukul kala⸣-[ga-z]u bi$_{2}$-dab$_{5}$-ba-še$_{3}$
ud me-da ud ul-⸢le$_{2}$-še$_{3}$ gu$_{2}$-bi gir$_{3}$⸣-su b[a-gub-be$_{2}$-en]

*Göttertypentext* col. II 9–10 (Köcher 1953, 66–67)
With his foot he steps on the Anzû-bird.
His Name: Ninurta.

GIR$_{3}^{II}$-*šu ša*$_{2}$ KAB *pu-ri-da* ⸢*pi-ta-at*⸣-*ma*
MU.NI $^{d}$*nin-urta*

Unfortunately, no image has hitherto come to my attention showing Ninurta in such a posture.[24]

Coming back to Anzû, initially this seemingly hostile bird figure depicted on Old Akkadian cylinder seals is clearly differentiated from the lion-headed Anzû bird known from fourth-millennium images onward.[25] Nevertheless, sometime within the

23. See also Kramer (1984: 233); and Alster (2006: 16–19).

24. The best comparable images are of Ishtar on Old Akkadian as well as Neo-Assyrian cylinder seals, e.g., Boehmer (1969: fig. XXXII no. 382) showing her with her foot set on a lion's back, her symbolic animal. Wiggermann (1992: 151–157) has already thoroughly discussed and analyzed the depictions of gods mounting their symbolic animals, which are in most cases defeated enemies, symbolizing the master-servant relation. Images showing Ninurta mounting a monster are frequent on Neo-Assyrian cylinder seals (see in general Braun-Holzinger 1998–2001); still in this case, the monster he is mounting represents his flood power, the monster *abūbu* and not Anzû; see Seidl (1998).

25. Note that the lion-headed Anzû bird is also known from two Old Akkadian cylinder seals with similar scenes (Boehmer 1965: 59 and fig. XXIX nos. 354–355). Since they show a giant Anzû bird flying and attacking a god next to an Anzû chick they may be connected to the Sumerian version of the Anzû story Ninurta and the Turtle; note also the god Enki facing a hero god on no. 354.

FIGURE 20.4. Old Akkadian cylinder seal, Tell Asmar; drawing by the author according to the photograph in Ornan (2010: 417 –fig. 15).

Old Akkadian period it became identified with him. This is known from a cylinder seal from Tell Asmar showing the same scene but with the well-known lion-headed Anzû bird (fig. 20.4). Though evidence is meager, we may hypothesize that different mythological material featuring a giant bird originating in the mountain somehow intermingled with each other in the course of the later third millennium BCE. During this process, characteristics and stories about Anzû might have been re-modeled and finally found their way into a written form, most probably in more than one instance. A waypoint in this development is marked by the Old Babylonian Akkadian Anzû story, which was extended to form the well-known Standard Babylonian version. It features an Anzû bird, whose existence, on the one hand, is indispensable for the world's natural order, since he exercises control over the world's flowing waters. On the other hand, he is hostile and threatens divine community and its order. This dichotomic nature of Anzû is only coherent against the background of the story's narration. There, his shift of character is connected to his betrayal, which is motivated by his desire to control all divine powers.

This is the time to shift to Ninurta, Anzû's defeater. This god, who was extensively studied by Amar Annus in his 2002 dissertation, is well known as the heroic son of Enlil and Bēlet-ilī. His conquests of monsters and evil demons achieved in the mountains are narrated in Sumerian poems, among them the well-known Angin and Lugale (Cooper 1978; van Dijk 1983). The Akkadian Anzû Epic extends his conquests even further, assigning to him the dominion over mountains, sky, and even the sea:

SB Anzû I 10–12[26]

It is he who in his fierceness bound and fettered the stone creature; → Mountain
Overcoming soaring Anzû with his weapon; → Sky
Slaying the Kusarikku in the midst of the sea. → Sea

26. Translation after Foster (2005: 561–562).

A frequent Akkadian title of Ninurta is "his father's avenger" *mutēr gimil abīšu* which expresses the basics for his acting in the Anzû Epic (Annus 2002: 121–122). For, explicitly in this story, he avenges his father whose *Ellilūtu*—manifested in the tablet of destinies—was stolen by the evil bird.

The Anzû Epic beautifully draws the career of this god from a silent mother's boy to a respectable and self-confident superhero. As we know, this is the intention of the text in the first place, the same as the *Enūma Elish* is for Marduk: it narrates Ninurta's advancement among the gods. Still it astonishes, that, apart from the prologue, the first time we read about Ninurta in the narration itself is only at the beginning of the second tablet:

SB Anzû II 28–29
The hero heard his mother's command.
He bend forward, bristled with rage and went off to his mountain.

*zi-kir um-mi-šu* ⸢*iš*⸣-[*m*]*e*-⸢*e*⸣ *qu-ra-du*
*ig-ru-ur ir*-⸢*ta*⸣-*ub ša*$_2$-⸢*du-us*⸣-*su* ⸢*ig*⸣-*guš*

And even then he is not really talkative and obeys his mothers demands without any comment. The few words he speaks within the course of narration increase toward the end of the story. This distribution of silence and speech apparently reflects his growing self-confidence.

In his very first speech presenting himself to the Anzû bird, he directly points to his adviser, Ea, and, of course, to his parental descent (SB Anzû II 45–47). It is this parental descent that sets him apart in the first place. In contrast to his collegues Adad, Šara, and Girra the theft of the tablet of destinies affects Ninurta personally. Only as the son, he may avenge his father.

A second and surely overwhelming reason for selecting him as Anzû's conqueror is his fighting power. Apart from his troops and his weapons consisting of the seven storms, bow and lightening arrows, his major force is, as is generally known, the flood. In the Akkadian Anzû Epic it virtually explodes at the moment of his final victory over Anzû in the mountain:[27]

SB Anzû III 17–20, 35
He slew the mountain, stirred and devastated[28] its meadows,
Ninurta slew the mountain, stirred and devastated its meadows,
He devastated the wide earth in his fury
He devastated the midst of the mountains, he killed evil Anzû.
. . .
As he soaked the bank? with water, he skinned the [mountain], (and) took the hide.

27. See also Wilcke (2007: 15–17 with n. 41).

28. Contrary to most translations (see, e.g., Hecker 1994: 757; Foster 2005: 573; Wilcke 2007); *raḫāṣu* A (*CAD* R:69–72) refers to the devastation and not the drowning caused by the flooding water.

Ninurta acting as a flood or in attendance of flooding waters is well known from several texts and also images (Annus 2002: 123–133). Passages describing the flood as his mighty weapon, the emanation of his powers, or his rage in battle are frequent. Neo-Assyrian cylinder seals and texts picture him mounting or riding the *abūbu*, depicted as a lion-dragon (fig. 20.1). Apart from combat, Ninurta's flood power is also well known for its productive side. As master of flooding water, he is responsible for all matters connected to water control, irrigation, and thus fertility of the land.[29]

Thus, Ninurta's natural force appears in two ways, productive and destructive. So far, the Akkadian Anzû Epic only narrates his military destructive power. It was especially welcome when directed against enemies and world-threatening monsters. Nevertheless, it could also change its target. This is a case of disaster generally feared by gods as well as humans.[30] Concerning humans, their methods of avoiding such a threat are—for example—the singing of appeasing and heart-soothing laments, such as *Eršema-* and *Šu'illakku*-prayers.

Coming back to our primary text, it is this unpredictable danger coming from the god that was the topic of the last broken portion of the Anzû Epic. Ninurta is seduced by his desire to keep all divine powers for himself and refuses to return the tablet of destinies to it's original holder, his own father. In contrast to the beginning of the text, this is the moment when our hero has transformed into a self-confident and self-speaking god expressing his own desires rather than those of his parents. Unfortunately, we do not know what happened further. However, I believe that the otherwise rather unknown god Birdu who appears in the last broken part of the Anzû Epic and whose name is obviously connected to the Semitic root *BRD* "cold; coolness" has played an important part in soothing and thus cooling down Ninurta's rage before his reentering the divine community.[31] All we know is that at the very end, all problems are solved: Anzû is installed at the temple's front (SB Anzû III 116) and Ninurta is exalted and receives kingship over the world (SB Anzû III 120–126 and the following).

## Synopsis

Reviewing the chain of narration, both, Ninurta and Anzû run through the same development.[32] Anzû is originally a positive figure, not only in a historical perspective but also reflected in the narrative itself. He actually represents a natural power, accomplishing an essential part for the world's natural operation. By changing his destiny, and bringing him to the god's temple, he sees the precious object and cannot resist betraying his new master. This turns him into an evil and dangerous creature.

A similar development is drawn for his opponent Ninurta. He is the heir of his father, the great hero of the gods. Dutifully, he goes to the mountain in order to defeat

29. See, e.g., Lugale 349–359 (van Dijk 1983: 95–96); Annus (2002: 127–128, 152–155).

30. See, e.g., Angin 83–91, 127 (*ECTSL* 1.6.1), Ninurta frightening Enlil and the Anuna, or the Ershema CT 42, 12+ (Cohen 1981: 143 No. 45).

31. Ebeling (1938: 31); since Birdu is further associated with the netherworld through equations with Meslamta'ea, we may hypothesize whether some part of the Anzû story took place in the netherworld or at least in the *apsû*, similar to Ninurta and the Turtle and other comparable compositions; see Shehata 2017.

32. Similarly already Vogelzang (1988: 133–134).

the evil bird and avenge his father. In any case, right after his duty's fulfillment, he changes in character. He catches sight of the tablet of destinies and formulates the same wishes for himself as Anzû did before him.

From the literary perspective, both Ninurta and Anzû, are treated as similar figures, they are captivated by the same desires, sharing the same point of inflection and undergoing the same change in character. This equal treatment in literary terms is comprehensible in view of their cosmological dimension. As I have recapitulated so far, both Ninurta and Anzû represent different manifestations of the same natural force, water. And natural forces are in general unpredictable, undergoing different conditions, bringing either benefit or destruction to mankind.

In the Anzû Epic, the loss of the tablet of destinies and thus the loss of supreme authority, the *Ellilūtu*, is described as *nadû parṣū* "the breakdown of divine order" (SB Anzû I 81, 108). Authority or command is closely linked to the care and assurance of functioning rules. Hence, disorder is determined as the end of all existing rules caused by the shift of authority into the hands of a hostile enemy. This picture fits very well with Anzû. He represents the traditional Mesopotamian enemy figure, coming from the mountain and threatening a well-organized city-state community. But, what empirical model does Ninurta represent? Is he the heir to the throne suffering from megalomania after success in combat and thus turning against his origin? Or is he simply the still raging and thus frightening and impure soldier coming back from the blood-moist battlefield?[33]

Whatever his actions remind of, the threat coming from him is not at all equivalent to the danger coming from the enemy bird. Apart from similarities between god and monster worked out on the literary basis, the only and essential difference between them, when it comes to handling them, is their origin. Ninurta, though capricious—and in contrast to Marduk in the *Enūma Elish* not unfailing—still was always part of the divine community and is therefore bound by familial and social rules. Leaving the question aside whether Ninurta kept the tablet of destinies for himself or not (see Annus 2002: 148–152; Shehata 2017), the situation he finds himself confronted with clearly reflects a typical and, for the ancient audience, well-known innerdynastic, generational transfer of power. The story thus records reflections of an empirical human perspective against the background of a mythological setting. And in view of his human counterpart, the earthly king, the threat coming from Ninurta does not affect divine order in its foundations, only its organization. Altogether he is an accepted heir apparent who has shown his efficiency in fighting back enemies. His excessive and seemingly dangerous ambitions concerning world dominion remain altogether controllable, namely through the grant of an increase in power and consideration—translated into ritual terms—through the increase of cultic attention at cult places, offerings, and prayers. Opposed to the god, there is the foreign and undomesticated animal Anzû. The only way to get control of him is via the god who has defeated him. And, though dead and fixed to the Ekur's front, Anzû's productive powers remain accessible for the world's benefit but—the same as Medusa's head by the Zeus-son—within the range of appropriate control by his defeater Ninurta.

33. Also according to Angin 76–97, Nuska is sent out by Enlil in order to receive the still-raging Ninurta with soothing words and presents, until finally Ninurta puts down his weapons and enters the temple.

A general feature of myths is to picture the given world from different perspectives and on different levels. The Anzû Epic is on the first level a poem of exaltation for Ninurta and hence legitimizes authority and earthly kingship. In case of Anzû, the same text further translates his historical shift of values into a mythological narrative setting. Subordinate to these primarily theological matters is the cosmological background of the myth. Reviewing the plot on the whole, it seems to retrace a whole year's water cycle. It starts in the dry summer, when water becomes scarce, which is reflected through the absence of Anzû's powers in divine and domesticated parts of the world. The story's events then pass through stormy and devastating autumn, pictured through the heavy battle of natural forces and the final victory and release of flooding waters, it then changes into a short but very cool winter, possibly the appearance of Birdu who tries to calm down the raging flood Ninurta. And it finally ends in spring, the time for New Year and Ninurta's (re-)entering into the temple, the arrival of controlled water streams bringing fertility to the land.

Within this cycle, disorder, be it foreign or partly domestic, appears as a recurring threat, which has to be overcome time and again. This leads us to the practical background of the text, which is—as is the *Enūma Elish*—the annual ritual assurance and renewal of the world's given order.

## BIBLIOGRAPHY

Alster, B.

2006 Ninurta and the Turtle: On Parodia Sacra in Sumerian Literature. Pp. 13–36 in *Approaches to Sumerian Literature: Studies in Honour of Stip (H. L. J. Vanstiphout)*. Edited by P. Michalowski and N. Veldhuis. CM 35. Leiden: Brill.

Annus, A.

2001 *The Standard Babylonian Epic of Anzû: Introduction, Cuneiform Text, Transliteration, Score, Glossary, Indices and Sign List*. SAACT 3. Helsinki: Neo-Assyrian Text Corpus Project.

2002 *The God Ninurta in the Mythology and Royal Ideology of Ancient Mesopotamia*. SAAS 14. Helsinki: Neo-Assyrian Text Corpus Project.

Aruz, J.

2003 *Art of the First Cities: The Third Millennium B.C. from the Mediterranean to the Indus; Catalog of an Exhibition Being Held at the Metropolitan Museum of Art, New York, from May 8 to August 17, 2003*. New Haven: Yale University Press.

Black, J. A.

1998 *Reading Sumerian Poetry*. Ithaca: Cornell University Press.

Boehmer, R. M.

1965 *Die Entwicklung der Glyptik während der Akkad-Zeit*. Untersuchtungen zur Assyriologie und Vorderasiatischen Archäologie 4. Berlin: de Gruyter.

1969 Zur Glyptik zwischen Mesilim- und Akkad-Zeit. *ZA* 59:261–292.

Braun-Holzinger, E. A.

1998–2001 Ninurta/Ninĝirsu. B: In der Bildkunst. *RlA* 9:522–525.

Cohen, M.

1981 *Sumerian hymnology: The Eršemma*. Hebrew Union College Annual Supplements 2. Cincinnati: Hebrew Union College.

Cooper, J. S.

1978 *An-gim-dím-ma: The Return of Ninurta to Nippur*. AnOr 52. Rome: Pontifical Biblical Institute.

Dijk, J. van
1983 *Lugal ud me-lám-bi nir-gál: Le récit épique et didactique des Traveaux de Ninurta du Déluge et de la nouvelle Création; Texte, traduction et introduction*. Leiden: Brill.

Ebeling, E.
1938 Birdu. *RlA* 2:31.

Foster, B.
2005 *Before the Muses: An Anthology of Akkadian Literature*. 3rd ed. Bethesda, MD: CDL.

Fuhr-Jaeppelt, I.
1972 *Materialien zur Ikonographie des Löwenadlers Anzu-Imdugud*. Munich: Scharl & Strohmeyer.

Hecker, K.
1994 Das Anzu-Epos. *TUAT* 3.4:745–759.

Köcher, F.
1953 Der babylonische Göttertypentext. *MIOF* 1: 57–107.

Kramer, S. N.
1984 Ninurta's Pride and Punishment. *AuOr* 2: 231–237.

Lambert, W. G.
1986 Ninurta Mythology in the Babylonian Epic of Creation. Pp. 55–59 in *Keilschriftliche Literaturen: Ausgewählte Vorträge der XXXII. Rencontre assyriologique internationale, Münster, 8.–12.7.1985*. Edited by K. Hecker and W. Sommerfeld. BBVO 6. Berlin: Reimer.
2013 *Babylonian Creation Myths*. MC 16. Winona Lake, IN: Eisenbrauns.

Lambert, W. G. and Millard, A. R.
1969 *Atra-Ḫasīs: The Babylonian Story of the Flood*. Oxford: Clarendon.

Livingstone, A.
2007 *Mystical and Mythological Explanatory Works of Assyrian and Babylonian Scholars*. Winona Lake, IN: Eisenbrauns.

Ornan, T
2010 "Humbaba, the Bull of Heaven and the Contribution of Images to the Reconstruction of the Gilgameš Epic", in Steymans, H. U. (Ed.), *Gilgamesch. Ikonographie eines Helden* (= OBO 245), Göttingen, Fribourg, 229–60, 411–24.

Porada, E.
1948 Corpus of Ancient Near Eastern Seals in North American Collections I: The Collection of the Pierpont Morgan Library, Washington.

Saggs, H. W. F.
1986 Additions to Anzû. *AfO* 33: 1–29.

Seidl, U.
1998 Das Flut-Ungeheuer *abūbu*. *ZA* 88: 100–113.

Shehata, D.
2017 Naturgewalt und (Un)heilsmacht im akkadischen Anzû-Mythos. Pp. 181–203 in *From the Four Corners of the Earth: Studies in Iconography and Cultures of the Ancient Near East in Honour of F. A. M. Wiggermann*. Edited by D. Kertai and O. Nieuwenhuyse. AOAT 441. Münster: Ugarit-Verlag.

Talon, P.
2005 *Enuma Eliš: The Standard Babylonian Creation Myth*. SAACT 4. Helsinki: Neo-Assyrian Text Corpus Project.

Vogelzang, M.
1988 *Bin šar dadmē: Edition and Analysis of the Akkadian Anzû Poem*. PhD diss., Rijksuniversiteit Groningen.

Wiggermann, F. A. M.

1982 On *bin šar dadmē*, the "Anzû-Myth." Pp. 418–425 in *Zikir Šumim: Assyriological Studies Presented to F. R. Kraus on the Occasion of His Seventieth Birthday*. Edited by G. van Driel. Leiden: Brill.

1992 *Mesopotamian Protective Spirits: The Ritual Texts*. CM 1. Groningen: Styx.

Wilcke, C.

1969 *Das Lugalbandaepos*. Wiesbaden: Harrassowitz.

2007 Vom altorientalischen Blick zurück auf die Anfänge. Pp. 3–59 in *Anfang und Ursprung: Die Frage nach dem Ersten in Philosophie und Kulturwissenschaft*. Edited by E. Angehrn. Colloquium Rauricum 10. Berlin: de Gruyter.

Zand, K. V.

2010 Zu den Schreibungen des Anzud-Vogels in der Fāra-Zeit. Pp. 415–442 in *Von Göttern und Menschen: Beiträge zu Literatur und Geschichte des Alten Orients; Festschrift für Brigitte Groneberg*. Edited by D. Shehata, F. Weiershäuser, and K. V. Zand. CM 41. Leiden: Brill.

CHAPTER 21

# When the Trial Does Not Work: Pathological Elements in the Judicial Procedure in the Old Babylonian Period

Cristina Simonetti

WHEN SPEAKING OF THE LAW of a people one immediately thinks of its procedural system; in a sense, we are all inclined to think that the law becomes more easily visible when something does not work, when there is the necessity that someone decide who is wrong and who is right, or whether an indicted person is guilty or not. Through the trial, in fact, a person believes he will obtain justice, and these very concepts of justice (*mišarum*) and truth (*kittum*) are the basis of the legislation of the Babylonian kings of the first half of the second millennium BCE. Naturally, we all know that one thing is the actual truth (historical truth) and another thing is the truth one can establish in a tribunal, and that what we call justice may not always win in court.

The Old Babylonian legal system has been thoroughly studied, from Edouard Cuq (1910: 65–101) to Eva Dombradi (1996), via many other important studies (e.g., Koschaker 1917; Walther 1917; Lautner 1922; Driver and Miles 1956; Leemans 1968), which have analytically described the system on the basis of procedural documents: Who were the judges, what were the ways for the discovery of evidence, what were the forms for taking an oath, what was the value of a judgment, and so on. From these data, although obviously within the limits of our available sources, we can see how the judicial machine actually did work. The picture cannot be but a fragmentary one due to the number of Old-Babylonian reigns, and naturally the administration of justice could not be homogeneous within the same kingdom. However, the procedural documents can offer a positive picture of the functioning of the justice system.

What I would like to briefly discuss here is what the ancients knew and thought about the possibility that the trials were sabotaged by one of the parties. However, since I must concentrate on the reign of only one king, the only one to offer enough material is of course Hammurabi of Babylon, and his famous code shall be my main source.[1] In order to do so, and since unfortunately we do not possess texts concerning false witnesses or corrupted judges, we must rely on laws or on edicts of debt release.[2]

1. See Leemans (1968: 128–129): "The finding of proceeding investigation is that the ancient Mesopotamian kings were, in fact, personally concerned with the distribution of justice and that especially Hammurapi's activities in this domain are well attested. . . . He showed much diligence in the distribution of justice. He not only gave judgments himself but he desired to be informed of the judgments in remitted cases as well."

2. I know two famous court cases involving false witnesses: TLB 1 231, studied by Leemans (1970: 63–66); and CBS 349, studied by Stol (1991: 333–339): they are very interesting, but unfortunately they are also broken and without a date, so I cannot use them here. Leemans (1968: 111) listed some cases where the judges were not prompt in giving justice, with lawsuits pending more than two years and one where a judge, the *kārum*, and the judges of Sippar had opened the house of someone without the consent of the

## Requirements to Start a Litigation

First, the Hammurabi Code opens with rules on certain procedural dysfunctions: accusation without proof (§§1–2), perjury (§§3–4), and alteration of a decision by the judge (§5). These first paragraphs are particularly important, if one also adds that, leaving aside §6, from §7 on Hammurabi keeps considering the requirements necessary to judicially enforce one's rights (having written evidence or witnesses), and it employs no less than five paragraphs (§§9–13) to explain how the evaluation of evidence should be made in a trial; we should conclude that, evidently, the problem of judicial malfunctioning was keenly perceived.

Let us start from what should be, according to Hammurabi, the requirements necessary in order to validly initiate a trial.[3] Paragraph 7 reads: "If a man should purchase silver, gold, a slave woman, an ox, a sheep, a donkey, or anything else whatsoever, from a son of a man or from a slave of a man without witnesses or a contract—or if he accepts the goods for safekeeping—that man is a thief, he shall be killed."

In this case, actually, Hammurabi is considering the situation from the viewpoint of the accused person: a man is charged with theft by the father or the master of the person who, according to the plaintiff, delivered to him a valuable good. If the defendant cannot bring a witness or a document exculpating him, he shall be considered as a thief (see Driver and Miles 1956: 80; 82–86). In two other paragraphs (§§122–123) the code takes into consideration a similar case (in these latter texts the code speaks of safekeeping in general, i.e., the goods are not delivered by the son of a free man—probably to be intended as a sort of the Roman *filius familiae*, i.e., someone who is submitted to his father's authority or a slave), but from the viewpoint of the plaintiff.

> §122: If a man intends to give silver, gold, or anything else to another man for safekeeping, he shall exhibit before witnesses anything which he intends to give, he shall draw up a written contract, and (in this manner) he shall give goods for safekeeping.
> §123: If he gives goods for safekeeping without witness or a written contract, and they deny that he gave anything, that case has no basis for a claim.

In other words, in a safekeeping it is necessary to deliver the goods before witnesses and in the presence of a scribe, otherwise one cannot claim back the delivered goods, if the keeper denies having received them: the burden of proof is therefore borne by the depositor, unless the keeper received the goods not directly from the owner, but from an employee of the owner. In this latter case, it shall be the keeper who bears the burden of proving the delivery, by showing a written document or witnesses, otherwise he shall be considered a thief.

There are also other cases in which it is necessary to conclude a contract in front of witnesses or scribes who draft a written document in order for such contract to be valid.[4]

---

competent authorities. I propose to search other evidences in trial texts and letters, dated by Hammurabi, in a future work.

3. The quoted texts are translated by Roth (1995).

4. §§ 96; 97; 104; 105; 106; 107; 124; 128; 150; 151; 165; 178; 179; 183. See also AbB 11 55, studied by Charpin (2000: 73–74).

## The Evaluation of Evidence

When the requirements to start a litigation do exist, the judge has to consider the evidence (see Boyer 1965: 181–200) in order to make a fair decision: in many cases, Hammurabi takes into consideration the various proofs, oral or written, and suggests the possible solution.[5] But there is a particularly interesting case, a dense group of five paragraphs, wherein Hammurabi distinguishes among the various possible situations.

> §9: If a man who claims to have lost property then discovers his lost property in another man's possession, but the man in whose possession the lost property was discovered declares: "A seller sold it to me, I purchased it in the presence of witnesses," and the owner of the lost property declares: "I can bring witnesses who can identify my lost property," (and then if) the buyer produces the seller who sold it to him and the witnesses in whose presence he purchased it, and also the owner of the lost property produces the witnesses who can identify his lost property—the judges shall examine their cases, and the witnesses in whose presence the purchase was made and the witnesses who can identify the lost property shall state the facts known to them before the god, then it is the seller who is the thief, he shall be killed; the owner of the lost property shall take his lost property, and the buyer shall take from the seller's estate the amount of silver that he weighed and delivered.
> §10: If the buyer could not produce the seller who sold (the lost property) to him or the witnesses before whom he made the purchase, but the owner of the lost property could produce witnesses who can identify his lost property, then it is the buyer who is the thief, he shall be killed; the owner of the lost property shall take his lost property.
> -§12: If the seller should die, the buyer shall take fivefold the claim for that case from the estate of the seller.
> §13: If that man's witnesses are not available, the judges shall grant him an extension until the sixth month, but if he does not bring his witnesses by the sixth month, it is that man who is a liar, he shall be assessed the penalty for the case.

It is really interesting here to see how Hammurabi lists the different possibilities (see Driver-Miles 1956: 95–105): if both parties bring witnesses, the seller is the thief (§9); if the (alleged) purchaser does not bring evidence while the alleged victim does, then the purchaser is the thief (§10); if the (alleged) victim does not prove his claim, then he committed perjury and must be convicted (§11); if the purchaser is dead (but then clearly there must be evidence that a sale did actually occur) then the purchaser shall receive an amount equal to five times the value of the claimed good (§12): this is in practice a variety of the second case, which explains how the purchaser can be reimbursed in case he cannot obtain satisfaction from the vendor of a stolen thing. Finally, if one of the parties tries to gain time in bringing his witnesses, then he cannot wait for more than six months; after such deadline, he is convicted (§13).

5. §§A; 178–179; 183–184; 251.

In short, in a few paragraphs we are offered a sort of subsystem to carry on the evaluation of a complex case involving three parties. Although we are far from the systematization found in Roman law, it is nonetheless interesting that even in such a source, often considered to be confused and incoherent, one could find this kind of provision.

## Accusation Without Proof

In the first two paragraphs of his code, Hammurabi considers two cases of serious accusations without proof.

> §1: If a man accuses another man and charges him with homicide but cannot bring proof against him, his accuser shall be killed.
> §2: If a man charges another man with practicing witchcraft but cannot bring proof against him, he who charged with witchcraft shall go to the divine River Ordeal, he shall indeed submit to the divine River Ordeal; if the divine River Ordeal should overwhelm him, his accuser shall take full legal possession of his estate; if the divine River Ordeal should clear that man and should he survive, he who made the charge with witchcraft against him shall be killed; he who submitted to the divine River Ordeal shall take full legal possession of his accuser's estate.

In the first case, we have a charge of murder: the accuser who cannot prove such a grave charge can be sentenced to death. One cannot make such a charge if there aren't proofs. We assume, as all commentators do (see Driver and Miles 1956: 58–61; Szlechter 1977: 19–24), that the charge be made in a process. In the second case (see Driver and Miles 1956: 61–65), the charge is grave as well, but the accuser is treated differently: he shall not be put to death, unless the defendant had not previously shown his innocence through an ordeal (immersion in a river). Only if he survives his accuser shall be put to death and his goods shall pass to the defendant. If, on the contrary, the defendant perishes, his goods should pass to the accuser.

The commentators believe that the different treatment reserved for the accuser are due to the fact that a charge of witchcraft is more difficult to prove than one of murder, and that only a direct divine intervention, through the Euphrates (the divine river), is capable of revealing the truth. Once the truth is revealed, however, not only shall the defendant lose his life, but his goods as well.

In certain cases, therefore, even without proof one can start a process, but the risk if one loses is quite high: even in the cases of §§9–13, in fact, if the accuser cannot prove his charge, he is considered as a liar, and therefore is sentenced to death. To be a liar recalls the perjuror of §§3–4, but in this case (§11) it is the defendant who lied, not a witness, and perhaps the penalty would be greater in any event.

In addition to these grave cases, however, the code also considers other, minor false charges. There is the case of §126, in which a man declares having lost something and accuses his district (*babtum*), but then the district swears before the gods that nothing was stolen: the false accuser shall pay twice what he declared having lost.[6] Thus in §127, for instance, whoever defames a priestess-*ugbabtum* or a married woman shall be beaten before the judges and half of his head shall be shaved.[7]

We have, then, hints at other cases where there is defamation, but its procedural importance is little. For example, in §161, when breaking a promise of marriage is due to the fact that the fiancé was defamed, the father shall nonetheless pay twice the value of the marriage gift received, but the defamer shall not be allowed to marry the girl.

## Perjury

> §3: If a man comes forward to give false testimony [*šībūt sarratim*] in a case but cannot bring evidence of his accusation, if the case involves a capital offense, that man will be killed.
> §4: If he comes forward to give (false) testimony for (a case whose penalty is) grain or silver, he shall be assessed the penalty for that case .

In this case, we are in front of witnesses who commit perjury in a trial: the penalty they face depends on what is at stake in the trial.[8] If it is a capital trial, perjury may obtain the acquittal or conviction of a person who, if convicted, faced the death penalty, the consequence is quite high: the perjurer shall die. If, instead, the penalty at stake is only a pecuniary one, then the penalty for the perjurer shall be proportional to the value of the case.

What is relevant, besides the logical consistence of the two paragraphs, is that they appear to be an abstract principle: they are a sort of a general rule. Obviously, we are speaking here of a perjury in the strict meaning, that is, a perjury in a trial. The proportionality principle, however, is also partially evident in the case of a false charge or defamation in the prior paragraphs: if charges are serious, the accuser shall be sentenced to death, but if he breaks a promise of marriage, he shall be forbidden to marry the girl who thus remains free to marry another man (§127), or if one defames a priestess or a married woman, then he is publicly humiliated by being beaten and shaved (§126).

## The Judge Who Alters His Judgment

> §5: If a judge renders a judgment, gives a verdict, or deposits a sealed opinion, after which he reverses his judgment, they shall charge and convict that judge of having reversed the judgment which he rendered and he shall give twelvefold

6. §126 "If a man whose property is not lost should declare 'My property is lost,' and accuse his city quarter, his city quarter shall establish against him before the god that no property of his is lost, and he shall give to his city quarter twofold whatever he claimed."

7. §127 "If a man causes a finger to be pointed in accusation against an *ugbabtu* or against a man's wife but cannot bring proof, they shall flog that man before the judges and they shall shave off half of his hair."

8. For witnesses, see Driver-Miles (1956: 65–68); see also Klengel (1960: 357–375).

the claim of that judgment; moreover, they shall unseat him from his judgeship in the assembly, and he shall never again sit in a judgment with the judges.

This is one of the most studied cases of the Hammurabi Code (see Lautner 1922: 25–67; Driver and Miles 1956: 68–80). It is the case of a judge who first renders a judgment and then alters it. If this is proven, the judge shall be obliged to pay twelvefold the value of the proceeding and he shall moreover be banned forever from the courts: he shall not sit as a judge in a process.

Naturally we have to consider that the alteration of the judgment must be thoroughly proven: probably it is implied that some pressure from a party upon the judge must have been made (in which case there would be a situation of bribery) or that some sort of interest of the judge himself must be involved (partiality in favor of one of the parties). In any event, the necessity to prove this alteration of a judgment officially rendered is stressed: only if proven, may such a charge lead to a perpetual ban of the judge and to the payment of the highest penalty in all the code.

Even aside from its actual application and the precise requirements for conviction, it is very significant that from the beginning of his code, Hammurabi takes into consideration a sanction for the judge who does not judge correctly. It is likely that such cases actually did occur. We know for certain that Hammurabi was often called to judge upon or to check the behavior of his officials in the legal field (see Leemans 1968, esp. 110–122): mistakes happen, but in some cases clearly it was possible to prove that what occurred was not a mistake but a rethinking, perhaps due to pressures from one of the parties. In this case it would have been up to other judges, or maybe to the king himself, to remedy by applying the appropriate penalties.

## Conclusions

To sum up, we may conclude that within the Hammurabi Code, but also elsewhere (e.g. Codex of Ur-Namma §§13; 14; 27; 28; Codex of Lipit-Ishtar §§22; 38; Edict of Ammiṣaduqa §§5; 7), there are provisions concerning cases that may render unfair the proceedings aimed at reestablishing justice (*misharum*): one goes to court to obtain justice, but when one party is disloyal, or when the umpire is unfair, it is necessary to consider these cases as crimes and to provide adequate penalties. They work as deterrents: accusing someone of murder without proof is very risky, as well as accusing someone of theft; defaming a man who is going to marry, perhaps the girl one is in love with, is not very effective, since in all events the girl shall never be allowed to marry the defamer. Stating that the penalty for perjury shall be the same for the crime where the perjury occurred is a strong deterrent. This is also probably the reason for giving so high a penalty and forever destroying the career of a judge who alters his decision, possibly because he has been bribed.

The king legislator's awareness is noteworthy: he immediately begins by taking into account the possible unfair behaviors that may occur in a trial. And thus he seeks to reassure his people, declaring that he shall try (that he had already tried), if and when possible, to correct the mistakes of the procedural system, adopting the correct measures. He tries, therefore, to restore order within the courts, such that justice and fairness reign. But alas, within the tribunal it is the justice of the men, not the justice of the gods, that rules: and the kings do only what they can.

**BIBLIOGRAPHY**


Boyer, G.
1965 La preuve dans les ancient Droit du Proche Orient. Pp. 181–200 in *Mélanges d'histoire du droit oriental*. Paris: Sirey.

Charpin, D.
2000 Lettres et procès paléo-babyloniens. Pp. 69–111 in *Rendre la justice en Mèsopotamie: Archives judiciares du Proche-Orient ancien (3.e-1.er millénaires avant J.-C.)*. Edited by F. Joannès. Saint-Denis: Presses Universitaires de Vincennes.

Cuq, E.
1910 Essai sur l'organisation judiciaire de la Caldée. *RA* 7: 65–101.

Dombradi, E.
1996 *Die Darstellung des Rechtsaustrags in den Altbabylonischen Prozessurkunden*. FAOS 20. Stuttgart: Steiner.

Driver, G. R. and Miles, J. C.
1956 *The Babylonian Laws*. 2 vols. Oxford: Clarendon.

Klengel, H.
1960 Zu den *šībūtum* in altbabylonischer Zeit. *Or* 29: 357–375.

Koschaker, P.
1917 *Rechtsvergleichende Studien zur Gesetzgebung Ḫammurapis*. Leizpig: Veit.

Lautner, J.
1922 *Die richterliche Entscheidung und die Streitbeendigung im altbabylonischen Prozeßrechte*. Leipziger rechtswissenschaftliche Studien 3. Leipzig: Weicher.

Leemans, W. F.
1968 King Hammurapi as a Judge. Pp. 107–129 in *Symbolae iuridicae et historicae Martino David dedicatae*. Edited by J. Ankum, R. Feenstre, and W. F. Leemans. Iura Orienti Antiqui 2. Leiden: Brill.
1970 Le faux témoin. *RA* 64: 63–66.

Roth, M. T.
1995 *Law Collections from Mesopotamia and Asia Minor*. WAW 6. Atlanta: Scholars Press.

Stol, M.
1991 Eine Prozessurkunde über "falsches Zeugnis." Pp. 333–339 in *Marchands, Diplomats et Empereurs: Études sur la civilisation mésopotamienne offertes à Paul Garelli*. Edited by D. Charpin and F. Joannes. Paris: Éditions Recherches sur les Civilisations.

Szlechter, É.
1977 *Codex Hammurapi*. Studia et Documenta 3. Rome: Pontificia Universitas Lateranensis.

Walther, A.
1917 *Das altbabylonische Gerichtswesen*. LSS 6. Leipzig: Hinrich.

CHAPTER 22

# The Ashurbanipal Library Project at the British Museum

Jon Taylor

IT WAS A REMARKABLE STROKE OF LUCK that the first large corpus of cuneiform texts to be rediscovered in Mesopotamia was the Library of Assurbanipal, king of Assyria (668–ca. 630 BC). It quickly became the foundation stone on which the modern study of Assyriology was built. The library remains a key Assyriological resource 160 years later. The British Museum's Ashurbanipal Library Project is working to make the entire library available in digital form. A digital catalogue is now publicly available; it will be updated and expanded regularly, keeping pace with the intensive research that continues to be undertaken on its texts. New, high-resolution digital images of the entire library are available, together with an extensive library of historical photos and line drawings dating back as far as the 1850s. We also include bibliography and as many transliterations and translations as possible. The catalogue is intended as a long-term resource to stimulate interest and facilitate teaching and research on the texts.

## History of the Project

The project was set up in 2002, following a request from the Iraqi Ministry of Higher Education and Research for support for their planned new Institute for Cuneiform Studies at the University of Mosul. Funding from the Townley Group of British Museum Friends (2003) enabled Dr. Jeanette Fincke to produce a new database classifying each of the three thousand five hundred library tablets in Babylonian script. Further funding (2005, 2006) allowed Fincke to focus on astrological fortune-telling texts in Assyrian script. The results of this work feature on a website (http://www.fincke-cuneiform.com/nineveh/index.htm), and were published by Fincke (2003/2004, 2004, 2014). A third tranche of funding (2008–2010) from the Townley Group brought the assistance of the foremost expert on the library, Professor Riekele Borger, Emeritus Professor of Assyriology at the University of Göttingen. His tireless and meticulous work in identifying and joining fragments proved invaluable. His work is being incorporated into our catalogue.

From 2009–2013, with the generous support of the Andrew Mellon Foundation, a new phase of activity saw the creation of high-resolution digital images of all the library tablets. The British Museum's founding mission is to make its collections freely available to the "studious and curious." As technology changed, new methods of engagement became possible. In 1852 Lord Rosse, Chairman of the Trustees, had declared: "I feel very anxious that some attempt should be made to Photograph the

FIGURE 22.1. The photograph of K 15 made by Roger Fenton in the 1850s.

inscriptions so as to place them conveniently within the reach of persons that have a taste for that line of research . . . and it seems to me to be a reproach to the Trustees . . . that the aids of modern Science should not have been called for sooner."

Thus the new technology of photography was put to use in imaging cuneiform tablets. Roger Fenton, pioneer photographer famous today for his work in the Crimea, was employed as the museum's first official photographer. In the 1850s he produced images of almost three hundred tablets recently excavated by A. H. Layard at Nineveh. But photography would remain prohibitively expensive for mass imaging of tablets until the turn of the twenty-first century. Finally, the ready availability of digital photography, cheap data storage, the internet, and widespread broadband access have made it feasible to make Rosse's vision a reality. Now for the first time, the entire library is available in new high-quality images. Each final image is a composite—comprising up to fourteen primary images—representing a virtual unfolding of the 3D object into a 2D facsimile with all faces of each tablet visible in a single image. Additional images of seal impressions were taken, since these require different lighting from the text. The images were released over the course of the project both on the British Museum Collections Online site: http://www.britishmuseum.org/research/search_the_collection_database.aspx; and on the CDLI website: http://cdli.ucla.edu/.

## Institute for Cuneiform Studies, Mosul

In 2002 plans were unveiled for a new Institute for Cuneiform Studies at the University of Mosul. Teaching and research were to focus on Ashurbanipal's Library, which had been excavated across the river from Mosul. Construction of the Institute for Cuneiform Studies is well underway, and its inauguration is due in 2015.[1] It will

1. This paragraph describes the situation at the time of the submission of the article, April 2014.

FIGURE 22.2. The photograph of K 15 made by the Ashurbanipal Library Project in 2009. © Trustees of the British Museum.

house departments of Archaeology, Assyriology and Ancient Near Eastern Civilizations, Excavation and Conservation. Archaeologists from Mosul are now excavating at Nineveh; it is hoped that the rest of Ashurbanipal's Library may soon be found there.

## The Online Catalogue

The Ashurbanipal Library catalogue remains a work in progress. It builds on the museum's acquisition registers, file cards and collections database, the printed catalogues of Carl Bezold and others, Erle Leichty's bibliography, additional cataloguing by Fincke and Borger, and the integration of various other resources, printed and electronic. An attempt is being made to bring it fully up-to-date and keep it up-to-date

FIGURE 22.3. Institute for Cuneiform Studies, University of Mosul. Photo by Ali Yassin Al-Jaboori.

as the ever-increasing flow of new publications continues. We warmly welcome the collaboration of colleagues.

We are continuing to update and improve the catalogue, now also adding a wide range of metadata relating to tablet and formatting features, colophons, and script types, as well as transliterations and translations (many of which are kindly shared by colleagues). The original images produced during the course of the project will continue to be available, as a record of the state of the library in 2009–2013. The availability of the images has resulted in a significant increase in the number of joins being made. As these happen, additional versions of the images will become available, so that scholars also have access to the latest state of knowledge.

The catalogue is intended to offer as wide access as possible to one of the most remarkable repositories of knowledge the world has ever known. The texts and translations are available through the standard Oracc Creative Commons terms. The images we have produced are available through the standard British Museum terms (http://www.britishmuseum.org/about_this_site/terms_of_use/free_image_service.aspx). They are thus freely available for scholarly use, including noncommercial publication and teaching and research presentations.

## Credits

The catalogue is the fruit of a wide-reaching international collaboration, and stands as a testament to the industry and kindness of everyone involved. It has been made possible through the hard work of many colleagues: Marieka Arksey, Lisa Baylis, Kristin Phelps, Sarah Readings, and Ana Tam, with the assistance of Frances Anderson, Elizabeth Bennett, Pippa Browne, Mary Bywater, Amy Davy, Joanna Derman, Eleonora Farris, Matt Fittock, Alberto Giannese, Chloe Higman, Nadia Jaglom, Gina Konstantopoulos, Aimee Laird, Nineb Lamassu, Alix Lowe, Sophie Major, Jana Matuszak, Willis Monroe, Michelle Parker, Anna Perdibon, Ryan Perry, Giulia Pieralisi, Ignatius Rautenbach, Holly Salisbury, Chiara Salvador, Johanna Tudeau, Karolin Ulbricht, Maeve Weber, and Heather Williamson. Prior to digitization, conservation

FIGURE 22.4. A glass lantern slide of display case "Table Case B" in the Kouyunjik Gallery of the British Museum, circa 1880s, containing the Gilgamesh tablets. Private collection. Top row: left (?), center K 3375 (Gilgamesh), right (?). Bottom row: left K 162 (Ishtar's Descent), center Rm 616 (Gilgamesh), right K 2252 (Gilgamesh).

work was conducted by Julia Barton, Bryony Finn, Hazel Gardiner, Denise Ling, Kathleen Swales, and Rachel Swift. The project also relied on many colleagues at the museum, especially Jonathan Whitson-Cloud in the documentation team, and Rebecca Green in the Information Services team.

The catalogue, available at the Open Richly Annotated Cuneiform Corpus (www .oracc.org), also brings together all available transliterations and translations of library texts. This includes a large amount of unpublished as well as published material. In particular, we have benefitted from the generous support of the State Archives of Assyria (courtesy of Simo Parpola and Karen Radner), the Digital Corpus of Cuneiform Lexical Texts (courtesy of Niek Veldhuis), the Royal Inscriptions of the Neo-Assyrian Period (courtesy of Grant Frame), Claus Ambos, Nicla de Zorzi, Sally Freedman, Erlend Gehlken, Ann Guinan, Enrique Jiménez, Ulla Koch, Wilfred Lambert, Alasdair Livingstone, Daniel Schwemer, JoAnn Scurlock, Henry Stadhouders, Lorenzo Verderame, and Martin Worthington.

Most library tablets are currently curated in the British Museum. There are tablets elsewhere, however. Reuniting them has been made possible by the kind collaboration of partner institutions around the world: the Hermitage, the Louvre, the Vatican Museums, Penn Museum, the Kunsthistorisches Museum Vienna, and the De Liagre Böhl Collection Leiden.

We are very grateful to all our colleagues for their hard work and kind cooperation. The project remains an open collaboration.

## Future Research by the Museum

The library will be a major focus of research at the museum for the long term. While a lot is known about individual compositions within the library, and about genres of text, our understanding of the nature of the library itself is still far from complete. Its sheer scale is daunting. We aim to understand the composition and functioning of the library. This will be achieved through a detailed study of palaeography, orthography, and materiality. We are also studying the colophons.

A second area of interest is the presentation and reception of the library and its contents in the modern era. From 1850s the museum produced detailed gallery guides, allowing us to reconstruct which tablets were on display in which case in which gallery. They also tell us what the museum saw as important to tell the visitor. Some photographs of the galleries as they stood in the nineteenth century are preserved, both official and unofficial. These are being gathered and will be made available. They allow us to chart the history of interpretation of the library tablets.

The discovery of Assyria caused an enormous media sensation. Visitors flocked to the museum to see the winged bulls and lions sent back by Layard from Nineveh in the 1850s. Similarly in 1873, news of George Smith's revelation of the flood tablet raced around the world, stimulating intense interest that has yet to subside over a century later. Fascination with Assyria was reflected in the spread of Assyrian motifs into the popular imagination, and manifested through their use in ephemeral materials: postcards (a Twitter-like obsession from the turn of the twentieth century up to the First World War), collecting cards from popular products of the time such as meat extract, margarine, or cigarettes, and newspaper advertising and the like. These materials are being collected and also made available through the project.

### BIBLIOGRAPHY

Fincke, J.

2003/2004 The Babylonian Texts of Nineveh: Report on the British Museum's Ashurbanipal Library Project. *AfO* 50: 112–149.

2004 The British Museum's Ashurbanipal Library Project. *Iraq* 66: 55–60.

2014 Babylonische Gelehrte am neuassyrischen Hof: Zwischen Anpassung und Individualität. Pp. 269–292 in *Krieg und Frieden: 52e Rencontre Assyriologique Internationale, International Congress of Assyriology and Near Eastern Archaeology, Münster, 17.–21. Juli 2006*. Edited by H. Neumann, R. Dittmann, S. Paulus, G. Neumann, and A. Schuster-Brandis. AOAT 401. Münster: Ugarit-Verlag.

CHAPTER 23

# The Sea and Monarchic Legitimation in the Ancient Near East

Joanna Töyräänvuori

THE SEA AND THE KING appear together in many ancient Northwest Semitic texts, dating back to the Mari of the Old Babylonian period, featuring in the epics of Late Bronze Age Ugarit, all the way down to biblical texts dating to the Persian period. The sea is also a staple of many Assyrian and Babylonian royal inscriptions, figuring in the feats of many, if indeed not most, of the kings following the Urukean Lugal-zage-si and Sargon of Agade.[1] While the sea is an important geographical feature on the shore of the eastern Mediterranean where ancient Ugarit was located, there is much less occasion for its prominence in the myths and royal inscriptions of inland empires like Yamḫad, Mari, and Assyria. What could explain its symbolic significance in these different types of texts spanning across such a long time and a vast area? It is my intention to discuss the use of the ancient Near Eastern myth of divine combat, or *Chaoskampf,* as an instrument of monarchic legitimation in the many kingdoms that seemed to have modeled their royal ideologies on the example of the great Akkadian Sargon and the mythologized narratives of his conquests, among which featured the important cult center of Aleppo, where the myth of the storm god's battle with the sea may have originated.

The myth of divine combat between the storm god and the sea first appears in the Old Babylonian period, although myths of divine battle between other contestants are known from earlier times. One of the first explicit mentions of the battle is in the letter of an Aleppan prophet to King Zimri-Lim of Mari, which mentions the weapons that the storm god of Aleppo had used in defeating the sea.[2]

1. Malamat 1965: 365. An older contemporary of Sargon's, Lugal-zage-si, also boasted of having dominion from the Upper Sea to the Lower Sea, and seems to have been the first king to unite all of Sumer under single rule. Note that in the Lugal-zege-si vase inscription RIME 1.14.20.01:I 36–II 9 (u$_4$ [$^{d}$]en-líl lugal kur-kur-ra-ke$_4$ lugal-zà-ge-si nam-lugal kalam-ma e-na-šúm-ma-a igi kalam!-ma-ke$_4$ si e-na-sá-a kur-kur girì-na e-ni-sè-ga-a utu-è-ta utu-šú-šè gú e-na-gar-ra-a u$_4$-ba a-ab-ba sig-<ta>-ta idigna buranum-bé a-ab-ba igi-dim-ma-šè; "When Enlil, king of the world, had given Lugal-zage-si the kingship of the land and had let the eyes of the land be directed toward him and had placed all the foreign lands at his feet and had made them subject to him from the rising of the sun to the setting of the sun, then from the Lower Sea of the Tigris and Euphrates to the Upper Sea") Lugal-zage-si claims that it was the storm god Enlil that gave him dominion from Upper Sea to Lower Sea. Regardless of the function of this terminology in Lugal-zage-si's ideology, it is possible that the Agadean Sargon, "fathered by no man," was utilizing language used by Lugal-zage-si to legitimate his usurpation. Unless otherwise noted, all translations are by the author.

2. Malamat 1998: 27, 34. "The other, recent evidence from Mari, touching on the mythological character of the Mediterranean, is to be found in a letter sent to King Zimri-Lim at Mari (the son of the aforementioned

**Letter** (A.1968:1–4′)[3]

| | |
|---|---|
| *a-na be-lí-ia qí-bí-ma* | To my lord say: |
| *um-ma nu-úr-*$^{d}$*su'en ìr-ka-a-ma* | "Thus Nur-Sin, your servant: |
| $^{I}$*a-bi-ia a-pí-lum ša* $^{d}$IM *be-el ḫa-la-a*[*b*$^{ki}$] | Abiya, the prophet of Addu, the Lord of Alep[po], |
| *il-li-kam-ma ki-a-am iq-bé-e-em* | he came to me and thus he said: |
| *um-ma-a-mi* $^{d}$IM*-ma ma-a-tam*$_4$ (TUM) *ka-la-ša* | 'Says Adad: "The land, in its entirety |
| *a-na ia-aḫ-du-li-im ad-di-in* | I had given to Yahdun-Lim, |
| *ù i-na* $^{GIŠ}$tukul.*meš-ia ma-ḫi-ra-am ú-ul ir-ši* | and with my weapons, an equal he did not encounter, |
| *i-ia-tam i-zi-ib-ma ma-a-tam ša ad-di-nu-šu*[*m*] | (yet when) he abandoned me, the land which I had given hi[m], |
| *a-na sa-am-si-*$^{d}$IM *ad-*[*di-i*]*n* | I g[av]e to Shamshi-Adad |
| [. . . $^{I}$]*sa-am-si-*$^{d}$IM | . . . Shamshi-Adad |
| (lacuna) | (lacuna) |
| *lu-t*[*e-e*]*r-ka a-na* $^{GIŠ}$[*gu.za* É *a-bi-ka*] | —let me r[e]store you! On the [throne of the house of your father] |
| *ú-te-er-ka* $^{GIŠ}$tukul.[*meš*] | I returned you, the weapon[s] |
| *ša it-ti te-em-tim am-ta-aḫ-ṣú* | with which I struck the sea |
| *ad-di-na-ak-kum* | I have given you . . ."' . . ." |

This brief mention has been connected to an earlier campaign to the Mediterranean coast by a predecessor of Zimri-Lim, the Amorite king Yahdun-Lim. In Yahdun-Lim's foundation inscription of the Shamash temple, the earlier king records his military campaign to the Mediterranean coast. In Yahdun-Lim's inscription (E4.6.8.2:34–37, 41–51, 60–63; Dossin 1955: 1–28) we find the following:

| | |
|---|---|
| *ša iš-tu u*$_4$*-um ṣa-at* | From the days of old, |
| *a-lam Ma-ri*$^{ki}$ DINGIR *ib-nu-ú* | when god (/El/Anu) had built Mari, |
| LUGAL *ma-ma-an wa-ši-ib Ma-ri*$^{ki}$ | no king seated in Mari |
| *ti-a-am-ta-am la ik-šu-du* | had reached the sea |
| . . . | . . . |
| $^{m}$*Ia-ah-du-un-li-im* | Yahdun-Lim |
| DUMU *Ia-gi-id-li-im* | son of Yaggid-Lim |
| LUGAL *ga-aš-ru-um ri-im šar-ri* | the mighty king, the wild ox of kings |
| *i-na le-ù-tim* | went to the shore of the sea |
| *ù ga-mi-ru-tim* | in irresistible strength and |
| *a-na ki-ša-ad ti-a-am-tim* | to the great sea he offeredthe sacrifices |
| *il-li-ik-ma* | of his great kingship[4] |

Yahdun-Lim and the last king of Old Babylonian Mari) by his ambassador to Aleppo in the days of its King Yarim-Lim."

3. Only the pertinent lines have been translated. For a full transliteration, translation, and facsimile, see Durand 1993, 43–45.

4. Malamat (1998: 34) parses the term "great royal sacrifices" and (1965: 376) "a multitude of royal sacrifices."

| | |
|---|---|
| *a-na* A.A.AB.BA *ni-qi šar-ru-ti-šú* | and his troops |
| *ra-bi-a-am iq-qi* | washed themselves |
| *ù ṣa-bu-šu i-na qé-re-eb* A.A.AB.BA | with water |
| *me-e ir-mu-uk* | in the midst of the great sea |
| . . . | . . . |
| *ma-a-tam ša-ti ša ki-ša-ad* A.A.AB. B[A] | The land that was on the shore of the great sea he |
| *ù-ka-an-ni-iš* | subjugated, |
| *a-na pí-im ù-še-ši-ib-ši* | he made it obedient to (the command of his) |
| *wa-ar-ki-šu ù-ša-li-ik-ši* | mouth, to follow after him |

Having reached the sea, Yahdun-Lim offers the sea "the sacrifices of his great kingship," and has his troops make a washing in the sea as a symbolic act. While the myth is not explicitly mentioned in the inscription, the ideology of it seems to underlie the inscription (Malamat 1998: 25).

The most complete iteration of this myth of divine combat between the storm god and the sea is known to us from the texts of the ancient city of Ugarit, on the coast of modern day Syria. The Baal Cycle, a collection of loosely connected texts of epic poetry, features the weather god Baal's battle against Yamm, whose name means "sea." The myth is in narrative form, complete with dialogue and action, and concerns the question of which deity, the sea or the weather god, should become the ruler of the assembly of the gods. The text of the Baal Cycle that was discovered in Ugarit dates to the Late Bronze Age, and is at least half a millennium later than the brief glimpses at the myth we have from ancient Mari. But the date that the text was originally composed is an open question, and it clearly draws from older material, either directly from Mari or Aleppo, as Ugarit had relations with both kingdoms harking back to the Old Babylonian period, or indirectly through an intermediary.[5] The prince of Ugarit is believed to have visited Mari, in awe of its palaces (A.186), so the suggestion that the two kingdoms may have shared some of the symbolic aspects of kingship, such as the storm god's defeat of the sea on behalf of the king, is hardly inconceivable. While the myth seems to have its roots in the Aleppan cult center of the storm god (which is rather curious considering Aleppo's inland location), it was through the acts of the kings of Mari that the myth blossomed, and it is in the Late Bronze Age Ugarit that we find it in full bloom.[6]

The Northwest Semitic or Amorite myth of divine combat was also likely perused in the fashioning of the Babylonian epic of Enuma Elish, which in its extant form dates to the Neo-Assyrian period. Its composition is a much discussed topic: some have dated it contemporary to the Mari letter, being the era of Hammurabi, which seems unlikely, while some, like B. F. Batto (1992: 35), date its composition later than the

5. The tablets of the Baal Cycle were discovered in the so-called library of the high priest (which was possibly the location of a scribal school) in the city of Ugarit, in the years 1930–1933 (Smith 1994: 1; 1997: 82). The first publication was made by Virolleaud (1929, 1932). Physically, the tablets were written between the years 1400–1350 BCE (Smith 1997: 81). The date of their composition however remains an open question, and Smith admits that there are layers present in the text that witness to a longer development.

6. On the Amorite origins of the myth, see Durand 1993; Bordreuil and Pardee 1993; Wyatt 2002: 35; 2003: 148.

Baal Cycle. Wherever the truth of its dating may lie, it seems that the Babylonian myth is a composite of different traditions, one of which is surely the Northwest Semitic myth. The Babylonian myth features aspects that are not found in the Northwest Semitic myth, such as the creation of the world and the creation of man, or the war between the generations of the gods, but the core function of the myth is to elevate Marduk, the god of Babylon, as the supreme deity. As defeating the sea was one of the staples of kingship, so Marduk had to defeat Tiamat to become the king of the gods.[7] But why had the defeating of the sea become symbolic of kingship in the first place?

There are several legends pertaining to Sargon of Agade that connect the monarch with the sea, and the king's life was connected to water in a number of ways. According to A. Malamat, the text of the so-called Sargon chronicle "doubtless indicates the sacred and purifying aspect of such a great body of water." In it, Sargon makes the campaign to the Mediterranean, and it seems that he was indeed the first Mesopotamian king to have made a military incursion there. According to Malamat, there seems to be no doubt concerning the historicity of Sargon's expedition. He entertains the notion that Sargon and his successors may have ruled the coasts of the Eastern Mediterranean and Cyprus, even maintaining a possible commercial relationship with Crete. And, during his voyage, Sargon appears to have made a stop at Tuttul, a city in Mari territory, to honor the storm god of the area, Dagan. Curious are also the Sargon omens discovered at Mari, popular also in later times While not direct evidence of Sargon's presence at Mari, his enduring legacy in the area is also witnessed by the Sargon omens discovered in the city, which seem to have been popular centuries after the death of the king (Green 2003: 68; Horowitz 1998: 77).

Sargon's predecessor Lugal-zage-si, the uniter of Sumer, mentions the Upper and Lower Sea in his vase inscriptions from the weather god Enlil's shrine at Nippur, and is believed to either have made a small raid to the Mediterranean coast, or to have exaggerated his conquests by claiming to have done so. But while Lugal-zage-si's inscription may have been the prototype upon which Sargon modeled his royal inscriptions, it is Sargon's conquests that set the standard on what a later Mesopotamian king was supposed have and projected as having accomplished. In another legend, preserved in several copies, Sargon is also presented as washing his weapon in the sea.[8] In the same text, it is mentioned that it was the storm god Enlil who gave Sargon the Upper Sea and the Lower Sea as his dominion, as with Lugal-zage-si. Similar language to the Sargonic passage is found in a cultic psalm dedicated to Shamash, possibly from

7. Dalley 1987: 329, in her treatment of the Enuma Elish, divided it into two parts: the creation story (which she called the "sacred marriage" part of the myth), and the *Chaoskampf*, clearly delineating the two strands in the narrative. Even Kramer 1943: 70–73, one of the most prolific early commentators on the myth, observed the Sumerian influences in what he called the "Semitic creation epic" (in 1944: 114)—although he was convinced that the epic was of Sumerian origin (p. 77: "even a surface examination of its contents clearly reveals Sumerian origins and influence"). I would go further and suggest that there are three distinct parts to the narrative: the creation, the war between the generations of the gods, and the battle between Tiamat and Marduk. The first has its origins in Sumerian mythology, the second in Indo-Aryan mythology, and the third in Amorite mythology. Weaving all of these narratives into the Enuma Elish served to increase the legitimation of Marduk as the supreme god and Babylon as the center of the universe.

8. RIME 2.1.1.1:50–52: $^{\text{GIŠ}}$TUKUL-*ni* A.AB.BA-*ka* Ì.LUḪ; 2.1.1.1:56–58: $^{\text{GIŠ}}$TUKUL-*ki-śu in ti-a-am-tim* Ì.LUḪ; 2.1.1.2:59–61: ⸢$^{\text{GIŠ}}$⸣ TUKUL-*kí-śu in ti-a-am-tim* Ì.LUḪ; 2.1.1.3:44–46: $^{\text{GIŠ}}$⸢TUKUL⸣ [-*ki-śu*] ⸢*in*⸣ [*ti-a-am-tim*] Ì.[LUḪ].

Sippar. In the reverse of the same tablet, the sea and the Euphrates River are contrasted, paralleling the storm god Baal's defeat of Prince Sea and Judge River of the Ugaritic myth. In SBH 23 obv. 19–25 and 23 rev. 1 (restored from R IV 26:4,5/SBH 47 19–22) we find the following lines:

<table>
<tr><td>dingir babbar é-ta dingir babbar šuš-aš ur-sa[g-gal]</td><td>From sunrise to sunset, grea[t hero]</td></tr>
<tr><td>im-gal-lu im ǵir-ra ur-[sag-gal]</td><td>In the south and north, [great hero]</td></tr>
<tr><td>a-ab-ba sik-šú [ur-sag-gal]</td><td>to the Lower Sea, [great hero]</td></tr>
<tr><td>a-ab-ba ši-nim- šú [ur-sag-gal]</td><td>to the Upper Sea, [great hero]</td></tr>
<tr><td>ki $^{giš}$ǵa-lu-úb da-ri-ta[ur-sag-gal]</td><td>in the land of eternal haluppu-tree, [great hero]</td></tr>
<tr><td>$^{giš}$ǵa-lu-úb $^{giš}$tir $^{giš}$erin-kud-da [ur-sag-gal]</td><td>the haluppu-tree, the cedar forest, [great hero]</td></tr>
<tr><td>$^{d}$en-bi-lu-lu $^{giš}$tir $^{giš}$erin [ur-sag-gal]</td><td>Marduk[9] of the cedar forest, [great hero]</td></tr>
<tr><td></td><td></td></tr>
<tr><td>ur-sag me-en a-ab-ba um-[mi-lal ab-ši ǵu-luǵ-ga]</td><td>You are a hero, if it[10] is directed upon the sea, [the sea shudders]</td></tr>
<tr><td>ur-sag me-en sug-ga um-mi-[lal sug-ga še-ám-du]</td><td>You are a hero, if it is directed upon the marsh, [the marsh moans]</td></tr>
<tr><td>a-ge-a íd zimbir$^{ki}$-ge [um-mi-lal]</td><td>if it be directed upon the Euphrates, [the Euphrates moans]</td></tr>
</table>

While it is difficult to ascertain what the original function of the hymn was, the vocabulary used in it is very similar to the Sargonic legend, and to what we find in later royal inscriptions. It is possible that the Sargonic authors—and it must be stressed that most texts pertaining to Sargon are not contemporary to his reign and are to be dated much later, and even the autobiographical text fragments are scribal copies—have borrowed their language of royal legitimation from temple liturgy. Sargon's grandson Naram-Sin also claims to have had dominion from the Upper Sea to the Lower Sea, master of the four quarters of the earth. And like his grandfather, he also washed his weapon in the sea.[11] Naram-Sin was also the first Mesopotamian king to elevate himself as a god, taking on not only the DINGIR-sign to his name, but also the horned miter of the gods in his royal iconography. In Naram-Sin, more than in any other Mesopotaman monarch before him, the god and king became one.[12]

Paralleling the Mosaic birth narrative, Sargon was also believed to have been cast into the river by his mother, as he had been borne illegitimately. In the Sargon Birth

9. Enbilulu is equated with Marduk and Adad of Babylon (Kutscher 1975: 50).

10. Langdon (1914: 56, 69) interprets "it" as the word of Enlil and Anu, as he connects the hymn to a series of hymns intended for the cult of Ur bearing the same catchline, *an-na e-lum-e*. However, there seems to be no connection between the texts. Some sort of offensive force or weapon is probably indicated. On the significance of the weapons of the storm god in relation to this ideology, see Töyräänvuori 2012.

11. RIME 2.1.4.3: 29–32: $^{GIŠ}$TUKUL-*kí-śu*$_4$ *i*[*n*] *ti-a-am-tim śa-píl-tim* Ì.LUḪ.

12. See Hallo 1987 for the changes over the centuries in the propagandistic justification of Mesopotamian kingship.

Legend, the river carries Sargon to Akki, "the drawer of water," who then raises him as his son. It might be speculated whether these aspects of Sargon's are later found in the figure of the biblical Moses informed by the latter's role as the "antiking"; the figure of Moses, it seems, possesses all the symbolic aspects of a king, but at the same time is emphatically *not* a king, transcending and subverting the role. While the historical basis of the Sargon narratives is somewhat questionable, it does remain that in later times these legendary tales were connected to Sargon, who was considered an exemplary king—a model on which later kings could base their kingships, both regarding the symbols of monarchic rule, as well as the narrative of kingship. Malamat (1965: 373) writes that the expeditions of the rulers of the Old Babylonian period were "doubtless" a source of inspiration for poets and narrators. The enduring popularity of Sargon's example is evidenced by the fact that the Sargonic legends were popular hundreds upon hundreds of years after his death—Nabonidus, who based much of his royal propaganda on the Neo-Assyrian kings, who in turn had used the figure of Sargon in their own political legitimation, even seems to have conducted archaeological digs at Sargon's palaces (Oates 1979: 162).

It bears repeating that most of the sources of the Sargonic legends do not date to his time, but are considerably later and anecdotal in nature, most dating to the Neo-Assyrian period. But the historicity of the Sargonic narratives is not the focus of the inquiry, but rather the effect of the legends, of Sargon's conquest of the sea on Enlil's behalf, and with the blessing of the Amorite Dagan, on the formation of the Northwest Semitic myth of divine combat and its later use in monarchic legitimation.[13]

Next I will discuss the witness of royal inscriptions from the Assyrian and Babylonian area. The Sargonic motif in the Assyrian inscriptions has been discussed previously by R. Rollinger in his 2012 paper entitled "From Sargon of Agade and the Assyrian Kings." What the Mesopotamian royal inscriptions offer us is a concurrent evolution of the motif of the myth of divine combat: whereas in the Northwest Semitic cultural area the motif was embedded in mythology and cultic poetry, becoming more and more removed from the concrete concept of the legitimation of power as time went by, in the Assyrian and Babylonian area it was explicitly forged into a rather secular facet of the royal ideology, and carved into stone in the many royal inscriptions from the area. I will present some examples of the conquest of the sea in Mesopotamian royal inscriptions.

Neo-Assyrian kings of the first millennium BCE often recorded their arrival at the Mediterranean coast and their offering of sacrifices on the seashore, undoubtedly fashioning this propagandistic practice on Sargon's precedent. The troops of the Neo-Assyrian kings dipped their weapons in the water of the sea, according to Malamat (1998: 25) thus symbolically purifying them, "with no further ceremony."

The sea is mentioned in a temple inscription of the Assyrian monarch Tiglath-pileser I in the eleventh century BCE, commemorating the rebuilding of a temple of Anu and Adad in the city of Assur. Tiglath-pileser, who made a campaign to the

13. Malamat 1965: 369–370. He writes, "It would be difficult, therefore, to assume that details of this kind are just figments of the imagination, while plagiarism is unthinkable, at least as far as our present information goes, since there is no document of the same or even similar contents that could have served as an archetype for the king's scribes." While this is possible, there would almost certainly have been at the very least oral accounts of Sargon and Naram-Sin's campaigns circulating in the ancient Near East.

Mediterranean Sea, was the first monarch to rule after Assyria was restored to power and, while his inscription may owe influence to the Sargonic legends, undoubtedly the following Assyrian inscriptions were at least partially also fashioned after Tigleth-pileser's inscriptions, making him one of the nexus points in the transmission of the tradition. The language of Tiglath-pileser's inscription is similar to the previous inscriptions, further mentioning the locale of Lebanon, cedar wood, and tribute, which he claims to have received from the Phoenician cities of Byblos, Sidon, and Arvad. It also features the line: "I killed a narwhal which they call 'sea horse' on the high sea." While there are many familiar elements to the inscription, the slaying of this peculiar creature is not mentioned elsewhere. The sea is also mentioned in the so-called Tiglath-Pileser cylinder, where the term "Upper Sea" and the "Upper Sea of the welcoming of the sun" are mentioned. This sea appears to be located in Anatolia. The sea is also mentioned in Tiglath-pileser's rock inscription of Sebeneh-Su, which speaks of the great sea of the land of Amurru, and the sea of Nairi.[14]

Assurnasirpal II made a campaign similar to Sargon and Yahdun-Lim, which is related in the annals (Badali et al. 1982). In it, reference is made to the washing of his weapon in the sea, and the offering of sacrifices by the sea. In the standard inscription (RIMA.0.101.30), Assurnasirpal also fashions himself as: "The glorious king, the shepherd, the protector of the whole world, the king, the word of whose mouth destroys mountains and seas." The Assyrian king Shalmaneser III, son of Assurnasirpal II, is also presented as sacrificing to the sea in a stele he set up on the shore of the Mediterranean. The Black Obelisk of Shalmaneser III, iv, 7–19, 26–30 reads: "I went to the mountain of Bali-Rasi, which is a promontory on the sea upon the land of Tyre. I set up there a stele of myself as king. . . . I crossed the Euphrates at its flood; I advanced to the shore of the sea of the setting sun; I washed my weapons in the sea; I offered sacrifices to my gods." The formulation of the Shalmaneser inscription is slightly different from other accounts, as it calls the sea "the sea of the Land of Amurru," while still referring to the Mediterranean. But Shalmaneser also washed his weapon in the sea. Malamat connected both Shalmaneser's and Assurnasirpal's inscriptions to Yahdun-Lim's foundation inscription, and to his campaign to the Mediterranean Sea. The so-called throne-base inscription of Shalmaneser III was found in Nimrud. Other Shalmaneser inscriptions mentioning the sea include the Kurkh monolith and the Balawat gates inscription.[15] There is also a mention in one of his inscriptions of the storm god Adad carrying the weapon or whip with which he punished the sea.[16]

Sennacherib was the son of Sargon II. The Assyrian monarch Sargon II, who was of uncertain ancestry, had no relation to Sargon of Agade, and only used the latter's name to legitimate his kingship. Many of the legends pertaining to Sargon of Agade may have been circulated or even authored during the reign of Sargon II, as the king

14. The Sea of Nairi and the washing of the weapons are also mentioned in Shalmaneser III's inscriptions: RIMA 3 A.0.102.1; A.0.102.2; A. 0.102.28. It is not entirely clear what body of water is meant by the term.

15. ALAM *ina* UGU A.AB.BA *šá* [KUR]*na-i-ri ú-šá-zi-iz* UDU.SISKUR.*meš ana* DINGIR.*meš* BAL-*qi*; "I erected a statue by the great sea of the land of Nairi; I made offerings to the gods."

16. Rollinger 2012: 730. He calls this text a "variant of the other texts" mentioning the washing of the weapons, implying that he thinks that all of the kings were performing the ritual of the washing of the weapons on behalf of their god. The washing of the weapon in the sea is only mentioned in a few of the inscriptions.

for obvious reasons encouraged his association with the earlier, legendary king. It is therefore not surprising that Sargon II's son would have employed the language of Sargon of Agade in the legitimation of his own kingship. Mention of the sea is also found in the Sennacherib/Taylor Prism, col. I 10–15 (Luckenbill 1926):

| | |
|---|---|
| $^{d}$*aš-šur* KUR-*ú* GAL-*ú* LUGAL-*ut la šá-na-*[*an*] | The god Ashur, the great mountain, an |
| *ú-šat-li-ma-an-ni-*[*ma*] | unrivaled kingship entrusted me [and] |
| UGU *gim-ri a-šib pa-rak-*[*ki*] | above all those who dwell in palace[es] |
| *ú-šar-ba-a* $^{GIŠ}$TUKUL.MEŠ-[*ia*] | he made [my] weapons powerful, |
| *ul-tu* A.AB.BA *e-le-ni-*[*ti*] | from the upp[er] sea |
| *ša šùl-mu* $^{d}$UTU-[*ši*] | of the setting sun |
| *a-di tam-tim šap-li-*[*ti*] | to the low[er] sea |
| *ša ṣi-it* $^{d}$UTU-[*ši*] | of the rising sun |
| [*gim-ri ṣal-mat*] SAG.DU *ú-šak-niš še-*[*pu-ú-a*] | he brought [all the black-headed people] to submit at my fe[et] |

The terminology in the Sennacherib prism has some added variation to the standard phrase of "from the Upper Sea to the Lower Sea." This expansion on the phrase may indicate that an earlier text employing the standard phrase was well known to the scribes who authored the inscription.

Esarhaddon, on his part, fought extensive campaigns on the coast of the Mediterranean, and there is almost certainly a historical basis for most mentions of the sea in relation to him (Leichty 2008). In Esarhaddon Cylinder A (I 9–18 ), he describes himself as:

| | |
|---|---|
| *ka-šid* $^{URU}$*ṣi-du-un-ni šá ina* MURUB$_4$ *tam-tim* | conqueror of Sidon which is in the heart of |
| *sa-pi-nu gi-mir da-ád-me-šú* | the sea, the overthrower of all its houses |
| BÀD-*šú ù šu-bat-su as-suḫ-ma* | its wall and its dwellings I tore down and |
| *qé-reb tam-tim ad-di-i-ma* | I threw them in the middle of the sea and |
| *a-šar maš-kán-i-šú ú-ḫal-liq* | its place I destroyed |
| *mab-di-mi-il-ku-ut-ti* LUGAL-*šu* | Abdi-Milku, its king |
| *ša la-pa-an* $^{GIŠ}$.TUKUL.MEŠ-*ia* | who before my weapons |
| *ina* MURUB$_4$ *tam-tim in-nab-tu* | into the heart of the sea he fled |
| *ki-ma nu-u-ni ul-tu qé-reb tam-tim* | like a fish out from the middle of the sea |
| *a-bar-šu-ma ak-ki-sa qaq-qa-su* | I drew him and cut off his head |

This inscription, though embellishing the incidents, has the pretension of being a historical document. It seems almost to bring us a full circle, from the narration of Sargon's campaign, to the utilization of an established trope by following kings, all the way down to the description of Esarhaddon's campaigns, where the motif is undeniably dissolved back into historical reality. What is more curious about Esarhaddon is that one of the inscriptions detailing his feats was authored by his West Semitic mother Naqia. In this building inscription he is also described as having gone from the Upper Sea to the Lower Sea.[17]

There are similar mentions in royal inscriptions not mentioned in this brief paper, as they had become a standard script that king after king had to repeat in their inscriptions, whether or not they actually conducted the feats enumerated in them.

And the tradition did not end with Neo-Assyrian kings. We find similar notions later in the Cyrus cylinder, suggesting that the tradition was alive and well even in Achaemenid times. The sixth-century Persian king Cyrus the Great, upon conquering the city of Babylon from Nabonidus declared himself "king of Sumer and Agade" and "king of the four corners of the world" in language reminiscent of earlier Mesopotamian kings. In the Cyrus cylinder (28–29), written in the Akkadian language and drawing heavily from Mesopotamian precedents, he also claims to rule all the kings from the Upper Sea to the Lower Sea, who brought him heavy tribute. In the Daiva inscription, Xerxes also boasts having conquered the people "on this side of the sea and on that side of the sea." Nabonidus himself, the last king of Babylon, in the Nabonidus cylinder from Sippar, mentions the Upper and the Lower Sea, claiming to have mustered his troops from them. The conquest of the sea also features in the later Alexandrine romances, which serve as an example of the later use of the myth in royal legitimation: Alexander's mythographers made use of the motif in order to make him appear as the legitimate king of Babylon, even though the underlying myth of divine combat between the storm god and the sea itself must have been completely lost on them.[18] There are also some hints of the tradition in certain biblical texts, but they are a topic unto themselves, and must be discussed at another occasion.

A few conclusions, then: From a review of the texts, it seems that there was a resurgence of using the myth in the legitimation of royal ideology in the Neo-Assyrian period, beginning with Tiglath-pileser I. The dynasty used the figure of Sargon of Agade and his reign quite openly as a source of the legitimation of their power, as the basis of their royal ideology and propaganda. One needs only to look at the figure of Sargon II, who certainly did not fashion his kingship after Sargon I of Assyria—who is known for little else than having himself been named after the Akkadian Sargon. What this goes to show is that we are dealing with an extremely long-lived tradition, borne at least in part from the political aspirations of Mesopotamian kingdoms toward the economies and resources of the eastern Mediterranean.

While "from the Upper Sea to the Lower Sea" is a phrase that could be used to invoke the idea of great kingship even without any mythological connotations, or without actual historical basis to the claim, the variation that we find in the expression of

17. Esarhaddon 2004/RINAP 4: [*maš-šur*-ŠEŠ]-SUM.NA DUMU *ṣi-it lìb-bi-ia ina* GIŠ.GU.ZA AD-*šú ṭa-biš* [I] [. . .] [*ul-tu tam*]-*tim e-li-ti a-di tam-tim šap*-[*li-ti*] [. . .] *it-tal-la-ku-ma*; "Esarhaddon, my son, offspring of my heart on the throne of his father they seated him from the Upper Sea to the Lower Sea they constantly went." (http://oracc.iaas.upenn.edu/rinap/rinap4/Q003406/html).

18. Rollinger 2012: 732. He mentions the texts Diodorus Siculus, *Bibliotheca Historica* 17, 95; Plutarch of Chaeronea, *On the Fortune or the Virtue of Alexander the Great*, 62; Curtius Rufus, *Historiae Alexandri Magni* 9, 4, 13; Justin, *Epitome of the Philippic History of Pompeius Trogus* 12, 8; Pliny, *Natural History*, 6, 49, 62; Philostratus, *Life of Apollonius of Tana*, 2, 43; Arrian of Nicomedia, *Anabasis Alexandri*, 5, 29, 1f. The works of Diodorus, Plutarch, Curtius, Justin, and Arrian are the main surviving accounts of Alexander's life and exploits.

this concept indicates that it entailed more than empty pomp. Not every Mesopotamian king employed the phrase in their inscriptions, so the use of the phrase may have implied actual presence in the coastal areas, at least some of the time. While it is possible that at least to a certain extent this language of legitimation employed the mythological backdrop of the battle of the storm god against the sea, what I suggest is that the opposite also held true. The formation of the myth was founded in historical reality. What we seem to find here is a sort of "legitimation loop": a mythology is sprung from an actual desire and necessity to conquer coastal regions, this mythology is then used to legitimize monarchic power, and is confirmed by the conquest of coastal regions—a symbolic conquest of the sea. But which came first? Was the conquest of the sea mythologized, or was it because of the myth that the sea needed to be conquered?

## BIBLIOGRAPHY

Badali, E., Biga, M. G., Carena, O., di Bernardo, G., di Rienzo, S. and Liverani, M.
1982 Studies on the Annals of Aššurnasirpal II. 1: Morphological Analysis. *Vicino Oriente* 5: 13–73.

Batto, B. F.
1992 *Slaying the Dragon: Mythmaking in the Biblical Tradition.* Louisville: Westminster John Knox.

Bordreuil, P. and Pardee, D.
1993 Le Combat de Baʿlu avec Yammu d'après les textes ougaritiques. *MARI* 7: 63–70.

Dalley, S.
1989 *Myths from Mesopotamia: Creation, the Flood, Gilgamesh, and Others.* Oxford: Oxford University Press.

Dossin, G.
1955 L'Inscription de foundation de Iahdun-lim, roi de Mari. *Syria* 32: 1–28.

Durand, J. M
1993 Le Mythologème du combat entre le dieu de l'orage et la mer an Mésopotamie. *MARI* 7: 41–61.

Green, A. R. W.
2003 *The Storm-god in the Ancient Near East.* BJSUCSD 8. Winona Lake, IN: Eisenbrauns.

Hallo, W. W.
1987 The Birth of Kings. Pp. 46–52 in *Love and Death in the Ancient Near East: Essays in Honor of Marvin H. Pope.* Edited by J. H. Marks and R. M. Good. Guilford, CT: Four Quarters.

Horowitz, W.
1998 *Mesopotamian Cosmic Geography.* MC 8. Winona Lake, IN: Eisenbrauns.

Kramer, S. N.
1943 Review of *The Babylonian Genesis: The Story of Creation,* by Alexander Heidel. *JAOS* 63: 69–73.
1944 *Sumerian Mythology: A Study of Spiritual and Literary Achievement in the Third Millennium B.C.* Philadelphia: American Philosophical Society.

Kutscher, R.
1975 *Oh Angry Sea (a.ab.ba hu.luh.ha): The History of a Sumerian Congregational Lament.* YNER 6. New Haven: Yale University Press.

Langdon, S.
1914 *Tammuz and Ishtar: A Monograph upon Babylonian Religion and Theology.* Oxford: Clarendon.

Leichty, E.
2008 Esarhaddon's Eastern Campaign. Pp. 183–187 in *Treasures on Camels' Humps: Historical and Literary Studies from the Ancient Near East Presented to Israel Eph'al*. Edited by M. Cogan and D. Kahn. Jerusalem: Magnes.

Luckenbill, D. D.
1926 *Ancient Records of Assyria and Babylonia*. 2 vols. Chicago: University of Chicago.

Malamat, A.
1965 Campaigns to the Mediterranean by Iahdunlim and Other Early Mesopotamian Rulers. Pp. 365–374 in *Studies in Honor of Benno Landsberger on His Seventy-fifth Birthday*. Edited by H. G. Güterbock and T. Jacobsen. AS 16. Chicago: University of Chicago Press.
1998 *Mari and the Bible*. SHCANE 12. Leiden: Brill.

Oates, J.
1979 *Babylon*. London: Thames & Hudson.

Rollinger, R.
2012 From Sargon of Agade and the Assyrian Kings to Khusrau I and Beyond: On the Persistence of Ancient Near Eastern Traditions. Pp. 725–743 in *Leggo! Studies Presented to Frederick Mario Fales on the Occasion of His 65th Birthday*. Edited by G. B. Lanfranchi, D. M. Bonacossa, C. Pappi, and S. Ponchia. LAOS 2. Wiesbaden: Harrassowitz.

Smith, M. S.
1994 *The Ugaritic Ba'al Cycle*, vol. 1: *Introduction with Text, Translation and Commentary of KTU 1.1–1.2*. VTSup 55. Leiden: Brill.
1997 The Baal Cycle. Pp. 81–180 in *Ugaritic Narrative Poetry*. Edited by S. B. Parker. WAW 9. Atlanta: Scholars Press.

Töyräänvuori, J.
2012 Weapons of the Storm God in Ancient Near Eastern and Biblical Traditions. *StOr* 112: 147–180.

Virolleaud, C.
1929 Les Inscriptions cunéiformes de Ras-Shamra. *Syria* 10: 245–255.
1932 Un poème phénicien de Ras-Shamra: la lutte de Mot, fils des dieux, et d' 'Aléïn, fils de Baal. *Syria* 12: 193–224.

Wyatt, N.
2002 *Religious Texts from Ugarit*. 2nd ed. BibSem 53. London: Sheffield Academic.
2003 What Has Ugarit to Do with Jerusalem? (Inaugural Lecture in the Chair of Ancient Near Eastern Religions, 3 October 2002). *Studies in World Christianity* 8:138–160.

CHAPTER 24

# Putting Life in Order: The Architecture of the New Excavations in Kamid el-Loz, Lebanon

Julia Linke and Elisabeth Wagner-Durand

In memory of our friends on the excavation who left us too early: Ali Aswad (d. 2012) and Akram An'a (d. 2009)

THIS ARTICLE WILL PRESENT selected architectural features of Kamid el-Loz by linking these with the phenomena of order and memory.

Ordering architectural space by restricting certain habitats to the conduction of cultic activities or to the representation of power has been a matter of fact in ancient Near Eastern studies.[1] Mostly temples, and to a lesser extent palaces, seem to be limited to a distinct spot inside settlements, forming part of the architectural order of a city. It goes without saying that these are matters connected with the sanctity of certain places, with the visibility or—in contrast—with the closure of these habitats, and with matters of protection, legitimation, and tradition.

These architectural orders, however, are also connected with the realm of the collective memory. The idea of linking structures with questions of memory is all but new, and thus many archaeologists and philologists have been dealing with this topic.

Focusing on the aspect of memory, this article deals especially with the architectural order of Kumidi during the Middle and Late Bronze Age referring to a combination of the new excavation results of the University of Freiburg, directed by Marlies Heinz, and the former excavations, conducted by the University of Saarbrucken, mainly directed by Rolf Hachmann.[2]

Treating questions of creation, maintenance, reestablishment, and disintegration of collective memories, we will concentrate on how architectural order—being the mirror of the social order of a community—acts upon the individual and collective

*Authors' note:* Our thanks go to the organizers of the RAI in Ghent for giving the opportunity to speak there and to publish the paper in this conference volume. Furthermore, our sincere thanks go to Prof. Dr. Marlies Heinz, Freiburg who gave us the possibility to work in Kamid el-Loz and to be engaged with the material of the site. She has been supportive ever since our first days on the excavations. Out of convenience the site's name is written here as Kamid el-Loz, however the correct transcription would be Kāmid el-Lōz.

1. Concerning the structuring of cities, arrangement of palaces and—to a lesser extend of temples—within see, e.g., Novák 1999. Concerning the persistence of temples and palaces in ancient Near Eastern contexts see for examples the temple of Eridu (Heinrich and Seidl 1982: esp. 23, 28-29) and the Old Palace of Assur (Novák 1999: 112–113).

2. For further information on the Freiburg excavations, see esp. Heinz et al. (2001); Heinz (2010); Heinz and Kirsch (2011) and the bibliography given there. For further information on the Saarbrucken excavations, see esp.: Metzger (2012); Hachmann and Adler (1996); Echt (1984); Adler and Penner (2001); Miron (1982). Most excavation results have been (pre)published in the volumes of the Saarbrücker Bände für Altertumskunde or in the Lebanese journal *Berytus*.

memory in Kamid el-Loz, and how this collective memory in turn affects the architectural order of the society.

## Theoretical Premises

Memory manifests itself not only by passing knowledge and stories but also through bodily actions and with the help of visual manifestations and their perception.[3] The more often certain practices are repeated, paths taken, cultic duties fulfilled, and visual features perceived, the more extensively social orders—linked with these practices and features—become written into the bodily system.[4] In this vein, architectural order is not only an order that is visually perceived at a certain moment in time, but also one that is permanently written into the body by constant repetition. Thus, the collective social memory—visible in a certain architectural order—is also created inside the human itself, it becomes embodied. This, in turn, relates to a terminology primarily presented by P. Connerton (1989) and later on adopted by Rowlands (1993) reshaping this terminology in respect of archaeological matters. Consequently, memory practices are divided into a dichotomy of inscribed and incorporated memory practices. Whereas inscribed practices are understood as the usage *of* and materialization *in* monuments, texts and representations with a clearly material visible access, the incorporated practices are defined by some kind of subtle, less material, obscure character that seems to be less materially visible, but to a greater extent bodily perceptible (Connerton 1989, van Dyke and Alcock 2003: 3-4). In this vein, Connerton uses the term "embodied" in the sense of bodily rituals with a less formularized character and ephemeral authority. In this contribution, however, the term embodied should by no means be restricted to some kind of ephemeral and undefined memory practices that are never related to archaeologically easily accessible monuments. Rather, these embodied memories are understood as all memories that are written into the bodily system by repetitive behaviors and that can be associated with daily routines as well as with unwritten and unspoken laws or by legal and religious obligations. In the end, body and brain, and therefore the human mind, are not able to differentiate between these categories. Although memory continues to be a phenomenon of individual nature in respect to body and mind, it rises to a collective level when certain actions are repeated by a distinct and defined group. Even though this collective memory does not become truly inheritable by means of genetics, it may have been transmitted to

3. For literature on memory (collective, cultural, social) in archaeological contexts, see, e.g., Assmann 2007; van Dyke and Alcock 2003; Rowlands 1993; and Harmanşah 2013. The overall concept of memory applied here draws close to Assmann's (2007: esp. 20 and 50) term of the communicative memory, since it refers to the memory shared by all inhabitants of Kumidi, communicated more or less explicitly and not refined to a distinct group. However, both terms—the communicative and the cultural memory—are very distinct and their meaning is predefined. Thus, these terms are avoided here.

One could also describe this visually manifested type of memory with the term of "mimetic memory" coined by Assmann, who describes it as a memory learned by mimetic actions (2007: 20). However, it should also be seen in combination with Assmann's term of the "memory of things" (20), since it's the world of things that surrounds us shaping our daily routines and experiences.

4. For a paradigmatic archaeological study on how daily routines affect memory and socialization see Hodder and Cessford 2004.

everybody in the group by having the same experiences and therefore sharing the same sets of memories and by mediating them to each other via communication. In this respect, the location of official buildings is more than a mere sign of secular and religious power, they draw near to what P. Nora called "*lieux de memoire*."[5]

To cut a long story short: buildings and their architectural order are part of the memory of a certain group, and therefore they may become part of a heritage that seems to be given and granted, and is consequently somehow unchangeable.

Therefore, we will argue—in case of the citadel of Kumidi—that apart from specific features initially determining the precise building spot, the citadel and especially the palace became part of the collective memory of Kumidi. This collective memory fostered the manifold return of certain official buildings like palace and temple during the Middle and the Late Bronze Age to their inherent building spot.[6] This memory was the reason why the palace had to return to its building spot, even after interruptions and phases of imbalance of power.

## The Tell: The Geopolitical Situation and Settlement History

The tell of Kamid el-Loz, the ancient Kumidi of the Amarna age, is situated in the southern Beqaa, in modern Lebanon, at an altitude of roughly 940 m above sea level (see fig. 24.1).[7] The settlement hill encompasses an area of 7 ha (Hachmann 1966: 12) and therefore it is one of the largest tells of the Beqaa Valley (8).

The Beqaa Valley is a high plain and lies between the Lebanon Mountains in the west, the Anti-Lebanon Mountains in the east and Mount Hermon in the south. As the valley is very fertile it is also called the "garden of Lebanon" and even today it serves as the center of Lebanese agricultural production. Above all, it is the Litani River that ensures the water supply for the Beqaa Valley.[8]

In addition to this advantaged agricultural setting, Kamid el-Loz has an ideal situation for trading with its position at the crossroads between the road leading from the sea via the mountain pass of Masser ash-Shouf to Damascus, as well as directly on the road that connects Egypt, Syria, and Anatolia in a north-south direction (see, e.g., Heinz 2000).

This geo-political location of Kumidi, as a communication center situated in direct vicinity to important overland routes, was one of the reasons for selecting the site for excavation and explains the city's importance and influence, especially during the later Middle Bronze Age and the Late Bronze Age (see, e.g., Heinz 2010: 9).

The settlement history can be very briefly summarized as follows: According to Leon Marfoe the earliest findings date into the Late Pottery Neolithic/Chalcolithic 2,

5. Nora 1990: esp. 11-33; Eril 2005: 25. Though, the national character which is primarily inherent to the term of the *lieu de memoire* shall not be embedded here.

6. For the purpose of this paper, we are confining ourselves to the citadel area. The temple (area), however, also provides an interesting and promising study subject.

7. Its first excavations started fifty years ago in 1963 by the University of Saarbrucken. After a longer break (starting in 1981) due to the civil war, the excavations were resumed by Marlies Heinz in 1997—again temporally interrupted right now by the current political situation.

8. Concerning the Beqaa and its geopolitical setting see also in short Hachmann and Kuschke 1966.

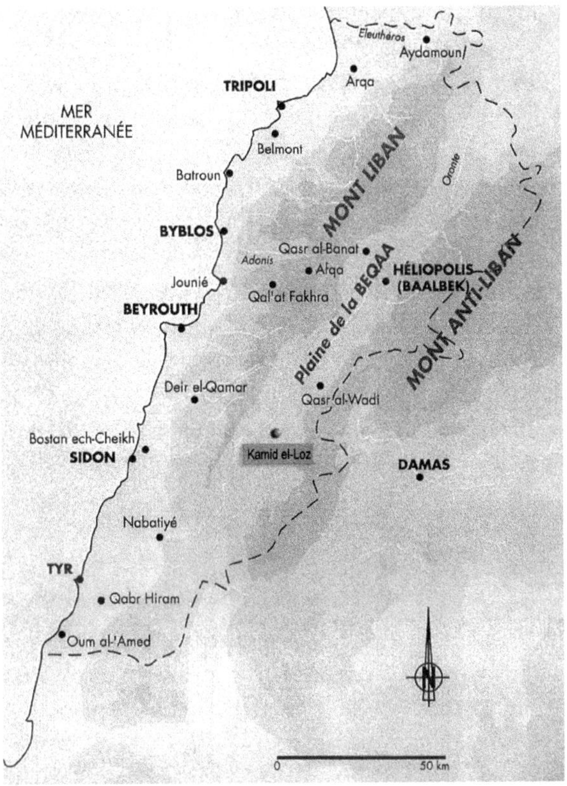


FIGURE. 24.1. Kamid el-Loz within Lebanon and the Beqaa.

the local Djsr stage.[9] Nonetheless, the first more substantial archaeological remains stem from the transition of the Early Bronze to the Middle Bronze Age and the early Middle Bronze Age (MB I–MB IIA).[10] During the course of the Middle Bronze Age the data known increase continuously, first through the still barely represented MB I and then throughout the MB II/III during which the settlement can be categorized as a city due to its mere size, its fortification, the appearance of certain official buildings, and the formation of distinct living quarters.[11] Throughout the following Late Bronze Age, Kamid el-Loz (known as Kumidi during the Amarna Age) continues to be a city, with a city wall, a temple, a palace, as well as different settlement quarters.[12]

Nevertheless, a fundamental change occurs in the Early Iron Age I, when the site loses important architectural features, not having a palace, a temple, or elite buildings

9. Marfoe 1995: esp. 59 and 109: "It can be assumed that level d is the oldest cultural level presently found at tell Kāmid el-Lōz. This is proved by the findings, which belong, without any exception, to the Djisr Stage (LPNC2)."

10. For an overview of the Saarbrucken excavations, see Echt 1984: 58–59; and Marfoe 1995: 103–105. For Freiburg, see mainly Weber 2010; and Walther 2010a.

11. For the Saarbrucken excavations, see Echt (1984), 58–59; and Marfoe 1995: 104–105. For the results of the Freiburg excavations, see mainly Linke (2011b). This by no means implies that the settlement did not reach city level before the MB II, but that the excavated areas are still not extensive enough to reveal this information.

12. Freiburg, see, e.g., Heinz, Wagner, Linke, Walther, et al. 2010: 31–63; Saarbrucken, see, e.g., Echt 1984: 49–54; and Marfoe 1995: 121–128.

of any kind. Corresponding to this, the following Iron Age II could also only very scantly be documented.[13]

Architecturally this also applies to the Persian period (Iron Age III) during which an extended cemetery stretched over most parts of the tell.[14] This cemetery was still in use in the Hellenistic period, during which the settlement definitely returned to the hill itself. From Roman and later times both a settlement and graves could be documented by excavation. In the end the sepulchral use won and even today a modern cemetery covers parts of the ancient Kumidi.[15]

Most probably already in Persian and Hellenistic times, but surely during the Roman and the Byzantine/post-Roman periods, the settlement of Kamid el-Loz extended to the hillsides mainly south of the tell. Several finds of graves and burials in the slopes around the modern village document this.

Nevertheless, before entering the more detailed discussion of the later MB II and LB-citadel, two additional remarks concerning the earlier settlement history relating to the so-called citadel should be made.

### *The Early Middle Bronze Age I and II Remains*

The first Middle Bronze Age I traces could be identified in the area of the citadel. In a deep trench north of the so-called Schatzhaus-area some structures were uncovered that contained MB I pottery (Linke 2011b). Use and formal attribution to an actual MB I citadel will be reappraised when enlarging the area.

It also should be mentioned that an early MB II occupation existed on the tell of which a fortification wall but neither a palace nor a temple have been located yet. This early Middle Bronze Age settlement was given up; a cemetery was constructed in these ruins and displaced the living. [16] After this sepulchral use, a period of urbanization, actually reurbanization, set in. With this urbanization phase, we have reached the core periods of our article. Therefore, we will now take a closer look at the architectural remains of the later Middle Bronze Age II citadel and the following Late Bronze Age remains, applying the already described theoretical approaches to the archaeological record. At the current moment, based on preliminary stratigraphical analyses as well as pottery studies, we can state that the late MB II is the time when a new fortification was built, when temple and palace were erected, and living quarters

13. For the results of the Freiburg excavations, see most recently: Heinz, Wagner, Linke, Walther, et al. 2010: 15–31. For an overview of the Saarbrucken excavations, see Echt 1984: esp. 42–49; and Marfoe 1995: 159–165. The separation between the end of the Iron Age I and the beginning of the Iron Age II seems to be difficult in Kumidi, and therefore the attribution of the later Iron Age settlement phases and levels by the Freiburg excavation mainly remains IA I/II. The Saarbrucken excavations date all Iron Age settlement levels (8–1) excavated by them to the Iron Age I. See Marfoe 1995: 159–165.

14. This cemetery is accompanied by contemporary burials on the neighboring Tell Krūm (Bertemes 1986: 33). Concerning the cemetery on the tell Kamid el-Loz, see Poppa 1978; Hachmann and Penner 1999; Linke and Wagner 2010b; Linke 2010b.

15. For the settlement history of Kamid el-Loz see Heinz 2016; for the Saarbrucken excavations in the form of summaries, see Weippert 1998; and Hachmann 1989/1991.

16. The cemetery, dating into the settlement hiatus on the northern slope following the very early MB II settlement there, raises serious questions whether during this hiatus a temple and a palace were likely to be found on the tell or whether the tell was settled during this period. Yet, all synchronization of the early MB building levels from the old and new excavations has to remain tentative and preliminary at the moment.

stretched over considerable parts of the tell. Hence, the settlement was structured in a certain order and showed all the markers needed to be called an urban environment.

### *The Middle Bronze Age II Palace(s) (See Fig. 24.2)*

The oldest identifiable MB II structure from the citadel, the highest known spot of the tell, is a multiroom stone-mud-brick building, henceforth called the older Middle Bronze Age palace (Heinz 2016, Wagner 2010a), but admittedly still excavated in a very narrow amplitude. It immediately precedes the younger extended Middle Bronze Age palace; wall sizes and pottery findings of both buildings resemble each other. Together with the tradition of the building spot this led to the decision to provisionally name this older building "palace." This palace fell victim to a fire, and directly on top of its debris and ruins the younger Middle Bronze Age palace was erected.

This younger MB II palace, most likely a multistory building according to wall size, height, and room fillings, consisted of several rooms and courtyards, eight of them being extensively excavated.[17] One courtyard, extended and representative, contained a wooden (mainly oak, partly cedar) pavilion-like roofing construction that could be uncovered on the trodden floor covered by heaps of burnt mud-brick. This courtyard or hall (R10) covering about 120 m² had first been considered to be the center of the palace, but the assumption now taken is that the palace extends far to the east and may be architecturally connected to the so-called Schatzhaus-area (also named an administrative area). The extension of the palaces to the east, north, and south are still to be uncovered, but the western bordering walls—at least for the most part—have been reached. Some of the rooms can be clearly assigned to specific activities, for example, room 8 seems to have been preserved for intensive, but elaborate storage functions, represented by earthen benches with embedded storage pithoi at the southern and western sides of the room. These pithoi were associated with juglets, some of them painted (mostly the so-called Levantine painted ware) and bulks of partly elaborately burnished or painted jars, bowls, and plates.[18] According to the find situation, wooden shelves could be reconstructed on which at least some of these dishes had been stored. Further findings inside the palace rooms and its fillings hint to a variety of activities, among them food processing and administration, proven, for example, by seal impressions and seals, which reoccur in other parts of the citadel, mainly the so-called Schatzhaus-area. One seal of Middle Syrian style was obviously in use both in the palace itself and in the eastern parts of the citadel, as the findings of the identical seal impression from both these areas show.[19]

One interesting feature of the younger Middle Bronze Age palace's architecture needs to be noted with respect of memory and tradition. Whereas most parts of the

17. The mud-brick filling from the heavily burnt palace, which had never been rebuilt, indicates the existence of a second story, as does a crashed down floor in room R7 (Heinz 2016: 85; Wagner-Durand 2011).

18. The Levantine painted ware has been described has "hallmarks of the beginning of Middle Bronze Age" in the Levant by Bagh (2002: 89). In Kumidi, however, this ware also occurs in the very late layers of the MBA and in contrast to most sites in the Levant, the pottery vessels in question also occur in the settlement context, and not only in graves (A. Catanzariti pers. comm.).

19. The seal impressions Fnr. 342 (from the palace) and Fnr. 396 (from the "Schatzhaus"-area) were both impressed on handles (Linke and Heinz 2012; Linke 2010c: 88; 2011a).

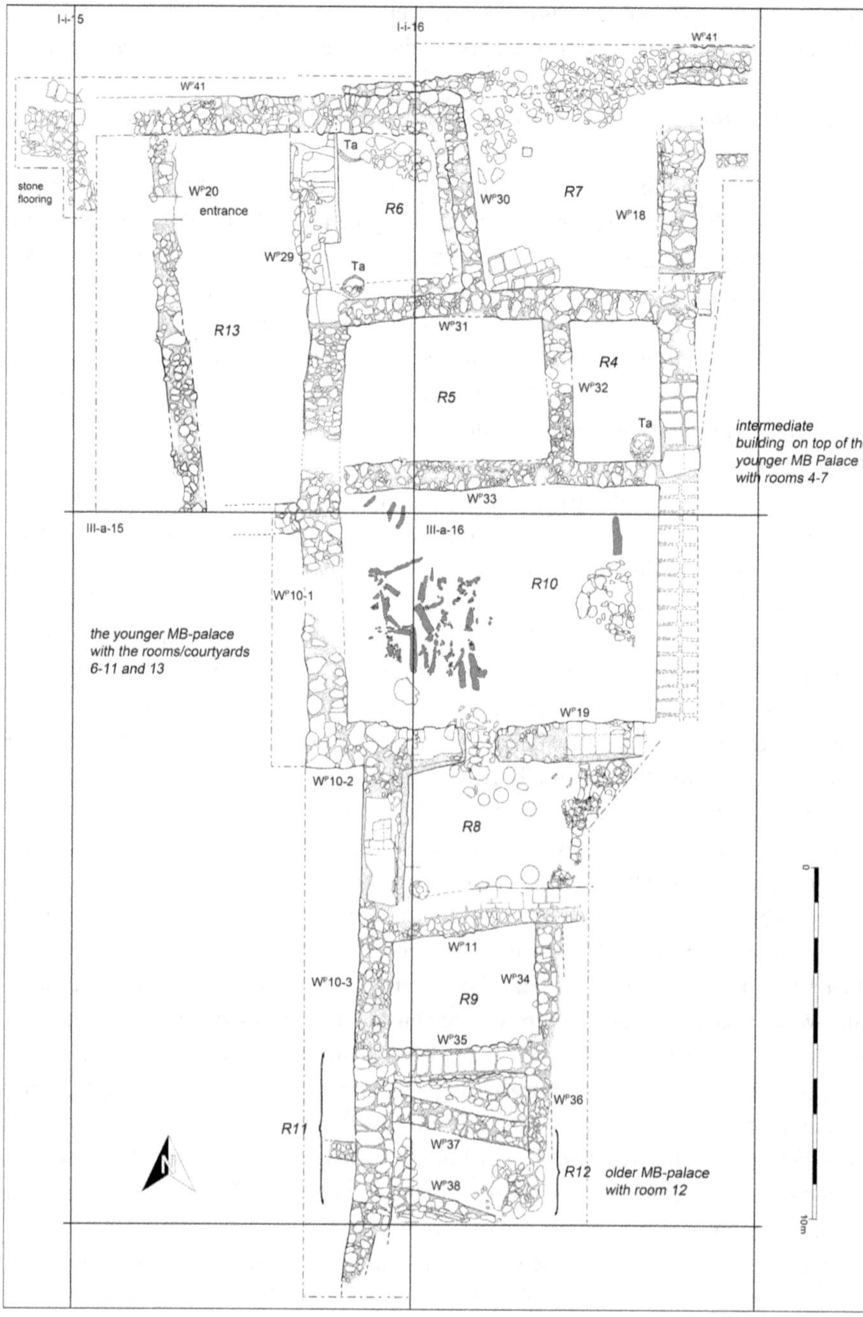


FIGURE 24.2. The Middle Bronze Age palace(s).

palace walls seems to be erected anew, and whereas its overall orientation differs from its predecessor (as far as can be determined now), some parts refer to the reuse of the old architecture (Wagner-Durand 2011) and therefore hint at a deliberate physical association with the predecessor, which not only concerns the locus as such but also the building itself.

### *The So-Called Schatzhaus/Treasury*

The eastern border of the citadel has not yet been reached. The eastern part of the citadel, the so-called Schatzhaus-area, is currently uncovered to a much lesser extent than the area of the palace. Excavations in the so-called Schatzhaus-area brought to light some massive walls from the Middle Bronze Age that obviously form the corners of two huge rooms or courtyards. The construction technique of these walls strongly resembles the ones of the palace: massive stone foundations with a mud-brick superstructure (see Linke 2011b). A solid terrace wall supports the foundations of the two rooms to the north and the stratigraphy suggests a very high elevation for these structures. The described Middle Bronze Age structures have been erected on heaps of massive burnt mud-brick rubble of an older building period at this part of the tell.

So far we are not able to assign any certain function to this part of the citadel for the Middle Bronze Age, but several finds of stamped pottery sherds as well as of pithoi point to storage activities (Linke 2011a; Walther 2010b: 68; Linke 2010a: 123 n. 350). A close connection to the palace can be discerned, based on the shape, building technique, closeness to the palace, and also the pottery findings.

### *The Middle Bronze Age Citadel* in Toto *(See Fig. 24.4)*

The citadel as a whole seems to have been segregated from the rest of the city. A very steep slope could be detected in the area immediately west of the palace—this part might have once formed some kind of defense area. This also refers to the visibility of the palace from the west and to the, at least partial, segregation from the sacral power in the form of the temple being segregated from the citadel. A similar slope could be recorded north of the eastern part of the citadel (Linke and Wagner 2010c: 156; Linke 2011b).

At some point during the final stages of the MBA II, the whole citadel had been heavily and fatally destroyed by fire. Remains of this destruction are represented by the massive layers of burnt mud brick that can be detected in all parts of the citadel (Heinz et al. 2010: 163; Wagner-Durand 2011; Linke 2011b). The blaze seems to have been set on purpose and reached a destructive intensity, which also led to the destruction of the massive mud-brick superstructures and the entire palace. The stone foundations were blackened and the mud bricks burnt to their core, adopting a crystalline structure. The organic binder between stone and mud bricks burned and formed a black layer between the superstructure and stone foundations. The plaster either flaked off the walls or fused inseparably with the collapsing mud bricks and rubble. The wood used for the roofing constructions or room installations burned heavily. Still, some cedar and oak balks could be exposed (Dr. Otto Cichocki: pers. comm.). They were preserved by the huge amount of mud bricks and burnt debris crashing into the rooms and serving as the foundation for later building activities. In storage room 8 the pithoi, some with oily content, burned heavily, bearing black traces of the flames engulfing the room. Potential wooden constructions like shelves burned and their load fell to the floor. The progression of the fire caused the collapse of the mud-brick walls, the rubble settling on the ashy destruction layer and filling up the rooms several meters high.

Whatever led to this fatal destruction, it was not only physically significant, but also ideologically.

### *The Intermediate Building (See Fig. 24.2)*

On top of the burnt mud bricks of the former Middle Bronze Age palace, a comparable small house was erected (Heinz 2016: 116–118), reusing at least some of the still-standing older Middle Bronze Age stone foundations. This building has been called "the intermediate building," relating to its position in between the Late Bronze Age and Middle Bronze Age period and in between the palace buildings. Neither size, nor installations, nor room inventory give witness of an administrative or elite character for this building, which shows signs of household activities, namely a *tannour* as well as specific pottery. If this interpretation is correct, a political crisis in Kamid el-Loz materially visualizes itself within the archaeological record of the palace building spot by the erection of the so-called intermediate building.

Like its predecessor, the extended MB II palace, this structure also fell victim to a fire. In the course of time—a longer hiatus has not yet been revealed by the stratigraphical record—the palace returned to its now *traditional* building spot. Materializing and visualizing the imbalance of power, the intermediate building challenges our ideas about the order of the town and the collective memory. According to our data, several options are available for explaining the interruption in time, place, and order. First option: the palace had not yet been part of a fully established collective memory by the time the intermediate building was built. Therefore, a deviating usage of the building spot was easily possible. Second option: The palace was indeed part of the collective memory, and the intermediate building formed a conscious and intentional break, visualizing the disempowerment of the once ruling elite addressing all the inhabitants of Kamid el-Loz. These questions so far remain unsettled, and both possibilities can be considered.

### *The Crisis of the Late Middle Bronze Age—Further Evidence*

It is not only the heavy fire blaze destroying the citadel's architecture, as well as the following intermediate building materializing and visualizing the downfall of the Middle Bronze Age (political) elite, that hint at a crisis destabilizing the city of Kumidi, but another archaeological feature uncovered west of the temple can be understood as a sign for this anomy:[20] At least ten individuals of different age groups and sexes have been laid to rest in quite an extensive pit situated underneath the later-dating Late Bronze Age house A west of the temple: the so-called graves G$^{t}$1–3.[21] The preliminary analysis of the graves revealed that at least two of the individuals died a violent death, hinting at an aggressive incident.[22] Furthermore, the dead seem to be

20. The term anomy in respect to this phenomenon in Kamid el-Loz has been introduced by M. Heinz (pers. comm.).

21. The stratigraphy reveals that the pit must have been established prior to the construction of the LB building A. The pottery found inside the pit, mainly two juglets, surely dates the complex into the late MB period. For the jugs, see Kulemann-Ossen 2010: 131, pl. 21.11, and fig. 131.1. Concerning the graves before 2011, see Linke and Wagner 2010a: 118–120, figs. 76–79; after 2011, see Heinz and Kirsch 2011.

22. One individual shows severe and most likely fatal cranial injuries; another individual had been hit by a bronze spearhead penetrating the rib cage (spear head = GF$^{t}$1).

buried in a quite hastily conducted ritual, once again suggesting a period of distress and disorder.[23]

Finally, yet importantly, the crises can be also observed in the temple area as well, where the temple itself fell victim to fire at the end of the Middle Bronze Age (Metzger 2012: 202–204).

### *The Late Bronze Age Citadel (See Fig. 24.3)*

The history of the succeeding Late Bronze Age citadel is rich and full of destructions and rebuildings, of singularities like the treasury (the "Schatzhaus") and of regularities like wall types and pottery. Returning to the question of ordering cities by visual markers of power, by sacral places and by living habitats, by streets and by fortifications, ergo by segregations and integrations, the question must again rise: Why did the palace—as did the citadel as a whole—return to their place? Certainly, the building spot must have been loaded with either meaning and/or by geological or geographic potential respectively.

If we consider this return as not only being the result of a mere functional decision, without any ideological or propagandistic or pious aspects, than this return shows clear connections to memory and order. Once again, two antipodal possibilities are present here: Either the palace returned because the collective memory, once established, was so strong that the imbalance of power—or better—the deviating usage of this spot of the tell seemed impossible, maybe even heretical. Or, there was no strong collective memory reclaiming the old order, but a new elite used the—at least remaining—memories to attach itself to the past: those building the Late Bronze Age palaces—maybe even a foreign elite, or an elite pushed by foreign powers like Egypt—established an "invented tradition," a term introduced by Eric Hobsbawm (1992), linking themselves to a past that was not their own. By using the already established memories and connecting these to themselves, they were able to create the illusion of a shared and common past, and therefore of legitimation. This legitimation was visualized in the order of the town, handed down from the past, somehow experienced by everybody living in Kumidi over the years.

The palace and other functional areas, however, remained in the same spot for the next several hundred years. Without doubt, the order of the city with its most likely segregated citadel and the integrated temple, neighbored—or more likely surrounded—by activities of living and handicraft, was maintained over years and became part of the memory of the inhabitants by daily centennial practices and experiences.

### *A Look into the Iron Age*

If we put these ideas into a broader context, it seems quite surprising that all this *lost* its place and meaning with the end of the Late Bronze Age.

23. The final stratigraphical attribution of the grave pit into the different levels and phases of the later MB period, however, is still under examination.

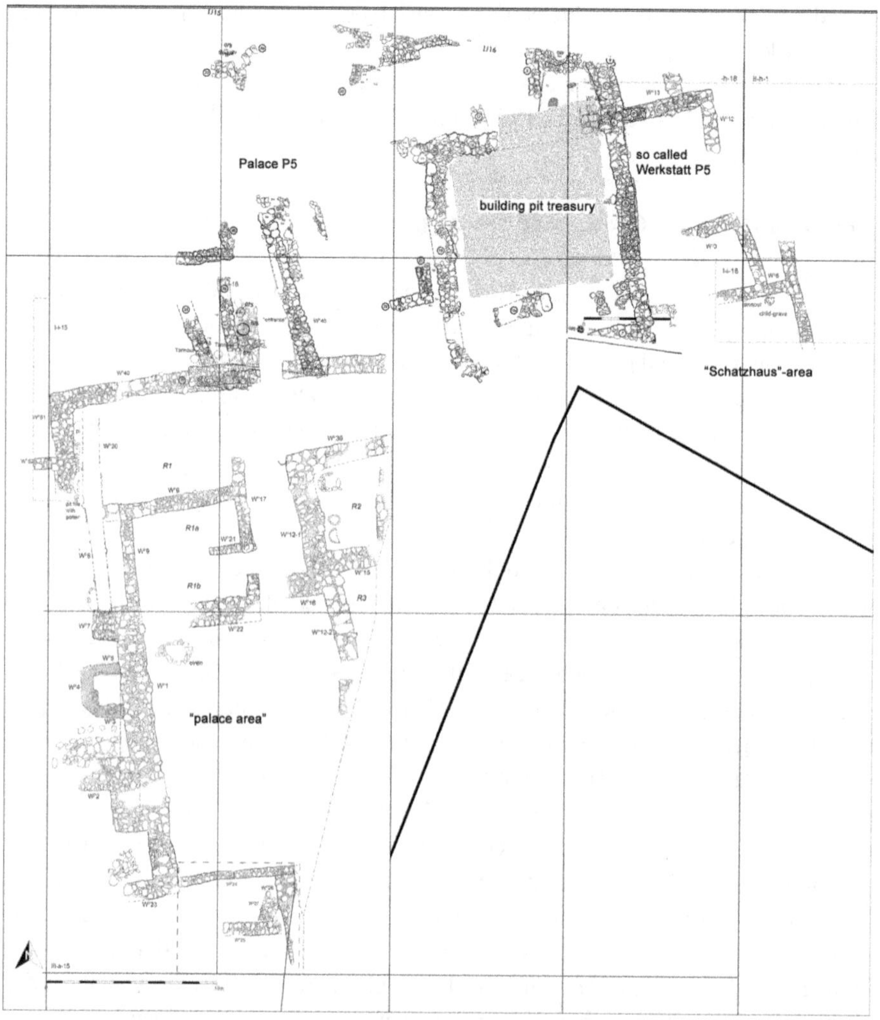


FIGURE 24.3. The remains of the oldest Late Bronze Age palace.

The end of the koine, of diplomatic transfers and military struggles, of communication and of gifts, coincides with the end of the architectural order of Kumidi.[24] There is no evidence whatsoever among the very numerous Iron Age I buildings excavated, which hint to a political or religious power, or to an elite, visualizing itself in the archaeological record via architecture.[25] The city seems to have lost its societal order. Of course, this is a current impression given by the structures excavated so far; we cannot exclude that an Iron Age palace (and temple!) existed at another place, away from the former citadel. Nevertheless, we certainly witness a change of position that should mark a change in the societal order.

24. For the end of the Late Bronze Age as an overall phenomenon, see Cline 2014.

25. Concerning the architecture excavated, see Echt 1984: esp. 42–49; Linke 2010d; Linke and Wagner 2010d.

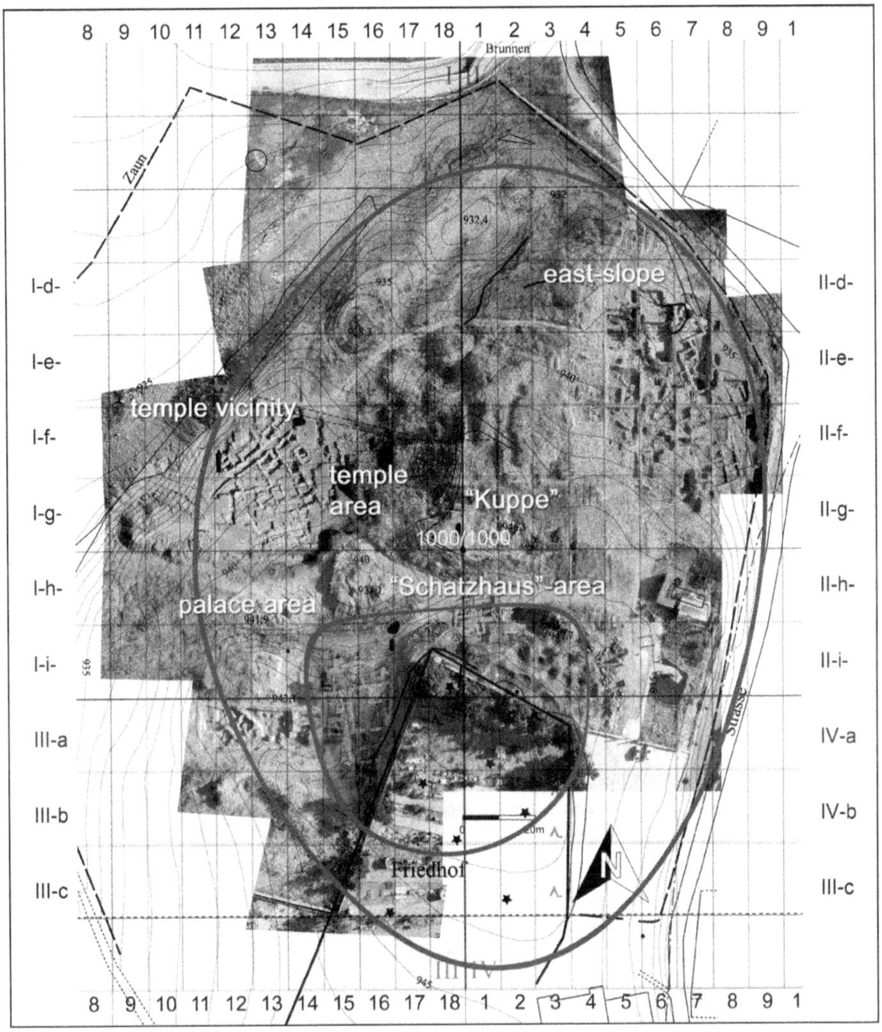


FIGURE 24.4. The MB citadel—a tentative reconstruction.

### *Summary and Outlook: The Citadel and the Collective Memory*

Considering the citadel and the temple area being part of a collective memory, perceived by bodily experiences, we must ask what the generation living during both phases (if existing) must have dealt with, and why there was no return. Was there a desire for a palace, but no elite available? Was there an imminent need to forget, recovering from the latest foreign rule, maybe reestablished by Ramses II?[26] Was the palace overbuilt by simple houses on purpose, rewriting memory and distorting order? Alternatively, was it a mere usage change? Did the inhabitants of Kamid el-Loz themselves change? Did the connected memory and order start to develop anew?

26. Kumidi might have once again become an important Egyptian city (namely Rameses) under Ramesses II, governed by an Egyptian *shakin mati*. See Morris 2005: 393 and 467.

These questions will be slowly answered when recovering more and more of the city's layout by new excavations and by the meticulous synchronization of both the Freiburg and the Saarbrucken excavation results. Incorporating pottery and other findings into these analyses, without falling into the pots and people trap, will also help to understand the developments in Kamid el-Loz concerning collective memory and mnemonic behaviors throughout the different periods. In this vein, further investigations are required to gain more and more detailed knowledge, especially about the Iron and Middle Bronze Age, answering the questions whether the palace, with respect to the citadel, disposed of a tradition going back to the MB I or further on into the Iron Age. Thus, the citadel as a "*lieux de memoire*" and the connected material culture as footprints of the bodily conveyed collective memory of the inhabitants of Kumidi will remain of particular interest for further studies in and about the tell Kamid el-Loz.

## BIBLIOGRAPHY

Adler, W. and Penner, S.
2001 *Kāmid el-Lōz 18: Die spätbronzezeitlichen Palastanlagen.* SBA 62. Bonn: Habelt.

Assmann, J.
2007 *Das kulturelle Gedächtnis: Schrift, Erinnerung und politische Identität in frühen Hochkulturen.* Beck Paperback 1307. 6th ed. Munich: Beck.

Bagh, T.
2002 Painted Pottery at the Beginning of the Middle Bronze Age: Levantine Painted Ware. Pp. 89–101 in *The Middle Bronze Age in the Levant: Proceedings of an International Conference on MB IIA Ceramic Material in Vienna 24th–26th of January 2001.* Edited by M. Bietak. CCEM 3. Vienna: Österreichischen Akademie der Wissenschaften.

Bertemes, F.
1986 Das frühe Neolithikum von Kāmid el-Lōz. Pp. 33–70 in *Bericht über die Ergebnisse der Ausgrabungen in Kāmid el-Lōz in den Jahren 1977 bis 1981.* Edited by R. Hachmann. SBA 36. Bonn: Habelt.

Cline, E. H.
2014 *1177 B.C: The Year Civilization Collapsed: Turning Points in Ancient History.* Princeton: Princeton University Press, 2014.

Connerton, P.
1989 *How Societies Remember.* Themes in the Social Sciences. Cambridge: Cambridge University Press.

Dyke, R. M. van and Alcock, S. E., eds.
2003 *Archaeologies of Memory.* Malden, MA: Blackwell.

Echt, R.
1984 *Kāmid el-Lōz 5: Die Stratigraphie.* SBA 34. Bonn: Habelt.

Eril, A.
2005 *Kollektives Gedächtnis und Erinnerungskulturen: Eine Einführung.* Stuttgart: Metzler.

Hachmann, R.
1989/1991 Kāmid el-Lōz 1863–1981: German Excavations in Lebanon. *Berytus* 37: 5–187.

Hachmann, R. and Adler, W., eds.
1996 *Kāmid el-Lōz 16: "Schatzhaus"-Studien.* SBA 59. Bonn: Habelt.

Hachmann, R. and Kuschke, A.
1966 *Bericht über die Ergebnisse der Ausgrabungen in Kamid el-Loz (Libanon) in den Jahren 1963 und 1964.* SBA 3. Bonn: Habelt.

Hachmann, R. and Penner, S.
1999 *Kāmid el-Lōz 3: Der eisenzeitliche Friedhof und seine kulturelle Umwelt.* SBA 21. Bonn: Habelt.
Harmanşah, Ö.
2013 *Cities and the Shaping of Memory in the Ancient Near East.* Cambridge: Cambridge University Press.
Heinrich, E. and U. Seidl.
1982 *Die Tempel und Heiligtümer im alten Mesopotamien: Typologie, Morphologie und Geschichte.* Denkmäler antiker Architektur 14. Berlin: de Gruyter.
Heinz, M., ed.
2000 Kamid el-Loz: Knotenpunkt überregionaler Fernstraßen und Sitz des ägyptischen Statthalters in der Beqa`a-Ebene; Archäologie im Libanon. *Antike Welt* 31: 359–368.
2010 *Kamid el-Loz: Intermediary Between Cultures; More Than 10 Years of Archaeological Research in Kamid el-Loz (1997–2007).* BAAL Hors-serie 7. Beirut: Ministère de la Culture, Direction Générale des Antiquités.
2016 *Kamid el-Loz: 4000 Years and More of Rural and Urban Life in the Lebanese Beqa'a Plain.* Archaeology and History in the Lebanon Special Issue. Beirut: Lebanese British Friends of the National Museum.
Heinz, M., Bonatz, D., Gilibert, A., Heckmann, H., Holzer, I., Jauß, C., Kirchhofer, F., Knötzele, P., Petersen, L., and Zaven, T.
2001 Kamid el-Loz in the Beqa'a Plain/Lebanon: Continuity and Change in the Settlement of a Region. *BAAL* 5: 5–91.
Heinz, M. and Kirsch, L.
2011 The Dead in the Residential Area West of the Temple. *BAAL* 15: 60–63.
Heinz, M., Linke, J., Catanzeriti, A., and Wagner-Durand, E.
2011 Kamid el-Loz: Report on the Excavations 2010 and 2011. *BAAL* 15: 29–108.
Heinz, M., Linke, J., Wagner, E., and Kulemann-Ossen, S.
2010 The Palace Area and Its Vicinity. Pp. 153–180 in *Kamid el-Loz: Intermediary Between Cultures; More Than 10 Years of Archaeological Research in Kamid el-Loz (1997–2007).* Edited by M. Heinz. BAAL Hors-serie 7. Beirut: Ministère de la Culture, Direction Générale des Antiquités.
Heinz, M., Wagner, E., Linke, J., Walther, A., Catanzariti, A., Müller, J.-M., and Weber, M.
2010 Report on the Excavations in Kamid el-Loz 2008–2009. *BAAL* 14: 9–134.
Hobsbawm, E. J.
1992 Introduction: Inventing Traditions. Pp. 1–14 in *The Invention of Tradition.* Edited by E. J. Hobsbawm and T. O. Ranger. Cambridge: Cambridge University Press.
Hodder, I. and Cessford, C.
2004 Daily Practice and Social Memory at Çatalhöyük. *American Antiquity* 69: 17–40.
Kulemann-Ossen, S.
2010 The Finds (Areas: I-f-12/13/14; I-g-12–14; I-e-14). Pp. 130–138 in *Kamid el-Loz: Intermediary Between Cultures; More Than 10 Years of Archaeological Research in Kamid el-Loz (1997–2007).* Edited by M. Heinz. BAAL Hors-serie 7. Beirut: Ministère de la Culture, Direction Générale des Antiquités.
Linke, J.
2010a Catalogue of the Small Finds. *BAAL* 14: 102–126.
2010b The Iron Age (Persian and Hellenistic Times): The Graves 2008–2009. *BAAL* 14: 16–26.
2010c The Small Finds. *BAAL* 14: 29, 38–40, 52–53, 60–61, 88–89.
2010d The Excavation Results 2008 and 2009 of the East Slope—The Iron Age I (II) Settlement. *BAAL* 14: 18–21.
2011a Selected Findings from the MBA Administrative Area. BAAL 15: 89-91.

2011b The So-Called Administrative Area East of the Palace. *BAAL* 15: 50–60.

Linke, J. and Heinz, M.
2012 Hyperculture, Tradition and Identity: How to Communicate with Seals in Times of Global Action; A Middle Bronze Age Seal Impression from Kamid el-Loz. Pp. 185–190 in *Materiality and Social Practice: Transformative Capacities of Intercultural Encounters*. Edited by P. Stockhammer and J. Maran. Oxford: Oxbow.

Linke, J. and Wagner, E.
2010a Stratigraphy and Architecture of the Buildings South of the "Main" Street: Buildings A, B, F, G, H. Pp. 117–122 in *Kamid el-Loz: Intermediary Between Cultures; More Than 10 Years of Archaeological Research in Kamid el-Loz (1997–2007)*. Edited by M. Heinz. BAAL Hors-serie 7. Beirut: Ministère de la Culture, Direction Générale des Antiquités.
2010b The Graves at the East-Slope. Pp. 74–96 in *Kamid el-Loz: Intermediary Between Cultures; More Than 10 Years of Archaeological Research in Kamid el-Loz (1997–2007)*. Edited by M. Heinz. BAAL Hors-serie 7. Beirut: Ministère de la Culture, Direction Générale des Antiquités.
2010c The Palace Area and Its Vicinity—The Deep Trench from 2002. Pp. 155–157 in *Kamid el-Loz: Intermediary Between Cultures; More Than 10 Years of Archaeological Research in Kamid el-Loz (1997–2007)*. Edited by M. Heinz. BAAL Hors-serie 7. Beirut: Ministère de la Culture, Direction Générale des Antiquités.
2010d The Stratigraphy and Chronology of the East-slope: Areas II-e-5/ II-e-6, II-e-7 and II-f-9. Pp. 35–49 in *Kamid el-Loz: Intermediary Between Cultures; More Than 10 Years of Archaeological Research in Kamid el-Loz (1997–2007)*. Edited by M. Heinz. BAAL Hors-serie 7. Beirut: Ministère de la Culture, Direction Générale des Antiquités.

Marfoe, L.
1995 *Kāmid el-Lōz 13: The Prehistoric and the Early Historic Context of the Site; Catalog and Commentary*. SBA 41. Bonn: Habelt.

Metzger, M.
2012 *Kāmid el-Lōz 17: Die mittelbronzezeitlichen Tempelanlagen T4 und T5*. SBA 71. Bonn: Habelt.

Miron, R.
1982 Die "mittelbronzezeitlichen" Gräber am Nordhang des Tells. Pp. 101–121 in *Bericht über die Ausgrabungen in Kamid el-Loz in den Jahren 1971 bis 1974*. SBA 32. Edited by R. Hachmann. Bonn: Habelt.

Morris, E. F.
2005 *The Architecture of Imperialism: Military Bases and the Evolution of Foreign Policy in Egypt's New Kingdom*. Probleme der Ägyptologie 22. Leiden: Brill.

Nora, P.
1990 *Zwischen Geschichte und Gedächtnis*. Berlin: Wagenbach.

Novák, M.
1999 *Herrschaftsform und Stadtbaukunst: Programmatik im mesopotamischen Residenzstadtbau von Agade bis Surra-man-ra'ā*. Saarbrücken: SDV.

Poppa, R.
1978 *Kāmid el-Lōz 2: Der eisenzeitliche Friedhof von Kamid el-Loz; Befunde und Funde*. SBA 18. Bonn: Habelt.

Rowlands, M.
1993 The Role of Memory in the Transmission of Culture. *World Archaeology* 25: 141–151.

Wagner, E.
2010a The Rooms of the Intermediate Building. *BAAL* 14:79–81.

2010b The So-Called Schatzhaus-Area—The Architectural Units. *BAAL* 14:63–68.

Wagner-Durand, E.

2011 The Palaces. *BAAL* 15: 34–50.

Walther, A.

2010a The Pottery. *BAAL* 14:29-31, 40-42, 53-56, 61-63, 67-68, 71-71, 78, 81, 89.94, 96.

2010b The So-Called Schatzhaus-Area—The Pottery. *BAAL* 14:68–69.

Weber, M.

2010 The "Oven". *BAAL* 14: 69–71.

Weippert, H.

1998 Kumidi: Die Ergebnisse der Ausgrabungen auf dem Tell Kāmid el-Lōz in den Jahren 1963 bis 1981. *ZDPV* 114: 1–38.

CHAPTER 25

# Enmity Against Samsu-ditāna

Elyze Zomer

THE TEXT EXAMINED HERE is HS 1885+ from the Hilprecht-Sammlung in Jena, provenience Nippur, which has now been successfully joined with two fragments from the collection of the University of Pennsylvania in Philadelphia. W. von Soden already made a few references to this text in his *Akkadisches Handwörterbuch* and in his 1959 (p. 231) article, qualifying HS 1885+ as a Middle Babylonian epic naming, interestingly, the last king of the First Dynasty of Babylon, Samsu-ditāna. What is even more of interest is the fact that Samsu-ditāna is not the protagonist king, but is being vividly antagonized by a rival king in this epic. The name of this hostile king is found on the reverse and has proven to be Gulkišar (*Gul-⌜ki⌝-šár*), the sixth king of the First Sealand Dynasty. This new synchronism between Samsu-ditāna and Gulkišar might offer us some new insights on the final moments around the fall of Babylon.[1]

The text itself can be classified as a so-called *Königsepos* and must have consisted of about ninety lines in total. The first lines of the tablet are broken, but the Gulkišar epic seems to start with an interaction between the protagonist king Gulkišar and the deity Ištar. Thereafter Gulkišar addresses his troops and speaks of going to war with his accompanying deity Ištar against his rival Samsu-ditāna. This speech is in first-person singular and is full of metaphors for destroying the enemy and its offspring. Of special interest is the emphasis on the flood similes within the text, in its vocabulary we find *abubu*, *agû*, and a new attestation for a simile with Errakal. When compared with other so-called *Königsepen*, HS 1885+ resembles more the notorious Zimri-lim epic in format than, for example, the later, more extravagant and abundant Tukultī-Ninurta epic. Recurring themes in both the Zimri-lim epic and HS 1885+ are the address of the troops, the concept of a companion deity or deities, the revelation of divine sign and the use of the divine epithet *narāmu/narāmtu*. In HS 1885+ we interestingly find the epithet *narāmti* A.AB.BA ("beloved of the Sealand") used for the accompanying deity Ištar.

We all know the famous statement that Muršili I sacked Babylon beginning the dark age in the second-half of the second millennium BC mentioned in the Chronicle of Early Kings and the Proclamation of Telipinu. We have always assumed that the Kassites filled the vacuum and took control over Babylon almost immediately thereafter. Could it be possible that—be it even for a very short period—there was another prominent party present at the fall of Babylon? Could this be the First Sealand Dynasty?

1. The Gulkišar-epic has now been published as TMH 12, 1. An extensive and up-to-date discussion can be found in Zomer 2016 and Zomer 2019: 3-28.

A temporary control of at least one Sealand king over Babylon might explain the position of the First Sealand Dynasty within the king lists. This theory was first proposed by Goetze (1957: 66) and has found more and more followers over the last decades.

Let us now consider the historical perspective of the following three groups concerning the fall of Babylon and the role of the First Sealand Dynasty.

## First Dynasty of Babylon

When we observe the Late Old Babylonian period, we find several indications and (in)direct synchronisms between the First Dynasty of Babylon and the First Sealand Dynasty. During the reign of Samsu-iluna, as we all know, the great rebellion in the south occurred. A disruption in the administration in southern Babylonia followed thereafter. Later, approximately around Samsu-iluna's thirtieth year, the authority over central Babylonia was gradually lost. In cities like Isin, Maškan-šapir and Nippur documentation disappears and five legal tablets found in Nippur bear the year-names of a king named Ilīma-ilum.[2] This king is known from the Babylonian King Lists A and B and is regarded as the founder of the First Sealand Dynasty. Yet, this is not the first attestation of the Sealand; in two texts from Larsa dating from the reign of Rīm-Sîn II a group of imprisoned Sealand soldiers is mentioned (OECT 15 10:10) and in the other one (OECT 15 78:18′) a Sealand king, whose name might be restored as [*Ilumma-i*]*lī* (Dalley 2009: 1). The synchronism between Samsu-iluna and Ilīma-ilum is also confirmed by an entry in the Chronicle of Early Kings.[3]

The rising First Sealand Dynasty seems to have had influence in Babylonia as far north as Nippur during the final decade of Samsu-iluna, whose kingdom was reduced to the heartland of northern Babylonia, such as the cities of Babylon, Dilbat, Kiš, Sippar, and their surroundings, but seems to have extended to the further northern regions, such as Ḫana, the Diyala, and the Khabur-triangle.

Ilīma-ilum occurs also in a synchronism with the successor of Samsu-iluna, Abī-ešuḫ. The Chronicle of Early Kings and yearname "o" (Ae 19) both refer to the event of damming up the Tigris against the threat of the First Sealand Dynasty.[4] Additionally, an extispicy report (George 2013: 13–19) and a later oracle inquiry emphasize the importance of this event.[5]

2. BE 6/2 68: MU GIBIL *ì-lí-ma*-DINGIR LUGAL.E; UM 55–21–239 MU *ì-lí-ma*-DINGIR LUGAL.E; ARN 123 ⸢MU⸣ *ì-lí*-⸢DINGIR⸣ LUGAL.E; PBS 8/1 89 MU.ÚS.SA [*ì*]-*lí-ma*-DI[NGIR]; TMH 10 54 *ì-lí-ma*-DINGIR LUGAL.E.

3. Grayson 1975: 156; rev (6.) [I]*Sa-am-su-i-lu-na* x [. . .] (7.) [I]DINGIR-*ma*-DINGIR ZI-*am-ma* $BAD_5$.$BAD_5$ ÉRIN[*me*]-[*šú im-ḫaṣ*].

4. The Chronicle of the Early Kings: Grayson 1975: 156; rev. 8. [I]*A-bi-ši* DUMU [I]*Sa-am-su-i-lu-na ka-šad* [I]DINGIR-*ma*-DINGIR *iš*-[*kun*[?]]-*ma* 9. [id]IDIGNA *a-na se-ke-ri lìb-ba-šú ub-lam*-[*m*]*a* 10. [id]IDIGNA *is-kìr-ma* [I]DINGIR-*ma*-DINGIR *ul* [DAB[*bat*]-*ma*]. The year name is in Horsnell 1999: 261; MU *a-bi-e-šu-uḫ* LUGAL.E USU MAḪ [d]AMAR.UTU.KA.TA [id]IDIGNA GIŠ BÍ.IN.KÉŠ.DA.

5. Lambert 2007: 57. *Tamītu* K 2556, Obv. II; K 4721 Rev.; ND 4393+4401+4405/26, Obv III; K 21542 26–38: "should the . . . soldiers, as many as Abī-ešuḫ, king of Babylon, son of Samsu-iluna, calls together and organizes, within this month up to 30th day, a day he knows, has consulted about, and has long been waiting for, the day he has set his face on, has made his mind up on, on the east side of the Tigris should they open the water-gate, should they turn it to 90°, by heaping up reed bundles and earth should they dam the river, should the (water) flow as it will)?"

Apparently, this was not the only measure that Abī-ešuḫ had taken in this area. In year-name "m" (Ae 21) Abī-ešuḫ is said to have built an eponym-fortress Dūr-Abī-ešuḫ on the banks of the Tigris.[6] Tentatively it has been suggested that this fortress was constructed against the territorial ambitions of the First Sealand Dynasty and to protect Nippur and central Babylonia from the east and the southeast against the threats of waterborne invasion (George 2009: 141).

There must have been a real concern about the protection of Nippur in the eleventh year of Ammī-ditāna; we know now with publication of the archive of Dūr-Abī-ešuḫ that the city was partially abandoned and suffered from enemy attacks.[7] We would expect that the so-called enemy behind these attacks on Nippur, considered from a geographic point of view, is the First Sealand Dynasty, here are the usual suspects, threatening the southern border of the Babylonian heartland.

At the end of Ammī-ditāna's reign, we find another synchronism, this time with the third king of the First Sealand Dynasty, Damqi-ilišu in the year-name Ad. 37.[8] Here the siege of Udinim is the last fact recorded in the year-names during Ammī-ditāna. The settlement is thought to be located in southern Babylonia (Pientka 1998: 227 n. 54). Unfortunately, we cannot say whether this was an expedition into southern Babylonia or was to protect the southern border of the Babylonian heartland or perhaps even both.

For the reign of Ammī-ṣaduqa we don't find direct conflicts with the First Sealand Dynasty, but they probably maintained their position in southern Babylonia up to Nippur, consolidating rather than expanding their realm.

Samsu-ditāna, the last king of his dynasty, struggled with enemies at the borders of the Babylonian heartland, that is, to the north: Hatti, Kassites, and Hanigalbat, and to the south: the First Sealand Dynasty. The enmity against Samsu-ditāna and the fall of Babylon are well-known topics in literary and historical texts, since this event must have had a great impact on the historical perception of later generations:

1. Prophecy of Marduk
2. The Agum-Kakrime Inscription
3. *Tamītu* ND 5492: concerning the safety of the city
4. The Proclamation of Telipinu
5. Chronicle of Early Kings
6. YBC 2242: *kudurru* Kadašman-ḫarbe (I)
7. HS 1885+ The Gulkišar epic

Both texts 1 and 2 refer to the exile of the statue of Marduk in the land of Hatti for twenty-four years, which coincides with text 5 where it is stated that at the time

6. Horsnell 1999: 262–263; MU *A-bi-e-šu-uḫ* LUGAL.E BÀD.DA *A-bi-e-šu-uḫ*.$KE_4$ BÍ.IN.DÙ.A LUGAL.E UGU GIŠ.$GI_4$.$GI_4$ $^{id}$IDIGNA.KA.TA BÍ.IN.DÙ.A.

7. Van Lerberghe and Voet 2009: 7. CUNES 51–02–138: "To our lord speak. Thus report your servants: the city and the troops of our lord are well. In the eleventh month on the twenty-eight day the citizens of Nippur who fled from Nippur to the banks of the river spoke to us as follows—in the eleventh month on the nineteenth day five hundred enemies with horses and regular troops invaded Nippur. They entered the Ekur-temple. (. . .) They resisted the enemies with horses and went away. In the eleventh month on the twenty-fourth day three hundred enemies with horses entered the Ekur- temple again. (. . .) The enemy has been defeated and the enemy has left Nippur. This is what they have told us so far."

8. Horsnell 1999: 319–320; MU *am-mi-di-ta-na* LUGAL.E BÀD.DA UDINIM$^{ki}$.MA (ÉREN) *dam-qí-ì-lí-šu*.$KE_4$ BÍ.IN.DÙ.A BÍ.IN.GUL.LA.

of Samsu-ditāna the land of Hatti marched against Akkad. This event is also attested in the Hittite sources, in text 4 where it is said that Muršili I went to Babylon and destroyed it. All these sources suggest that the Hittites were responsible for dealing the final blow to Babylon.

Text 3 is of a much later dating, but recovers the historical perspective of the turmoil before the fall of Babylon.[9] The text lists a number of rebellious enemies who threaten the security of the city of Babylon at the time of Samsu-ditāna. Noteworthy here is the absence of the First Sealand Dynasty, but one could conclude that since the oracle question is put for the duration of just one month, that a short-time northern coalition of the mentioned troops was expected against Samsu-ditāna, perhaps preceding the Hittite advance (Lambert 2007: 144).

Text 6 is a *kudurru* of Kadašman-ḫarbe I. This text was brought to light by S. Paulus in several publications (Paulus 2011: 4 n. 31; 2013: 441 n. 129; 2014: 296–304). The disorder that followed after Samsu-ditāna is ascribed in this text to the "fighting of the Amorites," "the insurrection of the Haneans," and the "army of the Kassites," clearly showing the Kassite influence in this matter.

Finally, we have text 7 HS 1885+ (the Gulkišar epic) where, as already stated above, we find the Sealand king Gulkišar antagonizing Samsu-ditāna.

It is clear that at the end of the First Dynasty of Babylon multiple groups were pressing at the borders of the Babylonian heartland and, as has been said, the Kassites are of great importance in this historical survey.

## Early Kassite Kings

When studying the early Kassite kings, we have to observe the dynastic genealogy of the Agum-Kakrime Inscription, the Babylonian King List A and the Synchronistic King List. The results are in table 25.1.

I follow F. van Koppen, who made a case for the chronology of the early Kassite kings during the Rencontre in Leiden (2012), in accepting that the Tell-Muhammad Kassite kings Ḫurbaḫ and Šipta-ulzi are likely to be indicated at the time of Samsu-ditāna. It is a powerful Kassite figure by the name of Agum, who claims in the Agum-Kakrime Inscription to be "one who settles the land of Ešnunna." This phrase is normally used to denote the reconciliation after warfare (Van Koppen 2010: 460). From the year-names of Tell-Muhammad we know that its kings must have exercised some control over the Diyala region.[10] So Agum in his inscription suggests that he took this region by force, explaining the omission of the Tell-Muhammad kings in his dynastic genealogy. It is this same Agum that is the first Kassite to explicitly state having control over Babylon.[11] Second, it is stated by Agum in his inscription that he refurbished

9. Lambert 2007: 25–26; *Tamītu* ND 5492 31–41: "The Elamites' army, the . . . -ratû army, the infantry corps, the Kassite army, the Idamaraṣ army that is stationed in Idamaraṣ and the foreign troops that are with them, the Ḫanigalbat army and the foreign troops that are with them, the Samḫarû army and the foreign troops that are with them, the Edašuštu army, all the 'hunters,' its auxiliary and reserve troops and the foreign troops that are with them:—the enemy troops [. . .] as many as there are."

10. IM 90606: MU DINGIR.DIDLI *ša áš-nun-na ḫur-ba-aḫ/zum ú-ud-di-šu.*

11. Oshima 2012: 242; col. i 31–43: "King of the Kassites and the Akkadians, king of the wide land of Babylon, the one who settles the land of Ešnunna, the wide-spread people, the king of Padan and Alman,

TABLE 25.1. Dynastic geneology of the early Kassite kings.

| Dynastic genealogy | Babylonian King List A | Synchronic King List |
|---|---|---|
| | Gandaš | Gandaš |
| Agum I | Agum I | Agum I |
| Kaštiliaš(u) I | Kaštiliaš(u) I | Kaštiliaš(u) I |
| | Ušši | |
| Abirattaš | Abirattaš | Abirattaš |
| | | Kaštiliaš(u) II |
| Uršigurumaš | Urzigurumaš | Urzigurumaš |
| | [. . .] x | Ḫurbaḫ/zum |
| | | Šipta-ulzi |
| [. . .]-kakrime | (broken) | Agum II |
| | | Burnaburiaš |
| | | [. . .] |
| | | Kaštiliaš(u) III |

the Esagila upon the return of the statue of Marduk to Babylon.[12] Both indications are solely based on the Agum-Kakrime Inscription and given the discussion on the authenticity of the text one might ignore them. However, even if the text is an ancient forgery, it could be assumed that the later priests and scholars of the Esagila were the inventors (Oshima 2012: 233), since they must have had access to its archives with the records of the ancient Babylonian kings leaving the historical value of the inscription still intact. One must stress that Agum does not explicitly mention his rule over Sumer in stating his hegemony. This corresponds well with the known presence of the First Sealand Dynasty in southern Babylonia, as we have seen earlier.

The tenth Kassite king listed in the Synchronistic King List after Agum II is Burnaburiaš. He is also attested in the Synchronistic History, where he is said to have established the boundary together with Puzur-Aššur III of Assyria. The reference to Burnaburiaš in both sources implies that he ruled at least over northern Babylonia. This would fit the theory of his predecessor Agum being the first Kassite king to have control over Babylon.

Eventually it came down to a confrontation between the early Kassite kings and the First Sealand Dynasty. Ulamburiaš, a king not preserved in the king lists is said in the Chronicle of Early Kings to have driven out the last king of the Sealand, Ea-gāmil, and conquered the Sealand.[13] This fits well with a mace head mentioning Ulamburiaš as a king of the Sealand and as a son of Burnaburiaš.[14] We might assume that Ulamburiaš had a special status among the early Kassite kings. He might not have ruled over

king of the land of the Gutians, the barbarous people, the king who subjugates the four-corners (of the world), the favorite of the great gods, am I."

12. Oshima 2012: 244; col. vi 40—vii 10: "(A prayer) for the king Agum, who made the cella of Marduk, renewed the Esagila, and brought back Marduk to his abode, exempted them (from tax for) the gifts of these workers as well as the house, field, and orchard for Marduk a[nd] Zarpanitu."

13. Grayson 1975: 15; . (12) $^{\text{Id}}$*É-a-ga-mil* LUGAL KUR *tam-tim a-na* $^{\text{KUR}}$*Elamti*$^{\text{KI}}$ *i[ḫ-liq]-ma* (13) EGIR-*šú* $^{\text{I}}$*Ú-lam-bur-áš* ŠEŠ $^{\text{I}}$*Kaš-til-ía*-ÍA $^{\text{KUR}}$*Kaš-[šu]-ú* (14) ERÍN-*šú id-ke-e-ma* KUR *tam-tim* KUR*ud* EN-*ut* KUR *i-pu-uš*.

14. Stein 2000: 129; BE 6405: (1) *pí-in-gi* $^{\text{NA4}}$ŠU.U (2) *ša Ú-la-bu-ra-ri-ia-aš* (3) DUMU *Bur-na-bu-ra-ri-ia-aš* LUGAL (4) LUGAL KUR A.AB.BA.

Babylon, hence his omission within the king lists, but was king over the Sealand alongside his brother Kaštiliaš, who ruled over Babylon (Van Koppen 2017). At least we can conclude that the downfall of the First Sealand Dynasty took place during Ulamburiaš, which is confirmed by the Babylonian King List A and B and the Synchronistic King List, where Ea-gāmil is listed as the last king of the Sealand.

Finally, another Agum is said in the Chronicle of Early Kings to have delivered the final blow to the First Sealand Dynasty by conquering Dūr-Enlil.[15] Interpreting this chronicle entry, we get the impression that Dūr-Enlil was the last stronghold of the First Sealand Dynasty. This brings us to the recently published archive of the First Sealand Dynasty by S. Dalley (2009) in CUSAS 9. The provenance of this archive is unknown, but we might deduce from its geographical contacts that it must have been in the vicinity of Nippur (Dalley 2009: 4). A large group of published and unpublished Middle Babylonian texts refer to a Dūr-Enlil and a Dūr-Enlillē in the vicinity of Nippur.[16] Furthermore, year-name H within the archive of the First Sealand Dynasty refers to building activities within Dūr-Enlillē.[17] It would not be unlikely that this stronghold of the Sealand in the vicinity of Nippur was in fact Dūr-Enlil or Dūr-Enlillē. What we should keep in mind is that the origins of the First Sealand Dynasty lie presumably in the far marshes of southern Babylonia, where according to the several king lists, the seat of residence of this dynasty was Uruku(g) or E'uruku(g), but its exact location is hard to determine (Dalley 2009: 5).[18] One could argue that the main seat of residence of this dynasty had shifted up north into central Babylonia, consolidating its power.

That the focus of power of the First Sealand Dynasty was not only directed toward the north, but also extended further south is shown from recently excavated texts from Bahrain to be published by A. Cavigneaux and B. Andre-Salvini mentioning the First Sealand king Ea-gāmil. Other texts bear (royal?) Kassite names indicating that the Kassites simply took advantage of the existing situation annexing the totality of the Sealand and dividing it up into several provinces (Højlund 1989: 12).

## Sealand Dynasty

I would like to conclude with the perspective of the First Sealand Dynasty. The new direct synchronism in HS 1885+ gives us new insight into the years around the fall of Babylon. It is said that the raison-d'être of the First Sealand Dynasty within the king lists was the fact that at least one of these kings must have ruled over Babylon.

15. Grayson 1975: 156; rev. (15) $^{I}$*A-gu-um* DUMU $^{I}$*Kaš-til-ía-àš* ERÍN-*šú id-ke-e-ma* (16) *a-na* KUR *tam-tim il-lik* (17) $^{URU}$*Dūr-*$^{d}$50 KUR$^{ud}$ (18) *É-galga-šeš-na* É $^{d}$50 *šá Dūr-*$^{d}$50 *ú-šal-pit*.

16. With gratitude to Prof. W. H. van Soldt.

17. Dalley 2009:12; MU A.A-DÀRA-GALAM.MA LUGAL.E É.ÚNU$^{KI}$ LIBIR.RA ⸢BÀD⸣-$^{d}$EN.LÍL.LE.KE$_{4}$.

18. In addition to Dalley, note that a lunar eclipse, which has been associated with the "fall of Babylon," might relate to the Sealand Dynasty, where the associated omen apodosis reads, following Roaf 2012: 158, "The prediction is given for Babylon: The destruction of Babylon is near. The scattering of the scattered land is near (?). Ellil will curse and revile the land in its entirety (?). The king to whom they said 'yes,' his people will be scattered. His reign will end. In the assembly of the gods his destruction is near. Ur will take away the rule of Babylon. Ur will take supremacy over Babylon." The possible connection between Ur and the First Sealand Dynasty has not yet been considered for this text.

In addition one should note that the Synchronistic King List chooses the First Sealand Dynasty over their Babylonian counterparts as contemporaries of the Assyrian kings.

**First Sealand Dynasty**

1. Ilīma-ilum
2. Itti-ili-nībī
3. Damqi-ilišu
4. Iškibal
5. Šušši
6. Gulkišar
7. ᴵDIŠ+U-EN (SyKL only)
8. Pešgaldarameš
9. Ayadaragalama
10. Ekurduana
11. Melamkurkura
12. Ea-gāmil

We have seen that Ilīma-ilum and Damqi-ilišu battled the kings of Babylon and that the kings of Babylon were seated in Babylon itself. This leaves us with the only possibility that the First Sealand Dynasty comes in view for the first time around the fall of Babylon. The new direct synchronism of Gulkišar and Samsu-ditāna seems to confirm this theory. Note that an indirect synchronism between these two kings was already suggested decades ago (Goetze 1957: 66; Jaritz 1958: 193). However, since we don't have any contemporary sources on Gulkišar, we will have to investigate later sources. Gulkišar is mentioned twice; first in a so-called *Distanzangabe* in a kudurru (BE I/1 83) stating the time elapsed between his reign and Enlil-nādin-apli and second in a colophon that dates the original copy of a glass-making text (BM 120960). Furthermore, the archive of the First Sealand Dynasty, dating the two successors of Gulkišar, can give us some new insights in the perception of the royal ancestors of the dynasty.

First of all, the elaborate Sumerian names of these two kings might be a tribute to their ancestor Gulkišar (Dalley 2009: 2). Pešgaldarameš can be analyzed as "Son of a stag" and Ayadaragalama "(My) father is the skillfull ibex."[19] These kings are both listed as son of Gulkišar in the Babylonian King List B, which could be taken literally, but could also implicate that they were son and grandson of Gulkišar. One offering list (Dalley 2009: 81 no. 83 MS 2200:15′) from this archive mentions the divine name Šamaš-ana-Gulkišar-kurub (Šamaš-bless-Gulkišar), which indicates the reverent position of Gulkišar and the ancestor cult of his successors. Interestingly, it seems that the kings of the First Sealand Dynasty continued the tradition of Sumerian throne-names and Gulkišar's name as well can be translated "Destroyer of the Universe" implying that he was not unsuccessful as a conqueror. If we believe the king lists, Gulkišar reigned for fifty-six years, which is respectably long. All this indicates that Gulkišar had a unique position within the First Sealand Dynasty and the historical perception thereof. We therefore propose the possibility of Gulkišar having had temporary control

19. Note small correction to reading of Dalley 2009: 2 of Ayadaragalama.

over Babylon. Temporary, possibly less than a year, based upon the evidence found in the archives of the First Sealand Dynasty. We cannot state that the First Sealand Dynasty, during the reigns of the successors of Gulkišar, was in control of northern Babylonia. What we do find is a certain interest and presence of this dynasty in this area, which could be an indication of former control or just an interest in trade (Dalley 2009: 9). We should keep in mind that in Tell-Muhammad, which was just north of Sippar, a Kassite dynasty was located shortly before and after the fall of Babylon. If the First Sealand Dynasty ever ruled over Babylon, however briefly it may have been, it must have been before Pešgaldarameš and Ayadaragalama. The First Sealand Dynasty must have had its heyday during the final years of Gulkišar and shortly after the fall of Babylon, which is also indicated by the flourishing economy of the archive of the First Sealand Dynasty (Dalley 2010: 61).

The fact that Gulkišar is now found as a contemporary and hostile king against Samsu-ditāna in HS 1885+ speaks in favor of this theory. The successors of Gulkišar must have faced the rise of the Kassites, who by this time, having settled their affairs in the north and united under Agum II, founded their capital in Babylon. The assumption that the First Sealand Dynasty in the person of Gulkišar ever controlled Babylon is only deduced from the fact that this dynasty was included in several king lists and that we now have a literary text written on behalf of Gulkišar speaking of his enmity against Samsu-ditāna. In any case, the always careful suggestion that the First Sealand Dynasty was present at the fall of Babylon seems now to be confirmed.

## BIBLIOGRAPHY

Dalley, S.

2009 — *Babylonian Tablets from the First Sealand Dynasty in the Schøyen Collection.* CUSAS 9. Bethesda, MD: CDL.

2010 — Administration in Texts from the First Sealand Dynasty. Pp. 61–68 in *City Administration in the Ancient Near East.* Vol. 2 of *Proceedings of the 53e Recontre Assyriologique Internationale*, Edited by L. Kogan, N. Koslova, S. Loesov, and S. Tischchenko. Babel und Bibel 5. Winona Lake, IN: Eisenbrauns.

George, A. R.

2009 — *Babylonian Literary Texts in the Schøyen Collection.* CUSAS 10. Bethesda, MD: CDL.

2013 — *Babylonian Divinatory Texts Chiefly in the Schøyen Collection.* CUSAS 18. Bethesda, MD: CDL.

Goetze, A.

1957 — On the Chronology of the Second Millennium B.C. *JCS* 11: 63–73.

Grayson, A. K.

1975 — *Assyrian and Babylonian Chronicles.* TCS 5. Locust Valley, NY: Augustin.

Højlund, F.

1989 — Dilmun and the Sealand. *Northern Akkad Project Reports* 2: 9–14.

Horsnell, M. J. A.

1999 — *The Year-Names of the First Dynasty of Babylon.* 2 vols. Hamilton: McMaster University Press.

Jaritz, K.

1958 — Quellen zur Geschichte der Kaššû-Dynastie. *MIOF* 6: 187–265.

Koppen, F. van.
2010 The Old to Middle Babylonian Transition: History and Chronology of the Mesopotamian Dark Age. *Ägypten und Levante* 20:453–463.
2017 The Early Kassite Period. Pp. 45–92 in *Karanduniaš: Babylonia Under the Kassites; Proceedings of the Symposium Held in Munich 30 June to 2 July 2011*. Edited by A. Bartelmus and K. Sternitzke. 2 vols. Untersuchungen zur Assyriologie und Vorderasiatischen Archäologie 11. Berlin: de Gruyter.

Lambert, W. G.
2007 *Babylonian Oracle Questions*. MC 13. Winona Lake, IN: Eisenbrauns.

Lerberghe, K. van and Voet, G.
2009 *A Late Old Babylonian Temple Archive from Dūr-Abiešuḫ*. CUSAS 8. Bethesda, MD: CDL.

Oshima, T.
2012 Another Attempt at Two Kassite Royal Inscriptions: The Agum-Kakrime Inscription and the Inscription of Kurigalzu the Son of Kadashmanharbe. Pp. 225–268 in *Babel und Bibel 6*. Edited by L. Kogan. Winona Lake, IN: Eisenbrauns.

Paulus, S.
2011 Foreigners Under Foreign Rulers: The Case of Kassite Babylonia (2nd Half of the 2nd Millennium BC). Pp. 1–16 in *The Foreigner and the Law: Perspectives from the Hebrew Bible and the Ancient Near East*. Edited by R. Achenbach, R. Albertz, and J. Wöhrle. BZABR 16. Wiesbaden: Harrassowitz.
2013 Beziehungen zweier Großmächte—Elam und Babylonien in der 2. Hälfte des 2. Jt. v. Chr. Ein Beitrag zur internen Chronologie. Pp. 429–449 in *Susa and Elam: Archeological, Philological, Historical and Geographical Perspectives; Proceedings of the International Congress Held at Ghent University, December 14–17 2009*. Edited by K. de Graef and J. Tavernier. Mémoires de la Délégation en Perse 58. Leiden: Brill.
2014 *Die babylonischen Kudurru-Inschriften von der kassitischen bis zur frühneubabylonischen Zeit: Untersucht unter besonderer Berücksichtigung gesellschafts- und rechtshistorischer Fragestellungen*. AOAT 51. Münster: Ugarit-Verlag.

Pientka, R.
1998 *Die spätaltbabylonische Zeit: Abiesuh bis Samsuditana; Quellen, Jahresdaten, Geschichte*. IMGULA 2. Münster: Rhema.

Roaf, M.
2012 The Fall of Babylon in 1499 NC or 1595 MC. *Akkadica* 133: 147–174.

Soden, W. von.
1959 Beiträge zum Verständnis des babylonischen Gilgameš-Epos. *ZA* 53: 209–235.

Stein, P.
2000 *Die mittel- und neubabylonischen Königsinschriften bis zum Ende der Assyrerherrschaft: Grammatische Untersuchungen*. Jenaer Beiträge zum Vorderen Orient 3. Wiesbaden: Harrassowitz.

Zomer, E.
2016 Game of Thrones: Koningen in Strijd in de Laat Oud-Babylonische Periode. *Phoenix* 62: 52–63.
2019 *Middle Babylonian Literary Texts from the Frau Professor Hilprecht Collection, Jena*. TMH 12. Wiesbaden: Harrassowitz Verlag.

# CONTRIBUTORS

**Netanel Anor** (PhD 2016) has held research and teaching positions at the Freie Universität Berlin, at the Hebrew University, and at Tel Aviv University. He currently conducts a study on the Babylonian Pantheon of the late third millennium BCE in the framework of the research project "GLAM: God-Lists of Ancient Mesopotamia." His research and publications—most recently, "The Seer and His Client in the Ritual of Extispicy" (2020)—focus on different aspects of scholarly knowledge.

**Dalila Bendellal-Younsi** is a doctoral student in History, Archaeology, and Literature of the Ancient World at the University of Lille (UMR 8164). She studies penalty law, and more specifically the penalties on theft, during the first half of the second millennium BCE.

**Yigal Bloch** (PhD 2013) wrote his dissertation about Middle Assyrian Chronology. He participated as a postdoctoral scholar in research projects at the University of California Berkeley, the Hebrew University of Jerusalem, and the University of Haifa. He is currently a curator at the Bible Lands Museum Jerusalem. Recent publications include studies on the Amorites (with Nathan Wasserman, in Hebrew) and on alphabetic scribes in first millennium Babylonia.

**Daniel Bodi** (PhD 1988) is Professor of History of Religions of Antiquity at the University of Paris 4, La Sorbonne. His research focuses on the context of literature and religion in the Near East. His most recent publication is "Two Animal Proverbs in Aḫiqar and in Aesop on Human Relationships: Mercilessness and Sharing" (2018).

**Daniel Bonneterre** (PhD 1991) is professor at University of Quebec (Canada). His research focuses on food consumption and ritual practices. His most recent publications are *Manger avec les dieux* (in press) and "De l'antiquité vénérable des repas sacrés. Enquête sur trois mythes mésopotamiens" (2019).

**Monica Bouso** (PhD 2012) works as a postdoctoral researcher in the Faculty of Arts of the Universitat de Lleida (UdL, Catalonia) and is professor and coordinator of the Interuniversity online Grade of History, History of Art and Geography, UdL-UOC

(Universitat Oberta de Catalunya). Currently, she is the secretary of the *Revista d'Arqueologia de Ponent* edited by the UdL. Her research interests, which range from the ancient Near East to the western Mediterranean, include cognitive archaeology, intellectual and religious history of the ancient Near East, formation of complex and textual communities, transmission of cultural memory and ritual performance; she has also published several articles on funerary practices.

**Katrien De Graef** (PhD 2004) is currently Associate Professor of Assyriology and History of the Ancient Near East at Ghent University. Her research focuses primarily on the socio-economic history of the Old Babylonian period (2000–1500 BCE) in general, and that of the cities of Sippar (Iraq) and Susa (Iran) in particular, including gender studies and sealing praxis, and the relation between Babylonia and Elam in the third and second millennium BCE. Recent publications include studies on female agency in the Old Babylonian economy, advance payments in the Ur-Utu archive, and biculturalism and bilingualism in Susa.

**Sophie Démare-Lafont** (PhD 1990) teaches history of law at the university of Panthéon-Assas and is director of studies at the École Pratique des Hautes Études, PSL. She has published extensively on the legal position of women in the ancient Near East; her most recent publication is *Debt in Ancient Mediterranean Societies: A Documentary Approach* (2019).

**Aline Distexhe** has worked on Neo-Assyrian linguistic phenomena at the Université Libre de Bruxelles.

**Lena Fijałkowska** (PhD 2005) is assistant professor at the Department of Studies in the Development of State and Law, Faculty of Law and Administration, University of Lodz, Poland, is a legal historian specializing in the history of ancient Near Eastern law. Publications include articles on the history of contract and family law in Mesopotamia and Syria, especially in the second millennium BCE, most recently, "I Was Swollen with Hunger and He Kept Me Alive" (2018).

**Steven J. Garfinkle** (PhD 2000) is Professor of Ancient History at Western Washington University, and editor of the *Journal of Ancient Near Eastern History*. His research focuses on the society and economy of early Mesopotamia, with emphasis on the intersections between commerce, state formation, and violence. He is the author of numerous studies on the kingdom of Ur and the history of the late third millennium BCE, including *Entrepreneurs and Enterprise in Early Mesopotamia: A Study of Three Archives from the Third Dynasty of Ur* (2012).

**Anne Goddeeris** (PhD 2001) is an Assyriologist currently affiliated with Ghent University. She has published two volumes with new Old Babylonian legal and administrative documents from Kisurra (now in the British Museum, 2009) and from Nippur (now in the Hilprecht Sammlung, 2016). Her research focuses on the social and economic history of Babylonia during the Old Babylonian period.

**Anna Gómez-Bach** (PhD 2011) is assistant professor at the Prehistory Department, Autonomous University of Barcelona, and researcher at GRAMPO (Grup de Recerca en Arqueologia del Mediterrani i Pròxim Orient). She has been head of the archaeological mission at Banahilk (Soran, Iraqi Kurdistan) since 2017 and codirector with Dr. Miquel Molist at Gird Lashkir (Erbil, Iraqi Kurdistan) since 2015. She is a specialist in prehistoric pottery and archaeometric analysis.

**Rodrigo Hernáiz** (PhD 2018) is a linguist and Assyriologist. After working as a researcher at the Institute of Near East Studies (IPOA), University of Barcelona (Spain), he received his PhD at the Philipps University Marburg (Germany). He currently works as lecturer of languages and linguistics at The Open University (UK). He has recently published a monograph in the AOAT series, *Studies on Linguistic and Orthographic Variation in Old Babylonian Letters* (2020).

**Krzysztof Hipp** (PhD 2017) is presently a postdoctoral independent researcher affiliated with the Institute of Archaeology of the Jagiellonian University. His research interests revolve around Assyro-Urartian relations, Urartian expansion toward north Syria and along the Zagros, and Urartian Archaeology. His PhD dissertation (unpublished), *The Assyrian Empire and the Kingdom of Urartu: Struggle for the Domination in the Near East in the First Half of the First Millennium BCE*, pertains to, among other things, the economic implications of the conflict, especially for the Assyrians. His publications are available on academia.edu and ResearchGate.

**Sandra Jacobs** (PhD 2010) is a research fellow at King's College, London, and currently teaches "'*inūma ilu awīlum*': When Gods Were Men—An Introduction to the Bible in Its Ancient Near Eastern Setting" at Leo Baeck College. She is the author of *The Body as Property: Physical Disfigurement in Biblical Law* (2014). Her research expertise is in ancient Hebrew, Aramaic, and Akkadian law, where she focuses on the areas of corporal and capital punishments, body image, and distinctions of gender.

**Daniele Umberto Lampasona** (PhD 2013) completed his dissertation, entitled "Letter-orders in the Ur III period," whose main results are summarized in this article, at the Università degli studi di Napoli—l'Orientale. In 2014 he held a postdoctoral DAAD scholarship at the Westfälische Wilhelms-Universität of Münster, focusing on prosopographical reconstruction during the Ur III period. During the 2008 season, he took part in the archaeological excavations in Tell Mozan, ancient Urkesh. His most recent article about letter-orders was published in *Libiamo ne' lieti calici* (2016).

**Julia Linke** (PhD 2018) is an archaeologist with a PhD from the University of Freiburg. Her main research interests are kingship and the communication of power. After several years of fieldwork in Lebanon and Turkey as well as teaching at Freiburg University, she has been working as a curator for archaeological exhibitions since 2015. Currently, she is curating digital contents for the collection of Ancient Cultures at the Badisches Landesmuseum Karlsruhe. She is the coeditor of the volume *Tales of Royalty: Notions of Kingship in Visual and Textual Narration in the Ancient Near East* (2020).

**Alex Loktionov** (Phd 2019) is currently the Lady Wallis Budge Junior Research Fellow at Christ's College, Cambridge. He is also an Affiliated Lecturer in the Department of Archaeology at the University of Cambridge, where he teaches Egyptian and Akkadian. His main research interests focus on justice, decision-making, and modes of social control in the ancient Near East, encompassing both Egypt and Mesopotamia, concentrating predominantly on hieroglyphic and cuneiform sources from the second millennium BCE. He has published several articles about judicial procedures in Egypt and Assyria.

**Kathleen McCaffrey** lives in Charlestown, West Virginia, where she pursues a quiet life dedicated to research and tending a large rose garden. With Mesopotamian religion as her primary focus, she has investigated issues of gender related to ancient religious personnel and is currently analyzing double messaging in Mesopotamian literature. She holds an MA in ancient religion from Claremont University and a second MA in Assyriology from University of California, Berkeley. Her most recent publication is *Gendering for Fortune and Misfortune* (2017).

**Virginie Muller** currently holds a permanent position as a lecturer in Assyriology at the University of Lyon (France) and she is a research fellow at the Laboratory Archéorient (UMR 5133), Maison de l'Orient et de la Méditerranée. Her main research topics and interests are anthropology of death and mortuary practices according to Sumerian and Akkadian texts, as well as omen and divination.

**Paola Negri Scafa** (PhD 1978) is a member of the Center for Studies on the Fondamenti del diritto antico (Fundamentals of Ancient Law), University "Suor Orsola Benincasa." She collaborates with colleagues from the Universities of Rome "La Sapienza" and "Tor Vergata," and continues her studies on issues related to the Mesopotamian world. These include studies and research on the kingdom of Arrapḫa, and in particular research on scribes and the scribal system, on the administrative, military, fiscal, legal structure of the kingdom, with a focus on the Hurrian ethnic-cultural component. Other topics of interest are Mesopotamian economics, with a particular focus on Nuzi and the fifteenth–fourteenth centuries BCE, studies on women and the female priesthood, and studies of Mesopotamian divination, with a focus on earthquake-related texts. Among her most recent publications she coauthored a publication of Old Babylonian contracts from a private collection.

**Reettakaisa Sofia Salo** (PhD 2017) studied Protestant Theology and Assyriology at the University Åbo Akademi (Turku, Finland) and the University of Münster (Germany). She wrote her dissertation on Judean royal ideology, comparing royal psalms in the Hebrew Bible with ancient Near Eastern sources (*Die judäische Königsideologie im Kontext der Nachbarkulturen: Untersuchungen zu den Königspsalmen 2, 18, 20, 21, 45 und 72* [2017]). Her research interests include connections between Israel and Judah with other ancient Near Eastern cultures, Ugarit, the book of Ezekiel, and textual criticism, on which she has published several articles.

**Christoph Schmidhuber** (PhD 2019) received his PhD from Cambridge and currently holds a postdoctoral position at the Collège de France in Paris. His research centers on the social history of ancient Mesopotamia, with a special focus on the Old Babylonian period (2000–1600 BCE). Wider research interests include divination, royal self-presentation, and Akkadian and Sumerian philology.

**JoAnn Scurlock** (PhD 1988) is the daughter of a law professor (John Scurlock) and a chemistry professor (Jean Scurlock). She holds a PhD from the Department of Near Eastern Languages and Civilizations of the Oriental Institute of the University of Chicago. She has published three books, with another on the way, on Mesopotamian medicine and magic, as well as over ninety articles on all aspects of Mesopotamian political and cultural history, as well as forays into Classics, biblical, and Ugaritic Studies. She has also published several articles on rituals in Mesopotamian jurisdiction.

**Dahlia Shehata** (PhD 2004) is an Assyiologist who specializes in Ancient Mesopotamian languages, culture, and society with particular emphasis on literature, religion, and music history. Her dissertation *Musiker und ihr vokales Repertoire* (2009) focused on the second millennium BCE, presenting professional musicians and the performance contexts of hymns and prayers. Her Habilitation (Würzburg 2018), exploring her second research interest, dealt with the Akkadian Epic of Anzu, a mythological cosmic bird. She has published several articles on both music and literature in Mesopotamia. Among her latest projects was the organization of the music exhibition "MUS-IC-ON! Klang der Antike" at the Martin von Wagner-Museum, Würzburg (2019–2020). She currently has the position of Assistant Professor at the University of Würzburg where she teaches Sumerian and Akkadian, as well as history courses.

**Cristina Simonetti** (PhD 1998) graduated in Ancient History in 1990 with Professor M. Liverani (with a dissertation on adoption in the Old-Babylonian Period), she discussed her PhD thesis, *La compravendita di beni immobili in Mesopotamia in età antico-babilonese*, in the faculty of Law at the University of Rome "La Sapienza" in 1998. Since 2007 she has been a researcher in Roman and ancient law in the Faculty of Law in the University of Rome "Tor Vergata." She teaches on ancient Near Eastern law in "Tor Vergata" and "La Sapienza," where she is also part of the board of teachers in the PhD program in Philology and History of the Ancient World. She has several publications on Mesopotamian law.

**Jon Taylor** (PhD 2001) is Curator of Cuneiform Collections in the Department of the Middle East at the British Museum. His research interests range from literacy and education in the ancient Near East, the palaeography of cuneiform, the nontextual features of clay documents, to uses of the past in the ancient Near East itself. Recent publications include an introduction to cuneiform culture, entitled "Cuneiform" (2016).

**Joanna Töyräänvuori** (PhD 2016) is a postdoctoral fellow at the Ancient Near Eastern Empires center of excellence at the University of Helsinki. Having graduated in Hebrew Bible Studies at the Theological Faculty of the University of Helsinki, Töyräänvuori's expertise centers on the political mythologies of the eastern Mediterranean. Among her publications, she edited the forthcoming *Die Welt des Orients* issue, *Construction of Identity in the Ancient World* (2020).

**Elisabeth Wagner-Durand** (PhD 2009) received her PhD from the Albert-Ludwigs-University, Freiburg. Her research focuses on visual culture, the history of emotions, and on narratives as a cultural means of expression. She is most recently the coeditor of *Tales of Royalty: Notions of Kingship in Visual and Textual Narration in the Ancient Near East* (2020).

**Elyze Zomer** (PhD 2017) is a Research Fellow at the Philipps-University Marburg in Germany. She received her doctoral degree in Ancient Near Eastern Studies from the University of Leipzig. Her main research focuses on Mesopotamian magico-medical texts, literature, religion, and divination. She is the author of a number of articles and books, most recently *Middle Babylonian Literary Texts from the Frau Professor Hilprecht Collection, Jena* (2019).

www.ingramcontent.com/pod-product-compliance
Lightning Source LLC
LaVergne TN
LVHW081939200926
848484LV00009B/2471